The Life of
Céline

BLACKWELL CRITICAL BIOGRAPHIES

General Editor: Claude Rawson

The Life of
CÉLINE

A Critical Biography

Nicholas Hewitt

Copyright © Nicholas Hewitt 1999

The right of Nicholas Hewitt to be identified as author of this work has been asserted in accordance with the Copyright, Designs and Patents Act 1988.

First published 1999

2 4 6 8 10 9 7 5 3 1

Blackwell Publishers Ltd
108 Cowley Road
Oxford OX4 1JF
UK

Blackwell Publishers Inc.
350 Main Street
Malden, Massachusetts 02148
USA

PQ 2607 .E834 Z697 1999

British Library Cataloguing in Publication Data

A CIP catalogue record for this book is available from the British Library.

Library of Congress Cataloging-in-Publication Data

Hewitt, Nicholas.
    The life of Céline: a critical biography / Nicholas Hewitt.
        p.   cm. – (Blackwell critical biographies; 11)
    Includes bibliographical references and index.
    ISBN 0-631-17615-2 (alk. paper)
    1. Céline, Louis-Ferdinand, 1894–1961 – Biography.   2. Authors, French – 20th
      century – Biography.   I. Title.   II. Series.
    PQ2607.E834Z697   1998
    843'.912
      [B]–DC21
                                                                            98–7229
                                                                                 CIP

Typeset in 10 on 11 pt Baskerville
by Best-set Typesetter Ltd., Hong Kong
Printed in Great Britain by T.J. International, Padstow, Cornwall

This book is printed on acid-free paper

To Helen

Contents

Contents

Illustrations

The illustrations appear between pp. 192 and 193.

Preface

Louis-Ferdinand Céline is now recognized, along with Proust, to whom he owed so much and with whom he remained fascinated until his death, as France's foremost twentieth-century novelist. He owes this reputation to an unusually rich combination of three elements. In the first place, he was always careful to emphasize his importance as a stylist, a linguistic innovator who created a new literary language through the infusion of spoken French into the written culture which had remained unchanged since Malherbe. In this, his project was remarkably similar to that of a near-contemporary, Raymond Queneau, and its originality can be judged from comparison with less successful imitators, like Céline's disciple in the post-war period, Albert Paraz. Secondly, this linguistic experimentation accompanied and reinforced a highly acute awareness of social and economic history, an awareness which, perhaps even more than the use of popular language, led to comparisons with Zola and the Naturalists. From the early thesis on *Semmelweis* to the final German trilogy, Céline's fiction is rooted in a tangible and recognizable society, from the Belle Epoque to the new France of the 1950s, to such an extent that society's economic dynamic and myths permeate the language and psychology of the characters: the gold standard which dominates *Mort à crédit*, for example, is the sole guarantor of the 'credit' of the title, as it is of the fragile psychological hierarchy in which Ferdinand is pitted against Auguste. Finally, in his complex manipulation of cultural reference and self-reference, Céline reveals himself as one of Europe's foremost Modernist novelists: in a study like Jack Murray's *The Landscapes of Alienation*,[1] he sits comfortably in the company of Franz Kafka.

This status as a major Modernist was not always recognized. Little was written critically on Céline during his lifetime after his return to France in the 1950s, and in the decade following his death in 1961, the increasing volume of studies of his work, to a greater or lesser extent hagiographic, concentrated largely on the thematic properties of the first two novels, *Voyage au bout de la nuit* and *Mort à crédit*, whilst steering carefully away from the anti-Semitic pamphlets, collaboration, and the later, more abstract, fiction. A non-French readership, for perfectly understandable reasons, was again led to concentrate on the thematic, specifically metaphysical and ethical, properties of the early novels. North American criticism has been symptomatic of this approach: faced with translations which still do not convey accurately the delicacy and complexity of Céline's stylistic 'petite musique', critics have concentrated on both the bleak vision and the rebelliousness of the novels' narrators, seeing in them the precursors of the heroes of the Beat Generation. In this context, a writer like Kurt Vonnegut stands out for having recognized, as early as *Slaughterhouse 5*, that the Naturalist depiction of disaster must go hand in hand with the fantasy that Céline called 'féerie' and which Vonnegut himself transformed into science fiction.

In fact, as Pascal Fouché reminds us in his summary of Céline research in the twenty-five years since the author's death,[2] more detailed long-term projects had already begun in the 1960s and were to lead to the important body of university criticism which emerged in the mid-1970s with the formation of the Société des Etudes Céliniennes. This was accompanied by the establishment of definitive texts of all the novels, undertaken in the *Pléiade* series by Henri Godard, and not completed until 1993. Not only do the four *Pléiade* volumes provide a firm base from which to analyse the fiction, their critical apparatus and variants establish once and for all how conscious a writer Céline was and how elaborate the 'lacework' of the fictional texts. Finally, the documentation established by Godard in his editions has drawn on and been accompanied by the systematic editions of unpublished works, interviews and correspondence in the *Cahiers Céline* and the volumes edited by Jean-Paul Louis. In their turn, these publications have made possible serious attempts at Célinian biography.

This work owes a considerable debt to existing biographical studies. As early as 1975, Patrick McCarthy published the first critical biography of Céline in English,[3] and although some of its factual data have been superseded by later work, many of the critical judgements remain highly valid. In France, François Gibault produced his ground-breaking three-volume study between 1977 and 1985,[4] making use of previously unpublished material, followed in 1988 by Frédéric Vitoux's *La Vie de Céline*, drawing heavily on the reminiscences of Lucette Destouches,[5] and by Philippe Alméras' penetrating biography, *Céline: entre haines et passion*.[6] Although Henri Godard, in *Céline scandale*,[7] expresses irritation at the changing attitudes of biographers towards Céline, alternating between admiration and denigration,[8] these three biographies are in fact largely complementary, drawing upon different sources and with Alméras adding a welcome degree of scepticism to the more readily accepted elements of the Céline myth.

Where Godard is undoubtedly correct, however, is in his identification of the major problem confronting biographers of Céline, which is the reconciliation of two apparently contradictory tendencies: the emphasis upon Céline as a great Modernist writer, and the exploration of his role of one of

France's most spectacular anti-Semites. The difficulty is that it is not sufficient simply to demonstrate, as does Alice Kaplan or Yves Pagès,[9] that the sources of Céline's anti-Semitism go back to French culture in the nineteenth century. What is more complicated is to determine why Céline, by the 1930s an urbane and successful writer with a considerable left-wing following and a number of Jewish acquaintances, should have suddenly and unexpectedly launched himself into violent anti-Semitic polemic in *Bagatelles pour un massacre* and *L'Ecole des cadavres*; just as it is more difficult to explain the close relationship between the increasingly sophisticated Modernist fictional output and the style and tenor of the pamphlets. Nor is the task of unravelling the sources of Céline's Modernist aesthetic an easy one, not least because, as a writer who abandoned, at least temporarily, full-time education at the age of 14, he presents all the enigma of the autodidact, with a rich but often arbitrarily assembled culture deriving from the French secondary syllabus, and also sources in Germany and Britain. Complex as the nature of Céline's cultural formation is, however, it is essential to reposition him in a definable and recognizable intellectual and artistic context, in which the post-First World War *nouveau mal du siècle*, the influence of Nietzsche and the role of Montmartre as a Parisian cultural centre are all key elements.

What further complicates the task of Célinian biography is the highly relative relationship which its subject has with the truth: from the very earliest interviews after the publication of *Voyage au bout de la nuit*, Céline was at pains to create a personality, often demonstrably at variance with the facts, but which corresponded to the expectations of the interlocutor and the imaginary biography he wished to create. As Robert Poulet cruelly put it, by the end of his life 'he lied a lot, convinced that he owed nothing to anyone, not even the truth.'[10] This process is not merely one of circumstantial fabrication, but of a consistent attempt to modify or deny reality: from the juvenile adoption of the pseudo-aristocracy of the 'Des Touches' lineage to the more sinister denial of complicity in collaboration. Here the biographical process of modification and denial corresponds to the procedure of transposition, so central to the novels: that bending of reality in order to create an aesthetically satisfying and plausible effect, outlined at the end of his career in the *Entretiens avec le Professeur Y*. It is precisely for this reason that the novels cannot ever be used as evidence in the construction of the Célinian biography, tempting as the possibility may appear in, for example, *Mort à crédit*. Even the final 'chronicle' which is *D'un château l'autre* consciously expropriates the possibilities of the medieval chronicle to deliver the 'real' truth through an invention or deformation of the historical facts. It is also why, in spite of the very rich results yielded by the work of, for example, Deleuze and Guattari, a psychoanalytical study of the author is fraught with difficulties.

For these reasons, it has therefore appeared appropriate to begin with the one firm ground which exists in both Céline's biography and his fiction, which is the sense of place and space. There are few writers in French fiction, including Balzac and Zola, who have such a precise and well-developed appreciation of the importance of urban space and who have been so gifted in its exploitation for their fictional needs. In particular, three loci recur: the artisanal and commercial heart of Paris in the second and third *arrondissements*, in which Céline was brought up and where he situated *Mort à crédit*; those industrial suburbs to the north and west of the capital, where he was born, where he worked and where he died: Courbevoie, Clichy, Sartrouville, Bezons and Meudon, which constitute the Célinian social heartland; and, back in the centre, yet not wholly part of it, the Parisian 'village' and artistic community of Montmartre, which played such a role in shaping his aesthetic, and to which due tribute is paid in *Voyage au bout de la nuit* and *Féerie pour une autre fois*. It is true that London is nostalgically evoked in *Guignol's Band*, and Germany in the trilogy, yet this narrow urban landscape of the imagination becomes Céline's fictional territory, just as powerfully as Faulkner's Yoknapatawpha County. The 'lieu de mémoire' becomes his 'lieu de création': the place where he began, where he ended his journey, and which serves as the foundations of the novels.

This study has benefited from the advice and help over a long period of time of members of the Société des Etudes Céliniennes, in particular Jean-Pierre Dauphin, Henri Godard, Colin Nettelbeck and Merlin Thomas, who guided me in my early work on Céline. I should also record my gratitude to the librarians and staff of the following libraries: the British Library, the Bibliothèque Nationale, the Institut Mémoires de l'Edition Contemporaine, the Institut de l'Histoire du Temps Présent, the Bibliothèque Historique de la Ville de Paris and the Bibliothèque Municipale de Clichy-la-Garenne. I should also thank the Librarian and staff of the Hallward Library at the University of Nottingham, and the University itself for its support for the project in the form of generous study leave and research funding.

1

A Parisian Childhood

I Courbevoie

Writing in 1957 from the semi-reclusion of Meudon, the narrator Céline of
D'un château l'autre ponders on the circularity and lack of success of his
life, recalling his birth just a kilometre down-stream in the suburb of
Courbevoie, just the other side of the Bois de Boulogne: 'To be honest, just
between ourselves, I'm finishing up even worse than I began . . . Not that I
began very well . . . I was born, as I've kept saying, in Courbevoie, Seine . . .
I'll say it again for the thousandth time . . . and after a lot of coming and
going I'm really ending up worse than ever.'[1] Céline was born at four in
the afternoon on 27 May 1894 as Louis-Ferdinand Destouches in the
family home at number 12 Rampe du Pont in Courbevoie, the son of an
insurance-company clerk, Ferdinand-Auguste Destouches, and Marguerite-
Louise-Céline Guillou, a lace-worker who ran a precarious fashion and
lingerie shop beneath the family apartment.

Courbevoie lies on the western side of the Pont de Neuilly and has now
been all but subsumed into the 1960s development of La Défense. In the
1890s it was in a state of transition: it still retained traces of its earlier life
as a rural village, with the vineyards, windmills and the *guinguettes* on the
banks of the Seine which had been visited by Parisians in search of rest and
entertainment, but it had also become a thriving commercial and industrial
suburb, a port about to be engulfed by the city on the opposite bank.[2] Thus
began a curious and possibly self-willed feature of Céline's career, which
was marked by frequent, in some respects constant, contact with the industrial suburbs which grew up in the last quarter of the nineteenth century
around Paris and which, as the *banlieue rouge* or *ceinture rouge*, constituted
the bastion of the French Communist Party until the 1970s: his work as a
doctor in Clichy, transposed as La Garenne-Rancy in *Voyage au bout de la
nuit*, from 1927 to 1936, his post in Sartrouville in 1940 and his subsequent

work in Bezons during the Occupation, and his retirement after exile in Denmark to Meudon, overlooking the Renault plant at Boulogne-Billancourt. Certainly Céline, as he suggests at the beginning of *D'un château l'autre*, was increasingly insistent on both his allegiance to the Parisian suburbs and his origins in Courbevoie. He was, for example, particularly proud that the actress Arletty, who became a close friend in the 1950s, had come from the same suburb. As he wrote in 1947 to Albert Paraz, 'Arletty, my friend, is also my neighbour: she was born in Courbevoie too, a bit lower down the Rampe du Pont.'[3] And Arletty herself returned the compliment: on hearing of the charges being brought against Céline for collaboration, she declared: 'Céline cannot be a traitor . . . he's from Courbevoie!'[4] although she was also careful to puncture Céline's depiction of the town as a working-class settlement: 'His origins were bourgeois. That must not be forgotten.'[5] Céline's emphasis on his origins in itself provides some clue to his anxiety to depict himself as an industrial suburban writer: not only were the Parisian suburbs a privileged locus of urban change and the subject of Impressionist painting, as, incidentally, was Montmartre, they were also the repository of authentic Parisian, artisanal and working-class values when the capital itself had become both gentrified and cosmopolitan. The claim to suburban credentials, therefore, is at one and the same time a claim to social and moral authenticity, with an accompanying language and voice.

If Céline was subsequently to exploit the connotations of his Parisian suburban connections, he was equally at pains to emphasize from relatively early on the Breton origins of both his parents, which enabled him to cultivate a Celtic mysticism and poetry resolutely at odds with the French classical literary tradition. Yet, if both parents had Breton origins, their backgrounds were very different. On his mother's side, the Guillou family, although originally Breton, were second-generation Parisians: Marguerite's father, Jean-Jacques Guillou, was born in the twelfth *arrondissement* on 6 April 1847, and became a coppersmith. He married Céline's grandmother, Céline Lesjean, a bootmaker, on 21 August 1868, and died in 1879, leaving her with two children: Marguerite, born on 10 September 1868, and Julien, always known as Louis, born in 1874. The family lived in Ménilmontant until the death of Jean-Jacques and then moved to the Rue de Provence in the ninth *arrondissement*, where Céline Guillou opened an 'antique shop specializing in old lace'.[6]

The grandmother was to be an important figure in the life of Céline's family: once widowed, her hard work enabled her to buy her own shop 'Antiquités, dentelles et porcelaines'[7] at the junction of the Rue Lafayette and the Rue de Provence and effectively to move her family from the working class to the petite bourgeoisie of commerce. As she acquired more money, she invested it in property: first in three new houses in the burgeoning suburb of Asnières and, in 1899, in an eight-roomed house in the Rue de Châteaudun in the same suburb.[8] Not only did this investment bring relative financial security to her and her children, but, on her death at the age of 57 in 1904, both Marguerite and Louis received a substantial inheritance. As Philippe Alméras reminds us,[9] this inheritance gave Céline's parents a financial security which is considerably at variance with the depiction of the economic state of the family in *Mort à crédit* and Céline's subsequent claims in the interviews and correspondence after the publication of *Voyage au bout de la nuit*, when it suited him to portray his childhood as impoverished and cruel. At the same time, the importance of the grandmother in Céline's emotional development can be gauged by his choice of her name as his literary pseudonym.

If the trajectory of the maternal side of Céline's family is resolutely upward, that of the paternal side is almost exactly inverse, from provincial bourgeois respectability to bohemian *déclassement*. Ferdinand-Auguste Destouches, always known as Fernand (although it is perhaps worth bearing in mind that his forenames provide the names for both central protagonists of *Mort à crédit*), was descended from the minor nobility of the Cotentin Peninsula, the Des Touches de Lentiellère, the owners of a farm near Coutances. The Des Touches were therefore technically Norman rather than Breton, although the family split in the eighteenth century, one branch moving to Germany, the other to Fougères in Brittany. Céline's father liked to think that the family was related to the Chevalier Des Touches, the counter-revolutionary hero of Barbey d'Aurevilly's novel of 1864,[10] and Céline himself in his twenties subscribed to this myth, signing himself Des Touches or des Touches, and writing to his family from Africa with the news that: 'I have received an interesting letter from the Société des Antiquaires de Normandie, congratulating me for being a descendant of the des Touches and inviting me to one of their meetings at my convenience.'[11] During the same African adventure, he wrote to his childhood friend Simone Saintu: 'the day when, like Tircis, I contemplate retirement, I will definitely go to Normandy. In the region of Coutances there is an old family château which will probably be able to shelter my family and a few faithful friends.'[12] In one sense, this fixation with a noble lineage is probably no more than the reaction of an awkward adolescent or young man to a milieu and parents of which he is slightly ashamed. On another level, however, it translates at a very early age a constant trait in Céline's character, which is an unalterable belief in both his own superiority and his own rightness: the author of a first novel convinced that it will win the Prix Goncourt, the signatory of the anti-Semitic pamphlets who never questions the justice of his cause. It is also this which makes it very difficult to classify Céline politically: paradoxically for a writer who adopts, or appears to adopt, a deliberately populist style, he is observing the world in which he lives from a position of some considerable superiority. Not that such an attitude implies aloofness: like one of the writers of his generation whom he most resembles, Georges Bernanos, described by Roger Nimier as a 'Spanish Grandee', his observation of the folly of the modern world can be expressed only through intense anger.[13]

The Breton side of the Destouches family eventually settled in Vannes, where Thomas Destouches, who had abandoned his first wife in Fougères, established himself as Administrator of the Department of the Morbihan. Among this branch of the family is to be found the distinguished pharmacist Théodore Destouches, whose career, as François Gibault notes, presents some uncanny similarities with the medical career of Céline, including common research projects on quinine,[14] and, in particular, Théodore's cousin and Céline's paternal grandfather, Auguste. Auguste was the most illustrious of the Destouches, the model of what the family was in its greatness and what it could be again. As Céline wrote to Simone Saintu: 'My family is proud to count among its members an *agrégé* in French Grammar, who has always been cited as an example to me, at a time when people bothered to.'[15] In the preface to *Guignol's Band*, the narrator confides to the reader:

> I must confess to you that my grandfather, named Auguste Destouches, taught rhetoric, was even a professor of that at the *lycée* in Le Havre around 1855 . . . I've got all my grandfather's writings, all his files and his drafts, drawers full of them! Ah, they're wonderful! He used to write the Préfet's speeches, in a wonderful style, I can assure you! . . . He won all the medals of the Académie Française. I keep them with feeling. He's my ancestor . . . that's how I know the French language![16]

Auguste Destouches was born in Vannes in 1835 and studied at the Collège du Havre, before obtaining the teaching post of *maître élémentaire* in Rennes. Here he became the private secretary of the Préfet of the Department of Ille et Vilaine and embarked on a successful career as a poet.[17] In 1860, however, he met and fell in love with Hermance Caroline Delhaye, who was to become Céline's grandmother, the daughter of a rich exporter from Le Havre. Since she did not wish to leave her native city, he agreed to leave his post with the Préfet, and went back to his old academic career at the *lycée* in Le Havre. Despite several failures in the *licence* examination at Caen, he passed in 1867 the newly instituted *agrégation de l'enseignement spécial*, and his place in Le Havre society was assured.[18]

This brilliant career, and indeed the success of the Destouches family, was cut short by Auguste's premature death at the age of 39 in 1874 from typhoid fever. Auguste and Hermance had one daughter and four sons, including Céline's father Fernand, born in 1865. After the death of Auguste, Hermance rapidly resumed her social life in Le Havre, and, not finding it exciting enough, decided to move to Paris in 1875, in order to cultivate a career in the capital's literary salons.[19] She left her four sons as boarders at the Lycée du Havre and took her daughter Amélie, who was an accomplished pianist, with her to Paris. Very rapidly Hermance's fortune was exhausted, and she was forced to live on hand-outs from her daughter's lovers, for Amélie, far from making her reputation as a pianist, led an increasingly scandalous life as a *demi-mondaine* across Europe, before marrying a Romanian diplomat, Zénon Zawirski. She died in Angers in 1950.[20]

Fernand, on the other hand, neglected by his mother and abandoned in the Lycée du Havre, showed little academic ability. In 1884, he left Le Havre for Paris, living with his sister Amélie in the house in Courbevoie rented for her by one of her lovers, and enrolled at the Lycée Condorcet, where he showed the same lack of aptitude as he had in Le Havre. He appears to have combined frequent truancy with academic weakness and passed only the first half of the *baccalauréat* before leaving school in 1885.[21] Céline's father, therefore, unlike Auguste in *Mort à crédit*, was not even a full *bachelier*, and certainly not a *licencié*, as Céline subsequently claimed. In 1960, in an interview with Jean Guénot and Jacques Darribehaude, he tried to explain why his father had never entered the teaching profession: 'The poor man, this is what happened: to go into teaching he needed to take the *licence d'enseignement*, whereas he only had a *licence libre*, and he couldn't take it because he didn't have any money: his father had died, leaving his wife with five children.'[22]

Embroidering on the known reality is a constant feature of Céline's public utterances, and one which has rendered the task of the biographer increasingly difficult. Right from the early interviews on the publication of *Voyage au bout de la nuit*, however, there is a very clear pattern which continues unabated: not only is Céline attempting to enhance an often more mundane reality so that it becomes more attractive, particularly to a specifically chosen audience, but there is also the need to deny the reality of the social situation in which he was brought up. In some cases, when it suits him to adopt a populist persona or the role of victim, he exaggerates the modesty of his upbringing; at other times, as with the 'des Touches' affectation in his early twenties, there is the need to assert a bourgeois or even pseudo-aristocratic identity. Either way, Céline was not comfortable with the undramatic reality of a modest but unthreatening petit-bourgeois family background.

Fernand Destouches left the Lycée Condorcet on 20 March 1885 to do his military service, signing on for five years in the 27th Artillery Regiment, a decision which appears to testify to a lack of ambition or clear ideas regarding a career. Two years later, he was promoted to the rank of *maréchal des logis* (the equivalent of sergeant in the cavalry and the artillery), which he retained until he left the army in September 1889. The following year, he entered the Phénix insurance company as a clerk, a post he occupied without interruption or promotion until his retirement in 1927. At the same time he met Marguerite Guillou, whom he finally married, against the strong opposition of her mother and brother, at Asnières on 8 July 1893. Although, as François Gibault comments, Fernand, the scion of Norman and Breton nobility and the son of a famous provincial *agrégé*, must have hesitated before marrying beneath him,[23] it was in fact the Guillou family, hard-working, thrifty and increasingly wealthy, who were horrified at the prospect of Marguerite's marriage with an amiable *raté*.

Nor did the early years of the marriage appear to prove them wrong. Desperate to have their own business in addition to Fernand's position with the Phénix, the couple bought the small *Modes et Lingerie* shop on the Rampe du Pont in Courbevoie where Céline was born. Since her family suspected that Marguerite might have incipient tuberculosis, and since Courbevoie was considered an unhealthy spot, the baby was sent to a wet-nurse, first in Voisines, near Sens in the Department of the Yonne, and then in yet another of Céline's Parisian suburbs, Puteaux, where the parents could visit him more easily. As Céline wrote to Paraz in 1947: 'I was brought up in Puteaux. Sentier des Bergères! With a wet-nurse. My mother was too ill. You could see all of Paris from there. Those are my first memories as a young child,'[24] though since he was not yet 3 years old when he left in May 1897, the memories may well have been acquired with hindsight. In fact, he was not to return to Courbevoie at all. Despite all Marguerite's efforts, a shop selling *Modes et Lingerie* on the Rampe du Pont in the rapidly industri-alizing port area of Courbevoie was doomed to failure, and in April 1897 the couple were forced to sell the business.[25] They moved into an apartment at number 19, Rue de Babylone, in the Left-Bank seventh *arrondissement*, where their baby came to join them in May, and Marguerite abandoned her independence for a job in a hat-shop in the Rue de Rivoli. She had not, however, given up her ambition for independence and, after a brief spell in the Rue Ganneron in Montmartre, from November 1898 to July 1899, the family took over the shop of a *Marchand d'objets de curiosité en boutique* at number 67, Passage de Choiseul, between the Opéra and the Bourse in the second *arrondissement*. In the Spring of 1904, they moved across the Passage to number 64, where Marguerite set up a shop specializing in lace, luxury lingerie and antiques. It was in the Passage de Choiseul, transposed into the Passage des Bérésinas in *Mort à crédit*, in the very heart of commercial Paris, that Céline was to spend his childhood.

II THE AUTUMN OF CENTRAL PARIS

As Philippe Alméras comments: 'Young Louis, who had spent three days of his life in Courbevoie and who had come to Paris at the age of three, now lived in a quarter bounded by the Salle Drouot, the Bourse, the Avenue de l'Opéra and the Palais-Royal, a village, of which the Passage was the high street.'[26] In fact, this 'village' into which Céline came in 1899 and in which he grew up was a significant geographical entity in the urban fabric of Paris at a particularly important moment in its development. More precisely, it was a district faced with irreversible change and the definitive loss of its traditional population, part of what Anthony Sutcliffe terms 'the Autumn of Central Paris'.[27]

It has become a commonplace to refer to the last half of the nineteenth century as a period in which Paris underwent a process of *embourgeoisement*. As early as 1948, Philippe Ariès, in his *Histoire des populations françaises et de leurs attitudes devant la vie depuis le XVIIIe siècle*, identified a shift in the demography of the capital from 1845 to 1931 by which the traditional artisanal and working-class population declined rapidly, replaced by non-industrial, white-collar workers needed to service an increasingly sophisticated and bureaucratic society.[28] This process, aided by Haussmann's planning policy during the Second Empire and by the growth of heavy industry, particularly the automobile industry, in the suburbs at the turn of the twentieth century, resulted in rises in rents and prices which definitively excluded the traditional inner-city population and transformed the capital from a bastion of political radicalism to one of conservatism.[29] Even a historian who contests this view as over-simplistic, like Lenard R. Berlanstein, cannot contradict the fact that, on the basis of the 1911 census, there had been an almost total colonization of the inner city, particularly the most central *arrondissements*, by white-collar workers, with a corresponding exodus of manual workers to the outer *arrondissements* like Ménilmontant or Belleville, or further, to the burgeoning industrial suburbs.[30] What is useful about Berlanstein's thesis, however, is his reminder that the *embourgeoisement* theory often depends on an overly rigorous interpretation of the *employé* as middle-class, when most of them were relatively lowly-paid white-collar workers in department stores and offices in both the public and private sectors.[31]

It is clear, however, that, by moving into the second *arrondissement* in the last year of the nineteenth century, Céline's parents moved into an unusually sensitive context, of which Céline himself was acutely aware, without necessarily being victimized by it, and which he exploited with considerable knowledge and dexterity in his work, most notably in *Mort à crédit*. Not only did they enter a city whose population was shifting, but they both exercised trades which were problematic and vulnerable to an accelerating population-shift.

Marguerite Destouches had chosen to set herself up as a shopkeeper, when her experience in Courbevoie should already have indicated just how fragile that trade could be. The Second Empire had seen the growth of the department stores: Boucicaut's Au Bon Marché, opened in 1852 and close to the family apartment on the Rue de Babylone, Chauchard's Le Louvre (1855), Jaluzot's Printemps (1864), Le Coin de Rue (1864), A la Belle Jardinière (1866–7) and the Cognacq-Jay's A la Samaritaine (1869).[32] These new arrivals undoubtedly had an effect on the stability and viability of *le petit commerce*, particularly since, by the turn of the century, they had introduced credit schemes, by which customers, in exchange for fixed monthly payments, could acquire credit coupons.[33] As examples of stores offering this facility, Berlanstein lists not only prestigious establishments like *Dufayel* or *Samaritaine*, but 'more mundane stores, like *Place Clichy*, *Ville de Saint-Denis*, *Petit Saint-Thomas*, *Aux Classes Laborieuses*, and several hundred smaller shops.'[34] The effect of this competition from the department stores with their system of easy credit would have been felt particularly in Marguerite Destouches' chosen trade, lace and lingerie. Ariès records that the traditional Parisian craft of *fils et tissus*, which included luxury lace-goods, was established in the capital around 1850[35] and had maintained a workforce of 160,000 until 1906.[36] Thereafter, the *fils et tissus* trade, like all Parisian artisanal crafts, effectively collapsed, falling by 80 per cent from 1906 to 1931, possibly as the result of the introduction of artificial fibres from 1891 onwards.[37] Berlanstein also connects this decline with the increasing de-skilling of the Parisian artisans, with the proliferation of *demi-ouvriers* and *petites mains* to undertake relatively unskilled work on an almost assembly-line basis.[38]

Nevertheless, as Yves Lequin reminds us, although the decline of the traditional Parisian artisan was a fact, the process affecting the Parisian *boutique* was a good deal more complicated: 'In 1887, A. de Foville announced that "the huge bazaar will kill off the small shop..." He was wrong, and to be able to live out a comfortable old age was already an image of success for most working-class people. With the *patronat* flexing its muscles and the *artisanat* disappearing, the shop remained the sole means at hand of upward mobility, of getting out of the working class.'[39] It was for this reason that 'from 1879 to 1939, the number of shops in France doubled.'[40] Yet this is in some way a misleading figure, for 'at least as many small businesses died as were born, and each economic crisis multiplied the bankruptcies.'[41] In other words, while the *boutique* remained a permanant feature of French urban life, it still constituted a highly risky career for those willing to undertake it. That there should have been so many willing to take the risk, including Céline's parents, is explained by Lequin's concluding comments on the crucial role of status within the inner city:

> The standard of living, the concrete working conditions, the block on upward mobility are of less importance than the hopes which shopkeepers cherish. In the heart of the cities abandoned by their traditional patriciates, the shop-keepers – and to a lesser extent the artisans who still stay there – are at the top of the heap and they tend to confuse the fundamental place which they occupy in their urban decor with the first place in the social hierarchy. Even if they dream of making their son a civil-servant...[42]

Marguerite Destouches dreamt of making her son into a floor-walker in a department store. Céline himself, by opting for medicine, had chosen what was still in the 1920s what Lequin calls 'the model of social success.'[43]

If Marguerite Destouches, as a shopkeeper concerned with the trade of *fils et tissus*, found herself at an important turning-point in the economic and social evolution of Paris, her husband, as an *employé*, occupied a no less significant social role. As we have seen, Fernand Destouches entered the Phénix insurance company, situated near the Passage de Choiseul, in 1890. He remained with the company until his retirement at the age of 58 in

1923, and was only promoted to the grade of *sous-chef de bureau* in 1922, with a salary of 625 francs per month.[44] In fact, that promotion itself may have been merely the result of a common practice in companies at the time to enhance their long-term employees' pension rights just before retirement.[45] Fernand Destouches therefore joined that army of white-collar workers who displaced the traditional Parisian artisans from the centre of the city, but who constituted not so much a new bourgeoisie as a white-collar working class. As Berlanstein argues, three-fourths of *employés'* posts in 1907–8 'offered less than 1800 francs a year, less than the wages a skilled labourer might have expected if he worked regularly'.[46] And Lequin concurs: in spite of the caricatural image of the lazy and well-fed civil servant,

> The condition of the *employés* was not uniformly enviable: amongst the conscripts of the 1880s, their height was barely greater than that of workers, the number of them rejected was greater, and the image of the humble and bent clerk does not just belong to literature . . . In Bordeaux, right in the middle of the Belle Epoque, there were more victims of tuberculosis amongst *employés* than amongst factory workers.[47]

If, as Lequin argues, the working conditions of the *employé* were often harsh and uncertain,[48] the jobs became more insecure at the turn of the century with the employment of women and the introduction of new technology. As Berlanstein points out:

> New office machinery had the potential to disrupt established clerical routines but drew fewer comments than did the entry of women. The impact of typewriters was to alter traditional channels of training and promotion, especially in small offices. Letter-copying had been the usual, entry-level post for a young clerk, and through it he was expected to learn about the business and advance to more important positions. With machine copying, this task became a permanent job, usually for women. Young men had to start in posts of greater responsibility, requiring more extensive preparation. Clerks who had little but good penmanship to recommend them had a new career barrier but failed to make their complaints heard.[49]

Similarly, the invention of the mechanical adding-machine threatened further the security of the *employé*, yet, as Berlanstein adds, often these new innovations were not systematically exploited and 'the problem of male employees was not competition from women or machines but decelerating growth in clerical employment and an increased hard-headedness among employers.'[50] Nevertheless, Fernand Destouches, as a *bachelier* (or at least half-*bachelier*) in a large Parisian insurance company, was potentially vulnerable, not merely to competition from women and the introduction of new technology, but also to the inflation of qualifications at entry which these implied. That Céline was acutely conscious of the importance of these developments among the *employés* at the turn of the century is evidenced by the depiction of Auguste's grappling with the typewriter in *Mort à crédit* and the rivalry with new graduate entrants into *La Coccinelle*.

If Celine was brought up in 'the Autumn of Central Paris', where both his mother and father constituted deeply sensitive indicators of social change, the very locus of that upbringing, the Passage de Choiseul, was highly significant. As Walter Benjamin points out, in *Paris, The Capital of the Nineteenth Century*,

> Most of the Paris arcades came into being during the decade and a half which followed 1822. The first condition of their emergence was the boom in the textile trade. The *magasins de nouveauté*, the first establishments that kept large stocks on the premises, began to appear. They were the forerunners of the department stores . . . The arcades were centres of the luxury-goods trade. The manner in which they were fitted out displayed Art in the service of the salesman. Contemporaries never tired of admiring them. For long afterwards they remained a point of attraction for foreigners.[51]

For Benjamin, these arcades were essential to Fourier's definition of a nineteenth-century utopia: 'In the arcades, Fourier had seen the architectonic canon for the phalanstery. Their reactionary transformation at Fourier's hands was characteristic: while they originally served social ends, with him they became dwelling-places. The phalanstery became a city of arcades.'[52] The observations are important for two reasons: Céline's parents moved into what had been the concrete expression of a boom in the luxury-goods trade which became a utopia. The problem is that they were indeed in an arcade become dwelling-place, but a dwelling-place that was no longer a utopia, only a relic of its decline. By the 1900s, it is by no means clear that the arcades were the 'high streets' of their quartiers, as Alméras asserts for the Passage de Choiseul; they were certainly well on the way to becoming those intriguing backwaters of old curiosity shops adopted by the Surrealists in the 1920s.[53]

III PASSAGE DE CHOISEUL

The Passage de Choiseul runs north from the Rue des Petits-Champs to the Rue Saint-Augustin in the *quartier* of the Bourse, a *quartier* characterized by a mixture of business activity, including the Bourse itself, the Banque de France and major financial institutions, the elegance of the Avenue de l'Opéra, the Rue de la Paix and the Grands Boulevards. It comprises a dense network of narrow streets housing the remains of Parisian artisanal and shopkeeping activity, and numerous types of entertainment. These ranged from the high cultural – the Opéra itself and the Comédie Française – to the popular: the Robert Houdin cinema on the Boulevard Montmartre, now the Musée Grévin, where Céline saw the early Méliès films with his grandmother, the music-hall L'Olympia, where he saw Harry Houdini in 1901,[54] and Offenbach's Théâtre des Bouffes-Parisiennes on the Rue Monsigny, whose stage-door opened on to the Passage de Choiseul. The Passage itself housed Emile Weil's gun-shop, two bookshops, the *pâtissier* Charvin, a pipe-shop, Dorange's carpet and furniture shop, and the Dones couple, who ran a business in rubber goods and surgical instruments.[55] Marguerite Destouches' shops, therefore, specializing in lace goods and antique furniture, were part of a small commercial community selling non-essential, often artisan-produced goods: the epitome of 'articles de Paris'.

Number 64 Passage de Choiseul, to which the family moved in 1904, consisted of the shop itself on the ground floor, with a cellar below. Above, was a kitchen-cum-dining-room, and above that the parents' bedroom, from which a small staircase led to a third floor on which were located Céline's bedroom and the toilet.[56] This bedroom, which was above the roof-line, was the only room in the establishment which had access to fresh air. These were admittedly relatively modest quarters, with no heating, but by no means exceptional for tradespeople of that period: indeed, for a child to have his own bedroom was something of a luxury. What is important is that the material conditions in which Céline was brought up at this period of his life are considerably at variance with the depiction of Ferdinand's childhood in the Passage des Bérésinas in *Mort à crédit*.

Nor is there any evidence that the relationship with his parents was anything other than affectionate or that the father-figure of *Mort à crédit*, Auguste, is directly derived from Fernand Destouches, though they may have shared conservative political opinions. As Philippe Alméras reminds us, this was the period of the Dreyfus Case, and:

> Paris was patriotic, and anti-Dreyfus amongst the working-class and the petite-bourgeoisie. The Case was an attack on the army and an excuse for doing away with the Deuxième Bureau. Staff officers resigned and the military schools saw a drop in intake. In the Municipal Elections of 1900, the lists of Edouard Drumont, the author of *La france juive*, gained a majority in the City Council. In the anticlerical struggle waged by the Radicals, with the *Inventaires* and the *Séparation*, the role of the Freemasons became clear. It became blindingly obvious with the *Affaire André*: the Freemasons were targeting the senior army officers, they were everywhere![57]

François Gibault describes Fernand Destouches as typical in his political opinions of the Parisian petite-bourgeoisie of the period: a reader of *La Patrie* and of Drumont and a fervent supporter of *revanche* against Germany.[58] There is no detailed evidence, however, of any further political views, and Céline would appear to have been raised in an ideological milieu fairly characteristic of its class and its time.

On 18 December 1904, the grandmother Céline Guillou died, the first major drama in Céline's life. She had been a frequent and close companion to her grandson, introducing him, as we have seen, to the early cinema and the music-hall, and guiding his first excursions into popular reading with *Les Aventures illustrées*, reflected in *La Légende du Roi Krogold* in *Mort à crédit*.[59] On her death she left him her dog, Bobs. In return, Céline's choice of his grandmother's name as a pseudonym reflects, not just a desire to position himself and his work in a particular class, the Parisian petite-bourgeoisie, and a particular period, the Belle Epoque, but a testimony of affection.

For the family as a whole, Céline Guillou's death had far-reaching consequences. She died a relatively wealthy woman, and her inheritance, divided between her son Louis and her daughter, enabled Fernand and Marguerite Destouches to enjoy a lifestyle and financial security which contrasts radically with the misery of the family depicted in *Mort à crédit*. Céline's later memories, often designed to protect a legend or establish a persona, dwell upon the financial hardships. In a letter to the pianist Lucienne Delforge of 1936, he evokes his mother: '[She] is still working. I remember the Passage when she was younger, the enormous pile of lace to be repaired, the huge mountain of lace which always covered the table – a mountain of work for a few francs. It was never finished. It was so we could eat. I had nightmares about it at night, so did she,'[60] and in the interviews with Jean Guénot and Jacques Darribehaude of 1960, he emphasizes: 'My mother always said to me: "You little wretch, if there weren't any rich people . . . we wouldn't have anything to eat. Rich people have got responsibilities." My mother venerated rich people.'[61] To Robert Poulet he confided: 'My mother was a repairer of old lace. That's why I've remained a worker, nothing but a worker.'[62] He came to believe this myth so that, towards the end of his life, he attempted to persuade his former wife, Edith Follet, that his mother had sold lace at Meudon station, to which she retorted: 'Really, Louis, who do you think you're talking to?'[63] The fact remains that at the end of 1907 Céline's parents were able to move to a bourgeois apartment at number 11 in the nearby Rue Marsolier and by 1908 Fernand Destouches' financial advisor, Louis Montourcy, estimated the family's fortune at 150,000 francs.[64] The family spent their summer holidays in Dieppe, and Fernand Destouches even had a small boat, *Le Tom* at Ablon. François Gibault's enticing formula: '[Céline] was brought up by bourgeois amongst the people, according to aristocratic principles and with proletarian means,'[65] was only half true after Céline Guillou's death: the aristocratic principles may have persisted and the *quartier* around the Passage may still have been artisanal, but after 1904 Céline was brought up in the less dramatic, but undoubtedly more comfortable security of the Parisian lower bourgeoisie.

An indication of the family's changed circumstances is to be found in Céline's education. At the age of 6, on 1 October 1900, he was enrolled at the State-run Ecole Communale in the nearby Rue de Louvois, opposite the Bibliothèque Nationale, and he remained in this bastion of the Third Republic's education policy until 1905. As François Gibault records, Céline's performance was not noticeably different from that of his father in Le Havre. The *Directeur* wrote in his report: 'An intelligent child, but with an excessive laziness fostered by the weakness of his parents. He was capable of very good work with firm guidance. He was taught well, but brought up very laxly,'[66] a comment largely confirmed by a reminiscence of a friend from days in Rennes, Marcel Brochard: 'It is true, Louis, that you were an uncontrollable child, undisciplined, drunk on freedom, and that you received slaps and beatings which were certainly deserved.'[67] In February 1905, however, the parents removed him from the State system and enrolled him in the private and Catholic Ecole Saint-Joseph des Tuileries in the Rue du 29 Juillet, ten minutes' walk from the Passage Choiseul. The fees were 50 francs a month, plus additional expenses. According to Gibault, this change of school was the brainchild of Marguerite Destouches, who wanted Céline, who was just approaching his First Communion, to have a good Catholic education.[68] At the same time, it guaranteed a highly disciplined environment with relatively small classes of eighteen or so. This seems to have had some beneficial effect, since Céline's performance improved and his marks were normally above the average for his class. Nor do there appear to have been any problems of discipline.[69] This bourgeois education was supplemented by private piano lessons after school, in the course of which he met the young girl with whom he was to correspond regularly during his African journey, Simone Saintu, and which furnished him with a knowledge of music which was to inform his later work.

At the end of the school year, however, in 1906, Céline's parents decided to return him to the State sector, and he completed his primary education at the Ecole Communale at number 11 Rue d'Argenteuil, just off the Avenue de l'Opéra. Quite why the parents should have taken this decision remains obscure: Gibault suggests that it may have been due to a combination of a renewal of financial insecurity, although this is unsubstantiated, and Fernand's insistence on a 'Republican' education for his son in the context of the triumph of the Third Republic's anticlericalism in the early years of the century.[70] It is also highly probable that the cessation of a cosseted private education and a return to the Ecole Communale conformed to Fernand's and Marguerite's plans for Céline's career, which did not involve continuation to secondary education or the university, but was directed instead towards commerce. Be that as it may, he received the *Certificat d'études* in July 1907, together with the *Marie-Amélie Debat prix de bonne conduite*, and completed his full-time education. It is important for an understanding of Céline's later work to bear in mind that, for a twentieth-century French writer, his formal education was rudimentary and brief, even though he was later to take an accelerated version of the *baccalauréat*. Commenting on *Féerie pour une autre fois*, for example, Henri Godard notes that the stock in trade of Céline's literary references 'comes from a common fund of culture which is in the main that of the old *Certificat d'études*, no doubt enriched by memories of reading done for the preparation of the first Baccalauréat.'[71] Unlike writers of the same generation and similar, albeit less fortunate, backgrounds, like Jean Guéhenno or Louis Guilloux, Céline did not acquire the breadth of formal literary culture obtained in the *lycées*. It is perhaps for this reason that a constant target of his formidable anger was that group of privileged people who had benefited from a *lycée* education, and that one recurrent form of his mythomania concerned working on the *lycée* syllabus at night, in spite of his parents and his employers, leading to his passing the *baccalauréat* in 1912 at the age of 18, when in fact he passed it much later.[72] In fact, his cultural formation is composed of the much more exciting mixture of the syllabus for the *Certificat*, comprising essentially the French classic authors, with the rogue acquisitions of the autodidact – not merely from French culture, but from Britain and Germany as well.

IV Germany and England

In an interview with Louis Pauwels and André Brissaud in 1959, Céline, who still insisted that his father had the *licence*,[73] and, incidentally, that he worked for the insurance company 'Le Pays' in the Rue Lafayette, remembered his parents' plans for his career: 'My mother's ambition was to turn me into a buyer for a department store. There was no higher job in her mind. As for my father, he didn't want me to continue my studies because he thought they led to poverty.'[74] What the parents did believe, however, was that the acquisition of foreign languages, particularly German and English, would be of inestimable value in a career in commerce, and in this they would appear to be no more than reflecting a reality of the time. In his study of *employés'* standards of living, Lenard Berlanstein comments: 'Yet, even jobs requiring experience and special expertise did not entail particularly large pay. A bookkeeper who knew both English and German 'perfectly' was offered only 150 to 200 francs a month,'[75] and the implication is that this information, taken from the magazine *L'Employé. Organe du syndicat des employés du commerce et de l'industrie*, reflects particular job specifications of the period, in which knowledge of German and English were requirements for certain types of white-collar post. With this in mind, Céline's parents decided that he should learn these two languages by spending periods of time upon leaving school in both Germany and England.

Thus it was that, at the end of August 1907, Fernand and Marguerite Destouches accompanied their son to the small town of Diepholz, near Hanover, where he lodged with the headmaster of the Mittelschule, Hugo Schmidt. The visit, which lasted an entire school year, until July 1908, appears to have been a success, and Gibault notes that: 'Hugo Schmidt was struck by the ease with which Louis learnt German which he spoke fluently after only a few weeks in Diepholz. He considered him an excellent child and praised his liveliness, his good health and his application at work.'[76] While this report may have been slightly exaggerated regarding the speed and extent of language acquisition, the image of a gifted linguist and a cheerful and hard-working pupil conflicts strongly with the depiction of

Ferdinand's disastrous stay at Meanwell College in *Mort à crédit*: he appears to have enjoyed himself and to have profited from his studies. Moreover, there is no trace of the breakdown of relations with the parents which characterizes the novel: Fernand and Marguerite accompanied Céline to Diepholz, Marguerite returning to visit him at Toussaint (1 November), and his father at Christmas.[77] Céline himself spent the Easter holidays in Paris. Similarly, Céline's letters to his parents throughout this year spent in Germany testify to an affectionate, normal relationship. His New Year's letter, for example, begins: 'Dear Parents, it is New Year's Day. It is a holiday which, even though I'm not here with you, should cheer you, for it is with this holiday that come my New Year's wishes, but not as banal as the others. I wish you good health for ever, and I thank you from the bottom of my heart for the sacrifices that you have made for my future.'[78] Nor is there a trace of the exasperation with the parents' stinginess which informs the novel. On the contrary, as Gibault reports: 'Louis' correspondence shows a constant concern on his part with money. To make savings, to spare his parents expenditure, will remain all his life one of his characteristics.'[79]

While the parents had been impressed with Céline's progress in German, an informal examination they set for him at Easter 1908 had shown some weaknesses in grammar and the written language which justified a further spell in Germany, and in September 1908 he set off for Karlsruhe, where he was enrolled at the Realschule at number 4 Risenlohrstrasse and where he lodged with Professor Rudolph Bittrolff. He stayed until the end of December, making considerable progress with his written German and continuing to take piano lessons. The correspondence with his parents during this visit to Germany remained affectionate, though tinged with some anxieties about the family's financial state,[80] and he was happy to return to Paris on 29 December.

Two months later, on 22 February 1909 the second phase of the parents' strategy took place, with Fernand Destouches accompanying his son to Rochester, where he was enrolled in University School, run by a Mr and Mrs Toukin. From the outset, it was clear that the school was a disaster for Céline: his letters complain of poor discipline and unstimulating teaching, and particularly of insufficient food.[81] Fernand and Marguerite decided that their son should leave the school immediately and, on the pretext that his mother was ill and had to convalesce in the south, Céline left Rochester at the end of March for Pierremont Hall in Broadstairs. This school was run by Gilbert and Elizabeth Farnfield and was everything that University School was not: the rations were adequate, the teaching professional and the environment congenial. Gilbert Farnfield's letters to Fernand Destouches report on considerable progress made by Céline in English, and also list a wide range of sporting activities, including swimming, hockey, cricket, tennis and running.[82] Céline's own letters to his parents testify to the same respect and affection as those from Germany, and there is none of the acrimony and stubbornness which characterizes the protagonist of *Mort à crédit*. When Céline returned to Paris in November 1909 he had a good mastery of spoken and written English, which was to mark his later work more than the German influence. Not only is there frequent recourse to Anglicism in his work, but the contact with England gave him an original and rich scale of cultural and political references: the setting of *Guignol's Band* in London, the ambiguous Anglophobia of the pamphlets, and the constant traces of English writers as diverse as Shakespeare, Defoe, Swift, Dickens, Conrad, H. G. Wells and Kipling. The fictitious quotation of the Monmouth episode from Macaulay's *History of England* in *Voyage au bout de la nuit* must surely be the only reference to the Whig historian in twentieth-century French fiction.[83] It is these foreign borrowings, however, laid over the classic syllabus of the Ecole Communale, which help make Céline's mature writing so rich and so complex.

V COMMERCE

When Céline later recalled his early years in employment, he characteristically chose to embroider the facts and to confuse the reality of his biography with the fiction of *Mort à crédit*. In an interview with Claude Bonnefoy for *Arts*, he stated: 'I was apprenticed to a lot of people . . . Apprentices weren't paid . . . I was even told that often apprentices had to pay their employers, to be shown the trade . . . So I couldn't complain . . . I climbed floor after floor, I carried the tools, I went to get the workers from the bistro opposite . . . But at the end of six months, I was given the sack . . . They took on someone else, always for nothing.'[84] The truth is more mundane, though it is possible that he received no wages for his early apprenticeships: in fact he had a small number of jobs, for the most part in the jewellery trade, which gave him increasing experience and responsibility. On 1 January 1910 he started work as a trainee in a large draper's store, Raimon, on the corner of the Rue de Choiseul and the Rue du Quatre-Septembre, a mere hundred yards from the family home, now in the Rue Marsollier. He left seven months later on 31 July, with a satisfactory certificate of employment, and in September started work with Robert, a jeweller's shop, on the corner of the Rue Royale and the Rue Saint-Honoré.[85] He remained with Robert until 31 March 1911, leaving with a further favourable certificate, in which his employer commented: 'I have only praise for his honesty, his application and his scrupulousness. In a word, this young man is to be recommended in every aspect.'[86] Yet again, we are far from the delinquent Ferdinand of *Mort à crédit*. On leaving Robert, he remained in the jewellery trade, but changed *quartier*, moving to Henri Wagner, 'Bijouterie, Joaillerie, Ciselure, Pièces de Commande', at number 114 Rue du Temple, in the third *arrondissement*, where, according to François Gibault, he undertook more responsible tasks, such as the transport of expensive items of jewellery.[87] Wagner's, however, was in itself only a stepping-stone to the pinnacle of Céline's success in commerce, which came with his employment by

Lacloche Frères, a highly prestigious jewellery chain with a shop at number 15 Rue de la Paix, and with branches in Bond Street, Madrid, San-Sebastian, Biarritz, Aix-les-Bains and Nice.[88] It was a career in such an establishment and with such an international company that Fernand and Marguerite Destouches had dreamt of when they plotted Céline's future.

In his interview with Claude Bonnefoy, Céline recalled his days in the jewellery trade:

> They gave me everything to do . . . Cleaning the silver, watching the custom-ers' hands, walking their dogs! . . . I especially ran errands . . . I went with the salesman . . . I carried the sample-case, an enormous chest containing the models in lead of tie-pins. These tie-pins were awful . . . very complicated, allegorical and symbolic . . . That was the fashion . . . We had to walk a great deal . . . From the Place de la République to the Avenue de l'Opéra, from the Odéon to the Seine, we did all the jewellers' shops . . . we didn't sell much . . . In the evening, we finished up on the steps of the Ambigu . . . All the salesmen fetched up there . . . all poor . . . They talked shop and ex-changed leads . . . But in the heat of July, it wasn't very pleasant . . . The sample-case was very heavy.[89]

This is clearly a conflation of all his experiences as an apprentice. With Lacloche in the Rue de la Paix, it was the dog-walking and the spying on customers that he remembered most.[90] In fact, he did not remain in the Paris branch for very long and at the end of December 1911 he was transferred to the firm's shop in Nice.

This was obviously a major step, not merely in Céline's commercial career, but in his life as a whole: the moment, at the age of 17, when he effectively left the family home. François Gibault quotes from the draft of a letter from Fernand Destouches to M. Lacloche on Céline's return from Nice, in which he expresses his concern at this new departure in his son's life: 'You will understand that it was not without considerable anxiety that I resigned myself to completely abandoning to his own devices and beyond any control a seventeen-year-old boy, with already a very independent streak.'[91] During his period in Nice, Céline stayed at the Hôtel-Pension du Congrès, run by the Carpatti couple and Madame Anna Lemplé. François Gibault notes that, while he earned only 150 francs per month as an apprentice (a figure which gives the lie to Céline's own claims in the interview with Bonnefoy), his expenses in Nice were at least double this figure, so that the parents effectively had to subsidize his employment.[92] The reason for the Lacloche branch in Nice was of course the town's role as a major winter resort for the European aristocracy, as Céline recalled for Albert Paraz, with characteristic exaggeration:

> I delivered jewellery all right when I was an apprentice at Lacloche, in the Rue de la Paix and in Nice, on the Bv Masséna (the Winter season). 60 francs a month I got (and no food). The treasures I carried, diadems for Russian princesses – to the Hotel Cimiez! Yes! Oh, I used to meet Grand Dukes all

right! And those wonderful carnivals! Those Vegliones! And Emilienne d'Alençon! And the Tsar's brother! And I was hungry, all right, on my sixty francs! In 1910![93]

And in an earlier letter to Simone Saintu, Céline claims to have met the Austrian Emperor Franz Joseph and to have asked for his autograph on the only thing he had at hand, one of Lacloche's business cards. According to the letter, the Emperor, with the words 'I, too, young man, have a business,' handed Céline his own card, with the words: 'F.-J. d'Habsbourg Empereur d'Autriche'.[94] Somewhat lacking in humour, François Gibault uses the archives to prove that Franz-Joseph never went to Nice in the winter of 1911–12 and that Céline's story is pure fabrication, though the episode does demonstrate a constant concern of Céline's, at least in his early life, to impress. Finally, in April 1912, he witnessed the celebrations commemorating the visits to Nice of Queen Victoria.

In addition to a certain fascination with the visiting aristocracy, Céline also experienced more popular entertainments, in particular the theatre and music-hall, the Eldorado Casino, which showed films on a giant screen and which, in the evenings, hosted some of the most famous music-hall stars of the period: Dickson, Polin, the author of *La Petite Tonkinoise* and *L'Ami Bidasse*, and the comedian Dranem.[95] This taste for music-hall, reinforced by his visits to London from 1916 onwards, was to inform an important element of Céline's work: not just figures like Sosthène de Rodiencourt in *Guignol's Band*, but a fascination with both the *féerie* and the style of this type of popular theatre.

The draft of the letter from Fernand Destouches to M. Lacloche, however, indicates that Céline may have overindulged in the attractions which Nice had to offer, and on 12 May 1912, at his father's request, he packed his bags and returned to Paris.[96] The return from Nice effectively marks the end of Céline's career in commerce. He had virtually terminated his apprenticeship, and M. Lacloche was willing to give him a full-time position in the firm. Before this could take place, however, Céline had to undertake his military service, just like Lacloche's own son, who was the same age. At the age of 18, therefore, on 28 September 1912, he signed up for three years in the cavalry regiment, the 12ème Régiment de Cuirassiers Lourds, stationed at Rambouillet. His childhood was over.

What is important about this childhood for the author's later work is not necessarily the experience itself but what it gave Céline the opportunity to observe. He was brought up on the frontiers of financial security and vulnerability, though the family's position became increasingly secure. Nevertheless, he was perfectly positioned to be able to observe the artisanal life of *fin-de-siècle* Paris, the pressures facing the vanishing Parisian petite-bourgeoisie, the trades they plied, and the tensions which such pressures could exert psychologically on families. All of this was to be incorporated into *Mort à crédit*. Comfortable as this milieu may have been, we also note an implicit dissatisfaction, taking the form of delusions of grandeur or separateness, much as a child dissatisfied with its parents might prefer to believe that it had been stolen from a much grander context by gypsies. This goes together with an incipient lack of discipline and growing independence, particularly sexually, as Fernand's anxious concerns at his son's life alone in Nice reveal. Finally, both the cessation of Céline's formal studies at the age of 14 after the programme of the *Certificat d'études*, and the unusual experience of an upbringing in Germany, Britain and Nice give to Céline's cultural formation a particularly rich texture which he would later exploit.

2

National Service:
The Army and the Colonies

I THE '12 CUIR'

The precise reasons for Céline volunteering for the army in 1912 are not totally apparent. Having suggested that it was convenient for Céline to do his military service before entering full-time employment with Lacloche, and at the same time as Lacloche's son, Gibault goes on to report a later but unreliable version from Fernand Destouches, in which he sent his son into the Army because he could no longer control him.[1] One important concern, however, of which Fernand, as a former *engagé* himself, would have been very much aware, was the fact that, whereas a conscript undertaking his military service had no say in the unit to which he was assigned, normally serving in the infantry, a volunteer could choose his own regiment. In signing on with the 12ème Régiment de Cuirassiers at its barracks at Rambouillet on 28 September 1912, Céline had in fact chosen a regiment of some considerable distinction, one in keeping with a descendant of the Chevalier Des Touches. The '12 Cuir' was not perhaps as prestigious as its sister regiment, the 1er Régiment de Cuirassiers, the main ceremonial regiment in Paris, and renowned for its homosexuality,[2] but it was still very much conscious of its standing and its traditions.

The army in the belle époque was often highly brutal and almost uniformly conservative, a conservatism exacerbated by the Dreyfus Case and its aftermath. The literature of the period abounds in anti-militarist fiction, concentrating upon the cruelty of the regime, which, as Christine Sautermeister reminds us, informed Céline's own writing on the Army, in both *Voyage au bout de la nuit* and *Casse-pipe:*[3] particularly Georges Darien's *Biribi*, Lucien Descaves' *Sous-offs* and Abel Hermant's *Le Cavalier Miserey* of 1887, which so antagonized the military that one, possibly apocryphal, account depicts the Colonel of the 12e Chasseurs, the Duc de Chartres, burning it in front of the assembled regiment.[4] Céline was to come across two of these writers later in his career: Descaves, who was a fervent supporter of *Voyage au bout de la nuit* on the Prix Goncourt jury in 1932, and Hermant, who became a major figure in the Vichy establishment during the Occupation. Additionally, as Yves Pagès notes, Darien's racist anarchism was a contributory factor in the development of Céline's own anti-Semitism.[5] It was no coincidence that Hermant's denunciation of the army's brutality should concern the cavalry: the point about the cavalry was that, whereas the riders were expendable, the horses were not, and the former were very much at the service of the latter. Quite apart from the actual fighting, cavalry service was essentially a countryman's job and a stable-boy's trade.[6] It was also politically loaded: cavalry soldiers were recruited from the countryside, not merely because of their skills and background as farm labourers, but also because, as country-dwellers from the provinces, they would have no sympathy for the urban, specifically Parisian, industrial workers they were employed to police, and whose strikes and demonstrations they were ideally equipped to break. Céline's own experience in action against strikers is part of a long military and literary tradition which goes back at least as far as Stendhal's *Lucien Leuwen*.

The major civilian function of the '12 Cuir' was to escort the President of the Republic and his guests when in residence at the Château de Rambouillet, while being able to intervene in disturbances to public order in nearby Paris. It was made up for the most part of Breton soldiery. The problem, however, was that, while Céline may have delighted in fabricating for himself an idealized Breton ancestry, the real Bretons were far from attractive to a young Parisian bourgeois who had travelled to Germany, Britain and the Côte d'Azur. He wrote later to Roger Nimier, who had served briefly in the *Hussards* at the end of the Second World War:

> And what bumpkins they were! They were specially recruited for the strikes in Paris – which were fierce! . . . They were melancholy people – *mystical*. I saw them charge towards their death – without blinking – all 800 of them – like one man and horse – a sort of attraction – not once – ten times! As if it were a release! They had no sensuality whatsoever – not one out of ten spoke French – they were gentle and brutal at the same time – idiots, in short.[7]

Surrounded by unthinking soldiers of peasant stock whom he could not even understand, deprived of companionship, Céline found it difficult to cope with the harshness of the routine, the brutality of the NCOs and, ironically for one who had deliberately chosen a cavalry regiment, the horses he was supposed to look after and ride. As he reminisced to Claude Bonnefoy: 'I had to learn to ride a horse. I'd never been anywhere near a horse. At the beginning it was terrible, I fell off all the time . . . It was hard, almost as hard as the prisons in Denmark.'[8] So bad was the situation that, as he recorded a year later in the *Carnet du Cuirassier Destouches*, he considered deserting,[9] and an anxious Fernand Destouches wrote to M. Lacloche: 'Since his arrival at the regiment, his attitude is causing me serious concern and in order to decide what measures to take, I should like an urgent meeting with you.'[10] Marguerite Destouches was dispatched to Rambouillet to talk to a lieutenant in the regiment, Dugué Mac-Carthy, an unusually enlightened officer, imbued with the principles of Lyautey's *Le Rôle social de l'officer dans le service militaire universel*. Dugué Mac-Carthy, who had established a choir and a theatre troupe for the men at Rambouillet, appears to have taken Céline under his wing and reconciled him to life in the regiment. Here again, however, it is important not to exaggerate Céline's despair or, indeed, the self-dramatization in the *Carnet du Cuirassier Destouches*: as Henri Godard points out, his military dossier shows him passing through basic training normally, being promoted to *brigadier* in the normal period of six months, in May 1913, and being further promoted to *Maréchal des Logis* in August 1914.[11] The well-known photograph of Céline in his full-dress uniform as *Maréchal des Logis* certainly does not depict a military victim, and we are far from *Le Cavalier Miserey*.

The *Carnet du Cuirassier Destouches*, however, is not so far removed from Hermant's work, and it is the essentially literary quality of the notebook which constitutes its interest: apart from the letters to the parents from Germany and Britain, the *Carnet* constitutes the first example of Célinian writing. And highly derivative writing it is too, often embarrassingly overwritten, with frequent recourse to 'hélas!' and the 'diaphanous paleness' of the text.[12] Composed on the first anniversary of Céline's arrival at Rambouillet, the *Carnet* looks back at his first year in the army and expresses a despair which may well have been real but which was also now highly derivative from, among others, Abel Hermant: 'How many horrible awakenings have I had at the sound so falsely cheerful of the bugle, which brings back to your mind the bitterness and disaster of a day in the life of a new recruit.'[13] Half of the *Carnet* dwells on the torture facing the new recruit, from the day of his arrival, at 'the guard-room, full of NCOs with a bullying appearance,'[14] throughout the period of basic training. The interest of the work, however, lies not so much in this traditional expression of 'servitudes militaires' as in the evidence that its author had also toyed with the 'grandeurs': 'I felt that the grandiloquent speeches which I gave a month earlier on youthful energy were mere boasting.'[15] The repeated use of the term 'énergie' places the young Céline in a particular intellectual and cultural context in the period just before the First World War, that of Barrès and, particularly, that of the 'Agathon' report of 1912, *Ce que pensent les jeunes gens d'aujourd'hui*.[16] It was this survey, conducted by authors close to Action Française, Henri Massis and Alfred de Tarde, which attempted to prove that the younger generation of French university students had not followed the previous generation in embracing rationalism, democracy, internationalism and pacifism, but were, instead, Catholic, militarist, authoritarian and staunchly nationalist.[17] Typical of this generation was the soldier-novelist Ernest Psichari, the grandson of the rationalist philosopher Ernest Renan, who, in *L'Appel des armes*, celebrated the military and patriotic values of 'énergie', and who was to die in the war he exulted in so fervently. The tone of parts of the *Carnet*, and the insistence on 'énergie', show Céline to have been inspired not merely by the sufferings of Hermant's protagonist, but also by the fervour of Psichari's.

The problem, however, as the author of the notebook discovers on reaching the regiment, is that 'énergie juvénile', when frustrated by routine squalor or brutality, turns to its counterpart, melancholia: 'a basic sadness is at the bottom of my heart'[18] and 'this deep melancholia loses no time in covering all my *ennuis* and joins with them to torture my soul.'[19] This 'tristesse' and melancholia not only place Céline alongside that other icon of pre-war culture, Alain-Fournier, but also indicate his debt to the French Romantic tradition, encapsulated precisely in Vigny's *Servitudes et grandeurs militaires*, in which the glory of the military ambition, once denied by the banality of peace, turns into despair, anxiety and melancholia.[20] Critics have been too reluctant to place Céline in a cultural or intellectual context, but the fragments of writing in the *Carnet* would appear to indicate that he certainly shared some of the cultural baggage of his more educated contemporaries and that his later writing can, at least in part, be read in the context of post-war Neo-Romanticism, the 'nouveau mal du siècle' which informed the writers of the 1920s. Why else should the final section of *Voyage au bout de la nuit* take place in Baryton's asylum in Vigny-sur-Seine?

Finally, what the author of the *Carnet* mostly recognizes, at least in the latter sections, is his 'basic pride', which scares him,[21] and which fuels a huge sense of ambition: 'I want to dominate, not through an artificial power, like military authority, but later, or as soon as possible, I want to be a complete man. Will I ever become one? Will I have the necessary fortune which enables you to educate yourself? I want to obtain by my own efforts a wealthy position which will enable me to indulge all my fantasies.'[22] He is also, accurately as it turns out, conscious that this pride will condemn him to some solitude: 'I believe that I have a heart which is too complicated to enable me to find a companion whom I could love for long.'[23] Nevertheless, this is a price which he is prepared to pay: 'In a word, I am proud – is that a fault? I don't think so, and it will create problems for me, or also, perhaps, *Success*.'[24] With the emphasis on pride and fortune, and with the italicized flourish of the ending on '*Success*', we are no longer in the world of Vigny but in that of Balzac, and the young Céline sees himself as a new Rastignac. Yet both Vigny and Balzac – and Stendhal, that other apostle of 'énergie' – are writing under the ambiguous shadow of Napoleon, and a long shadow it proves. That classic expression of the 'nouveau mal du siècle', Malraux's *La Tentation de l'Occident* of 1926, chooses to evoke an impossible heroism with a description of the morning of Austerlitz. The cult of Napoleon remained a potent intellectual force in France in the inter-war years, in-forming anti-democratic politics, views on France's international standing and the cultural fallout from the ending of the war, and it is not sufficiently recognized to what extent Céline was also subject to that force. There is a consistent strand of Napoleonic references in Céline's work, from *La Vie et l'oeuvre de Philippe-Ignace Semmelweis*, particularly the homage to Corvisart, the Surgeon-General to the Grand Army, via the complex use of the *Chanson de la Bérésina*, sung by Napoleon's Swiss Regiment as it acted out its doomed rearguard action covering the crossing of the Berezina, which introduces *Voyage au bout de la nuit*, itself punctuated by further Napoleonic references and debates, to the location of the family home in *Mort à crédit* in the 'Passage des Bérésinas' and beyond.

It would be foolish to place too much emphasis on such a juvenile and skimpy text as the *Carnet du Cuirassier Destouches*. It is an important document, however, in so far as it shows the young Céline adopting a highly formal French literary style, which he later chose to abandon for an equally artificial one, and for the first time working in an essentially cultural context: the anti-militarist novelists, but also the prophets of energy, who may also include Nietzsche, the poets of melancholy and the novelists of ambition, in all three of which the Napoleonic tradition is crucial. His curtailed formal education and his upbringing in the Passage de Choiseul by no means appear to have left him immune from intellectual and cultural currents affecting his contemporaries, which would, in part, feed into the mature fiction. Above all, the *Carnet* reveals that ambition and pride which formed powerful driving forces in Céline's subsequent career, and frustration of which had equally significant results.

Céline's period at Rambouillet coincided with the end of the belle époque and gave him a privileged view of its grandeurs and conflicts. The presidential property played host to grand hunting-parties which had continued unchanged since the Empire or the monarchy. In particular, Céline recalled the annual hunting-parties of the Duchesse d'Uzès: 'I very well remember the Duchesse d'Uzès, on horseback, the old cow, and the Prince Orloff, with all the officers of the Regiment, and my job was to hold the horses . . . That was it. We were mere cattle.'[25] He also remembered the last great cavalry manoeuvres of Western Europe and the last peace-time review at Longchamp, presided over by Poincaré.[26] At the same time, he witnessed opposition to the regime. As Alméras reminds us, near the presidential domain of Rambouillet, the anarchist Sébastien Faure had, with the aid of the Duchesse d'Uzès, set up an experimental establishment, La Ruche, half-commune, half-school, on which Céline evidently drew when inventing Coutrial des Pereires' colony at Blême-le-Petit, in *Mort à crédit*.[27] One of the tasks of the '12 Cuir' was to patrol the area and to keep a close watch on La Ruche: 'God, were we jeered at! La Ruche was defended by an earthen rampart and from the top of it all of Sébastien Faure's charges called us bloodthirsty traitors as we passed. When I was only a 'Cavalier 2e Classe', it wasn't too bad, when I became 'brigadier', it was awful, but when I was a 'Maréchal des Logis' that infuriated them. Yet they were pretty kids, and sturdy.'[28] More seriously, as noted before, Céline's regiment went into action against strikers in the capital: 'I remember a May Day on the Rue des Pyramides, where we came face to face with revolutionary workers throwing stones at us.'[29] What Céline recalled particularly was the lack of support for the strikers and their ineffectualness. The belle époque was still for law and order, and Céline himself appears to have seen no reason for departing from the established norms: 'Personally, I did not then believe that those strikers could achieve anything. No-one realized what was happening. People respected order and discipline. The question of revolt never even arose (when it does, it's all over).'[30] As Alméras concludes: 'Destouches was not a rebel.'[31] Indeed, as we have seen, after the first despairing period of basic training, the 'brigadier' and, especially, the 'Maréchal des Logis' Destouches became more imbued with the 'grandeurs' of the military than its 'servitudes', an itinerary followed by the hero of *Casse-pipe*, who, by one of the later fragments of the novel, has moved far beyond the new recruit's horror at the brutality of the cavalry barracks to a sense of regimental pride and solidarity. Evoking the regiment's journey from Rambouillet to Paris to participate in the last 14 July parade before the war, the narrator of the novel comments: 'We drank curaçao throughout the journey. The squad liked that with baked potatoes. A speciality of ours.'[32]

II THE WAR

There is every indication that this sense of regimental solidarity remained with Céline as he embarked for war. The '12 Cuir' had received its orders to move to the Meuse sector at 18.30 on 31 July 1914 and the regiment left by train early the following day. Before leaving, Céline wrote to his parents in conventional patriotic terms: 'Everyone is at his post, confident and calm, even though the frenetic excitement of the first moments has given way to a deathly silence which is the sign of a sudden surprise. As for me, I shall do my duty to the end and if by chance I should not return . . . be sure, to diminish your grief, that I die happy, thanking you from the bottom of my heart.'[33] On arrival, the regiment was assigned the task of covering the infantry in a sector bounded on the north by the Luxembourg border and to the east by the cities of Metz and Nancy.[34] Both Gibault and Alméras give detailed accounts of the regiment's first days on a shifting front, in particular its first casualties (the Capitaine de Malmusse and the Maréchal des Logis Le Conte) and its first experience of artillery fire, when it witnessed the destruction of the French town of Malavilliers on 22 August.[35] In September the regiment played a decisive part on the periphery of the Battle of the Marne by reinforcing the 6th Corps, and it was at this point that Céline discovered for the first time the reality of modern warfare. He wrote to his parents in terms very different from the earlier expressions of patriotism: 'The battle is fierce . . . I have never seen and will never see again so much horror. We are walking through this spectacle almost unawares, through being accustomed to danger and especially through the numbing tiredness which we have endured for a month.'[36] Yet the losses suffered by the '12 Cuir' on the Meuse were relatively light and, after the crisis of the Battle of the Marne had passed, the sector was no longer considered a priority. On 2 October the regiment was transferred by train to the more critical front of Flanders.

They arrived at Armentières at 10 in the morning on 4 October, after two nights in the train, and the '12 Cuir' was attached to the 7th Cavalry Division, with Céline in the 2nd Cavalry Squadron. Within the general context of menacing German advances in the Noyon sector, the regiment's mission was to cover the landing of British troops at Dunkirk from German cavalry attacks.[37] From 4 to 15 October, when it was reinforced, the Regiment was involved in heavy fighting along the River Lys and sustained more losses. It also experienced for the first time those elements of modern warfare, such as artillery, shrapnel and increased firepower from the infantry, which were to inflict heavy damage and rapidly render the cavalry redundant.

On the 15th, the '12 Cuir' was diverted to the Belgian front, to prevent the Belgian armies retreating to the Yser from being cut off by the Germans. There followed ten days of fierce fighting, until 25 October, when the regiment covered the 66th Infantry Regiment in its attack on Poelkappelle. It was in the course of this attack, on 27 October, that Céline and six other men were wounded.[38]

With the wound received at Poelkappelle a further element of mythology enters Céline's biography, alongside the poverty-stricken childhood and the meeting with Franz Joseph, and one which Céline himself did much to foster. The persona of a severely wounded war hero was increasingly useful to Céline in establishing his reputation as a writer, in asserting his patriotic credentials in the years immediately before and during the Second World War and, particularly, in establishing the role of victim and scapegoat after the Occupation. There is no doubt that Céline was an authentic hero: as Gibault records, in spite of withering fire around Poelkappelle, it was essential to maintain liaison between the 66th and 125th Infantry Regiments, and, when volunteers were requested, Céline 'spontaneously volunteered'.[39] Following Céline's wounding, the commander of the 2nd Squadron, Captain Schneider, wrote to Fernand Destouches in the most glowing terms: 'Your son has just been wounded. He fell courageously, rushing through the bullets with an enthusiasm and a courage which never left him from the very beginning of the campaign,'[40] and on 24 November 1914 Céline was awarded the Médaille Militaire by General Joffre. As Captain Schneider wrote again to Fernand Destouches: 'Your son has been awarded the Médaille Militaire for his fine conduct under fire.'[41] While there is no doubt about Céline's heroism at Poelkappelle, there is considerable confusion, often maintained by Céline himself, concerning both the nature of the act itself and the extent of his injuries.

Part of the confusion stems from a Parisian publication called *L'Illustré National*, which, in a number towards the end of 1914, devoted its entire final page to Céline's exploit, with a line-drawing of a cavalry sergeant on horseback and with sabre drawn charging through artillery and rifle-fire. As Alméras comments:

Below it, as a caption, was a text inspired by the official citation and illustrated by the drawing: 'The *Maréchal des Logis* Destouches, of the 12th Regiment of Cuirassiers, has received the Médaille Militaire for having spontaneously volunteered (when he was acting as liaison between an infantry regiment and his brigade) to deliver under heavy fire an order which the infantry messengers were reluctant to deliver. After having delivered this order, he was unfortunately seriously wounded as he returned from his mission.'[42]

This coverage of Céline's heroic act was probably directly prompted by Fernand Destouches, revelling in the role of proud father of a war hero,[43] but, as Alméras argues, it is unlikely that it corresponds to the truth. In the battle around Poelkappelle, the '12 Cuir' had dismounted and occupied trenches along with the infantry regiment it was supporting. It is most improbable, therefore, that any liaison between the cavalry and the infantry book place on horseback, especially given the nature of the terrain, pitted with shell-craters.[44] Indeed, Céline himself seems to acknowledge as much when writing in 1916 to Simone Saintu from Africa, two years after his injury: 'I remember that at that time between the first line of trenches and the command post, there were no cross-trenches. So, at night-fall, you could spend hours blindly searching for the command post which, obviously, was not shown by any light. We used to call that "looking after the cows". It was while "looking after the cows" that I was hit.'[45] It would appear, therefore, that Céline was wounded while undertaking his mission on foot. The legend of the heroic horseman persisted, resurfacing at Sigmaringen,[46] with the original design transposed through a montage on to the front page of *L'Illustré National* and even the much better-known and more prestigious *L'Illustration.*[47]

At the same time, the legend persists of Céline having received a serious head-wound, needing trepanation. Henri Mondor, in the preface to his Pléiade edition of *Voyage au bout de la nuit* and *Mort à credit*, talks of 'Céline's poor fractured head', and Marcel Aymé aserts in the *Cahiers de l'Herne* that 'Following trepanation necessitated by a head-wound received in 1914, and which he claimed had been badly done, he had always suffered from violent migraines.'[48] Nor did Céline himself do anything to correct this myth: indeed, it became increasingly useful to him, particularly after the collapse of the Vichy regime. As Philippe Alméras comments, the legend of the metal plate in Céline's head probably derives from a photograph of him when convalescing at the Val-de-Grâce military hospital in Paris, in which his head is covered in a copious bandage.[49] The likelihood, however, is that the bandage was the result of severe toothache rather than anything more serious. Certainly, the wound that Céline received was from a ricocheting bullet which hit his right arm, causing extensive and permanent damage.[50] Yet Céline, certainly from the 1930s onwards, complained of persistent migraines and buzzing in the ears, which have been variously attributed to abuse of quinine while in the colonies, an ear infection and high blood-pressure.[51] For François Gibault, there is another explanation: prior to the arm-wound which won him the Médaille Militaire, Céline had been injured 'at an indeterminate date'[52] by a shell which exploded near him, hurling him against a tree. It was from this earlier wound, which entailed a violent blow to the head, that came the persistent pains of which Céline later complained. What is interesting, however, is that Céline's own references to persistent headaches and their cause in the war do not occur until the 1930s. When writing to Cillie Pam in 1932, for example, although Céline refers darkly to 'being ill myself, chronically',[53] there is no reference to the head-wound. The question of the head-wound, therefore, is likely to tell us far more about Céline after the publication of *Voyage* than about his activity during the war.

After being wounded, Céline walked seven kilometres to find a dressing station, before transferring to an ambulance convoy going from Ypres to Dunkirk. He left the convoy at Hazebrouck, where he notified his parents and where the spent bullet was removed[54] by a civilian doctor, Dr Senellart, who diagnosed not merely a fracture but also a possibly permanent paralysis.[55] Céline refused anaesthetic, fearing that his arm might be amputated, and, in all, spent one month convalescing in Hazebrouck, in the Red Cross Hospital at the Collège Saint-Jacques. On 1 December, thanks to the intervention of his uncle, Georges Destouches, the General Secretary of the Faculté de Médecine de Paris, he was transferred to the military hospital of the Val-de-Grâce. Legend has it that he left the matron of the hospital in Hazebrouck, Alice D., pregnant.[56] It was at the Val-de-Grâce, in the Rue Saint-Jacques, that he received the Médaille Militaire and met a sergeant, Albert Milon, a model for Sergeant Brandelore in *Voyage*, a believer in survival, with whom he established a close and durable friendship. Céline tried in vain to entice Milon to the colonies with tales of fabulous wealth; he succeeded in enrolling him in the Mission Rockefeller when he returned from Africa and, although they lost contact, he still retained an affectionate memory of his wartime friend. When Milon, who had become a salesman for a wine company and had been involved in Radical Party politics, died in 1947, Céline wrote from Denmark to his widow: 'He takes away with him a good half of our dearest common memories from our most epic trials . . . He takes with him as well our poor hopes, our painful and oh! so wounded illusions . . . our sacrifices, our so useless heroisms . . . You see, Renée, the end really started at the Val-de-Grâce. It was only a respite, a reprieve: it wasn't life or happiness . . . That wasn't possible any more . . . A terrible fate hung over us.'[57]

This painful vision of post-war life would only become apparent with a particular hindsight. For the moment, Céline, with his Médaille Militaire, his uniform and his arm in a sling, could enjoy the immense prestige of a wounded warrior in wartime civilian Paris, where the War still inculcated fear and guilt and where the injured were still prestigious novelties. Not that he was completely cured: at the end of December, he had been transferred from the Val-de-Grâce to an auxiliary hospital at 121 Boulevard Raspail and then, on the same day, 31 December 1914, to the Hospice Paul-Brousse in the suburb of Villejuif, directed by the famous oncologist

Gustave Roussy.[58] On 19 January 1915 Professor Gosset operated on his arm, and on 24 February Céline was granted three months' leave, interrupted by one week's admission to the military hospital in the Lycée Michelet at Vanves to undergo subsequently controversial electric-shock treatment.[59] It was only later in March that, installed in his parents' apartment in the Rue Marsollier, he could profit fully from his leave.

From this period of Céline's life a number of ambiguities persist, in addition to the biographical confusions and the mythomania. In the first place, the parents' role still appears to be relatively non-problematic. They still showed considerable concern and support, running to his bedside in Hazebrouck as soon as they received news of his injury; he still expressed affection and respect, however conventionally articulated. At the same time, in spite of an explicable and rational response to the reality of twentieth-century warfare, there is no evidence that, at this time, Céline was anything other than orthodoxly patriotic: the letter to Renée Milon, on her husband's death, expresses a disillusionment which takes its significance, precisely, from hindsight. In other words, Céline in 1916 was certainly not the Bardamu of *Voyage au bout de la nuit*, nor did he have his protagonist's anarchist credo: he was a long way from the subversiveness of the narrator of Henri Barbusse's *Le Feu*, of 1917. Instead, he rather enjoyed the prestige of the hero who had survived what was increasingly becoming a massacre. In this, he was not untypical of other figures from his generation, with whom he was to have much greater contact twenty years later: the reactionary anarchist writers, painters and graphic artists of Montmartre, including Mac Orlan, Carco, Dorgelès, Daragnès, Gus Bofa, Chas Laborde and Vlaminck, of whom Georges Charensol comments: 'these ex-combattants . . . had returned sickened by the war which they had fought bravely. But, as patriots, they did not allow anyone to talk about the war lightly. For having made an innocent joke about it, Pascin was given a good hiding by the engraver Daragnès. Hating the war, they talked about it ceaselessly, very proud of the courage they had shown and of the cunning which had enabled them to survive.'[60] That combination of hatred of the war, pride in courage and celebration of cunning and survival, which he shared with the Montmartre culture of the inter-war years, were to be key elements of Céline's own stance on the conflict and were to regulate his depiction of it in his fiction and pamphlets.

III LONDON

Céline's convalescent leave ended in May 1915, and on the 10th he posted a card from Folkestone to his uncle Charles, signed 'L. Destouches, délégué du Grand Quartier Général au Consulat de France, Londres, Bedford sq.'[61] Impressive as the title may sound, the reality was more prosaic: he had been assigned to a desk job in the French Consulate processing immigration applications. His colleague in the same department, Georges Geoffroy, who, like Céline, had just come from the front, having served in the 8th Cavalry Division, described their work as that of 'giving military advice for the delivery of entry visas to France',[62] and hence technically part of the French counter-espionage service. Mundane though the work was, Geoffroy did recall that they processed the application of Mata Hari, who allegedly then invited them to dinner in her suite at the Savoy.[63] Céline characteristically played up the dramatic side of his new posting, writing to Albert Milon that 'I am here, as you know, in counter-espionage',[64] and telling an extraordinary tale to his cousin Charlotte Robic about a secret mission to Switzerland in the course of which, in Germany, he found himself in a railway compartment with an Uhlan officer whom he recognized as the son of one of his teachers in Diepholz. He reported breathlessly that he only managed to escape by leaping from the train as it slowed down.[65] Philippe Alméras, however, is surely right when he asserts that the real mystery of Céline's journey to London is how a lightly wounded and otherwise fit cavalry sergeant could obtain a desk job far from the conflict in the first place and how, ostensibly fully cured, he could be first provisionally and then definitively invalided out of the army, on 2 September and 16 December?[66] It certainly seems likely that the posting to this plum job was due to Fernand's search for patronage and, if so, it marks the beginning of a long process in Céline's career by which he was never afraid to cut corners and use influence, a case in point being the role of Selskar Gunn in his early medical career. The real importance of Céline's experience of wartime London lies elsewhere. He moved into Geoffroy's apartment at 71 Gower Street and, in addition to his work at the Consulate and his reading – Geoffroy remembers his reading German philosophers, including Fichte, Schopenhauer and Nietzsche[67] – had plenty of time to explore London. As Gibault comments, London was then one of the world's great ports, and Céline was to remain fascinated, like Mac Orlan, with the life – particularly the low life – of port cities,[68] a feature which emerges with considerable power and detail in *Guignol's Band*. Paul Morand, then a junior attaché at the French Embassy, paints in *Londres* a graphic picture of the British capital during the war: '*Nouveaux riches,* workers spoilt by high wages, men in safe jobs and war profiteers, all sorts of spies, microphones in the best hotels; fleeing Russian princesses, international adventurers, dowry-hunters looking for war widows, American arms salesmen at the Ritz, sending orchids and taking orders. The night-clubs are making a fortune.'[69] Céline's interests, however, took him to more popular entertainment, in particular the London music-hall, at that time the best in the world. Peter Dunwoodie has listed the music-hall acts that Céline could have seen during 1915 and their particular importance for *Guignol's Band*.[70] It is important to stress, however, that the interest in music-hall predates the visit to London and that it remained a powerful element in Céline's cultural background: the exaggeration, the often crude comedy, the patter – in essence the artificiality – inform his mature fiction and non-fiction alike:

the real meaning of the 'Bagatelles' of the anti-Semitic pamphlet *Bagatelles pour un massacre* is the patter used by fairground barkers.

At the same time, Céline and Geoffroy gravitated rapidly to the French criminal community in Soho. This quarter of London was traditionally French and already devoted to crime and prostitution by the 1870s. Jules Vallès, the ex-Communard exiled to London in 1871, and whose *Jacques Vingtras* trilogy had such a profound influence on *Mort à crédit*, was horrified at the way in which French crime had taken over the centre of London: 'I must confess that it was made to dishonour us, this Leicester Square, full of the riff-raff of France. Soho: infamous Soho!'[71] The articles Vallès wrote during his exile, collected in *La Rue à Londres*, with their evocation of the 'criminals who cast their nets in troubled waters'[72] and who 'in the evening loiter in Regent Street',[73] are as much the basis of *Guignol's Band* as Céline's own experience, as are a whole host of French evocations of London.[74] They concentrate on the world of crime and prostitution which Céline enjoyed frequenting and which he rediscovered in post-war Montmartre. Even though he was not to meet his real guide to the French underworld in London, Joseph Garcin, a possible model for Cascade in *Guignol's Band*, until 1929,[75] he had already acquired more than a taste for the city's less respectable pleasures.

In this context, the supposed 'mystery' of Céline's first marriage, to Suzanne Nebout on 19 January 1916, becomes readily explicable. François Gibault presents it as something of a drama, with Céline not informing his parents and Suzanne allegedly walking unannounced into the family shop with the words: 'I am Madame Destouches.'[76] Since the marriage was never declared to the French Consulate and since there is no subsequent record of 'Madame Destouches', Philippe Alméras is surely right in seeing this marriage, real as it undoubtedly was, as a marriage of convenience, performed to help a Frenchwoman obtain an identity card in Britain.[77] What is interesting, however, is that the marriage certificate should promote Céline to the rank of lieutenant, that it should still give him the aristocratic name of Louis des Touches, and that it should cite as his profession 'Private Secretary of Insurance Company':[78] even in what Alméras terms a 'practical joke', there is an important and consistent mythomania in operation.

It is also highly significant that one of the recorded witnesses to the ceremony was one Edouard Benedictus, an eccentric, an inventor specializing in gas warfare, financed by Paul Lafitte and, above all, a member of French occult circles. As Alméras records, he was in close contact with the 'Magus Papus' and the visionary Mme Fraya. Not only was he a successful inventor, who discovered Triplex safety glass, he also served as a possible model for Sosthène de Rodiencourt in *Guignol's Band*, and was an important link between Céline and other important figures of post-war French culture, including not only Blaise Cendrars and Abel Gance[79] but also Raoul Marquis, alias the Marquis de Graffigny, the model for Courtial des Pereires in *Mort à crédit*. Céline's knowledge of the occult and his frequenting of occultist circles, including Saint-Pol-Roux 'Le Magnifique' and the

'Sâr' Georges Peladon, is an important element in his subsequent work and one he shared with other writers of the period.[80] Once again, Céline's cultural development, though eccentric, is by no means totally removed from a more general context. The same is true of his brief career in the colonies.

IV Africa

Apart from his marriage on 16 January 1916, few details are known about Céline's life between his definitive 'réforme' of 2 December 1915 and his departure for Africa in May 1916. Leaving the army entailed leaving his job at the Consulate. Céline's own subsequent explanations of how he earned his living prior to leaving for Africa, such as 'making aircraft wings',[81] are unconvincing. What is known is that in the spring of 1916 he had come to Paris to sign a contract with the Compagnie Forestière Sangha-Oubangui (CFSO) to work as a trainee plantation manager in Cameroon, at a starting salary of 150 francs per month, rising to 200 on completion of a period of probation, with 325 francs a month subsistence.[82]

At the outbreak of war, Cameroon was a German colony and the object of a sea blockade and land invasion by a combined force of British and French troops. It was not until the spring of 1916 that the Germans were finally ousted and the territory was divided between the French and the British, with the French colony establishing its capital at Douala. The CFSO, created in 1910 with its headquarters in the Rue La Rochefoucauld,[83] took over the activities of the German colonists, in particular, trading for ivory and wild rubber and planting cocoa. As France's newest colony, it had urgent need of dynamic and ambitious young men who wished to make their fortune. Quite how Céline came to apply is unclear, but it was probably through either Fernand Destouches or Benedictus.[84] In any case, in early May 1916 he sailed from Le Havre to Southampton before proceeding to Liverpool, where, on 10 May, he embarked on the RMS *Accra*, a small freighter of the British and African Steam Navigation Company, which was to take him to Douala, via Freetown in Sierra Leone and Lagos in Nigeria.[85] Curiously, the arrival in Southampton appears to have been marred by some kind of undisclosed incident instigated by Céline's friend from London, Georges Geoffroy, the report of which to his parents gives an early insight into a more pugnacious personality: 'A lot of obstacles were put in my way at Southampton to prevent my disembarking, but, like Napoleon on his return from Elba, I soon got the opposition on my side. Nevertheless, I did recognize amongst this little coalition some of my friends, and especially Geoffroy, for whom I have prepared a little dog – which will bite its master.'[86] The Napoleonic sense of superiority goes alongside a desire for revenge, a desire which resurfaced later in the African correspondence when Céline complained to his parents at the apparent neglect of his uncle

Georges Destouches, the famous General Secretary of the Faculty of Medicine: 'Let my relatives or friends, who believe that they have made a mistake in taking up with me or who are not able to approve of my behaviour, know definitively that I could not give a damn about them, and let there be no doubt on that subject.'[87] Despite Céline's comment to Milon that 'I do not, as you know, bear eternal grudges,'[88] his capacity for animosity, so characteristic of his later career and so vital a fuel for his writing, was already clearly visible in his writing from Africa. In the event, he subsequently renewed his friendship with Geoffroy, who became a Parisian jeweller from whom he bought a number of expensive articles during the Occupation and after.

The journey was a disaster and very nearly convinced Céline to turn around on his arrival and return to Europe. He wrote to his father at his office at the Phénix, so as not to worry Marguerite Destouches, with the news that there had been two deaths on board, that he himself was suffering from fever and asking for 1000 francs so that he could return immediately.[89] Demoralized by fever and by the exaggerated tales of colonial passengers on the *Accra*, he wrote to Albert Milon that 'there was no future' in Africa and that life 'was absorbed by a sun which drowns everything and kills without fail everything which resists it'.[90] As Alméras comments, the demoralization also took the form of hypochondria, and Céline spent the voyage dipping into his medicine chest, particularly for quinine, that same quinine which left him with buzzing in the ears.[91]

Yet, with the arrival in Douala and the abatement of the fever, he recovered his self-confidence and the correspondence begins to take the form of a jaunty travelogue. He did not remain in the capital of the colony for long and, after only a few days in the Hôtel de France, he was assigned to Campo, in the newly conquered territories, where he was to set up a trading-post, to which he set off in the small coastal steamer, the *Fullah*. He established himself initially at Campo Beach, a military post on the mouth of the River N'Tem presided over by Max Delestrée, a lieutenant in the colonial infantry, and a sergeant, the models for Grappa and Alcide in *Voyage au bout de la nuit*. Céline's work consisted of collecting wild rubber, an essential war commodity, and ivory, by bartering relatively worthless European goods.[92] Having established this trading-post at Campo Beach, Céline was then put in charge of the former German 'Kampo Plantation Robert Guthman' at Bikobimbo, twenty-five kilometres up the N'Tem, on one of its tributaries, the Bongola, to harvest the cocoa crop. Here, in the settlement of Dipikar, accompanied until 20 August by a colonial sergeant, Harté, and then completely on his own, Céline was in charge of a large native workforce, paid in rice, tobacco and other commodities and, by European standards, a huge estate.[93] It was here that he was to remain until his sudden departure from the colony on 5 April 1917.

The first thing that life in the colonies appears to have taught Céline is a preoccupation with health which veered rapidly to hypochondria. He was particularly conscious that, whereas the north was conducive to good health, the tropics 'destroyed organisms and brains':[94] hence the possibilities of racial inequality, a commonplace theory he shared with many Edwardian writers on both sides of the Channel, including Kipling and Mac Orlan. One of his first impressions on arrival in Freetown was racial: he wrote to Simone Saintu that 'if all the negroes were exported to Europe, I would understand their intellectual inferiority,'[95] a comment which looks forward to the racism of the pamphlets and the illustrations to the wartime editions showing black leaders wearing grass skirts and frock coats. In order to preserve his health, he sent copious orders for medicines to his parents and consulted medical works, such as Boyce's *Mosquito or Man? The Conquest of the Tropical World*. Céline saw the life of the white man in the tropics as a constant battle against disease and infection, in which the slightest relaxation could be fatal: hence his emphasis in his correspondence home upon preventive measures such as quinine, solar helmets and veils, and especially upon abstinence from alcohol, which he saw as the major factor in the disintegration of the health and the morale of the white colonial. For Alméras, it was from this period that Céline's antagonism to alcohol dated, forged in a Manichean battle against infection.[96]

These preventive measures against sickness, however, reinforced rather than deterred Céline in his mission as a model colonist. The letters to Albert Milon, which tried to entice Céline's erstwhile sickbed companion to a career in Africa, emphasize both the financial rewards and the status. Describing his journeys on horseback around his territory, in 'impeccable white dress [to Milon he insisted on the importance of dress]',[97] he also stressed the wealth to be made: in his letters to Milon he boasted that he was putting aside 2000 francs per month and that, by the time he returned home in fourteen months, he would have saved 25,000 francs (the equivalent of 250,000 francs today).[98] As both Gibault and Alméras point out, this assertion raises the question of where this fortune was coming from: the CPSO, in its draconian contract, stipulated that there was to be no supplementary income whatsoever for its employees, on pain of instant dismissal.[99] Yet Céline, on a monthly salary of 150 to 200 francs, could not possibly have been in a position to save 2000 francs a month: either, as Alméras suggests, he was already acting as a doctor and charging for unofficial health care[100] or he was also trading on his own account and, perhaps in addition, falsifying the company's ledgers. It may be that it was as a result of discrepancies in Céline's book-keeping that the company, on the pretext of medical reasons, had him returned to France.[101]

In addition to playing the role of the model colonial, even down to the white suit, Céline used his time in Cameroon in building up his heteroclite fund of literary and intellectual knowledge. François Gibault lists the following authors mentioned in the copious correspondence from Africa addressed to the parents, Simone Saintu and Milon: Albert Samain, Jules Renard, Voltaire, Socrates, Pascal, the Prince de Ligne, Metchnikoff, Musset, Montluc, Talleyrand, Urbain Gohier, Claude Farrère, Oscar Wilde, Baldwin, Maeterlinck, Kipling, Brunetière, Jules Lemaître, Bergson and

Faguet.[102] What is interesting about this list, in addition to its breadth, is the concentration on philosophers and critics (Faguet, Brunetière and Bergson), together with 'classics' like Voltaire, Pascal, Musset and Socrates, and a predominance of turn-of-the-century figures such as Renard (the author, like Vallès in *L'Enfant*, of a famous account of child persecution, *Poil-de-Carotte*), Farrère (the great French adventure and colonial novelist), Maeterlinck and Kipling, for whom Céline had a special admiration.[103] Indeed, the narrative voice of *Plain Tales from the Hills*, often that of the subversive soldier Mulvaney, may well inform more than the colonial action in *Voyage au bout de la nuit*, just as Céline's 'petite musique' may owe much to the poetic vernacular of the *Barrack-Room Ballads*.

At the same time, the African episode is the first period in Céline's life when a consistent literary ambition begins to emerge. Much more than the correspondence from Germany and England, or the letters from the army and the front, the correspondence from Africa is essentially literary, striving for verbal pictures and, above all, effect. It is no coincidence, therefore, that this should be the period of his first attempts at formal creative writing, apart from the *Carnet du Cuirassier Destouches*. He allegedly sent a short story to Henri de Régnier at *Le Journal*, which he claimed had been accepted, but of which there is no trace,[104] and dispatched to Simone Saintu two poems dated 29 and 30 August 1916, entitled *Gnomographie* ('Gnomography') and *Le Grand Chêne* ('The Great Oak').[105] The first reads as follows:

> Stamboul est endormi sous la lune blafarde
> Le Bosphore miroité de mille feux argentés
> Seul dans la grande ville mahométane
> Le vieux crieur des heures n'est pas encore couché
>
> Sa voix que l'écho répète avec ampleur
> Annonce à la ville qu'il est déjà dix heures
> Mais par une fenêtre de son haut minaret
> Il plonge dans une chambre son regard indiscret
>
> Il reste un moment muet, cloué par la surprise
> Et caresse, nerveux, sa grande barbe grise.
> Mais fidèle au devoir il assure sa voix
>
> Et l'écho étonné, répète par trois fois,
> A la lune rougissant, aux étoiles éblouies,
> A Stamboul la blanche, qu'il est bientôt midi.[106]

The form of the poem is, by any standards, that of conventional Symbolism and, indeed, Orientalism, and is proof, if any were needed, of Céline's ability to handle the formal constraints of French literary writing, here the Alexandrine sonnet. What is perhaps more interesting for a reading of the later Céline, however, is the emphasis on voyeurism in line 8, a form of sexuality which he found particularly enticing and which he was to exploit fully in his fiction.

The second poem, whose title is only indicated in the margin, reads as follows:

> Mais, déjà lentement, le ciel se décolore
> Les rayons du couchant, purchassés par la nuit
> Luttent contre les ténèbres et résistent encore
> Pour voiler la retraite du soleil qui fuit.
>
> En haut du noir rocher qui domine les bois
> Le chêne retient encore la lumière qui décroît
> Cependant, peu à peu l'ombre remonte et le prend
> Et le plonge à son tour dans le tout inquiétant
>
> Chaque heure de notre vie apporte aussi son ombre
> Les illusions perdues, l'amertume qui monte
> En chassant l'espérance, qui ne reviendra plus
> Envahissent notre coeur, le détruisent et le tuent.[107]

This poem is still couched in a conventional format of late nineteenth-century poetics but, with its equally conventional equation of dusk and the onset of human disillusionment, it is far less successful. Both poems were sent to Simone Saintu, prefaced by a quotation from Théodore de Banville, and were no doubt designed to impress a well brought-up young girl with the sensitivity of the late Romantic poet. What both poems demonstrate, however, is an awareness of style and a gift for imitation, which Céline was to manipulate later in his fiction, albeit by subverting the conventional Romanticism of his earlier work.

A potentially more successful work is the complete short story, 'Des vagues', which concludes the African correspondence and is dated 30 April 1917, when Céline was on his way home on board the RMS *Tarquah*. It is a slight fragment, dealing with a small group of passengers on a colonial vessel, who finally learn the news of America's intervention in the First World War. The significance of the work for Céline's later production lies both in the successful creation of a light style of 'badinage', used later in the plays *Progrès* and *L'Eglise*, and in a highly competent manipulation of carica-ture, which was later to give him a common ground with the caricaturists of Montmartre and would constitute a powerful element of his fiction. The characters assembled in the *Tarquonia*'s smoking-room are a caricatural microcosm of Europe, as are the characters deployed in *L'Eglise*. There is a phlegmatic Scottish officer, Major Tomkatrick, the grey Swiss, M. Brunner, the greasy governor of a Portuguese colony, M. Camuzet, the very model of a modern French Republican, two Danish Protestant missionaries and a Romanian prince, Catulesco. This slight story contains the germs of Céline's later virtuoso caricatural verve, but also of the racial and national stereotyping which similarly inform the pamphlets.

It is perhaps important at this point, when considering Céline's reading and writing during his short spell in the French African colonies, to remind ourselves that, as with his childhood and military experiences, it was not just the lived experience which mattered, but its literary representation. When Céline comes to depict Africa in *Voyage au bout de la nuit*, he will do so, not just through the memory of his own lived experience, but through the cultural filter of those who wrote about the colonies; in this respect, authors such as Loti, Kipling, Farrère and especially Conrad are vital. The African episode of *Voyage* derives as much from Marlow's search for Mister Kurtz in *Heart of Darkness* as from Céline's lived experience in Cameroon, and the title *Voyage au bout de la nuit* is in itself a literal paraphrase of the French title of Conrad's novella, *Au Coeur des ténèbres*. Philippe Alméras' hypothesis that Céline could have become the one great French colonial writer, the equal of Karen Blixen, Conrad and Kipling, surely misses the point. Céline's greatness resides precisely in his ability to remain a French urban novelist while deploying the complex montage of colonial literature, and it is in this process that one of the sources of his Modernism is to be found.

The whole adventure appears to have collapsed very quickly and the ambition to stay fourteen months in Africa seems to have vanished. Officially, he was repatriated on medical grounds, complaining of pain from his arm-wound and of enteritis, as certified by a Dr Dreneau, who recommended his immediate repatriation.[108] In addition, the company had decided to suspend the cocoa operation in Campo as being unprofitable. Philippe Alméras is more circumspect, noting that the accounts for Céline's operation in Bikobimbo for 1916 have disappeared and arguing, as we have seen, that it was possible that his supplementary income had got the better of him, detected by a sharp-eyed accountant.[109] Either way, it is likely that the health clause was used to repatriate Céline at the company's cost and to avoid a potential scandal. As was so often the case in Céline's life, he appeared to have ended up exactly where he started. Certainly, he seemed to be living up to his description of himself to Simone Saintu, when he announced his precipitate departure for Africa: 'Everything about me: my decisions and my gestures, is capricious.'[110]

3

The Student of Medicine

In the interview with Claude Bonnefoy, Céline listed his various jobs before becoming a doctor: 'I had twelve trades, all of them miserable! I was a jewellery salesman and delivery-boy in Nice. In Paris, I pushed barrows around. I was a sales representative, a brick salesman . . . and even editorial assistant at the inventors' magazine, *Eurêka*.'[1]

Eurêka, revue de l'invention, was founded by Paul Lafitte in June 1916, with its offices in the Rue Favart between the Rue du Quatre-Septembre and the Boulevard des Italiens in the second *arrondissement,* in other words in Céline's own neighbourhood.[2] In November 1917, Céline joined the staff of the magazine as an office-boy and general factotum, probably as the result of an introduction from his friend from London days, Edouard Benedictus, still acting as advisor to Lafitte. While his own later description of the post as that of 'editorial assistant' may have been slightly exaggerated, it covered a broad range of activities, from criss-crossing Paris to collect articles to translation. The number of 9 February 1918 carried an article 'De l'utilisation rationnelle du Progrès: Passages les plus saillants d'un message de l'éminent docteur Nutting à l'Associated Engineering Societies de Worcester Mass. USA', translated from the English by Louis Destouches.[3] Not only, as Alméras remarks,[4] had the aristocratic 'des' vanished, but the periods spent in England had clearly paid off. Moreover, the title of the article looks forward to that of Céline's play of 1926/7, *Progrès/Périclès*. Marginal as *Eurêka* might appear, it brought Céline, both in his journeys across Paris and in the editorial offices themselves, into contact with a certain cultural milieu of the time. Blaise Cendrars recalled him working as 'office-boy' for the magazine, and Céline subsequently claimed in a letter to Charles Deshayes: 'Do I know Cendrars! I've known him since 1916! And the others! I know all those famous people! I tried to

scrape a living with Abel Gance in the misery of that period . . . Canudo!
. . . Vuillermoz! . . . I knew all these "Geniuses" when they were starting
out.'[5] To this group, in *Nord*, the narrator adds the painter Van Dongen.[6]
Yet again, it is important to be able to situate Céline, however marginally,
within a certain Parisian cultural context, in which he was not acting in
complete isolation.

Of all the figures whom Céline met in the offices of *Eurêka*, the most
extraordinary was the man who was to contribute massively to the portrayal
of Courtial des Pereires in *Mort à crédit*. Known either as Henri (or Henry)
Marquis or Raoul Marquis, he used his surname and his birthplace at the
village of Graffigny in the Department of the Haute-Marne to construct an
aristocratic persona as the Marquis Henri de Graffigny. A dedicated bal-
loonist and inventor, whose experiments included the pumping of electric
current into the soil to grow crops of monster vegetables,[7] he was also
a prolific popularizer of science and author of numerous playlets and
science-fiction novels in the style and tradition of Jules Verne: *Un drame
sous la mongolfière, A tout vapeur, Le Tour du monde en aéroplane* and the
four-volume *Aventures extraordinaires d'un savant russe*, written in collaboration with G. Le Faure, and prefaced by no less a person than Camille
Flammarion himself, the greatest popularizer of science in France.[8] The
Marquis de Graffigny also specialized in puppet-plays, which may have
inspired in Céline an interest in the Guignol tradition, culminating in
Guignol's Band, and in dramas which he called 'féeries': *Le Trésor du pôle,
comédie-féerie* and *Culotte rouge ou Les Vainqueurs du Kraden, drame-féerie.*[9]

It is important to recall the ambiguous and exciting status of invention
and science in the early years of the twentieth century. The possibilities
seemed endless, particularly when the rules of science were still expanding:
until an invention was proven either a definite success or an abject failure,
there was no clear dividing line between inspired scientific intuition
or reckless self-delusion. Thomas Edison, whose successes were the inspiration of thousands of small independent inventors, notched up his own
considerable share of failures and Edouard Benedictus, in spite of his
occultism, was still able to invent the 'unbreakable glass' which became
Triplex. Nor was Raoul Marquis (Henri de Graffigny) himself by any
means all charlatan. He was awarded a doctorate in physical science
from the Sorbonne in May 1904 for a thesis on *Recherches dans la série du
Furfurane* and, as late as the academic year 1928–9, he was appointed a
temporary lecturer in the science faculty of the University of Paris, where
he gave a series of lectures on organic chemistry.[10] The important point is
that at this period in the history of science, the boundaries of certain
knowledge were neither secure nor fixed, and apparent fantasy could, with
luck, become scientific law and make the fortune of its instigator. The
compelling feature in Edwardian science fiction, the novels of H. G. Wells
or Jules Verne, is the essentially plausible nature of all invention in this
period, in which Céline's early goal of 'success' could be achieved by one
flash of inspiration.

That Céline himself was by no means immune to the temptations of this form of success is evidenced by his precocious marine biology experiments at Roscoff when he was a medical student and by his invention of the drug 'Basdowine' in 1933 for the Gallier Laboratories.[11] More important, however, the blurred frontier between charlatanism and science, caused by the absence of firm knowledge and the very concepts which make a distinction between the two possible, would become an important theoretical consideration underlying his medical thesis on Semmelweis. Finally, it seems probable that Céline took with him from his short stay at *Eurêka* an interest in and facility for the popularization of science, which he fully exploited in his early medical career. *La Quinine en thérapeutique*, published at his own expense in 1925, is a popularization of a thesis on quinine written by one of his great-uncles;[12] *Semmelweis* itself, published a year earlier, relies, as we shall see, on no original research, no primary sources and no technical scientific data which would deter the lay person. Instead it is, ostensibly at least, an uplifting tale of scientific perseverance and frustration aimed at the average reader, the sort of writing already familiar to Céline through the magazine *Je sais tout*, illustrations from which supplement the text, often incongruously, of the wartime editions of *Bagatelles pour un massacre* and *L'Ecole des cadavres*. The short summary of the thesis published in *La Presse médicale* as 'Les Derniers jours de Semmelweis' in June 1924 is, in effect, the popularization of a popularization.

As François Gibault suggests,[13] the work at *Eurêka* could only be a temporary pause, and sooner or later Céline was bound to grow tired of working in this eccentric milieu and living in his parents' apartment. When the opportunity to leave both came, he took it, and in March 1918 headed for Brittany.

II THE MISSION ROCKEFELLER

The unlikely agent of this move from Paris and parental control was the American charity, the Rockefeller Foundation, founded in 1913. Even before the United States' entry into the First World War in 1917, American charitable organizations had given help to the allies. The main activity of the Rockefeller Foundation at this time was in the sphere of public health and hygiene and, in the case of France, was directed towards the battle against tuberculosis. In early 1917, a team had visited France to inspect the extent of tuberculosis, and the results were so alarming that a 'Commission américaine de préservation contre la tuberculose' was dispatched, better known under the name 'Mission Rockefeller.'[14] Until the development of the BCG vaccine after the Second World War, tuberculosis was the major killer disease in Western Europe. Although improvements to urban drainage and water systems in the late nineteenth century had helped to diminish outbreaks of cholera and, to a lesser extent, typhus, tuberculosis was endemic through poor living conditions both in the countryside and in the cities: indeed, migration from the countryside to the city was one of the major factors in the spread of the disease. Once contracted through an insufficient diet and unhygienic surroundings, the disease was extremely contagious, transmitted through coughing and spitting. France was particularly affected by the disease: as Alméras reminds us, not only did it have the lowest birth rate in Europe, at 18.7 per thousand in 1911, it had the highest mortality rate,[15] due in large part to tuberculosis, fostered in its turn by a high rural population occupying poor living conditions and an urban population whose housing was often no better. In both cases, the problem was accentuated by poor diet, alcoholism and a general lack of concern with hygiene, at both an individual and official level, with crippling implications for French medical care and for the French economy as a whole. In 1928 Dr Eugène Briau, writing in *La Presse médicale*, estimated that the entire French medical budget for that year of 560 million francs would be spent on treating tuberculosis and syphilis alone.[16] The Mission Rockefeller, therefore, undertook a campaign of preventive medicine, aiming to educate the French, and especially the rural French population, in the importance of hygiene and the dangers of neglecting it.

In practical terms, the Mission set up a number of propaganda teams, which operated, as Alméras indicates,[17] rather like touring theatre troupes, booking halls in advance and giving out advance publicity or, given the nature of the struggle, like Soviet agit-prop groups during the Russian Civil War. Each team had a lorry with a mobile cinema, a puppet theatre, exhibition material and a lecturer. The performances, set up in advance with the help of the local authorities, were directed at schoolchildren – hence the importance of the puppet theatre – and adults, where the lecture, with slides, was the central feature. The performances ended with uplifting songs set to popular tunes: *J'ai du bon soleil dans ma chambrette* set to *J'ai du bon tabac*, or *Va-t-en, va-t-en microbe!* set to *Il pleut, il pleut bergère*. Since the Mission had a quasi-official status as part of the Allied war effort, its participants wore uniform, loosely modelled on American army officers' dress.

It is not clear how Céline came to join the Mission Rockefeller, though he later claimed that it was as a result of having intercepted his director's mail at *Eurêka*.[18] There is certainly some plausibility in this, since, not only did the Mission employ Céline as a lecturer, but also his friend from the war, Albert Milon, as a courier, and Henri de Graffigny, with his experience as a playwright and Guignol specialist, as puppet-master.[19] The team to which Céline belonged was led by an American, Dr Livingston Farrand, the President of the University of Colorado, and by his deputy, Professor Selskar Gunn, through whose influence Céline was later to enter the League of Nations. It was Céline's future father-in-law, Dr Athanase Follet, head of the Medical School at the University of Rennes and Chairman of the 'Comité départemental d'Ille-et-Vilaine de lutte contre la tuberculose', who requested that the Mission's first tour should be to Brittany, which, as one of

France's poorest and most rural regions, was particularly vulnerable, and Dr Farrand's team set off in February 1918, passing through Chartres before arriving in Rennes early in March.[20] According to Dr Bruno, the Mission's secretary, the team's entry into the Breton capital was triumphal: 'The whole population, massed on both sides of the street, from the station to the town hall, cheered joyfully the arrival of these "new American forces . . . against the inner enemy: tuberculosis,"'[21] and they were greeted by the Préfet of the Department, General Amade, the region's military commander, the Mayor of Rennes and Dr Follet. The first lecture took place on 11 March 1918 in the Théâtre de Rennes, given by Dr Bruno, and on 12 March, in the Omnia cinema, Céline gave his first lecture. The regional newspaper, *Ouest-Eclair*, reported that: 'M. Louis Destouches, introduced in formal and uplifting terms by Monsieur Dodu, Inspecteur de l'Académie, gave an extremely interesting lecture. He spoke with considerable knowledge of the subject and with a skill appreciated by the connoisseurs.'[22] Thereafter Céline, now assigned to team number 2, spent the rest of the year 1918 travelling all over Brittany. Already, *Ouest-Eclair* had described in grandiose terms the activities of the Mission:

> Huge lorries have been constructed, which can carry their own generators, with film-shows, pictures, complete exhibitions setting out the main points from the theatrical performances; lecturers and women from the American Red Cross accompany them, speaking French, ardent apostles in an unprecedented crusade, skilled in that special eloquence which goes right to a crowd's heart. These 'kings of hygiene' from the other side of the Atlantic are the counterparts of the American 'kings of steel, oil, railroads and mines.'[23]

Céline's own memories are more mundane, but confirm the basic format:

> We went all over Brittany in a lorry. There was a Breton Canadian with us, who took his wife and five children. We gave lectures in schools on tuberculosis. We gave up to five or six a day. The peasants we were talking to and who mainly spoke patois couldn't always understand what we were saying . . . They listened politely, without saying anything . . . They mainly looked at the films . . . They were very instructive, the films . . . You could see flies walking on milk . . . The film broke every five minutes, or came off the reel . . . It didn't matter, we repaired it.[24]

All the press reports during Céline's tour of Brittany in 1918 are highly complimentary, emphasizing his hard work and his ability as a speaker.[25]

Like *Eurêka*, however, the Mission Rockefeller patently did not offer a permanent career and, after his last lecture of 1918, on 3 December, Céline temporarily left the team when it headed for the Morbihan and the Loire-Inférieure, and stayed in Rennes in order to prepare for the *baccalauréat*. The law of 10 January 1919 allowed ex-combatants to take the *baccalauréat* on the basis of a restricted syllabus and with no written examinations, and Céline, who had rejoined the Mission in his tour of the south-west, passed the first part of the examination in Bordeaux on 2 April 1919, with the following marks:

Explication latine: *Horace*	16/20
Explication française: *Les Pensées* de Pascal	13/20
Première langue vivante	18/20
Deuxième langue vivante	14/20
Géographie: La Champagne	11/20
Histoire moderne: L'organisation de la France par la Révolution	14/20
Mathématiques: volume de la pyramide	12/20

and the *mention* 'bien'.[26] After touring in Castillon, Saint-Emilion and Libourne, he took the second part of the philosophy *baccalauréat* in Bordeaux on 2 July 1919 and obtained the following marks:

Philosophie: le plaisir et la douleur	13/20
Histoire contemporaine: la République de 1848 à 1851	18/20
Géographie: l'Irelande	16/20
Sciences naturelles: le rein	14/20

with, again, the *mention* 'bien'.[27] With the *baccalauréat*, Céline's career since the *Certificat des études* – the journeys to Germany and England (the 'première language vivante' in which he scored so well in the first part of the *bac*), the apprenticeship in Parisian commerce, the spell in Nice, the army and the war, and the brief period as a colonial trader – resumed what appeared to be an orthodox bourgeois trajectory after a highly eccentric detour, and he was now able to envisage entry into that most respectable and apparently lucrative of professions: medicine.

If he could aspire to a career which seemed beyond the grasp of his parents in the Passage Choiseul, it was not merely due to the 'mad determination to be a doctor'[28] which he retrospectively attributed to himself in later interviews, when it suited him to insist on his vocation as a doctor, even though, as we have seen, he enjoyed dabbling in medicine whilst in Africa. The decision to become a medical student at Rennes, which temporarily postponed an intention to seek his fortune in America,[29] arose at least in part from his engagement and marriage to a young woman whom he met at a reception to welcome the Mission Rockefeller to Rennes on 11 March 1918. The precise circumstances of Céline's first encounter with Edith Follet, the daughter of the head of the Medical School of the University and President of the Departmental Committee against Tuberculosis, Athanase Follet, remain unclear,[30] but the courtship appears to have been extremely rapid and he soon became a welcome guest in the family home. The couple were married as soon as Céline had passed his *baccalauréat* in the summer of 1919, with the marriage contract being signed on 4 July and the marriage itself, with both a civil and religious ceremony, taking place in Quintin, in the Côtes-du-Nord Department, on 19 August.[31] As Alméras points out, the desire to enhance Céline's family status still persisted: his father, who had allegedly warned Follet of his son's previous marriage and tried to deter him,[32] was described on the marriage certificate as a 'chef de bureau' at the Phénix; Marguerite Destouches was 'sans profession' and Céline's uncle, Louis Guillou, became an 'industrialist'.[33]

If the marriage took place in a small town on the north coast and not in Rennes, it was mainly because Athanase Follet had become such a controversial figure in the city that he preferred to marry his daughter away from those who knew him.[34] Born in 1867, Athanase Follet, who also had the name 'Marin', which he shares with Courtial des Pereires, had come from a humble Breton background to achieve considerable success in the medical profession, due both to sheer hard work as a medical student in Paris and to an advantageous marriage with the daughter of a prestigious Breton doctor, Augustin Morvan.[35] When Céline met him in 1918, he had achieved a powerful position in Rennes through his scientific and academic work, his role on numerous committees, like the Departmental anti-tuberculosis one, but also through a highly developed political sense. He was hugely ambitious and willing to make any compromise, using Freemasonry and republicanism to ingratiate himself with the regime, and accepting posts in religious establishments to maintain his reputation with Brittany's Catholics.[36] In a letter to Milon quoted at length in Gibault's biography, Céline takes great delight in detailing the lengths to which his father-in-law would go to win his way back into the favour of the Archbishop of Rennes, Cardinal Dubourg.[37] Unsurprisingly, this consumate opportunism made a large number of enemies in the Rennes Medical School and, when Follet was appointed Director in June 1918,[38] his colleagues made a formal protest at the first meeting he chaired, ending with the words: 'If you still have the slightest sense of dignity, resign now, Monsieur,'[39] which left the arch-conspirator totally unmoved. The importance of Follet for Céline, however, is that, like Benedictus and de Graffigny, he was the latest in a series of eccentrics in Celine's early life and, coming from a modest background himself, he was not bound by bourgeois convention to the extent that he would refuse to allow his daughter to marry the son of petit-bourgeois Parisians, albeit promoted for the occasion. In this respect he played a major role in Céline's development and facilitated, even encouraged his entry into a profession which he was to exercise in numerous ways until the end of his life.

III MEDICAL STUDIES

After their marriage, Céline and Edith moved into an apartment on the ground floor of the Follet family house at number 6 Quai Richemont, in the centre of Rennes. They took their meals with Edith's parents, and Céline was able to use Athanase Follet's study and library, which he rapidly turned into his own room. It was here that he worked flat out on his medical studies, as part of an accelerated programme designed especially for demobilized soldiers and in which the Medical School at Rennes specialized.[40] Both Gibault and Alméras emphasize that, contrary to some accounts, Céline benefited neither from a reduced syllabus nor from undue patronage from his father-in-law, and that he, like many ex-combatants, merely availed himself of a law enabling him to complete his medical studies in two and a half years instead of the usual four.[41]

He began work on his premedical studies in October 1919, obtaining his initial qualification, the PCN ('propédeutique aux études de médecine') on 26 March 1920, and immediately registering as a medical student. On 7 April 1921 he took his first examinations, in anatomy, and passed with the *mentions* 'bien' and 'assez bien'; on 22 July 1921 he passed his examinations in histology, physiology, biological physics and biological chemistry with the *mention* 'bien', and on 16 November 1921 he took his final examinations at Rennes, with practicals in (1) operational medicine and topographical anatomy and (2) pathological anatomy, and oral exams in (1) operational medicine, topographical anatomy, external pathology and childbirth, and (2) general pathology, parasites, animals, vegetables, microbes and internal pathology, all of which he passed with the *mention* 'bien'.[42] In other words, between April 1919 and November 1921, Céline had succeeded in transforming himself from an unqualified wanderer without even the *baccalauréat* into a nearly qualified medical student: a considerable achievement, which testifies to determination and hard work, but also to that sense of ambition which was present as early as the *Carnet du Cuirassier Destouches*.

A further clue to the nature of that ambition is contained in a letter from the early Rennes period to Albert Milon. In the first place, Céline shows himself, perhaps deliberately, to be highly conscious of the precariousness of his position as a 'proletarian' Parisian in a bourgeois household and embarking on a bourgeois career. Describing his huge capacity for hard work, he writes: 'I was born amongst the people and the comforts of the gentle life have in no way diminished my decidedly plebeian constitution.'[43] He continues, reflecting on his life in the midst of

a comfort which makes me think of so many whom a less fortunate destiny leaves on their painful feet all day, travelling in suburban trains or working as salespeople in department stores. But poverty is only conceivable for those who have experienced it – and the bourgeois heart is something inconceivably lacklustre and insensitive to the poverty of others – I don't say this for Edith, who is charming, even though altruism is not her strong suit (where could she have learnt it?), but for that crowd of hideous egoists whom I encounter in the street, with their round and closed faces – Yes, my friend, I have successively climbed and descended a good number of rungs on the social ladder and I remain amazed at the lack of understanding of the clear barriers which exist between men – There's more difference between a French bourgeois and a poor Frenchman than between a rich Frenchman and an opulent German.[44]

Even if we discount a certain amount of this as a desire to impress and to give himself an exaggeratedly proletarian past, as if he were Julien Sorel in the Maison de la Môle, there remains that antipathy to the bourgeoisie which was to be a constant in Céline's life and work and which looks forward already to the metaphor of society as a slave-galley which opens *Voyage au bout de la nuit*. Nor would the 'round and closed faces' of the citizens of Rennes be out of place among Sartre's burghers of Bouville in *La Nausée*. Paradoxically, however, immediately after this denunciation and declaration of social war, there follows the by now familiar evocation of success: 'I am wallowing in the delights of studies – I'm enjoying myself – in every way – you just need to try – But I've got every ambition – and I'm especially drawn to discoveries.'[45]

In fact, it was literally through scientific discovery that the precocious medical student Céline aimed to achieve an easy and rapid success. The vocation was more towards success than specifically towards medicine. He explored the curative possibilities of 'snail extract' on tuberculosis, then worked on the survival of the typhus bacillus in a vacuum.[46] In the summer of 1920, while Edith sunned herself on the beach, Céline worked at the marine research station at Roscoff, in particular on the physiology of the *Convoluta*, a sea-urchin which took on the colour of the algae it absorbed[47] and which retained uric acid from its environment. The subject of the research itself has very few implications for Céline's future work, but what is significant is that this young medical student, on the basis of a very short research project, should publish his findings in a scientific paper for the Académie des Sciences and that he should enrol one of the most distinguished scientists of his day, Edmond Perrier, who had been on the board of *Eurêka*, to sponsor it: 'Observations physiologiques sur *Convoluta roscoffensis* – Note de M. Louis Destouches – présentée par M. Edmond Perrier' appeared in the *Actes* of the Académie des Sciences of 26 October 1920.[48] A year later he published, again in the *Actes* of the Académie, a study of the hibernation of caterpillars, 'Prolongation de la vie chez les *Galleria mellonella*,'[49] about which, according to Edith Follet, he had corresponded with another famous scientist, Alexis Carrel.[50] In other words, Céline's pursuit of 'success' was still designed to take place through a series of spectacular short cuts and the mobilization of as much patronage as he could muster. The problem is that this hasty and amateurish work was more at home among the inventors of *Eurêka* than the scientists of the Académie and has something in common with the efforts of Courtial des Pereires. As André Lwoff, himself a Nobel prizewinner, comments on Céline's scientific research: 'Both publications show evidence of a certain hastiness and a no less certain naivety both in thought and expression . . . No one could regret that he sacrificed the profession of researcher for that of writer. His contribution to science could never have equalled in value and originality his contribution to literature, which is considerable.'[51]

Céline's cosseted private life in the apartment in the Quai Richemont was dominated by hard work and by an accelerated reading programme, which included Rabelais, Ronsard, Du Bellay, Petronius, Dickens, Bergson, Tallemant des Réaux and, his favourite, Remy de Gourmont.[52] It also showed an increasing desire for independence, an independence which appears to have been respected by Edith. In his letter to Milon already quoted, Céline spells out his needs: 'It's only at the price of the greatest independence that this marriage is possible, and, thankfully, freedom is understood in its fullest meaning by the entire family.'[53] Not only did this give Céline a considerable freedom of action with regard to his father-in-law, with whom he appears to have enjoyed cordial relations and who totally respected his independence,[54] it also determined his rapport with Edith, 'of whom I see very little, since I am as much a loner as I am independent and I hate constraint, even in its most affectionate form'.[55] At the beginning of their marriage Céline and Edith, often in the company of Marcel Brochard, who had married Edith's best friend, or the Breton journalist Francis Vareddes, had travelled all over the region, using Céline's Indiana motorcycle and sidecar.[56] Yet, with the birth of the couple's daughter Colette on 15 June 1920, we start to see an assertion of that independence displayed in the letter to Milon and which was eventually to destroy the marriage. With the birth of their daughter, Céline showed a highly antagonistic attitude towards both his own parents and his parents-in-law. Colette was christened without any display of ceremony and with Céline's parents being excluded: 'Things will go off very simply, without any special meal – nor grandmother – I shall not go to the church and Edith will stay in bed,' he wrote to his parents,[57] and he added: 'the child's grandmother is kept, on my orders, away from caresses which would give her great pleasure but for which I have no indulgence.'[58]

What we see very clearly is a man unable to accept a close relationship or the responsibility of parenthood. Instead, he preferred to return to a bachelor life with his friends Milon and Vareddes, which involved a considerable amount of sexual freedom and adventure: a conference organized by the Fondation Rockefeller in Pau in July 1921 was the excuse for a group sexual encounter, of which Edith was by no means ignorant.[59] Céline wrote to a friend in Pau shortly before his arrival stating: 'You know my opinion on these things. You're free to invite any little cousins or female cousins. You understand.'[60] This sexual dilettantism was to continue for at least another fourteen years, until his relationship with Lucette Almansor, and was accompanied until the end of his life by the need for a relationship with male friends, the pattern of which had already been set by Milon and, in London, by Georges Geoffroy. It was to continue, crucially, with his entry into the essentially male community of Montmartre in the late 1920s.

In fact, Céline's commitment to independence was rapidly eroding his marriage, a process illuminated by his move to Paris at the beginning of 1923. The Ecole de Médecine of Rennes had only delegated status and was not authorized to award entire medical degrees. After the early years of study, the candidate was normally required to complete his or her training at the Faculté de Médecine de Paris, which oversaw the school at Rennes.

On 5 December 1922, Céline was authorized by Rennes to complete his studies in Paris. He took his exams on 15 February 1923, in which he failed 'Therapy, Medicine, and Pharmacology', with the *mention* 'mal', but passed 'Hygiene', with the *mention* 'médiocre' and 'Legal Medicine', with the *mention* 'bien'. He was forced to retake the 'Therapy' examination on 10 April 1923, which he passed with the *mention* 'bien', and then completed his studies with fifth-year examinations in 'Internal clinical studies' ('bien') 'External clinical studies' ('bien') and 'Obstetrics' ('médiocre').[61] As a student in Paris, Céline had originally envisaged renting an apartment for Edith, Colette and himself in the capital, but had rapidly decided to live by himself and commute from Rennes, helped by Athanase Follet's post as 'médecin des chemins de fer' to provide the necessary free transport.[62] He had already had some experience of Paris as a student on a course at the Tarnier Maternity Clinic in the Latin Quarter from 1 October to 16 December 1922,[63] and it was the Director of the Obstetrics Service, Professor Brindeau, who allegedly first suggested to Céline that he write his medical thesis, the only hurdle left before qualification as a doctor, on a literary rather than a scientific subject, the career of the Hungarian doctor and scientist Semmelweis.[64] It was while writing his thesis on Semmelweis, defended on 1 May 1924, awarded the *mention* 'très bien' by the jury, and later, on 22 January 1925, given a bronze medal by the Commission des Prix des Thèses, that he undertook his first practical work as a doctor. He worked as a locum in Rennes for a Doctor Porée from 1 June to 31 August 1923, and for his father-in-law at the Catholic clinic of La Sagesse from 18 August to 31 October 1923,[65] then in the town of Revin in the Ardennes, where he replaced a Doctor Boucher for the months of July and August.[66] As Alméras comments, the choice of the subject of Semmelweis appears paradoxical, in spite of the encouragement of Brindeau, since Semmelweis was an obstetrician and obstetrics was, as we have seen, Céline's worst subject in his final examinations in Paris. What we are probably witnessing with the thesis on Semmelweis, however, is, in a curious way, the end of Céline's pretensions to scientific research, and the resurgence of the old ambition of literary 'success'.

IV SEMMELWEIS

According to the official biography,[67] Ignác Fülöp Semmelweis, Hungary's greatest medical scientist, was born on 1 July 1818 in Budapest, the son of a prosperous grocer. After a successful career at the Royal Catholic University Gymnasium, he studied philosophy for two years at Pest University before enrolling at his father's instigation as a law student at the University of Vienna in 1837. He rapidly changed his mind, however, and decided to study medicine, returning to the University of Pest for two years before completing his medical studies in Vienna in 1844 with a thesis in Latin, the

Tractatus de Vita Plantarum. He stayed on in Vienna after obtaining his degree, attending courses by the young rising stars in Viennese medical circles, Skoda, Rokitansky and Hebra, who were proponents of 'the new trend of pathology',[68] which sought confirmation of diagnosis in dissection. Semmelweis was drawn to surgery, like his mentor Skoda, but there were no posts in Skoda's clinic at the time. He therefore decided to specialize in obstetrics and applied for a post in the clinic of Professor Klein, where he was finally appointed after a two-year wait in 1846. This was to be the turning-point in his career: the maternity clinic of the Allgemeines Krankenhaus of Vienna had a successful history of treatment from its foundation in 1784 until 1840, with a mortality rate as low as 1.25 per cent. This persisted, even with the creation of two clinics, one under Professor Klein and the other under his colleague Professor Bartsch. In 1840, however, a new regulation was introduced which separated the training of medical students from that of students in midwifery: the medical students remained in the First Clinic, directed by Klein, while the midwifery students were confined to the Second Clinic under Bartsch. Immediately, a huge rise in the mortality rate occurred in the First Clinic: between 1840 and 1846 it was 9.92 per cent, as opposed to 3.38 per cent in the Second Clinic, with horrifying peaks, as in October 1842, of 29.3 per cent.[69]

Semmelweis spent his first year in Klein's clinic attempting to resolve what, in terms of mid-nineteenth-century scientific knowledge, was inexplicable: 'everything seemed problematic, everything seemed unclear, everything was dubious, undecipherable, only the great number of dead was an undoubted reality.'[70] Rejecting the current explanations (an epidemic or rough treatment by medical staff) as illogical since the same conditions applied in the two clinics, with their markedly different mortality rates, he looked for a local cause specific to Clinic Number 1. He found it by chance on hearing the news of the death of his friend Kolletchka, a professor of forensic medicine, who had died as the result of a cut received while performing an autopsy. Semmelweis immediately saw the significance: the one specific local factor in the First Clinic which distinguished it from the Second was the presence of medical students who had come straight from the dissecting-room to treat the women in labour, as indeed had Semmelweis himself, and the 'infectious material which caused cadaver fever also caused puerperal fever'.[71] The solution was simple: if the 'cadaverous poison' was resistant to mere soap and water, it could be defeated by disinfectant and, after experimentation, Semmelweis opted for chlorinated lime as the best ingredient, making it compulsory for all doctors, medical students and nurses in May 1847. The results were spectacular: by July 1847 the mortality rate in the First Clinic had fallen to 1.20 per cent, and in March and August 1848 there were no fatalities in either clinic.

Semmelweis's great mistake was in not immediately publishing his findings and, instead of the expected acclaim, he was subjected to a sustained campaign of vilification from his jealous superior, Professor Klein, members of the 'old' Viennese School of Medicine and even the international community, including Simpson in Edinburgh, Scanzoni in Würzburg, Dubois in Paris and Kiwisch in Prague.[72] Semmelweis had, perhaps inadvertently, walked into the middle of a war between the 'old' school and the 'new', represented by Skoda and Hebra.

Semmelweis remained in Vienna during the 1848 Revolution in Budapest and the War of Independence against Austria, even though he had difficulty in obtaining appointment as a *Privat-Dozent* when his post at Klein's clinic expired, and he was not allowed to use cadavers for his practical demonstrations. In 1850, just after receiving his appointment, he suddenly decided to return to Budapest, where he frequented liberal Hungarian nationalist circles. He was initially appointed as honorary head of the Maternity Ward of the Saint Rochus Hospital, under the sympathetic but ineffectual Professor Birly, whom he succeeded as professor of theoretical and practical obstetrics at the University of Pest in 1855, a post he held until his death ten years later. This final period of his life was marked by the beginnings of recognition – he was invited to the University of Zurich and he published his major work *Aethiologie der Begriff und die Prophylaxis des Kindbettfiebers* in 1861 – but also by continued opposition and incomprehension which provoked increasingly unstable behaviour on his part. This included issuing open letters to colleagues, like the one to Scanzoni in Würzburg, which read: 'You have demonstrated . . . that in a new hospital like yours, which has been accommodated with the most modern furnishing and appliances, a good deal of homicide can be committed, providing one has the indispensable talent to carry it out.'[73] His mental health declined until, in the middle of July 1865, he became incoherent during a faculty meeting. His former colleague and supporter Professor Hebra travelled from Vienna and took him back to an asylum in the Austrian capital, where he died on 13 August 1865. Later evidence suggests that, while Semmelweis was suffering from both long-term psychopathia and a degeneration of the nervous system from 1861 onwards, the immediate cause of death was pyaemia, caused by an infected wound from the operating theatre. In other words, Semmelweis, who was only posthumously to be recognized as one of the great pioneers of antisepsis, along with Lister and Oliver Wendell Holmes, died from the same disease as his patients.

The *Thèse de Médecine* was the final hurdle which a medical student had to overcome before qualifying and its status was more akin to that of a final year undergraduate dissertation than a doctoral thesis requiring original scientific research. Céline's thesis, entitled *La Vie et l'oeuvre de Philippe Ignace Semmelweis (1818–1865)*, is remarkable for its lack of technical data and appears to have been compiled from the secondary material listed in the bibliography which, at the time, apart from Professor Pinard's 'Discours d'inauguration du monument de Semmelweis', published in *La Presse médicale* in 1906, was exclusively in German and English. Indeed, it may well be that the subject appealed to Céline precisely because it involved the use of the two foreign languages in which he was competent.

If it was obviously acceptable for the *thèse* to be based on non-technical secondary data and to be written in an ostentatiously literary style, it is still surprising to see a candidate submit, and indeed, a jury pass, a thesis so full of factual errors. When Céline published a summary of his work, 'Les Derniers Jours de Semmelweis', in *La Presse médicale* on 25 June 1924, just eight weeks after the *soutenance* on 1 May, a professor at the University of Budapest, Tiberius de Györy, replied with a number of basic corrections.[74] Céline had described Semmelweis, who was patently Hungarian, as a 'Viennese obstetrician'; he systematically referred to Semmelweis's arch-enemy as Professor Klin and not Klein, and put the mortality rate of his clinic at a scarcely credible 96 per cent. According to Györy, not only were Semmelweis's Hungarian colleagues right behind his discovery, but he never, as Céline alleges, put up posters around Budapest denouncing his enemies. Regarding the death of Semmelweis, Céline recounts a melodramatic scene in which the mad doctor deliberately stabs himself with an infected scalpel during an autopsy, and a no less fictitious, though, as we shall see, highly significant, episode in which the faithful Skoda rushes to take the mad and dying Semmelweis back to Vienna. Finally, Györy draws attention to a number of errors of dates, including those of his return to Vienna (31 July and not 22 June) and, more curiously, that of his death (13 August and not 16 August). It is also worth mentioning that, in order to portray Semmelweis's struggle with Klin as one against sheer human malevolence, Céline omits to mention that Klein, as a highly conservative Court doctor, had political reasons to be distrustful of Semmelweis, whom he regarded as a dangerous liberal. Similarly, his depiction of Semmelweis as an essentially lone fighter for truth is enhanced by the avoidance of all mention of his marriage and five children.

It might be argued that getting the date of Semmelweis's death wrong is at least symmetrical, since Céline contrives to get the date of his birth wrong as well, putting it as 18 July and not 1 July. Moreover, some attempt at rigour should have rendered Semmelweis's name correctly: he was Ignác Fülöp, and not, as Céline inverts it, Philippe Ignace. Or is he? Céline may have been skating on thin ice by introducing so many factual errors, and his jury, albeit packed with friends like Athanase Follet and Selskar Gunn, was overly tolerant or lacking in vigilance, but the point is elsewhere. The procedures of factual error introduced for the first time in *Semmelweis* were to become profoundly familiar to readers of his later work: the errors of dates which undermine *Voyage au bout de la nuit* as a realist novel, from the *Chanson des Gardes suisses* of 1793, when they were massacred in 1792, to Lola's ancestors having sailed with the *Mayflower* in 1677, only fifty-seven years out,[75] or Maréchal Moncey defending the Place Clichy against the approaching Cossacks in the wrong year;[76] and the curiously unbelievable statistics for Jewish mobilization during the First World War which tantalizingly call into question *Bagatelles pour un massacre* and *L'Ecole des cadavres*. For the first time the reader, with hindsight, has a privileged encounter with the cornerstone of Céline's fiction: the technique of transposition, central also to Modernist writing. As Alméras suggests, *Semmelweis* must be read as a novel, not necessarily exclusively in a Hugolian tradition,[77] but certainly as a complex and impertinent fictional gesture.

That *Semmelweis* constitutes the beginning of the formal Célinian *oeuvre* is confirmed by the fact that not only did he attempt to popularize the work in *La Presse médicale*, but that he republished it in 1936 as a means of padding out the very short and polemical text, *Mea culpa*. This is significant in itself: Céline, setting out on the very dangerous waters of inter-war polemic, accompanied his denunciation of the Soviet Union with the exemplary tale of a tragic polemicist. At the same time he was careful, in the preface to the 1936 edition, to emphasize the legendary and hence general qualities of the tale he had to tell: 'Here is the terrible story of Philippe-Ignace Semmelweis,'[78] a line which recalls the opening of Blaise Cendrars' tale of the no less exemplary hero of *L'Or*, of 1924: 'Here is the marvellous story of General Johann Auguste Suter.'[79] What that legend is about, ostensibly, is a duel with death and a struggle against human pettiness and cruelty. Céline's Semmelweis is appalled at the situation in Klin's clinic, where 'the two great joys of existence, that of being young and that of giving life',[80] are denied and inverted. In Klin's clinic, the act of birth becomes an act of death for mother and child alike, and, since the disease is transmitted by doctors and medical students, straight from contact with death itself; the nineteenth-century humanist image of the doctor as life-preserving is inverted so that he becomes 'the auxiliary of death'.[81] In both cases, the ground is laid for some of Céline's later work. In the novels, there is a contrast between the plastic beauty of the female body and an emphasis on it as an agent of death: in *Voyage au bout de la nuit*, sex ends in abortion, and abortion in haemorrhage and death. As Yannik Mancel writes:

> In the Célinian textuality, all women appear, not merely as under sentence of the menopause, but also, and perhaps especially, as carriers of a potential inflammation/decomposition of the genital organs. It is particularly as the carrier of a virtual death that the female sexual organs are presented in Céline's work: there is a danger of death for the mother, first of all, as evidenced by the very subject of Céline's doctoral thesis, and then an equal danger for the child, proven by the sequences of abortion, miscarriage and bungled deliveries which are dotted throughout the Célinian narrative.[82]

At the same time, the ambiguous attitude towards the traditional image of the humanist doctor looks forward to Céline's later reflections on social medicine and hygiene, to his portrayal of Bardamu, in *Voyage au bout de la nuit*, as a medical student and then doctor who discovers the impossibility of the practice of medicine in a divided society, and to the disillusioned narrator of *Mort à crédit*, who has 'not always practised medicine, that shit'.[83]

Part of the reason for the failure of Semmelweis in his struggle with death is that the doctors in Céline's narrative are all too often the repositories of that human pettiness and cruelty which, again, characterize the subsequent fiction. Semmelweis's allies, Skoda, Rokitansky and Hebra, are not adequate to the task of defending his discovery in the face of professional jealousy and sheer human stupidity. Once again, the beginnings of Céline's extreme scepticism regarding humanity and humanism are to be found in *Semmelweis*. The comment in *Mea culpa*, of 1936: 'Man is human to about the same extent as chickens fly,'[84] merely codifies the experience and realization of Semmelweis, recounted in the same volume.

Yet if, as Alméras suggests, *Semmelweis* is thematically dominated by a battle between good and evil, obscurantism and enlightenment,[85] it has an immensely broad field of concern. For Céline, the case of Semmelweis illustrates the complex process of the search for truth in a context where none of the subsequent rules or laws yet exist to enable that truth to be discovered or identified. Semmelweis does not benefit from the knowledge of bacteria arrived at by Pasteur and which retrospectively, but only retrospectively, validated his discovery. It is for this reason that Céline superimposes Semmelweis's quest for the truth upon a readily recognizable model, that of Descartes, and that he describes that quest in terms of the Cartesian dichotomy between light and darkness. Semmelweis, he writes, 'wants to see absolutely clearly',[86] but, before being able to do so, is obliged to wander round the truth he seeks without recognizing it. Compared with Semmelweis, however, Descartes was fortunate in that, in spite of opposition from the Catholic Church, his work achieved rapid and widespread recognition. The second major issue which Céline explores in *Semmelweis*, therefore, is that of persuasion. Difficult as it may be, with no rules to guide, to discover the truth, it is even more difficult to convince others of the rightness or usefulness of the discovery, particularly when there are additional factors such as professional jealousy. In this context, Semmelweis's discovery is a test both of his personality and of available means of communication. In personal terms, Semmelweis failed to adapt to the importance of his discovery and to find the right means of communicating it. As Céline concluded his thesis: 'it seems that his discovery went beyond the limits of his genius. That was, perhaps, the profound cause of all his sufferings.'[87] It was for this reason that he went mad. Yet, in the face of almost general incomprehension, Semmelweis's real tragedy was that he never, in Céline's narrative, found the appropriate form of communicating his discovery. With the successive failure of letters, of a personal emissary, Arneth, to the French scientific establishment, even of the solidly scientific *Aetiology*, he resorted to the polemical procedures of open letters ('Fathers, do you know what you are doing in calling to the bedside of your wife in labour a doctor or a midwife? What you are doing is deliberately making her run the risk of death')[88] or posters on the walls of the city. *Semmelweis*, therefore, is a study of polemic, but particularly of its counter-productive and destructive, even self-destructive, nature. It is highly significant in this context that it should be republished in 1936 together with *Mea culpa*, a deeply camouflaged piece of polemic, but only one year before the almost suicidal

Bagatelles pour un massacre. That Céline was aware of the dangers is confirmed by the preface to the 1936 edition, in which he recommends tact and cunning in the publicizing of a discovery:

> Just imagine that today, in the same way, another innocent should turn up with a cure for cancer. He wouldn't know what sort of dance they would lead him! It would be amazing! He would have to take extra care! He would have to be forewarned. He's have to keep his head down! He'd be better off joining the Foreign Legion! Nothing is free in this world. Everything is paid for, good, like evil, eventually. It's just that good is more expensive.[89]

Why Céline did not heed his own advice is one of the enigmas of his development in the 1930s.

If Céline's narrative of Semmelweis moves out from a narrow study of the discovery of a disease to more general reflections on human nature, the nature of scientific discovery and the role of polemic, he is oddly careful to set that narrative in a particular philosophico-historical context. The announcement of Semmelweis's birth in 1818 is immediately followed, not by an evocation of his childhood, which comes later, but by a long historical description which appears, at first sight, unconnected. We go back in time to 1805: 'On the 2 December, at four in the morning, action commenced in fog which rapidly dispersed . . . AUSTERLITZ . . . But that's not what we're really looking for . . . we're looking for a man like us, with our blood and our race, closer to Semmelweis: Corvisart . . . ! Corvisart.'[90] Céline's first work of fiction, if that is what it is, begins with a moving description of the Surgeon-General of the Grand Army, Corvisart, who, during the Battle of Austerlitz, took time off to work in Vienna on his translation of the classic medical treatise of Auenbrugger on auscultation, a vital work of medical research neglected for fifty years.[91] Not only does this place the doctoral thesis of the young Destouches in a familiar context of the intellectual history of the 1920s, when the cult of Napoleon and the 'nouveau mal du siècle' was at its height, as witnessed, for example, by Malraux's *La Tentation de l'Occident*,[92] it also, very neatly, places Céline as the author recuperating the 'lost' discovery of Semmelweis in an exactly symmetrical position to Corvisart discovering the lost manuscript of Auenbrugger. Destouches, or Des Touches, becomes Corvisart, right at the heart of the Napoleonic epic.

At the same time, the thesis itself opens curiously with a highly stylized evocation of the French Revolution, an evocation so stylized that its first line: 'Mirabeau criait si fort que Versailles eut peur,'[93] is almost an alexandrine. This poetic opening is followed by the description of a rapid alternation between uncontrollable violence and periods of calm:

> Death howled in the bloody foam of its disparate legions; from the Nile to Stockholm and from the Vendée to Russia, a hundred armies invoked at the same time a hundred reasons to be untamed. Frontiers ravaged, and reformed in an immense kingdom of Frenzy, men wanting progress and progress wanting men: such was this monstrous marriage. Humanity got

bored; we burned a few gods, changed our costume and paid History with a few new glories. And then, once the torment had been satisfied and the great hopes had been buried for centuries to come, each one of these furies went off as a 'subject' to the Bastille, came back a 'citizen' and went back to his pettiness.[94]

For Céline, the crucial moment in this process was 1793, the year of the *Chanson des Gardes suisses* and the execution of the king: 'The flower of an epoch was destroyed.'[95] The castigation of the 'butchery'[96] which followed, justified by the new sense of equality, leaves no doubt as to the author's hostility: Céline is still very much the descendant of the Chevalier des Touches, and although his political position may appear to oscillate, he remains passionately anti-republican.

The chaos which results from 1793 leads to a conflagration throughout Europe which can only be mastered through strength: 'In the course of these monstrous years . . . Europe needed a male. In the first glimmers of that storm, Napoleon took Europe and, willy-nilly, kept her for fifteen years.'[97] The Napoleonic period cannot last, however, and peace becomes fashionable again: 'People only wanted sweetness and tenderness . . . And Napoleon, who persisted in living, was shut up on an island with a cancer.'[98] It is at this time that sentimental Romanticism dominates in taste and in the arts, and it is the immediate post-Napoleonic period which sees the birth of Semmelweis.

It is a curious introduction, even more so in the context of an academic thesis, highly overwritten and apparently of dubious relevance to the subject. On closer inspection, however, in addition to the reactionary, monarchist and anti-republican perspective it establishes, it does provide a particular theoretical and cultural context for the story of Semmelweis and also constructs a sophisticated structural framework. Céline's view of history from the Revolution to the Restoration is clearly dialectical and anthropomorphic. A period of violence is succeeded by a period of peace which, in its turn, degenerates into violent chaos and is mastered by a dictator, only to return to sentimentalism. At the same time, both the violence and the degenerative periods of peace are expressions of a feminine historical principle, while the period of glory and control is clearly the expression of the masculine. This sexualization of history and its portrayal as a cycle appears to owe a considerable amount to Nietzsche, whom, according to Georges Charensol, Céline was reading in London, and to the German philosopher's doctrine of eternal recurrence as well as his championship of the masculine qualities of the Will. In this context, Céline's use of the disputed account of Skoda coming from Vienna to rescue the mad Semmelweis may well owe its origins to the famous journey of Franz Overbeck to bring back the mad Nietzsche from Genoa to Basle.

Nor is the historical material which opens the work so irrelevant as it initially appears: the French Revolution, for Céline, like Semmelweis's patients, died at birth, and this Napoleon of science was ultimately defeated by the human pettiness denounced in the introduction. At the same time the cyclical structure of history, in which the still-born Revolution of 1789 is repeated in the similarly failed Revolution of 1848, is reflected in the controlled symmetry which Céline detects in Semmelweis's own career: continually oscillating between the twin cities of the Dual Monarchy, Vienna and Budapest (itself divided between Buda and Pest); dying from the same infection which had killed his friend Kolletchka and which he had identified; brought back, in Céline's narrative, to Vienna by the physician Skoda who had initially seduced him away from law to medicine.

Although Alméras is surely right to point to the stylistic shortcomings in the text, Céline's first published work (it was printed by Francis Simon, in Rennes), quite apart from its thematic implications for his later work, shows an ability to handle a formal, high-register literary French style, to deploy a complex and rigorous structure and, finally, to establish a rich historical and cultural context. In the novels, that formal style is abandoned in favour of a richer but no less artificial literary language derived from the patterns and rhythms of spoken French, but the concern with structure and the wide range of cultural reference remain crucial components of Célinian fiction.

V CAREER

It is characteristic of Céline at this time that he should attempt to exploit the success of his thesis as rapidly as possible. As we have seen, he success-fully defended it on 1 May 1924, and published his résumé 'Les Derniers jours de Semmelweis' in *La Presse médicale* on 25 June. As Gibault notes, he had evidently already circulated a number of complimentary copies to influential figures, since in the newspaper article he quotes Romain Rolland's approving reaction: 'I thought I knew human stupidity and its evil, but decidedly it is limitless.'[99] Céline, now 30, was in a hurry: he needed to make his name known and to get as much influential support as possible.

He was also evidently undecided as to a future career, but one thing is quite clear: he was not at all tempted at that stage by general practice, and the mythology of his medical vocation was constructed later with the ap-pearance of *Voyage au bout de la nuit*. He wrote to Milon: 'I have no desire to take over the La Sagesse clinic or the Rue Duguesclin practice (from Dr Follet), either alone or with some other thief.'[100] Initially, he was tempted by research in Paris. In November 1923, thanks to Dr Follet, who recommended him to Emile Roux, he was supposed to work with Serge Metalnikov at the Institut Pasteur, but, in spite of later claims to the contrary, he spent very little time there, not even bothering to register for the course in microbiology, a lack of concern which soured relations be-tween Follet and Roux.[101] At the same time, he had planned to work at the Institut du Cancer in the suburb of Villejuif, and had even written to Milon asking him to find an apartment for himself and Edith,[102] but this plan had come to nothing as well. Other projects included psychiatry[103] and paediatrics.[104] Gibault records that, from 23 to 25 June 1924, he passed the examinations for becoming a ship's doctor,[105] a qualification which he was to make real use of during the mobilization of 1939 on board the *Chella*.

In fact, he still appears to have nourished his old ambition to go to America[106] and had kept in close contact with his old friends in the Mission Rockefeller. We have seen that Professor Selskar Gunn, presumably on Céline's nomination, had served on the jury for his thesis, along with Brindeau, Follet and Henri Maréchal, 'Chef de Clinique' in the Paris Medical Faculty, and it was Gunn who, in May 1924, introduced him to Dr Ludwig Rajchman, the Director of the Hygiene Section of the League of Nations in Geneva. On 14 May, Céline followed up this meeting by sending Rajchman a copy of the, as yet unpublished, *Presse médicale* article, having obviously previously given him a copy of the actual thesis: 'Here is an article for *La Presse médicale* which reasonably summarizes what I think on a number of levels and touches on subjects which we discussed during our interview in Paris. I thought that, in addition to my thesis, it would be nice for you to know what was going on in the mind of a possible colleague.'[107] The letter continues with an apparently favourable comment on the 1924 parliamentary elections, which brought in the Cartel des Gauches and launched France, briefly, on an internationalist, Briandist, foreign policy: 'Our elections will give to our country its real [role?] in the world and to the League of Nations a preponderant place in our affairs which it has not yet had.'[108] It ends with the news that he will be coming to Geneva in four weeks. A second letter, dated 12 June and posted from Rennes, in reply to what was evidently a highly positive response from Rajchman, shows that negotiations had become much more concrete. Agreeing to arrive at the end of June, Céline placed himself entirely at Rajchman's disposal for the length of his stay, and announced the news of his recent qualification as a ship's doctor as enabling him to 'have a qualification as a hygienist which will perhaps help you to some extent in pushing my candidacy'.[109] He also reminded Rajchman that Gunn had promised him a trip to the United States 'perhaps after my first stay in Geneva? Before my permanent appointment?'[110] Clearly, Céline had been offered a temporary posting to Geneva, with the possibility of foreign travel and the likelihood of a longer-term appointment. He left Rennes on 21 June 1924, with the promise that Edith and Colette would join him as soon as he was established.

Céline had moved a long way, and extremely rapidly, since his return to Europe from Africa. He had acquired academic qualifications and entry into what was considered, at least, a desirable and lucrative profession. He had married and become a father in a milieu which, in spite of his own nascent bohemianism and radical politics, was incontestably bourgeois. He had also acquired a culture which, whilst not uniformly orthodox, was rich and complex, with a certain stylistic virtuosity and the elements of a literary ambition. Politically, he was already the chameleon he would be in later life: anti-Semitic, according to Edith Follet,[111] Monarchist and Bonapartist in *Semmelweis*, Briandist and Republican in his correspondence with the Jewish Rajchman of the League of Nations. The search for 'success' is still strongly present: in the admiration for great men in the thesis, in its grandiose style, perhaps even in the veiled contempt for the jury enshrined in the number of factual errors, and certainly in the single-minded completion of the medical syllabus in four years. At the same time, that ambition is not initially, at least, going to take Céline into the humanitarian backwaters of an obscure medical practice: the myth of the 'médecin des pauvres' is more attractive than its reality. The newly qualified doctor is much more attracted to the glamorous life of an international medical administrator, albeit in his chosen field of hygiene, than to the practice of medicine.

4

The League of Nations

I Geneva

Céline began his work for the League of Nations on 27 June 1924, employed as a doctor in the Hygiene Section, Grade B, with a monthly salary of 1000 Swiss francs.[1] He was given a fixed-term contract until 31 December 1927 and his post was funded, not directly by the League, but by the Rockefeller Foundation. As Alméras points out, given the mythology surrounding Céline's departure from the League of Nations, these two facts are important. His appointment was always expected to terminate in 1927, and he was not directly employed by the League, still less by the Director of the Hygiene Service, Dr Ludwig Rajchman.[2]

Ludwig Rajchman was then aged 43 and had had a brilliant career.[3] He came from a well-known family of Polish Jewish intellectuals and took his medical degree at the University of Cracow. He then studied abroad, in Paris at the Institut Pasteur and in London at the Royal Institute of Health and King's College. In London, he became head of the Central Laboratory for Research into Dysentery. After the First World War he returned to Poland, where he was appointed Director of the National School of Hygiene and of the Polish Central Institute for Epidemiology, becoming a member of the Epidemics Committee of the newly established League of Nations. On 1 November 1921 the Secretary-General of the League, Sir Eric Drummond, appointed him as Director of the International Public Health Section, the forerunner of the World Health Organization. Drummond was a remarkable figure who survived the Second World War and went on to found the United Nations children's agency, UNICEF.

Some confusion remains as to Céline's relations with Rajchman, undoubtedly coloured by the malicious portrait of the Jewish administrator as Yudenzweck ('Jewish aim') in the play *L'Eglise* and as Yubelblat ('crowing newspaper') in *Bagatelles pour un massacre*. François Gibault wonders why

'this little man, excessively meticulous, should have recruited such a collaborator?'[4] Yet this is to invoke a later image of Céline's bohemianism and
casualness, even carelessness. At the time, in the summer of 1924, Céline
came to the League of Nations with excellent credentials: efficient and
successful medical studies at an accelerated rate; medical publications,
particularly in the area of hygiene; and especially, experience of working
with the Rockefeller Foundation which was funding the post and whose
senior administrator, Selskar Gunn, had personally recommended the candidate. It is essential to recall that, at this period in his life, Céline was very
much a not-so-young man on the make, still dominated by the ambition
expressed in the *Carnet du Cuirassier Destouches* and still dedicated to making
a reputation and a fortune. In 1924, as an appointee, he would have looked
a very reasonable prospect indeed. Nor have commentators got the relationship between the two men precisely right. Frédéric Vitoux comments
that 'it has often been noted that Ludwig Rajchman was like a father to
Louis Destouches-Céline, a Jewish father whom he was to betray cruelly.'[5] It
is certainly true that Céline had benefited from contact with and help from
a number of older men, Henri de Graffigny, Selskar Gunn and Athanase
Follet, and that he was certainly not averse to cutting loose from anyone, of
whatever age or gender, who had helped him but was no longer useful. But
there is no evidence that figures such as Graffigny, Gunn or Follet served as
'father-figures' in the technical, psychological sense which informs the
conscious deployment of characters like Uncle Edouard, Peter Merrywin
and Courtial des Pereires in *Mort à crédit*, written in the shadow of Freudian
psychoanalysis. Even if this were true, Rajchman hardly qualifies as a
'father-figure': merely thirteen years Céline's senior, he was not yet part of
an older generation, and was much more an example of a rapid rise to a
brilliant and powerful position, a rise which Céline himself was attempting
to replicate. In fact, the two men got on extremely well. As Gibault writes:
'He welcomed Louis with an enthusiasm which contrasted strongly with
the formal British-style courtesy which was traditional at the League of
Nations. He invited him to his home and introduced him to his wife, who
liked talking about literature and was dazzled by his conversation,'[6] and
Rajchman's daughter Irena remembers a 'handsome man, who kept
making the children laugh and loved talking with [my] mother, who was
a passionate reader.'[7] Later, Rajchman showed an amused tolerance of
Céline's absent-mindedness, and continued to fund his often transparently
spurious travel and research projects long after his departure from the
League. It was only the publication of *L'Eglise*, in 1933, which put an end to
this warm relationship, although even this is not completely certain. Marta
Aleksandra Belinska notes that, as late as 1944, Rajchman's address-book
still had Céline's address in it, albeit the out of date one at 98 Rue Lepic,
which Céline left in 1940.[8]

The work of the 'Grade B Doctor' consisted of the normal round of
duties of an international civil servant: 'interviews, reports, statistics, fore-
casts, contacts.'[9] In particular, Céline worked very closely with Rajchman, to

the extent that, as Alméras suggests, many of his own reports were probably published under his superior's name,[10] and he devoted much of his time to the preparation and undertaking of study tours. All the early evidence is that Céline loved the job. In a letter to Milon of 2 July 1924, he wrote: 'So this is where your old friend Louis has ended up – here, in the international bee-hive – I'm very obstinate, as you know – so here I am. This time I'm dealing with really big hygiene problems, and God!, I love it.'[11] At the same time, he appears to have had no difficulty in rapidly mastering both the attitude and the language of the senior civil servant, that same gift for formal discourse which we have noted earlier. In 1925, he handled the publication by the Hygiene Section of a booklet by Dr Abbatucci, the Under-Secretary for Health at the French Ministry of Colonies. His note to Rajchman reads confidently: 'Too short and not technical enough, but undeniably it seems to me to show on the part of the author those qualities of clarity, order and method which, I think, are exactly what we need for our monograph.'[12] His subsequent letter to the author has a barely concealed condescension: 'Cher confrère et ami ... Please begin with the corrections which we have discussed together, and then I shall call to see you around the 17 July and we can come to a definitive decision regarding publication.'[13] Dispensing orders and advice to Permanent Under-Secretaries: the Cuirassier Destouches has come a long way in his search for 'success'.

If Céline adapted rapidly to the world of administration and diplomacy of Geneva, he was still determined to make an impression by whatever means. The precocious scientific author of the papers on marine biology, who had rushed his thesis on Semmelweis into print as soon as it had been accepted and who had popularized it in *La Presse médicale*, resorted again to writing as a means of bolstering his reputation as a hygienist. In 1925 he brought out, on a no-royalty basis, a long treatise, *La Quinine en thérapeutique*, with the publisher Doin, in Paris. The fact that some disabused Breton colleagues saw in this work a barely disguised reworking of a thesis by Céline's great-uncle, Théodore Destouches, *Les Préparations pharmaceutiques du quinquina*,[14] testifies to a constant need on Céline's part at this time to maintain a rhythm of publication, even if the work itself is unoriginal or inaccurate. The name on the title-page is the vital ingredient, and this work is there to reinforce Céline's position in the League of Nations as an international hygienist. In fact, *La Quinine en thérapeutique* is of little interest for an overall study of its author, even if it does indicate a preoccupation with fever: Jean-Pierre Dauphin and Henri Godard do not even include it in their collection of Céline's medical writings. One episode in the study stands out, however, simply because it shows Céline's gifts as a story teller and a preoccupation, not with fever, but with what was to become a major Célinian theme: misplaced and comic enthusiasm. It concerns the sad tale of a Doctor Bazire, recounted in Guersant's *Répertoire des Sciences médicales*, who treats his wife's bout of intermittent fever with increasing doses of sulphate of quinine, persuaded that, if the illness is not abating, it is because the dose is too weak. As Céline describes him: 'The setbacks which he had suffered threw his already unstable imagination into despair; terrified, he saw the illness triumphant and the power of his remedy, which he believed infallible, too often ineffectual.'[15] Succumbing himself to a fever, he continued to increase the doses of sulphate of quinine until he finally died of his own remedy. As Céline laconically concludes: 'Mme Bazire only owed her life to the illness of her husband, who was no longer able to give her help.'[16] Bazire is the Molièresque counterpart of Semmelweis, but no less significant: in the absence of knowledge, all cures are plausible and sheer faith alone can too often become obsession and madness. It is perhaps for this reason that the doctors in *Voyage au bout de la nuit*, including eventually Bardamu, having understood this lesson, no longer have any pretension to cure.

Shortly after his arrival in Geneva, Céline moved into a comfortable apartment in a block called 'La Résidence'. It was from here, as Vitoux suggests, that he created an amiable social life:

> He was thirty years old, had a good job, an impressive calling card which he shamelessly abused – he was hardly going to spend his evenings, let alone his nights, going through dossiers or writing reports. He could dine in town, pursue the female personnel at the League with his impatient assiduity, fall into debt, have fun, act up and shock the bourgeois or diplomatic world between two migraines and two nasty fits of despair.[17]

There is considerable poetic licence here, but it does capture the sense of freedom which the 30-year-old Céline would have experienced in a prestigious and well-paid job in an international city full of opportunities for sexual encounters. Clearly, it did not accommodate what remained of his marriage: Edith and Colette, then aged 9, made the journey from Rennes to Geneva, but always as uneasy guests and with the prospect of moving permanently to Switzerland always being deferred. Vitoux records: 'Edith waited. And she ended up taking the train home with the girl. A few months later Louis wrote to her again, asking her to come back to him. She returned, docile, for a few days.'[18] More welcome female visitors were Germaine Constans, a friend from Rennes, often entrusted to bring Colette by herself without her mother, though Vitoux asserts that she was gay,[19] and Blanchette Fermon, who was, according to Céline, 'one of the rare girls to understand my immense lyricism . . . perhaps the only one.'[20]

With his marriage crumbling, Céline looked forward to punctuating his agreeable life on the shores of Lake Léman with what he had always wanted, a journey to the United States. As we have seen, the trip to America was the primary inducement in the initial negotiations with Gunn and Rajchman, and Rajchman was true to his word: Céline was chosen to lead a delegation of South American doctors on a five-month study tour of the United States and Europe. The formal proposal was submitted on 3 November 1924 and, on 14 February 1925, Céline boarded the American liner *Minnetonka* at

Cherbourg. A dream which he had nourished for ten years was about to come true.

II AMERICA

On his arrival, Céline booked into the Macalpine Hotel in New York, where he began preparations for what was to be a gruelling inspection tour. He met with representatives of the Rockefeller Foundation and then made a rapid visit to Washington to meet American officials, including Surgeon-General Cummings, who essentially dictated the programme of the visit. There is little evidence of the initial impression that America and its most famous city made on him, just a reference in a letter to Rajchman: 'Nothing I see here resembles anything I have seen before: it's mad, like the war,'[21] a comment which, at the least, is ambiguous. There is nothing at this stage to announce the extraordinarily stylized and sexualized descriptions of New York in *Voyage au bout de la nuit*, which are the product, not just of personal observation, but of a number of artistic and literary filters: avant-garde, particularly Italian Futurist representations of the modern city; works like Georges Duhamel's *Scènes de la vie future* and Paul Morand's *New York*; and caricaturists like George Grosz and his Montmartre equivalents, Gus Bofa and Chas Laborde. In fact, Céline's communications with Rajchman were less to do with the impressions of a tourist and more to do with a characteristic act of carelessness which had led him to leave behind in Geneva the addresses of the banks where the money to finance the tour was deposited. The Director replied in an affectionately bantering tone: 'I was not at all surprised to learn that you had left certain essential parts of your wardrobe at La Résidence, but I would never have thought that you would have forgotten the address of the bank where your fortune was deposited . . . Send us a long cablegram with a list of all the things you've forgotten and which you must have put down in a notebook.'[22]

On 1 March 1925, Céline landed in Cuba to rendezvous with the eight South American doctors he was to guide for the next five months around North America and Europe: Alba from Mexico, Alvarez from Cuba, Garira from Venezuela, Gubetich from Paraguay, Lerdes from San Salvador, Mattos from Brazil, Schiaffino from Uraguay and Valega from Peru.[23] François Gibault has meticulously traced Céline's journey throughout the United States and Canada in the spring of 1925.[24] Broadly the group, after visiting medical installations in Cuba, travelled to New Orleans and covered 4000 kilometres in three weeks through the southern states of Louisiana, Mississippi and Alabama, particularly investigating measures against malaria, a subject which coincided with Céline's own, if second-hand, interest in quinine. Céline's report to Rajchman on medicine in the south emphasized the civic pride of the small southern towns, praised the efforts to combat malaria and indicated a certain residual racism by commenting: 'We know that the Anglo-Saxon race is temperamentally hygienic.'[25] On 5 April they moved north to New York and on the 6 April travelled to Washington, where they were welcomed by Surgeon-General Cummings and Assistant Surgeon-General Long at the Federal Department of Health. On the 10 April the group was received at the White House by Calvin Coolidge, who had recently been inaugurated as President for a second term, and who probably, more than the Genevan Protestant, inspired the name of Bardamu's hotel in New York in *Voyage au bout de la nuit*, the 'Laugh Calvin'. As Céline somewhat petulantly reported to Rajchman: 'I was presented last and I was waiting wryly for someone to read out my official title, but I was disappointed, because they read out neither my nationality nor my title, just my name.' He added bitterly: 'I must have been taken for a South American!'[26]

South American or not, being presented to the President of the United States was a not unimpressive achievement for a child who had grown up in the Passage Choiseul. The important features of the journey for Céline's subsequent work were to come later: a visit in late April to the immigration centre on Ellis Island, later transposed in *Voyage au bout de la nuit*[27] and, crucially, inspections on 6 and 8 March of the Ford plant in Detroit and the Westinghouse factory in Pittsburgh.

A considerable amount of confusion surrounds Céline's visit to the Ford plant and its effect on his later work, confusion which, as so often, was largely sown by Céline himself. According to Gibault's timetable, the group spent only 6 March visiting the Health Service of Ford's factory, and probably not an entire day at that, given that they had the long journey to Pittsburgh ahead of them. While Céline's claim in *Mea culpa* that 'I was a doctor at Ford's'[28] is just technically correct (in that he was a doctor and had visited Ford's), he was never, as he suggested to Ernz Bendz and many other interlocutors, 'a doctor in the USA for four years,'[29] a myth which culminates in Henri Mondor's assertion that Céline 'had worked for the Ford Factory, in other words for super-capitalism.'[30] It was to be a constant feature of Céline's later polemical writing to establish spurious authority through the invocation of non-existent, or at least exaggerated, personal experience. Yet no European who was even mildly conscious of social trends, let alone one who specialized in public health, could be unaware of the significance of the Ford 'system' as the epitome of Americanization. The French distrusted it. The geography textbooks of the Third Republic attempted to play down the importance of the United States, but also uniformly portrayed American society as inhuman, robotic and a constant threat to the more humane lifestyle of Europe.[31] Industrialists, particularly Rimailho, Hyacinthe Dubreuil and André Citroën, toyed with Taylorism, but on the whole French manufacturing rejected American assembly-line techniques,[32] as did most French intellectuals, with the notable exception of Le Corbusier.[33] In the late 1920s and the 1930s, however, interest in American techniques was to grow, particularly on the political Right with

André Tardieu and the technocratic Ernest Mercier and his Redressement Français movement.[34]

Taylorism applied the rational principles of engineering to the manufacturing process by which each function was isolated and able to be performed on an assembly-line basis by workers whose skills were limited to the particular task to which they were assigned and the particular machine they operated. It was F. W. Taylor (1856–1915) who rationalized the process of de-skilling of the industrial workforce so visible in the world of the Parisian artisans. Instead of the artisanal craftsman, formed by a long apprenticeship and years of experience, the new industrial process called upon the 'ouvrier spécialisé', a specialist in only one, undemanding practice. The dehumanization this implied was summed up thus by Taylor himself, quoted by the social historian Olivier Targowla: 'One of the first characteristics of a man who is capable of doing the task of operating a die-casting machine is that he is so unintelligent and so lazy that he could be compared, concerning his mental aptitude, to an ox as much as to anything else. The man who has a lively and intelligent mind is completely unsuited for this work,'[35] a reference which foreshadows Céline's own comments on Ford. If Taylor proposed the reduction of the former artisanal worker to the role of an adjunct to a machine, Ford went further. Not only did he discover the vast commercial possibilities of workers who could also be customers, he extended the Taylorian mechanization of the worker to a global system, by which the employee would become constantly subject to the factory regime and ethos. Not merely did he extend Taylor's logic regarding the aptitude, or lack of aptitude, of the industrial workforce, by hiring and retaining men who were incapacitated, disabled and sick, he effectively established a localized corporate state around his plant, with its own health service, police force and ban on unions. It is perhaps for this reason that Gramsci, imprisoned by another corporate regime in Italy, saw the significance of Ford so clearly:

> It is from this point of view that one should study the 'puritanical' initiative of American industrialists like Ford. It is certain that they are not concerned with the 'humanity' or 'spirituality' of the worker, which is immediately smashed. The 'humanity' and 'spirituality' cannot be realised except in the world of production and work, in the 'demiurge', when the worker's personality was reflected whole in the object created and when the link between art and labour was still very strong. But it is precisely against this 'humanism' that the new industrialism is fighting.[36]

The consequence is the attempt to create a new kind of industrial worker who is no more than a 'trained gorilla'.[37]

Céline's own account of his lightning visit to the Ford plant betrays a mixture of bewilderment at the policy of hiring so many apparently disabled workers and a grudging recognition of the minimum of basic health care that such a system provides. After a short and not always totally

accurate account of Henry Ford's career and the economic factors which
compel him to sell ever-increasing numbers of cars in order to stay afloat,
he concluded that Ford's success was due to the creation of the most
sophisticated assembly-line system ever invented, by which 'anyone can
replace anyone to do anything without there resulting the slightest reduction in the number of parts produced in a day.'[38] It was this advance in
standardization which, for Céline, permitted Ford to indulge himself in the
bizarre social experiment of employing often the weakest workers, though
he forgot that even these weak workers could be considered as potential
purchasers of the Model T. He revelled in the statistics: a hundred blind
workers, 4000 to 5000 epileptics or paralytics, all receiving the statutory
Ford wage of 6 dollars a day.[39] The still-humanist doctor from Geneva
was appalled at the dehumanization this implied: 'the dream worker is the
chimpanzee.'[40] But the hygienist was intrigued by the positive social results:
a minimal turnover in the workforce, no sackings, and basic health surveillance and treatment through the Social Service and the Ford Hospital. Not
that Ford believed in health insurance. As Céline wryly commented: 'in
Ford's mind, the worker should save for medical treatment. Besides, it's
difficult to see what disease a worker could suffer from which would prevent
him from working at Ford's.'[41] Céline's conclusion, without being a ringing
endorsement, was nevertheless far from negative: 'This state of affairs, from
the health, and even the human point of view, is not disastrous. For the
present, it permits a lot of people to live who would not be able to do so
outside of Ford's.'[42] He is also conscious, however, of the inherent strangeness of the Ford system, which only survived because the assembly-line
technique was so perfected that it could tolerate the employment of a large
number of invalids. Other companies in Detroit, like Cadillac, had complete medical services and, as the note to the League concluded, somewhat
ambiguously: 'We came to Detroit with the intention of seeing whether
hygiene applied to industry increased the production of that industry: this
was proven by the experience of the Westinghouse Company of Pittsburgh.'[43] As for Ford, the economic and humane laws had been turned on
their head and the question was simply irrelevant: 'At Ford's, the health of
the worker is unimportant: it's the machine which does him the honour of
still needing him. The factors are reversed.'[44] Nevertheless, enough of the
Ford example stuck in Céline's mind for him to return to it in an apparently more positive way in Paris in 1928.

Biographers such as Alméras, Gibault or Vitoux have seen in Céline's visit
to Detroit a possible source of his anti-Semitism. It is undoubtedly true that
Henry Ford, in addition to his isolationism and hostility to unions, was also
violently anti-Semitic and used his newspaper, *The Dearborn Independent*, to
denounce 'How Jews gained American liquor control' and 'The Jewish
element in bootlegging evil', with claims that 'Popular music is a Jewish
monopoly.'[45] Céline arrived in America as a teetotaller in the midst of
prohibition and it is likely that the experience reinforced his perception of
the public heath risk constituted by alcohol, a theme which was to become

a frequent feature of the later medical pamphlets and the novels. It is improbable, however, that such a short visit to the Ford plants would have presented him with a sufficient knowledge of their owner's political philosophy to orientate his own views, although perceptions of a 'Jewish' underworld, founded to some extent on fact, as in the example of the Mafia banker Meyer Lansky, surfaced dramatically in 1933 during the break with Elizabeth Craig.

Unsurprisingly, the report on the visit to the Westinghouse factory in Pittsburgh on 8 March 1925 is less dramatic, though no less instructive regarding Céline's later reflections on medical insurance. If Ford was a dazzling and disconcerting display of eccentricity, Westinghouse was the epitome of 'a health institution which is both ingenious and logical.'[46] Here, 'the worker possesses almost universally a personal value.'[47] The reason is simple: Westinghouse had not achieved the degree of mechanization which pertained in Ford and was hence more dependent on the well-being and loyalty of the workforce. The loss of a worker, with the consequent retraining of his replacement, cost the company 60 dollars.[48] The loss of a worker through illness would have similar consequences. The company's response to the haemorrhage of its workforce which, according to Céline, had stood in the past as high as 125–150 per cent, was to introduce 'health insurance, a pension scheme and a workers' share option scheme,'[49] in addition to company housing and a company restaurant. Each worker payed a compulsory 1.5 dollars per month for health insurance, which provided for free medical treatment and sick pay of 40 to 50 dollars a month. What particularly interested Céline was the way in which this system provided for regular medical check-ups, leading, for example, to prompt diagnosis and treatment of tuberculosis. As he concluded, this was not a system motivated by philanthropy, but by sound business sense. Yet that very removal of what he was later to call 'la médecine bourgeoise' permitted a recognition of the importance of housing, diet and working conditions and a constant monitoring of the health of the workforce. The Westinghouse experience was probably more important than that of Ford in the later elaboration of Céline's theories on public health.

After seeing the Niagara Falls, the by now exhausted delegation left the United States for Canada, where they visited Ottawa, Montreal and Trois Rivières before ending up in Québec. In Montreal, Céline, described in *L'Evénement* as 'Secretary General of the League of Nations Hygiene Section' and 'son of the Secretary of the Faculty of Medicine of Paris',[50] which would have compensated for the lack of formal introduction at the White House and may owe something to his own desire to impress, made a speech which showed a perfect mastery of what Alméras terms 'after-dinner speaking':[51] 'You have emerged from the war more powerful than us, and fertile land and almost inexhaustible natural resources offer themselves to your sons.' He even concluded with a joke, adding that 'French medical practice was more successful in difficult things than in easy ones.'[52] The Céline of this period was a highly-confident and accomplished diplomat.

The group took the *Mont Royal* from Québec on 22 May and arrived in Liverpool on the 30th. Edith had come to meet her husband in London, but had fallen ill and been hospitalized. Significantly, while she remembered the illness as being mumps, Céline himself, in a laconic aside in a note to Rajchman, merely refers to 'flu, I think.'[53] It does not appear that the reunion led to any profound reconciliation. He was also met by a representative of the League of Nations, Captain Johnston-Watson, the administrator of the Hygiene Section, who had come to sort out the accounts of the American tour with Céline. In spite of certain irregularities, these were presumably satisfactory, since Céline received an excellent report from Rajchman on his handling of the American visit. The Director described him as 'a very intelligent and enthusiastic man' and raised his salary by 250 Swiss francs, to 1250. Once again, there is no indication whatsoever of Céline having anything other than a very successful career with the League.

After a brief respite in London, and a rapid journey to Geneva to brief Rajchman, the tour started up in Europe at the same remorseless pace: Holland from 18 to 24 June, Belgium from 25 June to 4 July, Switzerland until 11 July and then France.[54] In the course of the Swiss visit, Céline met with an Australian doctor, Doctor Park, to discuss health measures in the South Pacific. His recommendations were to constitute central planks in his later writing on health insurance: a ban on alcohol, the creation of health education centres and the supply of pure water from new tanks.[55] The group began their French tour in Lille on 12 July. They visited the north and Paris, including the Père-Lachaise, Les Halles and the Vaugirard slaughterhouses, before heading south for Lyons on 23 July. On the 26th they crossed the border to Turin.

The South Americans, by this point, had had enough, and Céline warned his Italian colleague in Turin, Dr Pantaleoni, to go easy with them: 'this exchange visit which began in exhaustion is ending in almost declared hostility.'[56] Most of the Italians did their best, providing a lighter programme in Turin from 28 to 30 July and in Ferrara on the 30th and 31st. However, in Ravenna on 1 August the Italians once more overloaded the programme, with Céline helpless and unable to do anything other than complain to Rajchman: 'We are seeing Italy in the worst possible conditions.'[57] On 3 August they moved on to Rome, where the delegation was received by Mussolini. However, as Alméras comments, this contact with Italian Fascism and the Duce seems to have had no durable influence on Céline, who was never particularly interested in the south and was culturally and temperamentally a man of the north.[58] The visit to Italy and the entire tour ended on 8 August, after a visit to the Pontine Marshes project and Ostia: the South Americans returned, it must be presumed thankfully, to their homes, and Céline went back to Geneva.

Here he became immersed in administration, in particular working on the preparations for a conference of Baltic and North Sea port doctors.[59] He also decided to move house: in December 1925, he left 'La Résidence' for a three-room apartment at number 35d Chemin de Miremont, in Champel, on the Left Bank of Lake Léman.[60] The rent was 1200 francs per annum, which gives a reasonable insight into the value of his annual salary of 15,000 Swiss francs: the 'Doctor Grade B' was, in effect, extremely well-paid and spent less than one-twelfth of his salary on housing. As Alméras comments,[61] with the additional 12,000 French francs paid annually by Dr Follet as his daughter's dowry, this constituted a very comfortable income indeed, quite sufficient to support a married couple and their child. It would never do so: the marriage, which had always tolerated Céline's own sexual freedom, had been fragile since the days of *Semmelweis* in Paris. Now it exploded. To letters from Edith, who complained of loneliness in Rennes and asked to join him in Geneva, he sent a definitive and brutal reply which left no possibility for any further illusions:

> You must find something which will make you independent in Paris. As for me, I find it impossible to live with anyone. I do not want to drag you around behind me snivelling and sorry for yourself. You bore me, and that's it. Don't hold on to me. I'd rather kill myself than live with you for ever: get that into your head and don't go on boring me with your attachment and tenderness ... I want to be alone, alone, alone: neither dominated, nor guarded, nor loved – free. I hate marriage, I loath it, I spit on it: it gives me the impression of a prison where I'm dying.[62]

A divorce petition was presented to the Court in Rennes on 9 March 1926, undefended by Céline. The divorce was pronounced on 21 June 1926, with Edith being awarded custody of Colette and the 12,000 francs annual allowance from her father. Céline was not in Rennes to hear the verdict: he was on a new mission for the League of Nations in West Africa, and besides, he had already met the woman who was to share his life for the next seven years, the American dancer Elizabeth Craig.

III Africa Again

Already in the autumn of 1925, Céline had begun preparations with Rajchman for a study tour of West Africa, similar in scope to the American journey. On 14 March 1926, he boarded the *Belle Ile* at La Pallice and arrived in Dakar six days later, on 20 March. He was guiding a delegation of three English doctors, three Belgians, two Spaniards, four Frenchmen, one Guatemalan, two Portuguese and one South African.[63] Their mission was to study health organization in the countries on the West Coast of Africa, culminating in a plenary conference in Freetown on the advisability of establishing a Hygiene Office of the League in West Africa. The journey appears to have been jinxed from the outset, though Doctor Lasnet, Inspector General of the Colonial Health Service, in his letters to Rajchman, blamed Céline for the tour's poor organization:[64] the timetables of the shipping companies made it impossible to visit Liberia and restricted the inspection of the Ivory Coast to one day;[65] nor was the budget sufficient to allow the entire delegation to visit all the countries. The delegation was immediately split up, therefore, with one group visiting the Gambia, one Portuguese Guinea, and the main group, led by Céline, inspecting Sudan and Guinea, a daunting journey involving 1500 kilometres on the Dakar–Niger railroad to Bamako, 300 kilometres by car across country to Kouroussa and finally another train to Conakry,[66] where they were joined by the other two groups who travelled by boat. The entire delegation then visited the Gold Coast, Togo, Dahomey and Nigeria, ending up in Freetown for the conference.

The conference was not a success, with each nationality arguing for its own sectional interests and no agreement whatsoever reached on the possibility, let alone the location, of a Public Health Bureau in West Africa. The delegation returned from Freetown on the *Eubée* with the issue unresolved, and arrived in La Rochelle on 9 June 1926. Céline travelled to Paris to make a verbal report on the mission to the 7th Session of the Hygiene Committee and then resumed a tour of Europe, similar to that undertaken by the South Americans, with his delegation: Holland, Brussels, Paris, Chartres, Geneva, Berne, Zurich, Basle and Leysin, ending up on 25 August with a round-table discussion at the Palais des Nations in Geneva on 'Social insurance and its relationship to hygiene', a subject rapidly becoming Céline's speciality.[67]

Frédéric Vitoux sees the fact that Céline only presented an oral report on his African journey as evidence of his 'utmost casualness' towards his 'administrative and editorial duties'.[68] There is no reason to deduce this at all, and Vitoux is probably extrapolating from the characterization of Bardamu in *L'Eglise*. Certainly, there is nothing inappropriate in an interim oral report on an ongoing mission to an official committee. Nevertheless, the journey had been another gruelling one and there is some evidence that Céline was no longer averse to the prospect of his contract with the Rockefeller Foundation and the League expiring at the end of 1927. As he wrote to Milon in 1926, he envisaged a possible career in Paris in one of his two specialisms, paediatrics or industrial medicine: 'I'm soon going to retire from the League of Nations in the course of next year. Do you know in the Paris area a clinic for industrial accidents which is for sale? Or a crèche or children's clinic?'[69] The importance of the second visit to Africa for Céline appears to lie here, in an acceptance that it was time to leave the League and move on to something else, rather than in literary exploitation. The African episode in *Voyage au bout de la nuit*, in addition to its intertextual borrowings from, notably, Conrad and *Heart of Darkness*, is clearly related to the first journey of 1916–17 and the impact of colonialism in the Dark Continent on the young Destouches, and does not derive from the mission of 1927. Nevertheless, Céline did attempt to capture something of his journey as a doctor in West Africa in the play which he wrote during the last year of his employment by the League of Nations, and which satirized it mercilessly: *L'Eglise*.

IV ELIZABETH AND THE PLAYS

It is difficult to situate precisely the first meeting between Céline and Elizabeth Craig, whether it took place before the African tour or after. In her interviews with Alphonse Juilland, over sixty years later, she recalled at one point that 'He then went to Africa on a medical mission for the League of Nations,'[70] but earlier she claimed that 'He had been recently divorced.'[71] Whether the meeting occurred in spring or summer 1926, it was dramatic:

> We met in front of books. He picked me up. We were both in Geneva. I had just come out of hospital for tuberculosis. My father and mother had come because I had been dancing and had had tuberculosis as a child. So, I had just got out of sanatorium and I was walking past a bookshop: I forget which one, it was a very fine bookshop – I've always loved books – I was walking around and looking at a book when this gentleman asked me: 'Do you like it . . . ?' I forget the name of the author. I replied: 'I don't know anything about the author, but it looks like a superb book.' He talked. We walked as far as the corner of the street, and there you are. When we parted, he asked me: 'Where do you live?' I replied: 'With my parents, at the hotel'. He asked: 'Can I come and see you?' I replied: 'Please do, I'd be delighted.' It was a Saturday.[72]

Elizabeth Craig was an attractive redhead and a dancer. Eight years younger than Céline (she was born on 12 March 1902), she came from a comfortably well-off family in California and had made a career as a dancer in the Ziegfeld Follies, with some walk-on parts in Hollywood films. In 1925[73] she joined the Albertina Rash company to come to Paris, bringing a new style of dancing based upon the Radio City Music Hall Rockettes, but on points: it was an instant success.[74] This career as a dancer was cut short by Elizabeth succumbing to a haemorrhage on the stage of the Moulin Rouge.[75] Her parents rushed from California to be with her and sent her for treatment to a sanatorium in Geneva, where she met Céline, before returning to Paris and her parents' rented apartment on the Boulevard Raspail. It was in Paris that they began their affair, and soon after Céline's visit Elizabeth decided to move in with him in his apartment in Champel. She was to stay with him, off and on, for the next seven years, though, as with the marriage to Edith Follet, the relationship was never intended by Céline to be monogamous. As Elizabeth Craig rather quaintly confessed to Alphonse Juilland: 'He was a sexual hornyrake'[76] and, until the mid-1930s, Céline's sexuality was not satisfied by any one partner, as his later relationships with Karen Marie Jensen, Erika Irrgang, Evelyne Pollet, Cillie Pam and others[77] and his activities with Henri Mahé, Joseph Garcin and John Marks testify.

It is difficult to assess the influence of Elizabeth Craig on Céline's career; it may well be that it was the traumatic loss of the redheaded dancer which was crucial. Undoubtedly, Alméras is right in pointing to the significance of the fact that they communicated in English and that this reinforced Céline's unusually strong Anglophone culture.[78] The notion that living with Elizabeth somehow guaranteed a permanent insight into America is less convincing. What she did provide was the first example in Céline's life of a certain appreciation of beauty which he derived from Nietzsche. As he wrote to Milton Hindus in 1947: 'I'm terribly sensitive to certain physical beauties – dancing girls, etc, and out of them I shape a sort of artificial paradise on earth. I've got to be close to Dancing to live. As I think Nietzsche wrote: "I'll have faith in a God only if he dances." Likewise Louis XIV had faith in ambassadors only if they were perfect dancers.'[79] She may also, as Alméras suggests,[80] have provided the optimism and drive necessary to give Céline the impetus to launch himself on a new career which had always been a possibility, from the precocity and self-consciousness of the *Carnet du Cuirassier Destouches* to the stylization of *Semmelweis*: literature.

Elizabeth Craig, like Edith Follet, destroyed most of her correspondence with Céline but a small number of letters survive from Christmas 1926 which bear witness to his first formal literary activities. Céline was in Paris, at a hotel at number 225 Boulevard Raspail, and he wrote to Elizabeth: 'I am back to my play . . . I think it will be funny.'[81] The letters recount his attempts to have the play performed, by a producer variously called 'Maggie' or 'Mayès', whom Eric Mazet identifies as Ladislas Medgyès.[82] Negotiations did not proceed well: Medgyès insisted on Céline covering the production costs of 50,000 francs. Only if it was a commercial success would he receive royalties. So desperate was Céline to have the play produced that he even offered to include Madgyès as co-author, a suggestion primly rejected by the Hungarian producer. Yet, if the play could be performed, there was a wonderful role in it for Elizabeth herself. Finally Medgyès, described as 'practical, sensual, cunning and asiatic,'[83] having read two acts, objected to the key female role and the project collapsed.[84] This episode is interesting, not merely because it enables us to date the completion of Céline's first play, which is almost certainly *L'Eglise* (although the composition of the much slighter *Progrès/Périclès* dates from the same period), at Christmas 1926, but because it exactly prefigures the experience recounted by the narrator of *Bagatelles pour un massacre*, who sees his ballet rejected by the no less Asiatic (read 'Jewish') Director of the Opéra. This initial rejection may well have cast a long shadow in Céline's career, not that he gave up. In September 1927 he submitted to Gallimard the manuscript of the play, which was returned the following month:[85] the reader noted: 'Some satirical vigour, but lacks continuity. Gifted portrayal of diverse milieux.'[86] There was still the burning ambition for recognition, evidenced by his attempt a year later to persuade Gallimard to publish *Semmelweis*.

Céline himself later had no illusions about his talents as a dramatist, though this did not prevent him publishing *L'Eglise* in 1933 in the wake of the success of *Voyage au bout de la nuit,* nor from striking up an acquaintance with Charles Dullin.[87] As he admitted in an interview with *L'Intransigeant:* 'I'm not a man of the theatre . . . , maybe they'll laugh at my dialogue . . . In any case, there's a special technique, tricks, a certain "crux" that eludes me.'[88] Why then should he have chosen the theatre as the initial vehicle for his literary ambition? It is probable, as he stated to the journalist from *L'Intransigeant,* that he was fascinated by drama: 'the theatre perturbs me,'[89] and very likely that the composition of *L'Eglise* and *Progrès* played an important part in his relationship with the dancer and would-be actress, Elizabeth Craig. In one of the letters, he promises her that ' "If I could be played" [*sic*], there would be a marvellous part for her.'[90] It is difficult to avoid the comparison with that nineteenth-century man of ambition, Balzac, who similarly, before discovering his true vocation as a novelist, was tempted by the immediacy of acclaim embodied in the theatre.

Of the two experiments with drama which Céline produced in 1926–7, the piece entitled *Progrès* is by far the slighter. The manuscript, bearing the initial title *PERICLES,* crossed out and replaced by *Progrès,* and with the subtitle 'Farce en trois tableaux et petits divertissements',[91] was given by Céline in 1933 to Cécile Robert Denoël, the wife of the publisher of *Voyage au bout de la nuit,* who finally allowed it to be published in 1978. In spite of its subtitle, the play in fact oscillates from farce to fantasy. The first tableau takes place in the household of Gaston, a frustrated insurance-company clerk, and Marie, his gentle but lame wife. The much shorter second tableau shows Marie's musical seduction by the neighbour M. Berlureau, and the third tableau takes place in a brothel, where all the customers are voyeurs, a sexual activity which, as we have seen, particularly attracted Céline himself. Here, Gaston's innocence is preserved through his meeting with a beautiful American dancer who deters him from being unfaithful to Marie. The final tableau is set in Heaven, with a benevolent God observing the reconciliation of Gaston and Marie. The play is an odd mixture, combining classic farce with the style of an operetta, and one can understand why Céline should have chosen not to proceed with plans for performance or publication, though, as Alméras is right to point out, it is not absolutely certain (albeit likely) that the play which is the subject of the Christmas 1926 correspondence is *L'Eglise* and not *Progrès.*[92] Nevertheless, the work is by no means devoid of interest in respect of Céline's later work. The first tableau, with the diatribes of Gaston, the lameness of Marie and the presence of her mother, Mme Punais, clearly looks forward to *Mort à crédit,* with Gaston as an early, comic, version of Auguste, Marie as a precursor of Clémence and 'Punais' as Courtial des Pereires' real name. At the same time, the second tableau, with the entry of 'four little children, dressed in coloured tunics, who dance a little ballet in the middle of the salon', prefigures the ballets which introduce and close *Bagatelles pour un massacre* and which make up the collection *Ballets sans musique, sans paroles, sans rien.* Similarly, the stage direction: 'They will dance to the music of Marie and Berlureau – but everything is a dream, a fantasy,' constitutes an early introduction to 'féerie', that heartland of Célinian writing. It is this, also, which explains the initial title *Périclès*: not only does Gaston, thanks to the American, remain as intact in his brothel as does Pericles' daughter Miranda in hers, but the play inaugurates a close intertextual relationship with Shakespeare which would last throughout Céline's work.[93] The farce and the fantasy do not totally preclude attempts to comment on post-war France. The title itself introduces what will become a familiar Célinian theme, that of the loss of innocence, and French prestige through progress: as the maid in the brothel comments, all prices in France have gone up because the English own everything. The fact that one of the principal characters, a musician and palmist, is called Mme Doumergue, who has taken no risks in her life so that she arrives in Heaven intact, is probably an attempt at political satire at the expense of the President of the Republic, the veteran politician Gaston Doumergue, who succeeded the mad Paul Deschanel in 1922. More seriously, the appearance of the American in the brothel, in addition to introducing a celebration of the dancer's body (looking forward to the day when 'women will be clothed only in muscles . . . and music,' and which will be a recurrent feature of Céline's subsequent work), also constitutes a damning indictment of poor diet and health in France, which looks forward in its turn to the medical writings and the anti-Semitic pamphlets. As Gaston rebukes the Madam in the brothel: 'You came into money so late that you couldn't grow any more when you got it. When you started to eat your fill, it was too late! That accounts for your vulgar, proletarian looks.'

L'Eglise has a number of features in common with *Progrès*, which plainly identify them as having been written, at least in part, in the same period, but it is altogether more complex. Whereas *Progrès* hovers between the influences of Labiche and Offenbach, *L'Eglise* is written in a style more reminiscent of the early Claudel, the Claudel of *L'Echange* or *Partage de midi*. Moreover, in spite of Céline's insistence in the preface to the 1933 edition that he had changed nothing since writing the play in 1927, the final version of *L'Eglise* shows signs of having been considerably reworked and, especially, lengthened, from the three acts announced to Max Descaves in March 1933[94] to the five acts which make up the published version.

The first act takes place in the French African colony of La Bragamance, whose health provision is being inspected by an American doctor, Gaige, working for the fictitious Barrell Foundation, and the French doctor, Bardamu, working for the League of Nations. The setting enables Céline to satirize colonial government through the administrator, Tandernot, and his drunken assistant, Pistil, who has obvious Shakespearean connotations of the character Pistol in *Henry V*. Throughout the act, Doctor Gaige remains motionless, and, unbeknown to the others, except Bardamu, has died of pneumonic plague. The French colonial authorities, however, prefer to deny the evidence and attribute his death to yellow fever, caught in British territory. Act II takes us to New York, where Bardamu has gone to break the news to Gaige's widow, Elizabeth, a dancer. He fails to meet

Elizabeth, but is captivated by the beauty of the dancers, using exactly the same terminology as that used in *Progrès*, and also agrees to a marriage of convenience with the owner of the theatre, Vera Stern, who is involved in shady underworld dealings.

What has subsequently attracted most attention, however, is the satire of the League of Nations in Geneva in Act III which, according to Céline, was the origin of the play's title: 'It seems to me that it sums up the League of Nations,' he said to Max Descaves. 'It's a church, with its directors and its personnel,' the church of 'the international religion of the reconciliation of peoples in the era of Briand'.[95] In Act III, Bardamu returns to Geneva to witness the futile and self-serving activities of myriad committees and finally to be dismissed as lacking in 'administrative spirit'.[96] Not only does *L'Eglise* satirize the bureaucracy of the League, it specifically lends an anti-Semitic note to the satire, through the crude portrayal of Bardamu's superiors, Yudenzweck, the all-powerful 'Director of the Service of Compromises', Moïse, 'Director of the Service of Indiscretions', and Mosaïc, 'Director of Transitory Affairs'. In other words, if the third act was a part of the original manuscript composed in 1926–7, then the anti-Semitism which Edith Follet claims was a constant in Céline surfaced specifically at the very beginning of his literary career and is, to some extent, inseparable from it. As Céline recalled to Jean Guénot and Jacques Darribehaude in 1960, it was the League of Nations which was at the origin of his anti-Semitism: 'I saw another exploiter. At the League of Nations, I soon saw that that was how things were fixed.'[97] The portrayal of Rajchman as Yudenzweck is cruel in itself, but has also led to some confusion among Céline's biographers, a confusion deliberately fostered by Céline himself. In *Bagatelles pour un massacre*, he describes how he showed the manuscript of *L'Eglise* to Yubelblat: 'he made a little grimace . . . he never forgot.'[98] This leads Vitoux and Gibault to claim that it was the origin of Céline's departure from the League: '*L'Eglise* had a terrible effect on Ludwig Rajchman and his wife.'[99] In fact, Alméras' version of events is much more plausible.[100] There is no evidence that Céline showed Rajchman the manuscript of the play. On the contrary, he continued to have cordial relations with his former superior, who treated his requests for funding for spurious research trips all over Europe with the same indulgence he had shown while Céline was in the League, until 1933, when *L'Eglise* was published and contact between them ceased. In fact, according to Elizabeth Craig, 'the only person he admired was his superior at the League of Nations in Geneva, a Jew who had given him the wonderful position he occupied when I first met him,'[101] and she detected no anti-Semitism in Céline, apart from highly significant light banter.[102] Certainly, to the end of his life Rajchman kept the autographed copy of *Voyage au bout de la nuit* sent him by Céline, with the dedication: 'To Ludwig Rajchman, a great voyaging human being'.[103] Yet Céline was no respecter of susceptibilities when it came to portraying even close friends in his writing: the depiction of a violently anti-Semitic Gen Paul in *Bagatelles pour un massacre*, which caused the painter considerable difficulties during the *Epuration*, is a case in point. The portrait of Rajchman as Yudenzweck/ Yubelblat is more sinister, however, since it enabled the anti-Semitic Céline to pose as a victim of Jewish persecution: 'Basically, I sacrificed myself, I'm a kind of martyr . . . I lost a very comfortable job for the violence and honesty of French literature.'[104] In this context, Rajchman's name, meaning 'man of revenge' in German, acquires an additional ironic significance.

The fourth and fifth acts take place in an industrial suburb of Paris, Blabigny-sur-Seine. In Act IV, set in a bistro run by the ailing Pistil and used by Bardamu as an unofficial surgery, Céline depicts the squalid exercise of social medicine (which he expands in La Garenne-Rancy in *Voyage au bout de la nuit*) and the departure of Vera Stern for America, unable fully to satisfy Bardamu's dreams. In the final act, Pistil's bistro has been taken over by Bardamu as a clinic. His discussion with a colleague on his botched delivery of a baby is interrupted by the arrival of Elizabeth Gaige, who silently undresses and begins to dance, ending the play on a note of balletic beauty.

It is certainly easy to see why the reader for Gallimard felt that the play 'lacked continuity'. *L'Eglise* seems to be, in fact, two plays, with the final two acts on urban medicine tacked on to the three acts, themselves hardly tightly organized, during which Bardamu works for the League of Nations. Indeed, Céline's assertion that the entire play was written in 1926–7, with only one modification in 1933, seems increasingly implausible. The external evidence points to an extension from the three acts originally announced to the five which appeared in the published version, whereas the internal evidence would again appear to confirm modifications supplied after Céline's work in Geneva. These include the depiction of the life of a 'médecin de banlieue' in the last two acts, too authentic not to be rooted in some personal experience, and the departure of Vera Stern for America despite Bardamu's pleas for her to stay, which must be grounded at least in part in the increasingly long absences of Elizabeth Craig in America in the early 1930s, leading to her definitive departure in the summer of 1933. In addition, there is an intriguingly detailed evocation of experimental theatre in Act II, again too precise not to stem from actual experience, and which may coincide with Céline's dedication of *Bagatelles pour un massacre* to 'Mes potes du "Théâtre en Toile"'. Declaring his long-term ambition to write for the theatre, Bardamu recounts to the dancer Flora:

> It's not easy; I tried, whilst I was doing medicine. There are two principal difficulties: the first is to find a theatre. You have no idea how expensive a theatre can be; I'm talking about a theatre where the public can go, because with a friend I found near to the city gates at Issy a little abandoned factory which could have made a theatre, but there was no road. We could have converted the factory, but you tell me what sort of public would have walked across fields to see modern theatre? Because our theatre was modern, needless to say. Nor, to be frank, were we very sure of our play: that was the other problem. So, to give ourselves confidence, we went to see all the bad plays that were on in Paris, and there really were some bad ones! Then we said to each

other: 'You see what they're playing? And yet, there are people there all the same!' That gave us courage, and we needed it, because I won't tell you what one square metre in central Paris costs. With the capital we had, we could have bought 6.25 square meters. But I had some friends who were geniuses: you always do when you're setting up a theatre. They told me that we had to cure that stupid habit of putting the audience one behind the other . . . that henceforth we ought to stack them up vertically; with our 6.25 square metres, we could have packed in three hundred people vertically.[105]

At the same time, the presence of Bardamu and the use of the same episode from Macaulay recounting the Monmouth uprising, though this time not transposed, may point to some overlap with the composition of *Voyage au bout de la nuit.*

The play may lack continuity and overall unity, but it does have a certain thematic coherence, particularly if Céline's original explanation of the title *L'Eglise* as uniquely signifying the League of Nations is supplemented by other interpretations. In particular, the play works well if it is seen as dealing less with the League and the religion of Briandism and more with the nineteenth-century secular religion of medicine. The play systematically demonstrates the vulnerability of the cult of humanist medicine to political considerations and social conditions: the reality of Gaige's death of pneumonic plague, with the real possibility of an epidemic, is dismissed in favour of colonial politics; in Geneva, the health of real people is subordinated to the proliferation of committees and the desperate search of their members for the best possible exchange rate; in Blabigny-sur-Seine, the efforts of the doctor are useless in the face of poor housing, appalling sanitary conditions and alcoholism. The preoccupations of *L'Eglise* are identical to those announced in *Semmelweis* and explored in the medical pamphlets of 1928 and later. In this way, the play can be viewed as a conscious descendant of Molière's *comédie-ballets*, not merely in style and the use of mime, but also in one of his principal targets.

At the same time the ballet itself, like *Progrès*, provides a counter-religion: the church of the female body enshrined in the dancer. The second act contains the same celebration of the female dancer's musculature as informs *Progrès*, and the play as a whole depicts the same sexualization of a metaphysical quest as that which begins *Semmelweis* and runs throughout *Voyage au bout de la nuit.* As Vera comments to Bardamu, in the often quoted line: 'Ferdinand . . . as long as you live, you will go between the legs of women to ask for the secret of the world!'[106] Yet she provides a qualification which is not without significance for the novel. Commenting on Bardamu's love of physical beauty, she adds: 'Pistil says that too now. You taught him that . . . the muscles . . . dance . . . no fat . . . But you don't go to the depths of yourself [jusqu'au bout de vous-même].'[107] It is perhaps for this reason that, alongside the perfection of the dancers, Flora, Vera and Elizabeth (with little phonetic difference between 'Craig' and 'Gaige'), there should be, as with Marie in *Progrès*, the important character of the 'boiteuse', the lame woman, in this case Janine, whose spiritual beauty and aspiration

imprisoned in physical imperfection become an image of the human condition, condemned to sadness and frustration, just as Claudel's limping
heroine Dona Prouhèze, in *Le Soulier de satin*, is condemned to sin.

The two plays demonstrate an ability to handle a lively style and, in
particular, a talent for choreography and mime which will inform the later
ballets. In particular, *L'Eglise*, which has received very little critical attention, is by no means negligible. The plays' weakness, however, is in their
transposition of autobiography, more suited to fiction than to drama, and
in the fact that Céline's talent is less for the construction of dialogue than
for the monologue which constitutes the text of the fiction. Céline obviously recognized this since he never returned to drama and, when he wrote
later for the stage, produced ballets 'without words'.

In fact, as his letter of 1926 to Milon indicates, Céline's secondment by
the Rockefeller Foundation was coming naturally to an end in December
1927, and there is no evidence to suggests, as Céline subsequently claimed,
either that he was sacked or that he resigned in protest at the 'Jewish'
corruption of the League.[108] His eyes were now firmly set on Paris and the
ever-obliging Rajchman sent him as a delegate to a conference on rabies
from 22 April to 6 May.[109] At the same time he applied and was rejected for
a post as medical advisor in the League's Health Section in Paris.[110] By the
summer of 1927, however, he appears to have virtually cut himself adrift
from his post in Geneva. On 2 July he registered as a doctor in the Department of the Seine, giving his address as Croissy-sur-Seine,[111] and, on
Rajchman's recommendation, he worked unofficially for Professor Léon
Bernard at the Hôpital Laënnec until September, learning clinical medicine.[112] It was Bernard, a highly distinguished doctor, a French representative to the Hygiene Section of the League of Nations and a Jew, who in
September provided a medical certificate for Céline, recommending sick
leave for a period of four months for malaria, which did not prevent him
being pilloried as 'that fat medical rabbi'[113] in *Bagatelles pour un massacre*.
This sick leave took Céline to the end of his contract with the League and
he never returned to Geneva, leaving the apartment in the Chemin de
Miremont and a string of debts. While most of these appear to be relatively
modest and connected with the decoration of the apartment and removal
expenses,[114] François Gibault mentions rumours in Geneva of much more
dramatic extravagance, including a brand-new Citroën 5CV convertible
and a set of crystal glasses, citing Germaine Constans, who lived with Céline
in Geneva for a month, who remembered lavish spending on furniture,
carpets and decorations.[115] If this were so, and it somehow does not ring
true, given Céline's characteristic parsimony and his declared dislike of
automobiles, it can be interpreted as both a rejection of the financial
restrictions of his childhood and a celebration of freedom with the end
of his marriage. In either case, it fell to Ludwig Rajchman to appease the
creditors.[116]

It was in the autumn of 1927 that Céline decided on general practice as
the branch of medicine he wished to work in. In October he registered as

a doctor practising at number 5 Rue des Saules, in Montmartre,[117] a *quartier* with which he was to be associated for the next seventeen years, and on 14 November he moved to 36 Rue d'Alsace in Clichy, with a plaque reading: 'Doctor Louis Destouches. General Practice. Childhood Diseases'.[118] He was to remain a general practitioner until just before his death.

Professor Robert Debré, who worked under Léon Bernard at the Laënnec Hospital, 'remembered Louis joining their team on occasion, wearing a faded raincoat and an unhappy look, his face already carved by suffering and by his life's myriad experiences'.[119] Professor Debré's memory has probably been overly clouded by the subsequent reputation of the anguished Céline, but the faded raincoat may be authentic. Céline had had a glittering and precocious career: a well-paid, glamorous and prestigious job; travel in Europe, Africa and America; and meetings with some of the most powerful leaders in the world, Coolidge and Mussolini. He had come a long way from the Passage Choiseul and, though he did not know it yet, this was, in conventional terms, the highest he was to rise. The smooth-talking international administrator was about to give way to the shabby doctor and the bohemian writer.

5

Clichy and Montmartre

In setting up in practice in Clichy, Céline returned to the northern indus-trial suburbs into which he had been born and in which all his subsequent medical career was to take place. Bounded on the west by the loop of the Seine, in the middle of which is the Ile Robinson, Clichy was one of those villages beyond the city boundaries of Paris which, from the last quarter of the nineteenth century onwards, had become progressively industrialized, the location of the capital's manufacturing industry subsumed into the city. This expansion of the Parisian suburbs accelerated during the inter-war years as a result of industrial growth, and whereas the population of Paris itself remained static at 2,900,000 in the period from 1921 to 1941, that of the *banlieue* rose during the same period from 1,400,000 to 4,200,000.[1] Nor could such a massive transformation occur without major social and public-health problems. As de Boisline emphasizes, 'At the end of the ninteenth century, the suburbs were a slum. The squalor engendered tuberculosis, venereal diseases and cholera,'[2] with the result that 'working-class life and the class struggle became part of industrial suburban culture.'[3] Clichy itself was typical of the northern suburbs. Berlanstein records that, by 1900, like Puteaux, it was a town with 'a high percentage of industrial craftsmen and metal workers'[4] and with attendant public-health problems, connected not least to the fact that Clichy was the outlet for the Paris sewer into the Seine.[5] After the First World War, the population grew steadily, if not dramatically, from 48,000 in 1914, to 49,000 in 1921, 50,400 in 1928 and 52,000 in 1939,[6] an expansion rendered more impressive when it is borne in mind that 2200 men from Clichy died in the war itself.[7] Hence, 'the population grew considerably: refugees, foreign workers or workers from the provinces necessary to the huge factory created during the conflict, the SOMUA, whose size had doubled and workforce considerably increased by the needs

of national defence.'[8] Clichy became the centre for other important industrial employers: the aviation suppliers Lioré et Olivier, the Société Alsatien
de Construction Electriques, the Câbles de Lyon with between 2000 and
2500 employees, Citroën with 4700, and Monsavon, which later became
L'Oréal.[9] This expansion compounded the two interrelated social problems common to the *banlieue* since the last quarter of the ninteenth
century: housing and health. Radical municipal administrations, often
dominated by Freemasons,[10] had attempted to improve living conditions,
particularly in the 'ragpickers' quarter' near the Paris fortifications, but in
1925 a Communist majority took control, under the mayor and député
Charles Auffray.[11] Auffray never achieved anything as dramatic in housing
reform as his famous colleague in Suresnes, Henri Sellier, with his 'cité-
jardin', but in 1922, prior to his election, he did use the establishment of an
Office Public des HBM for cheap public housing projects to build 117 municipal apparments, 94 of which were opened in 1928 in the Rue Simonneau.[12]
Private housing progressed more rapidly, with 139 apartments being
opened in 1925, 264 in 1926 and 300 in 1927,[13] though their impact on
Clichy's social problems was blunted by the fact that they were too expensive for workers. In 1930 it was estimated that 48.8 per cent of the population of Clichy was still 'badly housed', 29.4 per cent 'passably housed', with
only 21.8 per cent 'well-housed'.[14] What was interesting about the Rue
Simonneau development was that it combined a concern with modern
housing conditions with health provision and shopping facilities. Gaillard
notes that shops were installed in the basements of the new blocks, including a workers' cooperative bakery, 'La Fraternelle', and that the development also included public baths and showers and a municipal health clinic,
the 'dispensaire', placed between the Rue Simonneau and the Rue Fanny,
which was opened on 8 January 1929 and where Céline was employed as a
doctor after his practice in the Rue d'Alsace failed.[15] At the same time,
Auffray established a social work department and set up a Maison des
Pupilles du Patronage Municipal, which provided youth-club activities for
the children of Clichy, including annual summer camps by the sea, a major
innovation at the time and one to be fully developed by Léo Lagrange
during the Front Populaire government.[16] Clichy also played host to one of
France's largest public-works projects of the inter-war years, the building
of the huge Hôpital Beaujon, which had transferred from the Rue du
Faubourg-Saint-Honoré in Paris. All of these developments provided the
context in which Céline was to work as a doctor in Clichy, initially in private
practice, and subsequently as a 'médecin de dispensaire' from 1927 to
1937, and they constitute an indispensable background for an understanding of his writings on social medicine and public health from 1928 to 1933.
Nor was Céline alone at this time in his preoccupation as a doctor with
hygiene and preventive medicine. In 1937 two medical theses appeared
which used Clichy: Joseph Bordiga's *Fonctionnement d'une consultation de
médecine préventitive pour enfants d'âge scolaire*, and Julius Weber's *Un Centre de
triage de la tuberculose, fonctionnement du service et de la consultation de l'Hôpital*

Beaujon à Clichy.[17] The Depression of the 1930s accentuated the social
problems: there were long and bitter strikes at the Paul Dupont and Câbles
de Lyon factories, while Citroën put 1600 of its workers on short time,
leading to the first case of a factory occupation in France, on 28 March
1934, before closing down altogether, along with the accumulator manufac-
turer Fulmen and 'Clichy Ressorts'.[18] A symbolic victim of the Depression
was the workers' bakery, 'La Fraternelle', which was forced to close in
1934.[19]

   There is no doubt that, like all of the Parisian industrial suburbs in the
inter-war years, Clichy presented more than its fair share of social problems.
It is also true, however, that in his public statements and interviews after the
publication of *Voyage au bout de la nuit*, and in the transposition in the novel
itself of Clichy-la-Garenne into La Garenne-Rancy, Céline goes out of his
way to emphasize the social scandal. There is no mention of the fact that
the 'dispensaire' in the Rue Fanny is brand new and part of the innovative
housing development in the Rue Simonneau, no mention of the 'colonies
de vacances', no mention of the new park, the Parc Denain, later renamed
as the Parc Roger Salengro. While the official history is probably overly
optimistic in concluding that 'in 1935, Clichy rapidly took on the appearance of an agreeable estate, with many open spaces, and in the evening,
when the weather was good, the people would come to admire the electric
lights which were progressively replacing the old atmospheric gas-lamps,'[20]
there is little doubt that Céline dramatized the social problems of the town
in order to re-create a Zolaesque image of himself as 'médecin des pauvres'.
The same ambiguity is present in his depiction of the Communist municipality: the grandiose street-names in *Voyage au bout de la nuit* are used to
mock an administration manifestly more concerned with rhetoric than with
concrete policies. Similarly, the journalist Robert de Saint-Jean, who met
Céline after dinner at the home of Daniel Halévy after the publication of
Voyage au bout de la nuit, recalled him making scathing attacks on the Clichy
Communists:

> Céline says that he sees a lot of Communists in Clichy, and he notes that in
> general the members of the Party understand nothing about Marxist theories,
> even if they are translated as 'the rich man's house is yours: take it.' They are
> only led by their passions. At the town hall, Marx's books are never read, but
> *La Garçonne* is worn out and blackened with use. They are all sons of beggars.
> The French need to ask for favours, for crumbs, for privileges, even from
> a Communist 'député'. Moscow's decrees are Byzantine. Fundamentally,
> Moscow is a long way away, and is neither loved nor understood. Céline
> believes that the Russian Revolution is not for export, and that without it
> several countries in Central Europe, dominated by unemployment and
> poverty, would already have gone Communist.[21]

Nevertheless, if Céline's residual anarchism leads him to distrust Communism, his medical writings, particularly the article 'La Santé publique en
France', written for Henri Barbusse's *Monde* in 1930,[22] indicate a much

closer appreciation of what a Communist administration can achieve in the field of housing and public health, and bear clear evidence of his experience of such an administration in Clichy.

The Rue d'Alsace runs from east to west through the centre of Clichy, north of the main Boulevard Jean Jaurès. Céline's apartment was at number 36, on the corner of the present Rue Henri Barbusse, and on the first floor, just above a butcher's shop. Although it had three rooms, in addition to a kitchen and bathroom, it also served as Céline's surgery, and biographers describe it as poor accommodation.[23] It had its own character, however, as Céline's neighbour Jeanne Carayon remembers:

> this apartment somehow reveals the unexpected, the 'waiting room' is not like one at all. Above the windowed bay, against the plinth, a long box trailing clumps of marigolds, somehow artificial without being so, so well do they evoke a garden. Little furniture: ignoring it, the attention is drawn entirely towards the walls, which are hung with masks and objects such as 'colonials' bring back from Africa. A wooden statue – African too, no doubt – set right on the floor, extends a hand.[24]

This bohemian austerity, with its cheap African statuary, was a long way from the luxury of the apartment in Geneva.

François Gibault gives a somewhat lurid imagined account of Céline's clientele:

> Céline's surgery only saw queues of poor people, deprived children, cripples of all sorts, old people with no future. He saw them as so unhappy, so alone, grappling with sickness as well as injustice, that often he did not dare to ask them for money. Lots of times, he lent them money. Above all, he was concerned to understand them and to help them, talking to them about things in their lives, listening patiently to the tales of their suffering.[25]

In fact, opinion on Céline's abilities as a doctor was divided, particularly when he began to work in municipal medicine. One thing is certain, however, and that is that Céline had begun to practice general medicine at a particularly bad time for doctors in Paris. Although, as Berlanstein points out, medicine as a whole in France in the period up to the First World War was a secure and prosperous profession and the legitimate aspiration of the petite-bourgeoisie for their children, the situation was never as easy in the capital, and got worse in the inter-war years. As Theodore Zeldin explains, this was due in part to fierce competition from the paramedical professions of nurses, midwives and, especially, pharmacists, all able to undercut the doctor's fees, but much more to the uneven distribution of doctors in general practice throughout the country. In 1931, France as a whole appeared massively under-resourced, coming only seventeenth in the world for the number of doctors per head of population. Yet Paris had more doctors than any other city in Europe.[26] The implication is clear: while the life of the provincial, particularly the country doctor could be relatively comfortable (though *Madame Bovary* provides ample evidence for rural competition), the position of the doctor in Paris during the inter-war years often became untenable, threatened even further by rising inflation in the 1930s as the result of the Depression. The cost of a consultation rose from 20 francs in 1930 to 30 francs in 1938, and house-calls rose from 30 francs in 1936 to 35 or 40 francs by 1938.[27] It is hardly surprising, in this situation, that poor patients should attempt to avoid costly medical treatment altogether or prefer cut-price advice from nurses or pharmacists. Or else they availed themselves of the basic medical provision of the new municipal clinics, which, because they were free, constituted another powerful form of competition. What happened was that a small number of established doctors with a faithful clientele earned a comfortable living, while a mass of newly qualified practitioners failed to make an impact and almost invariably went bankrupt. What is interesting about this for Céline's career is that not only did it affect him personally, but it also had profound and far-reaching implications for the practice of medicine in the cities and its ability to reach those who needed it most.

One of Céline's first acts when he set up in practice in Clichy was to apply for membership of the Société de Médecine de Paris, the major research and academic body for doctors in the capital. In other words, he was not content simply to vanish into the world of general practice in the poor suburbs, but intended to continue to make an impact and maintain a high profile: the same ambition which motivated the precocious research papers from Roscoff and the publication of *Semmelweis*. In his report to the meeting of 24 March 1928, Dr Georges Rosenthal supported Céline's application on the grounds of 'both his military and civilian qualifications'.[28] Interestingly, among these civilian qualifications is the fact that Céline 'spent four years in the hygiene section of the League of Nations and founded an epidemiological bureau in West Africa':[29] clearly the doctor was up to his old tricks of embroidering the truth to make his case. More significantly, Dr Rosenthal reported that 'he wishes to study questions of the labour organization of the sick and workers,' concluding: 'Obviously, Dr Destouches' specialism is unusual; his life proves that he will be the man of daring initiatives and progress in social hygiene.'[30] He was elected as an associate member of the Society on 13 April 1928, by 21 out of 22 votes,[31] and lost no time in making his mark through a lecture to the Society on 26 May 1928, 'A propos du service sanitaire des usines Ford à Detroit', and an article in *La Presse médicale* on 24 November 1928 entitled 'Les Assurances sociales et une politique économique de santé publique'.

Essentially, both the lecture, subsequently published in the proceedings of the society, and the article, deal with the issue of public health care in an industrialized society, an issue which was the subject of considerable debate in France in the 1920s. From the Armistice onwards, the major trade union confederation, the CGT, had demanded the introduction of a State health insurance system to replace company insurance schemes and to offer a comprehensive provision of health care. The proposal had been adopted, even by the conservative parliament elected after the war, the 'Chambre bleu horizon', as early as 1921 and had passed into law in 1924. The monetary crisis of 1924–6 prevented its being enacted, however, and it was not until the stabilization of the franc under Poincaré in 1928 that the Chambre des Députés felt able to send the law for final ratification to the Senate. After bitter debate in the Senate and modifications to the law as a result of objections by the medical profession, the law was finally put into effect on 24 April 1930 by the government headed by the conservative André Tardieu, significantly a technocrat and one of the few French politicians to show enthusiasm for American techniques of industrial organization. It provided for health care for industrial workers, based on contributions from the State, the employer and the worker.

The law of 1930 effectively 'nationalized' existing company insurance schemes and brought health care for the workforce under the umbrella of the State. Yet, as such, it stopped far short of establishing the kind of national health service demanded by the Left, and it is significant that it was both sponsored and finally promulgated by right-wing governments. In fact, the entire issue of workers' health is a politically loaded one, as the participants in the debate in the late 1920s were all too well aware. The doctors held out for their independent status; the Left argued for a more general system of health provision, while the Right looked for a means of preserving a scheme of health insurance which effectively controlled the workforce. Public health in France began in 1826, when the Société Industrielle de Mulhouse introduced a system of sickness benefit for its employees. By 1852 the pattern had been adopted nationally and enshrined in a law prescribing the establishment of *caisses de secours mutuelles* in all factories, a system which remained in place until the Tardieu law of 1930 and which was based essentially on a compulsory health insurance scheme by which the sick worker consulted the doctor of his choice and was reimbursed by the *caisse*. While doctors liked the scheme, because it preserved their independent relationship with their clients and guaranteed immediate payment, it was inevitably less altruistic than it appeared and was loaded heavily in favour of the employers and the State. As Olivier Targowla points out in *Les Médecins aux mains sales*, the Mulhouse experiment was initially introduced to ward off more extreme demands by the workforce, a pattern visible throughout and in the origin of the 1930 law.[32] In addition, it allowed employers, and the State after 1852, to infiltrate workers' organizations and to ensure a compliant and productive workforce. For the basis of industrial medicine is not primarily the well-being of the worker in itself, but the need to guarantee a sufficient level of health for production to continue as efficiently as possible. As Targowla comments: 'To improve the hygienic state of the worker is to increase production. A strong state needs hygienists. Medical thought here has its origins in a general reflection on power. Social medicine, and hence industrial medicine, is above all a political project. At the origin of illness there is disorder, the slum, unclean-

liness, permanent danger. It is necessary to introduce order and rules.'[33]
For the medical hygienist, therefore, the worker exists only in relation to
his industrial production, a production which must be strenuously maintained, and that hygienist becomes part of 'a real sanitary and medical
police force' designed to 'control the workforce'.[34] In other words, the
medical hygienist, the specialist in public health and industrial medicine,
the branch of medicine chosen by Céline, was more naturally on the
political Right than the Left, the logical ally of the exponents of Taylor and
Ford and their dehumanization of the worker, their reduction of his significance to his productive output: 'the objective of industrial medicine . . . is
not health per se, but a sort of minimal health sufficient to keep the
machines turning.'[35]

It is no coincidence, therefore, that doctors who worked for insurance
companies should explicitly side with the employers against the workers,
and Targowla quotes from an article in *Le Journal* on 21 May 1909 by a Dr
Petitjean, an adviser to insurance companies and Senator for the Nièvre:

> Here we have invented lesions, unverifiable pains, strangely persistent
> lumbagos; it is so easy to remove a bandage and to put into the wound a
> splinter or a fish-bone . . . And even if the lesion really existed, even if it
> became permanent, does that mean that the patient has really suffered a loss?
> This worker has lost the end of a finger, this tool operator has a stiff leg; very
> probably, their capacity for work is not altered and their wage remains the
> same.[36]

Even more realistic is a Dr Rémy, professor of medicine in Paris:

> A split ear, a cut cheek, a broken nose, a scar running down the back or over
> other parts of limbs constitute deformities and sometimes infirmities, but
> they do not diminish the industrial value of the individual . . . When these
> lesions only affect the victim from the aesthetic point of view, however un-
> pleasant and offputting they may be, they should not fall under the scope of
> the law of 1898.[37]

In the immediate period of the debates on the introduction of a national
health insurance scheme in the late 1920s, the medical profession was
divided between those who wished to maintain the status quo in terms of
the strictly personal relationship between doctors and patients, those who,
with some reservations, were willing to opt for the provisions of the new law,
and those who saw this new legislation as far too modest and proposed in
its stead a radical extension of industrial medicine and hygiene in order
to bring the medical profession into the framework of an embryonic
corporatist state, a category into which Céline's own contributions to the
debate would appear to fall. The conservatives continued to express their
traditional distrust of working-class patients. The columns of *La Presse
médicale* abound in comments like: 'The poor like expensive medicines,
especially when they don't have to pay for them,'[38] 'he who doesn't pay is

abusing the system,'[39] 'in the majority of cases, it is the patient who is abusing the treatment,'[40] and 'the poor will henceforth insist on consultations, even if they are useless, to get their money's worth.'[41] The final phrase, 'to get their money's worth' ('pour leur argent') is a direct reference to Jules Romains' play *Knock, ou le triomphe de la médecine*, of 1926, to which Céline alludes in his preface to *Semmelweis*; Romains' play is a sharp satire on the commercialization of medicine.

The bulk of the profession appear to have followed Professor Balthazard, who represented the medical associations at a hearing of the parliamentary Commission d'Assurance et de Prévoyance Sociales. He noted that doctors already operated a third-party payment system in their dealings with the various company insurance schemes and friendly societies and assured the Chamber that they would be willing to act within the framework of the new State scheme, providing that the government accepted the continuation of freedom of choice of patients concerning their doctor and the payment of fees.[42] There were, however, more radical voices. Dr Eugène Briau, for example, writing on the two major plagues to affect modern France, tuberculosis and syphilis, complained that the budget set aside for the operation of the entire scheme, 560 million francs, would immediately be swallowed up by treatment of those two diseases alone:[43] 'in its haste to do good, the legislator is running the risk of ending up with a huge bankruptcy which will delay indefinitely the introduction of the genuinely social system which is essential.'[44] Similarly, radicals on the Right and Left joined in identifying the problem as that of the government's inability to guarantee the health of the nation in the first place. A Dr Specklin, in a speech at Bordeaux, declared:

> Instead of efficiently combating slum-dwelling and alcoholism, instead of checking sewers and drinking-water, instead of acting against the depopulation of the countryside resulting from the inheritance laws, the State is creating this enormous and costly apparatus of health insurance to treat those tuberculosis and typhoid patients who are precisely the victims of its own lack of care.[45]

Céline's lecture on Ford and his article on insurance placed him on the radical Right in the debate, though his ideas seem to have shifted to the left in the early 1930s. The Ford lecture uses much of the descriptive material present in the 1925 memorandum for the League of Nations: the problem of turnover in American industry and the desirability of a permanent workforce, leading to the Ford 'system' of reducing assembly-line tasks to such a minimum of skill that the physically and mentally sick can be employed and retained. As the company doctor told Céline, the ideal employee, as on the cotton farms in the south, was a chimpanzee.[46] What distinguishes the lecture from the previous memorandum, however, is that whereas Céline in 1925 looked with some distaste on the Ford experiment, seeming to prefer the more orthodox and humanist system of the

Westinghouse plant, in his lecture of 1928, in the context of the debate on health insurance, he now sees Ford as the prototype of an efficient public health system in an industrial society:

> As far as we are concerned as doctors and hygienists, from the Ford experiment we ought perhaps to ask ourselves whether it is not now time to apply serious modifications to the notions still currently in force concerning states of health and states of illness to revise them by seeing them from a really modern perspective, that of a world which is modernizing, Americanizing, if you like, a little more every day. There is little possibility of our escaping this evolution and there would probably be great advantages in not ignoring this process on more or less traditional, literary, pretexts which are always futile and practically disastrous.[47]

Realistically, France was now an industrial society and needed to explore rational systems of health care both for the economic strength of the nation and for an efficient public health service. The current system, and its planned extension through health insurance, was based on a fallacious notion of 'pseudo-philanthropy',[48] which was not merely extremely costly, but also failed to care genuinely for the sick, the old and the unemployed. For Céline, the only solution was to adopt a system similar to that of Ford: 'If we really wish to implement social hygiene, we must get hold of the men and the money where they are, where we can be certain to find them, and not waste our time constructing plans of action based on tendentious statistics.'[49] Hence:

> These people are either in the street or at home, or they are in a factory carrying out someone's orders . . . As far as their homes go, what have we done to improve their housing conditions? Nothing. What have we done to remove alcohol from the streets? Nothing. On the contrary. Is there any hope in Europe of seeing workers' wages rise, and by a lot? No. Not for a long time, if ever. The only choice we have left is to attempt to improve the public health and the condition of the sick at the moment when they are working and indirectly through the flexibility provided by well-organized work, by the modern factory.[50]

The article 'Les Assurances sociales et une politique économique de la santé publique', which appeared in *La Presse médicale* on 24 November 1928, took this argument to the extreme and gave it a specifically political gloss, to the extent that the editors felt the need to distance themselves: 'one of our young colleagues from Clichy has sent us an article which we feel obliged to publish below because of the original and new ideas which it contains, even though these ideas will seem to some readers a little theoretical and speculative.'[51] One originality of the article is that the author placed himself unequivocally on the political Right, as a defender of capitalism in France against the creeping scourge of Socialist collectivism, now threatening through health insurance legislation to create 'a monopoly of public health provision'.[52] Since it was too late to confront this threat head-on, the only solution was to adopt Disraeli's neo-conservative ploy of neutralizing socialist demands by introducing an even more collectivist system, but this time one favourable to capitalism. Here, the arguments used previously in favour of Ford take on their full political force, with Céline recommending a small number of 'wise precepts': '1. To admit that the insured person must work as much as possible and with the least interruption because of illness; 2. To admit that most sick people can work; 3. To admit that they must treat themselves and receive treatment whilst they are working and use all the possibilities on offer in modern industry for the employment of the sick.'[53] Even more than in the lecture on Ford, Céline advocates a work-based health-care system, beneficial both to the national economy and to the patients, and sounds the death-knell of that humanist medicine which has so failed the working-class: 'bourgeois medicine is dead, and rightly so, and it is its burlesque ghost which makes social insurance paradoxical and unworkable everywhere . . . Our humanitarianism is also out of date and damaging: it has no role in a society where social insurance operates.'[54] This 'ghost of bourgeois medicine' would re-emerge in *Voyage au bout de la nuit* in the character of Bardamu. For the moment, in Céline's brave new world, he is replaced by the industrial doctor, the 'doctor of the future'[55] who, like the policeman dealing with crime,[56] will go 'on patrol' where the sick people are, namely their place of work. In Céline's vision, Targowla's metaphor of an oppressive medical police force becomes reality. This celebration of the industrial doctor as a 'new man' is interesting for its implications in intellectual as well as political history, and once again Céline rejoins a mainstream current of French intellectual life in the 1920s. It is also politically significant that Céline's doctor will wage war, not merely against poor social conditions, but also against over-prescription of drugs, thus joining a post-war current of 'Neo-Hippocratism' which was the preserve of Action Française and the extreme Right.[57]

Céline's participation in the health insurance debate in 1928 places him unambiguously on the radical Right, and it is no coincidence whatsoever that his proposals should come into their own when the Vichy regime instituted medical services in factories in a circular of 28 July 1942, a year after the republishing of 'La Médecine chez Ford' and the same year as an interview for *Le Concours médical* on 'assembly-line medicine'.[58] The ambiguity, rather, lies in the discrepancy between the attitude to Ford expressed in 1928 and that which informs the 1925 account for Rajchman, the medical essays of the 1930s and, especially, the evocation of Detroit in *Voyage au bout de la nuit*, though the scarcely-veiled anti-Communism in the depiction of the municipality of La Garenne-Rancy would still place the author on the Right. It appears that Céline, in 1928, with his specialist interest in public health and industrial medicine, was tempted by a right-wing technocratic approach to society along the lines of Ernest Mercier's Redressement Français and its 'managerial elitism'.[59] It also appears that his subsequent experience as a doctor in Charles Auffray's municipal dispensary caused some doubts about the technocratic approach and led him, in the 1930s, to consider left-wing corporatism.

In point of fact, Céline himself, at the end of 1928, became a victim of 'bourgeois medicine': his practice in the Rue d'Alsace had never been able to compete with more long-established competitors. He attempted to raise a supplementary income by working for the pharmaceutical company 'La Biothérapie' as an advertising copy-writer and correspondent with the medical profession at a monthly salary of 1000 francs, a post he retained well after his literary success, until 1937,[60] but this was insufficient. At the beginning of 1929 a new municipal clinic was opened at number 10 Rue Fanny in Clichy, and Céline was appointed by the Direction de la Médecine d'Hygiène Populaire as a general practitioner, with surgery hours from five till six-thirty every evening, at a salary of 2000 francs a month:[61] a classic retreat from private to public medicine for the hard-pressed Parisian doctors in the inter-war years.

II Rue Fanny

The municipal clinics or 'dispensaires' were created in urban industrial centres in France in the 1920s to provide much-needed basic health care for those who could not afford to consult private doctors. The doctors who worked in these clinics were paid a salary and the patients were treated for nothing. Inevitably, the clinic's doctors saw the most deprived members of urban society, for the most part victims of diseases with social causes: syphilis, tuberculosis, alcoholism and typhus; they were made profoundly aware of the palliative nature of their work. No 'cure' could be offered for diseases arising from the effects of housing conditions, diet and lifestyle, which neither doctor nor patient could hope to influence. It is for this reason, as Céline indicated in his writings on health insurance from 1928 and later, that hygiene and industrial medicine immediately enter the political domain.

In order to gain more knowledge and experience of the diseases he was required to treat, Céline worked with the Institut Prophylactique, at number 36 Rue d'Assas, in the Latin Quarter. As François Gibault notes, the Institut was founded in 1916 by two doctors, Emile Chautemps and Arthur Vernes, with financial backing from the American millionaire Frank Jay Gould.[62] Céline became friendly with Arthur Vernes, and through the Institut and its benefactor he met Gould's wife Florence, one of the most important patrons of the arts in Paris in the inter-war years, with whom he was to have some contact subsequently.[63] His admiration for Vernes was confirmed by his use of a method of blood-testing for tuberculosis and syphilis, 'Vernes Resourcine', on which he wrote a paper for the Sociéte de Médecine de Paris in March 1930 and which provides a fascinating insight into the operation of the 'dispensaire' in Clichy.[64] Mindful of the human and economic need for rapid diagnosis of tuberculosis, Céline recounts the results of the analysis of 'those patients who *coughed or could be suffering from tuberculosis to various degrees,* chosen after a normally rapid examination amongst the *2200 new adult patients* in general medicine examined during the year'.[65] Out of this sample of 2200 new patients admitted annually, '860 coughed or presented more or less pronounced symptoms of possible infection.'[66] From this group, 648 could be eliminated as suffering from chest complaints such as bronchitis and emphysema, but 212 tested positive on the Vernes blood analysis for tuberculosis. In other words, nearly half of the annual intake of adult patients suffered from chest diseases, with one-tenth suffering specifically from tuberculosis. In addition, the tests threw up 32 patients from this sample suffering from syphilis, who were referred by Céline to the anti-syphilis clinic.[67] This was the medical environment in which Céline worked every day in the Rue Fanny.

More problematic than the clientele, however, were Céline's relations with his superior, the director of the 'dispensaire', a Lithuanian Jew called Grégoire Ichok. As Gibault records, Céline could never reconcile himself to working with a man whom he considered 'neither French, nor a doctor',[68] and who he felt had usurped his rightful position as director of the clinic in the Rue Fanny. In fact Ichok, born in 1892, had studied medicine in Königsberg, Leipzig and Heidelberg, before going on to Zurich and Basle. He came to France after the war, following a career not unlike that of Céline: the *baccalauréat* in 1925, followed by dispensation of the first four years of medical school as a result of his Swiss qualifications.[69] After only two years of study in France, he qualified as a French doctor in May 1927 with a thesis: *Sur la question des 'chambres d'allaitement'*, even though he did not receive French nationality until 6 March 1928. Céline's animosity was fuelled, therefore, by the fact that Ichok, two years his senior, was appointed over him even though he had graduated in France three years later, and had only held French nationality for nine months when the 'dispensaire' in the Rue Fanny was opened. In addition, Ichok, on the non-Communist Left, had powerful political connections: he had met Salomon Grumbach, chairman of the Foreign Affairs Committee of the Chambre des Députés, in a Swiss sanatorium in 1917; he knew Pierre Comert, press secretary at the Quai d'Orsay, and Charles Gombault of *Paris-Soir,* as well as non-political figures like Julien Cain, the head of the Bibliothèque Nationale, and Marc Chagall, whose name the 'dispensaire' currently bears.[70] Alongside his work in Clichy, he acted as technical adviser to the Ministère de la Santé Publique and taught at the Institut Statistique in Paris.[71] He was also an active member of LICA, the Ligue Internationale contre l'Antisémitisme. Like Céline, he published articles in both the popular and specialist press, writing the medical column in *Le Prolétaire de Clichy*, 'Hippocrate vous dit', on subjects like public health, mortality rates in Paris, and work for the sick and disabled. In one sense, it is difficult not to see in Ichok a man with similar ambitions to Céline's but apparently more successful in the world of public medicine, and it is probably this, as much as the 'usurpation', which accounts for Céline's hostility, a hostility cordially returned by Ichok himself.[72] It is probable that working with Ichok was one of the key steps on Céline's path to the overt anti-Semitism of *Bagatelles pour un massacre* and *L'Ecole des cadavres*. Certainly, in his personal mythology, as expressed in interviews with his friend Robert Poulet in 1958, Ichok (transformed into 'Idouc', just as Rachjman becomes 'Jubelblatt' in *Bagatelles pour un massacre*) is denounced as a Soviet spy and one of the interminable list of Céline's persecutors, the main reason for his leaving the 'dispensaire' in December 1937.[73] In the paranoid world of French anti-Semitism in the 1930s, a Lithuanian Jew, with powerful parliamentary connections and real family links with Soviet Russia, became all too easily an agent of the international Jewish conspiracy, dedicated to removing free-born Frenchmen from their rightful positions.

Eventually, Ichok fell victim to precisely this kind of paranoia. Deeply depressed at the declaration of war, he committed suicide by taking cyanide on the terrace of the Café des Sports on the Place Maillot at noon on 10 January 1940.[74] At his funeral at the Père-Lachaise on 17 January, Charles Auffray gave the funeral oration, concluding: 'We are called to live a precarious existence, within a society in which we alteratively come up against good and evil people. The evil person, who is more violent, intends to use every means to foster his interests, his passions and his madnesses. Against him, we must be armed with a similar violence. Woe to the meek, the gentle, the peace-loving, to loyal and honest souls!'[75] Needless to say, in his version to Robert Poulet, Céline imputed Ichok's suicide quite fictitiously to his panic at being summoned in 1939 by the intelligence service of the Military Governor of Paris, General Hering: the proof that he was a senior Soviet agent.[76]

Hardly had he arrived in the Rue Fanny, however, than Céline conceived another travel project for the League of Nations: this time, a return visit to London. On 8 February 1929, he wrote to the head of the Infectious Diseases section in Geneva, Dr Boudreau:

> Here is my request for a little study trip to London, which I would like to undertake at Easter. I have abandoned the study of the big problems of social organization, because they do not interest anyone. I would simply like to get the English perspective on the running of a 'dispensaire' like our own and the struggle against blennorrhagia – and also the *rational nourishment of the poor*. This should be extensively researched in England. I intend to go later in this context to Austria.[77]

Rajchman agreed to the project on 25 February, sending a cheque for 500 francs, and in a letter to Boudreau of 6 March, Céline replied with a more detailed plan, which is of interest both for the emphasis it contains on 'medical efficiency'[78] and for the information that, in Clichy, 'we have carried out 1000 consultations a month!' and 'effected 400 cures or improvements'.[79] He also announced his intention to leave on 26 March and return to France on 8 April. Little is known about this visit to London and no report was sent to Geneva. A letter to Dr Boudreau of 21 April, however, blames the Easter holidays for preventing him from seeing much, though he does comment on 'disastrous things in the English health insurance system'.[80] In fact, he had a meeting with a Professor MacCleary and had clearly visited both Stepney and the London Hospital, which appears in *Guignol's Band*.[81]

No sooner had he returned from London than he was planning his next journey: a three-week study trip to Antwerp, Oslo, Stockholm, Copenhagen and Berlin, in order to study the operation of municipal health and venereal-disease clinics in those cities.[82] At the end of August, however, he asked for the visit to be postponed until November, and announced a change of address to 98, Rue Lepic, in Montmartre.

III RUE LEPIC

The immediate reason for Céline and Elizabeth moving from Clichy was an outbreak of bedbugs at number 36 Rue d'Alsace. As Jeanne Carayon recalled: 'The invasion swept from one floor to another, from the fifth to the first.'[83] The couple moved into the top floor of number 98 Rue Lepic, under the eaves. As Vitoux describes it, it was: 'A little building, modern but already decrepit, whose streetside façade on the corner of the rue Giradon, on the heights of the Butte, bore a rather sad look, with its cream-coloured exterior pierced by only two windows per floor, without the least architectural whimsy, rather like a barn that had been converted into a residential building.'[84] Inside, Henri Mahé recalls its 'bourgeois décor, country doctor style, or perhaps a parson. Rustic table, gleaming polished Breton wardrobes, period armchairs, wide sofa, a high tapestry screen, rugs nicely arranged on the floor, on the wall a little pastel of a dancer by Degas, two or three decorative knick-knacks.'[85] The relative austerity of the Rue d'Alsace appears to have been temporary, probably caused by the debts in Geneva and Céline's lack of income as a private doctor. By the time he moved to Montmartre, he had an income of at least 3000 francs a month and could afford a more luxurious lifestyle. The apartment consisted of one long room, which also served as Elizabeth's dance studio, a small bedroom, a bathroom and a kitchen, which Céline turned into a study. What visitors remembered especially was the dramatic view from the 'studio' over Paris.[86] The Rue Lepic winds its way from the Place Blanche up the western side of the Butte de Montmartre right to the summit. With its street market, artisanal businesses and small shops it is, even now, a remnant of traditional Paris. When Céline moved there in 1929, it was unquestionably at the heart of the capital's most famous urban village, suspended between the 'Montmartre du plaisir et du crime'[87] on the Boulevard de Clichy and the industrial suburbs of Clichy, Saint-Ouen and Saint-Denis to the north.

While Montmartre may have been a convenient location for someone like Céline who worked in Clichy, his choice of it as a place to live was highly significant, and he was to remain there until going into exile in the summer of 1944. Not only did it replicate the artisanal milieu of his childhood in the Passage Choiseul, it had very specific cultural connotations which rendered it distinct from any other area of Paris, and particularly from avant-garde and intellectual centres on the Left Bank. Montmartre had become a pleasure centre for Paris with the construction of the Mur des Fermiers Généraux in 1786, which introduced tax differentials on, among other commodities, alcohol, between the capital and its surrounding villages. Immediately, all along the outside of the wall, and especially at gateways to the city, taverns and dance-halls sprang up serving cheap wine. Montmartre, which, with its windmills, vineyards and rural inns, had been popular with Parisians long before the construction of the wall, became the major beneficiary. As Paris expanded in the nineteenth century, however, extending its boundaries to the fortifications along the current Boulevards des Maréchaux, it engulfed Montmartre by the Law of 1886 and changed its character. Effectively, Montmartre found itself wedged between the industrial developments which accompanied the great railway networks running into the Gare du Nord and the Gare de l'Est (Batignolles to the west and La Chapelle to the east). Its southern borders along the Boulevard de Clichy and the Boulevard de Rochechouart were transformed into the marginal entertainment district of Paris, with the attendant mixture of 'pleasure and crime' centred on the Place Pigalle, the Place Blanche and the Place de Clichy, whilst the old 'village' of Montmartre retreated up to the Butte.[88] In the course of this development at the end of the nineteenth century, it attracted cabarets, dance-halls and music-halls, from Rodolphe Salis' Le Chat Noir to the Moulin Rouge and the Folies Bergère, avant-garde painters and writers, and political radicals of Right and Left, but especially anarchists.

Céline himself recalls the anarchist 'Bande à Bonnot' in *Mea culpa*,[89] and his description of Lola's black anarchist servant in *Voyage au bout de la nuit*, with his war-cry of 'liberta!' has echoes of the legendary Montmartre anarchist Libertad.[90] Bardamu himself establishes his claim to anarchism at the very beginning of *Voyage au bout de la nuit*, and many of the apparent ambiguities in Céline's own political position are resolved both if he is viewed as an anarchist and if we bear in mind that it was possible in Montmartre in the inter-war years for anarchism to assume radically right-wing colours when the Establishment appeared to be on the Left: the career of the veteran opposition journalist Jean Galtier-Boissière and his review *Le Crapouillot* is evidence of this. This radical subversiveness in the early days of Montmartre was at the base of its literary culture, through phenomena as diverse as Aristide Bruant and his fellow *chansonniers* who calculatedly insulted their bourgeois audience, the polemical tradition of Léon Bloy, and the poetry of figures such as Jean Richepin and Jehan-

Rictus. In other words, by moving to Montmartre, Céline was moving into a tight community with a radical political and artistic tradition.

That tradition was reinforced in the inter-war years, and Céline became a part of it.[91] The great days of Montmartre as capital of the Parisian avant-garde, orchestrated by Apollinaire and led by Picasso, were over. The inhabitants of the Bateau-Lavoir and the Butte in the heyday of Cubism – Picasso himself, Braque, Van Dongen, Modigliani, Max Jacob, André Salmon – had all moved away from Montmartre, mainly to the Left Bank and Montparnasse. They left behind them a very different artistic community, composed of personalities who were members of the great period of Montmartre bohemianism from 1900 to the war and who chose to remain associated with it, though not necessarily permanently resident there, in the inter-war years. Some of them were painters: Utrillo, constantly on the run from his mother Suzanne Valadon and often turning out Montmartre landscapes for the price of a litre of red wine; the Fauvist Vlaminck, increasingly embittered at the success of his erstwhile colleagues now in Montparnasse and accused of Collaboration during the Occupation; and the tortured Jules Pascin, who committed suicide in his studio on the Boulevard de Clichy in 1936. Most, however, were illustrators, engravers and caricaturists, rather than formal painters, continuing a Montmartre tradition which went back to the nineteenth century of Lautrec, Steinlen and Willette (whose huge fresco, *Parce Domine*, for Le Chat Noir, with its swarm of Parisian ghosts flying through the sky above Montmartre, must surely be at the origin of Bardamu's vision of the phantoms above the Butte on All Saints Night), and enjoying a new and lucrative lease of life with the creation of the luxury book market (or *livres d'artiste*) in the 1920s. There was Gus Bofa, the editor of *Le Sourire* and then *Le Rire* and founder of the important annual art-show L'Araignée; there was Chas Laborde, styled as the 'French George Grosz'; there was Francisque Poulbot, the creator of caricatural Parisian street-urchins; there was the Butte's master-engraver and book-illustrator, Jean-Gabriel Daragnès. In the same way that their Left-Bank counterparts congregated in the cafés of Montparnasse, the Coupole, the Dôme, the Sélect, or in the Flore, the Deux Magots and the Brasserie Lipp on the Boulevard Saint-Germain, these illustrators met in the bars and cafés of the Rue Caulaincourt, on the north side of the Butte, such as the bar Au Rêve or the Restaurant Manière. And these figures, all of whom go back to the belle époque, were joined in the inter-war years by new arrivals, such as the painter Gen Paul, who was to become Céline's close friend, and the violently anti-Semitic cartoonist for the fascist weekly *Je suis partout*, Ralph Soupault.

Similarly, the major novelists of pre-war Montmartre bohemianism, Pierre Mac Orlan, Francis Carco and Roland Dorgelès, remained closely associated with the Butte, though choosing to live away from it. Dorgelès, in addition to his major success with the description of life in the trenches in *Les Croix de bois* of 1919, had specialized in an often sentimentalized evocation of pre-war Montmartre, while Carco, right from his early depiction of male prostitution in lower Montmartre in *Jésus-la-Caille*, had continued to explore the seedy world of Montmartre's pleasure and crime. Of the three, it is probably Mac Orlan to whom Céline was most attracted, a fact he acknowledges in *Bagatelles pour un massacre*,[92] where he praises Mac Orlan's innovative style. In addition to the style, however, described in similar terms to that of Paul Morand,[93] there are other features which distinguish Mac Orlan from his two colleagues: his bitter and unsentimental memories of poverty in Montmartre before the war; a willingness to use fantasy and ghosts in order to create what he called 'le fantastique social', a sense of malaise at the very core of post-war European society; an early career as a pornographer, translated into a later sadistic attitude to sexuality; and an explicit racism built upon fear of invasion from the East. It was into this Montmartre literary culture that Céline arrived as a latecomer in 1929, preceded two years before by another newcomer, Marcel Aymé who, along with Gen Paul, was to be a central figure in Céline's circle. His portrait of Céline in full rhetorical flight in his piece 'Avenue Junot', in *Je suis partout* in 1943, captures vividly both Céline's own eccentric style of conversation and the milieu in which he moved. His evocation of Céline's diatribes in his short story 'En attendant', in *Le Vin de Paris* of 1944, was blamed by the author for his subsequent problems with French justice in *Maudits soupirs pour une autre fois*, an early version of *Féerie pour une autre fois*, in much the same way that the luckless Gen Paul blamed Céline for his caricatural anti-Semitism in *Bagatelles pour un massacre.*[94]

What is important about Montmartre culture in the inter-war years is that it was explicitly conservative, both politically and aesthetically. The bohemians who remained were quite aware that the avant-garde caravan had moved on, and Marcel Aymé's resentment at the lack of consideration they received is typical. Writing in his preface to Jean Vertex's volume, *Le Village inspiré*, he comments: 'Most of the witnesses to the heroic period seem convinced that life on the Butte, from 1920 onwards, ceased to be interesting. In other words, the village was no longer "inspired" from the moment when they emigrated to richer or more fashionable districts.'[95] This resentment towards those who had abandoned Montmartre was translated into a general resentment of artistic fashion, into which crept considerable anti-intellectualism, racism and nationalism. In other words, the 'village' became the symbol for its inhabitants of 'real France'. For one of the major memorialists of the great era of Montmartre, Paul Yaki, it was the rival artistic centre, Montparnasse, which had betrayed: 'Montparnasse has a monopoly of fashion nowadays amongst those foreigners who are on the lookout for famous taverns and hidden vices and amongst young artists looking for recognition.'[96] Yet, 'you begin to dream of rubbing shoulders amongst Frenchmen in a Montmartre on the summit, limited perhaps, but where the last gardens and some old dwellings have been preserved.'[97] The 'amongst Frenchmen' is significant, for if Montparnasse had betrayed, it was because it had sacrificed French national purity to a cosmopolitan racial mix. In an unpleasant sideswipe at Modigliani, another memorialist, Géo Cim, recalls: 'One night when he had been drinking in the Lapin Agile, completely disgusted, he abandoned the Butte, like most half-castes; not seeking to hide his Jewish origins, he went off to join the "wogs of Montparnasse" ["les bicots du Montparno"].'[98] It has already been indicated that one major feature which contributed to the general conservatism of the 'Ecole de Montmartre' was their experience of the First World War, which is identical to that of Céline: an uneasy mixture of pacifism and patriotism which, in the late 1930s, was often to find an easy alliance with the French extreme Right. As Georges Charensol records, the Montmartre Bohemians were openly proud of their war experience and Gus Bofa was unusual in keeping silent: 'he had been profoundly affected both morally and physically.'[99] Essentially, therefore, Montmartre culture in the inter-war years was composed of men of roughly Céline's age, or slightly older, who had been marked by the war, were strongly nationalistic to the point of racism, had pronounced anti-republican views, in so far as the Republic represented bourgeois politics and the modern, post-war world, and tended to be aesthetically conservative in their distrust of the avant-garde and Left-Bank intellectualism. In his memoirs, Jean Vertex recalls a rare journey to the Latin Quarter in the late 1940s: 'In the street, there processed before us samples of *Existentialism*, in uniform, unknown in Montmartre. Serious intellectuals discussed weighty matters on the edges of the pavements.'[100] Céline's oft-repeated distrust of and contempt for 'idéâs' and his instinctive hatred of Sartre coincide exactly with one of the main currents of Montmartre culture.

It is from this point onwards that it is possible to identify a marked bohemianism in Céline's lifestyle, manners and dress. Céline and Elizabeth Craig lived separate lives. The kitchen, as we have seen, was transformed into a study, so the couple ate their meals in local cafés and restaurants,[101] and after dinner Céline often wrote late into the night, though this did not prevent their going to the cinema, ballet, comic opera or the theatre, in which Céline maintained a semi-professional interest. Another Montmartre figure was the director Charles Dullin, whose Théâtre de l'Atelier was near the Abesses métro, and with whom Céline corresponded in 1929,[102] perhaps in the hope of having him perform *L'Eglise*. Elizabeth continued to dance, training regularly at Madame Egorova's studio in the Rue Rochechouart, and once appeared on stage at the Paramount cinema.[103] The relationship between the two, however, was increasingly unhappy, in spite of holidays in Normandy, Britanny, Pau and even Megève. As Elizabeth Craig recalled in her interviews with Alphonse Juilland just before her death, sixty years after the events she was describing, Céline underwent a major personality change in the late 1920s: 'Louis was such a different man while we were in Switzerland. I often wondered what made him so depressed and depressing when we came back to Paris. In Geneva we used to go skiing, he taught me how to ski and ice-skate, we had a great time. I can't understand why he changed so much. Even my parents noticed how much he had changed when they came for a visit.'[104] The reference to the parents is too precise for the reminiscence to be discounted, even with such a large time-gap. Her explanations for Céline's change of mood are also worth considering. First, she blames his work: 'he had been working in this welfare clinic and I guess it was all the misery and sickness he saw there that did it,'[105] a possibility reinforced in a letter to Joseph Garcin in June 1930, when, having complimented his correspondent on his grand contacts in London, he comments: 'My own contacts are quite different, as you will suspect. Hideousness and suffering: the all too common lot.'[106] As we have seen, given the mixed reality of public medicine in Clichy in the inter-war years, there may be more than an element of self-dramatization in this stance. Secondly, she singles out the novel: 'it all began when he decided to write this book, about two years after we met, when we moved to Rue Lepic,'[107] a comment which, again, coincides with the probable dates of composition of *Voyage au bout de la nuit*. It may also be that the new pessimism which Elizabeth Craig recalls was a reaction to the loss of 'the wonderful position' in Geneva, the first impediment to the unbridled ambition expressed in the *Carnet du Cuirassier Destouches*. He aimed to rectify this difficulty both morally and financially through the success of the novel. Philippe Alméras is surely right to contrast Elizabeth's portrait of a 'despairing' Céline in 1929–30 with the evident self-satisfaction and prosperity emanating from the photograph taken when he gave a speech in honour of Zola at Médan in 1933, yet the two are not contradictory and *Voyage au bout de la nuit* may well have fulfilled its purpose.

Certainly the mood-change in Céline noted in 1929–30 by Elizabeth Craig, even if only temporary, appears to have been accompanied by the adoption of eccentric, even Bohemian, dress and behaviour. As Gibault records of his life as a doctor in Clichy: 'Those who knew him at that period seem especially to have retained the memory of an eccentric who lacked neither personality nor zaniness.'[108] As for his dress, 'he was described as being strangely wrapped in bizarre pullovers, in suits which had been eaten by moths, whom he defended, saying: "They have to eat!"'[109] This is the first indication of that utter disregard for dress so familiar in the photographs of Céline in Denmark or Meudon, and with probably the same cause: the successful Céline has something of the dandy about him; the wounded Céline opts for rags and tatters.

Céline's bohemianism in this period was reinforced at the time of his move to the Rue Lepic by his meeting with the Breton painter Henri Mahé, introduced to him by Germaine Constans, acting through a journalist at *L'Intransigeant*, Aimée Barancy.[110] Mahé specialized in murals: he had painted the scenery for some of Abel Gance's films, had worked on the decoration of the liner *Normandie*, the murals on the Balajo in the Rue de Lappe, and the décor of the Rex Cinema on the Boulevard Poissonnière.[111] His real speciality, however, was brothels: he decorated, among others, the Sphinx in the Rue Montparnasse, the Joubert in the Rue Joubert, Charonne's Hotel and 31 Cité d'Antin, the subject of a short humorous sketch composed by Céline.[112] As Alméras records, with this in mind, Céline had considered commissioning him to decorate the bathroom in the Rue Lepic.[113] With his wife Maggy, who came from Rennes and knew Edith Follet, Mahé lived on a barge, the *Malemoa*, moored successively at Croissy-sur-Seine, the Quai de Bourbon and. finally, the Quai des Tuileries. Here he attracted a strange mixture of guests from the underworld, the *demi-monde*, the world of entertainment and the world of literature. Regular visitors included Céline and Elizabeth, 'Robert de Cotton, the son of a rich family, Jojo France, the owner of the "Balajo", the "grocer-poet" Roger Lécuyer, the clowns Antonet and Bébi, the Mayor of Bougival, Nane Germon, who played *ingénue* parts in the theatre, but was resting, Eliane Tayard, assistant to Carl Dreyer, and Abel Gance'.[114] In addition to this group of regulars, Roger Lécuyer remembers other visitors: Paul Belmondo, Maurice Cloche, Francis Carco, Mistinguette, Georges Simenon and the Fratellinis.[115] Sundays were the big days on the *Malemoa*: the regulars would go out on excursions to Bougival or simply stay on the barge. There was a lot of drinking, a lot of singing and a lot of sex, often leading the Vice Squad to inspect the Quai des Tuileries.[116] Indeed, Mahé's memoirs record a strong sexual complicity between himself and Céline in their chasing of women and young girls,[117] pursuits in which Elizabeth Craig played an ambiguous role. Mahé himself and Marcel Brochard, Céline's old friend from his days in Rennes, remember Elizabeth, described as a 'three-masted schooner', actively enticing women to the *Malemoa* and joining in the debauchery, though in her interviews with Juilland, perhaps unsurprisingly, she dismissed this.[118] Céline himself was to retain close contact with Mahé until the end of the war and they met frequently in Saint-Malo.[119] A reflection of the *Malemoa* is contained in the Toulouse episode of *Voyage au bout de la nuit*, when Bardamu, Robinson and Madelon come across a barge moored on the canal and spend an idyllic Sunday in peace and gaiety.

At the same time, in Montmartre, Céline made two important acquaintances, Joseph Garcin and Marcel Lafaye, who were to have a significant impact on his literary work. Garcin was a natural adventurer: born in the Department of the Gard in 1894, he had a distinguished war record, before moving to London in 1917 and 1918, where, much more than Céline, he became involved in the underworld.[120] After the war, he made a career for himself in hotels and restaurants, in addition to prostitution, and shuttled between London and Montmartre, before gradually retiring to the south. Between 1925 and 1930 he attempted to get into politics, apparently in the Senate,[121] and cultivated French Embassy officials in London and members of the British cabinet. Céline met him in 1929 and corresponded with him for the next ten years, often using him as a guide to the dives and brothels of London when he visited Britain. What is interesting about the correspondence with Garcin is that it shows that, at the time, Céline intended to include an episode on the London underworld in *Voyage au bout de la nuit* after the First World War section and needed authentic information. In a

letter dated April 1930, he writes: 'Decidedly, you need to teach me everything about the London milieu. I frequented it a little in 1915, superficially,
I was 20 and had too many memories of the Front.'[122] Throughout 1930, he
bombarded Garcin with requests for details on London, including maps,
and on his own experiences. In July 1931, however, he announced that he
was abandoning the London episode, though it would be the setting for the
next novel.[123] That novel would, of course, become *Guignol's Band*, though
it was not written until the Occupation, after *Mort à crédit* and the aborted
attempt at *Casse-pipe*, and Garcin, along with other legendary figures of the
London French underworld, like Jacques le Rouquin, will serve as a model
for the pimp Cascade. In addition to comments on the composition of
Voyage au bout de la nuit, the correspondence shows a considerable affinity
between the two ex-combatants, progressively convinced of an imminent
new conflict. Céline emphasized the indelible nature of the war experience: 'I will never recover from those weeks of 1914, in those viscous
downpours, in that terrible mud, in that blood and that shit and that
stupidity. That's a truth which I'm telling you again, and there are only a
few of us to share it.'[124] He provided a gloomy report of a recent journey to
Central Europe in 1930: 'I saw in Central Europe things you don't want to
see. The catastrophe is imminent, more specifically sadistic than anything
we have ever known – People are dancing and are blind and deaf.'[125]
Interestingly, the major difference between the two men is quasi-racial: as
Céline stated in a letter of October 1930, 'You know, I'm not a man of the
south. I need the cold of the north, the sun is fatal, and our flesh is already
so precarious.'[126] Céline claimed the same status as a man of the north as
did his fellow Montmartrois Mac Orlan.

In 1928 Céline met a friend of Garcin's, Marcel Lafaye, who lived in
Montmartre until 1934, when he emigrated to Algeria.[127] Lafaye was a
Parisian from the petite-bourgeoisie who, after a distinguished war in both
the infantry and the air force, went to manage a trading-post in Cameroon,
before going to work in America in 1929, for Pratt and Whitney in
Hartford, Connecticut, and then Ford in Detroit. The four years he spent
in Montmartre from 1930 to 1934 enabled him to frequent a number of
the Butte's personalities, such as Mac Orlan, Gen Paul and the painter
Foujita.[128] In his meticulous reconstruction of the relationship between
Céline and Lafaye, Pierre Lainé probably overemphasizes the importance
of the coincidences between the two men's careers, which are certainly
insufficient to confirm Lafaye as a model for Bardamu in *Voyage au bout de
la nuit*. To be petit-bourgeois and serve in the First World War was hardly
unusual, and there were many French ex-combatants who tried to make
careers both in the colonies and in America. Moreover, in spite of Lainé's
assertion that it was Lafaye who provided the name Bardamu for Céline's
protagonist,[129] it is important to remember that both the character and
some of the main lines of the narrative of the novel exist in dramatic form
in *L'Eglise* as early as 1926. In fact, rather than using Lafaye as a model,
Céline used him as a source of precise information, just as he used Garcin,

and exclusively on the one area he wished to include in the novel but on which he had only sketchy experience, the Ford plant in Detroit. Lafaye's daughter recalls him saying that 'he had given a lot of information to Céline, notably on Ford.'[130] As we have seen, Céline's own visit to Ford lasted at most forty-eight hours and, although his research had given him statistics, he still lacked the information on day-to-day working practices to be carried out by Bardamu. What this and the Garcin episode do show, however, is that Céline's fiction is considerably less autobiographical than it appears, that the transposition from his own lived experience has travelled a long way, and that the novels are a carefully constructed patchwork of testimony and invention.

Alongside the Bohemian life on the Butte and on board the *Malemoa*, and in addition to the composition of *Voyage au bout de la nuit*, Céline's major activity remained medicine. In addition to his full-time post at the Rue Fanny, he also worked at the 'Dispensaire Marthe-Brandès' at number 35 Avenue de Saint-Ouen, run by the Fédération Nationale des Blessés du Poumon et des Chirurgicaux, where, as Gibault notes, he treated many ex-combatants.[131] In spite of disagreements regarding Céline's clinical abilities, Philippe Roussin is right to stress the importance that Céline himself laid on his medical work, even, and especially, when he had become a famous novelist in 1932–3.[132] To be sure, this afforded him a public persona which was both intriguing and sympathetic, useful publicity for a new novelist, but the commitment goes deeper and remains constant, almost up to his death in 1961.

He was also constantly on the lookout for more means of making money, and in 1930 managed to extend his connections with 'La Biothérapie' to include medical research. The administrator of the firm, M. Gallier, had set up his own pharmaceutical laboratory at number 22 Avenue du Maine, and employed Céline as a researcher. It was here that Céline developed a drug called 'Basdowine', sold until 1971 in pill form to combat period pains, Basdow's disease and menopausal symptoms.[133] At the same time, he continued to do publicity work for 'La Biothérapie', in particular for their 'Sanogyl' toothpaste. He continued to work for the company until 1937, when he resigned following the publication of *Bagatelles pour un massacre*: the managing director of 'La Biothérapie' was Abraam Alpérine, a Jew and a friend of Grégoire Ichok's, who told Céline he could no longer employ him after such an anti-Semitic outburst.

At the same time Céline was exceptionally productive in his medical writings, both scientific and in the sociopolitical field of social hygiene. He published four technical articles in 1929 alone, 'L'Infection puerpérale et les antivirus', a 'Note sur l'emploi des antivirus de Besredka en pansements humides', a review article: 'L'Immunité dans les maladies infectieuses. A propos du livre récent de A. Besredka' and 'Deux expèriences de vaccination en masse et *per os* contre la typhoïde', followed in 1930 by the paper 'Essai de diagnostique et de thérapeutie méthodiques 'en série' sur certains malades d'un dispensaire' and in 1931 by the article 'Les Hémorragies minimes des gencives en clientèle'. The journals used were *La Presse Médicale, Paris Médical, La Gazette Médicale* and the *Bulletins et Mémoires de la Sociéte de Médecine de Paris*, and the articles and papers show a willingness to exploit previous research (on puerperal fever), the reading of one book (Besredka) and his own experience as a municipal doctor. Nevertheless, it is an impressive record and one which testifies to a continuing ambition in the field of academic medicine. Meanwhile Céline did not neglect the public health sphere, using his contacts in the League of Nations to fund further study tours: to Northern Europe and Scandinavia from 22 December 1929 for eight weeks, to Dresden, Prague and Vienna from 28 June to 17 July 1930, in which he detected the 'catastrophic atmosphere' reported in the letter to Garcin, and a visit to the archives in Geneva from 8 to 11 January 1931,[134] all funded by Rajchman. He also acted as group leader to a party of exchange researchers in Paris in May 1931, mercilessly lampooning one of the delegates, M. Wu, who 'visited the health institutions in Paris which he wished to inspect: including the Institut Pasteur, the Veterinary School at Maison-Alfort, the Folies-Bergères, the Verne Institut, the Dispensaire de Clichy, the Opéra, a . . . Chinese restaurant, etc.'[135] It is worth recording that, if the request for the Geneva visit was somewhat vague, concerning the 'consultation of documents in the Section relating to exchange visits and the work of committees, in order to be up to date and ready for all eventualities,'[136] the proposals for the Central European journey were well-informed and precise, citing specific areas of study in each city and named specialists he wished to observe. He concluded his proposal by stating: 'Here in Clichy I am continuing my work on the perfecting of an *assembly-line medical system* [médecine standard] and I intend to publish a book on the subject in a few months.'[137]

No book appeared as such, and no formal report was sent to Geneva, but two reflections on social medicine were published: an article in *Monde* in 1930, 'La Santé publique en France', and a polemical piece in *Le Mois* in 1933, 'Pour tuer le chômage tueront-ils les chômeurs?' to which can be added an unpublished memorandum of 1932 for the League of Nations, an extensive 'Mémoire pour le Cours des Hautes Etudes'. What is interesting about these papers on public health is that they appear to show a marked move away from the technocratic capitalism of the 1928 writings to a clear left-wing stance, indicated by Céline's use of the journal *Monde*, edited by the Communist sympathizers Henri Barbusse and Georges Altman. The preoccupations remain the same: housing conditions, alcoholism, unemployment; and so does the enemy: the bourgeois republican regime and its humanist myths. As Céline wrote in the memorandum, 'a pig-sty run like a republic would have gone bankrupt years ago.'[138] This time, though, the solution has changed: it is no longer the extension of Ford and Taylor to national political life along Mercier's technocratic elitist lines: 'This society would have to collapse to enable us to really talk about a generalized system of hygiene, which coincides only with a Socialist or Communist notion of the State.'[139] The article in *Monde* amplifies this argument. It constitutes a damning indictment of the state of health of the French working class, the 'classes laborieuses',[140] with the highest mortality rate in the industrialized world, at 16.6 per 1000 head of population, the worst wages, at 15 to 35 francs a day, the worst housing, along with the Russians, disastrous levels of tuberculosis and syphilis, and the highest level of alcoholism in the world, at a rate of consumption of 18.7 litres per inhabitant. This appalling situation is correlated with a poor education system, the power of the Catholic Church, crippling military budgets and an anarchic medical system fraught with sectional interests. What is interesting is that, having denounced the classic targets of the radical Left, big business, bourgeois doctors, the Church and the army, Céline has come round, at least grudgingly, to the idea of health insurance: 'health insurance has one essential advantage: it creates order, rules and clarity in a nation's medical system. It contradicts a lot of special interests, all to the common good.'[141] This is hardly a ringing endorsement, but it does express a modest faith in health insurance as a preliminary step on the road to medical justice before the revolution can install a Socialist or Communist State. It is not easy to detect what has moved Céline to this change of heart since 1928, nor is it completely unlikely that he is playing the same kind of complex polemical game in either the 1928 or the 1930–3 writings as he was to play in the anti-Semitic pamphlets of 1937 and 1938.[142] Ostensibly, however, the experience of municipal medicine in the Rue Fanny convinced him of the need for a left-wing regime to support his notion of rationalized medicine, or 'médecine standard'. His anarchism, at least at the beginning of the 1930s, appears to have pointed him towards the Left, and it was only really the disappointment with Soviet Russia in 1936 which finally pushed him definitively into the anarchism of the Right shared by many of his Montmartre acquaintances.

By the time *Voyage au bout de la nuit* was ready to be published in 1932, Céline appeared to have overcome some of the difficulties encountered on leaving Geneva: the loss of a prestigious position, a period of indebtedness, failure as a playwright and the depressing exercise of general medicine in a proletarian suburb. When he moved to the Rue Lepic he had recovered financially, living fairly comfortably on his earnings from the Rue Fanny, the Dispensaire Marthe-Brandès, 'La Biothérapie' and the Gallier laboratories: certainly three times the monthly income of the highest-paid worker he cites in the *Monde* article. He had also been able to create and maintain a high profile through medical research and published papers on public health and had successfully retained and fostered his League of Nations contacts, especially Rajchman, with whom he remained on excellent terms, to provide him with study tours throughout Europe. In Montmartre and with Mahé, he had made an entry into a congenial and stimulating bohemian artistic milieu, with pronounced anarchist and radical conservative views. At the same time, there is evidence of increased isolation, compounded by the effort required to finish the novel. His father died suddenly on 14 March 1932. As he wrote to Mahé: 'My father has died. I didn't ask you to come. I like to keep grief to a minimum. It's not easy. I'm of an age where you can't forget anything any more.'[143] There is little of the hostile relationship between Ferdinand and Auguste in *Mort à crédit* there, although probably the death of his father removed an inhibition which facilitated the creation of the novel. Moreover, the relationship with Elizabeth Craig was deteriorating. Every year she returned to the United States, and each time she remained a little longer. Céline, never committed to monogamy, had affairs: in April 1932 he met Erika Irrgang, a young German student who literally passed out from hunger on the terrace of a café on the Place du Tertre and woke up in a taxi taking her with Céline to the Rue Lepic.[144] She stayed until June but continued to correspond with Céline, of whom she left a fascinating account in the *Cahiers de l'Herne.*[145] No sooner had she left than he met an Austrian Jewish gymnastics teacher, Cillie Pam, on the terrace of the Café de la Paix: she stayed with him for a week.[146]

He could afford a break: by the spring of 1932, *Voyage au bout de la nuit* was finished.

6

Voyage au bout de la nuit

I COMPOSITION

Trotsky's famous comment on *Voyage au bout de la nuit*, that 'Louis-Ferdinand Céline walked into great literature as other people walk into their own house,'[1] is only half right. It is undoubtedly true that there have been few first novels which have shown such mastery and sophistication, even more so since both the book and its author appeared unannounced and as if from nowhere. At the same time, the circumstances of the novel's composition, and especially of its publication, remain unclear and are by no means elucidated by Céline's own comments in the first interviews he gave following publication in November 1932, in which that desire to invent, mislead and mystify which was to become a trademark first manifested itself.

In one of the first interviews Céline gave following the publication of *Voyage au bout de la nuit*, to Max Descaves in *Paris-Midi*, he claimed that the novel 'represents six years of work, at the rate of four hours a day',[2] and his neighbour in the Rue d'Alsace in Clichy, Jeanne Carayon, recalls him saying during his residence there from the end of 1927 to August 1929: 'I'm writing a novel. I've been working on it for four years, especially at night. If it's published, you can correct the proofs.'[3] Both assertions appear improbable: the comment to Max Descaves would put the genesis of *Voyage* in 1926 and Jeanne Carayon's reminiscence even earlier, in 1924 or 1925, although it is possible that Céline is referring, not just to the composition of the novel, but also to that of its theatrical prototype *L'Eglise*, which was written, as we have seen, in 1926. Elizabeth Craig's testimony, by which the novel's birth coincided with their move from Clichy to the Rue Lepic in August 1929, seems more reliable.[4] It seems much more likely that, after his failure to get *L'Eglise* performed or published, he decided to use some of the material in fictional form. Indeed, a letter to Gallimard in December 1931

announcing the completion of *Voyage au bout de la nuit* contains an indication that, after the rejection of *L'Eglise*, he had been encouraged to work on
another project: 'I sent you once before a manuscript, *L'Eglise*, which you
returned to me with the request that I submit something else.'[5]

The correspondence with Gallimard is also misleading as to the exact
date when the novel was completed. The first letter, of 9 December 1931,
announced: 'I have just finished a book, a sort of novel, whose composition
has taken me several years,'[6] yet, in a letter to Garcin at the same time, this
announcement seems premature: 'I'm exhausted, I'm finishing my book,
so many pages.'[7] In fact, in spite of Eric Mazet's assertion that both Henri
Mahé and Roger Lecuyer read the novel at the end of 1931,[8] it is unlikely
that this was the final version; its completion in typed form appears to have
occurred in the early spring of 1932. Instead of the six years of composition
which Céline claimed, therefore, the novel took at most three years to write,
a relatively rapid process, given its length and the fact that it had to be
written when Céline was free from his medical duties, mainly at night
and at weekends. Nevertheless, he was at pains in the early interviews to
play up the Romantic image of the nocturnal author, and the medical
duties were by no means as onerous as he and subsequent critics liked to
claim. According to Céline in the interview with Max Descaves, the manuscript of the novel ran to 50,000 pages,[9] though Robert Denoël recalled
only 20,000[10] and, like the subsequent manuscripts, it undoubtedly went
through several versions like, for example, the case of *Entretiens avec le
Professeur Y.*[11] As Vitoux comments, Céline worked quickly and intensively
but with immense care for composition, often preferring to jettison manuscript pages with which he was dissatisfied, as a film director uses many takes
for a particular scene:

> He wrote feverishly, in a single outpouring. His writing was not fastidious: it
> was flung onto the paper, often barely decipherable. He threw punctuation
> for a loop, he used hyphens like stepping-stones from one idea to another, an
> unexpected glissade . . . Céline was assuredly a stylist. But his style was end-
> lessly corrected, emerging by dint of retakes, repetitions, overhauls, addi-
> tions, or suppression, and not slowly, silently weighed and thought out before
> before consigning it to paper.[12]

At the same time, the remaining manuscripts show considerable evidence
of detailed revision, of a dedication to finding exactly the right word for the
rhythm to be maintained.[13]

In the course of the composition of *Voyage*, Céline also modified his
original plans. Initially, he had hoped to include a section on London,
coming between the war episode and Africa and using material supplied by
Garcin, but by July 1931 he had clearly realized that this would make the
novel unwieldy. He wrote on 24 July 1931: 'I'm giving up the London
adventure: a bit of the USA and the suburbs which I know only too well, and
that's it for the novel, for the immediate nocturnal labour,'[14] though he did

promise: 'The sequel later will have London as a setting,' thus announcing *Guignol's Band* ten years later. In other words, the novel nearing completion was the fruit of careful structural plotting as well as of constant stylistic revision.

If Céline misled his interviewers over the length of time he took to write *Voyage au bout de la nuit*, he was equally obfuscatory over his motivation in writing the novel. He insisted, right up until the end of his life, that his sole reason for writing *Voyage* was financial, either to help him pay the rent or to buy an apartment. In an interview with Madeleine Chapsal for *L'Express* on the publication of *D'un Château l'autre* in 1957, he stated: 'I wrote [*Voyage*] to pay for an apartment . . . It's simple: I was born at a time when people were afraid of the rent bill,'[15] and to André Parinaud's question in 1961, shortly before his death: 'Did you write any of your books with an intention other than that of earning money?' he replied: 'Not one! I don't do anything except to earn money.'[16] According to Céline, what gave him the idea of making money out of literature was the success of Eugène Dabit's novel *Hôtel du Nord* and the vogue for populism. Elizabeth Porquerol, who met Céline shortly after the publication of *Voyage*, recalled in her reminiscences of the meeting that 'what gave him the idea of writing was the success of the populists, and especially Dabit';[17] and to Claude Bonnefoy, who asked him why he became a writer, he replied: 'I would have done better becoming a psychiatrist! Why? Not through vocation. I'd never thought of it. But I knew Eugène Dabit . . . He'd just had a huge success with his *Hôtel du Nord* . . . And I thought: "I could do as well as that. It would help me to pay the rent."'[18] Vitoux adds that Céline had also been impressed by the fact that *Hôtel du Nord* had been awarded the Prix Populiste in May 1931.[19]

Neither of these explanations is particularly convincing and they read as part of a studied attempt on Céline's part to de-romanticize the role of the writer in general and his own activities in particular: the need throughout his life to adopt a camouflage for self-protection. Dabit's novel was indeed very successful, but it appeared in November 1929 when, even by the latest estimates, Céline had already started work on *Voyage au bout de la nuit* and had completed two plays by 1926 or 1927. Certainly, the award of the Prix Populiste in May 1931 would have come far too late to influence the composition of the novel, and it was, in any case, neither a particularly prestigious nor a lucrative award. It may well be, however, that Dabit's choice of publisher, Robert Denoël, influenced Céline when he came to look for a publisher for *Voyage*, and that the popularity of Dabit affected, not the composition of the novel itself, even the La Garenne-Rancy episode, but the persona and literary type Céline chose to adopt in his post-publication interviews. As for the purely commercial motivation, this, again, serves to contribute more to the public image of the author than to explain the reality. As we have seen, by 1932 Céline was relatively well off, with a reasonable salary from Clichy and additional earnings from his pharmaceutical work. At a period when the minimum annual wage was 9600 francs a

year, approximately £7500 in today's money, Céline's annual salary of
24,000 francs, about £18,000, in addition to the locum and laboratory work,
was not princely but certainly comfortable.[20] He was sufficiently well off,
indeed, to make over to his mother the royalties on 'Basdowine' when his
father died, and to take frequent holidays. While it is undoubtedly true
that, as Elizabeth Porquerol observed, 'the question of money has dominated him and still dominates him: a real sickness,'[21] Céline also carefully
fashioned and cultivated, as we shall see, an image of himself as a writer who
was desperately poor. Whilst this persona of an unsentimental and purely
commercial writer may have both given him favourable publicity and protected him from the effects of adverse criticism, it clashes with the quite
obvious professional pride in his writing which he occasionally allowed to
seep through. In the interview with Parinaud, for example, after claiming
never to have written anything without the aim of making money, he let
slip: 'Mind you, I **can** make the table turn.'[22] His letter to Gallimard of 14
April 1932 ends with an expression of quite extraordinary pride and confidence in the novel: 'It's money in the bank for a whole century of literature.
It's the Prix Goncourt on a plate for the lucky publisher who takes on this
unparalleled work, this crucial moment in human nature.'[23]

II PUBLICATION

If the story of the composition of Voyage au bout de la nuit is deliberately
obscure and contradictory, the history of its publication is even more so.
The novel was finished in manuscript form in early 1932 and was typed,
discreetly, by a secretary in the 'dispensaire' at Clichy, Aimée Paymal. As
early as December 1931, however, Céline had not merely announced its
completion to Gallimard, but had also offered it to Georges Altman, co-
editor, with Barbusse, of Monde, which had published his article on 'La
Santé publique en France' in March 1930. He also sent the typed manuscript to two small publishers, Editions Bossard and Eugène Figuière.
Bossard rejected the work because it did not fit their list, and Figuière, a
vanity publisher, agreed to publish the novel on receipt of 12,000 francs.[24]
On the face of it, these initial approaches to publishers are incomprehensible: Monde, a bi-monthly review, was in no position to publish a 500-page
novel, Voyage was manifestly unsuited to Bossard's list and Figuière was
similarly inappropriate. Indeed, as Gibault records, as late as June 1933,
when Voyage had won the Prix Renaudot and sold more than 50,000 copies,
Figuière, who had clearly not yet heard of it, wrote to Céline offering 'to
make a special effort in your favour, on condition that you agree not to
receive royalties until the 2001st volume sold'.[25] It does not seem sufficient
to explain these initial approaches, as Vitoux does, as the result of
'befuddlement' on Céline's part: rather, they are probably the consequence of the failure of L'Eglise, an insurance policy or bargaining chip in

negotiations with the big publishers who might well turn down the novel as they had turned down the play. Certainly, alongside the bravado which accompanied the approach to Gallimard, there was an uncertainty and timidity which led to obscure, but possibly more guaranteed, means of publication.

As we have seen, Céline's first approach to Gallimard dates from 9 December 1931, when the manuscript was not even typed, announcing 'a sort of novel, whose composition has taken me several years'.[26] On 14 December, Louis Chevasson replied on behalf of Gaston Gallimard asking for a résumé of the novel, and on 14 April 1932 Céline sent in both the manuscript and the résumé. At about the same time, he also sent the manuscript to the publishers Denoël et Steele, in the Rue Amélie. At this point, a mythology, which Céline did much to create and foster, and little to prevent, comes in to obscure events. In a letter to Milton Hindus on 28 July 1947, he claimed that 'I submitted the manuscript to Denoël and to the NRF [Gallimard] at the same time. Both accepted it the same day, but Denoël two hours before the NRF.'[27] In fact, Gallimard went through a lengthy process of reading the manuscript which severely tried Céline's patience. He wrote to Gaston Gallimard on 25 April, less than two weeks after submitting *Voyage*, asking for a report on progress. On 13 June, he wrote again, and was informed that the manuscript was still being read.[28] The reader at Gallimard, Benjamin Crémieux, who also held the Italian desk in the press service at the Quai d'Orsay, took his time over the reading and had his misgivings. As Vitoux records: 'at the literary committee that included, among others, Jean Paulhan, Ramon Fernandez, André Malraux, Gaston Gallimard and Emmanuel Berl, Benjamin Crémieux gave a summary of his [incomplete] reading of the work, a few pages of which he wanted to read to his colleagues. The manuscript then passed into the hands of Malraux and Berl,'[29] who were much more enthusiastic. Their opinion, however, failed to convince completely the rest of the committee, especially Crémieux, who insisted upon the manuscript being cut before it could be accepted. Eventually Gallimard agreed to publish the novel, but by this time, in late June 1932, it was too late and Céline had already accepted an offer from Denoël et Steele. In other words, Gallimard, after a perfectly reasonable delay of two and a half months, accepted this first novel, albeit on condition that certain cuts, admittedly probably unacceptable to the author, were made. Apart from one short text, 'Secrets dans l'île', in a collective volume *Neuf et un* of 1936, Gallimard had to wait until 1952 and *Féerie pour une autre fois* before they were able to publish Céline, a decision which Céline played up into a dramatic error akin to that of Gide's rejection of the manuscript of *A la recherche du temps perdu*.

The legend of Robert Denoël and *Voyage au bout de la nuit* is even more dramatic. Denoël was the son of a Belgian university teacher who had come to frequent Parisian artistic circles after the war and had established a small publishing house, the Librairie des Trois Magots, in 1928. In 1929 he achieved the coup of publishing Dabit's *Hôtel du Nord* and, in partnership with a rich American of Jewish origin, Bernard Steele, set up the new, albeit precarious, firm of Denoël et Steele which, in addition to literature (a recent success was the winner of the 1931 Prix Renaudot, Philippe Hériat's *L'Innocent*), also published an extensive field of psychoanalytical texts, including the *Revue Française de Psychanalyse*, taken over from Doin.[30] As we have seen, it was probably the connection with Dabit which influenced Céline in his choice of publisher. Yet there are contradictory versions of how Robert Denoël came to read *Voyage au bout de la nuit*. Céline himself told Paul Vialar in December 1932 that 'I left my manuscript with neither my name nor address on it';[31] Max Dorian, Denoël's assistant, tells a different tale, of an anonymous 'dame' who arrived at the publishers with the manuscript of *Voyage*, allegedly rejected by 'two large firms',[32] and accepted by Gallimard only if the author would pay the costs. As late as 1971, Robert Poulet was still retailing the myth of a 'lady painter' who had left her own manuscript with Denoël and had been confused with the author of *Voyage*.[33] Be that as it may, according to the legend, Denoël discovered the 900-page typescript on his desk one evening, read it overnight and convinced his partner that they should publish it, even getting Steele to telephone his mother in America to raise the extra capital. All that remained was to find the author. The manuscript of *Voyage* had been accompanied by that of a much shorter novel by a woman author in Montmartre, living at 98 Rue Lepic: Denoël's messenger quickly established that the real author of *Voyage* was a strange doctor living on the floor below.[34] Another version has the author absent-mindedly wrapping his manuscript in paper from a Montmartre laundry, from which he could be traced.[35] According to Jeanne Delannoy, who worked for Denoël and claimed to have read the manuscript first, the address was clearly marked, but Denoël, when he arrived at the Rue Lepic, found the author out and had to track him down at the clinic, where he made him sign a contract there and then, just beating Gallimard's acceptance by a few hours.[36] Philippe Alméras is quite right to question all of these melodramatic versions of the acceptance of *Voyage au bout de la nuit*, which, nevertheless, fulfilled an important purpose for the subsequent promotion of the book and the creation of a persona for its author. Céline was a highly organized and careful man, who never omitted putting an address on his correspondence, who gave both typescript and résumé to Gallimard and continued to bombard them with requests for reports on progress. It is unthinkable that he should have left the manuscript with Denoël without giving precise details of how he could be contacted. Yet the carefully constructed legend of the lost author comes to join other famous and probably equally apocryphal publishing tales, like that of Proust's manuscript and its secret knots which indicated that Gallimard had not even opened the parcel.

In fact, Céline signed a contract with Denoël and Steele on 30 June 1932, with a publication date set for October. The terms of the contract were standard: no royalties until the first 4000 copies sold, then 10 per cent on the next 1000, rising to 12 per cent from 5000 to 10,000 and 15 per cent from 10,000 to 50,000, with 18 per cent beyond that. Denoël retained first-refusal rights on the next five prose works.[37] On 29 June, Céline had written to Gallimard asking for the return of his manuscript, but this letter appears to have crossed with Crémieux's official reply, dated 2 July, offering to meet him to discuss possible cuts. Céline, apparently still wary of Denoël et Steele, did not dismiss this out of hand, putting off a meeting until late July or early August, and even received an offer from Louis Chevasson at Gallimard, promising that 'if he accepted cutting his manuscript, we would be very happy to envisage its publication.'[38] Steele, however, had raised the money from his mother, the publishing house was committed to the novel and, as soon as Céline saw that the production process had begun, he broke off contact with Gallimard. He had also definitively taken on a new identity: Louis Destouches had become Louis-Ferdinand Céline, taking his pseudonym, not, as he sometimes claimed, from his mother,[39] but from his grandmother, that formative influence on his childhood and a woman rooted in the belle époque to which he could never return.

As the novel went into production, Céline appeared both to distance himself and to involve himself closely. His promise to Jeanne Carayon that she was to be the one who corrected the proofs was kept, and he rarely went to Denoël's premises in the Rue Amélie. At the same time, he kept a close eye on the work of the editors and printers, constantly sending it back for revision when they tried to make his style and punctuation more orthodox: 'They want to make me write like François Mauriac!' he complained.[40] Once the initial tension of the signing of the contract was over, moreover, he showed an increasingly self-confident, even imperious attitude towards Denoël himself, writing on one occasion: 'Old man, I beg you, don't add one syllable to the text without telling me! You'd completely screw up the rhythm – I'm the only one who can relocate it,'[41] and giving detailed instructions on the cover design: 'No typographical sentimentality. A classical style . . . In my view, we need a fairly heavy and discreet cover. Beige and black. Or grey and grey, perhaps, and with equal, QUITE THICK letters. That's all.'[42] This attention to detail was to prove constant in Céline's literary career, but never with quite the same urgency as in the publication of his first novel, the novel he believed would win the Prix Goncourt.

III Literary Prizes

All the drama of the acceptance of *Voyage* and its publication took place without the presence of Elizabeth Craig, who had made one of her periodic returns to California at the beginning of 1932 and was to stay away for a whole year. Céline, as we have seen, rapidly consoled himself with Erika

Irrgang and Cillie Pam, and also, in the summer of 1932, made journeys to Marseilles and Brittany. In the meantime, Jeanne Carayon continued to keep a watchful eye on the production of the novel.

Voyage au bout de la nuit was published on 20 October 1932, and on 29 October it received its first review, a favourable one from Georges Altman in *Monde*. As a small publishing house, with limited resources, Denoël could not compete with his larger competitors, but he deployed those resources as efficiently as possible, both to ensure maximum sales and to make the novel a powerful contender for the 1932 Prix Goncourt. Prior to publication, he inserted advertisements in the major literary journals and persuaded some of them to publish excerpts. Céline himself was induced to send advance copies of *Voyage* to influential literary figures, especially members of the Goncourt jury, with obsequious dedications, like: 'To M. Jean Ajalbert, who lends us courage' or 'To Gaston Chérau, whose lessons we have tried to understand, a most respectful tribute.'[43] He was also dispatched by Denoël to make contact with Lucien Descaves, the author of the pre-war anti-militarist novel *Sous-Offs*, and a member of the Goncourt jury.

Descaves joined forces with Action Française's Léon Daudet, who had been greatly taken by the novel and was also a member of the Goncourt jury, to lobby for the award of the prize to Céline.[44] Initially, it appeared that their strategy had worked. At a preparatory meeting at the Restaurant Drouant on 30 November, Descaves and Daudet managed to put together an unassailable majority for *Voyage au bout de la nuit*, so much so that on 6 December Daudet published an article in *L'Action Française* apparently justifying in advance the award of the prize to Céline,[45] and Denoël already had printed red bands to go on the covers of the novel reading 'Prix Goncourt 1932'.[46] In the event, at the meeting to award the prize on 7 December, Descaves' and Daudet's coalition fell apart, the Rosny brothers defected, and the 1932 Prix Goncourt was awarded to a novel by Guy Mazeline, *Les Loups*, published by Gallimard. A furious Lucien Descaves stormed out of the meeting and denounced the betrayal to the waiting journalists outside in the Place Gaillon, thus transforming the 1932 Goncourt Prize into a major scandal, which, ironically, did far more for the sales figures of *Voyage au bout de la nuit* than the customary runner-up award of the Prix Théophraste Renaudot. Céline, who had waited outside the Restaurant Drouant with his daughter Colette, was clearly shocked by the whole experience, describing it as a 'nightmare' and a 'disaster' in a letter to Cillie Pam.[47] Even though he tried to put a brave face on it, claiming that 'with or without it, it's all the same to me,'[48] this was a set-back to Céline's ambition comparable to the rejection of *L'Eglise* or the failure of his medical practice in the Rue d'Alsace.

Paradoxically, due to the furore over Mazeline's victory, the novel became hugely successful. Denoël himself was the first to admit that, without the scandal, sales would probably have reached only 2000–3000;[49] as it was, in the two months following the award of the Goncourt, *Voyage* sold more than 50,000 copies, with more than 5000 newspaper and magazine articles devoted to it.[50]

The initial responses to *Voyage au bout de la nuit* were mixed and, as Vitoux reminds us, not easily classifiable on either Left or Right, though attracting considerable support from the anarchist press and from radicals at either end of the political spectrum.[51] *Le Cri du Jour*, *Le Canard enchaîné* and *Libertaire* all carried favourable reviews, and Galtier-Boissière's *Le Crapouillot* weighed into the controversy of the Goncourt Prize by libelling Rosny aîné.[52] On the extreme right, Léon Daudet, as we have seen, was a staunch supporter, though Maurras remained highly sceptical and, although Lucien Rebatet was enthusiastic, Robert Brasillach's classical tastes were offended by the novel.[53] Unsurprisingly, orthodox conservatives, like André Rousseaux in *Le Figaro*, were implacably opposed to it. It was the same on the Left: Georges Altmann gave a highly favourable account of the novel to the readers of *Monde*, but both mainstream Communists and Socialists remained hostile, attacking the novel's apparent pessimism and negativity.[54] Trotsky's enthusiastic account was tempered by the recognition that 'in Céline's book, there is no hope,'[55] and Paul Nizan's review for *L'Humanité* concluded: 'Céline is not one of ours: it is impossible to accept his profound anarchism, his contempt and his general repulsion which do not accept the proletariat.'[56]

In spite of this ultimately accurate distrust of Céline on the part of the orthodox Left, it was plainly to them that he made overtures in many interviews he gave following the publication of *Voyage au bout de la nuit*. Jean-Pierre Dauphin and Henri Godard may well be right in asserting that the newspaper interview had come to replace the nineteenth-century literary preface,[57] but there is a further and more obvious purpose to such interviews, in that they allow an author to position himself in the literary market-place and create the identity he wishes to have in the mind of the public. This is particularly true of an author who, like Céline, suddenly bursts on the attention of the public with no prior warning. Céline's early interviews contain a remarkably restricted and coherent number of motifs which work to create a powerful identity of a particular type of writer. The description of Céline given by the various interviewers consistently emphasizes his blonde or dark-blonde hair[58] and, particularly, his blue eyes. Elizabeth Porquerol refers to his 'sailor's blue eyes',[59] and Robert de Saint-Jean, recalling his meeting with Céline at Daniel Halévy's apartment, with Bernanos and Vallery-Radot also present, emphasizes his 'blue eyes: either like a sailor's (he is Breton) or like a psychiatrist's (he is a doctor)'.[60] This in its turn leads on to Céline's own accounts of his regional origins, where fiction begins to overwhelm fact: 'I was born of Breton and Flemish descent'[61] and 'My father was Flemish, from the north of Hazebrouck, my mother was Breton.'[62] The claim to both Breton and Flemish ancestry is interesting in that it enables Céline to establish links with a mystical and mythical European tradition which connects with his admiration for Brueghel. It is also, incidentally, a piece of significant mythomania which he shares with Malraux, who, in autobiographical statements throughout his life, wilfully confused Boulogne-sur-Mer with Boulogne-sur-Seine as his place of birth.

In the interviews, this Flemish Breton is also resolutely from the people, and his origins and childhood are shamelessly romanticized. To Paul Vialar, he claimed: 'I was born in Asnières in 1894. My father was a teacher; when he was sacked, he worked for the railways. My mother was a seamstress.'[63] And to Georges Altmann, 'my mother was a lace-worker; my father was the intellectual of the family. We had a shop, which we set up in lots of towns. It never worked. Bankruptcy, bankruptcy, bankruptcy.'[64] What is interesting here, apart from the mortifying dismissal of the family's hard-won petit-bourgeois respectability, is the constant valorization of the dead father, with the consequent subordination of Marguerite Destouches. It especially allows Céline to portray himself as authentically plebeian: 'I'm from the people, the real people,' he declared to Pierre-Jean Launay,[65] though the more perceptive Elizabeth Porquerol, perhaps benefiting from hindsight, corrects this: 'he was born in Courbevoie, but not from a working-class milieu (he does not have the self-confidence), rather from ordinary people between two classes, humiliated, who ought to have had another social position, failures, wounded and ashamed. No poverty (poverty is a big word), but something more painful.'[66] In this way, Céline, living in his 'leprous house',[67] can claim not merely to be the authentic witness of 'human misery',[68] but specifically the poet of the industrial suburbs. In a lyrical comment to Altman, he stated: 'They are close to me, these suburbs, I understand them, I feel them. I would even say that they exalt me, these sad suburbs beyond the city.'[69] As we have seen, Céline attempted to draw a consistent, although particular, self-portrait from his experience in Charles Auffray's Clichy, which did not always coincide with the reality.

One corollary of this affection for the suburbs, expressed twelve years later in his preface to Albert Serouille's *Bezons à travers les âges* of 1944, is Céline's cultivation of his role as a 'médecin des pauvres'. Although his initial reaction to press coverage of his medical work in Clichy was apparently hostile, he was, as Philippe Roussin observes, very careful to foster the image of an author-doctor in a poor 'dispensaire'. From as early as 7 December 1932, Max Descaves had revealed Céline's identity as a doctor, with the comment: 'I have the impression that Doctor Céline is well-liked by his patients.'[70] Similarly, when René Miquel, of *Je suis partout*, had the idea of simply turning up anonymously at the 'dispensaire' in the Rue Fanny, to see how Celine really operated as a doctor, he found a completely professional, caring physician.[71] What Céline is careful to do is to create the image of a 'fils du peuple', now a doctor in a poor industrial suburb, who has every credential to write about 'human misery'. Every credential? No, except that Céline was also gravely ill, the final element lacking in the romantic portrait of the working-class writer creating his work of genius in the hours left to him during the night. Merry Bromberger states: 'M. Céline . . . is ill,'[72] and later in the interview Céline claimed: 'I'm forty and

I'm ill.'[73] By the time Elizabeth Porquerol remembered her interview with him, Céline was 'seriously ill'.[74] In other words, Céline had done everything to foster an image which would be attractive to the left, with a working-class parentage, a job among the working class and traditionally poor health. It would also, of course, serve him in good stead when his anarchism moved from the radical Left to the radical Right. In the meantime, the biographical obfuscations do not help, particularly in a reading of what was one of Europe's major Modernist fictional texts, *Voyage au bout de la nuit.*

IV *Voyage au bout de la nuit*

If contemporary literary critics had paid as much attention to Céline's comments on the novel as the literary journalists had to his statements about his life, they would have avoided a lot of subsequent confusion regarding the status of *Voyage au bout de la nuit.* As early as his favourable review in *Candide,* Léon Daudet was fulminating against the widespread belief that the novel was barely camouflaged autobiography and that Bardamu was essentially Céline himself: 'that would be to assimilate Shakespeare to Falstaff, to make him responsible for the crime of Macbeth; it would be to accuse Sophocles of incest because of *Oedipus Rex,* or to identify Molière with Tartuffe.'[75] Yet the autobiographical interpretation of the novel has been deeply persistent, fuelled by obvious apparent similarities between Céline's own lived experience and the activities of his protagonist. This autobiographical interpretation has gone hand in hand with an equally resilient assumption that *Voyage au bout de la nuit* constitutes a brand of hyper-naturalism, a determination to paint the most degrading aspects of modern urban existence in a manner so uncompromising that it flirts with the obscene. It was this assumption, as we shall see, which led logically to the invitation to give the annual Zola address in Médan in 1933, and which was assisted by Céline's own, often clumsy, attempts to hitch himself to the populist bandwagon or the documentary-style First World War fiction of Barbusse. While both conservative and orthodox left-wing critics denounced this 'hyper-naturalism' as either vulgarity (as in the case of André Thérive in *Le Temps*) or as contempt for the proletariat, it gave rise to one of the most durable interpretations of both the novel and the author, particularly in the United States. Here Céline appears *par excellence* as a moralist, denouncing the corruption and hypocrisy of modern industrial society and reaffirming the values of the human individual: the spiritual father of Kerouac and the American Beat Generation.[76] The unifying principle between all three interpretations is the assumption of a lack of artifice upon Céline's part: that he writes as he speaks and speaks as he sees, with no compromise.

Admittedly, in his early interviews Céline himself sometimes found it useful to encourage such an innocent interpretation. To Pierre-Jean

Launay, he commented: 'It's not literature. So? It's life, life as it really is. Human suffering moves me greatly, be it physical or moral,'[77] and 'I wrote as I speak.'[78] Yet the bulk of the early interviews point in a very different direction, in which the fictive nature of the work takes precedence. To Merry Bromberger, he dismissed the autobiographical approach: 'My book an autobiography? Not at all! My life is far more simple and far more complicated that that.'[79] Instead, 'it's a narrative at three removes. Céline makes Bardamu hallucinate and he tells what he knows of Robinson'[80] and 'Bardamu is no more real than Pantagruel, nor Robinson more real than Picrochale.'[81] And, crucially, to Georges Altman he confided that 'it's a novel, but it's not the story of real "characters". Rather, they're ghosts.'[82] Finally, at the same time as he falsely invoked a Flemish ancestry, he revealed the reason for it in the hallucinatory process which the novel adopts: 'I have to enter into a state of delirium, I have to get to the level of Shakespeare, because I am incapable of constructing a story with *French* logic.'[83] In other words, the essence of the novel is to be found in its carefully theorized artifice, on which, significantly, Shakespeare is an important influence, which enables it to achieve the status of one of France's foremost Modernist texts.

While the novel clearly makes a major contribution to the expression of French inter-war metaphysical pessimism, the most obvious innovation in *Voyage au bout de la nuit* was stylistic, though towards the end of his career Céline was at pains to minimize this aspect of the novel in comparison with his later work. Talking to Madeleine Chapsal, of *L'Express*, in 1957, he admitted: 'In *Voyage*... I still made certain sacrifices to literature, to "good literature". You can still find the well-constructed sentence. In my opinion, from the technical point of view, it's a bit old-fashioned.'[84] Even though his first novel had not achieved the stylistic inventiveness apparent in *Mort à crédit* and the subsequent work, the use of a first-person narrator deploying the full armoury of the spoken French language was a significant step in Céline's conscious campaign, articulated at its most extensive in *Entretiens avec le Professeur Y* of 1955, to restore life and vigour to literary French, which had been in terminal decline since the death of Rabelais. In this task he joined Raymond Queneau, whose first novel, *Le Chiendent*, published in 1931, styled itself as an attempt to rewrite Descartes' *Le Discours de la méthode* in popular French. Yet, where Queneau cultivated the shock resulting from the collision between highly formal narrative and the transcription, often phonetic, of the spoken language, Céline, throughout his work, both fiction and non-fiction, chose to exploit the possibilities of the monologue and, in so doing, as Henri Godard demonstrates, to forge a genuine poetics.[85] Céline's claim in his interview with Pierre-Jean Launay that 'I wrote as I speak' has an important corollary which negates the image of the 'innocent' primitive: 'This language is my instrument.'[86] The style of *Voyage au bout de la nuit* consists of a carefully contrived poetic language in which the impression of popular speech is conveyed by the judicious use of slang from different periods and different professions involving, as Leo Spitzer recognized early on, the manipulation of only two common features of spoken French: the use of 'que' in popular reported speech and the repetition of pronoun and noun, as in 'J'ai cru longtemps qu'elle était sotte la petite Musyne' ('I thought for a long time that she was stupid, little Musyne').[87] What is interesting about the style this recipe creates, which is not readily conveyed in translation, is that, in spite of the views of some early critics, it is not essentially vulgar: the narrator is a cultivated doctor whose musings have been injected with the vigour and humour of the spoken language. In the same way that Céline's cultivation of Marcel Lafaye in order to create Bardamu contradicts any crude autobiographical interpretation of the protagonist, analysis of the novel's style points to a highly conscious orchestration of effects, which, in their turn, indicate that *Voyage* as a whole is immeasurably more complex and more ambitious than the work of hypernaturalism it was once assumed to be. This complexity is indicated by the 'mise-en-abyme' of the *Amiral Bragueton*, on which Bardamu sails to Africa, a journey which, in itself, is a mise-en-abyme of the novel as a whole[88] by which the various layers of paint which constitute the ship's 'second hull'[89] reflect both the 'artificial' relationship between the novel and the reality it ostensibly seeks to depict and the successive and irreducible layers of the text itself.

What constitutes a major strength of Céline as a novelist is that in his Modernist creation one of those textual layers, certainly in *Voyage au bout de la nuit* and *Mort à crédit*, is rooted in a precise and acutely observed social, political and economic reality. Indeed, apart from Zola, with whom Céline has an ambiguous relationship, there are few French novelists who possess such a sure and informed sense of social and economic history. Bardamu's 'vengeful and social prayer', *The Wings of Gold*,[90] introduces a sustained reflection on the role of gold in capitalist society, particularly the gold fetish, which underpins both the African and American episodes, most notably when Bardamu compares the banks of the gold quarter in Manhattan to churches,[91] and which, as in *Mort à crédit*, enters the poetics of the novel through the orchestration of the phoneme 'or'. At the same time, *Voyage au bout de la nuit* demonstrates the same consciousness of Parisian social history as that which, more dramatically, informs *Mort à crédit*, particularly in the depiction of the creeping urbanization of the once rural suburb of La Garenne-Rancy and the social and medical consequences for the new urban poor.

It is the irreverent and uncompromising depiction of both the social reality and its profound economic causes which makes the novel genuinely subversive and more than confirms both Céline's and Bardamu's claims to anarchism. Bardamu's anarchist prayer is followed by the no less anarchist fable of the nation-states as so many slave-galleys, with the masters on the deck and the workers in the hold until the workers are needed to attack the *Homeland Number 2*.[92] The traditional anarchist view of the First World War as a blood-letting deliberately organized by international capitalism to dispose of a militant working class is similarly conveyed by the allusion to the *Pied Piper of Hamelin* in the colonel and the regiment, with its band, who march past the cafés enticing out all the undesirables and leading them away into the countryside until they 'are caught like rats'.[93] It is this sustained anarchist perspective which renders the novel profoundly anti-republican, with its grim recognition that the fate of the republican citizen is identical to that of the colonized native, except that the native retains the dignity of working only when beaten, whereas 'the Whites, perfected by universal education, go of their own accord.'[94] Nor, as we have seen, is the obviously communist municipality of La Garenne-Rancy spared Bardamu's anarchist hostility: its grandiose street-names, the 'Place Lénine'[95] or the 'Coin de la Révolte',[96] cannot disguise the appalling conditions in which its population is living and which will kill the child Bébert with that traditional disease of the slums, typhus.

While it is undoubtedly true that the novel draws much of its power from the episodic 'snapshots' of the war, the colonies, America and the industrial suburbs, and the anger and despair that they engender, an anger and despair which coincide with mainstream preoccupations in French fiction in the inter-war years, the real subversiveness of the novel lies in the way in which it undermines those apparently realist conventions. It rapidly becomes clear that *Voyage au bout de la nuit* is not merely using the conventions of the picaresque or the eighteenth-century philosophical modification of the genre, as in *Candide*, but is undertaking a more radical experiment. The entire episode of the *Infanta Combitta* slave-galley which takes Bardamu from Africa to America, which Céline fought hard to have retained in the manuscript against Denoël's wishes and which patently conflicts with any possible realist interpretation of the novel, clearly points to a reading which is much more complex and which resides in the dream-world. The same is true of the historical dates given in the novel, which, as in *Semmelweis*, annex the domain of the historical to the fictional. The 'Chanson des Gardes suisses' which serves as an introduction is dated as 1793, though the Swiss Guard was massacred in the Tuileries in August 1792, and Lola's ancestors are recorded as having emigrated to America in 1677, on the *Mayflower*, which would have surprised the original settlers, who arrived in Plymouth, and not Boston, in 1620.[97] In this context, Céline's comments to interviewers on the novel's publication regarding the status of the characters as ghosts offer a powerful clue to a true reading. If the Swiss Guards who act as patron saints to *Voyage au bout de la nuit* were ghosts by 1793, then the novel as a whole, like their song, is a ghost novel, sung by survivors of a ghostly regiment killed in the First World War: in other words, it is a projection from the belle époque, in which the novel begins on the café terrace of the Place Clichy, into a wartime and post-war world in which the narrator no longer has a terrestrial reality. The narrator's first meeting with Robinson confirms this interpretation. He springs up out of the ground as a reflection of Bardamu's innermost thoughts, is identified strangely as a 'reservist' at a time when no reserve soldiers were mobilized and bears an uncanny resemblance to a dead cavalry major spotted outside Noirceur-sur-la-Lys.[98] He then reappears, improbably, throughout the novel. At the same time, Bardamu is willing to label all the other characters of the novel as 'phantoms', particularly in the epic scene on the Place du Tertre when they all appear as ghosts and fly off through the sky towards England[99] (an episode, as we have seen, clearly derived from Adolphe Willette's gigantic fresco *Carpe Domine*, painted for Rodolphe Salis' Le Chat Noir cabaret). He even identifies himself as a ghost, both in his compulsive departure from Molly in Detroit and in his assimilation of the persona of Proust during the Paris episode of the First World War: 'Proust, who was half-ghost himself, lost himself with an extraordinary tenacity in the infinite and diluting futility of the rites and customs which surround the members of high society, people of nothingness, phantoms of desires.'[100] Not only does this anchor the novel to a French Modernist tradition which combines the social overview with complex psychology and textual self-awareness, it also serves to remove it from the exclusively realist domain.

At the same time, it enables the reader to call into question the realist status of the narrative itself: does Bardamu's history really 'happen'? The novel begins in the Place Clichy, probably on the terrace of the Café Wepler as depicted by Bonnard in his painting of 1912: in other words, it is a novel whose starting-point is a painting, and not reality. The Place Clichy in particular, and Montmartre in general, then recur throughout *Voyage au bout de la nuit* as the uncanny geographical nexus of the work, which says more about the psychological composition of the narrator and the self-generative qualities of the text than about the reality being offered. Bardamu returns obsessively to the Place Clichy where his voyage began; all that remains to him when Robinson abandons him in Africa is a 'colour postcard of the Place Clichy',[101] and their final journey from Paris which leads to Robinson's death at the hands of Madelon begins from the same place. It is as if the passing of the military band which improbably conscripts the anarchist Bardamu constitutes not merely an echo of the Pied Piper, but also a reflection of that favourite Surrealist text, *Alice in Wonderland*, in which Alice's cat and the reading of her sister's book serve as the passage to an imaginary journey.

Here again, it is sometimes wise to take Céline's own pronouncements at their face value, and the preface to the novel (as opposed to the *Postface* of 1949 which is often wrongly included in the text) is of inestimable value, for here Céline warns the reader explicitly that *Voyage au bout de la nuit* is an imaginary journey: 'To travel is very useful, it makes the imagination work . . . Our journey is entirely imaginary. That is its strength.'[102] Previous interpretations have tended to read this pronouncement as a statement on the illusory nature of the human condition, but the rest of the preface makes clear that it is the imaginary qualities of fiction itself which are being underlined: 'People, animals, towns and things: everything is imagined. It's a novel, just a fictional tale. Littré says so, and he's never wrong.'[103] Specifically, *Voyage au bout de la nuit* fits literally into that eighteenth-century fictional category of the 'imaginary journey', whose most distinguished representative is *Robinson Crusoe* and its many derivatives. Like *The Swiss Family Robinson*, or Offenbach's operetta *Robinson Crusoë*, performed in the Théâtre des Bouffes Parisiennes, backing on to the Passage Choiseul, in 1900, the adventures of Bardamu and Robinson are one more 'Robinsonade'.[104] Not only does the preface emphasize the essentially literary, artificial quality of the work, it also concludes by drawing attention to its oneiric and ghostly characteristics: 'Anyone can do the same: you just need to close your eyes' and 'It is on the other side of life.'[105] In other words, the novel is to be read as a dream peopled with the ghosts of the soldiers who fell in the war and who pass insubstantially through the limbo of the post-war world, in the same way that the Swiss Guards continue to sing their ghostly song a year after their deaths, when the *ancien régime* has irreparably tumbled. The reader, like the narrator, is engaged in a journey to the end (literally) or depth of a night, and the novel ends with a cold dawn.

The emphasis on the 'fictional tale', however, also serves to establish the work's self-consciousness as a literary text. The novel's relationship to reality is mediated not merely through the dream-world but through a filter of intertextual references and allusions. The reference to Proust as a ghost himself depicting the decadent antics of a dead class indicates a similar relationship between *Voyage au bout de la nuit* and the post-war world in which its narrator no longer has a role. In the context of the dying Bébert, the parody of Montaigne's letter to his wife on the death of their child serves to undermine the credibility of humanist ethics.[106] More bizarre is the case of the extract from Macaulay's *History of England from the Accession of James the Second* dealing with the Monmouth uprising, which Bardamu uses to teach Baryton (the baritone to his tenor) and his daughter English:

> When we came to that supremely implacable passage when Monmouth the Pretender had just landed on the imprecise beaches of Kent . . . Just when his adventure started to dissolve . . . When Monmouth the Pretender no longer knew precisely what he was pretending to do . . . what he was pretending to want . . . When he started to say to himself that he would love to go away, but that he no longer knew where or how to go . . . When defeat rose up before him . . . In the pale light of dawn . . . When the sea took away his last ships . . .[107]

This 'history' is pure fiction and bears no relationship to Macaulay's account of Monmouth's landing in Dorset and his waging of a vigorous campaign in the south-west before defeat in battle.[108] Like the errors in *Semmelweis* and the wrong dates in the earlier part of *Voyage*, this deformation of Macaulay's narrative is an assault upon historicity itself and an assertion of the triumph of the imaginary and the fictional.

In addition to the direct references in the text, to which may be added the Freudian term in the name of the Abbé Protiste, *Voyage au bout de la nuit* is made up of a number of allusions to other works of literature, in particular, Browning's *Pied Piper of Hamelin* and, for the American episode,

Georges Duhamel's *Scènes de la vie future* of 1926 and possibly Paul Morand's *New York* of 1930. But the most striking extended literary allusion comes from the African episode and concerns Joseph Conrad's *Heart of Darkness*. Not only is the title of *Voyage au bout de la nuit*, as we have seen, a literal and deliberate paraphrase of the French title of Conrad's novella, *Au Coeur des ténèbres* ('in' or 'to the heart of darkness'), but the narrative, by which Bardamu goes up-river through the jungle in search of a mysterious trader (revealed as Robinson, who has 'gone native' and effectively disappeared) has clear parallels with Marlow's quest for Mr Kurtz. It is such parallels, however, and the tissue of direct literary references, which definitively demarcate Céline's novel from the Naturalist or populist works with which it was originally associated and place it in the tradition of Modernist fiction, of which Proust is an iconic figure.

As much may be gathered from a close inspection of the beginning and end of *Voyage au bout de la nuit*. Bardamu's opening words: 'This is how it began. I had never said anything. Nothing. It was Arthur Ganate who made me speak,'[109] with their emphasis on previous non-speech, are entirely appropriate to the narrator of a novel who, literally, does not exist before the first words appear on the page. In other words, it is a statement that can only be made by a fictional first-person narrator. Similarly, it looks forward to the last words of the work: 'so that no-one should speak any more'.[110] The novel is an eruption of fictional and linguistic activity into a silence to which it returns. At the same time, the circularity of the novel is conveyed by the sounding of the tug-boat at dawn which ends the work: 'In the distance, a tug-boat whistled; its call passed the bridge, another arch, and another one, a lock, another bridge, further and further away . . . It called towards it all the barges on the river, all of them, and the entire city, and the sky and the countryside, and us: it took everything away, the Seine as well, everything, so that no-one could talk about it any more.'[111] Not only does this passage close the novel with a return to the silence from which it sprang, it is a final echo of the Pied Piper's music which led Bardamu out on his nocturnal journey and which is now calling him back to eternal rest.

Voyage au bout de la nuit is an extraordinarily complex and sophisticated achievement for a writer at any stage of his career: as a first novel, coming virtually out of the blue, it is remarkable. The question, of course, is how Céline was able to construct with such self-confidence so variegated a work with so little prior experimentation with fiction. Not that it is an easy question to answer, particularly given Céline's status as an autodidact, benefiting not merely from the *baccalauréat* syllabus but also from less predictable and often English sources such as Macaulay. Elizabeth Porquerol's statement: 'He has read widely and is very cultivated,'[112] probably reflects accurately a wide and disparate culture which fed into *Voyage*, and which includes, according to one interview, figures as diverse as 'Balzac, Freud and Brueghel'.[113] Balzac is an obvious source for a novelist who possesses an uncanny sense of money and its operation in society. Brueghel he was to discover fully in a visit to the Kunsthistorisches Museum

in Vienna in 1933. Freud, as far as *Voyage* is concerned, is more problemati-
cal: apart from the reference to Protiste, picked up by Godard and Marie-
Christine Bellosta, there seems to be little direct Freudian influence on the
novel, though it may owe something to Freud's dream-theory, to his pessimistic writing following the First World War, such as *Civilization and its
Discontents* and, in the relationship between Bardamu and Robinson,
to Otto Rank's theory of the double.[114] Psychologically, Céline may also
have been influenced by his supporter at the time of the Goncourt battle,
Léon Daudet, and his essay *Le Rêve éveillé* of 1926, which proposed a dream-
theory without recourse to Freudian concepts of the unconscious. The full
Freudian influence, however, would not appear until *Mort à crédit*, where
the Oedipus complex appears in almost caricatural form.

Among the classics, Céline is more orientated to the non-classical and
often non-French tradition of Rabelais, Shakespeare and Dostoevsky, to
whom he refers frequently in the early interviews.[115] Regarding the French
Modernists, there is the evident debt to Proust, again to be fully exploited
in *Mort à crédit*, with a probable reading of Gide, especially the anti-colonial
texts. Among his contemporaries, he consistently singles out Barbusse,
probably due to the influence of *Le Feu* on the First World War episode,
Dabit, for the populist strain, and Morand and Ramuz for stylistic influence.[116] Indeed, Céline's stylistic innovation in *Voyage* derives not just from
Morand and Ramuz, but also from the French, and specifically Montmartre, *chansonnier* tradition of Richepin, Jehan Rictus and Aristide Bruant, as
well as late nineteenth-century novelists and polemicists such as Léon Bloy
and Jules Vallès, whose *L'Enfant* is one of the source texts for *Mort à crédit*.

In *Bagatelles pour un massacre*, Céline provides a highly personal review
of contemporary writers of whom he approves, though by this time Gide,
Wilde and Proust are rejected as part of the 'implacable continuity of the
Jewish programme'.[117] The Célinian pantheon includes Simenon, Marcel
Aymé, the Malraux of *Les Conquérants*, the art historian Elie Faure, wrongly
branded as half Jewish, Dabit, Morand, Pierre Mac Orlan, the great precursor of Céline's musicality in style and inventor of that fantastic narrative
space, 'le fantastique social', Aristide Bruant, Claude Farrère, the reactionary adventure novelist, Barbusse and Léon Daudet. Among the painters, he
singles out his Montmartre cronies Vlaminck, Gen Paul and Henri Mahé.

In other words, Céline arrived at *Voyage au bout de la nuit* with a considerable, if sometimes idiosyncratic, cultural baggage. It was a property he was
to exploit even further as he embarked on his second novel, announced
already in the interview to Victor Molitor, and as he began to come to terms
with the literary fame which had suddenly made him the equal of those
writers to whom he was indebted.

7

The 'House of Literature'

I Success

The period between the appearance of *Voyage au bout de la nuit* and the completion of *Mort à crédit* in February 1934 saw little in the way of publication on Céline's part, but considerable changes both in his own life and in the social and political situation in France and Europe. As a result of the furore surrounding the Prix Goncourt and the intrinsic interest in *Voyage au bout de la nuit*, Céline from the end of 1932 onwards found himself a public figure, suddenly placed at the centre of French literary life and with a much altered lifestyle. At home, he hosted the traditional lunch for the members of the Prix Renaudot jury on 16 March 1933[1] and became the jury's President at its next meeting on 7 December. He continued to develop close relations with those members of the Goncourt jury who had supported *Voyage*: Lucien Descaves, who invited Céline and his mother to lunch with Vlaminck and the Abbé Mugnier,[2] Léon Daudet, who remained a constant correspondent until 1936, and Jean Ajalbert, whom Céline and Elizabeth visited in Beauvais early in 1933.[3] Nor was he at all averse, despite his image as a loner, to literary dinner-parties, as Robert de Saint-Jean's account of the evening at Daniel Halévy's where he met Bernanos testifies. He was also cultivated, to no immediate effect, by leading members of Gallimard's stable. Jean Paulhan wrote to Denoël offering Céline space in the *NRF*, but was turned down;[4] Malraux, whose *Les Conquérants* Céline admired, asked him to write a preface for a novel translated by his wife, but again, without success.[5] The clutch of signed copies of *Voyage au bout de la nuit* which he sent out to literary personalities bore fruit, as in the case of François Mauriac, who sent Céline a letter of thanks and received in return an odd communication, containing the statement: 'We have nothing and can never have anything in common. You belong to another species, you see other people, you hear other voices. For me, a simpleton, God is a trick

to help us think more highly of ourselves and to avoid thinking of others.'[6]
An unknown figure until the publication of *Voyage*, by early 1933 Céline was
moving easily and self-confidently in elevated French literary circles. Hence
his ability to treat Eugène Dabit, who had nevertheless achieved considerable success before Céline with *Hôtel du Nord*, with unfailing condescension.
As he wrote in October 1933 regarding Dabit's new novel, *Un Mort tout neuf,*
'I am certain that your book will be quite remarkable. You do not try, like
me, unfortunately, to constantly overreach yourself, you are not weighed
down with pride, like me.'[7] Although Céline remained affectionate towards
Dabit throughout his life and recommended *Villa Oasis* to Milton Hindus in
1947,[8] the relationship between the two was clearly one-sided, and marked
by a sense of drama and anxiety on Dabit's part. Referring to 'this strange
friend of mine, Céline',[9] he recounted a subsequent visit to Saint-Germain-
en-Laye: 'for three hours, for him, for me, naturally, it's the atmosphere of
Voyage au bout de la nuit',[10] and in his last comment on Céline, he chose to
see him as a tortured soul: 'Céline lives alone, but he suffers without
admitting it, from his solitude, and his cry, his despair, are sometimes
terrible.'[11]

   In the years immediately following the publication of *Voyage*, Céline was
still assumed to be in the same populist category as Dabit and was consequently courted particularly by left-wing writers to join progressive causes.
In the wake of the Reichstag fire of 27 February 1933, Henri Barbusse
launched a campaign in France in favour of the accused, the Komintern
members Dimitrov, Popov and Tavev, and recruited Céline, who replied in
measured terms: 'Dear Barbusse, No one is better qualified than you to
draw up this protest, which, obviously, I am signing with you. I hope that in
the current situation it will not be too late for such a gesture to have a
positive effect. Unless Hitler uses Christmas to announce some kind of
political amnesty . . . Life is often owed to such stupidities. But you are the
best judge. Yours sincerely, L.-F. Céline.'[12] As Alméras points out, Céline's
signing of the petition seems to owe more to a personal admiration for
Barbusse than to any positive commitment to the accused, seen as the
victims of a universal fate. At the same time, the art historian Elie Faure,
whom Céline met for the first time on 25 February 1933 and with whom he
was to have a close friendship for the next two years, attempted to recruit
him into the newly formed Communist front organization, the Association
des Ecrivains et Artistes Révolutionnaires (AEAR). Céline fought back
as delicately as his friendship for Faure and his antipathy for left-wing
organizations would allow, citing Aragon and the AEAR's policy of collective composition as reasons for abstention: 'Can you see yourself thinking under the command of that arch-idiot Aragon?'[13] The real reason,
however, lies in Céline's essential anarchism: 'I'm an anarchist to the
depths of my being,' he wrote to Faure. 'I always have been and I will
never be anything else.'[14] And as early as May or June 1933, he expressed
complete disillusionment with the Left in terms which announce *Mea culpa*
and the pamphlets:

The left: what does that mean nowadays? NOTHING – *less than nothing.* We're going, we're flying towards fascism . . . *There's no-one on the left,* that's the truth. *Socialist thought, socialist PLEASURE, aren't even born yet.* People talk about them, that's all. If there were a left-wing *pleasure* there would be a left-wing body. If we become fascists, that's tough. This people will have decided to. IT WANTS TO. It likes the lash.[15]

Aragon himself, whose wife Elsa Triolet handled the Russian translation of *Voyage au bout de la nuit,* made an attempt to entice a gesture of commitment from Céline, though not, one suspects, with any great conviction. He launched a major survey in the AEAR review *Commune* in its October 1933 issue entitled 'Who do you write for?' and published Céline's reply in the January 1934 number. It was deliberately provocative and closed the door on subsequent attempts to recruit Céline as an *engagé* writer, at least on the Left: 'If you had asked why men, all men, from their birth to their death, drunkards or not, have the mania to create, to tell stories, I could have understood your question . . . But "Writer!!!", biologically, has no meaning. It is a romantic obscenity whose explanation can only be a superficial one.'[16] Aragon's conclusion: 'you can't make up your mind to take the side of the exploiters against the exploited. And the time has come, Céline, for you to take sides,'[17] was to be unexpectedly confirmed in 1936 and 1937: until then, Céline remained, or appeared to remain, neutral.

If Céline became a major literary personality in France in 1933, he also began to acquire an international reputation. *Voyage au bout de la nuit* was translated into German, though its serialization in the *Berliner Tagesblatt* and publication by Piper Verlag were banned by the Nazi regime.[18] The Czech edition, however, published by Borovy, was a success, and the novel had won a sort of 'mini Renaudot'.[19] In England, John Marks, the co-editor with Graham Greene of the *New Yorker* clone *Night and Day,* was working on the English translation for Chatto and Windus, which was also taken up by Little, Brown in the United States. Abel Gance's attempt to turn the novel into a film in 1933 was repeated by Jacques Deval in Hollywood the following year.[20]

All this turned Céline into a relatively wealthy man. By the end of January 1933, 50,000 copies of *Voyage* had been sold, compared with 100,000 copies of Mazeline's *Les Loups,* a figure which, incidentally, indicates the commercial impact of the Prix Goncourt. Céline's own claims, to Erika Irrgang and Cille Pam, were more fanciful (75,000 copies sold by February 1933, 100,000 by March), but Denoël's own figure of 112,000 sales by the end of 1938 still represents a considerable literary, and financial, success.[21] Alméras calculates Céline's earnings in royalties at 735,000 francs by June 1933, not counting fees from sales of translation rights[22] or deals, such as that with Galeries Lafayette, for 1000 francs an hour for a signing of the novel. And he still received his salary as a doctor in Clichy and his laboratory fees.

As such, this could not fail to have a radical effect on Céline's lifestyle. As Alméras acutely observes, the photograph of Céline giving the Zola address in Médan in October 1933 shows a relaxed figure in an elegant well-cut suit.[23] Through his friend Albert Milon, he invested some of his royalties in property, a three-roomed apartment on the fifth floor of a modern block in Saint-Germain-en-Laye, which he would occasionally use but more often let out:[24] the self-styled 'proletarian' author rapidly became a 'rentier'. Similarly, although Céline strove to maintain his image as a dedicated doctor of the poor in the industrial suburbs, his medical work declined markedly after the publication of *Voyage*, and he had frequent recourse to a locum. The immediate reason for this was that the success of the novel enabled him to indulge his passion for travel, though he was not averse to travelling at other people's expense if the opportunity presented itself. Thus, four days after the Prix Goncourt, on 11 December 1932, he set out on what was to be his last mission for the League of Nations: a journey to Germany to study medicine and unemployment. He called briefly at Geneva, where he met Rajchman and other League colleagues, and arrived in Berlin on 17 December, staying at the luxurious Hotel Hessler. His visit lasted a week and led to a short publication 'Pour tuer le chômage tueront-ils les chômeurs?' in *Le Mois* in its February–March 1933 issue. He then travelled on to Breslau on 25 December to see Erika Irrgang, before moving on to Vienna and Cillie Pam on 28 December.[25] He returned to Paris on 15 January 1933. Even though only a week of this thirty-five-day journey had been devoted to research into unemployment, Céline was at great pains to recover expenses for the entire trip. He wrote to Captain Johnston-Watson, who still handled the financial arrangements in Geneva, complaining that he had only received subsistence allowances for twenty-one days, at 6 dollars a day, rather than for the full thirty-five, and reminding him that he was obliged to pay his locum 70 francs a day. In fact, as Gibault points out, the League had already forwarded a further cheque for 2,505,20 francs, in addition to the original payment of 490,55 francs, making a total of 2,995,75 francs in all,[26] but the incident is further evidence of Céline's punctiliousness in financial matters which remained a constant throughout his life and was inevitably directed against his publishers.[27]

The real importance of this journey, however, in spite of the slight publication which resulted from the visit to Berlin, lies in Céline's introduction in Vienna to a predominantly Jewish psychoanalytic circle, including Freud's publisher, Dr A. J. Storfer, Annie Reich, the wife of Wilhelm, and Cillie's friend Anny Angel.[28] As Gibault reminds us, Céline's interest in Freud goes back at least as far as 1921, when he refered to him in two letters to Jean and Germaine Thomas,[29] and, as we have seen, he claimed Freudian influence on *Voyage au bout de la nuit*. In a letter to Joseph Garcin of 13 May 1933, however, he is at pains to dismiss the Freudian element in his work as pure 'packaging'. Having already given his recipe for dealing with interviewers: ('Lie and tell them anything'),[30] he wrote:

> You have to know what the reader wants, to follow fashion like shop-girls: that's the job of the writer, who is very constrained financially and that's the

condition without which there are no high sales (the only thing which counts). That applies to the war since Barbusse, and all those psychoanalytical plots since Freud. I choose the right direction, the direction indicated by the arrow, *obstinately*. If that's what the public wants, I'll kiss my mother and put shit everywhere.[31]

There is a great deal of assumed cynicism here, perhaps a desire to impress Garcin, which belies a more serious interest in Freud. In addition to the classic texts of psychoanalysis, Céline was probably familiar with Freud's post-First World War writing, in particular *Civilization and its Discontents* and *Beyond the Pleasure-Principle*, where a new pessimism based upon the death-wish replaces the earlier optimistic positivism. On 8 May 1933, before his next visit to Vienna, he wrote to Cillie Pam asking: 'Would you be kind enough to get me Freud's article "Mourning and Melancholia"? You can find it in *Collected Works*, Volume 5,'[32] and in July 1933 he wrote to Evelyne Pollet: 'Freud's works are really very important, in so far as the Human is important . . . In the years to come, I'm going to exploit them.'[33] There is no doubt that *Mort à crédit*, far more than *Voyage au bout de la nuit*, is a 'Freudian' novel, and that in the relationship between the mature narrator Ferdinand and the dead father Auguste there is an irreducible melancholia which results from unresolved grieving. Yet the cynicism of the letter to Garcin is not incompatible with this reading and, particularly in the exaggeratedly excremental elements of the novel and the caricaturally Oedipal assault on the father with the typewriter, *Mort à crédit* may also be seen as an ironic transposition of Freud's theories.

Céline was back in Paris for only three months before leaving in late May for London. Here he met John Marks and Joseph Garcin, who took him around the brothels and pubs of the capital's underworld.[34] He returned to France via Antwerp and his new mistress Evelyne Pollet. He came back to the Rue Lepic at the end of May, only to leave again on 6 June on a journey that would last until 25 June and which would take him to Basle, Zurich, Vienna, where he met up again with Cillie Pam and her psychoanalyst friends, and finally Prague.[35] August found him on holiday in Dinard, the first of a long line of Breton holidays. The same pattern of foreign travel was continued in 1934, with a further visit to John Marks in London, an extended stay during June and July in the United States, during which the relationship with Elizabeth Craig finally ended, and another holiday in Brittany. The following year, there was a further visit to John Marks in February and a long journey in July to Denmark, Finland, Berlin, Munich and Salzburg, in the company of the pianist Lucienne Delforge. What is significant about these journeys in the period between *Voyage au bout de la nuit* and *Mort à crédit* is that they all contain a sexual element, they take Céline towards North America and Northern and Central Europe, and not the south, and are an almost conscious assertion of both freedom and independence, particularly from the drudgery of medical practice. They also show his growing wealth: the correspondence emanating from Céline's travels in this period bears the letterheads of some of Europe's most prestigious hotels. Through the sales of *Voyage*, Céline had ostensibly become a successful man, a property-owner with an international reputation and lifestyle.

II PERSONAL LIFE

Yet, if Céline's material situation dramatically improved after the publication of *Voyage au bout de la nuit*, his personal life was dramatically more turbulent and marked by one event, the definitive break with Elizabeth Craig in 1934, which may have had lasting consequences.

Sexually, as Céline hinted in his 1960 interview with André Parinaud, he was a libertine.[36] With Garcin and John Marks, he toured the brothels of London. Henri Mahé's and Marcel Brochard's reminiscences reveal a man interested in sexual experiment, participating in group sex and particularly favouring voyeurism, especially where lesbian acts were involved, a theme present already in *Progrès/Périclès* of 1926.[37] The same trait undoubtedly explains in part his attraction to dancers: Elizabeth Craig, Karen Marie Jensen and his third wife Lucette Almansor. Nor, when with Elizabeth, did he have any pretension to monogamy, asserting the right to his own sexual freedom and, at least in theory, encouraging Elizabeth in her independence.[38] It was thus that, during Elizabeth's extended visit to the United States in 1932, he began his relationships first with Erika Irrgang, then with Cillie Pam. It is not clear for how long these relationships remained sexual: the correspondence contains an uneasy mixture of the downright licentious and the medically practical. Thus to Erika, in December 1932, just before his departure for Breslau, he wrote: 'Amuse yourself a little – be depraved – we'll see to that together – *but watch out for diseases*.'[39] Yet, instead of the promised four or five days with Erika, he spent only two.[40] Later that year, on 22 June 1932, he wrote: 'Use all your weapons at once, all of them, sex, theatre, education, work. But protect your health. No *sex without condoms*, OR ELSE FROM BEHIND,'[41] and on October 3: 'Preserve your health – your thighs, your mind . . . Make love (WITHOUT TAKING RISKS) because it's a stimulant.'[42] In the letter to Cillie Pam announcing his arrival in Vienna at the beginning of January 1933, he refused to stay with her, preferring a hotel: 'I shall go directly to the hotel and I DO NOT WANT to stay *with you*. For various reasons. It would first of all compromise you quite stupidly in the eyes of your friends and your boyfriend . . . I shall come round to your apartment often, *but not to sleep*.'[43] In both cases, it is likely that the sexual side of the relationship rapidly gave way to a close friendship which Céline was anxious to maintain. Anny Angel recalled meeting Céline with Cillie Pam in 1933 and the mixture of sadism and generosity of which he was capable:

I remember that, during his stay, he spent an entire night talking about all sorts of childish perversions, sexual practices involving corpses, etc. He had extraordinary gifts, and certainly gave the impression, at that time, of being a pervert and a psychopath. But otherwise he seemed capable of being a good and loyal friend. He was so to Cillie, undoubtedly, and at the time I believed he bore similar feelings towards me. For instance, he offered me his apartment in Paris in case I should have to leave Austria in a hurry with my son, for political reasons, and assured me that not only would I be welcome there, but that I could stay as long as I liked until I found something else – an offer that was certainly not to be taken lightly in those days.[44]

Anny Angel came across Céline unexpectedly in Brittany in the summer of 1938, when *Bagatelles pour un massacre* had made him one of France's foremost anti-Semites. She recalls him blushing and stammering: 'Where is Cillie?'[45] Cillie's husband had been imprisoned in Dachau, where he died in 1938, and she had fled abroad with her son. Céline's last letter to her, dated 21 February 1939, is a curious blend of concern and sheer tactless selfishness: 'This is terrible news! Still, now you're on the other side of the world. Did you manage to take some money with you? You will obviously rebuild your life over there. How are you going to work? . . . In my case, my little dramas are nothing compared with yours (for the moment), but tragedy is there . . . Following my anti-Semitic attitude, I've lost all my jobs.'[46] He last saw Erika Irrgang, who had emigrated to Cambridge, and was married with a small child, just after the publication of *Mort à crédit* in May 1936. The reunion was not a success. As Erika remembered: 'I don't know why our meeting in Cambridge, which was our last, was somehow depressing; there was something about it that's difficult to describe, something that is born with the instinctive feeling that there is nothing left to say.'[47]

In the immediate aftermath of *Voyage*, however, Céline was keen to keep up his international network of girlfriends and, indeed, to add to it. In January 1933, a 27-year-old Belgian mother of two, with literary pretensions, Evelyne Pollet, wrote to him expressing her admiration for *Voyage au bout de la nuit* and asking him to read one of her manuscripts.[48] Céline was unimpressed by the short story she sent him, although she went on to achieve a certain reputation in Belgium,[49] but he entered into a correspondence with her. Hence, on his way back to Paris from London in May 1933, he called on her in Antwerp and became her lover, beginning a relationship which lasted until 1941, and which Evelyne Pollet insisted remained sexual.[50] What is interesting about all these relationships is that Céline made no attempt to compartmentalize them and took pleasure in introducing successive new mistresses, like Lucienne Delforge or Lucette Almansor, to members of the network.

While this aspect of Céline's emotional life appears to have been relatively unproblematic, even highly supportive, his major relationship of the period, that with Elizabeth Craig, had severely deteriorated even before the

publication of *Voyage*. As noted earlier, Elizabeth had detected a considerable change in Céline's personality when they moved from Geneva to Paris
and particularly from Clichy to Montmartre. She was also conscious of
being neglected in favour of the composition of the novel. Accordingly, her
annual visits to her parents in California grew significantly longer, to the
extent that she had increasing doubts about returning to Paris. She was not
present in Paris for the publication of *Voyage au bout de la nuit* or for the
Goncourt affair, returning only in March 1933. She left again for the
United States in June, and during that time, in May, Céline had absented
himself in order to visit the London underworld with Garcin and John
Marks and to begin an affair with Evelyne Pollet in Antwerp. Indeed, the
relationship appears to have deteriorated to such an extent that when
Elizabeth left France on 7 June, Céline was already on his way to Switzerland and Austria, and it was a mutual friend, the dancer Karen Marie
Jensen, who accompanied her to Le Havre.[51] Probably to avoid admitting a
definitive break, Céline explained her precipitate departure as due to
financial worries: she will 'probably be in America for a very long time; her
affairs are going very badly there.'[52] As Alméras points out, the cover story
is an interesting one since it points unconsciously to one of Céline's major
and constant obsessions, financial security.[53]

Céline was not able to forget Elizabeth, however. In 1934, when he was
deeply into the writing of *Mort à crédit*, he sent her a postcard showing a
deserted Parc de Saint-Cloud, with the bleak message: 'That where I pass
my Sundays now sick of St Germain as you may well imagine,'[54] and, as
Vitoux somewhat luridly, but accurately, expresses it: 'Elizabeth still had
not returned. He suddenly decided to go get her. He was ready for anything, to humble himself, to storm, to beg her to return to their life
together.'[55] In fact, he had prepared the ground carefully: *Voyage* was about
to come out in America, in the John Marks translation, and Céline, who had
already given a preparatory interview to the *New York Herald Tribune* on 27
May 1934,[56] arranged to cross the Atlantic to help his publishers, Little
Brown of Boston, with the launch. He left France on 12 June on the
Champlain, of the Compagnie Générale Transatlantique, and arrived in
New York on 20 June, staying at the Vanderbilt Hotel. By the end of June,
having apparently failed to convince Elizabeth to join him in New York and
having completed his interviews with the American press, he left for the
West Coast, on the pretext of seeing Jacques Deval in Hollywood in order
to sell the film rights of *Voyage*.[57] It was in Deval's house that Céline's last
interview with Elizabeth took place early in July.

As Alméras comments, the number of conflicting accounts of the break
with Elizabeth rivals *Rashomon*. Jacques Deval, who witnessed the encounter, claimed that Céline was luke-warm in wanting Elizabeth back;[58] Céline
himself created a series of versions, each one more melodramatic than the
last. To Denoël, he hinted at an inexpressible disaster: 'Between us, I have
had an awful time which can never be described, not even by me,'[59] and to
Mahé, 'Things have come to pass here just as I predicted. An appalling

drama, so low, so vile, so degrading.'[60] To Cillie Pam, he was more explicit: 'I found Elizabeth in a semi-demented state that is neither describable nor explainable,'[61] and he rapidly developed a version which associated Elizabeth with gangsterism. He wrote to Mahé that 'Elizabeth has given herself to gangsters,'[62] though the painter was by no means deceived: 'There wasn't a damn thing in the way of gangsters!'[63] This version became common currency. To Milton Hindus in 1947 Céline wrote: 'She was living in a miasma of alcohol, tobacco, the police, and the lowlife among gangsters,'[64] and on September 2, 'she returned to the U.S. – to sink into low gangster circles and alcohol.'[65] It culminated in Lucette Almansor's account, by which Céline and Elizabeth met on a piece of waste ground and she was literally torn away from him by gangsters who suddenly appeared out of the darkness.[66]

The reality, necessarily, was much more mundane. Elizabeth, who was now living with an estate agent, Ben Tankle, had already decided not to return with Céline to Paris and, when he issued an ultimatum that he would leave without her, she simply did not turn up at Los Angeles airport the following day.[67] The relationship was at an end. Even Mahé's subsequent explanation, that she had 'married the Jewish judge in charge of her father's legacy',[68] was marred by the fact that Elizabeth's father was still alive and that Tankle was not a judge.

Why, then, so much obfuscation surrounding what was, after all, a banal event? On one level, in spite of Jacques Deval's dismissive comments, it may well be that the loss of Elizabeth Craig hurt Céline deeply. She herself claimed that during their first year together he begged: 'Don't ever leave me, don't ever leave me!'[69] Vitoux reminds us that in a letter of 10 September 1947 to Hindus, he concluded affectionately: 'What genius in that woman! I wouldn't have amounted to anything without her – What wit! what finesse . . . What painful and mischievous pantheism. What poetry . . . What mystery . . . She understood everything before you said a word. Rare is the woman who is not essentially a cow or a servant – she's a sorceress and a fairy.'[70] We have also seen ample evidence, in correspondence and interviews, of Céline's inclination to embroider the truth, particularly where such distortions give him a more dramatic aura. In this case, the rejected suitor becomes the heroic victim, with Céline able to exploit contemporary fascination with American gangsterism. John Dillinger was killed, betrayed by his girlfriend, in Chicago during Céline's stay there on his way back from Los Angeles, and gangsters were already the staple diet of popular culture on both sides of the Atlantic. It is also tempting to see in the myth of the 'Jewish judge' Ben Tankle at least a contributory factor in Céline's anti-Semitism.[71]

On leaving Los Angeles, Céline, at least superficially, appeared to recover his spirits, though his behaviour could be interpreted as unusually volatile. He arrived in Chicago on 15 July and stayed in the New Lawrence Hotel, which he claimed to be full of 'black pimps and gangsters':[72] the obsession with gangsterism, which he saw everywhere, had now become fused with racism. The reason for going to Chicago was to meet Karen Marie Jensen, the Danish dancer whom he and Elizabeth had met in 1931 and with whom they had formed 'an unusual trio of sexual complicity, anticipation, misunderstandings and thinly disguised jealousy'.[73] Karen was the daughter of a wealthy family in Copenhagen with an international career in variety: a better dancer than Elizabeth herself. Her relationship with Céline, ambiguous as it was, lasted until well after the war, and she was instrumental in his choice of Denmark as a place of exile following the Liberation. In the summer of 1934, she was playing in a Folies-Bergère-style show in Chicago when Céline visited her and asked her to marry him. At the time Karen Jensen turned him down, but a year later appeared to reconsider. It was now Céline's turn to backtrack, writing: 'I like you Karen, but I can't offer you much.'[74] The immediate vulnerability following the loss of Elizabeth had evaporated, though even in the summer of 1934 Céline was won over again by the sheer physicality of America. He wrote to Dabit on 14 July, just before leaving Hollywood: 'What flesh, my friend! I don't know if you could resist these delights? As far as I'm concerned, I just give in, I confess – Especially in California – where I nevertheless received an abominable lesson in distrust.'[75] Unable to oblige him, Karen Jensen introduced him to a dancer in New York, Irene McBride, who was unimpressed by Céline's courtship techniques. Through her, however, he met a number of other dancers, including, according to Gibault, one less than 15 years old.[76] He left New York on a one-class boat, the *Liberté*, and during the voyage to Cherbourg proposed marriage to a passenger, a sculptor called Louise Nevelson, to whom he wrote later from Saint-Malo: 'Dear Miss Nevelson, By now you must have been married over and over again. What passion will be left for me? I will be in Paris Saturday evening. Have lunch with me any day you say, but write one day before.'[77] The admonition to give a day's notice was standard practice with Céline in writing to his women friends, in case they disturbed a new or existing liaison unexpectedly.

It is difficult to assess properly this behaviour of Céline's following the break with Elizabeth. On one level, it appears to support Deval's scepticism regarding Céline's despair. Not only did he immediately resume his style of sexual independence, he also reasserted his role as an internationally famous novelist by signing an option on the film rights with Lester H. Yard, director of *Variety* magazine, gave a major interview to the *Chicago Daily News* and received generally copious press coverage.[78] At the same time, there is something more than a little frenetic in this behaviour, and repeated proposals of marriage may well be an indication of that same gradual divorce from reality evident in the accounts of the break-up with Elizabeth and without which the anti-Semitic pamphlets would not have been possible. Certainly the conclusion to a letter to Karen of 7 February 1935: 'I don't want to die alone,'[79] for all its banality and lack of tact, has a poignant depth.

Céline's appetite for new sexual encounters continued at least until his meeting with Lucette Almansor in 1936. Alméras recounts his meeting in

October 1934 with a 'Mme L.' at a concert in the Salle Pleyel, when he introduced himself by writing 'Louis-Ferdinand Céline' followed by '*Voyage au bout de la nuit*' on his programme.[80] In April 1935 he met the pianist Lucienne Delforge, with whom he spent a weekend in London before taking her to visit Karen in Copenhagen in July, followed by the long journey through Finland, Germany and Austria.[81] This relationship lasted until the spring of 1936, though they were to meet again in Sigmaringen in the winter of 1944–5.

The correspondence with Erika, Cillie and Evelyne Pollet is marked, not merely by precise medical advice, but also by expressions of a sustained pessimism. In her novel *Escaliers*, published in 1956 and a transparent account of her affair with Céline, Evelyne Pollet describes a scene in which the French writer and his Belgian mistress have just made love: ' "Don't you think it's fine, making love?" she asked in a caressing voice. "Don't you think it's very fine?" "Dying, that's what's fine," he said wearily,'[82] although it is possible that she, like Dabit, fell victim to Céline's self-dramatization. The question of Céline's personal pessimism in the inter-war years is a complex one and is not to be automatically confused with the bleakness of vision of the novels. The philosophical pessimism of French fiction in the inter-war years owes at least as much to purely aesthetic concerns connected with the search for a new tragic mode of expression as it does to either a psychological or a social reality.[83] In Céline's case, the pessimism, however genuine, was also part of the carefully created persona of the Dostoievskian writer, in the same way that he was able, chameleon-like, to impress a *mondain* dinner-party attended by the Abbé Mugnier with his proletarian speech[84] and strike other acquaintances with his quietly spoken refined discourse. In the letters to women friends, the sustained pessimism is an important weapon in the arsenal of seduction. Similarly, if Céline adopts a tone of cynical disillusion in the letters to Joseph Garcin, it can be read, at least partially, as the bravado of a writer trying to impress a man of the world.

The correspondence with Elie Faure, however, reveals a more reliable image and a clear divide between the humanist socialist art historian and the anarchist Céline. Even a letter from Dinard in the summer of 1934 reveals a profound sense of loss and impending disaster: 'Everything is pushing us and everything is changing. Even the dust is aging. There are fewer and fewer sails on the sea. The gentlemen with lorgnettes and rolled-up trousers are all already dead. That's what they were looking for on the horizon. So are we.'[85] Yet what underpins the pessimism of the correspondence with Elie Faure is the complete and profound rejection of humanism which lies at the basis of *Mea culpa* and its expression of political despair: 'Both Lenin and Napoleon failed.'[86] For Céline, any idealization of the working class, implicit in Faure's position, is impossible: 'The proletarian is a failed bourgeois. Nothing more.'[87] The reason is simple: Céline is able to view society from a proletarian perspective and with a proletarian language, whereas Faure is irretrievably bourgeois. In an impassioned letter of July 1935, Céline connects a general anti-humanist pessimism to this social perspective:

> You are not from the people, you are not vulgar, you are aristocratic: you say so yourself . . . You don't know what I know. You have been to lycée. *You didn't earn your bread before you went to school.* You have no right to judge me, you don't know. You don't know what I want. You don't know what I want, you don't know what I do. You don't know what horrible effort I have to make, every day, every night especially, to simply keep upright, to hold my pen . . . I'm speaking to you brutally, Elie, because you're on the other side, in spite of yourself. You don't speak our language and like to hear it.[88]

What is interesting about this outburst, in addition to its Romanticism and the fact that it is at variance with the biographical truth, is that Céline's intense philosophical pessimism ('We'll come to miss wars, Elie . . . Mankind is cursed')[89] is a conscious expression of class division, the privilege of those 'who have not been to lycée'. Unlike the abstract pessimism of Malraux or Drieu, Céline's pessimism, like that of his fellow Montmartre novelist Mac Orlan, proceeds from a concrete and definable social perspective with its own means of articulation.

III POLITICS

Politically, both domestically and internationally, events certainly appeared to justify growing pessimism. At home, France had enjoyed an extremely successful decade economically in the 1920s, due to the rebuilding of its industry, the return of the Alsace-Lorraine steel industries and the stabilization of the franc under Poincaré in 1926.[90] As Tom Kemp points out, however, this economic expansion of the 1920s concealed a number of contradictions regarding French industry which were to render the economy particularly vulnerable to the Depression which hit Europe in 1931[91] and were to delay recovery much longer than in other comparable European countries. The problem, essentially, was both structural and managerial. The 'franc Poincaré' which had been France's saviour in the 1920s, because it was both stable and undervalued in relation to other European currencies, thus facilitating exports, became a millstone round the French economy's neck after the sterling crisis of 1931 which led to the British abandonment of the gold standard. Thereafter, the franc was over-valued and France's capacity for export rapidly dried up. This in its turn led to a deepening stagnation of the economy, with decline in exports being accompanied by deceleration of domestic consumption. The crisis was compounded, however, by a lack of imagination or will on the part of both French industrialists and politicians. Politically, the maintenance of the 'franc Poincaré' became an article of faith, when all sense dictated that, like the British, the French should devalue. Alone of French politicians, Paul Reynaud advocated this logical step, but was universally derided. Instead, conservative politicians like Paul-Etienne Flandin or Pierre Laval pursued vigorous deflationary measures which simply pushed the economy further into stagnation. Thus, while other Western economies were beginning to come out of recession in 1935, the French economy was still in decline, and Léon Blum's belated recourse to devaluation in October 1936 was too little and too late. In the context of France's irrational clinging to the gold standard, Céline's anarchist prayer at the beginning of *Voyage au bout de la nuit*, 'The Wings of Gold' ('Les Ailes en or', which could also be phoneti-cally read as 'Les ££ en or'), evoking the worship of a golden pig, is unusually acute, as is his sustained reflection on the credit function and gold in *Mort à crédit*.

Significantly, this serious and prolonged economic crisis was accompa-nied by relatively low unemployment figures. 'In the course of 1932,' writes Kemp, 'those in receipt of benefit exceeded a quarter of a million and at its peak the annual average reached 433,700 in 1936.'[92] In Germany in 1932, the figure exceeded 6 million. The problem, however, was that these rela-tively low figures are a measure of France's fragile economic state and not of strength. The figures are low because France, at the end of the First World War, suffered a severe labour shortage and had recourse to the importation of large numbers of migrant and immigrant workers, all of whom simply returned home with the onset of the Depression. At the same time, the French workforce in the 1930s included large numbers of first generation city dwellers, who returned to the countryside, and older and unskilled workers who could not be easily reabsorbed into industry once recovery began. Above all, the low French unemployment figures in the 1930s are a glaring symptom of a dangerously primitive economy. In this respect, Céline's own work-base of Clichy is a case in point, and the rela-tively low growth rate in population throughout the 1930s may well have taken place against the background of migrant and provincial workers leaving the Parisian basin because of unemployment.

Politically, there was no sign of any concerted attempt to deal with the economy and the social consequences of its decline, although in this France was by no means alone, and Britain under Baldwin showed a similar paralysis of will. It is tempting to see the collapse of France in 1940, like the fall of the Fourth Republic in 1958, as somehow inevitable and preor-dained, the ineluctable consequence of constitutional weakness and politi-cal incompetence. There is no particular evidence, however, that the Third Republic, after it had weathered the storms of the late nineteenth century, was especially vulnerable or even generally despised. The riots of 6 Febru-ary 1934 toppled the Daladier government, but not the regime, which went on to survive the Front Populaire in 1936–7, the Munich crisis, with Daladier back at the helm, and the declaration of war in 1939. The defeat of France in 1940 (accompanied, we should remind ourselves, by the defeat of Britain in northern France and Belgium), while it may have been symptomatic of a failure to modernize in the 1930s and an underlying lack of nerve crystallized by the military and civilian rout which followed the German advance, can be explained in military terms alone.

French politics in the 1930s was dominated, as before, by the Radical Party and by the rivalry between its two leaders, Edouard Herriot, the mayor of Lyons, and Edouard Daladier. This party either led or participated in every government right up to the defeat of 1940, and Daladier's supporters were a vital ingredient in the Front Populaire coalition. Nor was there much sign of a widespread desire for a dramatic alternative. On the extreme right, Action Française, which constituted a destabilizing force in the 1920s, was less and less concerned with real political power and more with vituperative rhetoric, to the despair of its younger zealots, who were tempted by Fascism and even the Pretender, the Comte de Paris.[93] The paramilitary *Ligues*, like Colonel de la Rocque's Croix de Feu or Pierre Taittinger's Jeunesses Patriotes, mobilized impressively on the night of 6 February 1934, but docilely allowed themselves to be disbanded in 1936. The mayor of Saint-Denis, the neighbouring suburb to Clichy, the Communist Jacques Doriot, left the party in 1934 to set up the Fascist Parti Populaire Français (PPF), which enjoyed a huge popular membership in the mid-1930s, only to undergo a severe decline, though it remained an important expression of extreme right-wing French thought and a base for a number of writers and artists.[94] Many of the Montmartre community had close links with the PPF and Céline himself, during the Occupation, wrote approvingly of Doriot. On the Left, the Socialist SFIO was torn between a respect for the constitutional legitimacy of parliamentary elections and, particularly under its left wing led by Marceau Pivert, the temptations of revolution, while the Communist PCF, until the Front Populaire alliance of 1935, was a small party, 'pur et dur', on the margins of French political life. The Front Populaire government itself, which came to power in May 1936, dramatic as its initial legislation was, was enjoined by Léon Blum to remember that it had been legally elected and had not conquered power, and that its role was 'the loyal management' of the capitalist economy. It was the French Communists who attempted to persuade workers occupying factories the length and breadth of the country that 'you have to know how to end a strike,' and it was the Front Populaire government which unleashed the 'Battle of Clichy' on the night of 16 March 1937, when it sent its riot police against workers protesting at an extreme right-wing meeting.[95]

Internationally, the first half of the decade was dominated by models of social reorganization provided by New Deal politics in the United States and the continuing example of the Soviet Union, and by increasing international tension resulting from the activities of the Fascist powers, Italy and Germany, which elected Hitler as Chancellor in 1933. The Italian invasion of Abyssinia in 1935 marked the end of the ideal of 'Briandism' and of the effective role of the League of Nations, though without necessarily threatening peace in Europe. German rearmament and the reoccupation of the

Rhineland in 1936 were deliberate acts of self-assertion and defiance directed towards the hated victor of the Great War. The establishment of a totalitarian state and the exclusion and persecution of the Jews following the Nuremburg Laws of 1934 constituted further threats to the liberal-conservative republican regime in France. Even a visitor as enthusiastic as Robert Brasillach, in 1937, felt that Nazi Germany was, above all, '*strange*'.[96]

It was perhaps the growing threat of war which Céline's sensitive antennae picked up first. It is worth recalling that France already had a concept of an 'inter-war period': Léon Daudet's book *L'Entre-deux-guerres* had appeared in the 1920s and referred to the period between the Franco-Prussian and First World Wars. In other words, it had already entered the French consciousness that peace-time was merely a temporary interval between two wars. Certainly Céline, right from the beginning of his correspondence with Garcin, is conscious of the imminence of the 'catastrophe',[97] and it is an attempt to make France deviate from an apparently inevitable flight towards war which is the ostensible motivation for the writing of *Bagatelles pour un massacre*.

That being said, Céline, at least up until 1936, was remarkable for his political neutrality – even his lack of political interest. On one level, this is consistent with his avowed anarchism, as set out in the correspondence with Elie Faure, but it is also less systematic and conscious. When asked by a collaborator of Edouard Herriot, Paul-Yves Rio, to inscribe a copy of *Voyage au bout de la nuit* for the mayor of Lyons, who had just been elected President of the Chamber of Deputies and was greatly impressed by the novel, the scourge of French republican politics responded readily and jovially: 'Honour, Glory, a Lyons Sausage and a fanfare for the Big Man. Cordially, Louis-Ferdinand Céline.'[98] The banter continued when Herriot proposed awarding Céline the Légion d'Honneur, to which the novelist replied that he would prefer the 'cravate du poirot', the insignia of the Commander of the 'Mérite Agricole'. Nor, during the American journey of 1934, did Céline choose to make more than a passing, and purely personal, reference to the right-wing *cause célèbre* of the Stavisky affair. The *Chicago Daily News* interview of 18 July merely referred to Stavisky's outrage at the shocking qualities of *Voyage au bout de la nuit* and his attempts to establish a morally acceptable literary prize: 'Stavisky, guardian of French morality!, smiled the doctor.'[99] Irony, and literary concerns, evidently dominated in Céline's perspective. In conversation with the Abbé Mugnier just after the 6 February riots, Céline was similarly dismissive: 'It doesn't exist, it was a game. It was done by men devoid of ideas. The ex-combatants were afraid.'[100]

Nor do Céline's foreign travels in the period appear to have greatly affected him politically. The article for the left-wing journal *Le Mois*, 'Pour tuer le chômage tueront-ils les chômeurs?', is a very brief account of the state of unemployment in post-Weimar Germany, essentially based on an analysis of malnutrition, which blames a lack of political organization and will in peace-time, contrasted with Germany's performance during the First

World War. Indeed, the importance of the article may lie in the title, which, like the thrust of the social-medical pamphlets, relies upon an ironic exaggeration of logic derived from Swift's *Modest Proposal*. The conclusion, that 'it is possible that in Hitler's entourage there may be found the dictator for unemployment who will be finally be able to organize this anarchic poverty and stabilize it at a reasonable level . . . like a dead Hoover or a living Nansen,'[101] is no more a ringing endorsement of Nazism than the hope expressed in other medical writings that a non-republican, more authoritarian system of government, of Left or Right, may be more able to deal with chronic social problems. Nor is there any evidence that the German journeys of the 1930s significantly contributed to Céline's anti-Semitism. One of his few references to the fate of the German Jews is the naive and tactless query to Erika Irrgang in June 1933: 'Since the Jews have been run out of Germany, there must be some room there for other intellectuals? Heil Hitler! Take advantage of it!'[102] It is difficult to see how Alméras' conclusion that 'his antagonism regarding the Jews was a fruit of the German summer (of 1935)'[103] can be sustained. All the evidence is that Céline, in the first half of the 1930s, was relatively a-political, albeit with a residual anti-Semitism, and, in Vitoux's words, had 'withdrawn',[104] concentrating on his literary career and the composition of his next novel, *Mort à crédit*.

IV Literature

Céline published unusually little in the period 1932–6, particularly for a man who hitherto had made a point of rushing into print on a wide variety of subjects: a short article, 'Qu'on s'explique' for *Candide* in March 1933, the article on unemployment for *Le Mois* and a reply to a survey conducted by André Rousseaux in *Le Figaro littéraire* in June 1934. In addition to his travels and his love-affairs, all his energies were occupied by the composition of his second novel, *Mort à crédit*. After the failure of *Voyage* to win the Prix Goncourt, Céline appears to have momentarily considered abandoning literature. In a letter to Simone Saintu in January 1933, he wrote: 'I shall write nothing ever again – or at least I shall never publish anything again.'[105] Yet, by the summer of 1933 this momentary feeling of pique had passed, and he announced to Robert Denoël: 'I'm about to start my next huge book, *Mort à crédit*, shortly – but I'll need four or five years. It'll have 800 pages at least – *I want it in one single volume*.'[106] A letter to Joseph Garcin of July 1933, however, suggested that the book had already been started: 'I'm getting on with the next monster, another crazy enterprise.'[107] He still harassed both Garcin and John Marks for details of First World war London and appeared until relatively late to have planned the integration of both the war and London into *Mort à crédit*. He wrote to Denoël from Chicago in the summer of 1934 that he would publish the following year the first volume of *Mort à crédit*, dealing with 'Childhood, War, and London'.[108] As the novel progressed, however, the evocation of the narrator's childhood and its complex relationship to the well-being of the mature narrator came to dominate and the London episode was once again shelved, as it had been during the composition of *Voyage*. In fact, the 'war' subject-matter was to be dealt with speedily, albeit unsatisfactorily, in *Casse-pipe*, written in 1936, but the evocation of underworld London had to wait until the Occupation and the two volumes of *Guignol's Band*. Although Céline trimmed his fictional strategy to suit the demands of individual novels, from the very beginning his commitment to a complex transposition of autobiography was obvious, heavily influenced by Proust's *A la recherche du temps perdu*. In fact, in spite of numerous promises to Denoël that the completion of the manuscript was imminent, it was not completed until the beginning of 1936 and did not appear in the bookshops until 12 May 1936.

The composition of the work took its toll: Céline found it difficult to make sufficient progress in Montmartre and spent long periods in Saint-Germain-en-Laye, in the Pavillon Royal. In the autumn of 1935 he stayed in the Hotel Frascati in Le Havre, again to work on the novel and to profit from the attractions of the red-light district of Saint-Vincent.[109] Fortunately, he was able to arrange for his duties at the clinic in the Rue Fanny to be covered by a woman colleague, Dr Howyan.[110] By the beginning of 1936 the novel was still not finished and Céline was ill, claiming to be suffering variously from overwork, heart disease, intestinal problems and weight loss.[111] With the novel finally completed, as with *Voyage au bout de la nuit*, he needed the services of an expert secretary. Jeanne Carayon had emigrated to the United States, but before going had recommended a friend of hers, Marie Canavaggia, who was to produce the manuscripts and oversee the production of all Céline's works, with the exception of *Voyage*, the second volume of *Guignol's Band*, and the last novel, *Rigodon*, published posthumously.[112] As with the production of *Voyage*, Céline delegated a great deal to his secretary, who was not a typist and had considerable responsibilities for both pre- and post-publication arrangements, including research into the details and language of the novels,[113] but showed the same meticulous control over the details. He wrote to Marie Canavaggia from Le Havre on 12 April 1936, in response to a letter from her: 'Little details don't tire me at all! I WANT TO SEE THEM ALL! *The smallest comma obsesses me.*'[114] In the course of the composition of *Mort à crédit*, Céline definitively established a stormy relationship with his publisher Denoël, which was already incipient during the production of *Voyage au bout de la nuit*, but which became explicitly antagonistic and contemptuous. His letter to Denoël of July 1933 announcing the beginning of *Mort à crédit* contained a scathing attack on Bernard Steele: 'I sent Steele a letter really dressing him down over the accounts – He disgusts me. For three days now I've been asking him for two copies of *Voyage* which I need and I haven't received a thing,'[115] and concluded menacingly: 'You will need to draw up a new contract for me – I'll tell you later what I want.' The relationship between Céline and Denoël et

Steele proved to be typical of all his dealings with publishers. With an obsessive concern for accounts and percentages, he remained convinced all his life that his publishers: Denoël, Charles Frémanger or Gallimard, were trying to swindle him, a conjuncture of paranoia and avarice. Announcing the appearance of *Mort à crédit* in eight months' time, he spells out his demands: 'I assure you it's absolutely top quality. But I'm waiting for that letter from you. 12 percent from 1 to 20,000. 15 percent from 20 to 40,000. 18 percent over 40,000. All translations and adaptations to belong *solely to me*. Send the letter to Le Havre. If not, kiss *Mort à crédit* goodbye.'[116]

In fact, in the course of the long composition of *Mort à crédit*, Céline published only two significant texts, both in 1933. Denoël, anxious to maintain the momentum established by *Voyage au bout de la nuit*, brought out *L'Eglise* in the 'Loin des foules' collection on 26 September, with the blatantly commercial advertising band: 'In this astonishing drama, which no theatre dare produce, we see once again the savage spirit and epic inspiration of *Voyage au bout de la nuit*.'[117] The fact that no theatre had wanted to produce the play is thus transformed into an act of intriguing censorship. Céline had refused to have his photograph on the cover and instead opted for the famous nineteenth-century death mask, supposedly of an anonymous drowned working-girl, the 'Inconnue de la Seine'. As with the later illustrations for *Bagatelles pour un massacre* and *L'Ecole des cadavres*, this image is an experiment in allusiveness in that it does not immediately relate to the content of the text. In the same way that the illustrations for the pamphlets, often taken from the popular general-knowledge magazine *Je sais tout*, build up a pattern of belle époque and 1920s prejudice, the 'Inconnue de la Seine' is the portrait, above all, of a beautiful victim.

Reactions to the play were varied, and by no means uniformly unfavourable. Although Jean Prévost, in *Notre Temps*, dismissed *L'Eglise* as an *Ubu Roi* without the wit, René Lalou, in *L'Ecole libératrice*, and Pierre-Aimé Touchard, in *Esprit*, praised the text.[118] What is interesting about reactions to the play, however, is that, in spite of Denoël's drawing attention to the League of Nations episode in *Le Rempart*,[119] the anti-Semitism of the tableau did not arouse very much protest. Prévost, admittedly, referred to it, but not in very harsh terms: 'In Monsieur Céline's League of Nations, every director of arbitration services . . . *every one of them a 45-year-old Jew* – seems to me to have been born in the popular imagination at the very beginning of the Dreyfus Affair,'[120] while Céline's friend Ramon Fernandez, who had not yet moved to the extreme Right, mused in the left-wing *Marianne* that the play 'contains some singular surprises, most notable of which is the concept that the League of Nations is run by Jews, a theory which M. Céline shares with the Action Française and M. Hitler'.[121] As Alméras comments, '*L'Eglise* does not constitute an ideological break for Céline's contemporaries':[122] press coverage was largely favourable and even the left-leaning satirical *Le Canard enchaîné* greatly appreciated the third act, with Moïse, Mosaïc and Yudenzweck dominating the League. He concludes that 'there is a solid tradition of left-wing anti-Semitism.'[123] It is this which would account for the confused reactions on the left to the publication of *Bagatelles* and *L'Ecole des cadavres*. One person was not fooled. As we have seen, all contact between Céline and his friend and protector Ludwig Rajchmann ceased with the publication of *L'Eglise*, which may be interpreted as either an act of gross ingratitude on Céline's part or a more complicated failure to perceive the consequences of his actions, like his myriad proposals of marriage after the departure of Elizabeth Craig, his tormenting of Marcel Aymé or the publication itself of the anti-Semitic pamphlets.

The other major publication, short as it is, between the two novels was Céline's 'Hommage à Zola', the annual Zola lecture delivered in Médan on 1 October 1933. The invitation was in itself a considerable honour, though one which perpetuated a confusion between the style of *Voyage au bout de la nuit* and Naturalism. Céline himself complained to Evelyne Pollet that he 'did not like Zola at all'[124] and that he was only giving the address to please Lucien Descaves and his friends. Notwithstanding his reservations, however, he performed extremely well. Dressed, as we have seen, in an elegant suit, leaning nonchalantly against the doorway, he used the oratorical skills learnt while working for the Rockefeller Foundation to deliver a lecture which visiting journalists acclaimed. *Le Charivari* reported the reaction of one journalist: 'Céline has missed his vocation: he should have gone into the theatre, but as an actor.'[125] Nor does Céline's behaviour at the banquet following the lecture coincide with the image of the Dostoievskian prophet: 'We ate well, but the wine was not good,'[126] he announced on leaving, an intriguing reflection on his alleged teetotalism. In other words, alongside the death-obsessed writer, who attended a public execution just a fortnight later on the Boulevard Arago,[127] there was also a convivial, sociable and self-confident man.

The real significance of the 'Hommage à Zola', published later in the *Bulletin de la Société des Amis d'Emile Zola*, lies in its claim for the necessity of Modernism. Critics have been wrong to dismiss out of hand possible similarities between Zola and Céline, since in some crucial ways they can be seen as having the same aims. *Mort à crédit*, for example, like the novels in the *Rougon-Macquart* cycle, is exploring a real social milieu, geographically and chronologically confined, driven by strict economic laws and processes which impinge upon the psychology of its members. Like Zola's world, that of *Mort à crédit* possesses its own language, faithfully transcribed. At this point, however, Céline is painfully aware of the divide which separates him from Zola: not that Zola's model must be rejected, but that it is no longer attainable. The ambition to *tell the truth*, central to the Naturalist project, is no longer possible, and this for two reasons. In the first place, in the modern era, the truth is simply politically unpalatable: 'We have reached the end of twenty centuries of civilization, and yet no regime could resist two months of truth. I mean Marxist society as well as our bourgeois or fascist societies.'[128] Secondly, the Pasteurian faith in science on which Naturalism was predicated can no longer be retained, hence the savage satire on the Institut Pasteur as the Institut Bioduret-Joseph in *Voyage au bout de la nuit*. Instead, the rational, quantifiable world of the nineteenth century has been replaced by one which is post-Freudian, ruled by the death-wish and the unconscious. The creative writer must take refuge, not in social statistics, but in 'symbols and dreams! All transferences which the law does not reach, or at least not yet. For it is in symbols and dreams that we spend nine-tenths of our lives, since nine-tenths of our existence, of our living pleasure, are either unknown to us or forbidden.'[129] The generosity of spirit and confidence of Naturalism are now denied forever, for political and scientific reasons, and with them goes a huge artistic dignity, what Céline terms 'the great movements of the soul.'[130] Yet, beyond Zola, in the confines of the French inter-war years, Céline could still envisage the possibility of tragedy, but in a Modernist mode: 'If our music has turned tragic, it is because it has its reasons. Words today, like our music, go further than in Zola's day. Nowadays, we work through sensitivity and no longer through analysis, in a word, "from within". Our words go right to the instincts and touch them sometimes, but at the same time we have learnt that that is where our power stops, and forever.'[131] By recognizing the impossibility of 'truth' and analysis, the key weapons of Naturalism, Céline makes a fervent plea for Modernist aesthetics based upon 'symbols and dreams' and the primacy of the literary language. It is for this reason that, within his work and within the history of European Modernism, the address on Zola is a key text.

In the long and arduous composition of *Mort à crédit* and against the background of his tempestuous personal life, Céline was sustained by deepening roots in the Montmartre community. His circle of acquaintances on the Butte was enlarged by his meeting with figures such as the cartoonist Ralph Soupault, who was to become one of the pillars of *Je suis partout*; the playwright René Fauchois; the cabaret singer Max Revol; the painter Dignimont; the film actor and stunt man Pierre Labric, 'mayor of the free Montmartre Commune from 1929 to 1972',[132] in addition to occasional visitors like the artists Vlaminck, Dunoyer de Segonzac, Derain and Dufy, the Comédie Française star Marie Bell, with whom Céline was to maintain close relations until after the War, Damia and Florence Gould.

In Céline's Montmartre circle there were three key inner figures: Marcel Aymé, the actor Robert Le Vigan and the painter Gen Paul. Aymé's success with *La Jument verte* in 1933, although it type-cast him as a writer of ribald peasant novels, made him sufficiently well-off to become a full-time professional writer. Mostly silent and inscrutable behind dark glasses, he was a close friend of Céline's and remained unfailingly loyal, even if Céline did accuse him in an early version of *Féerie pour une autre fois* of having betrayed him by caricaturing his anti-Semitism during the Occupation in the short stories 'En attendant', in *Le Passe-muraille* and in 'Avenue Junot'.[133] Not that his loyalty protected him from Céline's bullying and ill-temper. As Lucette Almansor recalled to Frédéric Vitoux:

Louis would say very unpleasant things to him. He needed to. He had to have someone to bawl out. Marcel kept silent. He listened to Louis talk. Céline would light into him, like he did with the Jews, like Marcel was his whipping boy. He'd say to him: 'You're a filthy pig' and the like. Overhearing him, I'd ask: 'Why did you call him all those names?' He'd answer: 'Because he doesn't say a word and he knows very well that he has skeletons in his closet!' It was childish. Marcel would stay away for a couple of weeks. Louis would phone him and say: 'Why don't you come over?' Marcel Aymé understood Louis, that's why he put up with it all. He loved him. Céline often abused people.[134]

Another figure who remained a close friend of Céline's, throughout the Occupation, in Sigmaringen and finally in exile in Argentina, was the film actor Robert Le Vigan. Born as Robert Coquillaud, the son of a vet, in 1900, Le Vigan had been a highly successful stage actor, working for Gaston Baty and Louis Jouvet before going into the cinema with the onset of the talkies. Throughout the 1930s he worked with most of France's leading directors, particularly Julien Duvivier (*Maria Chapdeleine, Golgotha*, in which he played Christ, and the screen version of Mac Orlan's *La Bandera*) and Jean Renoir (in *Madame Bovary*, in which he played the moneylender Lheureux, and *Les Bas-fonds*). He also worked with Christian-Jacque and Henri Jeanson. Le Vigan, who was himself increasingly unstable psychologically, specialized in roles which took him to the very limit of sanity: one of his final and most memorable parts was that of that of the mad colonial soldier in Jacques Becker's *Goupi-Mains rouges* of 1943. Le Vigan would sit motionless and silent at gatherings in Gen Paul's studio, but it is clear that he was totally subjugated by Céline, whom he subsequently blamed for his paranoia.[135] As if to corroborate this, Céline himself turned Le Vigan into a fictional character, Le Vigan/La Vigue, in the *D'un château l'autre* trilogy, depriving him further of any psychological autonomy.

In addition to other meeting-places, like the Café Junot, Chez Pomme, Chez Canarie in the Rue Tholozé, or Chez Michou, Au Rêve and the Restaurant Manière in the Rue Caulaincourt,[136] the place where this Montmartre clan assembled, mostly on Sunday mornings, was the studio in the Avenue Junot of the painter Gen Paul.[137] Eugène Paul, who figures in Céline's work from 1937 onwards, either as the 'Popaul' of the pamphlets, which caused him some embarrassment, or the 'Jules' of *Féerie pour une autre fois*, was born on 2 July 1895, in a popular and Bohemian Parisian milieu. During the war he was wounded in the knee, which led to the amputation of his right leg. Afterwards, he became friendly with Utrillo and Juan Gris, learnt to paint with no previous training and established himself as a Montmartre 'character', drinking copiously and playing the trombone. His ad hoc band, the 'Chignole', paraded through Montmartre after the Liberation, to the irritation of most of its inhabitants, as a gesture of defiance at what Gen Paul took to be his sufferings from the *Epuration*, even though, as Gibault reminds us, his sales of paintings continued unabated.[138] Céline and Gen Paul had a close relationship, stemming from their shared upbringing in Paris, their experience of the First World War and their similar sexual proclivities. It was on a visit to Blanche d'Alessandri's dance studio on the Rue Henri-Monnier in November or December 1935 with Gen Paul that Céline first saw the dancer Lucette Almansor, with whom he was to spend the rest of his life.

After the Liberation, feeling put at risk by Céline's allusions to him in his pamphlets and wartime writings, Gen Paul was at pains to denigrate the writer, attacking his alleged stinginess, his sexual preferences for voyeurism and paedophilia, and disgusting habits like telling repulsive stories or carrying around in his pockets lumps of cheese, even Roquefort, which he would nibble during conversations.[139] While some of these claims may be discounted as the charges of a disaffected former friend, some of them ring true and coincide with a marked and obvious loss of self-esteem as the Occupation approached.

What is important about Céline's adoption of Montmartre as a cultural base is that it provided him with an artistic community which was, as we have seen, both politically anti-republican and reactionary and essentially non-intellectual. Although Céline would make forays into the Left Bank, he was essentially a Right-Bank man, and his friends were either fantastic writers, like Aymé, or actors and painters. It was from such a base that he was able to construct a literature which was resolutely non-abstract and non-philosophical. Although his hatred for Sartre cumulated with the perceived betrayal of *Portrait de l'antisémite*, to which he riposted with 'L'Agité de la bocale', the antagonism between the Montmartre bohemian and the 'Normalien' went back a long way, in spite of Sartre's use of the quotation from *L'Eglise* as the motto for *La Nausée*: 'C'est un garçon sans importance collective. C'est tout juste un individu.'

The period between the publication of Céline's first two novels had been highly charged. He became a relatively famous and wealthy writer, no longer dependent upon his medical practice for survival, but finding it useful as an image. He frequented famous figures in the worlds of literature, theatre, cinema and painting, even coming close to important politicians, in a way which would have seemed impossible prior to 1932. He became a *rentier* and an international traveller, a well-dressed, even suave figure at concerts or on Atlantic liners. He had a close circle of bohemian friends in the studios and cafés of Montmartre. At the same time, his personal life had been through a crisis. His companion since 1927, Elizabeth Craig, had broken with him in 1934 and, while on one level she was easily replaced, there was a frenetic and independent aspect of his personality in this period which was not entirely wholesome. It was not until the relationship with Lucette Almansor began in 1936 that some emotional stability would re-enter his life. Politically, all seemed to be quiet on the Western Front: he was not exercised by the great crises of the 1930s in the way that he was by those of the 1920s; Hitler seemed to hold no more temptation than Stalin, possibly less; the anarchist remained detached, albeit with a constant, but hardly dramatic, trickle of anti-Semitism. The main concern was literature: the completion, and then publication, of *Mort à crédit* – three years invested in solid work to produce what is undoubtedly his greatest novel. Yet the reaction of the public was to prove crucial to his subsequent development and course of action.

8

1936

I *MORT À CRÉDIT*

Céline's second novel is not merely the finest work he produced, it is also, together with Proust's *A la recherche du temps perdu* to which it owes so much, France's major fictional contribution to European Modernism. For the first time, there appears in all its inventiveness and complexity Céline's mature style: that careful blend of exclamation and the replacement of conjunctions and subordinate clauses by three dots which he was to refine throughout the rest of his career. This was the famous 'telegraphic' style which, in the introduction to *Guignol's Band*, he identified as the quintessence of Modernism: 'Jazz overthrew the waltz. Impressionism killed off "faux-jour", you'll write "telegraphically" or you won't write at all.'[1] In its most extreme form, it conveys perfectly the delirium and emotion of the narrator, as in the scene of the assault on the father:

> He comes back to breathe into my nostrils, more insults . . . still more . . . I too felt something rising in me . . . What with the heat . . . I passed both hands over my face . . . Suddenly I saw everything oddly! . . . I couldn't see at all . . . I just leapt at him . . . I was on him! . . . I lifted up his typewriter, the heavy, weighty machine . . . I lifted it right up in the air . . . And bang! . . . just like that, bang! . . . I smashed it into his face! . . . He couldn't push it away! . . . He fell over under the force of the blow, everything fell backwards . . .[2]

In part, this style was derived from the Communard writer Jules Vallès, whose novel *Le Bachelier*, the second volume of the *Jacques Vingtras* trilogy, Céline cites in his correspondence with his American publisher,[3] and which he praised to the Abbé Mugnier in April 1934: 'At table, Céline made a great eulogy to Jules Vallès. The end of *Le Bachelier*, he said, is splendid. It's a stroke of delirium. Never has anything been done better.'[4] In fact, *Mort à crédit* itself is more obviously indebted to the first volume, *L'Enfant*, a first-person narration of a persecuted child, as it is also to other novels of child-abuse, notably Renard's *Poil-de-carotte*.[5] What Céline is careful to do, however, as he does in *Voyage au bout de la nuit*, is to accentuate and valorize the 'petite musique' by adding a counterpoint in a formal register. Not only is the 'Legend of King Krogold' the mythologized account of Ferdinand's psychodrama, its mock-epic style is the language of reason from which the narrator and his father are exiled:

> The tumult of the battle grows faint with the last glows of the daylight . . . In the distance disappear the last of King Krogold's guards . . . In the dusk, there rise the death-rattles from the destruction of an entire army . . . Victors and vanquished alike give up the ghost as they can . . . The silence muffles both cries and death-rattles, increasingly faint and isolated . . . Crushed beneath a pile of soldiers, Gwendor the Magnificent is still losing blood . . . At dawn, death is before him. 'Have you understood, Gwendor?' 'I have understood, O Death! I understood from the beginning of this day . . .'[6]

Like the anarchist prayer at the beginning of *Voyage au bout de la nuit*, the Krogold legend serves to identify both the conscious and artificial nature of the 'petite musique', however much it is inspired by the rhythms of popular speech, and to emphasize the basic thematic concerns of the novel in betrayal and vengeance.

At the same time, again like the anarchist prayer, it introduces, through the 'gold' of Krogold, an essential socio-economic component of the novel. For *Mort à crédit*, like the Dickensian texts on which it is partly modelled, is rooted in an unusually precise historical and economic reality. The narrator Ferdinand is brought up in the Passage des Bérésinas in central Paris with a father who is an insurance clerk and a mother who sells fine lace. The father, Auguste, like Jacques Vingtras' father in *L'Enfant*, is a *bachelier*: he has passed the *baccalauréat*, once a prestigious examination, but now over-taken by the inflation of qualifications so that it is virtually useless on the job market. Auguste cannot rise above the position of junior clerk, his position constantly and increasingly undermined by a new intake of university graduates who torment him. His pathetic attempts to keep up with modernity lead to his purchase of a typewriter, which is, ironically, the weapon Ferdinand chooses in his attempt to murder him. The mother, Clémence, has a more subtle social status: as an independent shopkeeper, she commissions the lace goods and reproduction furniture which she sells from traditional artisans, and is thus superior to them. This spurious superiority and fragile status as a member of the petite-bourgeoisie, and not the working class, is as vulnerable as Auguste's empty prestige as a *bachelier*. The novel is about remorseless social change, the lingering death announced by the title. The artisans from whom Clémence buys her wares are driven out of central Paris by gentrification and rising prices. She herself cannot read the rapid changes in fashion, an example of the novel's obsession with time, and she cannot keep up with the newly dominant department stores, for whom she is forced to work. Auguste is the embodiment of the changes affecting Parisian white-collar workers at the turn of the century. Read as a social history, therefore, *Mort à crédit* is a fascinatingly accurate account of the traditional artisanal quarters of inner Paris during the belle époque and the inexorable decline of their natural population. In the same way that *Voyage au bout de la nuit* offers a hallucinatory vision of the horrors of the Western world after the First World War, *Mort à crédit* charts the extinction of the belle époque and the disappearance of its most faithful, if deluded, inhabitants, the petite-bourgeoisie, squeezed out between the dominant bourgeoisie and the rising proletariat. It is deeply fitting that Ferdinand, when asked his name by the policeman investigating the death of Courtial des Pereires, can only answer: 'Ferdinand. Born in Courbevoie.'[7] The petite-bourgeoisie have no future and therefore no surname.

At the same time, the novel is very well aware of the economic factors and symbolism instrumental in this decline. The 'crédit' in the title does not simply signify a long-drawn-out death, the 'death on the instalment plan' of its English version: it points to the very heart of the economic process which isolates and excludes Ferdinand's class. Small shopkeepers in France during the belle époque, and much later, used to display the popular Epinal print *Crédit est mort. Les mauvais payeurs l'ont tué* ('Credit is dead: bad debtors have killed him'). The problem for Ferdinand's family and his whole class is that, as shopkeepers, they are unable, unlike the department stores, to offer credit and hence increase their trade, and that, as individuals, they are prevented by their outdated morality from benefiting from the credit system as customers. They fall outside the economic system and hence must disappear. It is a rich and conscious irony of the novel that it should be Ferdinand, through the loss of the Çakya-Mouni gold ornament, who forces his parents to break the habit of a lifetime and pay Gorloge back in instalments.

The exclusion, however, also works on a symbolic level, that of the gold inherent in the name of King Krogold, and of the ubiquitous presence of the phoneme 'or' throughout the novel, in the title *Mort à crédit* and the names Gwendor and Nora Merrywin. If gold was the basis of the economy during the belle époque, the family and their class have none: not only are they excluded from the system, they literally lack 'credit', with no economic purchase but also no credibility. It is for this reason that Ferdinand spends the entire novel protesting his innocence and is never believed. Yet, if the family's ills in the belle époque stem from their exclusion from an economic system based upon the gold standard, the society in which the mature narrator finds himself in the 1930s suffers precisely from that same commitment to an outworn belief as the one that destroys his parents. France's economic crisis of the 1930s was due, as we have seen, in very large part to a refusal to abandon the gold standard when the rest of the world's major economies had done so, and the consequences were not just unemployment but the culmination of the process of decline of the petite-bourgeoisie. The paranoid hallucination of the mature narrator, in pursuit of the young girl Mireille who persists in telling stories about him, culminates in a pitched battle on the Place de la Concorde: '25,000 police cleared the Place de la Concorde. We couldn't hold on together. It was too hot. It was smoking. It was Hell.'[8] It would have been impossible for a French reader in 1936 to avoid the allusion to the riots of 6 February 1934 which toppled the Daladier government and which, to a major extent, constituted the last but futile act of protest from a petite-bourgeoise which had received its death-sentence in the belle époque.

If the socio-economic analysis of France in the belle époque is unusually well-informed and unusually acute, part of the richness of *Mort à crédit* lies in the fact that Céline, professionally, is also well aware of the psychological effects of financial crisis. Like Jacques Vingtras' father in *L'Enfant*, Ferdinand's father is driven by humiliation and anxiety to persecute his wife and son. Auguste himself launches into increasingly irrational and uncontrollable tirades, reduced by his frustration on occasion to retreating into the cellar and firing his revolver. His name encapsulates his dilemma: Auguste is the emperor and the tyrant, but also the 'Auguste' is one of the traditional clowns in French circuses. Within this neurotic and typically claustrophobic family unit, the major victim is the son Ferdinand, tortured to such an extent that he exhibits the classic symptoms of uncontrolled excretion and autism, before finally taking his revenge on the father-tormentor in the attack with the typewriter. We have already seen Céline's professional interest during the 1930s in Freud, and also his boast to Garcin that, if Freudianism was in vogue, he could turn it on like a tap. This mixture of genuine awareness and cynicism informs the treatment of the Oedipal theme in *Mort à crédit*. On one level, Céline provides a comic burlesque of the Freudian tragedy: the exaggerated and humorous depictions of Ferdinand's excretion, and the assault on the father, on the head with the typewriter, which may be felt to be too good to be true. At the same time, Céline has created a classic Freudian novel, in which other characters in the narrative reflect the family neurosis and are used to provide solutions to it. When Ferdinand stays in England at Meanwell College, he sidesteps the proprietor, Peter Merrywin, in order to spend his days walking in the grounds with Merrywin's wife, Nora, and the young idiot, Jonkind. This attempt to reorder the family trinity, with Ferdinand as father and Nora as wife, culminates in the confused episode before his return to France, when Nora comes to his bed and then drowns herself. In the same way, the novel provides a succession of alternative father-figures, all designed to neutralize or ameliorate the real father, Auguste: the ubiquitous Uncle Edouard is always available to resolve the conflict and concludes the novel by covering his nephew in layer upon layer of overcoats, just as Ferdinand is covered by layers of memory; the ineffectual and alcoholic Peter Merrywin, who constitutes no barrier to the pursuit of Nora; and Courtial des Pereires, who exhibits the same characteristic as Auguste in fleeing to the cellar each time trouble brews, and whose name Roger-*Marin* contains the father's frustrated ambition to be a seaman, but who is as playful, malleable and inventive as Auguste is threatening.

The most striking reflection of the father is *le roi* Krogold himself. Krogold is the hero of comic-books given to Ferdinand by his beloved grandmother Caroline (whose name itself has connotations of Charle-magne, the founder of the Carolingians) who subsequently forms the basis of the stories that he tells to *le petit* André which lead to his dismissal from Berlope, and the subject of the mature narrator's 'legend' which he reads to his cousin Gustin. Céline himself had planned a 'legend' as part of his programme of writing after *Voyage au bout de la nuit*, but in *Mort à crédit* the transposition of this ambition is more significant. As we have seen, Krogold introduces the theme of gold into the novel, but he also introduces the theme of *chronos*, of time, thus signifying the twin preoccupations of the novel, time and money, *mort* and *crédit*, both, incidentally, located in the father's profession in the insurance industry. This hint of a connection between Krogold and Auguste is made explicit in a reference later in the text to the father's watch: 'Father had a watch too, but his was in gold, a chronometer . . . He counted all the seconds on it right to the end . . . The big hand fascinated him.'[9] Yet, if Krogold is a reflection of Auguste, Krogold is also the supreme avenger of betrayal, the implacable destroyer of the traitor Gwendor. Céline once described *Mort à crédit* to Robert Poulet as 'the drama of bad conscience',[10] which can be read as both the false consciousness of the family and its class and the unresolved guilt of Ferdinand himself. It is essential to the operation of the novel that we realize that the mature narrator is psychologically sick, that he falls into delirium when unable to stifle Mireille's lies about him and that in his hallucinatory state he confuses memories of Auguste and Krogold, conclud-ing with his anguished exclamation to his mother: 'There wasn't a worse shit in the universe!'[11] If the novel, therefore, is the narration of a neurotic relationship between son and father, it is clear that the neurosis remains unresolved for the mature narrator, and may, indeed, be the motivation for the narration itself.

At this point, the reading of the text becomes complex and ambiguous, along the lines of the conundrum which concludes Carroll's *Through the Looking Glass*: did Alice dream the Red King or did the Red King dream Alice? In other words, is *Mort à crédit* the relatively simple Naturalist account of a childhood conflict which has left the mature narrator scarred, or is it the imagined past of a neurotic narrator, constructing a childhood from the elements of his own illness? Or is it a combination of both, in which the mature narrator attempts to exorcize the trauma of the past through liter-ary invention? This ambiguity is compounded by the fact that the novel's referential system is consciously and conspicuously cultural, and not merely psychological or social. The allusions to Freud may well point to a genuine theme of neurosis, but they are also knowing acknowledgements of a fashionable science. Similarly, the early part of the novel, as we have seen, is a clear gesture towards Vallès, while the English episode, set in the

Kentish countryside around Rochester, with its names like 'Merrywin', 'Meanwell College' and 'Hopeful Academy', is a homage to Dickens and also perhaps to that later, Edwardian chronicler of the Home Counties, H. G. Wells. Certainly, Dickens appears to be at the origin, not only of the Meanwell College episode, but also of the Micawber-like character of Courtial des Pereires, while the influence of Wells comes not only from his petit-bourgeois novels of the Edwardian south-east, but also from the science-fiction novels: Courtial recalls the jovial but eccentric inventor of *Tono-Bungay*, while the doomed experiment in Blême-le-Petit with the 'radiotellurique' waves has echoes of *The Food of the Gods*.

The essential referent, however, is Proust, never mentioned, as he is in *Voyage au bout de la nuit*, but omnipresent. *Mort à crédit* is a petit-bourgeois rewriting of *Du côté de chez Swann*, with Krogold and Gwendor playing the role of Golo and Geneviève de Brabant, Grand-mère Caroline in place of Proust's narrator's grandmother, and the openly conflictual family in the Passage instead of the discreet and cloying atmosphere of Combray. In both cases, however, there is a neurotic narrator, unable to resolve the conflicts of the past, to which he attempts to return through a state of half-consciousness. It is a measure of the social divide which separates Ferdinand from Proust's narrator that he should access the past through vomiting and delirium, whereas his earlier counterpart does so from a bedroom likened to a luxury hotel. What unites both protagonists, however, is a common problem in time: the search for an ideal world (cut off in the case of Proust by the First World War, in that of Céline by the 1900 *Exposition Universelle*), which triggered off his childhood narrator's first breakdown and which constituted the unbreachable barrier for the last century, which 'he saw end'.[12] Where Céline and Proust differ so crucially is in their concept of art. For Proust, it remains the sole salvation and the sole way back to the lost world. For Céline, that is no longer an option: the Krogold legend cannot prevent Gustin falling asleep and, as the narrator reflects wryly on the death of his concierge Madame Bérenge, 'all grief comes in letters.'[13] Rather than the Proustian transcendent mission of writing, Céline's narrator proposes one which is simply self-destructive but which has the virtue of achieving an ending – of the novel and of the narrator. Writing of his former patients, he concludes: 'I prefer telling stories. I'll tell such stories that they will come back on purpose to kill me, from the four corners of the world. Then it will be finished and I will be very pleased.'[14]

II REACTIONS

Céline, in one sense at least, was pleased that the novel was finished, not simply because of its inordinate length, but also because he was deeply proud of it, as indicated by the publicity slip which surrounded the volume when it was published on 12 May 1936 and which quoted Johann Sebastian Bach: 'I have put an enormous amount of work into this. Whoever puts in as much work will do as well as I have.'[15] Yet, even before publication there were warning signals that the novel's reception was not going to be as cordial as that of *Voyage au bout de la nuit*. When Robert Denoël first read the manuscript, he was horrified at the apparent obscenity of certain passages and demanded that Céline alter them. Céline refused to make any changes to his text and preferred instead to have the novel appear with blanks where the offending passages had been cut out.[16] Apart from a luxury edition published by Pierre Monnier in 1950, the 'censored' version of *Mort à crédit* was the only one available until Henri Godard's *Pléiade* edition of 1981. Denoël himself launched the same artful pre-publication publicity as he had for *Voyage*, giving puffs for the novel in *Bibliographie de la France* and *Paris-Soir*, where he wrote: 'It has been a long time since French literature has echoed to such sounds . . . *Mort à crédit* is the great book of the period.'[17]

Unfortunately, no one agreed with him, and the novel was roundly attacked from both Right and Left. François Gibault lists a number of critics who, partially at least, welcomed *Mort à crédit*, such as Eugène Marsan, Noël Sabord, Jacques Lejeune, Pierre Scize, Ramon Fernandez, André Gide, Emmanuel Berl and Marcel Arland, but overall the result was a disaster. Predictably, the Right was horrified. *Candide* concluded: 'Clearly, we are dealing with a maniac,'[18] and Brasillach, in *L'Action Française*, expressed a common high-cultural view: 'Books like this, which will be incomprehensible in twenty years' time, seem to me to be the opposite of art.'[19] If the Right was appalled by both the subject-matter and the style, the Left was alienated by Céline's obvious anti-humanism. Whereas *Voyage au bout de la nuit* could be read, possibly erroneously, as a denunciation of war and international capitalism and a celebration of the lone individual, *Mort à crédit* simply appeared as a gratuitous side-swipe at the working class, with left-wing readers failing to make any distinction among 'les petits gens' between petit-bourgeois and proletarians. Paul Nizan, who had already expressed doubts about Céline's nihilism in his review of *Voyage*, thundered in *L'Humanité*: 'In *Voyage* there was an unforgettable denunciation of war and the colonies. Today, Céline is denouncing only the poor and the vanquished.'[20] Even a reader as sympathetic as Elie Faure commented: 'There are some fine passages, but he gets bogged down in shit too much.'[21] Nor was Céline able to mobilize those writers who had so staunchly supported *Voyage*. Lucien Descaves, who had stormed out of the Académie Goncourt in 1932 and to whom *Mort à crédit* was dedicated, remained silent, as did that other defender of the first novel, Léon Daudet, even though Céline begged him to intervene on his behalf.

In fact, the situation was so bad that Denoël himself, most unusually, entered the battle with a pamphlet, *Apologie de Mort à crédit*, in which he attempted to counter the charges of obscenity and set out some of the important issues posed by the novel. Yet even this did not significantly increase sales. Céline attempted to put a brave face on it, writing to John Marks at the end of June: 'After a battle of insults with the critics, *Mort à crédit* has come out victorious, 8000 to 10,000 per day. We'll overtake *Voyage* if things settle down a bit . . . Tell the publishers all this,'[22] and to Herbert F. Jenkins, at Little, Brown, in Boston, on 1 June: 'At present we are selling very well in France. 30,000 (second week). It will probably be the same success as the "Journey" but slowly on account of the political situations.'[23] The main purpose of this was probably to drive up the rates for the English-language edition of the novel. As Alméras comments, Céline's sales-figures are 'pure fantasy'[24] and *Mort à crédit* sold conspicuously less well than *Voyage*, not reaching the magic figure when Céline's royalties would rise to 18 per cent.[25]

This critical rout and relative commercial failure culminated in a curious, but significant, personal attack on Céline in the satirical weekly *Le Merle blanc*. A reader from Biarritz, a M. Etcheverry, challenged the newspaper to publish his opinion of Céline: 'Céline is the darkness, hatred, madness, and ignoble, nauseating cowardice towards life,'[26] and concluded: 'Céline: to be eliminated – first.' Céline replied robustly: 'Whoever wants to kill me is free to do so – absolutely free! I don't have a militia to protect me. I even have a war-wound . . . Oh, I'm not afraid of Etcheverry! For people like that, I've still got a powerful boot up the arse.'[27] Yet Gibault is probably right in identifying the critical and commercial lambasting of *Mort à crédit*, and particularly the Etcheverry attack, as being at the origin of a major personality change on Céline's part. Although the narrator of the novel welcomes the self-destructive possibilities of his narrative, the letter to Etcheverry is the first example of a persecution complex which was to remain with him for the rest of his life.

In fact, Céline should not have been unduly surprised that *Mort à crédit* received such rough treatment. The sequels to phenomenally successful first novels by unknown authors fall victim as often as not to the jealousies and unfulfilled expectations of critics and readers alike and, after the huge publicity surrounding the publication of *Voyage au bout de la nuit*, it is quite understandable that the innovation and refusal to compromise in *Mort à crédit* should make enemies. Nor can Céline have been unaware that both his style and subject-matter were straying into territory which had seen violent literary battles previously. Although he was at pains to distance himself from Zola and Naturalism in the 1933 Médan address, the explicit sexuality, emphasis on excretion and apparently crude vocabulary in *Mort à crédit* laid the novel open to exactly the same charges as those levelled against *La Terre* barely fifty years earlier, leading to the *Manifeste des Cinq* and the break-up of the Naturalist group. Similarly, Céline's evocation of Vallès is by no means either coincidental nor innocent. In modelling the first part of the novel on *L'Enfant*, he can hardly have expected to escape a repetition of the furore after the publication of Vallès' novel in 1879 which followed him to his death. Even in his obituary notice, Brunetière began: 'It is of an evil man that I am writing.'[28] Like Vallès, Céline was seen as insulting that most sacred of French institutions, the family, and moreover, in what was perceived as thinly disguised autobiography, of denigrating his own family, the epitome of subversion and ingratitude. It is unlikely that Céline did not realize just how thin the ice was on which he was skating. Why, otherwise, should he expressly forbid his mother ever to read *Mort à crédit*, a promise she scrupulously honoured? Once again the possibility arises, as it would much more strongly in the anti-Semitic pamphlets, of the work of literature as an agent of the destruction of the author, of literature as suicide. Right from the thesis on Semmelweis, Céline had played games with the reader which could backfire and seriously wound him. On the verge of an unexpected medical career, the errors in *Semmelweis* could do him immense damage; as a courted left-wing novelist, he published *L'Eglise* in 1933, which cut him off both from his friendship with Rajchmann and his lucrative contacts with the League of Nations, and could have threatened his status and popularity as a writer. He was to go on to undermine definitively his left-wing credentials with *Mea culpa* at the end of 1936, and to cut himself off from the Left, without really gaining the confidence of the Right, with the publication of *Bagatelles pour un massacre*. In this process, both the aesthetic difficulty of *Mort à crédit* and its antagonistic subject-matter constitute an important stage.

There was, of course, a further crucial element in the failure of *Mort à crédit*, and one which was to have considerable implications for Céline's subsequent political evolution, the election of the Front Populaire government on the ballots of 26 April and 3 May 1936. The novel appeared just six days after Léon Blum was invited to lead a government made up of Socialists and left-wing Radicals, supported by Communist deputies. While the elections of 1936 saw a minimal shift in votes from Right to Left, the electoral pact between the three major parties in the Front Populaire ensured a major realignment of the parliamentary majority which gave to the Left the greatest parliamentary power they had ever had in the Third Republic and which resulted in the Republic's first Socialist prime minister. This election resulted in a spontaneous wave of strikes aimed at immediately securing major planks of the Front Populaire's electoral programme. These strikes led in their turn to the Matignon Agreements of June 1936 and, more important, a dramatic polarization of domestic politics. The Left debated the possibilities of introducing a full-blooded revolutionary programme, which it finally rejected in favour of parliamentary legitimacy, but in the meantime it celebrated a sea-change in political culture, by which the working population was given crucial welfare benefits such as a 40-hour week, basic trade-union rights and paid holidays. The Right saw its worst fears being realized. The decadence of the Republic had led finally to a Socialist-Communist government, intent on far-reaching social and economic changes and, moreover, led by a Jew. In the Chamber, during the installation of the Blum government on 6 June, Xavier Vallat, a *député* for the Ardèche department and a future Commissaire des Questions Juives under Vichy, declaimed that 'this old Gallo-Roman country was now being governed for the first time by a Jew.' In *L'Action Française*, Maurras vituperated that Blum 'should be shot, but in the back'. The exchange rate of anti-Semitic rhetoric had suddenly risen.

It is hardly surprising that, with the election of the Front Populaire government and the ensuing transformation of the French political culture, a novel which was both aesthetically incomprehensible and whose subject-matter seemed to hark back to a bygone age should have had difficulties in making a mark. In one crucial respect Céline, in carefully following his plan of transposition of elements of his own autobiography, had seriously misjudged his market. The past, and especially periods of the recent past, are fashionable, and indeed accessible, for only a very short time. The late 1940s, as one post-war period replicating another, saw a brief vogue for the culture of the 1920s. Roger Nimier became the Drieu la Rochelle of his era. In the same way, it was the 1920s, which oversaw the continued publication of Proust's *A la recherche du temps perdu*, which invented and consecrated the belle époque. By the 1930s, and particularly the period of the Front Populaire, attention was directed towards the present and the future, and not towards the past. Art Déco had replaced Art Nouveau, and the Exposition of 1937 replaced the Exposition Universelle of 1900 in the popular imagination. *Mort à crédit* did not simply get obscured by the political turbulence of the summer of 1936, as Céline hints in his correspondence, it was also, and wrongly, perceived as belonging to a different era. For a time at least, Céline was a victim of the novel's allegiance, not just to Vallés and Naturalism, but also to Proust.

In fact, 1936 seemed to see the failure of all of Céline's artistic projects: the poor reception of *Mort à crédit*, the difficulties in the composition of his next novel, *Casse-pipe*, based on his military experiences with the '12 Cuir' in Rambouillet, and his inability to have his ballet, *La Naissance d'une fée*, performed. This work, the first of five ballet choreographies written during his career, was the result of Céline's persistent and genuine love of classical dance and further evidence that he was a skilled manipulator of formal French in a dream-like plot and setting. It was further evidence of his debt to Shakespeare's comedies and a more formal example of his devotion to 'féerie'. He was also deeply committed to having his ballet set to music and performed, and he enrolled John Marks to use his influence in London, but to no avail. He approached the Danish ballet-director Barthollin, a friend of Karen Marie Jensen's, who worked at the Ballets de Monte-Carlo, run by René Blum, the brother of Léon Blum, but again without success.[29] As Alméras argues, this failure to have his ballet performed was anguishing and frustrating to Céline, who could only attribute the refusal to perform the work of a major writer to intrigue and betrayal.[30] He was to make a further attempt to have *La Naissance d'une fée* staged during his visit to Leningrad, but already the pattern of rejection had built up sufficiently for him to be able to use it as justification of his new-found anti-Semitism in *Bagatelles pour un massacre*.

As if this was not enough, Céline, as a result of his obsessive and micro-scopic inspection of his accounts, became convinced that Denoël was on the verge of bankruptcy. When Denoël reminded him that his advance royalties outweighed the sales and that, instead of the 23,000 francs Céline had peremptorily demanded, he would receive only 9164, Céline repeated his fears to Ramon Fernandez, who passed them on to Pierre Seligman, who, in his turn, wrote to Gaston Gallimard: 'L.-F. Céline is convinced that Denoël is going to go bust. He is prepared to deal with us on the basis of a monthly salary.'[31] Thus began protracted negotiations for the transfer of Céline to Gallimard which went on until the autum of 1936, after Céline's return from Russia, and which, in spite of Denoël's worsening financial situation and the departure of Bernard Steele in October, failed to materi-alize. Apart from a short piece, 'Secrets dans l'île' in a collection of writing by winners of the Prix Renaudot, *Neuf et une*, in November 1936, Céline was not to become a Gallimard author until the publication of *Féerie pour une autre fois* in 1952.

In the meantime, he needed a holiday. As was the case with the publica-tion of *Voyage au bout de la nuit*, he left France as soon as *Mort à crédit* appeared, making his unsuccessful visit to Erika Irrgang in Cambridge and following news of the novel's reception through correspondence with Marie Cannavaggia. In August, he set off on a sea-voyage which would take him to Denmark, Finland and, finally, the Soviet Union.

III RUSSIA

The history of the journeys of Western visitors to the Soviet Union in the inter-war years is well-documented, particularly by Fred Kupferman, Paul Gerbod and David Caute.[32] The American left-wing journalist Lincoln Steffens was one of the first Western sympathizers to visit post-revolutionary Russia, and his enthusiastic response: 'I have been over to see the future, and it works!' was the cue for literally hundreds of Western politicians, trade unionists, journalists, intellectuals and artists to follow him to see if he was right. And no country in the West was more interested in the Soviet Union than France: Kupferman lists 125 first-hand accounts of journeys to Russia in the inter-war years, not counting the novels or short stories inspired by the Soviet experience.[33] Most of these accounts were by un-known figures – often peasant organizers or minor trade unionists – who travelled at the expense of the Soviet Union and at its invitation. At the same time, the Russians were keen to attract prestigious writers and intellec-tuals who, if won over, could become valuable allies in the conflict both with the bourgeois state and its supreme example, Fascism. In this way, some of France's best-known writers, and by no means only those sympa-thetic to the Left, made the journey eastwards: Vitoux lists Romain Rolland, Henri Béraud, Georges Duhamel and Henri Barbusse as being among the first, with Béraud certainly an improbable sympathizer, followed by Malraux, Marc Chadourne, Roland Dorgelès and André Chamson.[34] Sometimes, there was the occasion for a mass visit, such as the 1934 Soviet Writers' Congress (which brought together a large number of Western writers and intellectuals and where, for the most part, they were roundly denounced as bourgeois by Gorki), or the famous delegation in the summer of 1936 led by Gide and including Louis Guilloux, the publisher Schiffrin and Céline's friend Eugène Dabit, who was to die of typhoid in Sebastopol on 21 August.

For left-wing personalities, these first contacts with the reality of Soviet society often placed considerable strain upon their loyalty and in many cases led to apostasy. To some extent, this was due to exaggerated aspirations. As Gerbod comments, the Russian Revolution

> took on a symbolic value for the 'capitalist' West: it was the dazzling signal for the emancipation of the struggling masses led by the Bolshevik elite; it was the starting-point for a new era, that of the Socialist City; it was the warning sign of a much greater revolution, destined to inevitably destroy those absolutist systems still operating in the world. This visionary optimism looked back to the example of France in 1793 and the dictatorship of the 'Mountain'.[35]

Unsurprisingly, some of the most fervent enthusiasts were disappointed by the reality. Gerbod refers to ex-communists, 'who saw the resurrection of the master-plan according to which the new state had simply assimilated the imperialist ambitions of the czarist regime, together with its bureaucratic and police methods,'[36] and Kupferman quotes from an otherwise favourable account by Emile Schreiber, the founder of *Echos*: 'the approval granted to Stalinist Russia consists for some commentators in discovering that the Soviet Union is really a bourgeois society.'[37] To these two accusations, which Céline was to take up in *Mea culpa* and *Bagatelles pour un massacre*, were added others, to which, again, Céline was to subscribe: the poverty of the regime, its inadequacies in wages and living conditions, and the inequality, by which the sole beneficiaries were the Party officials.[38] What is interesting, in the light of Céline's later criticism, is that many commentators saw in Soviet Russia a replica of capitalist society, in which the bureaucrat, but especially the engineer, held privileged positions, to the extent that there was no distinction between the West's assembly-line and time-and-motion techniques and what was going on in the industries of the Socialist City. Although a sympathetic reporter like Georges Friedmann could find clear water, though not entirely convincingly, between East and West ('there is a fundamental contrast between the Taylorism of the capitalist factory, where agreement has to be bought by bonuses and the brutal threat of dismissal, and the socialist example'),[39] Kupferman found examples of visitors 'who thought they could detect a similarity between the Bedaux System, denounced by the Communists in the West, and Stakhanovitism'.[40] All of which led the admittedly unsympathetic Alfred

Fabre-Luce to conclude that the USSR was 'an America which has not succeeded'.[41] Gide's famous and commercially successful *Retour d'URSS* was merely one of a succession of denunciations of Russia based on first-time visits, which came to constitute a minor polemical genre of the 1930s and in which Céline's own *Mea culpa* was to play an important part.

The origins, and indeed the details, of Céline's own journey to Russia are not totally clear, though the ostensible reason was, typically, financial: to collect the Soviet royalties from the Russian translation of *Voyage au bout de la nuit*. Soon after *Voyage* had appeared, Aragon and Elsa Triolet, convinced that Céline was on the Left, had persuaded the Soviet authorities to have the novel translated. Officially, the translator was Triolet herself, though she recognized that her text had been heavily 'revised', and Gibault contends that the translation was undertaken by a Soviet translator, with Triolet's role reduced to that of supplying details on French slang.[42] What is incontrovertible is that when the novel appeared in Moscow in 1934, it had only 296 pages in large print, compared with the 500 or so in the French edition. When he discovered this, Céline was furious and held both Aragon and Elsa Triolet responsible, the probable cause of their break.[43] The Soviet edition appeared with a highly laudatory preface from Ivan Anissimov, who praised it as 'a gigantic fresco of contemporary life',[44] and the novel sold extremely well, with three editions in Russian and an edition of 10,000 copies in 1935 in Ukrainian.[45] It also received excellent reviews and made a considerable impact on Soviet intellectuals.[46] The problem was that, in spite of the critical and especially commercial success of *Voyage* in Russia, Soviet law did not permit the export of royalties, which had to be spent in the country. Céline's decision to go to Russia, therefore, was based not merely on a wish to see for himself what the 'land of the Soviets' was like, but also on a desire to get his hands on the money owing to him. As he wrote to Cillie Pam, as he was travelling to Russia: 'I'm en route for Finland and Moscow . . . I'm going to Moscow to get a bit of money, if possible.'[47] This unusual mission had one other effect, however, in that it enabled Céline subsequently to portray himself as holier than his fellow-visitors: those who had been invited by the Soviets had had their expenses paid for, with the implication that their account was not wholly disinterested, whilst he, Céline, had borne all of his own expenses, and consequently his report was entirely reliable.[48] There is also an uncanny echo of Bardamu's experience on the *Amiral Bragueton*, in which all his misfortunes stemmed from being the 'sole paying passenger of the journey'.[49]

According to Vitoux, Céline had wished to take Lucette Almansor, who was not yet living with him in the Rue Lepic, but was already very close to him, as his travelling companion. As we have seen before, Céline enjoyed travelling with women. The couple were not married, however, and Soviet law did not permit them to share the same hotel room, a shadow of that same Soviet puritanism which was to strike Gide so forcibly in its treatment of homosexuality. He left Le Havre alone, therefore, towards the end of August on the SS *Polaris*, bound for Helsinki and Leningrad, stopping off in

Copenhagen long enough to see Karen Marie Jensen and deposit 11 kilos of gold in a Danish bank, part of the flight of gold reserves from France which the Front Populaire government was unable to stem. It was the presence of his gold in Denmark, which he had wrongly calculated as remaining neutral throughout the imminent world war, which was to act as a beacon for Céline throughout the Occupation and which led him into exile in 1945.

He arrived in Leningrad towards the beginning of September and stayed at the Evropeiskaya Hotel, described by Gibault as being the best in the city,[50] but which Céline dismissed later in *Bagatelles* as being 'second class, cockroaches and waterbugs on every floor' and costing the equivalent of 250 francs a day.[51] Despite the intention stated in his letter to Cillie Pam to go to Moscow, it is more than likely that he never left the Leningrad area and that he stayed in the Evropeiskaya until his departure, on the *Meknès*, on 21 September, arriving back in Le Havre four days later on the 25th.

Céline's recorded impressions of his stay in Leningrad are few in number in any case and mainly to be found in *Mea culpa* and, especially, *Bagatelles*. As such, they need to be treated with some caution, since they fulfil a polemical and, in the latter, quasi-fictional purpose. His reaction appears to have not been entirely negative, however. The city itself provides one of the most lyrical passages in *Bagatelles*:

> Just try to imagine . . . the Champs-Elysées . . . but now, four times as wide and flooded with pale water . . . the Neva . . . it stretches past . . . keeps on going . . . towards the pallid expanse . . . the sky . . . the sea . . . ever further . . . the estuary at the very end . . . goes on forever . . . the sea rising toward us . . . toward the city . . . the sea holds the city in its hand! . . . diaphanous, fantastical, extended . . . at arm's length . . . along all the banks . . . the whole city, a strong arm . . . palaces . . . more palaces . . . Hard rectangles . . . domed . . . marble . . . enormous hard gemstones . . . at the pale water's edge . . . To the left, a little canal, quite black . . . throwing itself there . . . against the colossus of the Admiralty, every slab a golden one . . . bearing a shimmering figurehead all in gold.'[52]

It is interesting, incidentally, that this description of Peter the Great's city should begin, as it were, where *Voyage*, with its canal, river, estuary and sea, leaves off, as if it is part of that 'féerie' which lies beyond language. At the same time, in *Bagatelles*, he writes lovingly of the Marinski (now Kirov) Theatre, where he claims to have seen Tchaikovsky's *Queen of Spades*, starring the ballerina Ulanova and in which, as a connoisseur, he appreciated the impeccable technique, especially in the 'pas de quatre'.[53] In his reminiscences of the theatre in the pamphlet, the ballet *La Naissance d'une fée* makes a further appearance, with the narrator attempting to get the director of the Marinski to perform it, only to be told that it was not sufficiently 'sozial'. If *Bagatelles* is to be believed, he also fell in love with his official guide and interpreter Natalie, who took him one afternoon to see the French tennis star Cochet play the Soviet champion Kudriakh, though, as

Vitoux comments, his claims to Karen Marie Jensen and Lucette Almansor that he succeeded in seducing her and that she wished to marry him, if only to leave the Soviet Union, need to be read as characteristic bravado.[54]

In general, however, he was appalled by his initiation into Soviet society. A postcard sent on 4 September to Jean Bonvilliers reads: 'Shit! If this is the future we had better just enjoy our miserable condition. What horror! In comparison, life in Gonesse takes on a certain charm!'[55] and the letters he wrote on his return show the same violent antipathy. To John Marks, on 25 September, he commented: 'I've just got back from Russia after a truly disgusting journey. What an awful country!';[56] to Cillie Pam: 'I've returned from Russia. What a horrible place! What an ignoble trick! What a sordid stupid story! It's all grotesque, theoretical and criminal!';[57] and to Karen Marie Jensen: 'I've been in Leningrad for a month. It's all abject, terrible, unbelievably dirty. You have to go there to believe it. It's horrible. dirty, poor – hideous. A prison of larvae. It's all police, bureaucracy and filthy chaos. It's all bluff and tyranny.'[58] And Robert Le Vigan's wife, interviewed many years later, recalls Céline's visit to Russia as having a profound effect on his and her husband's political orientation: 'At the beginning, he [Le Vigan] went with Céline and Gen Paul to political meetings. They put red scarves on round their necks. But when Céline came back from Russia, he told us: "Stop! We're going the wrong way!"'[59]

There are few details in any of his writing as to what caused this impression specifically, though *Bagatelles* records the outrage of the narrator Ferdinand at the insults heaped upon the dead czar during a visit to the Summer Palace at Tsarskoie-Tselo,[60] and his dismay as a doctor at the state of a hospital for venereal diseases.[61] Once again, the professional concern with standards of public health is a touchstone for Céline's vestigial political aspirations, and the modest optimism regarding a 'socialist or communist state formula' expressed in the 'Mémoire pour le cours des hautes études' in 1932[62] appears to have foundered definitively during the visit to Leningrad.

IV MEA CULPA

On his return from Russia, Céline stayed at the Hotel Frascati in Le Havre, where he discovered further evidence of Denoël's financial difficulties: a cheque for 35,977 francs signed on 31 July had been returned unpaid by the bank on 8 September.[63] In spite of Gallimard's attempts to poach his star author, Denoël held firm and was unusually forthright in his dealing with Céline: he informed him of Steele's resignation, and that the company not only owed 50,000 francs in taxes, but was also mortgaged for 200,000 francs.[64] In this situation, Céline had no choice: he was bound by his contract to Denoël, and if he did not grant his publisher time to refloat, then 'his books would be sold off at 80 francs a tonne.'[65] Céline backed down, but profited from the situation by imposing a new contract on Denoël. Henceforth, he would receive a royalty of 18 per cent on all copies sold, starting with a short pamphlet on Russia, *Mea culpa*, to be published together with *La Vie et l'oeuvre de Philippe-Ignace Semmelweis*, presumably to make up the weight.

In fact, as Alméras comments, Céline did well out of the deal: his royalties for the year 1936 were over 88,000 francs, more than four times his salary from Clichy.[66] He was also richly, and unexpectedly, rewarded by *Mea culpa*. Denoël appears to have been fairly pessimistic as to the pamphlet's sales, ordering an initial print-run of only 5000, though this was probably due more to financial prudence in a delicate situation. Céline, however, may have been conscious of the phenomenal success of Gide's *Retour de l'URSS*, published on 30 October 1936, which sold 146,300 copies in one year, going through nine printings, a success, incidentally, not repeated with his *Retouches à mon retour d'URSS*.[67] As it was, *Mea culpa*, in spite of Gibault's and Vitoux's assertion that it passed virtually unnoticed, sold well and had an excellent press, earning 9000 francs in royalties in its first two months.[68] While this may not have been the 'enormous success' that Céline announced to Karen Marie Jensen,[69] Philippe Alméras is surely right in his conclusion that it indicated to Céline that pamphlets could sell as well as fiction and that it thus paved the way to *Bagatelles pour un massacre*.[70]

It would not be accurate to conclude, as some critics have, that with *Mea culpa* Céline in some way burnt his boats, or that, as Alméras has it 'an uncertainty was removed.'[71] Certainly, for those who cared to read it, the pamphlet demonstrated that Céline was no longer a Communist, if he had ever been one, but the work is a characteristically Célinian piece of camouflage: a 'little chef-d'oeuvre'[72] perhaps, but a very dense and obscure one, and noticeably different from other recantations like that of Gide. In fact, the ostensible subject-matter, the Soviet Union, is so absent and details of the voyage to Leningrad (for which we shall have to wait for *Bagatelles pour un massacre*) so completely missing, that the reader can be forgiven for wondering just what guilt Céline's 'mea culpa' refers to.

In fact, before it can be read as a denunciation of Communism, *Mea culpa* must first of all be seen as a culmination of Céline's persistent attacks on bourgeois humanism: 'What is seductive in Communism, its great advantage, is that it will reveal to us Man.'[73] Yet the myth of Man is greatly exaggerated: 'Man is only about as human as chickens can fly. If they get hit in the arse, if a car bumps into them, they lift off up to the roof, but they come back straight away into the mud, to peck around in the shit.'[74] Hence the futility of a whole tradition of social thought based upon human happiness: 'the great pretension to happiness, that's the enormous imposture.'[75] The problem is twofold: the kind of society to which such a pretension to happiness leads; and the means by which such a society is created – revolution. Like so many travellers before him, Céline had seen in Soviet Russia the triumph of the machine, and with it the triumph of the engineer: hence the moving, if inaccurate claim: 'I've been a doctor at Ford's, I know what I'm talking about. All Fords are alike, Soviet or not.'[76] In other words, we are still on the terrain of the social hygiene writings, where the only alternative to the awful prospect of universal Taylorism was a Communist system. Now, that system is found to have embraced the very Taylorist principles which Céline was trying to avoid.

At the same time, the view of revolution propounded in *Mea culpa* is a disabused one of simple expropriation of the position of one class by another, in which the eternal victor is the bourgeoisie. 1917, therefore, is a mere repetition of 1789 in France, characterized as 'this stifling taking of power by the bourgeoisie',[77] but also of 1793, in which the 'thieves'[78] finally consolidated their position in blood. The problem, in 1917 as in 1793, is that the people believed themselves to be the masters when in fact they were being governed by the bourgeois. And the primary enemy of *Mea culpa*, and the common denominator with all the previous work, is an implacable hatred of the bourgeois. This is why the pamphlet begins with a celebration of spectacularly non-bourgeois heroes: 'Vive Pierre Ier! Vive Louis XIV! Vive Fouquet! Vive Gengis Khan! Vive Bonnot! la bande! et tous autres!':[79] from Peter the Great, the architect of Leningrad, to the scourge of pre-war Montmartre, the anarchist 'Bande à Bonnot'. Céline may have broken with Communism, but he has kept his anarchist, anti-humanist and anti-bourgeois credentials intact: hence the initial failure on the part of his contemporaries to detect a process of political change. In fact, there was no change at all, and it was no coincidence or act of commercial opportunism which led Céline to publish *Mea culpa* along with *Semmelweis*, which, as early as 1924, had made up its mind about the futile brutality of the Revolution, the execution of the king in 1793 and the doomed nature of the project to 'want to do too much good to people'. The publication of the two pieces in tandem serves to highlight the consistency in Céline's thought. *Mea culpa* also, however, looks forward to an otherwise incomprehensible act in the publishing of the anti-Semitic pamphlets, by concluding with the impreca-tion: 'I am! You are! We are thieves, hypocrites and bastards! No one will ever say those things. Never! Never! Yet the real Revolution would be the Revolution of Avowals, the Great Purification!'[80] For Céline, that revolution was around the corner, in 1937.

9

Anti-Semitism

I TRAVELS

After the dramas of 1936, Céline spent much of the following year travelling. In February he boarded the *Champlain* at Le Havre for New York. It was probably on this journey that he met Jean Gabin and Danielle Darieux, and on the return leg that he became friendly with Jane Bowles, the wife of the novelist Paul Bowles.[1] As Paul Bowles recalled in 1985: 'One day, on a ship, she had a little adventure with Céline . . . she was sitting one day reading *Voyage* in a deck chair on the deck of an ocean liner sailing from New York to Le Havre. A man came along, approached her and said, "Oh, you're reading Céline?" "Yes, as you see." And the guy answered, "Well, I'm Céline." They spent the rest of the trip talking. She found him very nice.'[2] What is interesting about the encounter and this aspect of Céline's travelling at this time is that, contrary to the popular image, often his own creation, of an anguished Bohemian, they show him to be perfectly at ease in the sophisticated and luxurious setting of a transatlantic liner. He had by no means yet adopted the role of the shabby outcast that was to typify him from the end of the Occupation onwards. Little is known about this visit to New York, though its one tangible result was an agreement by his publisher, Little, Brown, to bring out an American edition of *Mea culpa*.[3] Otherwise, a letter to Karen Marie Jensen shows that his enthusiasm for chorus-girls had not abated and that he was a regular member of the audience at Radio City Music Hall.[4] He was also less starry-eyed in his view of post-Depression America: 'I found New York greatly changed. Not nearly as arrogant as it used to be. Americanism has disappeared. They're following the same revolting path as Europe. They're completely in tow to Europe and the Jews, from strike to strike and the demagogy of revolution, which can't be far at this rate. The great American era is definitely over.'[5] In other words, in the same way that Céline's Communist aspirations, however modest, were destroyed by the visit to Leningrad, his ambiguous fascination with the American Dream was dispelled by the journey to New York in 1937. A powerful pattern was building up in his global vision, which would become fully articulated in *Bagatelles pour un massacre* at the end of the year: Europe was rotting away, and there was now no possible sign of an antidote in either West or East, because both had been corrupted by the insidious influence of the Jews.

When Céline returned to Paris this time, there was a significant and permanent change in his life. Lucette Almansor, the young dancer he had met at Blanche d'Alessandri's studio in the Rue Henri-Monnier towards the end of the previous year, had moved into the appartment in the Rue Lepic and was to stay with Céline for the rest of his life. She was born on 20 July 1912 near the Place Maubert in the fifth *arrondissement*. Her father was an accountant who had been separated from Lucette's mother for some years before Céline met her.[6] Lucette aimed initially for a career in the theatre and was a student at the Conservatoire, but, in spite of considerable dramatic gifts, she turned to classical dance. When she left the Conservatoire she joined the *corps de ballet* of the Opéra Comique, but was forced to abandon classical dance when she broke her big toe in an accident and turned to oriental dance instead, under the influence of the great Indian dancer Shandra Kali.[7] In 1935 she went to America, where she joined the same Folies-Bergère-style review produced by the impresario Fischer that Karen Marie Jensen had worked for a year earlier.[8] When Céline met her, she was following rigorous classes at Blanche d'Alessandri's studio, where she met major figures like Serge Lifar, Ludmilla Tcherina and Serge Perrault, who was to remain a close friend of the couple,[9] in addition to other women in Céline's circle such as Karen Marie Jensen and Irene McBride.[10] Céline was deeply impressed by her and, as Alméras records, courted her with the shyness of a young man, but also all his own impetuosity and impatience. Alongside gentle meetings by the lake in the Tuileries Gardens, there were hurried meals during which he forced her to order meat, but dragged her outside as soon as she was served.[11] When her parents divorced during Céline's visit to New York, she moved quite naturally into the appartment in the Rue Lepic, though even as late as September 1937, he was at pains to dismiss the relationship when writing to Karen Marie Jensen. Explaining that she was 'a poor little dancer he had taken in . . . who had hurt her knee in the street and whom he could not throw out,'[12] he concluded: 'She's not my mistress. You know me, she's just a woman down on her luck.'[13] In fact, the relationship was fast becoming profound and permanent, although this did not spare Lucette the same combination of apparent neglect and possessiveness as had so bewildered Elizabeth Craig. As she recalled to Frédéric Vitoux:

I had a tiny room overlooking the Rue d'Orchampt. The kitchen couldn't have been more than five feet long, and also served as the bathroom. A cleaning lady came every so often. Louis didn't want anyone to touch his papers. We didn't have a very bourgeois lifestyle nor a particularly comfortable one. We never went to the restaurant. No dinners with friends. I've never seen someone so possessed by his work, what with his practice and his books. Sometimes, on Sundays, we'd go to Saint-Germain-en-Laye. We'd take a walk, get back on the train, and he was back at work.[14]

At the same time, Céline, as with Elizabeth, was unable to bear Lucette's absence. When she toured abroad with dance companies, he wrote demanding that she return as soon as possible;[15] when, in the summer of 1937, they went to Saint Malo and Lucette was taken on as a dancer at the casino in Dinard, Céline was furious and distraught whenever the weather prevented her returning in the evening by ferry.[16] Nor was Céline uniformly tender. After what was to prove his last voyage to America, in 1938, he wrote disparagingly to Gen Paul from Le Havre: 'I've found *Pipe* [his name for Lucette] again with her cargo of customary disasters: the whole lot, the whole shitty avalanche that you know so well of my mother and my daughter: the same refrain with variants,' and thanked the painter for helping *Pipe* get out of the clutches of a 'little pimp': 'thefts, rapes and murders! . . . *Pipe*'s stupidity (and a little bit of viciousness),'[17] a refrain which echoes the break-up with Elizabeth Craig.

One person who was not pleased at this new relationship in Céline's life was Evelyne Pollet. When Céline, somewhat tactlessly, took Lucette with him on a visit to Antwerp in 1938, Evelyne was unable to meet her and took to her bedroom.[18] The following year, in June 1939, Evelyne, still recovering from a serious operation, visited Céline in Dinard and was so dismayed to find Lucette there, and sharing Céline's bed, that she took an overdose of digitalin. Céline treated her and the following day put her on the train for Paris. As she recalled much later, probably with some accuracy: 'Céline attracted women with one hand and drove them away with the other, through his intense fear of being possessed.'[19] She herself could never come to terms with her jealousy of Lucette Almansor, though she did meet Céline briefly in Antwerp in 1941 and corresponded with him until 1948. Céline himself remained gently affectionate, though, as Gibault records, he was typically and childishly ungrateful to her in a letter of 1951 to Albert Paraz (who, incidentally, had an affair with her in the summer of 1949): 'That bitch Evelyne never sent one single gramme of chocolate or anything! That damned hysterical, lying meddler. That bitch is mad with jealousy! . . . a 100% woman writer! . . . She's been haunting me for 15 years, the bitch! . . . desperate for publicity.'[20]

In May 1937, Céline went, without Lucette, to the Channel Island of Jersey, where a bizarre incident occurred. The coronation of King George VI was due to take place on 12 May and the whole of the United Kingdom, including the Channel Islands, was in a state of high security alert. The presence of a lone Frenchman on the island, with no obvious purpose to his visit, was evidently so suspicious that he was arrested by the Special Branch, interrogated and escaped being locked up only through the efforts of the French Consul, M. Delalande, with whom Céline remained in friendly contact.[21] As Céline wrote to Robert Denoël:

> You almost lost an author! I was deemed so suspicious on my arrival here that Scotland Yard put me in quarantine, practically under arrest, took my passport etc. Luckily the Consul was warned and identified me straight away. He recognized me from Rennes and Brittany! . . . My papers were scrutinized and, worst of all, deciphered, interpreted . . . and how! They suspected me of having accomplices on the island . . . a plot to kill the King![22]

This farcical episode, fully reported in *Paris-Soir* on 15 May 1927, concluded with a formal apology from the Governor of Jersey. What Céline was actually up to on the island is unclear, but it is likely that, as with previous visits to Denmark and his journey the following year to the island of Saint-Pierre-et-Miquelon, he was exploring possible places of refuge from the approaching war, in addition to testing the security and independence of the island's banks. Underneath the often exaggerated pacifist rhetoric and polemic of the pamphlets and the correspondence in the late 1930s, there was a very real appraisal on Céline's part of the inevitability of the impending conflict and the desirability, this time, of escaping it. It was this, combined with virulent anti-Semitism, which produced *Bagatelles pour un massacre*, written in the summer of 1937.

As with *Mort à crédit*, Céline found it easier and more agreeable to write outside Paris. As for his medical work in Clichy, although it often still suited him to adopt the role of the hard-pressed poor people's doctor, it was increasingly sporadic and part-time. In July, therefore, he left the Rue Lepic with Lucette and went to his favourite hotel in Le Havre, the Frascati, where, 'in a garret room overlooking the port',[23] the bulk of *Bagatelles* was written. Lucette Destouches recalled to Frédéric Vitoux both Céline's obsessive enthusiasm and commitment in writing the pamphlet and her own misgivings at the likely effect:

> 'But don't you realize, you're hanging a millstone around your neck.' He answered: 'Idiot! They're all going to kill each other, it's going to be an awful mess.' And Lucette: 'But you're the first they're going to knock off, the first to be assassinated.' He looked at her, incredulous. He imagined that the whole world, yes, the whole world would thank him for such a book. 'At least,' he told her after a pause, 'I'll have done something.'[24]

There is here the same inability to link cause and effect as was present in the publication of *L'Eglise* which ended the relationship with Ludwig Rajchman and formed an indispensable ingredient in Céline's paranoia. The pamphlet, unlike the previous novels, was composed very rapidly, completed over the rest of the summer, which Céline and Lucette spent in Saint-Malo as the guests of Marie Le Bannier, the mistress of his former father-in-law Athenase Follet, in her appartment on the Paramé road, just beyond the ramparts.[25]

Bagatelles, begun in July, was completed on Céline's return to Paris in September, and Robert Denoël prepared for its publication on 3 December 1937, with a red publicity wrapper reading 'For a good laugh in the trenches', and an advance notice in the *Bibliographie de la France*: 'The most atrocious, the most savage, the most hateful, but the most unbelievable lampoon the world has ever seen.'[26]

II *BAGATELLES POUR UN MASSACRE*

In fact, Denoël's entry in the *Bibliographie de la France*, emphasizing the 'savagery' but also the 'unbelievable' nature of the 'lampoon', points straight to the heart of Céline's text, which is the result of a complex political and, above all, literary project. The significance of the speed and facility with which the pamphlet was written, in contrast to the novels, should not be underestimated, particularly in the light of the intense difficulties Céline experienced in making progress with his next fictional project, the novel based upon his career as a *cuirassier* at Rambouillet, *Casse-pipe*. There is also evidence that Céline, who had experimented with po-lemic before in the medical writings of the late 1920s, which are themselves by no means devoid of ambiguity, was professionally intrigued by the genre. Vitoux records an incident in Montmartre just after Céline's return from the Soviet Union: 'In those days, recalls André Pulicani, a friend of Gen Paul's who had met Céline in the painter's studio, the pamphlets of the journalist Henri Béraud were all the rage. One day, Céline turned to Pulicani and asked him: "Do you think I measure up to Béraud?"'[27] In other words, quite apart from its identifiable targets, the war and the Jews, *Bagatelles* also has the status of an *exercice de style*, a stylistic experiment which moreover has the virtue of liberating Céline from his writer's block. In this process, the targets of persecution become the pretexts for an essentially aesthetic and formal project, and all the moral and political ambiguity of Modernism is to be found in it.

The complexity of the work is enshrined in its title, which was consistently misinterpreted from the pamphlet's publication as signifying 'a slight work without value to incite people to murder':[28] little *exercices de style* designed to whip up a persecution of the Jews. In fact, Céline is using two precise meanings of 'bagatelles', neither of which supports the standard interpreta-tion. In the first place, a 'bagatelle' is a musical term, meaning 'a light composition, a little piece of music which is both agreeable and easy, designed to please rather than edify' and 'a light and short piece of music, without any precise form'. Céline's Modernist aesthetic experiment, there-fore, is to adopt the musical qualities of the 'bagatelle', whereby the presence in the pamphlet of three ballet choreographies becomes quite natural, and to transfer them, through a *tour de force*, to the genre of polemic. At the same time, a more recondite meaning of 'bagatelles' signifies 'patter spoken by fairground barkers at the entrance to their sideshow to induce people to come and see their show'.[29] What Céline is doing, therefore, in *Bagatelles pour un massacre*, is inviting his audience to roll up and witness, not the massacre of the Jews by the French, but the opposite: the destruction of the French in a coming war instigated by the Jews. This theatrical aspect of the pamphlet is confirmed by the dedication of the work 'A mes potes du "Théâtre en Toile"' ('To my friends in the Theatre in the Tent') and, with its exaggerated violence and language, points us in the direction of one of Céline's favourite dramatic forms, that of the Grand Guignol puppet theatre which gave its name to his third completed novel, *Guignol's Band*. As Marc Angenot perceptively notes, in *Bagatelles pour un massacre* it is for this reason that 'the violence of the pamphlet is a spectacular violence.'[30]

On one level, therefore, the work must be read as a cry of warning of the impending massacre of the French, as Céline indicated when showing the manuscript to Lucette Almansor. As such, it contains all the stock-in-trade of French anti-Semitism.[31] The main beneficiaries of the First World War were the Jews, who participated in the conflict in infinitely small numbers, whereas the French male population was decimated, and who secured power in post-war France through international finance and the insidious influence of alcohol. The triumph of the Front Populaire was merely the culmination of this process, but also part of a wider global conspiracy linking the 'Jewish' bankers of New York with the 'Jews' who run Russia and whose Revolution, in 1917, was financed by the Loeb-Warburg Bank. At the centre of this conspiracy is England, with its 'Jewish' City pulling all the strings, and the all-powerful but shadowy Intelligence Service. Céline thus manages to unite hostility to America, fear of Soviet Russia, which, incidentally, helped to wipe out the French petite-bourgeoisie through its refusal to honour the Russian Bonds (Emprunts Russes), and traditional French Anglophobia. In so doing, he drew upon a staple of French anti-Semitism which went back to the belle époque. As Hannah Arendt comments: 'Catholic politicians were the first people to link anti-semitism to imperialism, to declare that the Jews were the agents of England, and hence to pass off their anti-semitism as Anglophobia,'[32] and Céline's polemic owes at least as much to the patron saint of French anti-Semitism, Edouard Drumont, and his pamphlet of 1886, *La France juive*, as it does to contemporary polemic.

In fact, it is what Céline does with his debt to Drumont that alerts the reader that something odd is going on in what, on one level at least, purports to be an anti-Semitic polemic. What he does is consistently to misspell Drumont's name as 'Drummont', as if to distance himself and the reader from a naive acceptance of the French anti-Semitic tradition and to annex the historical campaigner to a fictional and ironic purpose, just as he had done previously in *Semmelweis* by inverting the forenames of his hero

and transforming Klein into 'Klin'. For, even compared with such disorganized and discursive pamphlets as Bernanos' *La Grande peur des bien-pensants*
and *Les Grands cimetières sous la lune*, *Bagatelles pour un massacre* does not fit
easily into the mould of polemic. It contains three ballet choreographies:
La Naissance d'une fée, *Voyou Paul*, *Brave Virginie*, which open the pamphlet,
and *Van Bagaden*, which closes it. Although the ostensible reason for their
presence is to establish a Jewish conspiracy to prevent the narrator's work
ever being performed – in the Opéra, at the 1937 Exposition des Arts et
Techniques and in the Marinski Theatre in Leningrad – they are also there
to enrich the text and to contrast in their beauty with the violence of the
polemic. At the same time, Céline chooses to couch his pamphlet in a
fictional form and, moreover, one which is readily recognizable to his
readers. The pamphlet has the same narrator, Ferdinand, as *Mort à crédit*,
with the same interlocutor, his cousin Gustin, supplemented this time with
two other interlocutors, the Montmartre painter Popaul (whose imputed
anti-Semitism was to cause Gen Paul his alleged difficulties at the Liberation) and a Jewish doctor, Léo Gutman. The work concludes, apparently
inconsequentially, with the narration of Ferdinand's delicate love-affair
with his Intourist guide Natalie in Leningrad. In other words, the pamphlet
is also a sequel to *Mort à crédit*, in fact the sequel which Céline was unable
to complete in *Casse-pipe*, and where the mature narrator of the novel has
simply adopted the mindless imprecations of his dead father Auguste.

In addition, Céline is up to his old tricks of falsifying, not merely
Drumont's name, but the statistics commonly used in French anti-Semitism
in the 1930s. In this context it is necessary, not merely to identify Céline's
sources, as Alice Kaplan has done, but to explore their use. Here,
Emmanuel Mounier, in his hostile review of *Bagatelles* in *Esprit*, completely
misses the point in criticizing the ridiculously low figures given by Céline
for French Jewish participation in the First World War.[33] The figures resem-
ble the impossibly high mortality rate in 'Klin's' maternity ward cited in
Semmelweis and take the polemic either into the exaggerated world of
Guignol or in the direction of parody. In this context, it is worth recalling
that Céline uses the same technique of utterly inconsequential quotations
to introduce each chapter as Boris Vian would employ in *L'Automne à Pékin*,
and that the photographs which accompanied the editions of *Bagatelles* and
its successor *L'Ecole des cadavres* during the Occupation have apparently the
same bewildering irrelevance. Finally, Céline, like many an anti-Semite
before him, made frequent use of that old anti-Jewish war-horse, *The
Protocols of the Elders of Zion*, which surfaced just after the Russian Revolution
as 'evidence' of a worldwide Jewish conspiracy. The problem was that, as
early as 1921, the *Protocols* had been shown to be a hoax, deriving in fact
from a satire against Napoleon III in the 1860s. Yet, as late as 1937, Céline's
narrator was still invoking this hoax as if it were historical fact.

This implies, and probably quite deliberately, a significant problem
for Céline's reader. On one level, the work is a dazzling literary *tour de
force*, embodying an *art poétique*, in which 'a style is first of all an emotion,'[34]

and where non-Jewish practitioners are singled out for praise: Simenon, Aymé, Malraux (up to *Les Conquérants*), Elie Faure, Eugène Dabit, Paul Morand, Mac Orlan, Claude Farrère, Barbusse and Léon Daudet, backed up by the painters Vlaminck, Gen Paul and Henri Mahé.[35] As a polemic, although *Bagatelles* contains the basic elements of inter-war anti-Semitism, including grudging approval of Hitler, the reader is left uneasy by the way in which these elements are packaged, both in a fictional format and surrounded by mistakes. It is as if the 'unbelievable lampoon' alluded to in Denoël's advance publicity is directed not merely against the Jews but also against the professional anti-Semite. It may well be that, as so frequently occurred, Céline's auto-destructive urge was accompanied by a no less powerful quest for self-preservation, and that the violence of the pamphlet's anti-Semitism was deliberately camouflaged in a fictional and ironic form. This would not, by any means, be incompatible with sophisticated anti-Semitic propaganda. Walter Benjamin wrote tantalizingly of an apparently throwaway statement at the end of Baudelaire's *Mon Coeur mis à nu*: 'There would be a wonderful conspiracy to organize for the extermination of the Jewish race,'[36] and concluded that this was an example of what he termed the 'culte de la blague', an essential component in Fascist propaganda which consists of saying the unacceptable in such a way that it can be taken as a joke while still insidiously making its point.[37] *Bagatelles pour un massacre* certainly makes sense if read in this way.

This ambiguity of the text was reflected in its reception in the winter and spring of 1938. Unsurprisingly, politically partisan reviewers split along ideological lines,[38] yet both sides expressed some uncertainty. Lucien Rebatet recalled his and Brasillach's delight at Céline's unexpected recruitment to anti-Semitism: 'The surprise was extraordinary . . . I got into a race with Brasillach over who would be the first in with his article, him in *Action française* or me in *Je suis partout*. I think it was Robert who won, by a nose.'[39] Yet, as Vitoux points out, Brasillach's article in *Action française* on 13 January 1938 already cast doubt on the seriousness of Céline's enterprise,[40] and when Céline repeated his performance a year later in *L'Ecole des cadavres*, both Rebatet and Brasillach parted company with him, sensing an elaborate hoax. As Rebatet recalled: 'I must say . . . to be truthful, that if we Fascists danced a jig in 1938 when *Bagatelles* was published, *L'Ecole des cadavres*, a year later, took the wind out of our sails. Céline continued to exaggerate.'[41] Similarly, some writers on the Left could not bring themselves to see the pamphlet as a work of political apostasy, preferring, like Pierre Loiselet in *Marianne*, to read *Bagatelles* as a linguistic *tour de force*, or, like Châtelain-Tailhade in *La Patrie humaine*, as a richly comic work.[42] Moreover, the liberal and highly influential *Nouvelle Revue Française* was extremely reluctant to take *Bagatelles* at face value as a work of anti-Semitic propaganda. In his review, Marcel Arland concluded that Céline succeeded by 'expanding a fact out of all proportion until it took on the significance of a monstrous myth'[43] and that 'his virulence leaves far behind it all anti-

Semitic attacks.'[44] In a famous article in April 1938, André Gide provided a reading of *Bagatelles*, with all its distortions of data, as a sophisticated satire on traditional and contemporary French anti-Semitic writing, but a nagging doubt remained: 'If we had to see in *Bagatelles pour un massacre* anything other than a game, Céline, in spite of all his genius, would be inexcusable for stirring up banal passions with this cynicism and this careless frivolity.'[45] Similarly, Emmanuel Berl, in conversation with Patrick Modiano, recalled that 'unlike many people, I find it fairly innocent . . . Since we don't know very well what it means . . . He's very violent, but you don't know very well against whom.'[46] Paradoxically, if the publication of *L'Ecole des cadavres* confirmed the doubts of the Fascist right, it was to dispel those of the Left, who concluded reluctantly that Céline had indeed burnt his boats.

Commercially, *Bagatelles pour un massacre* was highly successful, with the first print-run of 20,000 selling out rapidly and necessitating a second edition. By the end of the War, 75,000 copies had been sold in France alone,[47] and the work was translated shortly after publication into German and Italian. This commercial success compensated for a loss of income from Céline's medical work. He resigned on 10 December 1937 from the 'dispensaire' on the rue Fanny in Clichy and shortly afterwards lost his post at the Biothérapie laboratory.[48] While it is likely that, as he wrote to Henri Poulain, trying to recruit him for *Je suis partout*, he 'had been sacked, directly as a result of the book, from a pathetic little job of 400 francs a month,'[49] the departure from the clinic in Clichy is less clear. Undoubtedly, the publication of *Bagatelles* would have made Céline's position, working for a Jewish doctor in a Communist municipality, untenable, which is why he resigned. Yet there is no evidence of the kind of persecution which he was often to evoke later and which *Je suis partout* reported on 4 March 1938 with the words: 'He is losing successively all his jobs and all his positions,'[50] and still less to substantiate Le Vigan's claim that 'everything changed a few weeks later [after the publication of *Mea culpa*], when a simple edict from Léon Blum's Chef de Cabinet sacked Dr Destouches from the post which he occupied at the dispensaire in Clichy. He had been devoting himself to medicine there for ten years. He was even briefly imprisoned. He then became victim of an irrational fury.'[51] Céline, however, believed in his persecution: François Gibault quotes from a friendly letter to a Jewish former colleague in Geneva, Dr Walter Strauss, written after the publication of *Bagatelles*: 'The persecution of the Aryans exists as well. I've just been sacked – in atrocious conditions – from my job at the Clichy clinic where I was a doctor for 12 years, because of my book. The Director is a Lithuanian Jew – naturalized for 10 years – Ichok, or Ozok or Isaac, and 12 Jewish doctors have immediately been appointed. As you see, in France we have Nazism in reverse.'[52] Yet, in fact, as Alméras reminds us, although Dr Ichok was a staunch supporter of the Front Populaire, Céline had kept his post throughout 1937 in spite of the anti-Soviet sentiments of *Mea culpa*.[53] Not that this stemmed in any way the advance of Céline's paranoia.

III THE ANTI-SEMITE

What perplexed Céline's readers in 1937, and has continued to puzzle critics ever since, is the unexpected and sudden nature of his anti-Semitism. It is true that Elizabeth Craig recalled a certain anti-Semitic discourse as early as the 1920s, yet there is nothing in the early medical polemic nor in *Voyage au bout de la nuit* to even hint at anti-Semitism on the part of the author, though the French anarchist and libertarian tradition had often assimilated Jewishness and capitalism into a composite enemy. In fact, in his opening dialogue with Arthur Ganate, Bardamu expressly rejects any concept of race: 'What you call race is only this great collection of losers like me, with watery eyes, covered in lice and shivering with cold, who ended up here pursued by hunger, the plague, tumours and the cold, coming defeated from the four corners of the earth. They couldn't go any further because of the sea. That's France and those are the French.'[54] It is true that *L'Eglise* contains its famous third act set in the 'Jewish' League of Nations in Geneva, yet *Mort à crédit*, apart from one passing reference to an imaginary bank, the 'Comptoir Judéo-Suisse',[55] reverts to the non-racist ideology of the first novel. Indeed, the anti-Semitic tirades of Auguste, including denunciations of all the traditional enemies of the petite-bourgeoisie, are held up to ridicule and textually subverted. Yet, one year later, Auguste's son Ferdinand is, apparently inexplicably, recycling the same tirades.

In this apparently sudden conversion to anti-Semitism, Céline was not alone. A year earlier than *Bagatelles pour un massacre*, the Christian writer Marcel Jouhandeau had published a diatribe against the Jews, *Le Péril juif*, in which he recounted the surprise evoked by his first unexpected anti-Semitic article: 'The day my first article against the Jews appeared, Marcel Aymé, whom I like deeply, expressed his surprise at seeing me become suddenly a raving xenophobe.'[56] And, in the same way that Céline's anti-Semitism is aroused in *Bagatelles* by his failure to have his ballets performed, so the ostensible reason for Jouhandeau's xenophobia is equally trivial: the number of Jews involved in the management of Gallimard. For Jouhandeau, the community of poor Parisian Jews living in the Rue des Rosiers 'would not present any danger for us in itself, were it not the nursery of the Jewish intellectuals who tomorrow will try to destroy us.'[57] Similarly, as Gibault and numerous commentators have pointed out, possibly rather too easily, not only was there a long tradition of French intellectual anti-Semitism going back to Voltaire and culminating in the belle époque with Gobineau and Drumont, this tradition was also extremely healthy in the inter-war years, with explicitly anti-Semitic authors such as Maurras, Léon Daudet, Brasillach, Henri Béraud, Bernanos, Rebatet, Georges Suarez and Jouhandeau having a wide readership. Throughout the twentieth century, some of the most distinguished names in French literature had expressed sometimes strong anti-Semitic feelings:

Barrès, Drieu la Rochelle, Valéry, Paul Léautaud, Claudel and even Gide.[58] Moreover, anti-Semitism was often a powerful element in right-wing libertarian thought: Galtier-Boissière's *Le Crapouillot*, for example, published a special number in September 1936, entitled *Les Juifs*.[59] Finally it is important to recall that the artistic community in which Céline lived, that of interwar Montmartre, populated by ex-combatants from the First World War, exhibited definite racist and specifically anti-Semitic sentiments, and that some of its members, like Ralph Soupault, the cartoonist for *Je suis partout*, were members of Doriot's PPF.

Nevertheless, if Céline found an intellectual home for his anti-Semitism, albeit a home which he occasionally and progressively disrupted, this is not sufficient to explain in itself the anti-Semitism he adopted publically after 1937. In his biography, Frédéric Vitoux conscientiously explores the possible origins of Céline's racism, looking successively at his family background and childhood, his record of personal vulnerability, his pacifism, his professional concern with public health, his anti-humanism and his fundamental isolation.[60] All of these arguments merit consideration, but none of them is entirely convincing. It is certainly true that the Parisian petite-bourgeoisie from which Céline came was, as we have seen, exceptionally vulnerable to social and economic change from the mid-nineteenth century onwards and a powerful feeding-ground for anti-Semitism. If we abstract the fictional portrait of Auguste in *Mort à crédit*, however, there is little factual evidence to identify Fernand Destouches with this petit-bourgeois anti-Semitism and, even if there were, there is no inevitable process by which the son should automatically espouse the values of the father. The contrary is often the case, and the portrait of Céline as a petit-bourgeois victim, assiduously created and cultivated by the author himself, should also be set against the image of the well-dressed and suave international traveller, the habitué of ocean liners and luxury hotels.

It is also undoubtedly true that Céline's career had lurched between dazzling success and humiliating failure, though here again the issues are by no means clear-cut. His unhoped-for medical career led him to the pinnacle of success in the League of Nations in Geneva, to be followed a year later by near-bankruptcy in Clichy and the sordid grind of the 'dispensaire'; his first novel was a huge success, but very publicly failed to win the Prix Goncourt; he had a long relationship with a beautiful dancer, only to lose her to an American rival; his second novel was a relative failure and he was unable to make satisfactory progress with its successor, *Casse-pipe*, to cap it all, there seemed to be a conspiracy to prevent his ballets ever seeing the light of day. None of these elements, however, is particularly conclusive: as we have seen, Céline left Geneva of his own free will and without rancour and, from 1932 onwards, his duties at the clinic in Clichy were spasmodic and perfunctory. The débâcle of the Goncourt Prize still left him famous and rich and there is no evidence of more than passing bitterness. The relationship with Elizabeth Craig had fizzled out before she returned to America and, contrary to the outrage expressed in his letters,

Céline appears to have consoled himself with some ease and rapidity. The failure of the ballets to be performed is a theme in the fictional narrative of *Bagatelles* and, again, there is no evidence that Céline himself took it particularly badly. Yet the very fictional nature of that narrative may point us in a particular direction: that of an aesthetic compensation for the failure of *Mort à crédit* and an aesthetic renewal after the difficulties with the composition of *Casse-pipe*, by which Céline's literary Modernism is obliged to annex the most dangerous and fatal of political programmes. In other words, Céline's isolation identified by Vitoux, however psychologically real it may be, is also the major attribute of a *narrator* and the indispensable fuel for his rhetoric. As Philippe Muray comments: 'Céline's anti-Semitism was logically and paradoxically led by his revolution in style.'[61]

We are on firmer ground with the thematic arguments. Pacifism in the inter-war years in France, including libertarian pacifism, often coincided with anti-Semitism, seeing the 'international Jewish financial community' as the main instigators of political, and ultimately military, opposition to Nazi Germany and the dispossessed Jewish refugees from Hitler as the immediate cause of tension. Céline's permanent horror of war, deriving from his experience in 1914, coincides perfectly with this tendency, though it is important to stress that this coincidence was by no means inevitable and that French pacifism in the 1930s, as figures such as André Chamson show, was by no means the prerogative of the Right. It is also true that Céline's medical specialism of hygiene and public health was by no means politically neutral. As Olivier Targowla shows, much of the tradition of French public-health medicine was on the Right, demonstrating a distrust of Louis Chevalier's 'classes laborieuses'[62] and, in particular, of alien ethnic groups, who were considered to constitute the major health risk.[63] Metaphorically, exponents of racialist theories, especially the ethnologist Georges Montandon, resorted to a public-health model of society as an organism beset by an alien infection as a powerful form of propaganda. There is evidence of both strands in *Bagatelles pour un massacre*. The racial purity of France is at risk from the increasing presence of the Jews who, in their turn, are attempting to undermine the health of the Aryan population through the proliferation of alcohol. Finally, the anti-humanism of *Mea culpa* and its denigration of the concept of progress can lead quite plausibly, not merely to anti-Communism but to a retrenchment in narrow racism.

This political anti-Semitism was reinforced by both global and domestic political circumstances in the 1930s. The increasing economic and cultural threat from the United States seemed to be joining in a pincer movement with the Soviet menace from the East to crush Europe and its traditional values, supported by the insidious power of England and its Jewish financiers. Here, all of France's right-wing phobias met: anti-Americanism, anti-Bolshevism and Anglophobia. The only European nation seen to be resisting this coalition was Hitler's Germany, yet, inexplicably, it was Germany which was now cast as the enemy. The reason could only be the power of the Jews, in sympathy with their dispossessed relatives in Germany, who, through the 'Jewish' Front Populaire government, were committed to the economic and social undermining of France and a European war which would reinstate them in Germany. In this way, the Jew becomes the master and the threat and the Aryan the potential victim, hence justifying persecution of the Jews as legitimate self-defence. This is crucial to Céline's anti-Semitism and to the ambiguity of the title, as well as the narrative, of *Bagatelles pour un massacre*. Céline's exhortations to come and watch the massacre of the Aryans by the Jews in fact disguises but also avoids blame for the more obvious incitement to persecution. It is worth recalling that Céline as victim, the author of the ballet *Voyou Paul, Brave Virginie*, rejected from the 1937 Exposition Internationale des Arts et Techniques, organized by the 'Jewish' Front Populaire (and a miserable imitation of the great 1900 Exhibition), is the exact counterpart of the familiar figure of Céline the bully, the tireless persecutor of Robert Denoël and insulter of his friend Marcel Aymé. The victim/bully duality goes some way to explaining psychologically Céline's anti-Semitism, as it does stylistically to illuminate the sheer exuberance of the polemic.

What complicates Céline's position on the French Right even more, however, is that he chooses to adopt a position which is in a minority even among anti-Semites, that of racism, a position which, in fact, brings him unfashionably closer to Nazi ideology. As he wrote to Lucien Combelle, Gide's secretary and the future editor of *L'Emancipation Nationale* during the Occupation: 'Personally, I believe in racism – it's only a medical belief – a biological mystique.'[64] The pamphlets make clear that their anti-Semitism is not merely the result of a personal and specific grudge, but part of a wider programme of racial cleansing. This would be one of the central tenets of the second pamphlet, *L'Ecole des cadavres*, in which Céline reverts to the specifically biological metaphor of infection, by Jewish 'microbes'[65] requiring vigorous surgery and antisepsis.[66] It is for this reason that Mussolini's Italy is doomed: having embraced an anti-Semitic policy, it stopped short of full-blown racism, whereas 'the Jews are only afraid of racism.'[67] The narrator of *L'Ecole des cadavres*, however, is one of the rare scientists, with Georges Montandon,[68] to have seen the danger and the cure: 'Racism first!'[69] he cries, 'Long live racism! We have understood that through having so many corpses.'[70] The only way to avoid the almost inevitable repetition of the First World War is a policy of racism throughout Europe which will restore the purity and mystique of Charlemagne's empire.[71] In this respect, Céline's largely fictitious Breton and Flemish origins are consistently evoked in the pamphlets as a guarantee of racial purity and Aryan mysticism. This does, however, serve to demarcate him from the mainstream of French anti-Semitism of the inter-war years, which, in spite of Xavier Vallat's description of France as a 'Gallo-Roman state', was more concerned with alleged Jewish economic and political power than with notions of race. Céline's anti-Semitism is part of an integral racism extending from his disparagement of the Blacks in Africa to later paranoia at a possible Chinese invasion of the West after the Second World War.

The same marginality is visible in Céline's relations with France's anti-Semitic milieu. As Alméras records, after *Bagatelles*, Céline was in close contact with the editor of the extreme right-wing *Au Pilori*, Henry-Robert Petit, who introduced him to Montandon.[72] At the same time, Céline wrote to the polemicist Henri Béraud, who had attacked the Blum government in *Gringoire*, placing both himself and Béraud in the same anti-Semitic camp: 'We don't hate the Jews as Jews . . . What we criticize them for is indulging in RACISM.'[73] Yet Céline's integration into the French anti-Semitic cause was at best only partial. As Gibault reminds us, Céline was never a member of any extreme right-wing political party or league: neither Action Française, Georges Valois' Le Faisceau, Pierre Taittinger's Jeunesses Patriotes, François Coty's Solidarité Française, Colonel de la Rocque's Croix de Feu, nor even the Parti Populaire Français. Vitoux reports Céline's anonymous attendance at a meeting organized by Darquier de Pellepoix, destined to become Xavier Vallat's successor as Vichy's Commissaire Général aux Questions Juives, in the Rue Laugier on 2 December 1938. When he joined the speaker and organizers at a nearby café after the event, he shocked them with 'his hopeless disillusionment. The *patrie* was done for, he kept repeating in his monologue. No, he had nothing left to say, nothing left to hope for, like some connoisseur of decay. Too bad if Darquier was scandalized by such defeatism.'[74] The same is true of his relations with Nazi Germany. Alméras records that, when in Canada in 1938 he met, at Montandon's suggestion, the right-wing academic Professor Victor Barbeau and put him in contact with the *Weltdienst*, the German international anti-Semitic propaganda organization.[75] At the same time, he appears to have had little to do with official organizations for Franco-German *rapprochement*, such as the Comité France-Allemagne or the journal *Les Cahiers Franco-Allemands*. When the left-wing press in 1939 accused him, with some plausibility, of contacts with Otto Abetz, the German cultural envoy to Paris, he denied all knowledge of Abetz and claimed never to have visited Germany for thirty-five years,[76] a characteristic denial which prefigured his public memory of the Occupation. This ambiguity in his dealings with the Reich was to persist during the Occupation and is central to his role as an anti-Semite. On one level, he appeared to relish his new-found role as a militant and the newly discovered verve as a polemicist. At the same time, the text of the polemic was carefully designed to provide any number of escape routes (satire, black humour, stylistic exercise) and, in so far as it was possible, Céline was concerned to be seen to keep his hands clean from either practical organization or committed journalism.

There may also be a profound psychological reason for this ambiguous relationship with official anti-Semitism, one which, paradoxically, takes us closer to the heart of the anti-Semite. In *Nous autres Juifs*, Arnold Mandel notes that, in *D'un Château l'autre*, Céline describes Berlin in 1945 as still being populated by Jews engaged in all manner of deals whereas manifestly by 1945 there were no Jews left alive in the capital of the Reich.[77] The explanation is to be found both in the 'delirium' necessary to Céline's stylistic verve, but also in a profound ingredient of anti-Semitism:

This process could be described as recourse to amnesia. The murderer forgets that he has killed, not in order to escape the feeling of guilt or to avoid horrifying himself, but because he still needs the person he has killed or had killed. Hence the dead person must still be alive. Consequently, the dead person is not dead and the murderer has not killed. The anti-Semite hates the Jew, the extreme anti-Semite hates him very strongly and, if he can, he exterminates him. Yet his hatred is not assuaged . . . Since the object of his hatred has disappeared and is irreplaceable, the anti-Semite ignores his disappearance by believing – and not just seeming to believe – that he is still there. If we could establish a frivolous comparison, we would have to compare this 'game', but inversely, to children playing at war with toy guns. One of the little boys brandishes his gun, aims at his friend, pulls the trigger – if there is one – and cries: 'Bang, bang! You're dead!' The exterminator of the Jews goes up to the Jew with a real gun, which is really loaded. He fires point blank at the Jew and kills him, and then says: 'Bang, bang! You're not dead!'[78]

This very subtle analysis coincides with a particular character trait of Céline's which we have seen before and which concerns his apparent inability to envisage consequences for his actions. In particular, it goes some way to explaining his apparently innocent response to Lucette Almansor's concerned reaction to her reading of the manuscript of *Bagatelles*. The need to retain the object of his hatred would become one of the constant features of his defence and writing in the post-war period.

IV *L'ECOLE DES CADAVRES*

If *Bagatelles pour un massacre* constitutes Céline's urgent warning of an approaching war, his activities following its publication were mainly concerned with finding a financial and geographical refuge from the imminent conflict. Shortly after the publication of the pamphlet, he went to Amsterdam to deposit 184 ten-florin gold coins in the Nederlandsche Bank, profiting from the journey to see Evelyne Pollet in Antwerp. In the summer of 1938 he went with Henri Mahé to London to withdraw some gold from Lloyds Bank and transfer it to a safe deposit box at the Privat Banken of Copenhagen.[79] 1938 was also marked by one of his more bizarre journeys, this time to the remote French colony of Saint-Pierre-et-Miquelon, off the Canadian coast. The reason for the journey was to explore the island's viability as a place of refuge in the coming war. As Henri Mahé recalled later: 'That year, a kind of foul whiff of Apocalypse hovered over Europe . . . It was high time to unearth some island that no one wanted or would fight over, where lovely peace was assured and you could get yourself some. Saint-Pierre-et-Miquelon would stand a chance.'[80] A friend of Mahé's, René Héron de Villefosse, remembered meeting Céline on board Mahé's new boat, the *Enez Glaz*, and listening to his enthusiasm for Canada: 'Only one country in the world will be left in a century, the one where parish priests are kings, and that's Canada, the most damned boring country there is.'[81] An additional attraction of Saint-Pierre-et-Miquelon which appealed to Céline's growing Celtic mysticism was that it was an essentially Breton colony. He sailed from Bordeaux on 15 April 1938 on the small cargo boat, *Le Celte*, which, in addition to Céline, had only three other passengers, and arrived in Saint-Pierre on 26 April, after a voyage of eleven days.[82] The visit probably inspired *Scandale aux abysses* and certainly re-emerged in *D'un château l'autre* in the episode where the narrator Céline, marooned among the exiled Vichy Government in Sigmaringen, asks Pierre Laval to make him governor of Saint-Pierre-et-Miquelon.[83] He went on from Saint-Pierre to Montreal, where, as we have seen, he made the acquaintance of Victor Barbeau and attended an extreme right-wing meeting.[84] Yet neither Saint-Pierre nor Canada lived up to his expectations as places of refuge. He wrote to Gen Paul:

> On the whole, a detestable impression. Never has Jewish propaganda been so implacable, vituperative and insatiable. There is no salvation for us in this direction. The defeats of the Japanese are acclaimed even here, and the Catholics, like the Benedictines, in fact, are all Freemasons, pro-Jewish, anti-French and urging us on to crime. They see us all as being at war. They despise us like dogs and see us only as quarry. On the whole, it's abject. As for Saint-Pierre-et-Miquelon, F 3 points as well, and pro-Jewish. At the top, obviously. The circle is drawing in.[85]

He concluded that the only possible refuge was Franco's Spain.[86] From Canada, he travelled to New York for the launch of the American edition of *Mort à crédit*, and returned to France on 18 May on board the *Normandie*, presumably transposed into the Jewish-dominated liner the *Youpinium* in *L'Ecole des cadavres*. He arrived back in Le Havre on 23 May to be met by Lucette, and, after a week in the port, returned to Montmartre, before taking his holidays with Marie Le Bannier in Saint-Malo in July.[87] It was here that he wrote the bulk of the second pamphlet, although he had by no means abandoned his exclusively literary projects. In a letter to Denoël of 26 May, he had set out his programme of books to be completed: '1) *Casse-pipe*, 2) *Abîmes, Fredaines Soucis*, 3) *"Honny soit"* (the original title for *Guignol's Band*), 4) *La Volonté du Roi Krogold*'.[88]

If *Bagatelles pour un massacre* was a success because of its unexpected nature and originality of style, *L'Ecole des cadavres*, which was published on 24 November 1938, was a disappointment and its sales were poor. This was hardly surprising: the book appeared less than a month after the Munich crisis and the public were no longer in the mood for another satirical evocation of a massacre. Nor, on the face of it, does the second pamphlet have much to commend it. Merlin Thomas calls it 'Céline's one real incursion into what one might call journalism' and 'by a very considerable distance his feeblest and least interesting book'.[89] *L'Ecole des cadavres* has little of the formal and stylistic inventiveness of its predecessor and, apart from a brief fictional introduction, designed to position the narrator Ferdinand, appears to consist of an almost interminable series of repetitive anti-Semitic fragments, literally 'bagatelles', before the text as a whole simply fades out with no conclusion.

Closer inspection, however, shows a grouping of themes and even an attempt at complementarity with *Bagatelles pour un massacre*: whereas the first pamphlet was turned primarily against the Soviet Union, the second takes as its main target the Anglo-Saxon world of the United States and Britain. Still fresh from his journey to North America in April and May 1938, Céline, through his narrator Ferdinand, savagely denounces the power of the United States, governed by a President, Roosevelt, who has changed his name from 'Rosenfeld'[90] and whose patron saint Uncle Sam derives in fact from 'Samuel Cohen'.[91] Not only do the Americans despise the French, confining their interest to 'French shows'[92] in their burlesque houses, they can only begin to feel some admiration 'when the bugle rallies all our bodies together'.[93] The real vitriol, however, is reserved for Britain, dominated by the Jewish City, to which court and government are in thrall, and, interestingly, its Intelligence Service. Like many French writers in the inter-war years, including Malraux in *Les Conquérants*, and Drieu la Rochelle in *Notes pour comprendre le siècle*, Céline adopted a traditional nineteenth-century fear of British imperialism, perceived to be cynically manipulating world affairs through the ubiquitous agents of its all-powerful Intelligence Service: the 'Great Game' of Kipling's *Kim*. Rather than the Soviet threat, it is the international plot being orchestrated from New York and London which will plunge the French into an unwanted and suicidal war with Hitler.

In fact, *L'Ecole des cadavres* is noteworthy for a reappraisal of Communism which complements *Mea culpa* and harks back nostalgically to the idealism implicit in the medical pamphlets of the early 1930s. The ideal of Communism remains admirable: 'You don't become a Communist. You have to be born a Communist or resign yourself to never becoming one. Communism is a quality of the soul'[94] and 'Communism should be madness and, above all, on top of everything, poetry.'[95] In practice, however, 'Communism without poets, in the Jewish manner, scientific, rationalist, materialist, Marxist, administrative, shabby, nit-picking, at 600 kilos a sentence, is nothing but a very irritating means of prosaic tyranny . . . a cure which is much worse than the illness.'[96] If the 'Jewish' Soviet Union has failed to implement the poetry of Communism, Ferdinand turns to the one successful practitioner of Communism in the world, Hitler: 'a very good raiser of peoples, he is on the side of Life, he cares for the life of peoples, even our's. He is an Aryan.'[97] Like many on the extreme Right in France in the 1930s, Céline transformed his disappointment with Soviet Communism into a belief in Hitler as the sole repository of collectivist ideals and racism. He has merely switched to the other totalitarian option outlined in the *Monde* article of 1930. The reason, however, is as much spiritual and aesthetic as it is political, and Céline would reinforce this argument in the final pamphlet, *Les Beaux Draps*. Under Jewish domination, the French have lost all spirituality,[98] as evidenced by their artistic production, and their dominant class, the petite-bourgeoisie, unable to see further than its own limited morality, will happily lead the nation to slaughter.[99] The attraction of Hitlerism is that it promises to take Europe away from the petty, squalid and divided present, back to the Golden Age of Charlemagne's empire, united in faith and mysticism. Hence, starting with an apparently gratuitous news report: 'The Government of the Reich inaugurated yesterday the Rhine–Danube Canal, begun by Charlemagne,'[100] *L'Ecole des cadavres* embarks upon a comprehensive reflection on Charlemagne's empire, the disaster of its fragmentation with the Treaty of Verdun,[101] and the need to repeal the Treaty and rebuild a united Europe: 'What I want is an alliance with Germany.'[102]

There is nothing here to antagonize or alienate the French extreme Right, and at first sight Rebatet's and Brasillach's dismay at Céline's 'exaggeration' seems misplaced. Yet, although *L'Ecole des cadavres* appears a less ambiguous text than *Bagatelles pour un massacre*, it contains enough complexity to sow doubts in the most committed reader and to provide a possible disinculpation of its author. In the first place, the title itself, while primarily signifying a 'school for corpses', in other words 'how to become a corpse', also looks forward to a time in the near future when all Frenchmen will be corpses and will need to be taught how they became so. Frustrated at his fellow-citizens' failure to understand the threat, Céline proclaims: 'Since they don't want to understand, since they don't want to learn, since they want to go on endlessly repeating the same stupidities, very well! They'll get what they want! They'll take the exam anyway . . . in the fabulous school!'[103] In the same way that all of Ferdinand's fellow-pupils in *Mort à crédit* pass the Certificat d'Etudes, so all of the pamphleteer's generation will pass the ultimate examination in the great school of war. Yet, by looking forward to their deaths, and beyond, Céline is redeploying the technique introduced into *Voyage au bout de la nuit* by the 'Chanson des Gardes suisses, 1793', that of the ghost story, with a ghostly narrator. The pamphlet begins with Ferdinand walking along the Seine between La Jatte and Courbevoie (the industrial suburban landscape from which he came and which remains the heartland of his writing), when he is accosted by his muse, an ageing mermaid. As they trade insults, the mermaid ripostes: 'Corpse yourself!':[104] the pamphlet, written in 'the ink of the Seine',[105] is a warning from beyond the grave.

Not only does it begin with this ambiguity, which casts doubt both on its meaning and its literary status, but *L'Ecole des cadavres* proceeds immediately to define itself as an *exercice de style*. Ferdinand quotes from a letter he has just received, signed 'Salvador, Jew',[106] which presents all the qualities of Céline's own style but which somehow lacks its effect. Ferdinand is disturbed at the implications of this apparent pastiche and defines his own style, concluding that what separates him from Salvador is that 'passion has rendered him impossible'[107] and that 'he irritates me, he gets on my nerves, but he doesn't excite me.'[108] From then on, alongside the anti-Semitic polemic, there is a continued reflection on the creation and sustaining of that polemic itself: a school, not just for corpses, but also for polemicists.[109]

Finally, if the sympathetic reader were alerted by these aesthetic considerations, would he remain sympathetic in the light of Céline's continued blurring of categories? What is he to make, for example, of the attacks on right-wing leaders like Doriot or La Rocque, or the criticism of Maurras' 'Jewish' style, or again, the writing of Drumont as 'Drummont'?[110] It is difficult to see how the insertion of a lengthy list of anti-Semitic nonentities, with useful addresses and journals,[111] can be taken totally seriously, nor the assertion that the all-powerful Intelligence Service is led by 'Moses Sieff, Mark Spencer and Sassoon',[112] with previous luminaries being 'Mirabeau, Danton, Robespierre, Borodin, Trotsky and Lawrence'[113] even if, in Céline's world-view, anti-Semitism joined his repudiation of the French Revolution. There is ample evidence that the author who can provide a political programme reading: '1. Expulsion of all the Jews; 2. Prohibition and closure of all Masonic Lodges and Secret Societies; 3. Hard labour for life for all people who are dissatisfied or hard of hearing, etc.'[114] may be simply compiling a latter-day *Dictionnaire des idées reçues* which shows as much contempt for his fellow anti-Semites as for the ostensible enemy. It is this which accounts for the disorientation of Rebatet's Fascist colleagues: 'the fervent Célinians in *Je suis partout* veiled their face and shrugged their shoulders. Ferdinand was exaggerating. He had become a monomaniac of insult. He was clearly an anarchist.'[115]

It is this, perhaps, which explains the dedication of the work to Julian the Apostate, the Emperor who attempted to turn back the tide of Christianity and restore the golden cult of Mithras, but who failed and was murdered by his enemies. Like Julian, and indeed like Nietzsche, Céline envisages a repudiation of the present and a return to Charlemagne's Europe. Yet there is little hope of this: the weakness of the French petite-bourgeoisie and the awesome power of the Jews render his gesture suicidal. As the pamphlet ends: 'Here is Ferdinand, naked. We'll have to kill him. I can't see any other solution.'[116]

Denoël printed 25,000 copies of *L'Ecole des cadavres*, which proved wildly optimistic, since sales were disappointing. When, in April 1939, the government brought in legislation to ban racist articles in the press (though not in books), the Décrets Marchandeau, Denoël withdrew both pamphlets from the shops, a move widely interpreted as a way of saving face and gaining some publicity.[117] In fact, there was an additional, and painful, reason for the withdrawal of the pamphlets. On page 302 of *L'Ecole des cadavres*, Céline had quoted from an article in *L'Humanité* on the opening of a clinic for the Syndicat des Métaux de la Région Parisienne, in which he had characteristically added his own gloss '(All Jews)' to the list of speakers: Kalmanovitch, Oppmann, Rouquès, Lecain and Bli. He was subsequently sued, along with Robert Denoël, by Dr Pierre Rouquès, who was not a Jew, for defamation, on the grounds that, in the context of the violence of Céline's polemic, this constituted libel.[118] Céline and Denoël were summoned to the 12th Chambre of the Tribunal Correctionnelle of Paris where, on 21 June 1939, they were found guilty, fined 2000 francs damages and ordered to delete the offending passage.[119] The incident was also to surface in the charges brought against Céline after the Occupation, when Rouquès alleged that Céline's attack on him had led to his being persecuted. It was in this context that the pamphlets were withdrawn from sale, even though they reappeared shortly after the outbreak of war in the autumn of 1939, *L'Ecole des cadavres* bearing a disclaimer reading: '*L'Ecole des cadavres* is not directed against individuals. It is attacking a policy. To avoid any specific polemic, both author and publisher have decided to cut pages 17–18, 121–2, 301–2 from this edition and all subsequent ones.'[120]

The importance of the Rouquès case was that it undoubtedly accentuated Céline's paranoia. Coming on the heels of the Abetz affair, 'the Correctionnelle [Tribunal] for the son of Fernand and Marguerite, was humiliating and deeply wounding'[121] and proof of the immensity of the coalition arraigned against him, involving the Jews, the Masons, the Communists and the courts. It also coincided with the adoption of the persona and appearance of a victim. As early as December 1938 a sympathetic journalist, Marcel Sauvage of *L'Intransigeant*, had described meeting Céline in Montmartre, dressed in 'an old scarf around his neck, with a worn woollen overcoat, grown green through wear'.[122] The tramp-like image was now born which was to stay with Céline for the rest of his life. Yet he still continued to fulminate against the Jews in interminable tirades to his friends in Gen Paul's studio, and when war was finally declared in September 1939, first by Britain and then by France, he saw himself as entirely vindicated.

10

Phoney War

I CASSE-PIPE

The declaration of war in September 1939 effectively coincided with the end of Céline's attempts to complete his third novel, *Casse-pipe*. After the war, it served Céline's purpose to exaggerate both the size and state of completion of the novel's manuscript, which he left in his apartment in the Rue Girardon in Montmartre when he fled to Germany in 1944 and which he claimed had been destroyed, or at any rate lost, when the apartment was requisitioned at the Liberation.[1] To both Pierre Monnier and Roger Nimier, he referred to a manuscript of 600 pages which had been lost, and Robert Poulet, in *Mon ami Bardamu*, claims that the novel was 'finished, corrected and ready'.[2] Yet, as Henri Godard points out, this was contradicted by Céline himself in the correspondence with Milton Hindus, and there is no evidence that the novel had ever progressed beyond the initial fragmentary stage concerning episodes in the life of a cavalry recruit in the years just before the First World War.[3] In fact, the composition of *Casse-pipe* seems to have taken place over the winter of 1936–7: Céline probably started it in the autumn following the publication of *Mort à crédit* in 1936, and certainly interrupted it by the summer of 1937 in order to begin work on *Bagatelles pour un massacre*.[4] Although Robert Le Vigan had recollections of Céline returning to the novel in Paris in 1940, at the same time as he was writing *Les Beaux Draps*, this seems improbable. Céline was then at work on *Guignol's Band*, and Le Vigan was probably confusing the novel with Céline's oral reminiscences of a First World War cavalry charge to P. Ordioni in 1939.[5]

According to Robert Poulet, the main thrust of the novel was concerned with a cavalry squadron in 1914, which became detached from its regiment and, in its isolation, completely demoralized, to the extent that they took to idleness and drink and finally broke open the money-chest which they were supposed to be guarding. It is only then that the adjutant in charge realizes the enormity of the crime they have committed and the extent to which they have lost honour: 'Panic-stricken, in despair, he leads his men to the most dangerous point of the battle, and they charge, head down, men, horses, wagons, into the throng, which crushes them.'[6] In fact, what remains of the novel is its extended introduction, describing the volunteer Ferdinand's first night in the cavalry barracks of Rambouillet, followed by four fragmentary episodes detailing Ferdinand's apprenticeship in his first platoon, his learning to ride, the equestrian skill of Captain Dagomart and, finally, day-to-day life in the predominantly Breton platoon, commanded by Le Meheu. In addition, there are two further fragments, published by Dominique de Roux in the *Cahiers de l'Herne*, detailing Ferdinand's promotion to *Brigadier* (corporal), his participation with the regiment at the 1913 *quatorze juillet* parade in Paris and his subsequent treatment of new recruits. There is certainly no evidence that Céline ever got as far as setting down the catastrophic experience of the regiment in the early months of the war, culminating in the squadron's suicidal charge.

If this final charge into the 'Valley of Death' plainly evokes Tennyson's poem, the description of life in the cavalry barracks has very clear literary antecedents, including Courteline's *Les Gaîtés de l'escadron,* Jean Drault's *Soldat Chapuzot,* Charles Leroy's *Le Colonel Ramollot,* Lucien Descaves' *Sous-offs,* Georges Darien's *Biribi* and, especially, Abel Hermant's *Le Cavalier Miserey,* which allegedly so outraged orthodox military opinion when it appeared in 1887 that, as we have seen, the Duc de Chartres, Commander of the 12e Chasseurs, had it publically burnt.[7] It is also likely that Céline made use of Kipling's *Barrack-Room Ballads* and *Plain Tales from the Hills,* particularly the character of Mulvaney, as well as exploiting echoes of earlier French military fiction, such as Vigny's *Servitudes et grandeurs militaires,* Stendhal's *Lucien Leuwen* and Erckmann-Chatrian's *Histoire d'un conscrit de 1812.* In fact, in addition to its linguistic virtuosity, *Casse-pipe* is arguably Céline's most extended adventure into intertextuality, relying not merely on military fiction from a number of periods and cultures, but also upon a careful exploitation of Greek mythology, in particular the equation of the cavalry barracks, with their piles of horse-dung, with the Augean Stables, and the Theseus-like quest of Meheu's platoon through the labyrinth of the compound at night.

Indeed, *Casse-pipe,* even in its fragmentary form, is far more than an exercise in the genre of military fiction from which it derives, and Céline is at pains to emphasize the inherent strangeness of the military environment to the new volunteer Ferdinand right from the beginning of the novel. To the sentry's cry to Meheu, 'Brigadier, it's the volunteer!' comes the unexpected reply, 'Let the silly fool in!'[8] which is unexpected, not because of its rough aggressivity, but because it deliberately seeks to exclude the recruit from a closed military world – as closed linguistically, as Godard comments, as a cavalry barracks is confined by its walls.[9] The strangeness of the barracks at night immediately becomes threatening when Ferdinand meets the *Maréchal des logis*, Rancotte, who uncannily singles out the new recruit for persecution and does so by repeating the same accusations as those made throughout *Mort à crédit* by Ferdinand's father Auguste: 'But, my God, he stinks, this fellow!'[10] Indeed, if *Casse-pipe* is seen as a sequel to *Mort à crédit*, Ferdinand's search for refuge from the extended persecution of his father merely leads him to an extreme image of that persecution in the person of Rancotte, with much the same sexual psychoanalytical implications. As Jean-Pierre Richard suggests, in his remarkable essay on the novel, 'Casque-pipe', the military helmet or *casque* is a symbol of castration, and the piles of horse-dung in which Ferdinand and the platoon hide from the vengeful Rancotte constitute a powerful image of a search for non-being.[11]

Not only is Ferdinand distinguished from the rest of the regiment by the fact that he alone is wearing civilian clothes, a Raglan, no doubt borrowed from Uncle Edouard's pile of 'pardessus' at the end of *Mort à crédit*; he also stands out because he is a Parisian in a regiment predominantly made up of Bretons. This distinctiveness is compounded by the literal incomprehensibility of the cavalry barracks at night, in which vision and hearing are seriously impaired. When Ferdinand first meets his tormentor Rancotte, he records that 'I couln't see his eyes, because of the smoky lamp and, especially, because of his képi';[12] Brigadier Meheu 'has difficulty in opening my docket . . . and then in reading my name';[13] and Ferdinand is unable to hear what the others are saying: 'They spoke harshly together, they made comments. I couldn't understand what they were asking me . . . just bellows.'[14] This incomprehension leads Céline into an extended picture of the cavalry barracks in one night which corresponds to a nightmare, punctuated by the eruption of frantic, unreal horses, and dominated by the fear of authority. Nor is Ferdinand the only victim of this. For only half-explained reasons, Meheu's platoon is forced to leave its stables and set off through the dark and driving rain in a quest for the password which they have all inexplicably forgotten but which remains tantalizingly close. In this way, the fragment rapidly rises above conventional military comedy of the belle époque period. The stock comic cast of the members of an incompetent platoon who have forgotten that most basic military prerequisite, their password, becomes something much more complex and elusive. Like Bardamu's cavalry platoon in *Voyage au bout de la nuit*, Meheu's men are forced to wander in a strange quest through the night of untold nightmares, like Theseus through the labyrinth, and the search for the *word* which will release them, and which they never discover, reflects the increasing difficulty imposed upon the reader by a more complex textuality. At the same time, the forgetting of a password which will permit them to complete their mission is also a Freudian slip which reinforces the quest for nonbeing by hiding from Rancotte in the dung-heap of Arcile's Augean Stables. It is a significant act of unconscious abdication which indicates a refusal of their role and their own identity. A year after *Mort à crédit*, Céline had still not forgotten his Freud.

What is interesting about this major fragment of *Casse-pipe*, however, is that, like *Voyage au bout de la nuit*, night is followed by a dawn, but, unlike the first novel, this episode concludes more positively. After the night of initiation in which Ferdinand is uniformly persecuted and in which the platoon fails ever to discover the password, Rancotte finally brings an end to proceedings by ordering the sounding of the *diane*, reveille. All at once, the atmosphere, and the writing, change: 'Then, all around us, things came out like eyes . . . things in the mist . . . thousands of windows looking at us . . . reflections, I think . . . reflections . . . It was almost day now . . . it got paler from above . . . the roofs . . . and the whole barracks . . . the walls . . . the whitewash.'[15] In other words, the first fragment of *Casse-pipe* can be read as a drama of initiation or as a *veillée d'armes*, which, in spite of, or perhaps because of, the torment inflicted on the narrator, enables him to enter the real world more positively than any of his previous fictional counterparts: after the 'servitudes' come the 'grandeurs militaires'. And this pattern is sustained throughout the remaining fragments of the novel. In the riding-school, Ferdinand, portrayed as a burlesque Theseus in the opening section, emulates Captain Dagomart, a 'veritable Centaur'[16] on his mount Rubicon (itself an intratextual nod towards Bardamu's comment, 'Not every one is Caesar' in *Voyage*)[17] and finally becomes susceptible to the mystique of the regiment, accessible through dreams and not through language. The Bretons accede to this mystique through their animal-like simplicity: 'I was the only one from Paris. The others came from Finistère, and perhaps two or three from the Côtes-du-Nord. They didn't have very honest eyes, they were half shut, clear blue.'[18] And 'they had come to be soldiers, and that made them dreamy, with an animal-like dreaminess.'[19] Similarly, Ferdinand's officer, Lieutenant Portat des Oncelles, whose death he will witness in 1914, has exchanged language for the mystique of the army. Witnessing the chaos of the riding-class, he says nothing but the slightest of orders: 'it all left him in a dream.'[20] In spite of its brutality, the world of the regiment has its own enticing *féerie*, announced in the misty dawn after the first night. *Casse-pipe* is thus a novel of apprenticeship, though, in its original conception, leading towards self-inflicted death in the doomed cavalry charge.

This apprenticeship will culminate, in the later unpublished fragments of the novel collected by Dominique de Roux, in Ferdinand's complete assimilation into the regiment. In the episode describing the 1913 *quatorze juillet* parade, Ferdinand notes that he is now now longer a *bleu*, but has been promoted to *brigadier*: 'As a result of all the knocks I took, I became a perfect soldier.'[21] This even has the effect of reconciling him with his parents: 'I told my uncle and my parents that we could celebrate, and they paid for me to give drinks to the men.'[22] At the same time, as we have seen, this promotion coincides with a new sense of group identity, unseen in any of Céline's previous writing, at least in a positive sense: 'We drank curaçao all along the road. The squadron liked that with baked potatoes. A combination of ours.'[23] The inevitable consequence of this assimilation is that once Ferdinand, formerly the terrified new recruit persecuted by Rancotte and his platoon *brigadier* Meheu, becomes a *brigadier* in his own right, he too turns tormentor of the *bleus*: 'In the hut where I was in command, there was no God or hope[?]. I'd finally understood. At the heart of discipline there must be absolute discipline!'[24] and as his superior Lacadent comments: 'So, you're terrifying the new men? It seems that you're the biggest bastard in the regiment?'[25] Céline's recognition of the unrealizable nature of the ideal of Communism leads him to a simple anti-humanist dialectic in which individuals are either victims or persecutors, but cannot live in harmony together. It is this bleak vision which informs the anti-Semitic writing as well: Jew and Aryan are naturally antagonistic and are condemned to mutual persecution.

It remains unclear why Céline found it so difficult to make progress with and complete *Casse-pipe*, particularly because the initial fragment is one of the most complex and linguistically dense pieces of writing he produced. Henri Godard is probably correct in noting that the project was the victim of a shift in ideology around 1936. Whereas until then, pacifist denunciation of the army, in its belle époque shape, was still a powerful mode of writing, as evidenced by the success of *Voyage*, after 1936 the perception of the army was very different. In any case, the target had shifted, or at least conflated, into a mixture of pacifism and racism.[26] In other words, the receptivity of the public was likely to be different and Céline himself had turned his attention from the army to the Jews. Nevertheless, it is also likely that Céline found considerable difficulties in the composition of his third novel, which were resolved by the incursion into the new stylistic experience of polemic. In particular, the structural problems posed by the integration of the long opening section in the barracks, followed by the various fragmentary episodes showing Ferdinand's rise in the military hierarchy, into the finale of the war-time cavalry charge which constituted the book's main purpose, may well have proved insuperable. As it is, however, *Casse-pipe* still marks a progression in Céline's fictional output over *Voyage* and *Mort à crédit*, in particular stylistically and in the introduction of the notion of 'féerie' which would become one of the centre-pieces of the later fiction, as well as providing a fictional demonstration of the victim turned bully which parallels the anti-Semitic writing.

II 'DRÔLE-DE-GUERRE'

It would be a mistake to believe that the French entered the Second World War with anything like the defeatism which was subsequently imputed to them. Marcel Déat's famous newspaper article 'Mourir pour Danzig?' on 4 May 1939, while it may have translated a certain public bewilderment at France's treaty obligations, was distinctly unusual in expressing a refusal to fight. Rather, as Jean Crémieux-Brilhac demonstrates in *Les Français de l'année 40*, while the euphoria of 1870 and 1914 was absent in 1939, the French, almost unanimously, set about the task of war with calm determination.[27] Even the extreme Right, from Maurras' Action Française to La Rocque's PSF and Brasillach's *Je suis partout*, marched to the beat of the Republic's drums once war was declared, however much they had opposed it before September. There were several contributory reasons for this almost unanimous response: the triumph of patriotism or nationalism, and especially anti-Germanism, over international ideology; the comforting belief in France's military invincibility, fostered by the cult of the Maginot Line and the size of France's army, the biggest in the world, and summed up in the soon-to-be-ironic slogan: 'Nous vaincrons parce que nous sommes les plus forts'; and the fact that the government in power in 1939, while dependant upon the same parliament as that elected in 1936, was no longer the 'Jewish' Front Populaire, but made up of Radical, even conservative, stalwarts. In 1939, paradoxically, there was no 'Union Sacrée', because, unlike in 1914, it did not need to be invented or forged. The French marched together, calmly, against their traditional and, on the Left, ideological, enemy. Indeed, the only group to be severely discomfited by the outbreak of war were the Communists, who, right up until the signing of the Molotov–Ribbentrop Pact, had been the most vociferous advocates of an anti-fascist coalition. With Soviet Russia now the ally of Nazi Germany, members of the PCF twisted and turned to depict the war as a purely imperialist conflict in which French workers had no role. It was an argument which did not convince everyone. Paul Nizan left his prestigious post in the Party hierarchy and resigned; the Party itself was banned by Daladier, and its leaders either went underground or, like Maurice Thorez, deserted and fled to Moscow. But the bulk of the Party membership, however reluctantly, obeyed their conscription orders and joined their units to fight the ally of the socialist homeland.

Céline's own experience was in many ways typical of that of the French as a whole, including the extreme Right, during the unreal period of armed hostilities from September 1939 to April 1940, known as the 'Phoney War'. Initially, he decided to keep his head down. In September 1939, he and Lucette left the apartment in the Rue Lepic, possibly through fear of bombing, and moved to Saint-Germain-en-Laye, where he opened a medical practice. Céline had long been attracted to the elegant suburban town set in a forest and had invested in property there, though he never lived in the apartment he bought from the proceeds of *Voyage au bout de la nuit*. As Frédéric Vitoux points out, however, the project to return to general practice in Saint-Germain-en-Laye was ill thought out and quite unrealistic. Céline and Lucette rented a little house at 15 Rue de Bellevue, a quiet provincial cul-de-sac, far from the beaten track, the most inauspicious place for an unknown doctor to build up a clientele from scratch, even if he did put on his visiting-cards: 'Dr Louis F. Destouches, Graduate of the Paris Faculty of Medecine, War Invalid, *Médaille Militaire*, General practice,

Consultuations every day from 1 pm to 3 pm'.[28] Unsurprisingly, after a
month the new doctor had not attracted one single patient, and the dream
of a new life in Saint-Germain, so different from proletarian Clichy, where
Lucette could have taught at the local *conservatoire*, was quickly dashed. In
October, the couple returned to Paris and moved in with Céline's mother
in the Rue Marsollier.

It was from here that he embarked upon one of the more bizarre adventures of a career which was certainly not lacking in excitement. On 9
November 1939, the Commission de Réforme had confirmed his invalid
status at 70 per cent, though it was not to do so definitely until 22 July
1942.[29] Yet Céline was keen to serve in some capacity. As we have seen, way
back in 1924 he had taken the exams qualifying him as a ship's doctor, and
on 1 December 1939 he was employed by the Paquet steamship company as
ship's doctor on board the *Chella*, a civilian passenger boat, though recently
armed for warfare, sailing on the Marseille–Casablanca run. This was
only a temporary appointment, replacing the permanent ship's doctor, but,
in time of war, it entailed Céline's promotion to the naval rank of sub-
lieutenant, which gave him inordinate pleasure because of both the salary
and the status. He wrote to his friend Jean Bonvilliers enthusing at the
modest salary of 1700 francs per month and particularly at the rejuvenating
effect of the appointment: 'It takes me back 25 years, to when I was in the
12e. There hasn't been a service doctor since the days of wooden ships –
Not only that, but they've transferred me to the navy with one stripe! And
with a salary, unfortunately, which goes with the rank . . .'[30] Céline was back
to one of his favourite themes, complaints about his poverty. Presumably
the loss of his medical posts and the drying-up of his royalties had coincided
with the transfer of all his liquid assets into gold to make him temporarily
short of money, and in his letters to Jean Bonnevilliers he prays for the
posting to last, for financial and emotional reasons: 'I'd cut off an arm to
make it last . . . Still, I'll have lived!'[31]

Unfortunately, the experience was all too brief. On the night of 5 and 6
January 1940, at 10 p.m., the *Chella*, with 200 Moroccan troops on board,
collided with the British torpedo-boat, HMS *Kingston Cornelian*, just off
Gibraltar. The British vessel sank in 17 seconds, with the loss of 27 crew, and
the *Chella* was badly damaged in the prow. Céline spent the night performing emergency surgery on the injured, with a professionalism appreciated
by the rest of the *Chella*'s crew. One of the ship's officers wrote to him
shortly after, praising his work: 'Your behaviour during the "heroic" night
was much commented on.'[32] As for Céline, he wrote a graphic and highly
populist account to Jean Bonnevilliers, before narrating the event in more
flowery terms to his friend, the medical Colonel Camus: 'it goes without
saying that your friend, throughout this tragic night, between the dead, the
drowning and the wounded, brought honour to those who taught him the
profession of arms and acts, and courage and discipline.' He concluded:
'Between you and me, I've never had such fun.'[33] The *Chella* limped into

Marseille for a complete refit and Céline was paid off. His subsequent attempts to find another posting with the Paquet company all failed, and his short career as a naval officer was at an end.

He still needed work, however, and, against an international backdrop of a growing military threat with the German occupation of part of Norway and Denmark (where the bulk of his gold was deposited), he took over as head of the municipal clinic of Sartrouville, where he had worked temporarily in October 1939, replacing the permanent doctor, Dubroca, who had been mobilized.[34] Once again, Céline was back in the northern industrial suburbs. Sartrouville lies on the north bank of the Seine, between Clichy, where he had begun his career in general practice, and Bezons, where he was to continue it later in 1940. It was in Sartrouville that he experienced the invasion.

The German offensive began on 10 May with General Heinz Guderian's panzers streaming unexpectedly through the Ardennes, supported by almost complete air superiority. They were followed by the infantry and moved rapidly to the west and the south, isolating Belgium and Holland and splitting the British Expeditionary Force and part of the French army, which was evacuated through Dunkirk, from the bulk of the French troops. Belgium and Holland surrendered, the British dug in on the other side of the Channel, and the French army, hampered by poor communications and a seeming lack of any air support, broke and fled. The *Exode* had begun: a disorganized retreat by the French army to the south of the Loire, accompanied and hampered by a headlong flight of the civilian population, intent on escaping the oncoming Germans and salvaging what they could of their belongings. In one month the Germans had reached the Seine, the French Government had retreated, first to Tours and then to Bordeaux, and French military and civil order had all but broken down. Rather than the simple fact of military defeat, similar to that at Sedan in 1870 and to the one so narrowly avoided on the Marne in 1914, it was the breakdown of civil order, the panic of the northern population, which gave the French collapse in 1940 its traumatic quality.

In Sartrouville, as in other northern municipalities, the mayor had decided to evacuate part of the population, along with strategic and administrative resources like the town archives and the town fire-engine.[35] As head of the municipal clinic, Céline took command of the town ambulance and, with a driver and Lucette as unofficial nurse, evacuated two newborn babies and their alcoholic grandmother. The plan was for the municipal convoy to head for Pressigny-les-Pins, south of Montargis, prior to crossing the Loire at Gien, where they arrived on 15 June.[36] Like all the towns on the north bank of the Loire, Gien was blocked by refugees from the north and the panic-stricken crowds made the bridge impassable. Céline and Lucette decided to spend the night in a cinema, the Artistic, full of the evacuated patients from a Parisian mental hospital, and to wait until morning before attempting to cross the river. But during the night there was a fierce air-raid which destroyed much of the town centre, and Céline abandoned plans to cross at Gien, deciding instead to move on to Cosne-sur-Loire. This bridge was still intact when Céline and his ambulance crossed the Loire in late morning on 16 June, but was destroyed by German aircraft towards 3 o'clock in the afternoon.[37] It was this action which he transposed into the bombing of the bridge of Orléans which begins *Guignol's Band.*

At Cosne-sur-Loire they were welcomed at the former school, which had been turned into a military hospital, where the commander, Colonel Rehm, and his assistant, Dr Bruel, an admirer of Céline's work, took care of the two babies, leaving Céline and Lucette the freedom to sleep in the open on the banks of the Loire, now peaceful again.[38] The following day, they drove on with the grandmother and the babies to a little village on the Allier, Le Guettin, where they slept in a barn, and on 18 June they moved on to Issoudon, where Céline had hoped to set up permanent camp. The town was the target of another enemy air-attack, however, and, after handing over the two babies to a local crèche, Céline and Lucette continued on their way to La Rochelle, arriving on the evening of 19 June. It was here that they handed over the grandmother into safe keeping and, on 20 June, Céline reported to the Préfecture of the Department of the Charente-Inférieure. He was sent to the port of La Pallice (from which he had left for Africa on his League of Nations mission to Africa in 1926) with a note from Dr Detrieux, the departmental deputy public health official, stating that 'this doctor, who is a naval public-health doctor wishing to be used, would be happy to accept any post, if there were one, either on a ship or for anything else.'[39]

Little seems to have come of this, and the whole episode on the west coast is murky. Céline subsequently claimed that he tried to get away by boat, and Lucette remembered trying to persuade him to go to England:

> Boats were leaving for England. I said to Louis, 'Let's go!' Louis loved England, he thought about it. He would have found some medical work there, I would have been a dance teacher in London – why not? And everything that followed would have been different. But no, he said to himself: 'The kids, the old lady, I have to take them home.' After the Exodus, the panic, people were returning to their homes. Louis also said: 'You don't leave your country because things are going bad.' And then, he was curious, he wanted to see what was going on. And how could he forget his mother, who was still in Paris?[40]

As it was, Céline moved south and inland, to the town of Saint-Jean-d'Angély, where he was assigned to the French air force, working in an impromptu refugee camp as a doctor for the evacuated workers of the south-western aircraft company SNACSO.[41] It was here, on 30 June, that Céline's war ended, and he and his colleague, Dr Leconte, were released with the testimonial that they had 'fulfilled their mission with all the zeal, competence and devotion which was to be expected of them'.[42] By 14 July 1940, he and Lucette had returned the ambulance to the municipality of

Sartrouville, along with its cargo of the two babies and the alcoholic grand-mother, still clutching her bottles of red wine.

It was France's first *quatorze juillet* of the Occupation. In Bordeaux on 18 June, Paul Reynaud's government had resigned and had asked Marshal Philippe Pétain to seek an armistice with the victorious Germans, an armistice signed on 22 June at Rethondes in the same railway carriage in which the Germans had surrendered in 1918. The terms of the armistice were crippling, both economically and politically. Economically, they amounted to the expropriation of most of France's economic resources and production and, through rationing, the slow but inevitable starvation of the French population, forced to have recourse to the black market to supplement their meagre allowance. Politically, they divided the country into two, the occupied northern zone and, south of the Loire, the ironically named 'Free Zone', ruled, under German influence, by Marshal Pétain and a cabinet of conservative politicians, headed by Pierre Laval. Dire as the armistice was, it seemed to be France's sole choice. Her only ally, Britain, who many believed had led her into this doomed military adventure in the first place, only to abandon her at Dunkirk and subsequently destroy her fleet at Mers-el-Kébir, looked set to suffer the same fate, and few Frenchmen had even listened to de Gaulle's historic broadcast from London on the BBC on 18 June, much less been convinced by it. France was in the hands of the Germans and the extreme Right who had never liked the Third Republic and were determined to expunge the memory of 1936 and the 'Jewish' Front Populaire.

Céline, back in Paris after his picaresque journey to the west, found himself in an odd position. In one sense, as an accurate prophet of defeat, who had warned of the danger posed by the Jews, he found himself for once aligned with the party in power. In another, he was unemployed again. The doctor he had replaced as head of the clinic in Sartrouville had been demobilized and had resumed his post. It was at this point that Céline learnt that there was a vacancy as head of the municipal clinic in Bezons, the neighbouring suburb to Sartrouville. The incumbent, Dr Hogarth, was Haitian and, as a citizen of a country which was still on the side of the Allies, was no longer allowed to practise in France. Not only that, but the Communist Mayor of Bezons, M. Ferdonnet, had been disenfranchized and was replaced by a 'National Administrator', Frédéric Empeytaz. Céline was extremely anxious to have the post, and lobbied hard to get it, using the influence of M. Blanqui, the regional health director at Versailles, who hinted that if Céline were not appointed, the Minister would intervene in person.[43] On 3 November, Céline wrote again to Empeytaz, invoking anti-Semitic and anti-Masonic arguments at a time when exclusion of Jews and Masons from public office was official Vichy policy, in a letter which was a scarcely concealed threat: 'I do find that there are rather too many Jewish and Masonic doctors in Bezons – currently outlawed, by the way – I think it would be harmonious if a native of Courbevoie – *médaille militaire* and a war invalid – were to find his natural place there.'[44] This campaign, from a

Figure 1 The son: Céline and his parents (Archives L.-F. Céline/Collection François Gibault/IMEC)

Figure 2 The Passage Choiseul in the belle époque (Roger-Viollet)

Figure 3 The soldier: Céline as *Maréchal des Logis* of the '12 Cuir' (Archives L.-F. Céline/ Collection François Gibault/IMEC)

Figure 4 The secret agent: Céline in London, identity photograph (Archives L.-F. Céline/Collection François Gibault/IMEC)

Figure 5 The colonialist: Céline's cabin in Bikobimbo

Figure 6 Céline's marriage with Edith Follet, Brittany, 1917 (Archives L.-F. Céline/Collection François Gibault/ IMEC)

Figure 7 The civil servant: the Mission Rockefeller, led by Céline, meets Mussolini, 1925 (Archives L.-F. Céline/Collection François Gibault/IMEC)

Figure 8 The doctor: the *Dispensaire* in the Rue Fanny, Clichy

Figure 9 The Ile Robinson at Clichy

Figure 10 *Voyage au bout de la nuit*: 'Looking at the ladies in the café': Pierre Bonnard, *La Place Clichy*, 1912 (Photo Giraudon, Musée des Beaux-Arts et d'Archéologie, Besançon/© ADAGP, Paris and DACS, London, 1998)

Figure 11 The writer: Céline in 1932 (Collection of C. W. Nettelbeck)

Figure 12 Céline and Elizabeth Craig (Archives L.-F. Céline/ Collection François Gibault/IMEC)

Figure 13 Success: the Zola lecture at Médan, 1933 (Roger-Viollet)

Figure 14 Lucette Almansor (Archives L.-F. Céline/ Collection François Gibault/IMEC)

Figure 15 The *Exode* of 1940: Céline, Lucette and the Sartrouville
ambulance (Archives L.-F. Céline/Collection François Gibault/IMEC)

Figure 16 The anti-Semite: Céline at the Institut d'Etudes des
Questions Juives, Paris, 1941 (Roger-Viollet)

Figure 18 . . . and exile: Céline in Denmark (Archives L.-F. Céline/Collection François Gibault/IMEC)

Figure 17 'From castle to castle . . .': Sigmaringen

Figure 19 Back in favour: the recording session with Arletty and Michel Simon in Meudon (*Paris Match*/M. Simon)

Figure 20 After Bébert: Céline and Toto the parrot in Meudon (*Paris Match*/F. Pages)

Figure 21 Céline in Meudon shortly before his death (Roger-Viollet)

Figure 22 The funeral: Gaston Gallimard, Roger Nimier and Marcel Aymé (Paris Presse)

personality who was not afraid to hint at powerful official support, led to Céline's appointment as head of the Bezons clinic on 21 November 1940 at a salary of 36,000 francs per annum, and on 21 December he was registered as a doctor in the department of the Seine-et-Oise. He was to remain in this post until his departure for Germany in June 1944. Céline cut by no means an orthodox figure as the director of a municipal clinic: his dress became increasingly unkempt and he commuted from Paris to Bezons on an old moped, on which he did his rounds. Moreover, he was entirely consistent with his very earliest medical writings of the 1920s in subordinating clinical concerns to preoccupations with living conditions and diet. From the very beginning of his work in Bezons, he bombarded Empeytaz with complaints about the effects of rationing and the poverty of his patients. It was not enough to provide food and fuel vouchers, it was important to guarantee the means to purchase these necessities: 'To "receive" the voucher is valuable, but the purchase of the food to which the voucher entitles the patient is even more indispensable,'[45] and he quoted a mother of a 5-year-old child, the wife of a prisoner of war: 'The day I buy coal, we don't eat.'[46] In this battle against the deprivation of his patients, he enlisted the help of his highly placed acquaintances, making frequent visits, for example, to the offices of Fernand de Brinon, Vichy Ambassador to the German Occupation forces.[47] Such was his concern at the combined effects of diet and climate that, in the harsh winter of 1940, he filled the clinic with all the neighbourhood tramps.[48]

In Bezons he maintained good relations with Dr Hogarth and, particularly, with his wife, also a doctor, who acted as Céline's locum during his frequent absences. He also remained on good terms with Empeytaz and used his influence with de Brinon, Pierre Pucheu and Pierre Laval to get him a coveted post as *sous-préfet*, finally succeeding in February 1942, when his friend was appointed to Saint-Dizier in the department of Finistère.[49] One particular friendship that he made was with a former schoolteacher appointed by Empeytaz as municipal librarian of Bezons, Albert Serouille, whom he was treating for tuberculosis. He wrote later to Empeytaz that he was encouraging Serrouille to write a history of Bezons, which 'he was over the moon about,'[50] and when *Bezons à travers les âges* appeared in 1944 Céline provided the preface, in which he acknowledged his debt to the industrial suburbs in which he had lived for so much of his life. Living with his mother in the small apartment in the Rue Marsollier was not proving easy and, in particular, there was friction between Marguerite Destouches and her daughter-in-law. Gen Paul came to the couple's rescue by finding them a three-room apartment at number 4 Rue Girardon, just round the corner from the apartment they had occupied in the Rue Lepic. The apartment was on the fourth floor and looked out in one direction on to the Moulin de la Galette and in the other all over the north and west of Paris.[51] Céline and Lucette moved in in March 1941. Céline had a study, which he had criss-crossed with washing-lines on which he hung pages of manuscript with clothes-pegs. The rest of the apartment was decorated with quotations from Shakespeare which Céline wrote on the walls, together with a few objects such as African sculptures, a Dutch copper lamp and a wooden angel suspended from the ceiling. All around were piles of books.[52] Every evening, he carried his moped up the stairs and hung it on the wall. This Bohemian atmosphere was accentuated, according to some witnesses like the ever-malicious Gen Paul or Marie Bell, by stocks of coal in the bath and black-market produce in the cupboards.[53] It is certainly true that, throughout the Occupation, Céline kept up a remorseless search for black-market goods, soliciting food shipments from his friends in the countryside and prospecting ever deeper into Brittany to get supplies.

Céline and Lucette were to stay in the Rue Girardon until their departure for Germany in June 1944, and it was here that he wrote the two volumes of *Guignol's Band.* Just before moving in, however, in the autumn of 1940, he wrote his third and last pamphlet, *Les Beaux Draps*, in which he poured out his reactions to France's defeat, the new world in which she, and he, found themselves, and the daily misery facing the population of the industrial suburbs as the first winter of the Occupation set in.

III *LES BEAUX DRAPS*

The third pamphlet was published in March 1941 under the imprint of a new company set up by Denoël in the early days of the Occupation, the Nouvelles Editions Françaises, whose headquarters were next-door to Editions Denoël in the Rue Amélie, and which specialized in politically loaded texts, possibly to ensure a regular supply of paper in days of severe paper-rationing. Denoël was desperate to reopen his publishing house as soon as possible,[54] and *Les Beaux Draps* appeared in a newly invented collection called 'Intérêt National: Le Juif et la France', which also included Georges Montandon's *Comment reconnaître le Juif?*, a pamphlet by a Dr Querrioux, *La Médecine et les Juifs*, and two works by Lucien Rebatet, *La Presse*, and *Les Tribus du cinéma et du théâtre*, written under his regular pseudonym of François Vinneuil.[55] It was, incidentally, the technicality that all of Denoël's politically charged books were published under the imprint of the Nouvelles Editions Françaises which accounted for the acquittal of the Denoël publishing house on charges of printing work favourable to the enemy or of a racist nature in April 1948.[56]

Initially, Céline's pamphlet seems to fit into the general heading of 'Le Juif et la France'. *Les Beaux Draps* consists of an extended sequence of 'bagatelles', fragmentary reflections on the current state of France after the defeat of 1940 and the continuing threat posed by the Jews, followed by a concluding narrative which finally positions a narrator, the Ferdinand of *Mort à crédit* and the two preceding pamphlets, in a sequence which rapidly becomes one of the most impressive stylistic *tours de force* ever accomplished by Céline.

The book begins by justifying its title and recounting the *beaux draps*, the 'right mess' in which the French find themselves after the ignominious events of the summer, witnessed self-righteously from the perspective of a hero of the First World War. As the narrator confesses with mock regret, with allusions to Céline's own journey in the Sartrouville ambulance: 'I ran after the French Army from Bezons to La Rochelle, but I could never catch up with it';[57] and he quotes the contemporary jibe directed at the recruit of 1940: 'Hey, what have done with your rifle? It fell on the field of honour.'[58] In fact, the self-righteousness goes almost too far to be credible. When Ferdinand evokes the memory of the great Poincaré: 'This would never have happened if he had been alive,'[59] the reader may wonder if this is the same Poincaré so contemptuously referred to at the beginning of *Voyage au bout de la nuit* as going to open a 'little dog's show'.[60] As with *Bagatelles pour un massacre* and *L'Ecole des cadavres*, a strong possibility exists that Céline is compiling a Flaubertian *dictionnaire des idées reçues*, a possibility reinforced by the presence at the end of the pamphlet of Ferdinand's interlocutor, a Doctor Divetot, with connotations of the town Yvetot, at the heart of Flaubert's imaginative geography.

What is curious about Céline's third pamphlet is that, while on one level it is clearly about France in 1940 and 1941 and the 'very serious mess'[61] it is in, he is very careful, unlike Rebatet in *Les Décombres* of 1942, to avoid any specific historical references, either to Hitler or to Pétain. In other words, *Les Beaux Draps* takes place in a sort of political vacuum in which Céline's recurrent obsessions are allowed to dominate, in particular his anti-Semitism. Yet the anti-Semitism is removed from any form of historical specificity and elevated to what appears to be a timeless threat. Looking round at French society after the arrival of the Germans, the narrator notes that nothing has changed: 'There are more Jews than ever in the streets, more Jews than ever in the press, more Jews than ever in the law, more Jews than ever in the Sorbonne, more Jews than ever in medicine, more Jews than ever in the theatre or the Opera or the Comédie Française, in industry, in the banks. Paris and France are more than ever given over to the Masons and the Jews, who are more insolent than ever.'[62] This was plainly untrue: although Vichy's notorious *Statut sur les Juifs* was not promulgated until 2 June 1941, the new regime acted swiftly, and without the prompting of the Germans, to exclude both Jews and Freemasons from the professions and public office. A law of 13 August 1940 outlawed Freemasonry, and on 3 October 1940 a further law was passed excluding Jews from public office, positions in the army and the law, and the theatre and the cinema.[63] What Céline is doing is what he would do later in *D'un château l'autre* and what is identified by Arnold Mandel as that essential feature of anti-Semitic psychology by which the anti-Semite desperately needs the continued existence of the object of his persecution.

Hence Céline, after the German victory of 1940, and with the collapse of Britain apparently imminent, continued the same litany as that which ran through *Bagatelles* and *L'Ecole des cadavres* in 1937 and 1938. In France, the

Jews dominate all walks of life, and internationally they still pull all the strings through the Warburg Bank in New York and, especially, the insidious City of London which, under Pitt, brought down the French monarchy.[64] The only solution, as in *L'Ecole des cadavres*, is an extreme form of racism, and Céline adopts a racial definition of the Jew which is radically more extreme than that adopted later by Vichy. Whereas Vichy defined a Jew as a person having three Jewish grandparents,[65] Céline trumpets: 'By Jew, I mean any person who counts among his grandparents one single Jew,'[66] and he moves on to an explicit incitement to violence: 'String the Jew up, there's not a moment to lose!'[67]

In fact, Céline's main strategy against the Jews is to mount a revolution before they do, and one from which they will be excluded: 'The Jew is afraid of nothing . . . He's only afraid of one thing, of Communism without Jews.'[68] Much of *Les Beaux Draps* is therefore taken up with Céline's blueprint for a 'Communisme Labiche'[69] or 'Communisme petit-bourgeois'[70] which, with its minimum salary of 100 francs a day, full employment and comprehensive nationalization, together with motorways leading to the sea, is often read as a utopian political vision. In fact, not only does it bear an uncanny resemblance to Nazi social policy, it especially represents the triumph of that petit-bourgeois ideology so derided in *Mort à crédit*. What Céline is doing in *Les Beaux Draps* is what he had already done in the medical pamphlets of the 1920s, and specifically in 'Les Assurances sociales', in which he prescribed Disraeli's policy of pre-empting a threat by introducing a lesser evil. In public-health terms, the Ford system is portrayed as better than a socialist revolution and the sole means of pre-empting it, but the target of the pamphlet remains the parlous state of French urban living conditions. In *Les Beaux Draps* the choice is between 'Communism Labiche or death!':[71] the triumph of those very same petit-bourgeois who marched so readily to war or that of the Jews. Either way, the real problem is the misery of France in 1940.

What is important for the pamphlet, however, is that this misery is not purely material but is essentially spiritual, and here Céline takes up a theme introduced in *L'Ecole des cadavres* linking culture and race. He writes: 'A nation . . . can recover admirably from the greatest military defeats and the cruellest occupations, but only on one condition, the essential and mystical condition of remaining faithful, through victories and defeats, to the same ethnic group, the same blood, the same racial roots.'[72] And the specific culture of France is mystical and not intellectual. Currently, 'We're dying from being without legends, without mystery, without grandeur.'[73] Yet salvation is at hand: 'Every person who has a heart which beats has also his own song, his own little personal music,'[74] and the privileged expression of that music is in the Nietzschean celebration of dance: 'We must learn to dance again . . . We'll never dance in the factory, we'll never sing there either.'[75] Once again, the ideal of a pre-industrial world emerges in Céline's writing, accessed through man's innate musicality and fostered by the author's own cultivation of the 'petite musique' in his style. Not only does the cultivation of 'legend' lead back to the medieval world of Krogold and Charlemagne, it also expressly excludes a culture based upon the intellect, a culture in which Céline singles out Montaigne as a crucial originator: 'What do I care for preacherman M. Ben Montaigne, the sly old rabbi? . . . He's hardly the joy I'm seeking, fresh, roguish, mischievous, passionate . . . I'd like to die laughing, but gently . . . Du Bellay is more dear to me than Racine . . . M. Montaigne lacks all lyricism and that's a great crime in my eyes, he constructs his cunning Talmuds, his fat manuals on the "Perfect Jew".'[76] As we have seen, speculation on Montaigne's Jewish ancestry was widespread in France in the 1930s and Céline's adoption of 'Ben Montaigne' casts a specifically racial light on the reference to Montaigne in *Voyage au bout de la nuit*, while enabling him to divide French literature into two strands. There was the arid, intellectual one, beginning with Montaigne and Racine, whose 'Jewish' ancestry he also investigated, and culminating in Céline's post-war denigration of Sartre and Robbe-Grillet, and the creative, emotive culture, beginning with the Middle Ages and Rabelais and surviving into the twentieth century in such diverse figures as Bernanos, Conrad, Drieu and Malraux: all in the Nietzschean tradition. Céline's debt to Nietzsche, visible from *Semmelweis* onwards, cannot be underestimated.

It is at this point that the narrative proper takes on its full significance. It opens with a description of that cruel first winter of the Occupation:

> Oh! It's a hard winter . . . you can say that . . . the Seine will be full of ice-floes . . . I'm waiting for it . . . I saw that from the Pont de Bruyères . . . it's blowing a gale . . . nature isn't kind to people in need . . . Such a cold wind! . . . It's so cold! . . . The little mountain of Argenteuil is all frozen . . . with its windmill . . . It's covered in a big cloak of snow . . . Oh! It's a hard winter! The plain is covered in white as far as the distant hills, far away, all in white . . . It's playing at being Russia in the wind coming from the steppes . . . in whistling dancing whirlwinds and snowflakes and dust.[77]

It is a very rich descriptive passage, with medieval allusions to Villon and the opening of the *Testament*, and visual connotations, in the swirling flakes of snow, of Impressionist painting, which used the Seine at Argenteuil as a recurrent subject. At the same time, with this reach of the Seine, crossed by the Pont de Bruyères, we are back in the essential locus of Céline's writing: La Garenne-Rancy in *Voyage*, and the Ile de Robinson, just opposite Clichy, Ferdinand's origins in Courbevoie in *Mort à crédit*, and his cousin Gustin's practice beyond Asnières, and the narrator Ferdinand of *L'Ecole des cadavres*, who evokes his walk by the Seine at the island of La Grande Jatte, where he is insulted by the mermaid. This intratextuality is compounded by the very precise topographical notation: Argenteuil, the Mont Valérien, La Folie, Charlebourg and Gennevilliers, together with more fanciful names: the Rue des Bouleaux-Verts, the Rue des Michaux, the Venelle des Trois-Soeurs, the Impasse du Trou-de-Sable and the Ruelle des Bergères.[78]

This industrial landscape is dominated by the factory which provides Ferdinand the doctor with the bulk of his patients. Yet in this harsh winter being a doctor for the poor is no easy task: 'Good will is no longer enough! . . . Nor science or knowledge . . . things happen inevitably which are harsh and terrible!'[79] These 'terrible things' have more to do with deprivation than with sickness, and in the Occupation far more of the doctor's time was spent in giving out fuel and food coupons than in prescribing medical treatment: 'that's the rhythm . . . one . . . two . . . three vouchers . . . one prescription . . . That's the rate since yesterday . . . fewer and fewer prescriptions, more and more vouchers.'[80]

It is at this point that the narrative loses its realist credentials and departs into fantasy. Ferdinand is summoned to issue a death-certificate for an old lady who lives, mysteriously, 'on the limits of the town'.[81] When he arrives, he discovers that she is not dead, but has merely left, spirited away by a mysterious music. Previously, when he was talking to his colleague Divetot on the bridge, Ferdinand had heard a strange music: 'Can't you hear it? . . . Taa! . . . too! . . . too! . . . too . . . too . . . Taa! . . . Taa! . . . carried by the winter wind?'[82] When he later recounts his visit to the old lady to Divetot, he amplifies: 'You hear it like waves . . . sounds which pass . . . symphonies . . . The cry of the Swans is a thing which grasps you!'[83] The sequence is rich in resonances: the 'Appel des Cygnes' refers not merely to a 'Swan Song', the music of a dying France, but is also geographically specific to the 'Ile des Cygnes', on this reach of the river. As an island with music, 'full of noises', it has echoes of Céline's favourite play, *The Tempest*, fully developed in *Guignol's Band*, which leads to a new form of reading, in which the 'petite musique' of the Célinian style is transformed quite literally into musical notation. The word becomes sound, and in so doing ushers the author and reader into the privileged state of 'féerie', 'where melody led us'.[84] That this 'féerie' should be likened to a defeat to which the reader should surrender, and that it takes the ultimate form of a diabolical vision of betrayal, suicide and evil, is less important than the fact that the crucial transition has been made. In this respect, *Les Beaux Draps* encapsulates the process of the pamphlets as a whole: their polemic serves as a bridge between the 'realism' of *Mort à crédit* and *Casse-pipe* and the 'féerie' of the Shakespearean *Guignol's Band* and the operatic *Féerie pour une autre fois*. The narrator Ferdinand can say with pride: 'I shan't say anything more.'[85] The mission announced by the ending of the first novel has been more than accomplished, and the road between the 'voyage imaginaire' of *Voyage au bout de la nuit* and its sister genre, the 'féerie', is now open.

11

The Occupation

I GERMAN TIME

The most potent symbol of total German domination and the Nazis' intention simply to incorporate France into the new European order was the immediate imposition of German time, previously one hour ahead of the French. As Jean-Louis Bory was to show in his classic Liberation volume, *Mon Village à l'heure allemande* of 1945, it was the change in time which signified an entire change in lifestyle and political regime, enshrined in the terms of the Armistice agreement of June 1940 and confirmed as a result of Pétain's meeting with Hitler at Montoire in October 1940, which launched him 'on the road to Collaboration'. As we have seen, the Armistice agreement provided for the division of the country into three zones, in addition to the annexation of Alsace and Lorraine by Germany and of a small territory on the south-eastern border by Italy. These were a militarized zone comprising the Channel ports and the northern industrial basin centred on Lille, to be governed by the German military authorities in Brussels; an Occupied Zone covering all of France north of the Loire, together with the western and south-western coastal region; and, separated from the Occupied Zone by a *Ligne de Démarcation*, a 'Free Zone', with its capital in the spa town of Vichy. In addition to the division of the country and its loss of political coherence, the Armistice imposed draconian conditions on the defeated power. These included the dispersal of the French armed forces, apart from a small Armistice Army to patrol the Demarcation Line, and the transfer of a huge number of French prisoners of war to Germany. This was accompanied by a policy of deliberate economic spoliation, involving imposition of vast financial costs for the war itself and for maintaining the Occupation forces on French soil, together with expropriation of industrial products, raw materials and food, accompanied by a rationing policy which reduced French citizens, including children, to a daily intake of calories less than that which the German army itself recognized as insufficient for the nutrition of its own men.[1] The effect of this was not merely severely to weaken the health of the French population as a whole, but to provide the preconditions for a flourishing black market, often supplied from stocks requisitioned by the Germans themselves, which was a powerful weapon against any residual or resurgent French solidarity. In fact, in spite of French collaborationist hopes to the contrary, this economic policy was symptomatic of Germany's aims towards France as a whole: to subjugate her definitively and to use internal divisions and uncertainties as the most efficient short-term means to this end.

Much of that uncertainty stemmed from the status and operation of the Vichy regime itself. Led by Marshal Pétain, and with governments headed variously by Pierre Laval, Pierre-Etienne Flandin and Admiral Darlan, the regime in Vichy was not merely the executive power over the 'Free Zone', but also constituted the civil and administrative authority over all French citizens. When Céline wanted to boost his friend Empeytaz's application to become a Sous-Préfet in the department of Finistère, it was to his contacts in Vichy, Pucheu and Lehideux, that he went, and who finally delivered. The problem was that Vichy, although united in its hatred of the Third Republic, was hopelessly divided in terms both of personnel and policy. The 'Men of Vichy' constituted a disparate group, including parliamentarians and former ministers from the Third Republic, like Laval and Flandin, military men like Pétain himself, Weygand and Admiral Darlan, a host of journalists and propagandists, like Paul Marion, who became Minister of Information, and Fernand de Brinon, Vichy ambassador to the occupying power, pre-war Fascists, conservatives and Catholics. One significant group were the industrialists and technocrats who gathered round the director of the Worms Bank, Gabriel Le Roy Ladurie, including Jacques Le Roy Ladurie, Pierre Pucheu and François Lehideux, and who wielded considerable power under Darlan, to the extent that they were attacked by ardent collaborationists in Paris for constituting a 'synarchy' of businessmen taking over the state in order to pursue policies favourable to the big business 'trusts'.[2] Over them all hovered the presence of the Marshal, with an immense personal prestige in 1940 which had still not totally evaporated by the Normandy landings in 1944, and who, above all, remained ambiguous to his fellow-countrymen to the end. The myth of Pétain's 'double game' persisted at least until the British and American invasion of North Africa in November 1942 and often survived in the form of a belief in a patriotic Marshal who was maintained in ignorance and powerlessness by unscrupulous politicians. It was this heterogeneous nature of Vichy's corporate leadership, compounded by Pétain's own apparent inconsistencies, which led to wide divergencies in policy, essentially between traditionalism, a return to a pre-Revolutionary regional France, and modernization, in which Darlan's 'synarchic' technocrats held sway.

Part of the ambiguity arose from the fact that, amid conflicting policies, Vichy leaders had one overriding aim, which was to maintain an essentially

French national identity and protect exclusively French interests come what may. It was this which was at the basis of the Armistice itself, quite apart from the opportunity it provided for a radical realignment of domestic politics, as it was of Montoire and all subsequent policies of collaboration. For this reason, France technically remained neutral until the North African landings, and the United States, for example, retained an ambassador in Vichy, where there was continued discussion as to the merits of entering the war against Britain on Germany's side. Indeed, until the occupation of the 'Free Zone', Vichy exercised, or claimed to exercise, considerable autonomy, even going so far as to hunt down and execute German agents.[3] Even after the invasion of the 'Free Zone', Vichy leaders still deluded themselves that they retained freedom of movement. It is this illusion of independence which explains much of Vichy's policy and which lies at the base of the charge of its *attentisme*, its desire to wait and see how the war turned out. In fact, throughout the conflict Vichy comforted itself in the belief, increasingly at odds with the evidence, that it could negotiate for itself a privileged position, in the early years as a founder member of the new European order, and later, when German defeat appeared likely and then inevitable, as an honest broker between the belligerents. The fact that Nazi Germany saw France as a future protectorate and that 'total war' could result in nothing other than total defeat and unconditional surrender, not requiring a broker, honest or not, was irrelevant to Vichy's aim of 'France first'.

It was this retention of French nationalism, together with the persistence of parliamentary practices and political intrigue, let alone the suspicion of the continuing power of big business, which repelled the extreme Right. Very rapidly after the opening of the Demarcation Line, the 'Ultras' returned to Paris, under the direct presence of the German occupier and where the real integration of France into the new Europe could be plotted.

It was therefore Paris which was to be the real seat of collaboration, because it was in the capital that all the strings of German power were to be found. The ambassador in the Rue de Lille was Otto Abetz, a pre-war liberal who had converted to Nazism and enjoyed close relations with Hitler. His wife, Suzanne, was French and, as we have seen, he had worked actively in the German Embassy before the war in fostering Franco-German relations, to the extent that he had been expelled by Daladier. When he was rewarded with the post of ambassador (though, significantly enough, to Paris and not to Vichy) in 1940, he brought with him a genuine love of France and considerable knowledge of French personalities in all spheres of influence, including especially literature and journalism. This enthusiasm for France, however, often blinded those who had dealings with him to the fact that, underneath, he was coldly calculating in his determination to see France as a vassal power in Europe and to subjugate her through exploiting and fostering her internal divisions. Abetz played off Vichy against Paris, faction against faction, holding out carrots, be they a single party or a more privileged relationship within the Reich, but always ready to wield the big stick. It is significant that, right from the beginning, he saw Laval as Germany's best bet, and it was Abetz who imposed Laval's return to power in April 1942. His most important members of staff were his assistant, Rudolph Schleier, in charge of management, war veterans and prisoners of war, Ernst Achenbach, in charge of the political section, and Rahn, who headed an increasingly important information section, dealing with the press, radio and propaganda.[4] The area of the Embassy's influence which was most important for writers was the German Institute, directed by Karl Epting. His job was to 'attract French intellectuals and diffuse German culture by organizing language courses, lectures and exhibitions',[5] and in this he was assisted by Friedrich Sieburg and Friedrich Grimm. The focal point of German power in France, however, was not the Embassy but the Militärbefehlshaber in Frankreich (MBF), the Military Command in France, situated in the Hotel Majestic, headed throughout most of the Occupation by two cousins, Otto and Karl Heinrich von Stülpnagel. The MBF consisted of two major departments. The military section was responsible for 'repairing communication routes, guarding prisoners, army security, military justice',[6] and was under the command of Hans Speidel, assisted by the writer Ernst Jünger. The administrative section was subdivided into an economic section under Elmar Michel and a strictly administrative department under Werner Best, and together they supervised every aspect of French life.[7] There were two other departments under the MBF, but they received their orders directly from Berlin. The Propaganda-Abteilung, responsible to Goebbels, was headed by Heinz Schmidtke, and was in charge of both propaganda and censorship.[8] As such, it overlapped with the Embassy's own information section and Abetz fought hard to prise literary and artistic censorship away from Schmidtke, succeeding only in the summer of 1942. The officer in charge of literature at the Propaganda-Abteilung was Gerhard Heller, who had close and sympathetic contact with many French artistic figures during the Occupation. The other department nominally under the MBF, but really a power of its own, was the SS. Initially a small unit of twenty-five, led by Helmut Knochen, it had the responsibility to 'seek out, keep under surveillance and oppose "ideological enemies of Nazism": Jews, Christians, Communists and Freemasons'.[9] Knochen's reign was not an unqualified success and he resigned in the spring of 1942, making way for the appointment of Karl Oberg, who retained Knochen as deputy, and who took on the task of wholesale repression with a force of some 5000 SS, which, nevertheless, still needed the help of French auxiliaries and the French police.[10]

In Paris, the official representative of the Vichy government was Fernand de Brinon, who established himself in the former Ministry of the Interior on the Place Beauveau. Initially, there were protracted negotiations with the aim of bringing Pétain himself to Paris, or possibly Versailles, but the Marshal's conditions – that he would need his own neutral territory and military guard, on the lines of the Vatican and the Swiss Guards – were finally unacceptable to the Germans. Alongside the official representative of Collaboration were the leaders of France's pre-war Fascism: Jacques Doriot, Marcel Déat, the former Socialist député and now close to Pierre Laval, the Francisque's Marcel Bucard and the *Cagoulard* Eugène Deloncle, all jockeying for position, all lured on by the enticement of the 'single party' which would transform France, like Italy and Germany, into a totalitarian state, and all carefully kept dangling by Otto Abetz. At the same time, Paris was supplied by a highly collaborationist press. Daily newspapers ranged from the very popular pre-war titles, albeit often under new management, such as *Le Petit Parisien*, selling 505,000 copies in 1943, *Paris-Soir* (380,000) and *Le Matin* (263,000), to new publications like *Le Cri du Peuple* (58,000) and Jean Luchaire's *Les Nouveaux Temps* (57,000).[11] The weekly press saw the rapid return of some pre-war extreme right-wing journals, like Brasillach's *Je suis partout* (125,000 copies in 1943) and Jean Lestandi's *Au Pilori* (65,000), together with a host of new titles, representing every collaborationist tendency, one of the most significant of which was *La Gerbe* (140,000), directed by the former Goncourt prize-winner Alphonse de Châteaubriant. In the field of monthly periodicals, the Germans were particularly anxious to see prestigious literary and intellectual periodicals reappear, and they devoted especial effort to persuading Drieu la Rochelle to take over the editorship of the *Nouvelle Revue Française*.[12]

It was also Paris, naturally, which became, as the centre of German power, the locus of the most intense collaborationist activity, with the occupier being particularly keen to recruit professional groups. Among those groups who responded particularly positively to German overtures were doctors. Philippe Burrin explains this by the fact that Vichy had met a large number of long-standing demands from the medical profession and by an often shared interest between French and German doctors in hygiene. The Nobel prize-winner Alexis Carrel's interest in eugenics and his openly racist *L'Homme cet inconnu* led him quite naturally to extreme right-wing politics and support in the 1930s for La Rocque and Doriot.[13] The ethnological research of Georges Montandon, as we have seen, resulted in overt racism. Small wonder, therefore, that, when the Germans canvassed support for professional exchanges and study visits, the Minister of Education, Jérôme Carcopino, reported that 'it is in the faculty of medicine that it has most chance of success,'[14] and a number of such excursions took place throughout the Occupation, in one of which Céline himself participated. There was also considerable interest in collaboration emanating from autonomist groups in the French provinces, notably in Flanders and Brittany, where Olier Mordrel and the Parti National Breton attempted to secure a separate place in the new Europe.[15]

The one sphere the Germans were particularly interested in cultivating was the artistic world, especially the world of literature. Not only did discreet control over books and writers afford massive opportunities for careful propaganda and censorship, but the fostering of culture in general in France was one of the easiest and most immediate ways of asserting the return to normality after the defeat and, at least temporarily, giving the lie to the myth of German barbarism. It was this subtle form of propaganda which Vercors was at pains to counter in his classic *Le Silence de la mer*. The occupier was also acutely aware of the privileged status of writers and intellectuals in France and of their very real influence and political power. In their tactical willingness to accommodate the world of literature and the arts in general, however, they were met by a similar eagerness on the part of writers who wished to continue to publish and publishers who wished to resume business as soon as possible. In order to effect this, French publishers had few qualms about meeting any conditions imposed by the German authorities. Hence, they acquiesced in the 'Aryanization' of 'Jewish' companies, particularly Calmann-Lévy and Nathan; they accepted the expropriation of Hachette; and, when in difficulties, they were not above having recourse to German capital. Cluny became half-owned by a German company; Sorlot sold shares worth 800,000 francs to the German firm List; and Céline's publisher, Denoël, solved his chronic financial difficulties, no doubt exacerbated by the constant demands of his star author, by obtaining a loan of 2 million francs from a certain Audermann, to whom he sold 360 out of 725 shares in the company.[16] Subsequently, the German shareholding in both Sorlot and Denoël reverted to the Hibbelen Trust, which also controlled fifty French periodicals.[17] Nor were Parisian publishers slow to cooperate with the Germans in an exercise of self-censorship by compiling the 'Liste Otto' which included subjects and authors, usually Jews, Freemasons and Communists, unacceptable to the regime and which they agreed not to print. As Céline told Madeleine Chapsal with relish in 1957: '[Gallimard] has a catalogue which would justify his being shot every day.'[18] Finally, in their attempts to obtain as much paper as possible from the stringent rationing, most publishers, by no means the most extreme supporters of collaboration like Grasset or Denoël, but also liberal companies like Gallimard, proposed titles or collections designed to appeal to the Occupier: translations from German, writings or speeches by Hitler, works by known French right-wing writers. Denoël's new series, *Les Nouvelles Éditions Françaises*, with a specifically racist content, launched by *Les Beaux Draps* and including a volume of Hitler's speeches, was undoubtedly part of this strategy.

Nor was there any shortage of French writers willing to be published under this German-dominated system or even eager to express their support for the new regime. The literary history of France in the inter-war years tends to privilege the committed writers of the Left and to ignore the fact that the French literary community was evenly split between Right and Left.[19] Indeed, contrary to popular perception, on the subject of the Spanish Civil War France produced far more pro-Franco novels than pro-Republican ones. During the Occupation, while some right-wing writers, most spectacularly the Catholics Bernanos, Claudel and Mauriac, opposed Vichy, the literary Right as a whole flexed its muscles and profited as much as it could from being, for once, on the inside. In addition to the committed writer-journalists, like Brasillach and Rebatet on *Je suis partout*, Châteaubriant on *La Gerbe*, or Drieu on the *NRF*, writers occupied powerful positions in the Vichy administration, like Abel Bonnard, Minister of Education, or Paul Morand, official film censor, then ambassador to Romania and Switzerland, from which he prudently failed to return at the end of the war. An older generation of publicists, like Abel Hermant, the once radical detractor of the cavalry, and Henri Béraud, wielded considerable influence. In the 'Free Zone', the *Action Française* team around Maurras, Daudet until his death in 1942, Pujo and Thierry Maulnier attempted to reconcile their hatred of Germany with admiration for Pétain and the French State until their stance became irrelevant in the 'Guerre Franco-Française' of 1943–4. In addition, convinced anti-democrats like Montherlant, or members of pre-war anti-republican circles like Cocteau, gave the regime tacit support, in exchange for considerable lionizing, without offering overmuch commitment.

The measure of German success in cultivating French writers, and artists in general, is the fact, now become a cliché, that the period 1940–4 saw an extraordinary explosion of Parisian cultural activity in all areas of the arts, but particularly in literature, theatre and cinema. What is remarkable about this cultural activity is that it included, not merely artists sympathetic to the regime or essentially neutral, but also figures who were prominent in the Resistance: Camus, who published *L'Etranger* and *Le Mythe de Sisyphe* with Gallimard, and was willing to accept the cutting of the section on the 'Jewish' Kafka in the latter; Sartre, who published *L'Etre et le néant* and had *Les Mouches* performed; and known Communists like Aragon and Elsa Triolet, who continued to publish with the German-financed Denoël. The number of writers who simply abstained from publishing altogether, like Guéhenno, considering it to be an insidious form of collaboration, were few indeed, and Vercors' fable, *Le Silence de la mer*, which is a warning against communication in any form with a deceptively humanist enemy, went mostly unheeded. In fact, most of the writers who contributed to the clandestine *Les Lettres Françaises* also wrote and published freely in a German-dominated community of letters: Jean Paulhan, one of the directors of *Les Lettres Françaises*, also had such close relations with Gerhard Heller that Céline once mischievously put a sign reading '*NRF*' on Heller's door.[20]

Diverse as the world of collaboration was, there were two areas of policy which united all tendencies and to which they remained committed, to greater or lesser degrees, until the very end: one was anti-Semitism and the other was anti-Communism. As we have seen, one of the first acts of the Vichy Government, in the autumn of 1940, was to bring in legislation barring Jews, Freemasons and Communists from public office and professions like the law and medicine. The government then proceeded to set up a Commissariat Général des Questions Juives, headed first by Xavier Vallat, who had made the attack on Blum as France's first 'Jewish' leader in 1936, and then by Céline's old anti-Semitic sparring partner, Darquier de Pellepoix, a Paris municipal councillor. It was this Commissariat Général which promulgated the *Statut sur les Juifs* in June 1941, entailing, among other measures, a loss of civil rights, confiscation of property and a detailed census of all Jews on French territory – both 'foreign' and 'French' Jews. Not only was this anti-Semitic policy initiated without German prompting, and based upon a definition of 'Jewishness' more draconian than that pertaining in Nazi Germany, it was implemented with enthusiasm by the quasi-totality of the Vichy apparatus, particularly by the police chief René Bousquet. When the SS began to make demands regarding the census and concentration of the Jews in France, they found a system already in place, through the Union Général des Israélites de France (UGIF), by which, essentially, the French Jews cooperated in the census of foreign émigré Jews in the hope and belief that it was these non-French Jews who constituted the German target.[21] In fact, the French Jews were doing no more than playing the same game as the government. Laval was perfectly willing to surrender first foreign Jews, then French Jews to the Germans in exchange for concessions elsewhere. The road was open to the obligatory yellow stars, the Rafle du Vél d'Hiv in June 1942, and the deportation to Germany of 13,000 Jews, including 4000 children: only 400 of the whole 13,000 ever returned.[22] In other words, from the very beginning of the Occupation, and certainly by the summer of 1942, there was no longer any 'Jewish Question' in France.

This 'Jewish Question' was clearly linked in the minds of the Right with the struggle against Communism: Léon Blum and his 'Jewish' ministers were forever associated with the 'revolution' of 1936, backed by the PCF and, behind them, the Soviet Union. By 1939, however, and the Molotov–Ribbentrop Pact, this antagonism had become much more confused, with the pacifist extreme Right and the Communists at least nominally on the same side. Indeed, even in 1940, Abetz was negotiating fairly sympathetically with the clandestine PCF with a view to authorizing open publication of *L'Humanité*, on the grounds of its 'criticism of Vichy, denunciation of the war, and attacks against England, de Gaulle, and "other agents of English finance" who "would like to see the French make war for the benefit of the City"'.[23] Apart from the absence of anti-Semitism, there was considerable convergence from 1939 to 1941 between Communist and extreme right-wing thought, and their targets were exactly the same as Céline's in the pamphlets and his Occupation journalism. The ambiguity was dispersed, however, with the German invasion of Russia in the summer of 1941. The French Communists joined the Resistance and the collaborationists hailed the German army as the liberators of European civilization, under threat from the barbarians in the East. This was the context of Laval's infamous radio broadcast of 22 June 1942 in which he explicitly voiced his hope for a German victory, without which Europe would be overrun by Bolshevism, a broadcast which deeply shocked French public opinion and definitively isolated the Prime Minister. It was also the context for French armed collaboration. French troops fought alongside Germans on the Eastern front, first of all under the auspices of the Légion des Volontaires Français (LVF), founded in June 1941 by the Fascist leaders Doriot, Déat, Deloncle and Costantini, and particularly exploited by Doriot, who fought with them, and later, as the Division Charlemagne of the Waffen-SS.[24]

As the war progressed, some of the ambiguities concerning Vichy, and particularly the role of Pétain, were dispelled. Successively, the survival of Great Britain in the summer and autumn of 1940, the German invasion of the USSR, the entry of the United States into the war and increasing repression on the part of the occupier, particularly through the execution of hostages, cast doubts upon both the good intentions of Germany and its long-term chances of total victory. The Allied landings in North Africa and the subsequent occupation of the 'Free Zone' in November 1942 showed up the real powerlessness of the French government, as well as constituting a major step on the road to German defeat. From 1942 to 1944, as German power internationally contracted, with defeats in Russia and the Western Desert and the loss of Italy from the Axis in 1943, the hopes of the Vichy Government, paradoxically, grew: France saw itself as an intermediary between a weakened Germany and the Allied powers. The illusory nature of those hopes, however, was underlined by the intransigence of the Allies, committed solely to unconditional surrender, and by the escalation of Resistance internally, fuelled by the *maquis* resulting from the introduction of the compulsory labour scheme, the Service du travail Obligatoire (STO). The 'Guerre Franco-Française' had begun in earnest. The Gaullist Radio Londres broadcast threats of revenge on prominent collaborators; in France itself, the Resistance began sending little wooden coffins to known German or Vichy sympathizers; in Algiers, Admiral Darlan had been assassinated on 26 December 1942 by a young royalist; and in 1944, the former Interior Minister, Pierre Pucheu, who had abandoned Vichy, was executed by firing-squad. Darnand's Milice attacked anyone suspected of being an enemy of the regime and entered, alongside SS and Wehrmacht troops, into pitched battles with the *maquis*, with summary executions taking place on both sides. By June 1944, with the Allies successfully landed in Normandy and Paris preparing for insurrection, collaborators turned their thought to escape, either by hiding or by fleeing the country. The most fortunate and most privileged left for Germany.

II CÉLINE AND COLLABORATION

Charles Maurras, famously, experienced the assumption of power by Pétain and his successful wielding of it as a 'divine surprise'. More prosaically, Céline, in the summer and autumn of 1940, was in the position of a maniac who has suddenly discovered that his mania has become orthodoxy; as a result, he was a person of consequence, when yesterday he had been an outcast. Characteristically, Céline reacted to his new-found prominence with a mixture of satisfaction, self-importance and bullying. He immediately took pleasure in his new high profile, if not necessarily importance, in collaborationist circles, which brought him into contact with powerful personalities on both the French and German sides. He wrote to Empeytaz in Bezons, apologizing for his absence from the clinic: 'I have been asked to lunch tomorrow by Laval. I fear I may be late back, so, with your permission, I have asked Mme Hogarth to replace me,'[25] and it was at the home of Laval's daughter, Josée, in late 1942, that Céline first met Arletty, with whom he was to remain close until his death.[26] Similarly, as we have seen, he kept in close contact with Vichy's ambassador, Fernand de Brinon, whom he regularly lobbied when he needed official influence. He also knew the French Fascist leaders Costantini, Déat and Doriot, although, in spite of his admiration for Doriot as a man of action and a number of meetings at the home of his friend Dr Bécart,[27] it was, as Gibault suggests, Déat's pacifism which attracted him most.[28] He was also in regular contact with the major collaborationist journalists in Paris: Drieu had seriously considered him as a potential member of the new editorial team of the *NRF*.[29] He also met Alphonse de Châteaubriant of *La Gerbe* and the *Je suis partout* team of Brasillach, Laubreaux (with whom he tried to mediate in a violent dispute with Cocteau),[30] Henri Poulain, Henri-Robert Petit and especially Lucien Rebatet, whose *Les Décombres*, which had a considerable stylistic debt to Céline's own pamphlets, was the literary success of 1942. His relations in the press also included Lucien Combelle, formally Gide's secretary, who worked on *Le Fait* and *La Révolution Nationale*, before becoming its editor in 1944, and who was among the closest of collaborationist journalists to Céline; and, finally, Jean Lestandi, editor of the highly virulent weekly *Au Pilori*. Indeed, it was under the auspices of *Au Pilori* that an odd event occurred in December 1941 which reveals both the extent of Céline's self-importance and his range of contacts. In the 11 December number there appeared an unsigned article 'Prologue au parti unique?' which consisted primarily of a statement by Céline: 'As an anti-Jew from the very beginning, I sometimes have the impression that if I have not been overtaken by events, there are at least people who have entirely different conceptions from me on the Jewish question. This is why I have to meet them and talk with them.'[31] A high-level meeting was set up, to which the major figures of French collaboration were invited, including Xavier Vallat and Darquier de Pellepoix, Jean Luchaire, most of the *Je suis partout* team, Drieu la Rochelle, Alphonse de Châteaubriant, Georges Montandon, Marcel Déat, Eugène Deloncle, Anatole de Monzie and Ramon Fernandez.[32] In fact, only twelve of those invited attended, but some of the most important: Pierre Constanti, Pierre-Antoine Cousteau, Marcel Déat, Georges Montandon, Henri Poulain and Georges Suarez.[33] The 25 December number of *Au Pilori* reported that 'Céline spoke and summarized dramatically and pithily the drama confronting the French nation,' and that there was general agreement on three basic policies: the regeneration of France through racism; the need for the Church to commit itself on the question of racism; and a socialist policy of a minimum wage, which would restore to France a 'taste in the beautiful' and would replace 'sordid materialism' with idealism.[34] Nothing came of this meeting, but it places Céline at the centre of the debate on the elusive single party and reminds us that he was prominent enough to have been an outside candidate for the post of Vichy Commissaire Général aux Questions Juives instead of Vallat.[35] He continued to support collaborationist and racist enterprises, notably the Institut des Questions Juives in the Rue La Boétie, directed by Captain Sézille,[36] and the exhibition 'Le Juif et la France', organized by the same captain in the Palais Berlitz in November 1941, though his support did not prevent him complaining that none of his books were on sale.[37]

However 'paradoxical' Céline's behaviour during the Occupation may appear,[38] he never wavered on the two central planks of extreme collaborationist policy: anti-Communism and anti-Semitism. The threat of 'Jewish' Communism is one of the central themes of *Bagatelles pour un massacre* and *L'Ecole des cadavres* and is resolved in a peculiarly French way in the 'Communisme-Labiche' of *Les Beaux Draps*. Céline despaired of his countrymen's indifference to the threat, warning that it would serve them right when Kaganovitch was in power in France,[39] and he was enthusiastic about the German invasion of the USSR on 22 June 1941 and the French contribution to the anti-Bolshevik crusade through the formation of the LVF. He strongly supported Doriot's departure for Russia at the head of a division and was tempted to go himself, though in a medical capacity. He wrote to Châteaubriant that what was needed was 'a medical corps . . . a corps of transfusion experts . . . a corps of surgeons . . . of nurses, male and female . . . As I know Russia – with winter they'll have as much need of medical help and epidemiologists as they will of gun reinforcements! If this idea took hold, I'd willingly join up myself – but killing – and frankly I've killed a lot – no longer attracts me.'[40] In fact, whilst applauding from the sidelines, he always had an excuse not to go. Although he wrote to Karen Marie Jensen that 'I might even go to Russia in the end. If things there get serious, everyone should get involved – it'll be a question of life or death – if what we're doing is living,'[41] he had already confessed to one of Doriot's lieutenants, Ivan-Maurice Sicard, editor of *Les Cahiers de l'Emancipation Nationale*: 'I would have liked to have gone over there with Doriot, but I'm more of a seaman, a Breton.'[42] He never went, but the threat from the East, encompassing the Jews, the Communists and, in the post-war writing, the Chinese, remained essential to his xenophobia.

It was anti-Semitism, however, which exercised Céline most during the Occupation and which accounted for most of his occasional writing. In order to express his ideas, in addition to signing manifestos, like the one in the *Petit Parisien* of 9 March 1942 denouncing the Allied bombing of French cities,[43] giving interviews or replying to questionnaires, he had hit upon a device which afforded maximum impact with minimum responsibility, the informal, unpaid letter to journals which they were 'allowed' to publish.

The same prudence which prevented Céline from fighting on the Eastern Front and which made him introduce the 'literary' ambiguities into the pamphlets, led him to invent a form of polemic which, in the event of a German defeat, he could claim, as indeed he did in his defence against charges of treason in the post-war period, did not constitute Collaboration at all, since it entailed purely 'private' and unpaid correspondence. Replying to a request for an article from Combelle, he fulminated: 'Once and for all I NEVER write articles. I didn't write you an article, but a letter and a free one at that.'[44] Not that this prevented him from continually complaining that his writings had been mangled by the editors, leading to requests to see the proofs of these 'private' letters.[45] These letters build up to a substantial body of writing: in addition to three interviews, two replies to question-naires, one manifesto signature, and three extended quotations from speeches, Henri Godard identifies twenty-five of them, addressed essen-tially to the most extreme collaborationist journals: *Au Pilori* (seven times), *Je suis partout* (six times), *La Gerbe* (four times), *L'Appel* (four times) and *L'Emancipation Nationale* (three times).[46] The themes of these letters are remarkably, indeed obsessively, similar. Like many of his fellow-collaborators in Paris, Céline was deeply distrustful of Vichy and of the French will to participate in the new Europe in general. Writing to Charles Lesca of *Je suis partout* on the subject of the war in the East, he attacked the favourite target of the 'ultras', the Worms Bank 'synarchy':

> Will no one amongst you have the courage to go against orders, to break the censorship! Shit, no one will dare cry out against this confidence-trick of a crusade which leaves the Jews more than ever in every position of power whilst they're sending the last Aryan Frenchmen off to the Steppes! No one says anything, no one even thinks of it! The shamefulness of it! In that case, long live Worms![47]

In this scatter-gun approach to French irresponsibility, he even turned gratuitously on one of the icons, not just of French radicalism, but of French patriotism, Charles Péguy. He wrote to Costantini's *L'Appel*: 'I would point out to you that Péguy never understood anything, and that he was at one and the same time a Dreyfusard, a monarchist and a ham.'[48] Céline's real invective, however, as his letter to Lesca shows, was reserved for the Jews, whom he saw as still orchestrating the war and still flaunting their power in France. His first letter, on 13 February 1941, was to Châteaubriant's *La Gerbe*. In it he wrote: 'A hundred thousand shouts of "Long live Pétain!" aren't worth one little "out with the yids!" in practice. A little courage, in God's n . . . !'[49] This is a message which hardly varies throughout the Occupation. His last letter to Lestandi's *Au Pilori* in the edition of 10 September 1943 registers no change whatsoever: 'I weighed you all under Blum! . . . and I'll weigh you all again! In your little box! At a dawn which isn't far off. Ex-members of LICA [their French anti-Semitic league], eternal Freemason-pimps. Tomorrow they'll be racists with the

Jews. A new conformism and new guard dogs. A State anti-Semitism 90%
Jewish . . . People reproach me for not attending meetings . . . I only find
Jews there.'[50] Yet, by September 1943 all the great round-ups had taken
place and the majority of the French Jews, along with the immigrants, had
been deported, so why did Céline's obsessive vision see France even more
than ever under their domination? It is as if his mania kept him imprisoned
in a time-warp of the late 1930s, the period of the pamphlets, when there
were still Jewish ministers. Yet, as Arnold Mandel so perceptively observes,
it is the persistence of that very mania which guarantees the continued
identity of the anti-Semite. Critics of Céline's fiction, particularly Albert
Chesneau, have commented on his use, in *Voyage au bout de la nuit* and *Mort
à crédit*, of a Freudian 'repetition fantasy', by which a trauma is finally
mastered by endless repetition of its effects.[51] In the pamphlets and in the
publications during the Occupation, that obsessive repetition was constantly at work to exorcise a perceived Jewish threat which goes back to the
Front Populaire Government of 1936 and, possibly, even further back to his
childhood in the Passage Choiseul.

The most obvious form that repetition took was the successive reprinting
by Denoël of *Bagatelles pour un massacre* and *L'Ecole des cadavres*, including
new editions of both in late 1942, with a preface supporting the new
European order in the latter and illustrations for both. The preface was to
be one of the major pieces of evidence against Céline in the proceedings
brought against him after the war, even though Céline was careful to place
all the blame on Denoël's cupidity.[52] But the illustrations are more interesting: most of them come from the belle époque, from the magazine *Je sais
tout*, aimed at an aspiring petite-bourgeoisie, and show images of an 'eternal' France, unaware of the social and political forces eating away at it and
leading to its downfall at the hands of the Russians and the Jews. In other
words, the illustrations to *Bagatelles pour un massacre* and *L'Ecole des cadavres*
play a vital semiotic role in linking the world of Céline's own childhood,
and that of *Mort à crédit*, with the *beaux draps* in which France now finds
herself. The photograph of an early lady cyclist, labelled 'Une Précurseuse',
looks innocuous enough, but is intended to be symbolic of an entire
degeneration of social order; the cheerful group portrait of Frenchmen in
a bistro is in fact a reference to a Jewish plot to undermine the nation
through alcohol. The belle époque and the triumph of Dreyfus were, for
the anti-Semite, the beginning of a process which ended in 1940 and, for
Céline, still persisted into the Occupation.

In this context, it is useful to record Céline's return to his earlier preoccupations with hygiene during the Occupation. In February 1942, he gave
a lecture to the Ecole Libre des Sciences Médicales on 'La Médecine
standard', in which he took up the themes of the 1920s writings on Ford
and medical insurance. As we have already seen, hygiene was a favourite
topic, both literally and metaphorically, for collaborationist medical scientists, and Céline's recycling of his earlier theories, with emphasis on the
benefits of 'Taylorization' in medical practice, coincided, not merely with

the popularity of Carrel and Montandon, but also with Darlan's technoc-racy.[53] At the end of 1942, on 20 December, he gave another speech to his medical colleagues, but this time avoided any technical theory in favour of a by now familiar diatribe against the Jews and a regime which still refused to eradicate them.[54] In passing, he denounced 'the stupidities of a regime which maintained a Jewess in a suburban clinic in the place of an aryan doctor who was obliged to travel as a consequence fourteen kilometers every day by bus and on foot'.[55] A report of the speech was published in *Le Cri du Peuple* on 23 December, with the consequence that Céline's locum in Bezons, Dr Howyan, in fact an Armenian Christian, was visited by the German authorities. Rebarbative as Céline's general fulminations against the Jews may be, there is an even darker side which touches on individual denunciation. The previous year, in an interview on *Les Beaux Draps* with Henri Poulain of *Je suis partout*, Céline had commented: 'I did all I could on the Jew in the other two books . . . For now, anyway, they're less arrogant, less swaggering . . . Still, we shouldn't kid ourselves. The secretary of physi-cians of Seine-et-Oise is called Menckietzwictz.'[56] The luckless Pole had to write to the journal protesting that Céline had misspelt his authentically Polish, and not Jewish, name. In both cases, however, the intention, or at least the irresponsibility, is there, and had Howyan and Menckietzwictz been Jews, they would have found themselves in the deportees' transit-camp at Drancy.

Like most of the extreme collaborationists, Céline was distrusted by Vichy (*Les Beaux Draps* was banned in the 'Free Zone' in late 1941, possibly as a result of Céline's attempt to entrap Vallat in the *Au Pilori* meeting),[57] and gravitated naturally to the German authorities. He certainly had some contact with Abetz and the staff of the Embassy in the Rue de Lille, though it is possible, as we shall see, that this was exaggerated. Vitoux comments that 'there was no chance of finding him at the soirées held by Otto Abetz at the German embassy – he only went once or twice, out of contemptuous curiosity,'[58] and Alméras records his distrust of Suzanne Abetz, who had merely taken on the role of Paul Reynaud's mistress, Hélène de Portes.[59] He certainly lobbied Achenbach, the press and propaganda counsellor, on occasions when he needed help, but always through third parties like Châteaubriant. His main German contact was Karl Epting of the German Institute, who was not only a devoted fan (Cocteau reported that he was 'bewitched' by Céline),[60] but was also extremely useful: multiplying his contacts with German personalities, arranging an official invitation to Berlin in 1942, and intervening to secure a priority allocation of 15 tonnes of paper for the new edition of *L'Ecole des cadavres*, Denoël's German co-owners apparently proving inadequate. It was also through Epting that Céline met the medical figures Dr Knapp, of the German Office of Public Health,[61] and Dr Haubold, a senior Reich health official who was to be very useful to Céline in Germany at the end of the war.[62] The Institute was also the scene of cultural encounters: most notably with the sculptor Arno Brecker, whom Céline knew from the 1930s,[63] and Ernst Jünger, in addition to a host of French artistic personalities.[64] He also came to know Gerhard Heller, the literature censor, who, like Epting, was fanatically Francophile, but for that very reason was shocked by the ferocity and vulgarity of Céline's anti-Semitism.[65] Céline had also made the acquaintance of more sinister figures in the SS: Dr Pfannstiel, who had translated *Bagatelles pour un massacre* into German, and, in his office on the Square Rap, was in charge of intelligence gathering on secret societies,[66] and Hermann Bickler, SS head of political intelligence for the whole of Western Europe, who had his offices on the Avenue Foch.[67] Céline would often call in to chat with Bickler on his way from Montmartre to Bezons and invited him to dinner several times to the Rue Girardon. The SS officer clearly enjoyed his company, though probably did not benefit over-much from his visitor's political information, which, according to an affidavit prepared for François Gibault in 1979, consisted mainly of warnings about Suzanne Abetz and denunciations of 'that Jew', Laval.[68]

All in all, Céline emerges as a moderately important French collaborator, who was even tempted to work as a doctor in Germany caring for French emigrant workers,[69] and whom the Germans were keen to cultivate, in spite of some considerable distrust. His position within the hierarchy of collaborators is clearly indicated by the French SS leader Helmut Knochen's list of possible French members of an Advisory Committee for the Office Central Juif, which reads: 'Léon de Poncins, Georges Batault, Bernard Fay, Vacher de la Pouge . . . Darquier de Pellepoix, Montandon, and, with reservations, Serpeille de Gobineau, Céline'.[70] The reservations were reflected on the German side by Ernst Jünger's intense dislike of Céline, in whom the aristocratic officer detected 'the monstrous power of nihilism'.[71] This dislike had unexpected consequences when Jünger published his wartime journals, *Strahlungen*, just when Céline was preparing his defence against charges of treason. Whereas in the German edition, the outrageous and bloodthirsty anti-Semitic writer whom Jünger comes across in Parisian salons is called 'Merline', in the French edition the disguise was inadvertently omitted and Jünger's account took on the proportions of a denunciation. It was not only Jünger, however, who felt more at ease in the company of a fellow First World War combatant and aesthete like Drieu la Rochelle, who despised Céline. Bernard Payr, an important official in the Amt Schrifttum in Alfred Rosenberg's Ministry in Berlin, in a report of 28 January 1942 seriously questioned Epting's judgement in sponsoring a writer whose first novel had celebrated conscientious objection and whose latest work was unable to distinguish between 'robustness and filth'. Two weeks earlier, Payr had reviewed *Les Beaux Draps* in *Das Reich*, complaining of its 'total absence of morality', and had received for his trouble 'an abusive letter from Monsieur Céline, a letter which is one of the finest examples of this sort in my collection'.[72]

Céline, for his part, was careful to keep his distance from German contacts which might prove too compromising. He refused to attend the two Weimar writers' congresses of 1941 and 1942, which figures like

Jouhandeau and Drieu did attend,[73] and he also declined to take part in the delegation led by Fernand de Brinon in 1943 to visit the LVF on the Eastern Front, in the course of which the party went to see the exhumed bodies of the Polish officer corps at Katyn. This, incidentally, was the journey which, more than anything, cost Brasillach his life: confusing him in a photograph with Doriot, wearing a German uniform, de Gaulle refused to commute his death sentence. Céline also demanded that his name be withdrawn from the list of Honorary Members of the Cercle Européen.[74]

This mutual distrust has given rise to an alternative mythology of Céline during the Occupation, whereby he is portrayed as essentially subversive. While some of the evidence appears plausible, much of it is designed either to serve his defence during the post-war trial or to aid the process of rehabilitation. A number of stories abound, for example, which portray him as a dangerous embarrassment to Germans and fellow-collaborators alike. In 1941, Céline was at a reception at the Café de la Paix given by the Japanese journalist Kuni Matsuo, celebrating his departure for the post of secretary to the Prime Minister. Not only did Céline turn up so ill-dressed that the head waiter took him for a tramp and tried to throw him out, he then proceeded to 'ask a colonel of the Wehrmacht how many months he thought it would be until Germany's defeat'.[75] This story looks forward to a more famous and more dubious one, alleged to have taken place at the Embassy in the presence of Abetz. During a dinner-party which included Gen Paul, Jacques Benoist-Méchin and Drieu la Rochelle, Céline, after remaining silent for most of the meal, suddenly exploded and prophesied an imminent German defeat. In an attempt to stem the tirade, Abetz remarked: 'But it is well-known, Monsieur Céline, that you do not like the Germans,' to which Céline riposted that not only did he and Gen Paul like the Germans, but they liked them so much that they even imitated Hitler: at which point, with Céline's encouragement, Gen Paul did his celebrated impersonation of the Führer, in front of a panic-stricken ambassador.[76] For Gibault, this story is probably a conflation of several events, with or without the ambassador, while, more plausibly still, Alméras records Epting's opinion that Céline and Gen Paul were not of sufficient status to visit the embassy and that the entire narrative is a fabrication after an evening's drinking.[77] Nevertheless, the story served its purpose in demarcating Céline from mainstream collaboration, as do Rebatet's reminiscences, published in *L'Herne*, of Céline's comments in October 1940 that 'the Fritz have lost the war,'[78] his heckling of the speaker at the opening of the Institut d'Etude des Questions Juives on 11 May 1941,[79] or the story, reported by Céline himself as part of his defence, of a speech he was forced to make to French workers during his visit to Berlin in 1942: 'French workers. I'm going to tell you something really good. I know you well. I'm one of you, a worker like you. These guys [the Germans] are *lousy*. They say they're going to win the war. Maybe so. I don't know. The others, the Russians, on the other side, are no better. They may even be worse. It's a question of choosing between cholera and the plague. Not much fun. So long!'[80] As he added: 'The Club's dismay was great. There was again serious talk of incarcerating me (Laval, too, could think of nothing but incarcerating me . . .)'[81] As Rebatet laconically put it: 'Céline . . . did not share our optimism.'[82]

In his subsequent defence, both Céline and his supporters also drew attention to his far from clear-cut attitude on a personal level towards opponents and dissidents. The most authentic example of this concerns a simple-minded young Breton, Noël L'Helgouarch, who, after a drunken evening in Langoz, entered into a stupid dare with five friends to cut the telephone cable leading to a German post. L'Helgouarch was caught and sentenced to death, at which point Céline's friends Dr Desse and Dr Tuset asked him to help. In spite of his lobbying the Préfet of Finistère and Fernand de Brinon, Céline was unsuccessful and the young Breton was executed on 27 June 1941.[83] The episode left a deep impression on Céline, who remembered it particularly clearly when he was in prison in Denmark, awaiting possible extradition to France. There are also examples cited of Céline providing medical certificates excusing young men, like the Breton Marcel Plazannet, from joining the STO.[84] In fact, Céline was alleged to have not merely been of service to candidates for work in Germany, but also to actual members of the Resistance. The evidence for this comes from Céline's neighbour on the floor below in the Rue Girardon, Robert Champfleury, who lived there with his mistress Simone Mabille, and was a member of the same Resistance group as Roger Vaillant. After the war, not only did Champfleury remember the group discussing whether to assassinate Céline and his collaborationist friends, he also recalled that the writer was perfectly aware of what the group were doing and even gave medical help to the wounded: 'I came knocking on your door one day, accompanied by a Resistance fighter who had been tortured by the Gestapo. You let me in, you examined my friend's bruised hand and, without asking a single question, you bandaged it in the appropriate way, having rightly guessed the cause of the wound.'[85] Genuine acts of kindness appear to have co-existed with acts of spite or irresponsibility.

In spite of these possible anomalies, however, Céline's trajectory throughout the Occupation was broadly typical of that of the most extreme collaborationists. As Alméras comments, in his refusal to fight in Russia for the Worms Bank or Cardinal Gerlier, the pro-Vichy, anti-German Archbishop of Lyons, he was close to the 'attentisme' of Laval and Déat.[86] Yet, at the same time, summer and autumn 1941, as for many collaborators, constituted the high point of his commitment to the German cause: he believed firmly in a German victory[87] and his confidence was eroded relatively slowly. In a letter to Empeytaz after his journey to Berlin in March 1942 (in other words, after the first and unexpected winter spent by the Germans in Russia), he revised his opinions on a lightning campaign, but nevertheless remained optimistic in the long term: 'I'm just back from Germany – bluntly, I think we're in for fifteen years' war, even if it goes in our favour! we are not at the end of our hopes: or our waiting, or our winters! We must hold on!'[88] By 1943, however, and especially after the German defeat at Stalingrad on 2 February, he had become reconciled to Germany losing the war, and, as Gibault comments, the tone and content of his writing changed in consequence. There is considerably less polemic in any case and that is more moderate in tone, less specifically anti-Semitic and more concerned with general social issues or, as we have seen, a generalized, almost metaphorical racism.[89] At the same time, this 'deliberate disengagement'[90] took the form of a rejection of polemic in favour of a return to fiction. In an interview in March 1943 with R. Cardine-Petit, of *Panorama*, he spoke only of his new novel, set in London in 1916.[91] Not for Céline the almost suicidal defiance of the *Je suis partout* team, who, in the last days of the Occupation, held a mass meeting under the banner: 'Nous ne nous sommes pas dégonflés!' ('We haven't chickened out!')

III Personal Life

In fact, throughout the Occupation, Céline had been deeply preoccupied by personal concerns which had nothing to do with politics or the war. Chiefly, these concerns had to do with money, and it was, indeed, a severe test of his commitment to Germany when he discovered that the occupiers had designs on his savings by opening his deposit box at the Paris branch of Lloyds Bank on 14 March 1941[92] and, particularly, later that year, by requisitioning the gold he had deposited in the Amsterdamsche Bank in The Hague.[93] Céline moved heaven and earth in an attempt to save his gold. He travelled to Holland in July in a vain attempt to recover the deposit (a journey, incidentally, which took him to Antwerp and his last visit to Evelyne Pollet), and furiously lobbied Fernand de Brinon and Alphonse de Châteaubriant. In spite of Châteaubriant's intervention with Abetz and Achenbach, all these attempts failed and 185 golden guilders were confiscated, replaced by worthless paper money.

The loss of the Dutch gold became an obsession and Céline came to fear that the same fate would befall his deposits in Copenhagen, similarly under German occupation. It was this fear which lay at the origin of his bizarre journey to Berlin in 1942: he desperately needed to meet Karen Marie Jensen so that he could give her the keys to his safe deposit box and arrange for her to move the Danish gold to a place of safety.[94] To do this, he resorted to the same device as he had used in the 1920s and early 1930s with Rajchman, but this time with the ever-helpful Karl Epting: an official study tour to 'visit the medical facilities of a factory and a suburban clinic in Germany, and to visit a few physicians working in public health'.[95] He set out on 8 March 1942, accompanied by two doctors, Bécart and Rudler, and, curiously, his friend Gen Paul. This was a relatively high-level delegation, and they were received by Dr Conti, the Reich Minister of Public Health, at a soirée where they also met officers from the Eastern Front who convinced Céline that the war was going badly: he even confided on the way home to Dr Rudler: 'These people are washed up, the others are going to win.'[96] The real purpose of the visit, however, was to meet up with Karen, for whom he still felt a very real affection, and to give her the key and the combination to the safe deposit box, while agreeing on a simple code devised to trick the German censors. When, two months later, Karen withdrew the gold deposit, divided it up and hid it in various properties in the country, she wrote frequently to Céline throughout the rest of the Occupation with news of 'the children'. In one such letter, she informed Céline that 'the children' were in the country and that 'the papers and the jewels' were with a friend, hidden in a safe behind the fireplace. No further mention of the jewels was made, although Karen Marie Jensen was to prove a faithful and useful friend: not only did she preserve Céline's gold, she also made over to him her apartment in Copenhagen, where he and Lucette were to stay in 1945 until their arrest.

As in the 1930s, this obsession with money and security coincided during the Occupation with a period of relative wealth. Alméras, who lists all the regular royalty payments from Denoël, calculates that in 1942 Céline earned 422,882 francs from his books, in addition to 32,988 francs as salary from the Bezons clinic, making a total of 455,870 francs for the year.[97] Not only does this represent roughly 600,000 francs at today's value, or roughly £65,000, it compares with an annual salary of 106,200 francs for a provincial newspaper editor and between 180,000 and 300,000 francs for a senior civil servant.[98] In other words, he was extremely comfortably off, though this did not prevent him, like any miser, from dressing increasingly badly, with a dirty fur-lined coat and motorcyclist's gloves knotted on a string around his neck.[99] Most of his money went into the typical miser's occupations – conversion of liquid resources into gold or jewels, and stockpiling of black-market goods. Friends, perhaps maliciously, claimed that the apartment in the Rue Girardon was an Ali Baba's cave of useless treasures, like spades and barbed wire, and, more plausibly, black-market food. Certainly, there is a copious correspondence testifying to the motivation behind Céline's frequent journeys to Brittany and to his soliciting supplies of food. He wrote often to Henri Mahé's father until his death in December 1941, placing orders for butter, *rillettes* and roast meats, and thanking him for shipments of cheeses and ham. As Vitoux concludes: 'Céline was no sensualist, no Lucullus, no glutton, as we know. He was a man of anxieties. If the past rhymed with nostalgia, then the future was in tune with every sort of danger. *Rillettes*, ham and butter in the cupboard could no doubt go a little way toward dispelling the fear of tomorrow.'[100]

Yet the attraction of Brittany was not simply due to its role as a source of food: Céline had returned to it time and again during the 1930s, and throughout the Occupation it remained a place of delight and tranquillity, of escape and relaxation. Indeed, some of the correspondence of the period from Brittany shows a carefree quality which seems to have driven the war and its threats into oblivion. In particular, he loved Saint-Malo, but, since the Port of the Corsairs was in the forbidden militarized zone, he had to make do with Finistère and the west coast, staying frequently at Camaret, Beg-Meil and once, in 1942, in a mental sanatorium run by a friend, Dr Mondain. Lucette Destouches recalled the cottage they rented in Beg-Meil as being idyllic: 'a little house . . . with a fireplace and a marvellous kitchen garden where green peas were growing. On the beach, no one, I was by myself all day, half naked on the beach. Louis was working,'[101] and Céline's own letters to his friends in Montmartre were similarly enthusiastic: 'La Pipe is bathing – she's in the water all the time – It's beautiful weather here.'[102] He wrote again to Gen Paul: 'You're wrong not to come to Brittany – I assure you it's magical at the moment . . . La Pipe is giving orders and we've found a deaf housekeeper who can't hear anything but does the work of ten – Everything's going well, and we miss you.'[103] Only the lunatic asylum in Quimper, founded coincidentally by Athanase Follet, was sinister, but in an oddly compelling way: as Lucette recalled to Frédéric Vitoux, 'The loonies watched me. A little like ghosts – they appear, you don't know how, they vanish, they're lost souls, they're everywhere.'[104]

It was Saint-Malo, however, that was his real goal and he frequently evaded the German checkpoints or persuaded de Brinon to give him a visa. On one occasion even this failed and, on the advice of Olier Mordrel, he approached the German Kommandantur in Rennes and a local Gestapo officer, Hans Grimm, who, on the basis of a false residence permit delivered by the Saint-Malo police chief, allowed him to proceed.[105] This subsequently led to an article in *L'Humanité* on 2 January 1950, just before the opening of Céline's trial, accusing him of being a Gestapo agent.[106] After these difficulties in reaching Saint-Malo, Céline became much more conscious of how fragile his position was on the northern coast, and he no longer encouraged his Parisian friends to visit.

Throughout the war he retained and extended his circle of Breton contacts. These included the Desse couple, both doctors in Quimper, Dr Tuset, the Director of Health Services for the Finistère prefecture, who introduced him to Max Jacob,[107] the Breton autonomists in the PNB, including Mordrel, and the Breton 'bard' Théo Briant, whom he visited at Paramé and who returned his visit at the Villa Franklin, remarking on the view from Céline's window: 'we can see the steeple of Saint-Malo and a patch of the beach of the Fort National. The high tide sends us its scent and its murmurings.'[108] He also noticed Céline's unkempt appearance and apparent ill health: 'Pretty badly dressed, with his feet in old sandals and wearing a pair of stoker's trousers. His hair is still messy, his eyes hollow and blazing, his lips dripping with saliva.'[109] The inevitable outcome of the war was beginning to obsess him, with its likely purges. It was for Briant, the Celt, that he intervened with Henri Poulain of *Je suis partout* regarding a possible new edition of *La Légende de la mort*, by Anatole Le Braz, a contemporary Breton classic, out of print for thirteen years,[110] and that he composed a piece in medieval style on the subject of the neglected Le Braz for the review *Le Goéland* in its February 1944 issue.[111] In this he resumed the interest in medieval style evident in 'La Légende du Roi Krogold' of *Mort à crédit* and in the projected work of the mid-1930s, overtaken by the pamphlets, *La Volonté du Roi Krogold*. It was an interest which was to re-emerge in the cultivation of the medieval genre of the chronicle in the *D'un château l'autre* trilogy.

Céline's personal life during the war was marked by two events: a quarrel with his daughter Colette and his marriage to Lucette. On 10 June 1942, Colette Destouches married Yves Turpin, whose child she was expecting, without asking her father's permission. In spite of, or rather because of, his obsessive and possessive relationship with his daughter, Céline was deeply offended, refused to attend the ceremony and broke off all relations with her, even after the birth of his grandson, Jean-Marie, on 3 August 1942. He did not bother to inform Colette of his departure for Germany in the summer of 1944 and did not see her again until his return to France in 1952.[112] The marriage with Lucette took place at the *mairie* of the eighteenth *arrondissement* on 15 February 1943 with only two witnesses present: Victor Carré, in charge of food distribution at the *mairie*, and Gen Paul, who was furious that no meal had been arranged.[113] Lucette herself admitted to Vitoux that she had not wished to get married[114] and the wedding took place in the strictest secrecy, with Céline's mother finding out only two weeks later. The reason for the ceremony was purely practical. It took place just after the defeat of Stalingrad, when the balance of the conflict had tipped definitively in the Allies' favour. The relationship needed to be legally regularized (the marriage contract was signed on 10 February, five days before the ceremony, and Céline made a will leaving everything to Lucette), and Céline probably remembered that when he had wanted to take Lucette with him to Russia in 1936, he was unable to do so because they were not married. In 1943 it seemed likely that they would be travelling again.

If Bezons was his work, collaborationist Paris his sounding-board and Brittany his refuge, it was Montmartre which remained the village where he lived and where he relaxed with his regular friends, Daragnès, Marcel Aymé, Ralph Soupault, Antonio Zuloaga and Robert Le Vigan, mostly at the Sunday morning gatherings in Gen Paul's studio in the Avenue Junot. As Gibault reminds us, although the general tenor of the conversation was anti-British, anti-Semitic and also anti-German, it did not exclude figures with Resistance sympathies, like the two doctors, Marcel Rivault and Morchain.[115] Céline also, unlike in the 1930s, received visitors in the apartment in the Rue Girardon, albeit unwillingly: the most bizarre visit was that of Marie Bell and Florence Gould, who was drunk and fell down the stairs on the way out, breaking her leg.[116] It was in Montmartre that he acquired one of the most faithful and durable companions of his later years, the cat Bébert, who had originally belonged to Le Vigan and his mistress Tinou. The cat was to travel with Céline and Lucette through Germany to Denmark before finishing his life in Meudon, and plays a privileged role, which Vitoux explores, in the trilogy.[117] It was also from Montmartre that Céline was the witness of the Allied air-raids which dominate the second volume of *Féerie pour une autre fois*: the bombing of Billancourt on 3 March 1942[118] and the raid on La Chapelle on 21 April 1944, during which Montmartre itself had been hit.[119] Céline, who had already witnessed the bombing of Bezons by the RAF,[120] was determined to exploit the privileges of a new Pliny the Elder, who died observing the eruption of Vesuvius and to whom the second volume of *Féerie* is dedicated, without suffering the same fate.

Yet, as the war went on, this seemed by no means certain. Like all prominent collaborators, Céline began to figure in blacklists, like the one published by *Life* on 2 August 1942, and among lists of personalities to be punished at the Liberation read out by Radio Londres, which may be why he was so keen on banning its reception in France.[121] In the winter of 1943–4 he began to receive death-threats, either in letters or in the form of miniature coffins,[122] and he seriously feared assassination – not unreasonably, as his neighbours' 'plot', the murder in 1944 of Philippe Henriot, and the assassination attempt on Georges Mantandon show. It was for this reason that he asked Hermann Bickler to provide him with a pistol and a permit. Subsequently he never left home unarmed[123] and, to avoid the fate of Henriot and Mantandon, he forced his visitors to follow an elaborate code of knocks on his front door before he would open. He and Lucette also began to look seriously for a place of refuge: Brittany, where they considered hiding with false papers,[124] or Spain, where they could stay with the Montmartre painter Zuloaga, and where Karen Marie Jensen urged them to go.[125] In the end they rejected Brittany as too dangerous and Spain as too difficult and opted for what had always been the first choice: Denmark and the 'children'. Yet time was pressing, and in the aftermath of the Normandy landings there reigned a strange, proto-revolutionary atmosphere in Paris. A popular rumour on the evening of 6 June 1944 had Céline, Rebatet and other collaborators taking refuge in the German Embassy.[126] Céline made his decision: on 8 June he obtained his *Fremdenpass* from the German authorities, together with a vetinary certificate for Bébert. He also collected together all his royalties which had been in the safe deposit box in Lloyds Bank: 1.44 million francs, according to Alméras,[127] or 900,000 present-day francs, some of which were converted into gold and literally sewn into a special waistcoat by Lucette. On 17 June he and Lucette went secretly to the Gare de l'Est, accompanied only by a fellow-Montmartrois Pepino Morato, who helped carry their copious luggage: Céline's manuscript and papers, his cyanide and his money; Lucette's costumes and castanets, a tea-pot and a supply of tea.[128] They crossed the border *en route* for Baden-Baden, where they were to be the guests of the German government in the Brenner's Park Hotel, the most luxurious in the resort. They were not to see France again until 1951.

III GUIGNOL'S BAND

Alongside his occasional polemical writing, Céline had been concerned both with his literary persona and his purely literary production, reminding his readers increasingly frequently that he was not merely a political militant, but essentially a creative writer. The luxury edition of *Voyage au bout de la nuit* in March 1942, followed by that of *Mort à crédit* in October, both illustrated by Gen Paul, were not merely lucrative financial enterprises on the part of Denoël, they were also designed to consecrate Céline as a classic. Nor had Céline by any means abandoned his novelistic output, reverting to his original timetable for subjects to be treated by finally exploiting the experience of London during the First World War that he had meant to include in *Voyage*. Indeed, Henri Godard dates the beginning of the composition of *Guignol's Band* as early as the end of 1940, when Céline was still writing *Les Beaux Draps*: fragments of the manuscript of the novel are written on the other side of that of the pamphlet, and vice versa.[129] In 1941 work on the novel, known provisionally as *Honny soit* (from the motto of the Knights of the Garter) or *English Bar*,[130] slowed down, and Céline admitted to Marie Canavaggia that he had lost the thread of the story.[131] By the spring of 1943, however, he had completed the draft manuscript, and in June began the task of revising the first typed version.[132] On 21 August 1943, he wrote to Victor Carré that he had revised only 300 out of 760 pages[133] and it was this slow progress, coupled with the deteriorating military situation, which led him to envisage publishing the novel in two parts. There was a further third part projected, during which the experiment with the gas masks would kill Colonel O'Colloghan and Sosthène, Virginie would give birth in the London Hospital, assisted by Clodowitz, now inexplicably called Yudenzweck (the transposition of Rajchman in *L'Eglise*), before going mad and dying in a fire during the bombing of London, with Cascade being murdered by a jealous rival Moncul.[134] The first volume, *Guignol's Band* I, appeared in late March 1944,[135] and Céline continued working on volume II. When he left Paris in June 1944 there was a complete typewritten version, but with various parts in different stages of revision. Céline continued to work on it in Germany (even naively envisaging a prompt return to Paris to deliver the final text in September 1944)[136] and particularly in Denmark until 1947, when it was overtaken by a project called *La Bataille du Styx*, which was to become *Féerie pour une autre fois*.[137] After Céline's death, the copy of the second part of *Guignol's Band* which had been left with Marie Canavaggia in 1944 was passed by Lucette Destouches to Robert Poulet, who published it under the title *Le Pont de Londres*.[138] It was only after meticulous comparison of the different manuscripts and typed texts that Henri Godard was able to publish a quasi-definitive version of *Guignol's Band* II in 1988.[139]

The first volume of *Guignol's Band* was not well-received by critics in the collaborationist press, although, as Godard points out, they were careful to record every publication by Céline, whom they still considered the most prestigious of right-wing writers.[140] There was, however, general disappointment that, at such a critical historical moment, he should have chosen to publish an obviously apolitical work. The general view was that, in some way, Céline was about to jump ship, summed up in the article in *Le Réveil du peuple* of 24 May, entitled 'Bye bye Môssieu Céline'. Similarly, Charles Lesca, in *Je suis partout*, and Jacques de Lesdain, in *Aspect*, criticized the lack of polemical content.[141] *L'Echo des étudiants* even went so far as to compare Céline unfavourably with Sartre, and Genet's *Notre-Dame des Fleurs*, also published by Denoël.[142] Nevertheless, Céline continued to receive solid support from friends like Henri Poulain, Ramon Fernandez, Jean Fontenoy, Jullien-Courtine, Lucien Combelle and the faithful Karl Epting, who wrote a highly favourable review in *La Chronique de Paris*.[143] In particular, Céline appreciated the comments of Claude Jamet and Roger de Lafforest in articles in Lucien Combelle's *La Révolution Nationale*.[144]

Undoubtedly, part of the problem stems from the fact that, as Alméras puts it, '*Guignol's Band* in fact inaugurates the abstract period during which Céline sees himself as above all a stylist – a mirror-image of Proust, as some would say,'[145] a period which extends to the two volumes of *Féerie pour une autre fois* and which does not disappear entirely with the trilogy. The pamphlets had liberated Céline, both structurally and stylistically, from the impasse in which he found himself after *Mort à crédit*, and an implicit acknowledgement of this is to be found in the intratextual debts of *Guignol's Band* to *Bagatelles pour un massacre*: the character of the 'real archangel in the declining years of his adventure,'[146] the anarchist Borokrom, whom the narrator of the pamphlet had first met in Leningrad; the character Van Bagaden, of the ballet of the same name which concludes *Bagatelles*, who looks forward to Titus Van Claben in *Guignol's Band*; and the second ballet in *Bagatelles*, *Voyou Paul, Brave Virginie*, which not merely announces the name of the adolescent heroine of *Guignol's Band*, but also provides a common link in their debt to Bernadin de Saint-Pierre's *Paul et Virginie*, the idyllic quality of which Céline both exploits and subverts in his novel.[147]

What Céline also perfected in the pamphlets, particularly in the concluding section of *Les Beaux Draps*, which, as we have seen, he was writing at the same time as the opening of *Guignol's Band*, is an abstract, percussive quality of language which becomes, literally, musical: the 'petite musique' of Célinian stylistics is by no means exclusively metaphorical. It is on the contrary a concrete device to transform words from signifiers to sound. The opening description of the bombing of the bridge over the Loire at Orléans, with its liberal use of onomatopoeia: 'Braoum! Vraoum!'[148] 'Brouang! . . . Valmg!'[149] 'Vloumb! Vloumb!'[150] 'Hua! . . . Wraago! . . . Hua! . . . Wroong!'[151] and 'Ffrrou!'[152] is not merely an attempt to convey the noise of the attack, it is designed to initiate the reader into a Modernist world where language has become concrete.

This technique is derived in part from Céline's reading of Jules Vallès' *La Rue à Londres*, written by the ex-Communard in exile in the British capital, who, like Céline, resorts to onomatopoeia to convey its musicality: his 'Zim! malaboum, boum, boum'[153] looks forward to the bombing of Orléans and the evocation of Borokrom's grenades. At the same time, the use of Vallès introduces a sustained intertextuality in *Guignol's Band* which reinforces its Modernist status. Although, as Godard reminds us, 'a reading of *La Rue à Londres* before the composition of *Guignol's Band*, if not ruled out, is not confirmed,'[154] Céline had certainly heard of Vallès' book on London, since he asked Marie Canavaggia to obtain a copy for him in 1945.[155] The geography of London exploited by both writers is in some respects remarkably similar: both Céline and Vallès emphasize Soho and the docks at Wapping. Yet, whereas Céline evokes the essentially fairy-tale and intriguing quality of both, Vallès, the politically conscious ex-Communard, remains critical. As we have seen, of the French community in Soho he writes scathingly: 'I must confess that it was made to dishonour us, this Leicester Square, full of the riff-raff of France: Soho, infamous Soho!'[156] and, where Céline sees in the docks of London a magical cornucopia, Vallès is conscious only of this accumulation of goods as the external sign of a brutal and sordid imperialist aggression.

In fact, Vallès was only one of a considerable number of French authors who described the British capital. Jill Forbes lists Paul Féval's *Les Mystères de Londres*, Paul Morand's *Londres*, Flora Tristan's *Promenades dans Londres*, Taine's *Notes sur l'Angleterre*, and *Le Sadisme anglais* by Villiers de l'Isle-Adam.[157] In addition to these French evocations of London, and little nods in the direction of other writers, like the Norwegian anti-Semitic novelist Knut Hamsun, alluded to in the name of the sailing-ship, the *Kong Hamsun*, *Guignol's Band* remains highly conscious of a number of English sources: probably Dickens, especially the criminal gang in *Oliver Twist*, and, more significantly, Conrad and Shakespeare. We have already seen how the African episode of *Voyage au bout de la nuit* is indebted to *Heart of Darkness*, to the extent that Conrad's novella has even bequeathed its title to the novel. By the same token, *Guignol's Band*, with its band of criminals and anarchists pursued by the indefatigable Sergeant Matthew and a plot dominated by the murder of the pawnbroker Van Claben, presents considerable similarities to Conrad's *The Secret Agent* of 1907, in which the seedy Soho shopkeeper Adolf Verloc and his anarchist friends, including the bomb-making 'Professor', are hunted down by the representative of Scotland Yard, Inspector Heat. Verloc, in his attempt to strike at the nexus of capitalism by blowing up the Greenwich Observatory, the centre of Greenwich Mean Time, succeeds only in blowing up his idiot adopted son, Stevie, and dies, murdered by his wife, Winnie. In order to evoke London during the First World War, therefore, Céline has recourse to one of the great Edwardian novelists' descriptions of the city and, in addition to his own memories and documentation received from figures like Garcin, constructs his narrative from part of the plot of *The Secret Agent*.

By far the most important and self-conscious grounding of the novel, however, is in Shakespeare, Céline's constant literary guide.[158] It opens with a disparaging reference to Denoël and his reservations about the scenes of violence: 'All I can see is fights in your book!'[159] on which the narrator comments: 'If I brought him *King Lear*, he'd only see massacres in it,'[160] and the book is full of Shakespearean references: the pub *The Moor and Cheese*, which combines the Fleet Street tavern the Cheshire Cheese with *Othello, The Moor of Venice*, the actress Delphine's interruption of a performance of *Romeo and Juliet*, which, in itself, reflects the adolescent love-affair between Ferdinand and Virginie, her allusion to *The Merry Wives of Windsor*, and her crazed assumption of the role of Lady Macbeth in the murder of Van Claben. Above all the novel is modelled on *The Tempest*, Céline's favourite play. The fantastic world of London is presided over by Prospero Jim, the lugubrious landlord of the tavern La Croisière de Dingby, in which all the characters are exiles, is acceded to through the storm constituted by the bombing of Orléans, and normality is restored, at the end of *Guignol's Band* II, only with a further bombing – this time a Zeppelin air-raid, and another bridge – that over the Thames which replaces the bridge over the Loire. In the intervening fantasy world, peopled with Calibans and Trinculos in the form of Cascade's gangsters and anarchists, and punctuated by snatches of ethereal music in the form of children's songs, the narrator Ferdinand, who shares the same name as the young hero of *The Tempest*, conducts his love-affair with Virginie, who, at 15, was the same age as Miranda, under the auspices of the magician-engineer Sosthène de Rodiencourt.

With this complex intertextuality at the heart of the novel, it is unsurprising that its very title should take the form of a multilingual pun: *Guignol's Band* has connotations of 'Guignol's Gang', as in the belle époque Montmartre anarchist 'Bande à Bonnot', a 'gang of Guignols', clown-like and grotesque, enacting scenes of stylized violence, and 'Guignol's jazz-band', which connects with the admonition: 'Jazz has overturned the waltz,'[161] in addition to the sexually explicit allusion to the verb *bander*, to have an erection.

What is interesting about the novel, and what disconcerted its committed readers, is that, like the progression of the text itself, from the bombing of the Loire towns to First World War London, it is able to escape from the troubled present into an essentially unreal world of 'féerie', as if Céline himself is taking refuge from the Occupation in the idyllic memories of his time with Georges Geoffroy, whom he met frequently in Paris during the war, in 1915–16. The London of *Guignol's Band* is not a real city, any more than the Paris of *Voyage au bout de la nuit* and *Mort à crédit* is real in a naturalistic sense, and he employs the same dislocation of topography to create an autonomous space. The 'Elephant' and the 'Castle', for example, instead of being in their rightful position in South London, are described as being at the two extremes of Mile End. When Cascade's gang take flight after Borokrom's bomb has destroyed the Croisière de Dingby, their journey takes them improbably through a random selection of place-names: 'High Way Lambeth! . . . Moorgate, le Square, les Docks, Marylebone, Mint Place.' In fact, what Céline is more interested in is the sound of the words and not topographical precision: street-names like Blossom Avenue, Orchard Alley, Lavender Street, Daffodil Place, Plymouth Street, Falmouth Cottage and Neptune Commons, while connecting with echoes of the sea or with Sosthène's wife Pépé, described as 'the marvellous flower', have a primary importance simply as names: we are back in the Proustian world of 'Noms de pays, le nom'.

Yet, if *Guignol's Band* constitutes a flight into the abstract, through the murder of Van Claben and the love-affair with Virginie it also leads to an exorcism of some of the ghosts left floating after *Mort à crédit*. If the second novel was described by Céline to Robert Poulet as 'the drama of a bad conscience,'[162] *Guignol's Band* is the story of guilt. The murders of Mille-pattes and, especially, that of Van Claben (whose death, following being forced to eat his own gold and then being bounced upside down on his head) constitutes a reworking of the assault on Auguste in *Mort à crédit*, are followed by the spectre of retribution in the form of the ubiquitous Sergeant Matthew. What is important, however, and highly paradoxical given the historical circumstances in which the novel was written, is that, whereas in *Mort à crédit* the guilt is unresolved (in spite of the multiplication of father-figures in the narrative), in *Guignol's Band* the murder of Van Claben, the repository of gold and authority, is exorcized through the intervention of Cascade, another avatar of Oncle Edouard from the previous novel, who disposes of the body in the Thames – 'full fathom five thy father lies.' Although the bombing of London by the Zeppelins prevents Ferdinand from fleeing on the anachronistic sailing ship, the *Kong Hamsun*, it restores him to a reality which is far from negative, and the novel ends with the narrator, unlike Bardamu in *Voyage au bout de la nuit*, being able to cross his bridge and moving into the future with Sosthène and his pregnant child-bride Virginie.

The fact that in the projected third volume two of these characters were destined to die, along with Cascade, testifies not so much to a renewed pessimism on Céline's part after the Liberation as to a working-out of the genre of *Guignol*, in which Ferdinand has become a clown himself.[163] The violence of the action, as in the bombing of Montmartre in the next novel cycle, has been neutralized and immobilized in the realm of *féerie*. At the point of greatest danger, when Céline's life was at greatest risk, he broke through to a state of aesthetic security.

12

Exile

Céline's precipitate departure from Paris on 17 June, less than two weeks after the Normandy landings and when the Allied invasion was by no means obviously secure, was not to the taste of everyone. Indeed, it was some time before Parisian journalists, like Jean Galtier-Boissière, realized that he had gone. On 13 August he noted in his diary that 'Céline is said to have retreated to Switzerland,'[1] and as late as 1 September recorded that 'Céline took to the *maquis* since June.'[2] Unsurprisingly, Ernst Jünger's Prussian *hauteur* had nothing but disdain for sordid panic. He wrote in his diary that it was amazing how 'people who can coldly demand the heads of millions of men are so worried about their miserable little lives'.[3] Lucien Rebatet, who was subsequently more favourable in his judgement on Céline, was at the time equally dismissive: 'Bardamu was an honest cavalry-man at the age of twenty, but a complete failure at fifty. He was a loud-mouthed writer who became a right arse-hole as soon as things got difficult.'[4] And, indeed, Céline's flight to Germany preceded by some two months that of the rest of the French collaborators, who did not leave until the Battle of Normandy was definitively lost, Patton's tanks were advancing towards eastern France and Paris was preparing for the insurrection which would lead to its liberation.

As it was, Céline and Lucette had an untroubled journey on a scheduled train and arrived, as guests of the Reich Foreign Ministry, in Baden-Baden, where they were put up in the resort's finest hotel, the Brenner's Park. This first period in Baden-Baden, before the influx of further French 'guests', was idyllic. Céline, Lucette and Bébert were installed in a luxurious first-floor suite and gorged themselves on an abundance of food undreamt of in occupied Paris. Apart from a few political visitors, the clientele of the hotel was substantially that of a rich spa resort: Céline and Lucette made the acquaintance of the widow of General Hans von Seeckt, who had been Commander-in-Chief of the German army from 1920 to 1925.[5] In this gentle atmosphere, it was possible to forget for the moment the seriousness of the military situation, to the extent that Céline unrealistically envisaged a short visit to Paris in September and embarked on new reading projects. At the end of July he wrote to Karl Epting,[6] thanking him for his help in getting him out of France and enclosing a list of books to be sent from the Librairie Tschann, on the Boulevard du Montparnasse, including *Mémoires d'outre-tombe* by Chateaubriand, Ronsard's poems, and the Pléiade edition of the *Chroniqueurs du Moyen-Age*, a volume which was to have considerable significance for the composition of his own 'chronicle', the *D'un château `l'autre* trilogy.[7]

However idyllic life in the spa hotel was, with fine meals, luxurious accommodation and leisurely walks in the grounds, it was impossible to ignore the fact that the Brenner's Park was also a gilded prison, presided over by Dr Joseph Schlemann, a former Vice-Consul in Marseille, whose first act was to confiscate the passports and travel-passes of the residents.[8] He also reminded Céline that, as a guest of the Reich, he had a duty to repay Germany's kindness, in his case, as a writer, through propaganda work on the radio.[9] Céline, who had steadfastly maintained the fiction throughout the Occupation of refusing any formal literary collaboration, was certainly not going to endanger himself and his future at this point by broadcasting for the Germans, but the situation, with no travel documents and increasing pressure from Schlemann, was becoming threatening under the veneer of the hotel's tranquillity. He decided to put into practice as soon as possible his plan to reach Denmark and the gold, and, in the last fortnight of July 1944, was authorized to travel to Berlin, with a German woman doctor to keep him under surveillance. There he met Dr Knapp, of the foreign section of the German Public Health Department, whom he had known well in Paris, and who passed him on to the Foreign Ministry, where his request for authorization to travel to Denmark was listened to sympathetically, but without any immediate decision. Céline and Lucette were told to return to Baden-Baden to await the Ministry's ruling.[10]

They were not to enjoy the calm and abundance of the Brenner's Park for long. By mid-August, the influx of high-ranking and prominent collaborators from France had begun. Robert Le Vigan arrived on the 16th, followed a week later by the stars: the Luchaires,[11] the Abetz family, Marcel Déat and his family, Pierre Costantini, Alphonse de Châteaubriant, Fernand de Brinon and his mistress, Simone Mitre, Hérold-Paquis, Rebatet, Pierre-Antoine Cousteau and Ralph Soupault.[12] Among this group, composed essentially of Parisian collaborators (although, as Hérold-Paquis commented, in its spa setting it reassembled Vichy),[13] was Lucienne Delforge, whom Céline had not seen since 1936, with her lover, the Radio Paris announcer Henry Mercadier.[14] The most immediate consequence for Céline of this wave of arrivals from France was a change in living conditions.

He and Lucette were moved out of their first-floor suite to make way for more distinguished guests, and were put in much less comfortable quarters higher up, where, incidentally, their neighbours were a Swiss couple called Bonny whom they met later in Sigmaringen and through whom they hoped to be able to settle in Switzerland.[15] At the same time, the standard and quality of the food began to decline, and relations with Joseph Schlemann, and particularly his secretary Fräulein Fischer, deteriorated disastrously.[16] In addition to the physical constraints, to which, as we have seen before, Céline was particularly susceptible, Baden-Baden came to present one signal disadvantage: it was visibly and unambiguously the assembly-point for France's most notorious collaborators and, with the Allied armies moving rapidly towards Germany's western borders, it was an exceedingly dangerous place to be. Céline decided to distance himself from these highly dubious associations and to make a further effort to reach Denmark, with or without the Foreign Ministry's authorization. He contacted Karl Epting, now back in Berlin, who travelled immediately to Baden-Baden at the end of August and arranged the necessary authorizations for Céline, Lucette and Le Vigan to travel to Berlin to meet the important health official Dr Haubold.

Once again, contacts which Céline had made in Paris during the Occupation paid off: Haubold had visited Epting's German Institute to give a lecture on hygienic measures employed in the treatment of German refugees in the winter of 1939–40 and had talked with Céline on that occasion. He was a high-ranking official, with the SS rank of Standartenführer and a civil post as head of foreign relations of the Reich's Medical Council. It was as such that he was represented in Paris throughout the Occupation by Dr Knapp,[17] and he had the authority to permit Céline to practise medicine in Germany. In fact, Haubold offered him a well-paid medical post, which Céline, by now extremely wary of any paid employment under the Germans, declined. Céline, Lucette and Le Vigan spent a week in Berlin whilst Haubold tried to find an alternative solution, in the course of which they stayed in a modest hotel and had dinner on 10 September 1944 with Karl Epting in a restaurant on the Wilhelmstrasse, at which Alain Laubreaux was also present.[18] Finally, Haubold offered to lodge Céline and his party with some friends on their small estate in the village of Kränzlin, some eighty kilometres to the north-west of Berlin, near the town of Neuruppin. Céline accepted. He did not want to return to the collaborators in Baden-Baden and he could not stay in Berlin, which was under intense aerial bombardment. Moreover, Kränzlin was in the right direction, towards Denmark. They moved there around 15 September.[19]

In reconstructing Céline's experiences in Germany in 1944 and 1945, it is important to distance them from the narration of the 'chronicle' embodied in the trilogy, with Baden-Baden, Berlin and Kränzlin being evoked in the second volume, *Nord*, Sigmaringen being the subject-matter of *D'un château l'autre*, and the third volume, *Rigodon*, dealing with the final journey through Germany to Denmark. As in all of Céline's novels, there is considerable transposition from the autobiographical to the fictional, even, and indeed particularly, when the narrator is now called 'Céline'. In other words, while the trilogy exploits and captures the inherent strangeness of being an exile in Germany in the last months of the war, it is, in the medieval sense, a chronicle and not a factual record. Nowhere is this more apparent than in the contrast between the reality of Kränzlin and its portrayal, under the name Zornhof ('Place of Rage'), in *Nord*, which led to a posthumous lawsuit. Kränzlin was a small Prussian estate with a manorhouse inhabited by Haubold's friends, the Scherz family: the 80-year-old Erich Scherz, a former cavalry captain, his late wife's sister, his son Erich, paralysed by polio, his wife, Asta, and their two children, Ugo and Anne-Marie.[20] Céline appears to have had distant, but correct, relations with the family, nothing like those described in the Zornhof of *Nord*, in which the countess is depicted as a pyromaniac and nymphomaniac (an interesting echo, incidentally, of the hallucinatory end of Nora Merrywin in *Mort à crédit*) bent on murdering her crippled husband. The house was also inhabited by members of Haubold's medical services, who regarded the French arrivals with considerable distrust and hostility. Céline, Lucette and Bébert were put into a tiny room without running water or heating on the first floor, while Le Vigan slept in the basement, next to the kitchens.[21] This lack of comfort was compounded by the poor diet. As Gibault notes, whilst the Scherz family ate reasonably well on produce from the farms on the estate, Céline shared the basic regime of Haubold's staff, which consisted essentially of potatoes.[22] Moreover, the hostility of Haubold's employees was shared by other groups of workers living on the estate, 'French prisoners, German conscientious objectors (*Bibelforscher*) who were building barracks, Ukrainian and Polish refugees, former Berlin prostitutes recycled in forced labour, and even a group of Gypsies housed in the barracks or in caravans,'[23] none of whom were likely to be overly impressed by the visits of Céline's high-ranking patrons in their SS uniforms and official cars. Once again, the distinction between refuge and prison turned out to be a fine one, and Céline set his mind to ways of moving on.

In fact, it was Haubold again who offered a possible solution, by suggesting that Céline take a job as a doctor in an arms factory in the Baltic port of Rostock, with Le Vigan as nurse.[24] While Céline had no more intention of accepting this highly compromising post than any other, he was tempted by the fact that Rostock, and especially the fishing port at the mouth of the estuary, Warnemünde, were only some fifty kilometres from Denmark. Accordingly, he pretended to accept Haubold's offer, with the proviso that he be allowed to inspect the area first. Here accounts differ slightly. Le Vigan claimed in a letter to Albert Paraz that he accompanied Céline and Lucette to Rostock and Warnemünde,[25] whereas both Céline himself and Lucette insisted that they travelled alone, leaving Le Vigan at Kränzlin in charge of Bébert.[26] By both accounts, however, the expedition to Rostock was a failure: the beach at Warnemünde was swarming with soldiers and police and it was impossible to bribe a fisherman to take them clandestinely to Denmark. They returned disillusioned to Kränzlin.

In conversation with Frédéric Vitoux, Lucette Destouches provides a fascinating insight into Céline's state of mind at this time, which goes a long way to illuminating his subsequent nervous collapse when arrested in Denmark. She recalled:

> Louis was in anguish. For him, every second was a contemplation of horror. That's what people can't understand . . . With Louis . . . it was a tireless agitation. And since he wasn't writing, he concentrated that enormous strength, that intelligence, on thoughts of escape. Every second brought him a new idea for escape, by train, by boat. He couldn't help himself. I told him to sit still and wait – a kind of fatality – that we should let ourselves be carried along, wherever. Louis wasn't willing.[27]

One particular reason for Céline's anxiety was the fear that Kränzlin, near the Eastern Front, might be vulnerable to a rapid advance by the Red Army. This fear, coupled with the lack of warmth and near-starvation diet, made it impossible to envisage staying in Kränzlin much longer and, if the north and Denmark were no longer an immediate possibility, the only course of action was to retreat south, in the hope of crossing into Switzerland. At the end of September he wrote to Paul Bonny and his wife, who had been their neighbours in Baden-Baden, setting out the failure of the northern expedition in Kränzlin and Rostock, and concluding: 'We would certainly be delighted to come back to you! We have had some abominable experiences here! Agonizing ones!' More precisely, he went on: 'In short, I'm writing immediately to de Brinon that I want to rejoin your group, with the intention of crossing into Switzerland, with Le Vigan, of course.'[28] In the south, however, things had changed: the exiled French community was no longer in Baden-Baden, too close to Strasbourg and the Rhine, and had been moved to the Hohenzollern castle of Sigmaringen on the Danube, some thirty kilometres North of Lake Constance and Switzerland. There they had been joined by those leaders of the Vichy regime, notably Pétain and Laval, who had refused to continue to cooperate with the Germans and had been arrested. In this situation it was Fernand de Brinon, former Vichy ambassador to the German occupying forces, who now headed the governmental mission which had legal jurisdiction over the exiled French community, and who was therefore admirably placed to issue an authorization to Céline to come to Sigmaringen.

The decision, however, took tantalizingly long to come. Céline's and Le Vigan's letters to the Bonnys became more and more desperate as the deadline of 20 October for their move to Rostock approached. Finally, de Brinon gave his permission for them to move to Sigmaringen, where a doctor was needed, and Céline obtained the necessary authorization to leave Kränzlin from Dr Haubold. After a miserable six-week stay in northern Germany, with the frustration of coming so close to Denmark without being able to reach it, Céline, Lucette, Le Vigan and Bébert left the Scherz's estate and headed south, through Berlin, Leipzig, Fürth, Augsburg and Ulm,[29] arriving in Sigmaringen on 28 October 1944.[30] Like the rest of the French community, Lucien Rebatet was shocked at Céline's appearance:

> One morning in early November [*sic*] 1944, the rumour spread through Sigmaringen: 'Céline has arrived.' The guy was coming straight from his Kränzlin. A memorable stage entrance. Still shaken by his trip through devastated Germany, he wore a bluish canvas cap, like a locomotive engineer's circa 1905, two or three of his lumber jackets overlapping, filthy and ragged, a pair of moth-eaten mittens hanging from his neck, and under the mittens, in a haversack on his belly, Bébert the cat, presenting the phlegmatic face of a native Parisian who's seen it all before. You should have seen the faces of the hard-core militants and the rank-and-file militiamen at the sight of this hobo: 'That's the great fascist writer, the brilliant prophet?' I was speechless myself.[31]

II SIGMARINGEN

Sigmaringen was the setting for one of the most unreal and bizarre episodes in recent French history.[32] In the castle and the dwellings which surrounded it were to be found most of the major personalities of collaborationist politics: ministers, leaders of political parties, journalists and propagandists, and that motley band of camp-followers who had flourished in the *demi-monde* of collaboration in Vichy and Paris and were now in fear of their lives. Only two prominent groups were not housed in Sigmaringen: Joseph Darnand's Milice, camped on the shores of Lake Constance, and the remains of Doriot's LVF, billeted in Mengen, some twenty kilometres to the south-east. From here, Doriot planned to form a 'liberation army' of two million men, made up of his own LVF troops, members of the Milice and French prisoners of war, to drive out de Gaulle and his provisional government. Whimsical as this plan was, it was no less realistic than de Brinon's 'Mission Gouvernementale', a fully-fledged government in exile, backed up by a press and radio under the control of Jean Luchaire. Only some former members of the Vichy Government, including Pétain himself, Laval, Jean Bichelonne, who had been Minister for Industrial Production, and the ex-Information Minister Paul Marion, recognized that the game was up and refused to cooperate, consigned to virtual house arrest by their 'hosts'.

These grand personalities, along with the 'active' members of de Brinon's government, were lodged in the château itself, while the smaller fry were spread among the town's hotels. Céline and Lucette were housed in the Löwen, which was small but one of the best hotels in the little town, while Le Vigan went to the Bären, where Lucienne Delforge and Lucien Rebatet were lodged. This separation from Céline led to innumerable quarrels, based on Le Vigan's suspicion that the original project of a doctor and nurse partnership had been rejected and that Céline and Lucette were planning to abandon him,[33] though this did not prevent him testifying generously in his friend's favour after his arrest. In the Löwen, in addition to French émigrés like Jean Luchaire's daughter Corinne,[34] there was the brooding presence of the SS officer Boemelburg, former head of the Paris Gestapo and now Gauleiter of Sigmaringen,[35] with a literal power of life or death over the expatriate community.

As in Baden-Baden, the Germans insisted that all French 'guests' work for their living: Le Vigan, refused a post as nurse, was obliged to work as a radio announcer on Luchaire's station; Céline was more fortunate and was able to practise medicine, joining the Marcel Déat supporter André Jacquot as the French community's doctor. As such, he had a privileged view of all levels of this state in exile, subsequently transposed in *D'un château l'autre*, from the humblest militiaman to the grandest ministers and former ministers. He was never, as is sometimes alleged, Pétain's doctor, who was in reality Doctor Ménétrel until he was arrested by the Germans at de Brinon's instigation and replaced briefly by a prisoner of war, Dr Schillemans.[36] Yet he was on good terms with Pierre Laval, and particularly with Paul Marion and Abel Bonnard, whose 90-year-old mother he nursed in her final illness.[37] This purely medical role within the French community was subsequently essential to the non-political myth of Céline's wartime activities exploited by him and the supporters in his defence: unlike Le Vigan, he could claim, rightly, to have steered clear of any propaganda role which gave support to the Germans, acting instead as a devoted and disinterested doctor in difficult conditions. He treated 'influenza, consumption, and otitis . . . not to mention lice and fleas, scabies, and every possible variety of venereal disease'.[38] In the same way that he had issued medical certificates exempting young conscripts from the STO during the Occupation, he now issued them for members of the Division Charlemagne to save them from certain death on the Eastern Front.[39] Moreover, in an echo of a recurrent theme in Céline's life, he carried out treatment with drugs that he bought with his own money, often on the black market.[40] Finally, Céline appeared to continue to cultivate the role of a subversive which he had allegedly adopted during the Occupation at the German Embassy and at the opening of the Institut d'Etude des Questions Juives, and which served him well in his subsequent defence. According to Lucien Rebatet, when Karl Epting organized a one-day conference of French intellectuals on 6 November 1944, attended by de Brinon and Déat, Céline rapidly plunged it into chaos,[41] an event he was not slow to exploit in his defence. Writing in 1949 to his lawyer Jean-Louis Tixier-Vignancour, he emphasized that 'I *shouted* at that conference: "*I think that all this propagandist nonsense is disgusting!*"'[42] As

Déat himself observed: 'He sows defeatism at full volume, and people who spend an hour with him end up utterly depressed.'[43]

Although Céline and Lucette were now among their own countrymen, their living conditions had not noticeably improved since Kränzlin. The Löwen Hotel was built for fifty guests but had five times that number, and was both overcrowded and unhygienic. The diet, the *Stammgericht*, consisted of 'a hideous gruel of red cabbage and rutabaga',[44] although, as he had done in Paris, Céline supplemented it through black-market produce like 'hams, sausages, smoked goose breast'.[45] Moreover, Sigmaringen was every bit as threatening as the Scherz's manor-house had been: their German 'hosts' were notoriously unpredictable, and when Jacques Doriot died in a mysterious air attack on his car on the road from Mengen in February 1945, many in the French community saw it as a German measure to rid themselves of someone who was becoming an embarrassment.[46] Overhead, squadrons of RAF and USAF bombers passed daily on their way to pulverize the great cities of the Reich, while on land the British moved towards the Rhine, and the Americans and French towards Germany's western borders. In particular, Leclerc's 2nd Armoured Division had liberated Strasbourg on 23 November and now stood uncomfortably close to the Black Forest and Sigmaringen itself. Since the liberation of Paris in August, the exiled Frenchmen in Germany had been obsessed by reports of the *Epuration* back in France: the myths of the massacres in the south and south-west, the prison of Fresnes bulging with suspected collaborators, often victims of denunciation, and the first celebrity victim of the post-Liberation trials, Robert Brasillach, executed by firing-squad on 6 February 1945. There was every sign of retribution being both real and close. Even the German advance in the Ardennes on 15–16 December 1944, which had raised hopes of a lightning reversal of fortunes, had been broken by Patton's tanks at Bastogne.

Nor was Céline himself, prone as he was to paranoia, unjustified in panicking. Although the technical charges brought against him subsequently for extradition from Denmark and for collaboration were relatively slight, he had acquired in the public imagination a reputation as one of the most prominent and extreme collaborators. As such he ran a very real risk of assassination: Vitoux quotes the Resistant Pierre Petrovitch as claiming 'L.-F. Céline did well to flee Paris at the Liberation, not because he had anything to fear from *résistants* who knew him, but because certain hotheads were capable of anything. Some obscure commando would have unthinkingly shot him down and nobody would have been able to prevent it. Paris was in revolution.'[47] Even had he not been assassinated, Céline, had he been captured in the early days of the Liberation, would, like Brasillach, have run the risk of a rapid trial and a harsh sentence; even when the machinery of *Epuration* justice operated in a more impartial manner, writers and journalists still received heavy penalties. Many of Céline's companions in Sigmaringen ended up executed, like Luchaire and Hérold-

Paquis, or with death sentences, subsequently commuted, like most of the *Je suis partout* team.

Unsurprisingly, he remained obsessed by escape, and attempted to put into effect his original plan, communicated to Paul Bonny in the correspondence from Kränzlin, to enter Switzerland, whose proximity was rendered all the more tantalizing by the fact that it was linked to Sigmaringen by a regular rail service. Vitoux even records how Céline and Lucette went regularly to the station to watch the trains and came close to stowing away successfully on one,[48] though Alméras is surely correct in suggesting that if this was all that was needed to escape, 'three-quarters of the Sigmaringen colony would have vanished in January.'[49] What is certain is that on 22 January 1945, Céline made a formal request to the Swiss Consul in Stuttgart for an entry visa, and also hired a lawyer in Lausanne, Maître Savary, to approach the federal government,[50] in both cases without success. As Gibault remarks, Céline appears to have been unaware that Paul Morand, formerly French ambassador to Switzerland, was still in the country. At any rate, he never approached him for help. Apparently he still considered Spain a possibility, accessible through the Italian airfield of Mérano, though since this was the route taken by Laval and Abel Bonnard to Spain, which resulted in their being returned to France, he was perhaps right not to take the scheme further.

His favoured solution remained Denmark and he now moved everything in his power to obtain the necessary authorization, mobilizing Karl Epting and Gerhard Heller[51] and especially his SS friend from the Avenue Foch, Hermann Bickler, who was close to Werner Best, now German ambassador to Denmark. Through him, Céline and Lucette received the necessary entry visa, and Bickler also convinced Boemelburg to renew the couple's *Fremdenpass* and provide them with a travel document.[52] He also authorized Céline's nurse, Germinal Chamoin, to deliver Céline and Lucette to the border town of Flensburg and to make the return journey. On 22 March 1945, at 7.30 in the evening, Céline, Lucette and Bébert, accompanied by Chamoin, left the station at Sigmaringen for the long journey north.

Once again, this exercise in prudence hardly endeared Céline to his former collaborationist colleagues, though Marcel Déat, who remembered Céline's attempts to escape to Italy,[53] was more understanding: 'We were very pleased for Céline,' he noted.[54] Lucien Rebatet subsequently remembered Céline's nocturnal departure with unambiguous loyalty: 'We embraced for a long time, we laboriously lifted up the baggage. Ferdinand unfolded and waved for one last time his incredible passport. The train started, like a little local train. The rest of us stood there, anguished, in the infernal boiler. But there was no jealousy. If we were going to get punished, at least the best and the greatest of us would have escaped.'[55] But the reaction of Jean Hérold-Paquis, who was to be executed in 1948 for his role as a broadcaster on Radio Paris, probably summed up more accurately the view of the hard-liners in the French community at what he regarded as the 'flight of L.-F. Céline'.[56] Hérold-Paquis had concluded that Céline, as soon as he was convinced of the inevitability of a German defeat, had simply reneged on his former beliefs and had 'disavowed the author of *Bagatelles*, *L'Ecole des cadavres* and *Les Beaux Draps*':[57] 'in this German town, in front of millions of Frenchmen, Céline was undertaking himself his "journey to the end of shame". Then one day he disappeared.'[58]

Céline was at great pains subsequently to exaggerate both the length of the journey and its dangers. To Tixier-Vignancour, he wrote of a journey of eighteen days on foot,[59] and to his friend Dr Camus he recalled walking at one stage for thirty-five kilometres between two warring armies, 'under fire worse than that of 1917'.[60] In fact, the journey was quite horrific enough, but lasted no more than five days and never once came closer than 200 kilometres to either the Eastern or the Western Front.[61] The little narrow-gauge train from Sigmaringen took them first to Ulm, where they changed for Augsburg, and then headed north: to Nuremberg, Fürth, Bamberg, Lichtenfeld, Eisenach, Bebra, Göttingen, Hannover, Kleefeld, Lerthe, Hamburg and finally Flensberg, which they reached at midnight on 26 March 1945.[62] They passed through cities in ruins and in flames; their train was sometimes attacked by aircraft and had to take refuge in a tunnel; they came across strange travelling companions: a crippled Englishman and an Italian. At times, Céline was so depressed that he complained: 'If I had known, we would have committed suicide in Sigmaringen,'[63] but as they moved north, under the expert care of Chamoin, whom Céline encouraged with the cry: 'To the north, Chamoin, to the north!' he became more optimistic and more convinced that they would succeed. At Flensberg, he wrote letters for de Brinon and his colleague Dr Jacquot, and gave the remainder of his German money and his food coupons to Chamoin.[64] All that remained was to cross the border and get to Copenhagen, yet this was to be one final barrier. At 6 a.m. on 27 March, a Swedish Red Cross train carrying Swedish refugees steamed into Flensberg station, but the colonel in charge of it initially refused to allow Céline and Lucette to get on board. In spite of the melodramatic account conveyed by Vitoux, involving Lucette fainting from exhaustion and nearly falling under the train's wheels,[65] it is more likely that it simply took most of the day to persuade the Swedish colonel to take an additional two passengers. Chamoin, who then immediately left on the return journey to Sigmaringen, arriving on 31 March, noted laconically: 'Entry into Denmark at 18.38.'[66] For the present, Céline was safe.

III COPENHAGEN

On arrival in Copenhagen, Céline, Lucette and Bébert went first to the smartest hotel in the city, the Angleterre, where he had always stayed before the war. After resting, he then made contact with a friend of Karen Marie Jensen's, Madame Lindquist, a photographer, who passed him on to

Karen's cousin, Hella Johansen, with whom they stayed in the country before installing themselves, as previously agreed, in Karen's apartment at number 20 Ven Stranden.[67] It was an attractive apartment, on the top floor of a building which had once housed Hans Christian Andersen, in the centre of the old city. It was luxuriously furnished in Louis XV style, with antique porcelain, though its curtains, its chairs and its bowls were to be severely damaged by Bébert in the coming months. For Céline and Lucette, however, after the deprivations and dangers of the last nine months, it was a haven of security and relative plenty. The shops were full of food, even though Céline constantly complained of the high prices, and it was possible to lead a semblance of a normal life, especially for Lucette, who started to give Spanish and oriental dance lessons with the Danish ballet-master Birger Bartholin and even at the Opera, in spite of the hostility of its choreographer Harald Lander.[68] Céline himself, although he rarely went out of the apartment, even resumed writing, completing the manuscript of the second part of *Guignol's Band*, which he had brought with him from France, composing most of a ballet choreography, *Foudres et flèches*, and beginning work on the project initially entitled *La Bataille du Styx*, which was to become *Féerie pour une autre fois.*[69]

There were still plenty of clouds on the horizon. The first blow to strike was news of the death of Céline's mother, Marguerite Guillou, which had occurred on 6 March 1945, long before their departure from Sigmaringen. As Vitoux records, Céline was crushed by the news: 'he collapsed in tears. He spent hour after hour prostrate on his bed, holding Lucette's hand,'[70] and his grief was also compounded by guilt at the harshness with which he had often treated her. As he wrote to Marie Canavaggia: 'I feel horribly guilty for my hardness to her.'[71] At the same time, the end of the war and the capitulation of the German occupying forces in Denmark led to a new regime dominated by the Resistance and the Communists, and Céline's position as a French collaborator on the run was by no means secure. In particular, his only papers were those issued by the German authorities, Boemelburg and Best, and he urgently needed to regularize his situation in Denmark with the post-liberation regime. To do this, through Mrs Lindquist and Ottoststroem (a local pharmacist friend of Karen's), he contacted a lawyer, Thorvald Mikkelsen, who remained in charge of Céline's affairs throughout his stay in Denmark and who was to suffer the same fate as everyone else who attempted to help the writer. Mikkelsen, who had become a highly successful lawyer only after a failed business career, was a Francophile lover of literature whose French wife had only recently died. What was of considerable importance for Céline's case was the fact that he 'had also been very close to the Danish Resistance, he knew the Minister of Justice and many other members of the government.'[72] Mikkelsen wrote to his friend Bergtrup-Hansen, head of the national police force, vouching personally for Céline and Lucette and requesting residence permits for them, which were issued after a meeting with the Aliens Department on 20 June.[73] Their presence in Denmark was now official, although

Céline and Lucette felt by no means secure. Lucette thought that the Danes took her for a spy,[74] and Céline lived in constant fear of assassination by Communists, Danish Resistants or even a hit squad sent from France. It is unclear whether he knew that an arrest warrant under Articles 75 and 76 of the Penal Code, relating to treason and intelligence with the enemy, had been issued on 19 April 1945 in Paris,[75] or that his pamphlets had been banned by the French military censor along with Hitler's speeches and Rebatet's *Les Décombres*,[76] but he was certainly aware of the progress of the *Epuration*, both official and unofficial, especially the trials of Pétain and Laval in July–August and October, and the assassination of Robert Denoël on 2 December, shortly before his own arrest.

The circumstances of Denoël's death have never been fully explained. He went into hiding after the Liberation of Paris, but on 2 December decided to go to the theatre with his mistress Jeanne Loviton, who wrote under the pseudonym of Jean Voilier and was to take over the company on Denoël's death, inheriting from her murdered lover a role as Céline's *bête noire* in the 1940s. On the corner of the Rue de Grenelle and the Boulevard des Invalides a tyre burst, and Denoël started to change the wheel while Jeanne Loviton went to the police station on the Rue de Grenelle to call a taxi. It was there that, at the same time as the police, she heard the radio report that Denoël had been found dead by his car, shot in the back. It remains unclear whether robbery was the motive, though the 12,000 francs in Denoël's pocket were untouched, whether he was assassinated by the Resistance or whether he died as part of a more shady settling of accounts. Céline himself even became convinced that Jeanne Loviton was to blame.[77] His publisher's death was a cruel blow, though Céline saw it primarily as an indication of the noose tightening around his own neck. He wrote to Marie Canavaggia after the funeral: 'Here, it's one more tragedy. If you knew what we've been through these last eighteen months ... we're like animals who've been beaten too much ... you wonder if a heavier blow than the others wouldn't be a mercy.'[78] As it was, the blow was about to fall.

The French Legation in Copenhagen had known of Céline's presence as early as the end of September 1945, and its head, Guy de Girard de Charbonnière, later to be a full ambassador, requested advice from the French Foreign Minister, Georges Bidault.[79] Discussions between the Quai d'Orsay and the French Legation in Copenhagen continued throughout the autumn, culminating in Bidault's directive of 23 November to seek extradition. Nothing appears to have been done immediately, however, and it was a press leak which finally precipitated events. On 15 December in Paris, the newspaper *Samedi Soir* carried a story revealing Céline's presence in Denmark, which was picked up the following day by the major Danish newspaper *Politiken* with the headline: 'A French Nazi is Hiding in Copenhagen – The Writer Céline, who Escaped with the Vichy Government.'[80] This prompted a news-vendor, who recognized Céline as one of his regular clients, to contact the police, and on 17 December de Charbonnière formally approached the Danish Foreign Ministry asking for Céline's arrest pending extradition procedures. The Foreign Minister himself, Gustav Rasmussen, ordered the writer's arrest that very evening, and three plain-clothes police went to the apartment at 20 Ved Stranden. Their arrival caused complete panic. Both Céline and Lucette initially took the police-men for French assassins and refused to open the door. Only when Birger Bartholin, summoned by Lucette, confirmed that the men were indeed police officers was the door opened, but the couple were at the end of their tether. According to the newspaper *BT*, 'M. et Mme Destouche [*sic*] were very nervous and were in tears,'[81] and the arresting officer testified that 'an unbelievable chaos reigned in the room. Destouches and his wife were in their night-clothes, showing signs of the most extreme agitation.'[82] Céline and Lucette were taken to the Prefecture and then transferred to the Vestre Faengsel prison. Lucette was released on 28 December and returned to Karen's apartment, but Céline was to remain in prison until 26 February 1947, with a brief period in Sundby Hospital from 8 November 1946 until 24 January 1947.

Throughout this period, Céline had two major preoccupations: one, which receded with time, concerned the threat of extradition to France, and the other, which increased and led to his hospitalization at the end of 1946, was to do with his health. Both the Quai d'Orsay and de Charbonnière showed considerable energy in prosecuting the case for extradition, to the extent that Céline, himself never slow to identify a potential persecutor, saw the French ambassador as the Hudson Lowe to his Napoleon. Nevertheless, de Charbonnière was under considerable pres-sure both from his own ministry and from sections of the French press.[83] Moreover, Céline's position was weakened further by the fact that his lawyer, Mikkelsen, was on a business trip to the United States, although in retrospect this may have acted in Céline's favour by slowing the process down. Initially, the Danish government was sympathetic to the French request and was prepared to hand Céline over. The problem, however, was that, as Mikkelsen's friend Aage Seidenfaden, the head of the Copenhagen police, who knew Céline, reminded the Ministry of Justice as early as 28 December 1945, Céline and Lucette were in possession of perfectly legal residence permits, and moreover, the extradition request was based on charges of treason, which were expressly excluded from the extradition treaty between France and Denmark of 28 March 1877.[84] This argument was taken up in the Danish cabinet by another friend of Mikkelsen's, Per Federspiel, the Minister of Special Affairs in charge of all questions con-cerning the Resistance and the purges, who insisted on a decision being taken only at cabinet level and effectively blocked Céline's extradition. By 1 May 1946, the French chargé d'affaires, Jean de Lagarde, reported to Bidault that, because of Federspiel's opposition, the cause was effectively lost.[85] Mikkelsen's own activity on his return from America, which consisted essentially of reminding the Danish government of the international conse-quences of handing over Céline and this breach of Denmark's tradition of asylum, reinforced a process which was already running in the writer's favour. In the absence of any hard evidence of serious collaboration on Céline's part, the Danes gradually gave up and, on 26 February 1947, released him from prison to house arrest in Copenhagen's Rigshospitalet.[86]

Yet, as the two spells in hospital indicate, this prolonged period of intense anxiety, compounded by a prison regime and separation from Lucette, took its toll both psychologically and physically. In terms of physical deterioration, however, there is, as might be expected, some discrepancy between Céline's own accounts, motivated by a combination of self-dramatization, self-pity and a need to put pressure on his captors, and reports of other witnesses. From Sunby Hospital in November 1946, for example, he drew up a detailed medical report on his condition for Mikkelsen, in which he referred to severe head pains, ringing in the ears, rheumatism, paralysis of the arm, heart disease, an intestinal condition, eczema, pellagra, weight loss and the loss of all his teeth.[87] The report is grossly exaggerated but contains a core of truth. He did not, as he claims, spend six out of eleven months of incarceration in hospital, having been transferred to Sundby only on 11 November 1946 and discharged on 24 January 1947, and many of the conditions mentioned go back to the Célinian mythology of the early interviews after *Voyage au bout de la nuit*: the head wound, the ears, the paralysis of the arm and the dysentery, for example. Some of the comments are new, like the claim of cardiac weakness which 'had made it impossible for me for several years now to climb a staircase with several floors',[88] which hardly accords with the lifestyle of a man who had lived throughout the Occupation on the fourth floor of the Rue Girardon and had carried his moped up the stairs every day as well. The same is true of the weight loss, where Céline even contradicts himself, complaining one moment about the starvation diet in the Vestre Faengsel, then praising its copiousness. As Alméras observes, Céline's claim to have lost between forty and fifty kilos in prison is neither supported by any of the photographs taken of him shortly after his release nor particularly plausible: normally weighing about eighty kilos, losing over half his body-weight would have made him look like 'someone out of the concentration camps'.[89] Nevertheless, there was clearly sufficient physical deterioration in Céline's condition to justify his transfer to hospital, even though this appears to have been as much a result of Mikkelsen's pressure to make the regime of his client more palatable as of concrete medical needs. An objective witness at the end of his period of imprisonment, Tage Jensen, who was a young doctor in another Copenhagen hospital and who visited Céline at the Rigshospitalet, found him 'prematurely aged' and without teeth, but not unusually thin.[90] The major damage was probably psychological. François Gibault may exaggerate when he claims that Céline, on leaving prison in 1947, 'was completely ruined physically', but he is undoubtedly correct in stating that his imprisonment had 'humiliated him and destroyed his morale for the rest of his life'.[91] Coming after the anxieties of the last months of the Occupation in Paris, the community of condemned men in Sigmaringen, the epic journey through Germany in the last days of the

Reich and the nine months in hiding in Copenhagen, the arrest, imprisonment and constant fear of extradition to France led to a nervous collapse
from which Céline never fully recovered. It is undoubtedly from this period
that the final image of him, which was perpetuated by so many photographs
from his last period, stems: the bent back and hunched shoulders, the thin
unshaven face with the toothless mouth and staring eyes, the tramp-like
dress – though even here it would be unwise totally to discount the assumption of the clothes and persona of the martyr.

The long period of imprisonment was troubled still further by domestic
and financial problems. In June 1946, Karen Marie Jensen had returned to
Copenhagen from Spain, and was appalled to find her apartment so badly
treated by her guests. She remained sympathetic to Céline, interceding in
his favour with the Minister of Justice, but asked Lucette, who had returned
to the apartment after her release from prison in December 1945, to look
for somewhere else to live. In fact, one of Céline's warders, a painter called
Henning Jensen, wished to live in the south with his wife for a long period,
and Lucette was able to arrange for the couple to stay with her parents in
Menton in exchange for the use of his own apartment, a tiny studio near
the Kongens Have Park.[92] She moved in in September and, on his release
from the Rigshospitalet in June 1947, Céline was to join her there until the
Jensens' return in May 1948. Relations quickly deteriorated with Karen
Marie Jensen, who began to complain to Céline about Lucette's financial
extravagance, which was seriously diminishing the stock of gold held by
Hella Johansen. Initially, Céline believed Karen and in November 1946
wrote two violent letters to Lucette, in which he held her profligacy responsible for the position in which he now found himself, claiming to have
written *Les Beaux Draps* only because of financial difficulties, and concluding with a vicious attack on her appearance which is a measure of his
extreme psychological state: 'You no longer have a human shape, you're
like a skeleton, you're old, you frighten everyone – you'll make them laugh
– you've lost your skill – you've lost your hands, you're destroying yourself
and you're destroying me.'[93] Lucette, however, was able to convince him
that her extravagance alone could not account for such a drain on the gold,
and Céline, mercurial and distrustful, immediately concluded that Karen
and Hella Johansen had been stealing from him. In an emotional scene
worthy of a nineteenth-century melodrama, he summoned Lucette,
Mikkelsen, Karen and Hella Johansen to his bedside in the Sundby Hospital, where, according to Lucette in conversation with Vitoux, Karen finally
admitted to spending half of it.[94] In any event, Céline pronounced judgement: Karen and Hella were to hand over the gold to Mikkelsen, who would
pay an allowance to Céline and Lucette of 350 crowns a month, and Karen,
like so many people in Céline's life, passed from favour to rejection immediately and definitively. He had nothing more to do with the dancer who
'would have made a perfect Duchess of Brittany to his Duke' and who had
effectively saved him by looking after his fortune and giving him her

apartment to live in at the beginning of his exile. All the familiar abuse was heaped on her: she was henceforth 'an idiotic malevolent drunk',[95] who had led him into 'a trap laid by the Jews where they want me to die slowly',[96] and Denmark was similarly vilified: 'We're dealing with terrible Danish hypocrites: all the ferocity of the Vikings, the lies of the Jews and the hypocrisy of the Protestants.'[97] Mikkelsen himself was by no means immune and would eventually suffer the same fate.

The confrontation with Karen Marie Jensen took place in November 1946, while Céline was in Sundby Hospital, where he remained until 24 January 1947. By this time, however, as we have seen, the Danes were tiring of the extradition process and the French had effectively given up hope. On 26 February 1947 he was transferred to the Rigshospitalet, under a form of house arrest which allowed him to go out into the city, or beyond, during daytime. On 24 June he was finally released, joining Lucette and Bébert (who in his absence had undergone an operation for cancer) in Henning Jensen's apartment at 8 Kronprincessegade. Although it was centrally situated, the apartment, which consisted of two small rooms, was effectively cramped student accommodation, under the eaves again, and difficult to heat in winter or keep cool in summer. Nevertheless, in comparison with the traumas of 1946 it was a haven of normality, and Lucette resumed her routine of dance lessons, while Céline began to write seriously again. In prison, he had worked on the final version of *Guignol's Band* II, and had written most of the ballet choreography, *Foudres et flèches*. In the Jensens' cramped apartment, he completed these works and abandoned the project for a *Guignol's Band* III in favour of the more immediate narrative of Montmartre during the Occupation: the original title of *La Bataille du Styx* gave way to *Maudits soupirs pour une autre fois*, and this essentially memorialist work was finally transformed into *Féerie pour une autre fois*, the first volume of which was published in 1952, marking Céline's official entry into the house of Gallimard. This resumption of work was not without physical cost. To continue the composition of *Féerie*, Céline came to rely more and more on a diet of coffee and the sleeping drug Veronal, an echo of Balzac's frenetic literary work, which was eventually to contribute to his death.

This isolated existence was relieved by a small number of visitors from Paris: René Héron de Villefosse, whom Céline had known on Henri Mahé's boat, the *Enez-Glaz*, in the 1930s, and, shortly before his death, Jean-Gabriel Daragnès.[98] He was also visited by new acquaintances from the French community in Copenhagen: Denise Thomassen, who ran a French bookshop in the city, and the pastor of the French Reformed Church, François Löchen, who was to be a constant support until Céline's departure from Denmark.[99] At the same time (as he had done in prison and as he was to do in Korsör), Céline conducted a copious correspondence with people in France, mainly intended to orchestrate support, but which also brought news of old friends.[100] Not all of it was pleasant: he heard of the sentence of Le Vigan, who had stoutly defended Céline throughout his trial, to ten years' forced labour in November 1946,[101] and the death of Albert Milon, whom he had known since their meeting in 1914 in the Val-de-Grâce hospital, in December 1947.[102]

The bulk of the correspondence, which was to continue in Korsör, was directed towards, if not actual rehabilitation, at least re-entry into French literature. In addition, he returned to his habitual game of the reluctant interview in the press: with *France-Dimanche* on 29 June 1947, in which he made the common ex-collaborator's promise to go and fight in Indochina;[103] with Robert Massin for *La Rue* in November 1947, where he complained of the light treatment of Sacha Guitry and Montherlant;[104] and with *Samedi-Soir* on 22 November 1947, which was a non-interview, because Céline refused to open the door to the journalist, while nevertheless letting drop a few key points in the resulting shouting-match: his poverty, the title of his next novel and his refusal ever to talk about the Jews again.[105] He also negotiated with Jean Paulhan, who had just started up *Les Cahiers de la Pléiade* with Gallimard as a post-war version of the *Nouvelle Revue Française*, and was anxious to publish a new piece by Céline. In this, Paulhan was motivated not merely by admiration for Céline's work, but particularly by his growing disaffection with the policy of exclusion practised by the former Resistants in the Comité National des Ecrivains in the form of the 1944 blacklists. The project nearly came to nothing, since the work submitted by Céline was a ringing and literally scatological denunciation of Sartre: 'A l'agité du bocal'. It was Albert Paraz who drew Céline's attention to an apparently off-the-cuff reference in Sartre's *Réflexions sur la question juive* of 1947, which had, incidentally, previously appeared as 'Portrait de l'antisémite' in *Les Temps Modernes* in December 1945: 'If Céline was able to support the Nazis' socialist theses, it was because he was paid.'[106] For Céline, still facing charges of treason in France, this was a particularly vicious denunciation and he was understandably furious. In his riposte, he likened 'Jean-Baptiste' Sartre to a parasite in his own bowels: the 'agité du bocal' of the title.[107] Paulhan was appalled and refused to publish the pamphlet, which eventually appeared in 1948 in Paraz's own book *Le Gala des vaches*. Céline then offered him *Foudres et flèches*, which Paulhan found too slight, and finally the first chapter of what remained of *Casse-pipe*, which appeared in *Les Cahiers de la Pléiade* in the late summer of 1948, when Céline was in Korsör.[108]

What exercised him particularly, however, throughout the whole exile in Denmark was the resumption of normal publishing of his work in France, and here his fate was dependent on that of the Denoël company as well as on the CNE and the French Ministry of Finance, who were claiming the taxes which Céline had failed to pay during the Occupation.[109] On the death of Denoël, the publishing house, which was still the subject of a criminal prosecution for collaboration, was put into the hands of an administrator, Maximilian Vox (formerly Monod), pending the outcome of the litigation between the publisher's widow, whom he had allegedly been about to divorce, and his mistress, Jeanne Loviton, whom Denoël was allegedly about to marry. With the victory of Jeanne Loviton, the company was now able to resume business and, as Alméras reminds us, was keen to exploit the vogue for foreign, particularly American writers.[110] They also wished to republish Céline's novels, which they felt would rapidly rise to pre-war sales figures. The impediment to this, in addition to Céline's innate animosity to Jeanne Loviton, whom he distrusted as a woman and whom he rapidly came to accuse of complicity in Denoël's murder, was the tax situation. Since anything he earned in France would immediately be impounded by the French authorities, what he was interested in, before anything else, was payment of his arrears in royalties, to be paid into foreign accounts, and maximizing the US translation rights. Here, as we shall see, he found an unexpected ally in the (Jewish) literature instructor at the University of Chicago, Milton Hindus, later to move to Brandeis.[111] From 1947 onwards, as François Gibault sets out in detail, Céline fought a lengthy and increasingly acrimonious campaign with the house of Denoël, represented both by Jeanne Loviton and her literary director Guy Tosi, to retrieve the royalties he felt were owing to him and eventually to break free from his contractual obligations so that he could find another publisher, probably Gallimard.[112] What prolonged an already long drawn-out dispute, however, was the fact that, against all expectations, the Société Denoël was acquitted on 30 April 1948 of the charges of collaboration. On the face of it, this was extraordinary: the subsidiary of the company, Denoël's Nouvelles Editions Françaises, had published not only *Les Beaux Draps* but also patently collaborationist works such as Rebatet's *Les Décombres* and works by Montandon and other French racist writers. Clearly, Jeanne Loviton had acquired powerful political leverage, which sheds considerable light on the process of the *Epuration* in literary France. For Céline, the acquittal of Denoël had two implications, one negative, the other positive: while it continued to tie him to a newly viable publishing house from which he hoped to escape, it also provided him with an important trump card in his legal defence. If his publisher had been found innocent of collaboration in publishing Céline's works during the Occupation, it was difficult to see how the author of those works could be found guilty of the same accusations.

This period following Céline's release from prison, which saw some hardship in living conditions but also the possibility of rehabilitation as a writer, was threatened by the return of Henning Jensen and his wife. They had not had a happy experience in the south of France: Lucette's parents, the Piralozzis, had given them only an uncomfortable maid's room in their apartment in Menton and had been decidedly unfriendly. In the spring of 1948 they decided to come back to Copenhagen, and they wanted Céline and Lucette to vacate their apartment. The problem was that there was an acute housing shortage in Copenhagen, prices had risen astronomically, and the couple were obliged to accept the only possibility on offer: accommodation on Mikkelsen's estate at Klarskovgaard, eight kilometres from the port of Korsör, on the western coast of the island a hundred kilometres from Copenhagen. They moved there, still accompanied by Bébert, on May 19 1948.[113]

IV KLARSGOVGAARD

As Alméras records, it was Mikkelsen's father who had originally bought the property as the site for an educational colony for deprived children – an ironic echo of Courtial's project in *Mort à crédit* – ten hectares of land on the Baltic coast, with a number of houses on it.[114] His son had taken it over in the early 1920s,[115] planted it with apple orchards, and used it as a summer and weekend residence ever since. Apart from the main house ('Hovedhuset'), an attractive thatched, half-timbered building dating from the nineteenth century, there was a more modern house for guests ('Gaestehuset'), a bailiff's house ('Bestyrer Bolig'), and two smaller houses, further from the main settlement: 'Skovly', a three-roomed building 200 metres to the west of the main house, with a single cold-water tap, and last of all, 'Fanehuset', at the southern end of the property, an eighteenth-century thatched house with a beaten earth floor, no running water and only a peat-burning stove for heating.[116] Opinions differ as to the level of discomfort which Céline suffered during the three years he spent on Mikkelsen's property, not least because, from the outset, Céline was determined to hate it. He loathed the countryside and, apart from the experience of Cameroon, Klarskovgaard was his only period of extended contact with it. He wrote to Pastor Löchen: 'My hatred for the countryside has always been intense; now, it is beyond imagination.'[117] And to Dr Camus he complained, with no apparent sense of irony: 'I find the countryside completely tragic . . . and cruel! All you hear is the cries of sparrows murdering each other, a thousand murders every minute. What savagery!'[118] Nor did this self-styled Breton mariner take the Baltic seriously, claiming that it was not even 'watchable': 'The Sepulchral Sea, I call it, and the rare boats, the coffins, and the sails, the weeds.'[119] Moreover, he was acutely conscious of being in exile, of having found his own St Helena. He wrote to Dr Camus in 1949: 'I've got other things to do than to look at the countryside. Whether it's cold, hot or wet, it always stinks of fennel . . . Exile, you know, has nothing in common with holidays.'[120]

We have also seen that Céline was extremely sensitive to lack of comfort, deprivation and perceived humiliation, and the arrangements which Mikkelsen made at Klarskovgaard could only inflame such sensitivities. When they arrived on the estate in May, Mikkelsen had them installed in his own main house, which was extremely comfortable, and then transferred them to the guests' quarters in the 'Gaestehuset', which were still relatively luxurious. Frequently, however, Mikkelsen invited friends to stay on the estate, which meant that Céline and Lucette were forced to move. The first such occasion occurred in July 1948, when the British ambassador arrived, occupying the 'Gaestehuset', accompanied by the Danish Minister of Education, who took over the cottage 'Skovly'. Céline and Lucette moved to the smallest and most distant cottage, 'Fanehuset'.[121] This game of musical chairs continued throughout the couple's stay in Klarskovgaard, with occasional periods in the two luxurious houses, but generally alternating between 'Skovly' in winter and 'Fanehuset' in summer. This was not calculated to satisfy Céline's sense of dignity, nor his sense of comfort. Both cottages were undoubtedly quite primitive, though probably by no means to the extent that Céline complained. In particular, the lack of running water in 'Fanehuset' and the poor heating in 'Skovly' during the winter, not improved until 1950, were constant sources of irritation, as was the frequent moving around. At the same time, Céline found the food both scarce and unpalatable. He wrote to Le Vigan: 'Nothing grows here – *no vegetables*, it's too cold – We get meat once a week, astronomically expensive and *bad*. The eggs are tasteless – the fish is tasteless. Fortunately, we're not difficult. But *smoked herring with oatmeal*: I don't want any more, and the cats don't either.'[122] Mikkelsen did what he could to supplement this diet by bringing provisions from Copenhagen on each of his visits, and he also attempted to alleviate the couple's solitude by inviting them to dinner with his guests, such as the Danish Nobel laureate Johannes V. Jensen. Céline interpreted this, perversely perhaps, as a ploy on the part of his host to entertain his distinguished visitors by showing them the wild French Fascist novelist.[123] More and more distrustful of human beings, the couple took increasing refuge in their love of animals: in addition to the aging Bébert, they acquired four other cats in the course of their stay in Klarskovgaard, and a dog, Bessy, who had been left behind by the Germans and had run wild, and whom they tamed.[124]

Meanwhile, Céline continued with work on *Féerie pour une autre fois* and pursued his campaign for rehabilitation, both through correspondence and, increasingly, through visits. His major concern was the republishing of the 1930s novels, *Voyage au bout de la nuit* and *Mort à crédit*, which, he felt, would not merely remind the public of his literary status but bring in much-needed finance. One element in Céline's life at least had remained constant: his belief in the quality of his work, its classic status and its inevitable commercial success. Relations with Denoël, now under the control of Jeanne Loviton, had completely broken down, in spite of Guy Tosi's visit to Denmark at the end of 1947.[125] Since Tosi was unable to provide the 1000 crowns which he had promised, Céline wrote to Jeanne Loviton on 8 December 1947 invoking the clause in his contract which stipulated that if Denoël failed to publish or reissue his works over a particular period, he was free of his obligations to the company.[126] In fact the situation was more complex, and after the company's acquittal they were prepared to publish Céline again. The problem was that, with his ongoing dispute with the French over his back-taxes, Céline insisted on being published outside France so that his royalties could not be impounded. Into this stalemate came a young cartoonist for the journal *Ecoutes*, Pierre Monnier, who toured Denmark in the late summer of 1948 as press officer for an Auvergnat folk-group called *La Bourrée*[127] and was able to meet Céline at Klarskovgaard. From this meeting, a lengthy correspondence ensued, subsequently published by Monnier as *Ferdinand furieux*,[128] in the course of which the two plotted Céline's return to publishing. Monnier did the rounds of Paris publishers, but got nowhere with established firms like Flammarion or Plon.[129] He then approached the young publisher Charles Frémanger, who had set up a new company, Editions Jean Froissart, whose finances were based on the popular best-seller *Caroline chérie*, written by Jacques Laurent under the pseudonym of Cécil Saint-Laurent. Frémanger's office-boy was Antoine Blondin, whose first novel, *L'Europe buissonnière*, with many direct echoes of *Voyage au bout de la nuit*, was to be published by the company in 1949. Frémanger agreed to publish both *Voyage* and *Mort à crédit*, but in fact had neither the financial resources nor the administrative talents to carry out the task efficiently, despite visiting Céline in January 1949:[130] *Ferdinand furieux* is full of letters complaining about delays, denouncing Frémanger as a crook, screaming at the absence of royalty payments and often blaming the innocent Monnier for the entire enterprise.

In the meantime a small publisher, Charles de Jonquières, had produced an edition of *Foudres et flèches* in late December 1948, though again with little financial success.[131] Faced with this situation, and increasing aggressivity from Céline, Monnier decided to set up his own company, Editions Frédéric Chambriand, to publish the extant fragment of *Casse-pipe*, which appeared in December 1949 and sold relatively well.[132] He went on to publish a new edition of *Mort à crédit*, which sold considerably less well, and *Scandale aux abysses*, but he was not equipped to mount a major publishing operation on all of Céline's work. Negotiations continued, particularly via Jean Paulhan, for Céline's entry into Gallimard, although this did not happen until his return from exile in 1951.

In this campaign for rehabilitation, a new privileged correspondent emerged, who worked alongside Monnier and replaced Gen Paul, now permanently disgraced and disaffected. Albert Paraz was a right-wing anarchist, like Galtier-Boissière and a number of Montmartre figures, who had published extensively, on Céline's recommendation, with Denoël from the mid-1930s onwards, though Monnier questions whether he and Céline knew each other well previously.[133] He became an important figure in postwar right-wing literary circles, writing for journals such as *Rivarol*, and was committed to the rehabilitation of Céline, whose style he imitated, without always absorbing the talent. He worked hard as a lobbyist on Céline's behalf, corresponding with him regularly and publishing the correspondence, with Céline's agreement, along with 'A l'agité du bocal', in two volumes: *Le Gala des vaches* of 1948 and *Valsez saucisses* of 1950. What is interesting about this published correspondence is that Céline employed the same procedure of disinculpation as he did with collaborationist journals during the war. He wanted the message to get across but did not wish to be personally responsible, even going so far as to write in 1948 that 'I think we should stop the tune of published letters,'[134] though, as with the collaborationist press, he insisted on seeing the proofs. What is curious about the correspondence with Paraz is that, as in so many of Céline's relationships, it sometimes shows an extraordinary self-obsession and a commensurate lack of feeling for the interlocutor. Paraz, who had been accidentally gassed and who was suffering from the tuberculosis which was eventually to kill him in 1957, occasionally exceeded Céline's patience. On 5 April 1952, obviously in response to a request from Paraz to see a lady-friend, he replied viciously: 'As you know, I don't see anyone: can you get that into your head once and for all. So: neither Monnier, nor this person, no one, NO ONE. Is that clear enough? What a load of idiots you are! As for your X-ray – obviously, only a *very competent* radiographer can interpret it. Not me, for God's sake, not me! It's ridiculous – All this is inept – You're alive, and to be alive, as I see it, is the main thing.'[135]

Yet Paraz, with his contacts in *Rivarol*, the leading right-wing weekly of its day, and Gallimard, was an important instrument in Céline's rehabilitation, a rehabilitation which, it must be said, was not an easy task in the immediate post-war years. The sales figures were not particularly encouraging: slow sales of Monnier's 5000 run of *Mort à crédit*, though with better returns on the 8000 copies of *Casse-pipe*.[136] In April 1949, the journal *Carrefour* undertook a survey as to who would be the most widely read French author in the year 2000: Céline figured seventh, between Mauriac and Sartre,[137] and, in May 1950, a survey to find the twelve best French novels of the first half-century failed to place Céline in the final group, preferring Anatole France, Barrès, Gide, Proust, Valéry Larbaud, Duhamel, Lacretelle, Mauriac, Bernanos, Romains and Malraux.[138] It is interesting that the literary 'establishment' rejected, not only the 'Existentialists' like Sartre, Simone de Beauvoir and Camus, but also formal and stylistic innovators like Queneau. Immediate rehabilitation was not an obvious option in France.

It was a possibility, however, paradoxically, in America. Already, at the end of 1946, a New York lawyer, Julien Cornell, had circulated a petition against Céline's extradition from Denmark to France, signed by a disparate group including Henry Miller, Edgar Varèse, Céline's Boston publisher James Laughlin, Edmund Wilson and Will Rogers.[139] Laughlin himself had done much to relaunch Céline through new editions of the novels, and even visited the writer in Denmark, but the major American support for Céline came from Milton Hindus. The relationship between Céline and Hindus is exhaustively documented in Hindus' memoirs and the collected correspondence published under the title *The Crippled Giant*,[140] and sheds considerable light on Céline's personality. Hindus began corresponding with Céline early in 1947, while he was still in prison; Hindus had become convinced that not only was Céline a major writer, but that he had been unjustly persecuted because his anti-Semitism was metaphorical rather than real. He wrote from Paris: 'it seems to me that, regardless of what is true of the origin or nature of anti-semitism in others, in Céline it is due to hasty generalization, doubtful analogy, unhistorical empiricism, and quack science.'[141] As such, Hindus was immensely useful to Céline, particularly when he was considering emigration to the United States, and Céline initially responded in kind, particularly before his release, playing down his anti-Semitism in what Alméras terms his 'philosemite' period[142] and inviting Hindus to Denmark. The correspondence, however, shows the two men to be on different wavelengths: Hindus bombarded Céline with often naive questions about his literary influences and contemporary writing, while Céline, in between reflections of a general cultural nature, replied with precise instructions as to how Hindus could aid his rehabilitation and orders for coffee and nylons.[143] Hindus took up Céline's suggestion that he visit him in Korsör and travelled to Europe in the summer of 1948, passing through Paris, where he met members of the Montmartre community, and arriving in Korsör on 20 July. Already, Céline's letters show second thoughts about the visit. He claimed to be unable to have Hindus as a guest at Klarskovgaard, booking him into a shabby guest-house in Korsör, and refused to meet him on the night of his arrival, due to the veronal he was taking for his insomnia.[144] The visit itself was a disaster for Hindus and reduced him to a virtual nervous breakdown. As he recorded in his diary on 11 August: 'He's made me as crazy as himself. My eye tics, the muscle in my right leg pulls and gives me pain. This afternoon I could hardly stand on my left foot because I had such an itch in the sole of my foot, and the forefinger of my right hand is almost paralysed.'[145] The problem was that, in the course of his month-long visit, Hindus discovered that his hero was not the ideal-ized figure he had constructed through the correspondence, but was capa-ble of inflicting great pain on those with whom he was irritated, and that, moreover, Céline's anti-Semitism and anti-humanism were rather more real than metaphorical. Hindus returned to America, where he took up a new post at Brandeis, completely disillusioned. It was unfortunate that his record of the relationship and the disastrous visit should appear at a delicate stage in the prosecution in France of Céline, who reacted with fury, heaping insults on Hindus as soon as he saw the manuscript, and even writing to Brandeis University informing them that their new professor could not speak French.[146] What frightened him was that Hindus had scrupulously recorded, not merely Céline's continued and unrepentant anti-Semitism, but also his highly derogatory remarks against Mikkelsen and the Danes in general.[147] If his private response had been to lash out violently at Hindus, his public one was by now familiar. He had never invited Hindus to his home, he had barely talked to him, Hindus had made everything up: in short, Hindus no more existed than did the Germans during the Occupation, with whom Céline similarly claimed to have had had no contact.[148] Céline retained an almost schoolboy-like ability to deny the truth when it suited him and to believe in his own self-reinforcing version.

Part of the problem was that Céline, in exile, was deprived of his natural power-base, Montmartre, and, cut off from his old cronies, was obliged to enrol new supporters, some of whom, like Paraz or the painter Jean

Dubuffet,[149] served very well, while others, like Hindus, became trouble-some. In particular, he had fallen out seriously, and, it would transpire, definitively, with Gen Paul, who now blamed Céline for having compro-mised him during the Occupation by using him as an anti-Semitic mouth-piece in the pamphlets and, as he saw it, for having dragged him to the German Embassy and to Berlin.[150] It is certainly true that Gen Paul had some difficulties during the post-Liberation purges (though this did not seem seriously to affect the saleability of his paintings) and he adopted a policy which was both defensive (blaming Céline for having blackened his name) and offensive (defiantly leading a cacophonous brass band, his 'chignole', around Montmartre, much to the annoyance of the local resi-dents, to show that he had not gone to ground).[151] As it was, he moved to New York for two years, from 1946 to 1948, and broke off contact with Céline, though he did subsequently blame Céline's letters to his wife for the break-up of their marriage.[152] Céline, for his part, jeered at the rich lifestyle of 'Popol' and his return to drinking.[153] Gen Paul did, however, make some gesture of reconciliation by sending his new mistress, Gaby, to Korsör to meet Céline in November 1950, though her mission was never clear and the two friends never met again. In the meantime, Céline contin-ued to maintain contact with Montmartre, chiefly through letters and visits, involving principally Marcel Aymé, whom he seems to have forgiven his caricatures in 'Avenue Junot' and 'En attendante', and Daragnès.

He was particularly outraged at what he saw as a literary *coup d'état* by writers coming from the Resistance, in particular the group around Sartre with the loose label of 'Existentialists', and the compliance of centrist writers in this revolution. Much of his bile was reserved for François Mauriac, to whom he sent a number of insulting letters,[154] and his admira-tion went to writers of the New Right, like Maurice Bardèche, Brasillach's brother-in-law, whose *Lettre à François Mauriac* in 1947 and *Nurembourg ou la Terre Promise* in 1948 attacked the hypocrisy of the Resistance during the post-war trials, or Claude Jamet, whose *Fifi roi*, in particular, denounced the injustices of the new hegemony.[155] In return, a new generation of right-wing writers, rebelling against the new left-wing literary establishment, embraced Céline as their champion. Two of these were Antoine Blondin, who worked for Frémanger and wrote *L'Europe buissonnière* as a transposition of *Voyage au bout de la nuit* into the new post-war period, and his fellow 'Hussard', Roger Nimier, who sent Céline a copy of *Le Hussard bleu* in 1950, beginning a friendship which would last until Céline's death, just a year before Nimier's own.[156]

The monotonous routine in Klarskovgaard was enlivened by the extraor-dinary correspondence – Vitoux calculates that 4000 letters were sent dur-ing this period, mainly to Le Vigan, Paraz, Löchen, Daragnès, Paulhan, his lawyer Albert Naud, Dr Camus and Marie Canavaggia,[157] with Céline signifi-cantly never bothering to save the letters he received – and by the occa-sional visitor. In particular, he received in 1948 the Swedish writer Ernz Bendz, who was instrumental in arranging another distinguished Swedish

visit, in January and March 1949, that of Raoul Nordling, the famous
Swedish Consul in Paris during the Occupation, who had helped broker
the Liberation of the capital without the destruction of all its monu-
ments.[158] Both Swedes were to play a powerful role in Céline's defence
during his pre-trial period. Céline and Lucette were also visited by friends
like Daragnès, Henri Mahé and Marcel Aymé, and by relatives like Lucette's
mother and stepfather, the Pirazzoli couple who had lodged the Henning
Jensens in their villa in Menton.[159] The period was also marked by worries
about illness. Céline's daughter, Colette Turpin, with whom he had broken
temporarily over her marriage, was now reconciled with her father, though
he was still dismayed at her repeated pregnancies. He was distraught when
she had to undergo surgery for a fibroma in 1950, and even dispatched Dr
Camus to observe the operation.[160] Even more worrying was the state of
Lucette, who, like her daughter-in-law, suffered a fibroma in May 1950 and
needed emergency surgery in Copenhagen. In fact, she required extensive
treatment, some of it seriously botched, and the couple could not return to
Korsör until 15 July.[161]

During the months punctuated by these dramas and the occasional visits,
Céline concentrated on his correspondence, the composition of *Féerie pour
une autre fois*, and on reading: Gibault identifies references in the letters to
Chateaubriand, Tallemant des Réaux, the Goncourts' *Journal*, the *Revue des
Deux Mondes*, which he had enjoyed reading in Sigmaringen, *Les Trois
Mousquetaires*, *Madame Bovary*, *Le Père Goriot*, *Les Misérables*, lots of 'Classiques
Larousse', along with the obscure *Manuel du départ à l'étranger et aux colonies*,
which presumably brought back memories, and the pacifist Louis Rougier's
Pour une politique d'amnistie, which struck much closer to home.[162] In addition to his own writing and this reading, which owes much to the arbitrary
selection on offer to the exile, he concentrated on the one issue which
preoccupied him above all others: the legal case being brought against him
in France, the outcome of which would determine the end of his exile.

V THE TRIAL

The process of the prosecution of Céline, which lasted from 1945 to 1951,
is instructive, both regarding the conduct of France's post-war *Epuration*
and for the light it sheds on Céline's real culpability as a collaborator. As we
have seen, an arrest warrant was issued in Paris against Céline on 19 April
1945, under Article 75 of the Penal Code. This in itself highlights some of
the problems inherent in the process of the purges in newly liberated
France, which, in common with most European countries, had not legis-
lated for the highly exceptional conditions which pertained during the
Occupation. In order to sanction 'collaboration', the regime which resulted from the Resistance was obliged to try its perpetrators for 'treason',
using an existing law, Article 75, aimed at 'Any French person who, during

time of war, has intelligence with a foreign power or with its agents, with a view to favouring the enterprises of that power against France'[163] and which carried the death penalty. This law had been applied reasonably successfully during the First World War and the occupation by German armies of France's northern territories, but it was suited much less well to the complexities of life in France from 1940 to 1944. Not only did a large portion of the population consider, rightly or wrongly, that the war, as far as France was concerned, had ended in the summer of 1940, but many of those charged subsequently under Article 75 could not understand how expressly domestic activity, particularly in the area of literature and publishing, could come under the category of treason. The problem with Article 75 was that it was all too often a sledgehammer used to crack a nut: employed legitimately against leading politicians, major publicists, members of the Milice or volunteers in the German armed forces, it looked much less convincing when directed against crimes of opinion, however unpleasant those opinions may have been. Implicitly, post-Liberation regimes quickly realized this and, in addition to the Haute Cour, an essentially parliamentary tribunal which had been used before during the Third Republic to judge high-ranking politicians, and the Cours de Justice, set up mainly to try cases under Article 75, they introduced retrospectively a new charge, 'Indignité Nationale', with a new tribunal, the Chambres Civiques, with powers to inflict, not custodial sentences, but the more invidious punishment of 'dégradation nationale', which carried severe financial and other implications.[164]

The case of Céline is a classic illustration of how, in post-war France, the perception of collaboration outstripped hard evidence. There is no doubt that in the public and judicial consciousness, Céline was assumed to be one of France's most notorious collaborators, whereas, due partly to the facts of the case and partly to Céline's own skill in avoiding responsibility, his guilt was very difficult to prove. The Juge d'Instruction in charge of Céline's case, Zousman, who also investigated the *Je suis partout* team, issued the arrest warrant and began the extradition procedure from Denmark,[165] but very quickly found it difficult to obtain sufficient evidence. François Gibault records that he was unable to get copies of any of the pamphlets, either from Céline's apartment or from Denoël, and was reduced to photographing the preface to *Bagatelles pour un massacre* in the Bibliothèque Nationale.[166] It was for this reason that the extradition procedure foundered for sheer lack of evidence, particularly when some of the meagre evidence which was produced was patently wrong: the assumption, for example, in de Charbonnière's letter to the Danish Foreign Minister of 31 January 1946, that *Guignol's Band* and *Bezons à travers les âges* were 'works favourable to Germany'.[167] Zousman worked slowly, a fact which, in itself, was favourable to Céline, and finally established a dossier in which the following evidence could be used against him: his pre-war anti-Semitic views; his 'very infrequent' writing for *Au Pilori*, *Germinal* and *Le Cri du peuple*; his speech to French doctors in 1942 when he expressed anti-Semitic views; his membership of the Cercle Européen, from which he subsequently resigned; his journey to Germany in 1942; Abetz's list of possible French collaborators in the Bureau Central des Questions Juives; his preface to *L'Ecole des cadavres*, in which he was alleged to have 'denounced' his old enemy Dr Rouquès; and the allegation that he went with de Brinon to visit Katyn.[168]

This dossier was finally forwarded to the prosecution office in May 1949 and was entrusted to Jean Seltensperger, who, like Zousman, was relatively favourable to Céline's case. In the meantime, Céline had been marshalling his defence and assembling his own legal team. In particular, on the advice of his friend Antonio Zuloaga, he had approached the lawyer Albert Naud, who had had a distinguished career in the Resistance and had acquired a reputation for defending those whom the *Epuration* threatened to deprive of a fair trial, notably Henri Béraud, Pierre Laval and, later, members of the Cagoule.[169] Right from the beginning, however, Céline threatened to sour his relationship with Naud by bringing in, at Pirazzoli's suggestion and through the mysterious intermediary of 'a friend of President Auriol', another lawyer, Maître Fourcade.[170] Naud was understandably furious at this interference, and Céline had to write an ingratiating letter on 12 May 1947 placating him.[171] Nevertheless, this episode did not prevent him from doing the same thing in October 1948, when he engaged, at the suggestion of his millionaire friend Paul Marteau, the flamboyant right-wing lawyer Jean-Louis Tixier-Vignancour.[172] Whilst Naud was initially, outwardly at least, amenable to this reinforcement of Céline's legal team,[173] relations rapidly deteriorated, and a year later Naud was writing: 'Could it be understood between us once and for all that I am your sole lawyer?'[174] with Céline, rather petulantly this time, having to grovel again.[175] Throughout the long drawn-out legal process, Céline played off his legal team one against the other, criticizing Naud to Tixier, Tixier to Naud and both of them to his essential Danish lawyer, the tireless Mikkelsen. At the same time as this legal bickering, he was keen to do all that he could to conduct his own defence, producing as early as 6 November 1946 a 'Réponse aux accusations formulées contre moi par la justice française au titre de trahison et reproduites par la police judiciaire danoise au cours de mes interrogatoires, pendant mon incarcération 1945–1946 à Copenhague'[176] in which, predictably enough, he denied all charges, even those clearly supported by the evidence. In addition, he carried on a copious and lively correspondence with the Juge d'Instruction, the prosecutor, and even the Minister: so lively, in fact, that one prosecutor at least saw it as evidence of Céline's insanity.[177]

Seltensperger finally concluded, on the basis of Zousman's dossier, that Céline could really only be charged on the basis of two acts during the Occupation: certain passages in *Les Beaux Draps* and permitting the republication of *Bagatelles pour un massacre*.[178] He discounted all the other evidence, concluding that 'neither in his attitude, nor in his writing, do we find the trace of any sympathy, whether for Germany or for the Vichy

regime. It seems as if, in reality, he was never bothered to please anyone.'[179]
It followed from this that there was a case to answer, but that it did not merit
a trial before the Cour de Justice and that Article 75 was not applicable.
Rather, Céline should be tried by a Chambre Civique, and Seltensperger
recommended the lifting of the arrest warrant.[180] Unfortunately, the recommendation was leaked to the press before it could be implemented, with
L'Aurore reporting on 28 October 1949 that Céline's case was about to be
referred to the Chambre Civique.[181] Naud blamed Tixier while Tixier, who
knew Seltensperger well and claimed the credit for his decision, blamed
Mikkelsen.[182] In any event, the effect was disastrous: the public outcry
forced the Parquet to take Seltensperger off the case and give it to a new
prosecutor, Charasse. For his part, Céline blamed this reversal in his fortunes on the new Minister of Justice, René Mayer, whom he saw as yet
another Jew come to persecute him.[183]

In fact, while the dismissal of Seltensperger delayed the outcome of the
case, it did not greatly affect the result. Charasse was reasonably well-
disposed to Céline and, like his predecessor, concluded that Article 75 was
inappropriate. Unlike Seltensperger, however, he decided to forward
Céline to the Cour de Justice, but under Article 83, which sanctioned 'acts
prejudicial to national defence' and which, unlike Article 75, carried a
maximum penalty of one to five years and a fine of between 360,000 and
3,600,000 francs.[184] After a series of false starts and adjournments, due to
Céline's absence from the court, the trial took place on 21 February 1950,
with Judge Drappier presiding, and an impressive array of friends and
supporters testifying in Céline's favour.[185] The sentence was as lenient as it
could be, as even Céline grudgingly accepted: one year's imprisonment, a
fine of 50,000 francs, 'dégradation nationale' and the confiscation of half
his present and future property.[186]

The case should by now have been over, and Naud should have been able
to convince the authorities that the period spent by Céline in a Danish gaol
had effectively purged the one-year sentence imposed in France. The problem seemed inexplicably intractable, however, and it was left to Tixier-
Vignancour to find a technical solution. Profiting from the fact that the
Cours de Justice had been wound up on 1 February 1951 and had been
replaced by military tribunals, he devised a strategy with the head of military prosecutions, Colonel René Camadau. Céline was to apply to the
military tribunal for the quashing of his sentence. The refusal of the French
authorities in Denmark to grant him a passport would legally justify his
absence from the court, which could then decide his case in secrecy. At the
same time, Tixier made a formal request for an amnesty for Céline under
the law of 16 August 1947, which provided for amnesty for serious war
invalids who had not been sentenced to more than three years' imprisonment and were not guilty of denunciations or acts leading to deportations.
On 20 April 1951, the military tribunal met to consider the case of Louis-
Ferdinand Destouches and, while upholding the original judgement,
nevertheless granted him an amnesty as an ex-combatant of the 1914–1918

war, who had been wounded on 25 October 1914.[187] No mention was made of the fact that Dr Destouches was also Louis-Ferdinand Céline and, when the resultant furore came, it was too late to change the judgement. The incessantly trumpeted 75 per cent invalidity had finally paid off, and this time Céline was on his way home.

On 1 July 1951, Céline, Lucette, their dog Bessy and four cats, including Bébert, boarded an SAS flight to Nice. It was his first flight, and he enjoyed it immensely.[188]

The trial of Céline shows up many of the deficiencies of the purge system in post-war France. It is worth pointing out that he did have a case to answer. There were generalized imprecations against the Jews, especially in the early part of the Occupation and incitements to retribution. Occasionally these incitements came close to specific denunciations. Even though his contributions to the collaborationist press were studiously indirect, they were to some of the most extreme journals and supported, or indeed initiated, specific collaborationist policies, as in the case of the grand meeting of anti-Semites at the offices of *Au Pilori*. Céline maintained high-level contacts with German and pro-German officials and, as a prominent writer, brought a particular prestige to those contacts. He did express publicly his support for Doriot and the LVF. Throughout the Occupation, he urged the Vichy regime to more extreme measures of persecution of the Jews. It may be that Céline's collaboration was less extreme than that of, for example, the *Je suis partout* team, but the discrepancy in sentencing is by no means justified by the charges or the activities themselves: sentences to death or to life imprisonment against a one-year sentence.

Part of the problem, as we have seen, was to do with the gathering of evidence, but the main factor was a combination of the public perception of guilt and the time-frame in which the charges were brought. The sooner after the Liberation the trial, the more severe were the sentences likely to be. Céline's policy of remaining in Denmark until the final amnesty undoubtedly paid off. It did so particularly since, even at a late date, there were remarkable variations in the Republic's will to prosecute suspected literary, and indeed non-literary, collaborators – often due to personal relations or political considerations. As Céline kept reminding his lawyers and his judges, he was being unfairly treated in comparison with known collaborationist writers, like Cocteau, Motherlant and Morand, all of whom, in his lifetime, went on to be elected to the Académie Française.[189] For this alone, Céline's case is illuminating: Cocteau, Montherlant and Morand escaped serious prosecution because they fell into a recognizable and respected category of traditional writers, while Céline did not. From *Voyage au bout de la nuit* onwards, he was the victim, literally, of his style.

In these circumstances, it is not surprising that he should have organized his defence with a single-mindedness which, as in so many of his ventures, cut across normal considerations of friendship, gratitude or loyalty. The enticement and subsequent destruction of Hindus is but one example. His attitude to his lawyers is another: he played them off, as we have seen, one against the other, apparently despising all of them. None of them was paid. Naud, who had worked so hard on what was a highly unpopular case, was occasionally promised rewards, like Céline's apartment in Saint-Germain-en-Laye;[190] Tixier, whose dexterity with the law brought Céline back to France, appears to have received nothing. As for Mikkelsen, who probably saved Céline's life, who housed him on his estate and who travelled indefatigably to Paris to lobby for support, Céline became convinced that, like Karen Marie Jensen, he had robbed him of his gold. Convinced that he owed him 8000 crowns, Céline never forgave him, and Mikkelsen passed into that strange Pantheon of Céline's voluntarily forgotten enemies.[191] Mikkelsen himself remained strangely sanguine about his relationship with Céline, surmising that 'Céline was a curious mixture of excellent and, indeed, exceptional qualities, an intellectual aristocrat of the highest calibre, who despised the bourgeois, the épiciers [in French] and the hommes politiques [in French], but he was also a boor who only thought about himself and played the martyr as soon as his own skin was threatened.'[192] He concluded: 'He is incapable of seeing things and events, especially his own misfortunes, from a detached position. He is unaware that there is something called destiny, connected to the personality which has been given to him in exchange. One regrets that his fury lacks "dignity" . . . He lets himself be carried away by his hatred – Céline, who is so self-pitying, is madly in need of revenge.'[193] Although Mikkelsen maintained friendly relations of a sort with Céline when he had left Denmark, his judgement points to one constant feature in Céline's personality and an indispensable ingredient in his creativity.

13

Meudon

Céline's plane left Copenhagen at 6.25 in the evening, local time, and arrived in Nice at 11 p.m. Lucette's mother and stepfather, M. and Mme Pirazzoli, were not at the airport to meet them and the couple had to hire a taxi to take them, their animals and their luggage the thirty kilometres to Menton. At this point, accounts differ. Céline, in a letter to Paul Marteau, claimed that the Pirazzolis were not expecting them: 'Mind you, they'd been warned seven years earlier! They're very nice, but they're feeling the effects of age, extreme comfort and very small mental faculties!'[1] According to Lucette, however, in conversation with Frédéric Vitoux, her parents were waiting for them in the entrance-hall of the Bellevue, the luxurious apartment building where they lived on the Boulevard de Garavan, and had organized a sumptuous reception, with champagne, crystal glasses and a horde of guests, including journalists.[2] Céline, furious, stormed off to his room and refused to meet anyone. Whichever version is true, the couple's arrival set the tone for what proved a disastrous visit. After the privations of Korsör, Céline himself could not adapt to the excessive luxury of the Pirazzolis' apartment, especially since he was separated from his beloved animals, who were housed on a plot of land on the other side of the road. Nor could he stand the Pirazzolis, whom he referred to as the 'couscous', on account of Ercole Pirazzoli's alleged greasy complexion. In particular, he resented their addiction to gambling, which he saw as diminishing Lucette's inheritance, and Madame Pirazzoli's rapaciousness. He claimed to have seen her about to steal her daughter's fur coat, whilst Lucette accused her mother of planning to sell a manuscript of *Féerie pour une autre fois* in order to install the couple in another apartment.[3] In short, relations broke down completely, with Céline and Madame Pirazzoli competing for

Lucette's attention: in one violent dispute, Lucette claimed, her mother even brandished a revolver.[4]

In addition to the problems posed by this enforced cohabitation, Céline suffered greatly from the intense heat of the south of France in high summer. He wrote to Paraz, who lived close by in Vence and whom, interestingly, Céline never attempted to visit: 'I can't bear the climate and nor can Lucette – it's too heavy. But I've got no possibility of emigrating again. I'd love to live alone again in Brittany, but where would I get the money from?'[5] Yet in the same letter, he announced his attention to travel to Paris in September 'for a few days',[6] with air tickets which he had already bought in Denmark. In fact, he was able to make his escape much earlier, after a stay of only three weeks in Menton. The industrialist Paul Marteau, a patron of the arts who had founded a publishing house, 'La Connaissance', with René-Louis Doyon, and who had supported Céline during his exile in Denmark by purchasing the beginning of the manuscript of *Féerie pour une autre fois*,[7] invited him to stay in his house in Neuilly. On 23 July 1951 Céline, Lucette and the animals, accompanied by Pierre Monnier, took the afternoon flight from Nice to Le Bourget, from where they travelled by coach to the air terminal at the Invalides.[8] Here they were met by Paul Marteau and his wife, Pasqualine, who drove them to their house at 66b Boulevard Maurice-Barrès, which looked out on the Bois de Boulogne.[9] Céline, Lucette and the animals were housed in a small apartment on the second floor, in relative peace and luxury.

If Marteau was flattered to have a great writer under his roof, he and his wife paid heavily for the privilege. Céline as a guest was no more respectful than he had been in Denmark or in Menton. The animals caused havoc with the antique furniture; Lucette was encouraged to undertake strenuous exercises which threatened to bring the chandelier in Madame Marteau's bedroom, just below, crashing down; their hostess was unceremoniously thrown out of their apartment when Céline was working, and, moreover, forbidden from holding dinner parties: 'So the Marteaus, who received all the Paris highbrows at their table every day, had to warn off their friends and stop entertaining them.'[10] Nevertheless, Céline and either Paul or Pasqualine Marteau would go walking with their dogs in the Bois de Boulogne, and Marteau was at least permitted to enjoy visits by Céline's friends: Marcel Aymé, Dr Camus, Jacques Deval, Jean Bonvilliers and Jean Perrot.[11] Gen Paul, however, refused all blandishments, and would never see Céline again, except on his deathbed.[12] Not that Céline himself was any more flexible. He allowed his daughter Colette to visit, but refused to see his five grandchildren or to have anything to do with his son-in-law, Yves Turpin. In fact, Turpin made an effort to strike up an acquaintance by accosting Céline when he was out walking on the Boulevard Maurice-Barrès with the words: 'I'm your son-in-law,' receiving as the sole reply: 'Quite possibly.'[13]

The Marteaus left for their summer holidays in Cannes in mid-August, but left their cook in Neuilly, together with two cars and the chauffeur. Not only did this allow Céline and Lucette to spend a luxurious summer in an unusually and delightfully cool Paris, it also gave them the facilities to explore the suburbs looking for a house where they could live permanently. Initially, they had thought of Saint-Germain-en-Laye, which had always been a favourite spot of Céline's and a frequent refuge, but house prices in general had risen sharply, and they finally settled for a run-down Louis-Philippe villa on the slopes of Meudon, to the south-west of Paris, at 25 Route des Gardes. The house, once the property of Eugène Labiche, had a large garden for the animals and a splendid view of the Seine and Paris, but it was by no means an obvious choice. Built on four floors, its kitchen was in the basement, Céline's study was to be on the first floor, while Lucette planned to turn the upper two floors into a dance studio. As Alméras comments, with the garden being on a slope as well, 'both inside and out, it was necessary to go up and down continually, a strange situation for someone who claimed to be a semi-invalid.'[14] Céline himself, in a letter to Le Vigan, still in exile in Argentina, was hardly enthusiastic in his description:

> I'm sorry I don't have anyone to take a picture of the house. It's not too dilapidated, even though it's 150 years old, but it needs four servants. And Lucette and I are the lackeys, the gardeners, the teachers, the writers, the doctors, the tax-payers, and we're starving to death. It's on the side of the Côteau de Meudon: four identical houses built at the same time as the one owned by Bassano, Napoleon's secretary, next to it. It's got a view all over Paris: the Eiffel Tower, the Mont Valérien, Montmartre, the bridges over the Seine, and the Renault factory: a very good shack, with 500 thousand francs worth of upkeep per year, alas! It's going to kill us, Lucette and me, from overwork and old age.[15]

Jean Paulhan, from his apartment by the *Arènes*, in central Paris, wrote to Etiemble expressing his incomprehension at this 'absurd three-story house which he has rented [*sic*] at Meudon and which has been more or less renovated at a cost of more than a million' and concluding: 'But why Meudon?'[16]

In order to buy the house, Lucette sold two farmhouses in Normandy which she had inherited from her grandmother, and it was for this reason that, at a cost of 2.5 million francs, it was in her name. Although the purchase was completed on 1 October 1951, work needed to be done before Céline and Lucette could move in, and they were only finally installed towards the end of the month,[17] having spent a brief period with Lucette's father and his wife in the Rue Dulong in the seventeenth *arrondissement*.[18] The house was by no means comfortable. The kitchen was dark with bars on its windows; the central heating never worked, so it was atrociously cold during the winter; and there was very little furniture. The furnishings from the apartment in the Rue Girardon had been put in storage by the new tenant, Yvon Morandat, head of the Charbonnages de France, who had paid the costs up until 31 December 1951, but refused to pay any more. Céline's characteristic response was to position himself as victim, claim he had been robbed and invoke his lawyer Tixier, all of which ended in a friendly settlement, with Morandat bearing even more of the costs and the furniture being put up for sale.[19]

Céline turned the house into a fortress, with its railings topped by barbed wire and its garden guarded by the dogs, who slept in a kennel at the front of the house.[20] Lucette, however, went ahead with the conversion of the two upper floors into a dance studio and soon had a thriving school, mainly based on friends and acquaintances like Louise de Vilmorin's sister-in-law, Renée Cosima, Madame Gwen-aël Bolloré, Claude Maupommée, Judith Magre, Roger Nimier's wife, and two of Marcel Aymé's granddaughters.[21] It took Céline until September 1953 to practise medicine again, and he continued to look after his few patients until 31 March 1959, when he became eligible for a retirement pension. The pattern of their days was established early on. Céline rose early, drank a pot of weak tea, fed the dogs and began work. Lucette got up much later, around 9.30, and, after a cup of coffee prepared by Céline, began her classes. In the course of the morning Céline would go down to the gate to collect the mail and *Le Figaro*. They rarely went out: Céline himself walked twice a week down to Bas-Meudon to the shops, although the meat for the dogs was delivered. Every Tuesday afternoon Lucette went into Paris, where she bought fruit, cakes and croissants from Fauchon. Céline prepared the meals, closing the down-stairs shutters regularly at 6 in order to make dinner. They had little help: a gardener came in twice a week and, in 1957 or 1958, they employed a housekeeper.[22]

Politically, Céline's return to France passed off relatively quietly. *L'Humanité*, on 10 July 1951, had signalled Céline's presence in the south, though it had located him wrongly in Vence.[23] Initially, there had been some hostility among the inhabitants of Meudon: Lucette recalled that some shopkeepers refused to serve them and that there were 'little hand-bills nailed to the telephone poles and trees of lower Meudon calling on them to leave'.[24] For the most part, however, Céline seemed a forgotten man, until the case of Ernst Jünger's diaries erupted in September 1951. As we have seen, Céline the foul-mouthed anti-Semite represented everything which the aristocratic Jünger loathed and he recorded his antipathy faith-fully in his diaries. When he first published them in Germany he was careful not to identify Céline by name, for reasons of either caution or humanity, using instead the transparent disguise of 'Merline'. In the course of the French translation for Julliard, however, the original text citing Céline by name was used, with some of the most damning observations, such as the one on bayoneting the Jews, included.[25] Jünger himself was appalled at the mistake and wrote to Marcel Jouhandeau, asking him to convey his apolo-gies to Céline, who was not mollified in the slightest. Breaking definitively with Albert Naud, he instructed Tixier-Vignancour to take legal action against the publishing house of Julliard and the journals *Preuves* and *L'Aurore* which had reported Jünger's references to him. Tixier himself was not convinced of the wisdom of a lawsuit, particularly when Julliard brought out a revised edition of the diaries in October 1951 with the name 'Merline' reinstated, but Céline pressed ahead, appearing before the examining magistrate twice, on 26 October 1951 and on 17 July 1952, before he was finally persuaded to withdraw his action.[26] As Vitoux points out, what was significant about the Jünger case was not merely Céline's sensitivity and willingness to go to law over any statement he judged defamatory, but his by now familiar amnesia when it came to the events of the Occupation. Once again, he denied any contact with the Germans, any knowledge of Jünger and ever having said what he had reported.[27]

In addition to Lucette's inheritance, what had decided Céline to buy the house in Meudon was the fact that he now had a new publisher and, apparently, a secure income again. Pierre Monnier had continued to negotiate with Gallimard in the last months of Céline's exile and appeared to be close to success when, in early July, he received a letter from Jouhandeau saying that Jean Paulhan had an important message from Gaston Gallimard.[28] Céline's reaction was characteristically pessimistic, but on 16 July Monnier met Paulhan in Gaston Gallimard's office. Gallimard went straight to the point: 'I would be glad of the chance to publish Céline. I've had all the great names of literature here, Gide, Claudel, Faulkner, Valéry. All of them! And the only one I missed was Céline. Yes, I missed Céline. It was a mistake, a slip-up. So you can understand that now I'll do whatever I must to get him.'[29] What he did was to offer a contract for the republication of all the novels, with 18 per cent royalties and 5 million francs advance, plus a contract for *Féerie pour une autre fois* and an option on Céline's next five works. Monnier was dispatched with the contract on the first plane to Nice and, with its signature on 18 July 1951, a seven-year hiatus in the publication of Céline's work was at an end. Not that he proved any more grateful to his new publisher than he had been to Denoël. As soon as he was installed in Neuilly, he sent Paul Marteau to Gallimard to renegotiate the terms of the contract, asking for an additional 5 million francs advance, to which Gallimard agreed, even though the two men had not spoken to each other since Gallimard's mistress, Valentine Tessier, had left him for Marteau.[30] From then on, the familiar litany of insults and accusations of theft continued, much as they had with Denoël, even though Céline's account with Gallimard remained in deficit for the rest of his life.[31] Part of the problem was that Céline, in the France of the 1950s, was largely forgotten as a writer, and the work on which he placed his hopes for his literary return, *Féerie pour une autre fois*, was his least obviously accessible novel.

II *Féerie pour une autre fois*

As we have seen, the composition of the novel dates from the autumn of 1945, when Céline and Lucette were still in Karen Marie Jensen's apartment and he had not yet been imprisoned. Letters from this period to Marie Canavaggia mention a project called *La Bataille du Styx*, described as a 'short memoir'[32] aimed at recounting his departure from Montmartre in 1944 and his wanderings through Germany, but also serving as a defence document. As Henri Godard points out, the reference to the Styx and its boatman Charon (or Caron as Céline invariably wrote it) would re-emerge in *D'un château l'autre*.[33] At this point, Céline was still revising the second volume of *Guignol's Band* and still planning a third volume. With his arrest and imprisonment in December 1945, however, two factors altered his plans. In the first place, the experience of prison and exile had made Céline unbearably nostalgic for Montmartre, and the fictional re-creation of life on the *Butte* became a major preoccupation. Secondly, as the correspondence with Lucette shows, he had become increasingly concerned about his literary reputation in France and the need to produce a new book which would make an impact.[34] *Guignol's Band* II, self-evidently a mere sequel, could not serve this purpose and a new work was needed. As he wrote to Lucette: 'I've got to make my come-back with something up to date which will bring my readers back.'[35] That work was *La Bataille du Styx*, now referred to variously as 'Du côté des maudits', 'Au vent des maudits', 'Au vent des maudits soupirs pour une autre fois', before becoming definitively *Féerie pour une autre fois*.[36]

The fragments of Céline's prison notebooks published in the Pléiade edition of *Féerie pour une autre fois* show the complex development of the novel from its conception, but also serve to remind us, as Godard comments, that '*Féerie* I is, from start to finish, a novel written in a prison':[37] the nostalgic evocation of Montmartre has poignancy only because of the narrator's reflections on his own state in exile and prison. At the same time, because of the physical and legal limitations on Céline's opportunities for publishing, the novel had the longest period of composition of all of Céline's works, including *Voyage au bout de la nuit*: nine years in total from its inception in September 1945 to the publication of the second volume in July 1954. One consequence of this long period of composition is a succession of different versions of the novel, categorized by Henri Godard in the appendices to the Pléiade edition,[38] which mirror the successive changes in title. What is interesting about these different versions of the novel is that the early ones introduce a further narrative, after that of *Féerie* II, which describes Ferdinand wandering through Montmartre on the day after the bombing, and which indicates that Céline had clearly already envisaged a continuation of the novel, dealing with Sigmaringen.[39] In other words, the two volumes of *Féerie* and the three volumes of *D'un château l'autre* were originally conceived of as one work,[40] leading from Montmartre to Germany and ending in Denmark and the Vester Faengsel: the sister castle to Sigmaringen in the original concept of *D'un château l'autre*. What happened, of course, was what happened with all of Céline's fictional projects. As in the case of *Voyage au bout de la nuit* (whose original outline included the episode on London which was to become *Guignol's Band*), the material

simply expanded to the extent that it could not be accommodated. Moreover, as Godard comments: 'It is a law of writing with Céline that each time
he takes up a story of which he has already written one version, in order to
write another one, he spends longer and longer on the opening,'[41] a
comment which also explains the reasons for the non-completion of *Casse-
pipe*. In *Féerie I*, as with *D'un château l'autre*, the stuff of the 'memoir' itself
becomes subordinate to the positioning of the present-day narrator. On the
other hand, it is perhaps insufficient to qualify *Féerie pour une autre fois* as
simply 'unfinished'.[42] As Marie-Christine Bellosta points out in a perceptive
analysis, the two volumes form a unit, with each one having a definite role.[43]
The first volume, moving from Montmartre to Copenhagen, and back to
Montmartre, has the specific purpose of drumming up an audience for the
'spectacle' in the second volume, initially known as *Normance*. Not only does
the narrator deploy all his skill to entice the reader, but he lapses into
authentic sales patter: 'Buy Féerie! Buy Féerie! The book which rejuvenates
your soul . . .'[44] promising the work as a miraculous cure for all ills. In other
words, the first volume consists of that succession of 'bagatelles', or the sales
patter employed by a fairground barker outside his theatre, with which we
are already familiar in Céline's first anti-Semitic pamphlet, enticing us to
view the highly theatrical spectacle constituted by the second volume.
Céline's fictional projects may have changed in the course of the composition of his novels, but that does not necessarily imply that their final version
is incomplete.

As we have seen, and in keeping with all his novels, Céline attached
particular importance to the title and used several versions before settling
on *Féerie pour une autre fois*. 'Féerie' itself is a privileged Célinian term,
implying 'a confusion of place and time'[45] which has connotations of
Shakespearean comedy and the musicality so important to his later style.
Significantly, it begins to appear in the pamphlets, with the ballet *La
Naissance d'une fée*, which opens *Bagatelles pour un massacre*, and the 'Chant
des Cygnes' which closes *Les Beaux Draps*: 'A flight of stars! . . . all around
ring little bells! . . . it's the ballet! . . . and everything embraces, passes by,
pirouettes, a delightful farandole! . . . silvery refrains . . . the music of the
fairies! (musique de fées)'[46] and which finishes with the narrator Ferdinand
and his reader in a privileged state 'where melody led us'.[47] In Célinian
terms, the 'féerie' has connotations, not merely of enchantment, transcribed in theatrical terms in Shakespearean comedy, but of musical theatre, the ballet, in which words are either replaced by the movement of the
human body or conscripted into a primarily musical function, which also
occurs in opera and operetta. At the same time, as a literary sub-genre, a
'féerie', like the 'utopia' which appears half-ironically as the 'Communisme
Labiche' of *Les Beaux Draps*, is specifically and technically related to the
eighteenth-century genre of the 'voyage imaginaire', the best-known example of which is Defoe's *Robinson Crusoe*, and which was consciously adopted
as the form for *Voyage au bout de la nuit*.[48] In other words, Céline's fictional
and non-fictional output forms a coherent whole centred on non-realist

production. In this context, it is highly significant that *Féerie* I is conscious of its intratextual debt to Céline's first novel. Not only is the narrator Ferdinand, as in all the works from *Mort à crédit* onwards, the self-proclaimed author of *Voyage*, there is a common use of characters between the two works, such as the 'Colonel Des Entrayes',[49] demoted from General since his appearance in *Voyage au bout de la nuit*. In particular, the introduction to *Féerie* I: 'The horror of realities! All places, names, characters, and situations presented in this novel are imaginary! Absolutely imaginary! No connection with reality! It's only a 'féerie', and, at that, for a bygone era!'[50] takes up the beginning of *Voyage au bout de la nuit*: 'Travelling is very useful, it makes the imagination work. Everything else is disappointment and fatigue. Our journey is entirely imaginary. That's its strength. It goes from life to death. Men, animals, towns and things, everything is imagined. It's a novel, only a fictional tale.'[51] In other words, not only are we dealing with a novel which is extremely complex textually and intertextually, but *Féerie* is fully conscious of its position as a descendant of *Voyage*.

As Céline's preface states, this anti-realist, enchanted and musical writing is here to evoke a bygone era, 'une autre fois' – a further example of Céline's persistent reinventions of Proust's 'recherche du temps perdu'. As such, it is, as we have seen, a work fuelled by nostalgia: for the world of the belle époque, for idyllic periods spent in Saint-Malo[52] and particularly for the Montmartre where Céline lived for an almost uninterrupted period from 1929 to 1944. The topography of Montmartre is lovingly re-created in both volumes: its street-names and Métro stations; its landmarks, like the Moulin de la Galette, from which Jules signals to the enemy bombers; the headquarters of its artistic community, the bar Au Rêve and the Restaurant Manière ('Beaunière' in the text); together with the leading figures of Montmartre's Bohemia, thinly disguised: Marcel Aymé (Marc Empième), Daragnès (Lambrecaze), Max Revol, Jean Noceti (Ottavio) and, in particular, Gen Paul, transposed into the diabolical legless Jules, and Robert Le Vigan (Norbert).[53] Moreover, the links with an earlier Parisian Bohemia, and the reminder that the great Montmartre 'Bohème' was also now of 'a bygone era', are established in *Féerie* II by the introduction into the middle of the bombardment of two characters dressed as Rodolphe and Mimi from *La Bohème*,[54] who connect the novel, not merely with Puccini's opera but also with Murger's novel *Scènes de la vie de Bohème*.[55]

Féerie pour une autre fois constitutes the swansong for that Montmartre culture, from which Céline is by now irremediably cut off. This is the significance of the long 100-page section of *Féerie* I, in which the narrator evokes his prison cell and its noises and dreams of the past: it cuts through the reminiscences of Montmartre themselves and stands as an uncrossable barrier between Ferdinand and the 'potes' on the Butte. At the same time, the bombing of Montmartre, rising to a crescendo in *Féerie* II, which is dedicated to Pliny the Elder, who died observing the eruption of Vesuvius in AD 79, a victim of his curiosity, produces a fictional destruction of the world from which he is now excluded. In fact, the description of the bombing of Montmartre in *Féerie* is typical of Céline's fictional practice in being grossly exaggerated, historically inaccurate and transposed from a number of events. Montmartre was never the subject the object of an air-raid of the sort described by Céline, and bombing in *Féerie* is a transposition of the raids on the Renault factory at Boulogne-Billancourt in March 1942 and April 1943, which Céline could see from his window in the Rue Girardon,[56] and the attack on the La Chapelle goods-yards on the night of 21–22 April 1944. Not only could Céline clearly see the bombing from his apartment, but several bombs fell on residential areas near the goods-yards, including some on Montmartre itself.[57] What the experience does permit, through transposition, is the creation of a powerful spectacle of 'féerie' in the form of an apocalyptic destruction of the Butte, consigned forever to 'une autre fois'.

Critics of Céline have tended to accept Henri Godard's conclusion that 'never as much as in the 200 pages devoted in *Féerie* II to the single vision of a night-time bombing raid, has the narrative thread of a novel been so reduced; never did Céline place so much emphasis on style alone and upon the sole pleasure which the reader could gain line after line.'[58] To a certain extent, this is clearly true. In *Féerie*, particularly in the second volume, Céline went to the limits of his 'abstract style' and made fewest concessions to his readers, though in point of fact, much of the difficulty of reading *Féerie* II comes not so much from an absence of narrative as from a surfeit. There is too much going on, an accumulation, even a superimposition of frenetic events, such as one would find in a dream or nightmare. In this respect, *Féerie* II follows on directly from the orgy in the Touit-Touit Club in *Guignol's Band* II, though the readership in 1954 would have been unaware of this, since the volume was not published until after Céline's death. It is undoubtedly true, however, that the novel breaks new bounds in the con-text of Céline's work as a whole, in stylistic virtuosity, and particularly in the technique of onomatopoeia: the subject of considerable experimentation in the bombing sequences of *Guignol's Band* I. As Godard observes, an air-raid is essentially an aural experience: 'an air-raid is . . . at the time a paroxysm for whosoever lives through it.'[59] From here, it is but a short step to Céline's 'petite musique', the essential language of 'féerie': 'these echoes of distant explosions are part of the music of our era.'[60]

In fact, the novel is carefully and extensively based upon musical models. Godard lists, in addition to the obvious reference to *La Bohème*, quotations from *La Périchole*, *La Chanson de Fortunio* and *Louise*, with more minor allusions to *Werther*, *Manon*, *On ne badine pas avec l'amour* and *Véronique*, in addition to operettas like *Rip Van Winkle*[61] and grand opera like *Don Giovanni*.[62] Moreover, *Féerie* I is accompanied by a song which Céline wrote in 1936, and which he later recorded, called *Règlement*, which runs through-out the novel, together with musical notation. The song takes the form of insulting and vengeful verses with a more nostalgic refrain, which in them-selves serve as a 'mise en abyme' of the novel as a whole: its recognition of loss, together with a desire to lash out at the perceived cause. The first verse runs:

> Je te trouverai charogne
> Un vilain soir
> Je te ferai dans les mires
> Deux grands trous noirs!
> Ton âme de vache dans la trans'pe
> Prendra du champ!
> Tu verras cette belle assistance
> Tu verras voir comment que l'on danse
> Au grand cimetière des Bons-Enfants,

whereas the refrain is both populist and nostalgic:

> Mais voici tante Hortense
> Et son petit Léo
> Voici Clémentine
> Et le vaillant Toto
> Faut-il dire à ces potes
> Que la guerre est finie?
> Au Diable ta sorte!
> Carre! dauffe! m'importe!
> O malfrat tes crosses
> Que le vent t'emporte!
> Feuilles mortes et soucis![63]

In other words, the 'féerie' becomes specifically an opera or operetta, an extraordinary musical extravaganza, in which the luckless Ferdinand moves from being in front of the curtain in the first part of the novel to being immersed, and nearly killed, in the action in Part II. The fairground barker becomes the victim, just as the observer Pliny the Elder becomes the actor in the drama he is watching.

As we have seen, Céline had high hopes for *Féerie pour une autre fois* and had abandoned the sequel to *Guignol's Band* in order to 'burst through the ceiling a second time',[64] to wipe out the reputation of a collaborator and to be recognized once again as a major novelist. If this were his ambition, it was perverse in the extreme to forbid Gallimard to undertake any advance publicity before the novel was published on 27 June 1952, just before the summer holidays.[65] As it was, sales were slow and disappointing, and the reviews few and far between and largely hostile, in spite of favourable notices by Albert Paraz and Roger Grenier. Even friends and supporters of Céline, such as Théophile Briant, Roger Nimier and Robert Poulet, could hardly contain their disappointment. For them, in comparison with the previous work, *Féerie* was 'precious' and 'boring'.[66] Yet, if *Féerie* I had attracted twelve reviews in the first six months after its publication[67] *Féerie* II fared far worse, even though its title had been changed to *Normance* to distance it from its predecessor. The critics, even those close to Céline personally, were few in number and almost universally hostile.[68]

It was important for Céline to have a success with his first novel after the war: important financially; important emotionally because, since the *Carnet du Cuirassier Destouches*, he needed success; and, above all, important because he required immediate rehabilitation and immediate re-establishment of contact with 'his' readers. Yet his innovation in style and his revolutionary concept of the novel, although they are now recognized, had moved beyond the comprehension and tolerance of his readers, even those friendliest to him among the ranks of professional writers and critics. Characteristically, Céline lashed out: principally at Gallimard, whom he accused, as he had Denoël, of not bothering to market the books.[69] At the same time, he decided on a new strategy: a 'defence and illustration' of his method in what would become *Entretiens avec le Professeur Y*, and a new approach to the remaining material in the *Féerie* project. The reminiscences of Germany at the end of the war, with the French collaborationist community in Sigmaringen, would be marketed as commercially as possible, as the dramatic memoirs of an eye-witness to this shameful, but highly intriguing, period of France's recent past. Céline jettisoned the 'abstract' qualities of *Féerie*, and was about to begin the last phase of his career, as a chronicler. Until the success of *D'un Château l'autre*, however, Céline remained in literary purgatory.

III Purgatory

Part of Céline's problem was that the France to which he had returned in 1952 was very different from the one he had left eight years earlier. Politically, there were still plenty of reminders of the recent past. The 'Guerre Franco-Française' which had precipitated Céline's departure to Germany was still in the collective memory, the indispensable ingredient in the success of the trilogy, kept alive by the succession of trials which lasted well into the 1950s. At the same time, France under the Fourth Republic turned increasingly towards the future and away from the past. Although its colonial wars impeded the process, Marshall Aid, the nationalization of the banks and the planning policy had contributed to the creation of an increasingly urban society, beginning to enjoy the beginnings of modest affluence and the joys of consumerism, a shift of which Céline was very aware, as his disparaging comments in *Entretiens avec le Professeur Y* and the trilogy show. Culturally, the map had changed in a similar fashion. Literature was now, or was perceived to be, in competition with forms of commercial popular or mass culture, such as the cinema, radio, television and popular music. In its own domain, while many figures from the inter-war years had survived (generally castigated by Céline for being at least as guilty as he, but escaping scot-free because of influence), there had been new developments, in particular what the literary Right considered to be a cultural *coup d'état* by Sartrean Existentialists who had subordinated creativity to didacticism. It is certainly true that 'Existentialism', broadly, constituted a powerful force and that it overshadowed a number of writers, principally Queneau and Vian, who were concerned with fantasy and the ludic exploitation of language and were to be obscured again by the rise of the formal experimentation of the *Nouveau Roman*. Céline's literary base after the war was threatened not merely by his political exclusion but also by his incompatibility, like that of Vian and Queneau, with prevailing literary fashion. For a long time his popularity, and that itself by no means secure, lay with the former intellectual collaborators who had served their sentences and joined the anti-Republican 'Opposition Nationale' and its journal *Rivarol*, and the younger generation of right-wing writers, the 'Hussards', who reacted against the orthodoxy of Existentialism and adopted Céline as a privileged forebear.[70]

The project of *Entretiens avec le Professeur Y* began in October 1953, six months before Céline completed the second volume of *Féerie pour une autre fois*. Recognizing that it was likely to meet with the same hostility as its predecessor, Céline, still smarting from what he considered as a lack of commitment on the part of his publisher, wrote to Claude Gallimard that 'with the next book, I will be obliged to defend myself in the *Nouvelle NRF*,'[71] an idea which was taken up by its editor, Jean Paulhan. The first instalment duly appeared in the June 1954 number of the *NNRF*, but there then ensued a protracted and increasingly bitter series of negotiations regarding subsequent publication, culminating in Paulhan's definitive break with Céline on 14 January 1955. The problem was that Céline, uncharacteristically, had allowed the first instalment to appear without having written the rest of the text. Hence, when he came to complete the work, it had, as Paulhan complained, 'become much longer than we were led to believe'.[72] This difficulty was compounded by Céline's insistence that, in addition to its serialization in the *NNRF*, the work be published in volume form. Although Gaston Gallimard agreed to this and a contract was signed on 30 October 1954, the second instalment did not appear until November. An increasingly irritable Paulhan suggested publishing the rest of the work in one final instalment, but only on condition that he be allowed to cut the text.[73] It was Céline's vituperative response which finally precipitated the break with Paulhan, and which led to an intermittent publication of the remaining sections, in December 1954 and February and April 1955, while the volume itself finally appeared in March 1955.

The *Entretiens avec le Professeur Y* constitute the most extensive and explicit explanation of Céline's literary project, though the essay builds on earlier statements of his poetics in the 1932 article 'Qu'on s'explique', certain sections of *Bagatelles pour un masasacre* and the preface to *Guignol's Band* I, and was reiterated in an interview with Robert Sadoul for Radio Suisse-Romande in March 1955.[74] The substance of this fictitious interview, which takes place in the Square des Arts et Métiers, is well enough known, and has as its starting-point the assertion of modernity and aesthetic change found at the beginning of *Guignol's Band*: 'Jazz overthrew the waltz, Impressionism killed off "faux-jour", you'll write "telegraphically" or you won't write anything else again!'[75] with the corollary: 'It's up to you to understand! Cultivate your emotions!' Thus, Céline's first claim to his luckless interviewer is that he is an inventor, the inventor of 'emotion in the written language!'[76] He explicitly compares himself to the Impressionist painters excluded from the Salon of 1862, who had understood the need to distance themselves from photography and popular representation, the 'chromo', just as Céline sees the need to distance himself from cinema.[77] In the same way that the Impressionists adopted 'the illusion of the open air',[78] Céline, fully conscious of the technical sleight of hand involved, manipulates the *illusion* of spoken French in the context of the literary language. He does this in particular through the deployment of the first person singular, the 'law of the lyric genre' and, what is more, the law of the comic lyric,[79] which, in its turn, exploits 'argot' or 'the language of hatred'.[80] These, however, constitute only the preliminaries to Céline's real discovery, which came to him with the force of the revelation to Pascal on the Pont de Neuilly[81] but which he encountered on the steps of the Pigalle Métro station.[82] On the journey from Montmartre to Issy-les-Moulineaux on the Nord–Sud line, all the distractions of the surface, all the traffic-jams on the Boulevard Sébastopol, and all the hindrances are avoided and the goal is attained rapidly and directly.[83] In other words, whereas the dead 'literary' prose of fiction moves cumbersomely through a welter of superficial detail, Céline's style, because it is able to harness the emotions of the reader, takes that reader directly to 'the heart of the matter'. At the same time, Céline is fully conscious of the essentially technical nature of the enterprise. If the readers are to be carried along at breakneck speed, Céline's Métro must 'never come off the emotive rails'.[84] That is the true mark of his genius[85] and is achieved through the use of the 'trois points', his trademark, which constitute the sleepers holding the rails together.[86]

What is interesting about the *Entretiens avec le Professeur Y* is the way in which it confirms Céline's consciousness of the complexity of his technical innovation and of the tradition from which it derives, and the way in which it provides further proof of his immense self-confidence. The very notion of the author as the driver of an emotive Métro in which the readers are passengers unable to leave until the end of the journey is a highly authoritarian one, and is reinforced by Céline's quite serious claims to 'genius', both in the text itself and in the publisher's blurb, written by Jean Dutourd and corrected by Gaston Gallimard at Céline's insistence.[87] In this sense, Céline's bullying of the interviewer, the Professeur Y, reflects the relationship between author and reader. What is also remarkable, and considerably less well-explored, is the debt to Céline's first novel, *Voyage au bout de la nuit*. In the first place, the *Entretiens* adopt the same urban geography as the novel. The narrative ends with Céline sitting on a bench at two o'clock in the morning in the Place Clichy, where *Voyage au bout de la nuit* began and to which it constantly returns; the entire conceit of the Métro is constructed on a journey from Montmartre, the locus of *Voyage*, to the south, to the Mairie d'Issy, the end of the Nord–Sud Métro line, from which Bardamu discovers a ticket in a box abandoned by Robinson in the trading-post in Africa. More significantly, Céline's ambition in the *Entretiens* is couched in language which is remarkably similar to that of the ending of *Voyage*. When his interviewer asks: 'So, you're going to take everything away?' Céline replies: 'Yes, colonel . . . everything! . . . seven-story apartment buildings! . . . the ferocious growling buses! I'm not going to leave anything on the surface! I'm not going to leave anything! Neither the Colonnes Morris, nor nagging old ladies, nor tramps under the bridges! No! I'm taking everything away!'[88] an echo of the narrator's conclusion to the first novel in which he evokes the wail of the tug-boat's siren: 'It called towards it all the barges on the river, all of them, and the entire city, and the sky and the countryside, and us: it took everything away, the Seine as well, everything, so that no one could talk about it any more.'[89] We have already seen how, in this conclusion to *Voyage au bout de la nuit*, there is a doubling of the narrator, by which the actor Bardamu is led away to the silence from which he came by the writer, in the same way that he was enticed into his adventures by the Pied Piper-like Colonel of the Regiment. In *Entretiens*, which, incidentally, features another colonel, the writer as Pied Piper is still there, not in the guise of a tug-boat but as the driver of an emotive Métro.

At the same time, although in more compressed form, the narrative of *Entretiens avec le Professeur Y* serves the same purpose of illustration of the precept of emotion as does *Guignol's Band* in relation to its preface. The narrator is the same victim of his rapacious and lazy publishers as the narrator of *D'un château l'autre* and, in order to boost the sales of his books, agrees to an interview, on the neutral ground of the Square des Arts et Métiers, with one of the few available personalities not on holiday. The interview takes the form of a ritual humiliation, uncomfortably reminiscent of the treatment of Hindus in Denmark. Professor Y, who suddenly and unaccountably reveals himself to be the clandestine Colonel Réséda (ironically, the colour of the uniform worn by the German army of occupation) and who suffers from a prostate condition, begins to urinate uncontrollably. He then goes completely mad and insists on being taken directly to Gaston Gallimard. The subsequent journey, by taxi and on foot, across Paris, accompanied by hostile onlookers, during which they overshoot their target and end up near Boucicaut's Bon Marché store, is not merely reminiscent of a number of previous Célinian narratives, but also demonstrates in fictional form the advantages and the directness of the Métro. As a final but by no means totally affectionate gesture towards his publisher, Céline ends the narrative by depositing the unconscious but still mad interviewer in Gaston Gallimard's office, perhaps as unexpected and unwelcome an arrival as the manuscript itself.

If *Entretiens avec le Professeur Y* was supposed to relaunch Céline's post-war literary career and to counteract the unfavourable reception of *Féerie pour une autre fois*, it failed. Apart from favourable reviews by Pascal Pia in *Carrefour* and Roger Nimier in *Le Bulletin de Paris*, the reaction was best summed up by Kléber Haedens, writing in *Paris-Presse*, who exclaimed: 'Oh, if only he could write another *Mort à crédit*!'[90] In fact, the *Entretiens* had little impact upon either Céline's literary reputation or his way of life. According to Philippe Alméras, in March 1955 the sum total of his sales throughout the entire period he had been with Gallimard (in other words, since the signing of the contract in July 1951) amounted to only 16,100 copies, including 2900 copies of *Voyage au bout de la nuit*, 2000 of *Mort à crédit* and 6300 of *Féerie pour une autre fois*, a far cry from the 40,000 copies of the novel's first print-run.[91] As with Denoël in the past, Céline's instinctive response was to blame his publisher, even though, as we have seen, he was responsible for the lack of publicity surrounding the launch of *Féerie*. Relations up until the publication of *D'un Château l'autre* in 1957 remained tense, with Céline going so far in 1952 as to demand that Gallimard pay his back taxes.[92] While the sheer aggressiveness of Céline's correspondence over the publication of *Entretiens avec le Professeur Y* finally alienated Paulhan, who, as a distinguished former Resistant, had played a major part in Céline's rehabilitation, the relationship with Gaston Gallimard himself remained relatively stable, in spite of the flow of insults and tirades directed from the Route des Gardes to the Rue Sébastien Bottin. In fact, Gallimard, who no doubt saw Céline as a highly profitable if troublesome investment, was remarkably indulgent. He even finally agreeed in principle to his demand, formulated as early as 1954, to be published in the prestigious Bibliothèque de la Pléiade, between Bergson and Cervantes, and, with Malraux and Montherlant, the only living French authors in the collection.[93] This became a recurrent obsession of Céline's, an article of faith in his own genius and his status as France's foremost writer. In fact, negotiations over the Pléiade edition of the first two novels continued throughout the rest of his life, and the volume, edited by Jean Ducourneau and with a preface by Henri Mondor, did not appear until 1962. However, Gallimard did readily agree to the publication by Hachette of *Voyage au bout de la nuit* in the paperback Livre de Poche edition in 1956,[94] to be followed by *Mort à crédit*.[95] Only one misdemeanour on Céline's part seriously troubled the relationship, and that concerned his submission in 1955 of a manuscript to a rival publisher, Fasquelle. On this occasion Gallimard's indulgence was exhausted, and he tersely reminded Céline of the terms of his contract and of the extent of his debt with the publishing house: 11 million francs.[96] Relations were not to improve until Roger Nimier took over as Céline's editor at Gallimard in 1957.

Part of the problem stemmed from Céline's actual or perceived poverty, in spite of the advances received from Gallimard. In 1955 he earned just 822,528 francs from literature, the equivalent of 84,000 francs or roughly £10,000 today.[97] Alméras, however, is careful to note that the advance of 1.5

million francs (150,000 francs today) that Céline received for *Féerie pour une autre fois* II compared favourably with the annual salary of a young engineer just graduated from the Ecole Polytechnique – 120,000 current francs.[98] In addition, Céline and Lucette still had savings deposited with the Marteaus, and still received rent from their properties in Saint-Germain-en-Laye, Saint-Leu and Dieppe. Moreover, Gallimard continued to make regular and substantial advances on each new book and while, as he reminded Céline over the Fasquelle affair, this amounted to a 'debt' of 11 million francs, in a period of high inflation the value of this deficit was effectively reduced every year.[99] In fact, the effect of this perceived poverty was psychological rather than economic. It reinforced and confirmed Céline's chronic avariciousness; it bolstered his hatred of the rich, evidenced by disparaging references to Gaston Gallimard's fortune in *Entretiens avec le Professeur Y*; and it pushed him further into his self-adopted role, already dominant in the years of exile in Denmark, of an eccentric and despairing tramp. Robert Poulet, in *Mon ami Bardamu*, describes him, not without malice, as 'a ruined man, morally and materially . . . protected by childish precautions: the appearance of a tramp, a pack of dogs and a barrier of lies'[100] while Paulhan described him to Etiemble as 'a man who has been struck down, who doesn't leave his bedroom, who can't sleep, who suffers incessantly'.[101]

A recluse he remained, rarely leaving the house except for his short shopping trips to lower Meudon, and decidedly ill at ease on those rare occasions when he was enticed further afield. Marcel Aymé did succeed in luring him to his country house in Montfort-l'Amaury, when Céline was photographed playing *pétanque*. When he took him later to visit Vlaminck, however, Céline demanded to be taken home as soon as they arrived.[102] Nor could be bear Lucette being away from him: her weekly visits to Paris were a torture until she returned. Once, when Marcel Aymé and his wife persuaded her to attend the première of the Peking Opera at the Théâtre du Châtelet, they were disturbed in their box by a telephone call from an anxious Céline.[103] Like most recluses, he preferred the company of animals, to whom *Féerie* I is dedicated, along with the sick and the prisoners. Bébert the cat had died at the end of 1952, after a life full of adventures which had taken him from Montmartre through Germany to Denmark and back, and another cherished survivor from the Danish exile, the dog Bessy, died in 1954 or 1955.[104] By now the couple had a vast collection of dogs and cats. In addition, to console him for the loss of Bébert, Lucette bought Céline a West African parrot from La Samaritaine, called Toto. Initially, Céline was furious and insisted that she take it back, but within two days he and Toto were inseparable. Céline taught it to talk and sing; they would scream and shout at each other; the bird sat on Céline's desk as he wrote and was totally possessive, attacking any visitor who stayed too long.[105]

Not that there were many visitors in this period. Lucette's parents were allowed to call, but at fixed times; Céline himself renewed contact with Edith Follet, with whom he became very close during the last years of his life, and saw his daughter Colette regularly, but he refused to meet any of his grandchildren on the grounds that he was too sensitive. On the one occasion that Lucette and Colette arranged for a surprise visit from his eldest grandson, Jean-Marie Turpin, the experiment was a disaster. Instead of looking shy and child-like, the 15-year-old Jean-Marie arrived wearing a bow-tie, smoking a pipe, the very epitome of the intellectuals that Céline hated so much, and announced his ambition to be a writer. His grand-father's sole reply was that he should come back when he had passed his *baccalauréat.*[106]

Most visitors were old friends from the Montmartre days, though Gen Paul still remained aloof. Marcel Aymé called every Sunday morning,[107] and other friends with whom Céline kept more or less in contact included Jean Perrot, René Héron de Villefosse, André Pulicani, Henri Mahé, Dr Camus, Pierre Duverger, Lucien Rebatet, Jacques Deval and Pierre Monnier.[108] Marie Bell also made the journey to Meudon, although relations had been strained for a time when she became a member of the Commission d'Epuration du Théâtre in 1945.[109] In 1955, at the suggestion of Albert Paraz, Paul Chambrillon arranged a recording of extracts of Céline's work, with Michel Simon reading from *Voyage au bout de la nuit* and his old friend Arletty reading from *Mort à crédit.* The first attempt failed because of an echo, but a second version was made and released in 1956, in which Céline was persuaded to sing his two songs, *A noeud coulant* and *Règlement.*[110] As the correspondence shows, the relationship with Albert Paraz fluctuated be-tween guarded warmth and extreme coldness. He did not make the journey to Meudon until June 1956, when both Céline and Monnier were waiting to greet him. As Monnier records: 'we saw Paraz appear at the garden gate. He was walking with little steps, leaning on a friend's arm. His face was beam-ing. He was still very handsome despite his illness, and with a smile of happiness on a face that tuberculosis had not managed to ruin . . . I think Paraz experienced one of the greatest joys of his life that day.'[111] He visited Céline again in May 1957, and for one last time in August of the same year, shortly before his death in Vence on 2 September. Yet, as François Gibault concludes, it is probable that Céline was embarrassed by Paraz's effusions and never fully reciprocated his friendship.[112] Certainly the correspond-ence, often restricted to sometimes outdated medical advice on Paraz's tuberculosis, often shows considerable impatience and always a conscious-ness of superiority, as in the earlier correspondence with Dabit. It is curi-ous, and perhaps indicative of the nature of their relationship, that Céline's last letter to Paraz dates from 9 September 1957, five days after Paraz's death, of which he was obviously unaware, in spite of an obituary in *Rivarol* on September 5.[113]

Another figure from the past with whom Céline's dealings were, at the very least, ambiguous, was Thorvald Mikkelsen who, in spite of his rough treatment at Céline's hands, nevertheless corresponded regularly and vis-ited him in Meudon every time he came to Paris, bringing supplies of medicine. On one occasion, however, witnessed by a new acquaintance, Dr André Willemin, who had been introduced by Serge Perrault, Mikkelsen arrived at the gate unexpectedly. Céline conducted the entire conversation from his balcony, refused to invite Mikkelsen into the garden and, before going back into his study, told Mikkelsen to leave the parcel of medicine by the gate.[114]

If Céline's visitors were composed for the most part of old Montmartre friends or former collaborators, he had been, as we have seen, enthusiastically adopted by the group of young right-wing writers loosely known as the 'Hussards', comprising particularly Roger Nimier, Antoine Blondin, Stephen Hecquet, Albert Vidalie and Kléber Haedens.[115] While some of these writers had a common background in pre-war royalism or relatively minor collaboration, they were brought together in their outrage at the domination of the Resistance in post-war France, politically and legally through the *Epuration*, and intellectually and aesthetically through Existentialism. Adopting the tradition of the 1920s 'nouveau mal du siècle' and its predecessor in the post-Napoleonic era, they cultivated, in the case of Nimier, the insolence of a Stendhal and the despair of a Drieu la Rochelle, and, in that of Blondin, a comic wistfulness which, in the case of *L'Europe buissonnière*, owes much to *Voyage au bout de la nuit*. Nimier had sent a copy of his first novel, *Les Epées*, to Céline in Denmark in 1948, and had received a enthusiastic response, as he had to his second novel *Le Hussard bleu*. When Céline and Lucette moved to Meudon, he was taken to meet them by Marcel Aymé and soon became a regular visitor. Nimier captivated Céline by his charm and his sense of humour, and even succeeded in getting him to admire his new acquisition, the famous Aston-Martin in which he was to die in 1962.[116] In his turn, Nimier brought his friends to see Céline: Haedens, Vidalie, Hecquet and Blondin, to whom he said: 'Ah! You're little Blondin? Your books are so ethereal, so light, that when they fall through my hands they don't hurt my feet.'[117] In other words, although often ignored or considered burnt out by the French literary mainstream, Céline was at least able to count on solid support from the younger generation of French anti-establishment writers, who all held important roles in the literary press and, in the case of Nimier from 1957 onwards, in publishing. It was to be largely Nimier's enthusiasm, energy and commercial sense which were to make such a success of Céline's final trilogy, and were ultimately to gain him the rehabilitation and recognition he had been searching for since the end of the war and even earlier, since the semi-failure of *Mort à crédit*.

IV *D'UN CHÂTEAU L'AUTRE*

Céline began work on *D'un château l'autre* in the summer of 1954, in other words when *Féerie* II appeared, but while he was still working on the *Entretiens avec le Professeur Y*. The manuscript was completed in March 1957, and the book was published on 20 June of the same year.[118] He immediately began work on *Nord* in the spring of 1957, completing the manuscript by the end of 1959 and seeing the novel published in the week of 20–26 May 1960.[119] The third volume, *Rigodon*, was started in December 1959 and completed in draft form on 30 June 1961, the day before Céline's death, though his correspondence with Roger Nimier indicates that he had not planned the publication of the final version until 1964, when he would have been 70.[120] As it was, the novel did not appear until 1969.

There is every indication that the trilogy marks a change in strategy in Céline's fictional output, even though it follows on chronologically from *Féerie pour une autre fois* and is part of the same project. *Féerie* had offended because of its abstract technical difficulties and what was perceived as an exaggerated self-preoccupation. The readership was simply not interested in the novel's subject-matter. Céline was conscious, however, that his un-usually privileged experience in Germany in the last days of the Reich was commercially marketable. As he told Louis-Albert Zbinden, in an interview for Radio Lausanne on 25 July 1957, which echoes some of the interviews after the publication of *Voyage au bout de la nuit*, his motivation in writing *D'un château l'autre* was primarily economic:

> I've been the object of a sort of interdiction for a certain number of years, and, in bringing out a work which, in spite of everything, is in the public domain, because it speaks about things which are well-known and which, after all, interest the French – since it's a small part, very small, but, even so, a small part of the history of France: I speak about Pétain, I speak about Laval, I speak about Sigmaringen, it's a moment in the history of France, whether people like it or not. It may be regrettable, and we may regret it, but it's still a moment in the history of France. It existed and, one day, people will teach it in schools.[121]

It is for this reason that much of the novel's success was due to its image as a factual account of the last days of the Vichy government in exile. As Godard notes, many of the reviews had titles along the lines of: 'Sigmaringen told by an eye-witness'.[122] That Céline consciously exploited this historical interest on the part of his readers is evidenced by his constant adoption throughout the trilogy of the role of 'chronicler'. Yet here, as he reminded Madeleine Chapsal in the famous interview for *L'Express*, if he cites Froissart, Joinville or Commines, these 'immense names', it is not 'to show off, but because they come to mind'.[123] We have already seen that one of the books which Céline ordered from Paris when he was in Baden-Baden was the Pléiade edition of the French chroniclers, and what he exploits in his own 'chronicle' is the genre's highly ambiguous relationship to histori-cal fact, its ability to convey historical truth without necessarily replicating historical reality. This is the significance of the reaction of Otto Abetz, cited by Karl Epting in the *Cahiers de l'Herne*, to a scene in *D'un château l'autre* in which he figures and which cannot possibly have happened, whereby 'cer-tain inner realities of that period became transparent in that scene, through the grotesqueness of the situations and the characters, including himself.'[124] It is this significance of the chronicle which also demonstrates the futility of the, albeit successful, posthumous libel action brought against *Nord* by Asta Scherz and Dr Haubold, and which incidentally coincides with one of Céline's oldest aesthetic precepts: 'One must blacken, and blacken oneself.'[125]

It is perhaps also for this reason, in addition to purely practical ones, that Céline rejects a linear narrative. The first volume rightly chooses to deal with the most appetizing subject-matter: the French exiles in Sigmaringen, but the reader must first digest a hundred-page long introduction on the narrator's life at Meudon. In *Nord*, however, the narrative reverts to the period before Sigmaringen, with Céline in Baden-Baden, Berlin and then in northern Prussia, ending with the authorization to travel to Rostock. The final volume, which again begins with an introduction set in Meudon, opens on the Baltic before describing the journey south through Berlin and Ulm to Sigmaringen, where Céline and Lili are immediately turned round and sent north, until they reach safety in Denmark. In evoking the last days of the Third Reich, a period when, as Godard reminds us, 'time is out of joint,'[126] the dislocation of the chronology of the narrative becomes a powerful metaphor. Indeed, it is through this procedure, and through the deployment of the grotesque, as noted by Abetz, that Céline's chronicle is able to capture the inherent strangeness of Germany in 1944 and 1945. It also accounts for the use of comedy in a narrative about a human and historical disaster, such as the fight between Alphonse de Châteaubriant and Otto Abetz in *D'un château l'autre* over the orchestration of *The Ride of the Valkyries*[127] or the scene in *Rigodon* when the mad Le Vigan holds up Field Marshal Von Runstedt's car in Ulm during Rommel's funeral.[128] In the *Entretiens avec le Professeur Y*, Céline uses an image to explain the technique of the Impressionists: when painting a stick in water, in order to counteract the effects of refraction, you have to 'break the stick yourself! before you put it in the water! what a joke! it's the entire secret of Impressionism!'[129] In other words, distortion in art is the only way to the transmission of reality.

In his preface to the Pléiade edition of the trilogy, Henri Godard rightly emphasizes the continuity between the *D'un château l'autre* trilogy and the body of fictional work which preceded it,[130] and nowhere is this more apparent than in the Proustian quest for the past which informs all of Céline's fiction. The chronicle is not deployed merely to satisfy the reader's voyeurism; it constitutes the historical base which the narrator is attempting to retrieve and understand, in the same way that the narrator of *Mort à crédit* is attempting to seize the elusive past which has so marked him. Why else should the novels be so concerned to position the narrator in a present from which the past can only appear as peopled by ghosts? In *D'un château l'autre*, the phantoms who constitute the characters of *Voyage au bout de la nuit* return as the ghostly passengers on the 1900 'bateau-mouche', *La Publique*, whom Céline encounters at night on the quayside at Meudon, victims of the *Epuration* all, prisoners on Charon's barque.[131] Nor is the allusion to a ghost ship by any means gratuitous. It takes up the similarity which Bardamu bears to the hero of *The Flying Dutchman* (whose French title was *Le Vaisseau fantôme*), connects with the Wagnerian dispute between Abetz and Châteaubriant, and also reminds us that it was in Meudon that Wagner composed the opera. In other words, if the novel is composed in the shadow of Wagner, Céline is careful not to concentrate solely on the more obvious references to *Götterdämmerung*, but to use the allusions as an intratextual device posing the continuing problematic relationship between past and present, fact and memory.

At the same time, Céline is aware that the solution to the problem is in the present rather than the past, which is imprisoned in repetition and stasis. The title of *D'un château l'autre*, referring as it does to the passage from one prison to another, from Sigmaringen to Vestre Faengsel, is a gloomy affirmation of endless and inescapable repetition, just as a *Rigodon* is 'a dance to a tune in two-time, in one place, without going forward or backwards, nor moving to the side'[132] and the very image of stasis. At the same time, however, a 'rigodon' is a bell rung on a firing-range when a bull's eye is scored and, if the trilogy consists in part of the chronicle of a merciless imprisonment in history, it also can take definitive delight in hitting its present-day targets: the victims of the contemporary narrator's polemical rage, and ultimately the aesthetic perfection of the 'pure lace-work' which Céline announced proudly to Gaston Gallimard on the completion of *D'un château l'autre*.[133]

The publication of the novel received a belated consecration and definitively removed him from the obscurity in which he had been held since the end of the war. *D'un château l'autre* proved a major critical and commercial success and more than vindicated Céline's change of strategy after *Féerie* II. In part, this was due to Nimier's publicity master-stroke in setting up an interview with Jean-Jacques Servan-Schreiber's left-wing weekly *L'Express*, in which, almost for the first time since the war, Céline was able to reach a wide audience no longer confined to political sympathizers in the 'Opposition Nationale'. The interview with Madeleine Chapsal, followed by the one with André Parinaud in *Arts*, succeeded in finally re-establishing Céline in the literary mainstream.[134] At the same time, French critical opinion, so hostile to the experimentation of the two volumes of *Féerie pour une autre fois*, was enthusiastic, almost unanimous in its recognition of a 'resurrection' of Céline.[135] This process of rehabilitation was assisted, rather than hindered, by the one jarring note which came from his former comrades on the extreme Right. In the same way that he had been dismayed by his precipitate departure from Paris in the summer of 1944 and his no less hasty retreat from Sigmaringen, Pierre-Antoine Cousteau, for the old *Je suis partout* team, denounced in two articles in *Rivarol* the betrayal implicit in both the novel and the interview in *L'Express*.[136] Céline, however, was defended by both Paraz and Robert Poulet, and more half-heartedly by Rebatet, in an article in *Dimanche-Matin*.[137]

Céline, who had been largely ignored by the literary press until the publication of *D'un château l'autre,* now became the subject of a series of major interviews which lasted until his death.[138] He was also increasingly sought out for television appearances, including Pierre Dumayet's *Lectures pour tous* programme on 17 July 1957, though the interview with Louis Pauwels and André Brissaud in the spring of 1959 was banned at the request of anti-racist organizations and shown in part only ten years later.[139] On 12 October 1957 he was interviewed by Jacques Chancel on *Télémagazine,* although it would be an exaggeration to claim, as Vitoux suggests, that he had overnight become a television 'personality'.[140] This critical and popular acclaim was accompanied, for the first time since the war, by a modest upturn in Céline's finances. Although the sales of *D'un château l'autre* were still comparatively low, amounting to nearly 23,000 copies sold in the first year, they enabled him to reduce his deficit with Gallimard from 58,731 new francs in 1959 to 47,262 new francs a year later.[141] This trend, both critical and commercial, was reinforced by the success of *Nord,* launched with a prestigious interview in *Le Monde,* which, as Godard comments, emphasized the stylistic importance of the novel: 'Regarding his second book of memoirs on the Nazi defeat, Céline tells us how he "changed the place of words".'[142]

The final years after the publication of *D'un château l'autre* were marked by what Céline undoubtedly considered a belated recognition of his importance. In May 1959 Gallimard published his ballet choreographies, which had never been performed, under the title *Ballets sans musique, sans personne, sans rien.* Preparations for the Pléiade edition of the first two novels continued, though with frustrating delays,[143] and Gallimard agreed to one of Céline's long-standing demands, the publication of an academic study on his work, by commissioning a young Belgian scholar, Marc Hanrez, to prepare a book in the *Bibliothèque idéale* series, which appeared in 1961. Further, unsuccessful attempts were made to produce a film version of *Voyage au bout de la nuit,* to be directed by either Claude Autant-Lara or Louis Malle[144] and, in his constant thirst for the recognition he felt was his due, Céline proposed himself for the Grand Prix de la Ville de Paris.[145]

With his new-found semi-respectability, old friends, sometimes from the highly unrespectable past, made contact. Karl Epting, the director of the Institut Allemand during the Occupation, and Hermann Bickler, Céline's old SS friend, both wrote in July 1960,[146] and visitors in the last years included the Montmartre singer Max Revol, an old comrade from the '12 Cuir', André Neufinck, who had saved the *Carnet du Cuirassier Destouches,* Marie Le Bannier, the mistress of Anthanase Follet, whose house he stayed in at Saint-Malo, his fellow-collaborationist Dr Bécart, Fernand de Brinon's secretary and mistress Madame Mitre, his colleague in Sigmaringen, Dr Jacquot, and the sculptor Arno Breker.[147] Yet friends had been lost, in particular Robert Le Vigan, in exile in Argentina, who dated his break with Céline from 1955, claiming that it had nothing to do with his portrayal as a mad eccentric in *D'un château l'autre* and *Nord*, but was due to Céline's mania for 'torturing his friends . . .'[148] – in this case, writing to impoverished exiles in South America telling them to seek help from Le Vigan, now a prosperous landowner, when in reality, as he well knew, the actor was in terrible poverty.[149] Céline's gratuitous cruelty to his friends remained a constant character-trait until the end.

And the end was not far off. Shortly after sending the manuscript of *Nord* to Gallimard, Céline wrote to Roger Nimier in January 1960: 'I'm afraid of the future, Roger . . . get on with the printing, quickly!'[150] Céline's health was failing, probably due to a chronically poor diet. As Alméras notes, he kept going on bread and butter and biscuits, tea and coffee, and the indispensable veronal sleeping tablets,[151] and Dr Willemin was horrified by his diet of 'Véronal in the evening, coffee in the morning and anti-depressants in "enormous quantities"'.[152] In 1960 he had suffered a minor stroke, from which he apparently recovered,[153] but the effort of writing *Rigodon*, so soon after the completion of *Nord*, was taking its toll. Lucette Destouches confided to Frédéric Vitoux that he was 'more short of breath, sickly, and exhausted than ever,' with increasingly bad head-aches,[154] but that he insisted on overworking in order to complete *Rigodon*, so that she would have something to live on.[155] He duly completed the second draft on 30 June 1961, and wrote to both Gaston Gallimard and Roger Nimier to prepare the pre-publication contract.[156] The summer of 1961 was appallingly hot. On 31 June Céline rose early as usual, but by the time Lucette came down he was clearly unwell. She took him upstairs to bed, where he lay all day, naked, while she gave her usual dance-lessons, as he had wanted. 'I want to be left to die quietly,' he told her[157] when she suggested calling Dr Willemin. At six o'clock in the evening he died, of a haemorrhage in the left side of the brain. The press was not informed, but his friends were allowed to file past the body: Gen Paul, who had not seen Céline since 1944, came with Marcel Aymé.[158] The funeral took place in the cemetery of Meudon on the morning of 4 July. As Arletty recalls: 'I remember his wife, a doctor, a cat wandering around his grave. He wanted a holly-tree beside him, and a holly-tree was in flower; a small child with a check apron straight out of a 1912 catalogue was watering the flowers on the next grave. The child, the animal, the flower: the things he loved to finish the journey.'[159] Later that year, Lucette Destouches had a head-stone engraved with a sailing-ship and bearing the inscription: 'Louis-Ferdinand Céline. Doctor L.-F. Destouches. 1894–1961. Lucie Destouches. Née Almansor. 1912– '.

Conclusion: Céline and Power

Céline's death in 1961 passed largely unnoticed, overshadowed by the suicide of Ernest Hemingway the same week. Yet, as Alméras reminds us, Céline 'never underwent a literary purgatory, though it is true that he spent a long time in purgatory when he was alive'.[1] The comment, in fact, is only half-true. There was, as we have seen, a constant flow of books and articles on Céline from the 1960s onwards but, both in France and overseas, these were overwhelmingly devoted to the early fiction, and in particular *Voyage au bout de la nuit*, where, as Céline admitted to Madeleine Chapsal, he was still making concessions to 'good literature'.[2] Work on the later novels, and especially the 'abstract' *Guignol's Band* and *Féerie pour une autre fois* only came much later. In other words, by concentrating on *Voyage au bout de la nuit*, and incidentally ignoring for the most part its function as an 'imaginary voyage', early Céline criticism gave precedence to his presumed role as an outcast and rebel over his importance as a fictional innovator.

Nor, it must be admitted, was such a perception totally without foundation. As we have seen, Céline's writing is grounded in a definable social reality towards which both he and his narrators are frequently antagonistic. More specifically, as he proclaimed in his correspondence with Elie Faure, he was an anarchist, and the anarchist vision and style permeate his writing, from Bardamu's 'prière vengeresse et sociale' to the recurrent character Borokrom in *Bagatelles pour un massacre* and *Guignol's Band*, a novel whose introduction also celebrates the 'Bande à Bonnot' of the belle époque. This consistent anarchist stance sets Céline, albeit with some profound ambiguities, against the 'bourgeois' Third Republic and its successors, together with its institutions: the army, the Church, the political system and dominant professions such as medicine. In the same way, and perfectly consistently, his anarchist antagonism to organization and control leads to a rejection of his vestigial and transitory faith in the Soviet experiment, and takes him ultimately, along with many of his fellows, to a French anarchism of the Right, which is anti-progressist, anti-bourgeois and anti-Semitic and which, again temporarily, can make common cause with Nazism.

Neither is Céline's anarchism an exclusively literary phenomenon, the conscious adoption of the tradition of the great Montmartre anarchist poets of the 1890s like Jehan Rictus or Richepin. It stems from a careful and emotive observation of social change in France throughout the Third Republic and beyond. His social, political and aesthetic perception is rooted in the period of the belle époque, the period of his Parisian childhood and adolescence, of which Proust is the definitive chronicler. Yet here all the ambiguity comes into play. The belle époque is the period of the coming to power of the industrial bourgeoisie and the urban proletariat, who together begin the irreversible process of strangulation of the Parisian petite-bourgeoisie to which Céline himself belongs. The depiction of the *Exposition Universelle* of 1900 in *Mort à crédit*, and its paranoid hallucinatory reflection in the scene of the 'grande cliente', testify both to the cruel social divisions in Third Republic France and to the threat which modernization poses to those sectors of society which are functionally unable to adapt, those 'urban villagers' who, like Céline himself, finally seek sanctuary in Montmartre, the last redoubt of the belle époque. Yet, if he is alert to the threat, he is also doubly conscious of the charm exerted by this society which is no more, from the loving evocation of the 1900's 'bateaux-mouche' in *D'un château l'autre* or the port of London in *Guignol's Band* to his admiration for the skill of the vanished lace-makers. In a sense, Céline's entire development is contained in the growing perception that the progress of the twentieth century merely accentuates the alienation of the underclass already present in the belle époque, while at the same time diminishing its aesthetic qualities to the point of disappearance. The belle époque at least had its 'féerie', immeasurably enhanced by nostalgia; the inter-war years, as Céline desperately records in *Les Beaux Draps*, have driven 'legend' out of people's lives, with fatal consequences. It is for this reason that the acerbic social criticism directed at France in the medical polemics of the 1920s is replicated by the disappointment expressed regarding the Soviet Union in *Mea culpa* and *Bagatelles pour un massacre*: Not only did France in the inter-war years maintain its urban population in unacceptable housing conditions, with hygienic consequences which 'bourgeois medicine' and its 'burlesque ghosts' were incapable of solving, it refused the world of 'féerie' by symbolically rejecting Céline's ballets. In the same way, the appalling conditions in the hospital for venereal diseases in Leningrad, described in *Bagatelles pour un massacre*, show that Soviet doctors have nothing to learn in callousness and inefficiency from their bourgeois counterparts, and the Russians' inability to perform the ballet *Van Bagaden* shows that the Communist experiment is as devoid of imagination as Ford's assembly-line. The *beaux draps* in which the French found themselves in 1940 were the result of a parallel collapse of the imaginative powers of both Capitalism and Communism, by no means confined to France itself. For this analysis alone, Céline figures as an important chronicler of the progress of his century.

Important as this social and historical awareness is, of course, the essential question concerning Céline is the writing, particularly the fictional creation, and its origins. As we have seen, contrary to earlier biographical images of Céline as an untutored primitive, a Douanier Rousseau of the novel, his work is, in reality, the product of considerable, if not always orthodox, erudition. He makes constant use of the French classics, particularly those which figured on the *certificat* and *baccalauréat* syllabuses. His adolescent experience of Germany and England gave him access to both the German and English languages and their literatures: from Georges Geoffroy's reminiscences of Céline's reading of German philosophers while in London during the First World War to the enduring influence of English Edwardian writers, like Kipling, Conrad and Wells, and, crucially, Shakespeare, the probable origin of 'féerie'. At the same time, these multicultural literary sources are unusually enriched by Céline's subsequent scientific and medical training, from the early amateur biological research, giving rise to the metaphor of the later 'agité de la bocale', through the concern with obstetrics and hygiene which inform *Semmelweis*, the medical polemics and the anti-Semitism, to the crucial professional interest in Freud, which permits the semi-parodic play on the Oedipus myth in *Mort à crédit*. Finally, Céline is exceptionally if again selectively informed on aspects of painting and music which are exploited both in the fiction and the illustrations of his technique, as in *Entretiens avec le Professeur Y*. Here, the high cultural meets the popular or at least the middle-brow, the choice of the petite-bourgeoisie on its way to extinction. Echoes of Couperin, Mozart and Puccini are joined by those of Offenbach and popular song; recurrent images from Brueghel, Bosch, Impressionist technique and Modernists like Jongkind are supported by reflections of popular painting such as *Crédit est mort*, Millet's *Angélus* or Willette's *Parce Domine*.

It is essential to emphasize not merely Céline's cultural knowledge, awareness and exploitation, but also the fact that he was by no means as isolated or monstrous a figure in French literature as he is often portrayed. In fact, in many respects, his writing was a product of a particular era and typical of a certain style. He was hardly untypical of French cultural production in the immediate aftermath of the First World War, in which, like Drieu la Rochelle, Bernanos, Barbusse, Mac Orlan, Cendrars, Dorgelès and so many others, he had served, and whose peace-time disorientation was joined by that of a younger generation, that of Malraux, Marcel Arland and Saint-Exupéry. In this respect, Céline's writing up to and including *Voyage au bout de la nuit* is symptomatic of the French 'nouveau mal du siècle', that neo-Romantic response to a lost world of military heroism which reflected in the 1920s the despair felt by the generation of 1815 at the disappearance of Napoleon. The presence of Napoleon is a powerful one in Céline's early writing, obvious particularly in the introduction to *Semmelweis* and in

Parapine's reflections on the Emperor in *Voyage au bout de la nuit*. Once again, the emblematic Place Clichy, with its statue of the heroic Napoleonic Marshal Moncey, defines the cultural shadow under which the novel operates. Moreover, in *Semmelweis*, Céline shows himself to be perfectly aware of the two directions which the Romantic response to the Napoleonic downfall can take: the apparent sentimentalism of a Musset, present in Semmelweis' visit to Venice, or the Nietzschean exercise of the Will, illustrated by the confusion between Semmelweis' and Nietzsche's biography, and by the hero's unswerving quest for the truth. In his early pursuit of a Nietzschean project, visible in his own Napoleonic ambition for 'réussite', Céline reveals himself to be writing and thinking in the French cultural mainstream, a mainstream which would only fall apart with the confusions of the 1930s.

In this context, Céline is thematically quite recognizable as the contemporary of Malraux and the 'Absurde' and of Mac Orlan and his 'inquiétude' and 'fantastique sociale'. It is worth recalling Céline's admiration for Malraux's early fiction, especially *Les Conquérants*, reciprocated by Malraux's enthusiasm for *Voyage au bout de la nuit*.[3] At the same time, in his developing exploitation of fantasy and Freudianism, Céline coincides with the Surrealist project; in addition, as a would-be chronicler of the First World War, he joins more established figures such as Barbusse or Dorgelès; and, as a writer of 'voyages imaginaires', he shares the terrain with Cendrars, Paul Morand's *Bouddha vivant* and Malraux's *La Tentation de l'Occident*. These thematic concerns, however, are driven by a stylistic imperative. Yet, here again, Céline is by no means isolated, drawing on the earlier transcriptions and manipulations of the vernacular to be found in Vallès, Zola, Richepin and Jehan Rictus and the war novelists like Barbusse, and on the musical syncopation which he claimed to find in Morand and Mac Orlan, let alone the more radical experimentation of a James Joyce. It was his construction of a style which Céline, early on, claimed to be his abiding originality, a style which, like that of Proust, to whom he bears such an ambiguous and conscious affinity, is also the perfect means for the transcription of a particular world. Yet if Céline in the 1920s and 1930s forged his style from a blend of social, psychological and quasi-philosophical themes which he shared with many of his contemporaries, and from linguistic devices which go back to the last quarter of the nineteenth century (and, of course, further in their medieval and Shakespearean origins), he also created it crucially through his anti-Semitism from the mid-1930s onwards. Even in *Mort à crédit*, the mature Célinian style is not fully apparent. It emerges, disturbingly, only with *Bagatelles pour un massacre* and *L'Ecole des cadavres*, to the extent that Gide himself, in his review of the first pamphlet, saw it as a *tour de force* in the genre of the *exercice de style*, a polemical linguistic game, like Baudelaire's tirade against the Belgians. It is indeed here that we approach the crux of the Célinian 'scandale': it is not merely a case of a man who is at one and the same time a great writer and the holder of unacceptable political opinions, a situation which is, after all, banal, but of a great writer who sustains and furthers his literary experimentation through, and not in spite of, anti-Semitic polemic.

The empirical evidence of Céline's anti-Semitism is incontrovertible, but not particularly helpful by itself. There was undoubtedly a French anti-Semitic tradition throughout the nineteenth century which he draws on in the pamphlets; he was born and brought up when the Dreyfus Case was at its height; anti-Semitism was rife among the Parisian petite-bourgeoisie to which he and his family belonged, although there is no concrete evidence, outside of *Mort à crédit*, of anti-Semitism on the part of Fernand Destouches. It is also true that anti-Semitism was fashionable in intellectual circles until the end of the Second World War, that it constituted a powerful current of the French Left as well as the Right, and that it was intimately connected to libertarian thought, particularly of the Right. The discreet and jocular anti-Semitism of Céline in the 1920s recalled by Elizabeth Craig, therefore, would have had nothing particularly unusual or outrageous about it in his social, political and cultural context, and nor would the racism which first appears directed at the Africans in the letters from 1916 and 1917, and which is last seen in the threat of the Chinese invasion of Europe invoked in the final trilogy.

The problem is that, while these elements demonstrate the context, sources and opportunity for Céline's anti-Semitism, they do not provide any motivation for it. Nor, in this respect, are the number of psychoanalytical studies devoted to Céline, such as those by Nicole Debrie or Willy Szafran, as illuminating as one might hope.[4] More promising are the psychoanalytic readings of the texts themselves, beginning with Albert Chesneau's approach derived from Charles Maurron in *Essai de psychocritique de Louis-Ferdinand Céline*, and extending to the work of Deleuze and Guattari. One recurrent image, to be found in both Yannik Mancel and Serge André, is that of castration, to be found at its clearest in *Semmelweis*. Thus, for Serge André: 'the denial of castration is thus distributed on the two slopes of the man and his style: in saving language, in transforming it into a dancer, Céline identifies, in an increasingly theatrical way, with the invalid mother and, beyond her, with decomposition itself. Like Semmelweis, he can only finally save his mother by infecting himself mortally.'[5] Similarly, for Mancel, Céline, like Semmelweis, infects himself with his own 'écriture'. In the same way, the anti-Semitic literary project can be seen as the ultimate stage in the process of self-infection.

Attractive as this hypothesis is in its assimilation of the anti-Semitism to the self-destructive literary ambition already unveiled in *Mort à crédit*, where the narrator vows to tell such stories that his characters will return from the four corners of the world to kill him, it over-privileges the suicidal nature of the writing and, in particular, of the anti-Semitism. In fact, one of Céline's earliest North American critics, Bettina Knapp, was correct in identifying hatred as the dominating motive force in both Céline's life and work[6] and, while hatred can also imply self-hatred, it is also directed towards the dialectic identified by Arnold Mandel between the destruction and preservation of the Other. Hatred and thirst for revenge are central to both what we can perceive of Céline's own personality and, in particular, to his writing, beginning with his famous dictum that 'slang is the language of hatred.' In a letter to Albert Paraz, he confessed: 'An immense hatred keeps me alive. I'd live for a thousand years if I was sure of seeing the world go under,'[7] and we have already seen an early sign of Céline's unforgiving nature in his references to Georges Geoffroy's 'plot' in 1916. The centrality of revenge is also apparent in the anti-Semitism, with the 'quotation' from the *Almanach des Bons-Enfants* which introduces *Bagatelles pour un massacre*: 'He is naughty and he won't go to Heaven, the child who dies without settling all his accounts.'

Powerful as hatred and revenge are as fuel for Céline's survival and literature, they are in fact only components of a wider preoccupation, which has to do with power. Throughout his life, Céline was fascinated by men of power, however much he later attempted to disguise it through irony: from the early letter to Simone Saintu from Nice describing his fictitious encounter with the Emperor Franz Joseph to his depiction of the grandees of Vichy in exile in Sigmaringen. In the early years, it goes hand in hand with the Napoleonic ambition for 'réussite', translated into the careful cultivation of patronage, both in the scientific and medical career of the 1920s and in his literary début. In sexual terms, it also coincides with Céline's predilection for voyeurism, since the voyeur, as a detached observer, is in the position of supreme power. Yet Céline's relationship with power is characteristically ambiguous. He is mortified, humiliated and outraged when power is exercised against him: socially, as a member of the belle époque petite-bourgeoisie or as a failed doctor in Clichy; personally, in the cases of the Prix Goncourt, the loss of Elizabeth Craig, his relations with Grégoire Ichok, the failure of *Mort à crédit* and, most spectacularly, the *Epuration*. At the same time, and in compensation, he wields power remorselessly against his enemies and his victims: the letter breaking off his marriage to Edith Follet, the even crueller letter to Lucette Destouches from his Danish prison, his constant tormenting of Marcel Aymé and the dramatic persecution of Milton Hindus. Like the protagonist of the various fragments of *Casse-pipe*, who evolves from vulnerable new recruit to brutal NCO, the scourge of the regiment, Céline exhibits many of the characteristics of the classic bully or, in technical terms, of the Authoritarian Personality, who defers to authority when exerted from above, and exercises it ruthlessly on those below.[8] In this context, as Adorno and his team discovered in their American research of the 1940s, anti-Semitism is a key manifestation of authoritarianism. The deference of the authoritarian to those in power is compensated by a vigorous persecution and rejection of the outsider and the infiltrator. Yet, as in the case of Céline, the process is still more complex, for the Jew, for the anti-Semite, must first be perceived as a figure in authority, wielding unlimited economic, political and sexual power, so that the subsequent persecution may be portrayed as legitimate resistance. This is the logic behind Mandel's assertion that the anti-Semite *needs* the continued existence of the imaginary Jew in order to maintain his identity and deny his authoritarianism. It is for this reason that, in the pamphlets and the newspaper contributions during the Occupation, Céline is at pains to depict himself, as a typical Frenchman, as a *victim* of the Jews and, as a consequence, only reluctantly their persecutor. In other words, Céline's anti-Semitism and broader racism are symptomatic of his general power-relations and the instinctive urge to bully is legitimized through the transformation of the object of persecution into a figure of power.

While this may go some way to integrating Céline's anti-Semitism into a broader context, it is of little interest by itself unless it can also shed some light on his fictional writing. Yet it so happens that the exercise of power is crucial to Céline's concept of writing and, particularly, his notion of language. His violence is verbal and not physical: the extraordinarily exaggerated scenes of mayhem which fill *Guignol's Band* or *Féerie pour une autre fois* are stylized episodes which derive from Grand Guignol, and they exist only in language. In other words, in Céline's world, it is language which is the instrument of power, and not physical force. Why else should Ferdinand, in *Mort à crédit*, attempt to kill his father using a typewriter, a 'machine à écrire'? It is for this reason that Céline, both personally in his Sunday-morning sessions in Gen Paul's studio, and in literature in the pamphlets, used the tirade as the perfect tool of violence. Slang is not merely the language of hatred – properly used, it can be the expression of power. Nor is the access to power confined to language itself: it is at the heart of Céline's Modernist project. The description of the 'Métro émotif' in *Entretiens avec le Professeur Y*, with its emphasis upon the author/narrator who forcibly abducts and controls an entire readership, and sustains their docility through all the tricks of his style, is an unambiguous expression of literature conceived of as power. It is worth recalling in this context that not only is Modernism the language of that élite which Céline is unable socially to join in any other way, but that historically it is intimately connected with Fascism: Marinetti's Futurism provides the aesthetic blueprint for Mussolini's Italy.[9] The real 'scandal' of Céline is that his assault on 'bourgeois medicine' and its 'burlesque phantom' is also an assault on the bourgeois humanist faith in the inherent morality of art. While liberal bourgeois literature could not possibly accept that it could coexist with expressions of anti-Semitism, Céline's career is an uncomfortable reminder that great Modernist art can not merely coexist with it, but can actively exploit it.

Notes

Preface

1 Jack Murray, *The Landscapes of Alienation. Ideological Subversion in Kafka, Céline and Onetti* (Stanford, CA, 1991).
2 See: Pascal Fouché (ed.), *Vingt-cinq ans d'études céliniennes, L.-F. Céline, 5, Revue des Lettres Modernes* (Paris, 1988).
3 Patrick McCarthy, *Céline* (Harmondsworth, 1975).
4 François Gibault, *Céline I, 1894–1932: Le Temps des espérances* (Paris, 1977); *Céline II, 1932–1944: Délires et persécutions* (Paris, 1985); *Céline III: Cavalier de l'Apocalypse* (Paris, 1981).
5 Frédéric Vitoux, *La Vie de Céline* (Paris, 1988), trans. Jesse Browner as *Céline: A biography* (New York, 1994). Vitoux had previously published a study of *Voyage au bout de la nuit, Louis-Ferdinand Céline: Misère et parole* (Paris, 1973), a volume on *Bébert, le chat de Louis-Ferdinand Céline* (Paris, 1976) and another general study, *Céline* (Paris, 1978).
6 Philippe Alméras, *Céline: Entre haines et passion* (Paris, 1994).
7 Henri Godard, *Céline scandale* (Paris, 1994).
8 Ibid., pp. 24–5.
9 See: Alice Yaeger Kaplan, *Relevé des sources et citations dans 'Bagatelles pour un massacre'* (Tusson, 1987); *Reproductions of Banality: Fascism, literature and French intellectual life* (Minneapolis, 1986); Yves Pagès, *Les Fictions de politique chez L.-F. Céline* (Paris, 1994).
10 Robert Poulet, *Ce n'est pas une vie* (Paris, 1976), p. 158.

Chapter 1: A Parisian Childhood

1 Louis-Ferdinand Céline, *D'un château l'autre, Romans* II (Paris, 1974), p. 3. See Vitoux, *Céline: A biography*, p. 3.
2 See, for example, François Gibault, *Céline I, 1894–1932: Le Temps des espérances*, p. 36.

3   Letter to Albert Parz, 4 October 1947, *Cahiers Céline*, 6, p. 35, quoted in Gibault I, p. 37. In a later letter to Paraz, dated 9 December 1947, he refers to Alfred de Vigny's residence in Courbevoie, suggesting that the Vigny-sur-Seine of *Voyage au bout de la nuit* was transposed from the suburb in which he was born. See *Cahiers Céline*, 6, p. 46.

4   Quoted in Vitoux, p. 4.

5   Interview with Marc Laudelout, *Bulletin Célinien*, quoted in Alméras, p. 344.

6   Gibault I, p. 32.

7   Ibid., p. 33.

8   See ibid., p. 33.

9   See Alméras, pp. 11–12.

10   See Gibault I, p. 22.

11   Alméras, p. 57.

12   Letter to Simone Saintu, 30 October 1916, *Cahiers Céline*, 4, p. 144, quoted in Alméras, p. 55.

13   See Roger Nimier, *Le Grand d'Espagne* (Paris, 1950).

14   See Gibault I, pp. 24–5.

15   Letter to Simone Saintu, 28 October 1916, *Cahiers Céline*, 4, quoted in Gibault I, p. 26.

16   Louis-Ferdinand Céline, *Guignol's Band*, I, in *Romans*, 3 (Paris, 1988), p. 85.

17   See Gibault I, p. 27.

18   Ibid., pp. 29–31.

19   Ibid., p. 19.

20   Ibid., pp. 53–4.

21   Ibid., pp. 20–1.

22   'Entretiens avec Jean Guénot et Jacques Darribehaude', in Jean-Pierre Dauphin and Henri Godard (eds), *Cahiers Céline*, 2, *Céline et l'actualité littéraire, 1957–1961*, (Paris, 1976), p. 165, quoted in Gibault I, p. 21.

23   See Gibault I, p. 31.

24   Letter to Albert Paraz, 4 October 1947, *Cahiers Céline*, 6, p. 35, quoted in Gibault I, p. 40 and Vitoux, p. 24.

25   Ibid., p. 41.

26   Alméras, p. 13.

27   Anthony Sutcliffe, *The Autumn of Central Paris* (London, 1970).

28   Philippe Ariès, *Histoire des populations françaises et de leurs attitudes devant la vie depuis le XVIIIe siècle* (Paris, 1948), pp. 293–4.

29   Ibid., pp. 294–5.

30   See Lenard R. Berlanstein, *The Working People of Paris, 1871–1914* (Baltimore, MD and London, 1984), pp. 12–13.

31   Ibid., pp. 5–9.

32   See Maurice Crubellier (avec la collaboration de Maurice Agulhon), 'Les Citadins et leurs cultures', in Georges Duby (ed.), *Histoire de la France urbaine*, 4, *La Ville de l'âge industriel: le cycle haussmannien* (ed. Maurice Agulhon), (Paris, 1983), p. 395.

33   See Berlanstein, p. 49.

34   Ibid., p. 49.

35   Ariès, p. 292.

36   Ibid., p. 302.

37   See Guy P. Palmade, *Capitalisme et capitalistes français au XIXe siècle* (Paris, 1961), p. 237.

38 See Berlanstein, pp. 15–19.
39 Yves Lequin, 'Les Citadins, les classes et les luttes sociales', in Maurice Agulhon, p. 539.
40 Ibid., p. 541.
41 Ibid., p. 543.
42 Ibid., p. 547.
43 Ibid., p. 557.
44 Gibault I, p. 49.
45 See Berlanstein.
46 Berlanstein, p. 65.
47 Lequin, p. 552.
48 Ibid., p. 552.
49 Berlanstein, pp. 120–1.
50 Ibid., p. 121.
51 Walter Benjamin, 'Paris, the Capital of the Nineteenth Century', in *Charles Baudelaire. A Lyric Poet in an Age of High Capitalism*, trans. Harry Zohn (London, 1973), pp. 157–8.
52 Ibid., p. 160.
53 See, for example, George Melly and Michael Woods, *The Paris of the Surrealists* (London, 1991).
54 Gibault I, p. 51.
55 Ibid., pp. 47–8.
56 Ibid., pp. 46–7.
57 Alméras, p. 12.
58 Gibault I, pp. 57–8.
59 Vitoux, p. 44.
60 Letter to Lucienne Delforges, 26 August 1935, *Cahiers Céline*, 5, p. 263, quoted in Gibault I, p. 49.
61 'Entretiens avec Jean Guénot et Jacques Darribehaude', *Cahiers Céline*, 2, p. 163, quoted in Gibault I, pp. 69–70.
62 Robert Poulet, *Mon ami Bardamu. Entretiens familiers avec Louis-Ferdinand Céline* (Paris, 1971), p. 22.
63 Quoted in Vitoux, p. 549.
64 Gibault I, pp. 47, 69.
65 Ibid., p. 34.
66 Robert Faurisson, 'A quand la libération de Céline', *Les Nouvelles littéraires*, 28 May 1973, quoted in Gibault, p. 59.
67 Marcel Brochard, 'Céline à Rennes', *L'Herne*, 3–5, 1972, p. 204.
68 Gibault I, p. 59.
69 Ibid, pp. 59–60.
70 Ibid., p. 62.
71 Henri Godard, 'Notice', Louis-Ferdinand Céline, *Romans*, IV (Paris, 1993), p. 1197.
72 See Robert Poulet, *Mon ami Bardamu*, pp. 130–1.
73 L.-F. Céline, 'Interview avec Louis Pauwels et André Brissaud', *Cahiers Céline*, 2, p. 121.
74 Ibid., p. 123, cited in Vitoux, p. 39.
75 Berlanstein, p. 65.
76 Gibault I, p. 75.
77 Ibid., p. 73.

78 Quoted in ibid., p. 77.
79 Ibid., p. 77.
80 Ibid., p. 88.
81 Ibid., pp. 91–2.
82 Ibid., p. 95.
83 L.-F. Céline, *Romans,* I (Paris, 1981), pp. 436–7.
84 L.-F. Céline, 'Interview avec Claude Bonnefoy (*Arts*)', *Cahiers Céline*, 2, p. 209.
85 See Gibault I, pp. 105–6.
86 Quoted in ibid., p. 106.
87 Ibid., p. 107.
88 Ibid., p. 109.
89 L.-F. Céline, 'Interview avec Claude Bonnefoy', p. 210.
90 See Gibault I, p. 109.
91 Quoted in ibid., p. 110.
92 Ibid., p. 112.
93 L.-F. Céline, Letter to Albert Paraz, 5 April 1951, *Cahiers Céline*, 6, pp. 319–20, quoted in Gibault I, p. 113.
94 Letter to Simone Saintu, 5 November 1916, *Cahiers Céline*, 4, pp. 147–9, quoted in Gibault I, p. 113.
95 Ibid., pp. 112–13.
96 Ibid., p. 116.

Chapter 2: National Service: The Army and the Colonies

1   See Gibault I, p. 117.
2   See Alméras, pp. 22–3.
3   See Christine Sautermeister, 'Lecture théâtrale et cinématographique de *Casse-pipe*', Sociéte des Etudes Céliniennes, *Colloque de Paris, 1979* (Paris, 1980), pp. 126–7.
4   See Jean Roman, *Paris 1890s* (London, 1961), p. 51. The problem is that, whereas Hermant's novel was published in 1887, the Duc de Chartres retired as colonel of the regiment in 1883.
5   See Yves Pagès, 'Les Précédents de "l'Anarchisme du mépris"', in *Les Fictions de politique chez L.-F. Céline* (Paris, 1994), pp. 371–88.
6   See Alméras, p. 23.
7   L.-F. Céline, 'Lettre à Roger Nimier du 1er novembre 1950 sur le 12e Cuirassier', *Romans*, 3 (Paris, 1988), p. 76.
8   L.-F. Céline, 'Interview avec Claude Bonnefoy (*Arts*)', p. 211.
9   See L.-F. Céline, 'Carnet du Cuirassier Destouches', in *Romans*, 3 (Paris, 1988), p. 74.
10 Quoted in Gibault I, p. 128.
11 See Henri Godard, 'Notice', in L.-F. Céline, *Romans*, 3, p. 881. Gibault I, p. 133, puts the date of promotion to *brigadier* as 5 August 1913 and to *Maréchal des Logis* as 5 May 1914.
12 L.-F. Céline, 'Carnet du Cuirassier Destouches', p. 73.
13 Ibid., p. 74.
14 Ibid., p. 73.
15 Ibid., p. 74.
16 'Agathon', *Ce que pensent les jeunes gens d'aujourd'hui* (Paris, 1912).

17 See Richard Griffiths, *The Reactionary Revolution* (London, 1966); for an excellent fictional evocation of the shift from the previous generation to that which would make the war in 1914, see Roger Martin du Gard's novel *Jean Barois* (Paris, 1913).
18 *Le Carnet du Cuirassier Destouches*, p. 75.
19 Ibid., p. 75.
20 See Nicholas Hewitt, *Les Maladies du siècle* (Hull, 1988), p. 12.
21 *Le Carnet du Cuirassier Destouches*, p. 75.
22 Ibid., p. 75.
23 Ibid.
24 Ibid.
25 Interview with Jean Guénot and Jacques Darribehaude, *Cahiers Céline*, 2, p. 164, cited in Vitoux, p. 63.
26 See 'Interview with Claude Bonnefoy (*Arts*)' p. 212.
27 See Alméras, pp. 28–9.
28 Letter to Louis Lecoin, Klarskovgaard, 1950, *Textes et Documents*, 1 (Paris, 1979), p. 114, quoted in Alméras, p. 30.
29 L.-F. Céline, 'Interview avec Claude Bonnefoy (*Arts*)', p. 212.
30 Ibid., p. 212.
31 Alméras, p. 31.
32 L.-F. Céline, 'Fragment inédit de *Casse-pipe*', in Dominique de Roux (ed.), *Louis-Ferdinand Céline*, 3, *Cahiers de L'Herne* (Paris, 1962), p. 167.
33 Quoted in Gibault I, p. 137.
34 Alméras, pp. 34–5.
35 Gibault I, p. 139; Alméras, p. 35.
36 Quoted in Gibault I, p. 140.
37 Alméras, p. 37.
38 Ibid., p. 39.
39 From the official record of the 7th Cavalry Division, 25 November 1914, quoted in Gibault I, p. 146.
40 Ibid., pp. 148–9.
41 Ibid., p. 154.
42 Quoted in Alméras, p. 42.
43 Ibid., p. 42.
44 Ibid., pp. 42–3.
45 Letter to Simone Saintu, 29 October 1916, *Cahiers Céline*, 4, p. 140, quoted in Alméras, p. 43.
46 See Alméras, p. 43. A copy of the final page of *L'Illustré National* from the Sigmaringen period survives, with Céline's own handwritten comment: 'Extracts from *L'Illustré National*, Paris, December 1914. If only I'd known! LF Céline'.
47 Alméras, p. 43.
48 Quoted in Gibault I, p. 159.
49 Alméras, p. 42.
50 Ibid., p. 41.
51 Ibid., p. 42.
52 Gibault I, p. 161.
53 Letter to 'N' (Cillie Pam), October 1932, in Colin Nettelbeck (ed.), *Lettres à des amies*, *Cahiers Céline*, 5 (Paris, 1979), p. 75.
54 Alméras, p. 40.
55 Ibid., p. 41.

56 Gibault I, p. 153.
57 Quoted in ibid., p. 155.
58 Ibid., pp. 157–8.
59 Alméras, p. 43.
60 Georges Charensol, *D'une rive l'autre* (Paris, 1973), p. 223.
61 Quoted in Alméras, p. 44.
62 See Georges Geoffroy, 'Céline en Angleterre', *Les Cahiers de l'Herne* (Paris, 1963), pp. 11–12; and Alméras, p. 44.
63 Ibid., pp. 11–12.
64 Quoted in Gibault I, p. 167.
65 Ibid., pp. 170–1.
66 See Alméras, pp. 44, 45.
67 See Georges Geoffroy, 'Céline en Angleterre', *L'Herne*, p. 202, quoted in Alméras, p. 45.
68 See Gibault I, p. 167.
69 Paul Morand, *Londres* (Paris, 1933), p. 65, quoted in Gibault I, p. 168.
70 See Peter Dunwoodie, 'Merveilleux, étrange et fantastique dans les romans de Louis-Ferdinand Céline', *Les Lettres Romanes*, 37/1–2 (Feb.–May 1983), pp. 82–111.
71 Jules Vallès, *La Rue à Londres* (Paris, 1951), p. 103.
72 Ibid., p. 107.
73 Ibid., p. 106.
74 See Jill Forbes, 'Symbolique de l'espace: le "Londres" célinien', *Actes du Colloque International de Paris* (Paris, 1976), pp. 27–40.
75 L.-F. Céline, *Lettres à Joseph Garcin* (Paris, 1987), p. 12.
76 Gibault I, p. 169.
77 Alméras, pp. 45–6.
78 Ibid., p. 45.
79 Ibid., p. 46.
80 See André Derval, 'Céline et les écrivains mages', *Actes du Colloque de Toulouse (5–7 juillet 1990)*, (Tusson, 1991), pp. 87–100.
81 Gibault I, p. 172.
82 Ibid., p. 177.
83 Alméras, p. 47.
84 Ibid., p. 48.
85 Gibault I, p. 176.
86 Letter to parents, 9 May 1916, *Cahiers Céline*, 4, pp. 26–7, quoted in Gibault I, p. 176.
87 Quoted in ibid., p. 189.
88 Letter to Milon, 5 February 1917, *Cahiers Céline*, 4, p. 180.
89 See letter to Fernand Destouches, Freetown, 25 May 1916, *Cahiers Céline*, 4, p. 30, quoted in Alméras, pp. 50–1.
90 Letter to Albert Milon, Lagos, 2 June 1916, *Cahiers Céline*, 4, pp. 35–6, quoted in Alméras, p. 51.
91 Ibid., p. 51.
92 Ibid., pp. 52–3.
93 Ibid., pp. 52–3.
94 Ibid., p. 51.
95 Letter to Simone Saintu, Freetown 25 May 1916, *Cahiers Céline*, 4, p. 31. In addition to a generalized racism, the correspondence from Africa contains one specific early example of Céline's anti-Semitism. In a letter to Simone

Saintu of 25 October 1916, he comments favourably on an article by Urbain
Gohier containing the reference: 'The French literature of tomorrow must be
purely French, in other words alive, healthy, carefree and comforting. It will
be more Jewish than ever, in other words morbid, mercenary, and hysterically
patriotic' (*Cahiers Céline*, 4, p. 134).

96   Alméras, p. 53.
97   Ibid., p. 59.
98   Ibid.
99   Ibid., p. 48.
100 Ibid., p. 58.
101 Ibid., p. 60.
102 Gibault I, p. 183.
103 Ibid., p. 183.
104 Ibid., pp. 180–1.
105 See letter to Simone Saintu and his parents, 30 August 1916, *Cahiers Céline*, 4,
     p. 79.
106

> Istanbul is asleep under the pale moon.
> The Bosphorus reflects a thousand silver lights.
> Alone in the great Mahomedan city
> The old muezzin is not yet in bed.
>
> His voice, repeated and accentuated by the echo,
> Announces to the city that it is already ten o'clock.
> But, from his high minaret, through a window
> He casts an indiscreet glance into a bedroom.
>
> He remains a moment dumb, struck by surprise
> And nervously caresses his long grey beard.
> Yet, faithful to his duty, he raises his voice
>
> And the astonished echo repeats three times,
> To the blushing moon and to the amazed stars,
> To Istanbul the white, that it will soon be noon.

107

> But, already slowly, the sky loses its colour.
> The rays of the setting sun, pursued by the night,
> Struggle against the dusk and still resist
> In order to veil the retreat of the fleeing sun.
>
> At the top of the black rock which dominates the woods,
> The oak still retains the fading light.
> Yet, little by little the shadows rise and take it,
> Plunging it in its turn into the all-embracing anxiety.
>
> Every hour of our lives brings also its shadow.
> The lost illusions, the rising bitterness,
> Whilst driving away hope, which will never return,
> Invade our hearts, destroy them and kill them.

108 Alméras, pp. 59–60.
109 Ibid., p. 60.
110 Letter to Simone Saintu, end April/beginning May 1916, *Cahiers Céline*, 4, p. 20.

Chapter 3: The Student of Medicine

1 L.-F. Céline, 'Interview avec Claude Bonnefoy (*Arts*)', p. 209.
2 Alméras, p. 62.
3 Gibault I, p. 202.
4 Alméras, p. 63.
5 L.-F. Céline, letter to Charles Deshayes, 29 July 1947, in *Tout Céline*, 2 (Paris, 1983), p. 92, quoted in Alméras, p. 62.
6 L.-F. Céline, *Nord*, in *Romans*, 2 (Paris, 1974), p. 519.
7 Alméras, pp. 63–4; Gibault I, pp. 192–204.
8 Gibault I, pp. 199–200.
9 Ibid., p. 200.
10 Ibid., p. 203.
11 See *Cahiers Céline*, 3 (Paris, 1977), pp. 250–2.
12 See Jean-Pierre Dauphin and Jacques Boudillet, *Album Céline* (Paris, 1977), p. 81.
13 Gibault I, p. 205.
14 Ibid., p. 206.
15 Alméras, p. 65.
16 Eugène Briau, 'Assurances sociales et tuberculose', *La Presse médicale*, 11 January 1928, p. 44.
17 Alméras, p. 65.
18 Gibault I, p. 205.
19 Alméras, p. 66.
20 For a complete account of Céline's activities in Brittany, see Jacques François, *Contribution à l'étude des années rennaises du docteur Destouches (1918–24)*, unpublished thesis for the Faculté Mixte de Médecine et de Pharmacie de Rennes, 1967.
21 Quoted in Alméras, p. 66.
22 *Ouest-Eclair*, 14 March 1918, p. 3, quoted in Gibault I, p. 209.
23 Ibid.
24 L.-F. Céline, 'Interview avec Claude Bonnefoy (*Arts*)', p. 214, quoted in Gibault I, p. 211.
25 Ibid., p. 210.
26 Ibid., pp. 212–13.
27 Ibid., p. 213.
28 L.-F. Céline, 'Interview avec Claude Bonnefoy (*Arts*)', p. 211.
29 Gibault I, p. 184.
30 Alméras, p. 67.
31 Gibault I, pp. 222–3.
32 Ibid., p. 222.
33 Alméras, p. 71.
34 Ibid., p. 71.

35   Alméras, p. 67; Gibault I, pp. 214–15.
36   Gibault I, p. 215; Alméras, p. 67.
37   Gibault I, pp. 215–17.
38   Alméras, p. 69.
39   Quoted in ibid., p. 68.
40   Gibault I, pp. 225–6; Alméras, p. 71.
41   Gibault I, p. 227; Alméras, p. 71.
42   Gibault I, p. 228.
43   Letter to Albert Milon, undated, quoted in Gibault I, p. 226.
44   Quoted in ibid., p. 226.
45   Ibid., pp. 226–7.
46   Ibid., pp. 231–2.
47   See André Lwoff in *Le Figaro littéraire*, 7–13 April 1969, pp. 4–5, quoted in Gibault I, p. 232.
48   The full text of the article is printed in *Cahiers Céline*, 3, pp. 242–4.
49   Printed in *Cahiers Céline*, 3, pp. 245–6.
50   Gibault I, p. 232.
51   André Lwoff, pp. 4–5, quoted in *Cahiers Céline*, 3, p. 242.
52   Gibault I, p. 235.
53   Quoted in ibid., p. 226.
54   Ibid., p. 226.
55   Quoted in ibid., p. 226.
56   Alméras, p. 73.
57   Gibault I, p. 236.
58   Ibid., p. 236.
59   Alméras, p. 73; Gibault I, p. 235.
60   Quoted in Alméras, p. 73.
61   Gibault I, pp. 228–9.
62   Alméras, p. 75.
63   Gibault I, p. 229.
64   Ibid., pp. 229–30.
65   Ibid., p. 229.
66   Alméras, p. 76.
67   See József Antall, 'The Life of Ignác Fülöp Semmelweis (1818–1865)', in *Pictures from the Past of the Healing Arts. A Guidebook to the Semmelweis Museum, Library and Archives* (Budapest, 1993), pp. 15–25.
68   Ibid., p. 17.
69   Ibid., p. 18.
70   Note in Semmelweis's diary, quoted in ibid., pp. 18–19.
71   Ibid., p. 20.
72   Ibid., p. 21.
73   Quoted in ibid., p. 23.
74   See Tiberius de Györy, 'Remarques sur "Les Derniers jours de Semmelweis"', *La Presse médicale*, 10 September 1924, pp. 1531–2, in *Cahiers Céline*, 3, pp. 94–6.
75   *Romans*, I, p. 51.
76   Ibid., p. 350.
77   See Alméras, p. 77.
78   'Préface à la réédition de 1936', *Cahiers Céline*, 3, p. 96.
79   Blaise Cendrars, *L'Or* (Paris, 1960), p. 21.

80   *Cahiers Céline*, 3, p. 52.
81   Ibid., p. 36.
82   Yannik Mancel, 'De la sémiotique textuelle à la théorie du "roman": Céline', *Dialectiques*, 8 (1975), p. 56.
83   *Romans*, I, p. 511.
84   *Mea culpa, suivi de Semmelweis* (Paris, 1936), p. 25.
85   Alméras, p. 77.
86   *Cahiers Céline*, 3, p. 44.
87   Ibid., p. 78.
88   Ibid., p. 72.
89   'Préface à la réédition de 1936', *Cahiers Céline*, 3, p. 96.
90   *Cahiers Céline*, 3, p. 22.
91   Ibid, p. 23.
92   See André Malraux, *La Tentation de l'Occident* (Paris, 1924), p. 95. 'Nous avons tous senti la fraîcheur et la brume d'Austerlitz.' Céline's extended reflection on Romanticism in *Semmelweis* includes evocations of both its heroic, Hugolian mode and its sentimental current exemplified by Musset, to whom he makes constant reference in the correspondence from Africa with Simone Saintu. Indeed, Semmelweis' 'sentimental journey' to Venice in Céline's narrative has precise echoes of Musset's own travels.
93   Ibid., p. 19. 'Mirabeau shouted so loudly that Versailles was afraid.'
94   Ibid., p. 19.
95   Ibid., p. 20.
96   Ibid.
97   Ibid., p. 21.
98   Ibid.
99   L.-F. Céline, 'Les derniers jours de Semmelweis', *Cahiers Céline*, 3, p. 82.
100 Quoted in Gibault I, p. 240.
101 Ibid., pp. 240–1.
102 Ibid., p. 241.
103 See 'Interview avec Claude Bonnefoy (*Arts*)', *Cahiers Céline*, 2, p. 215.
104 Gibault I, p. 241.
105 Ibid., pp. 241–2.
106 Ibid., p. 242.
107 Quoted in ibid., p. 243.
108 Ibid.
109 Quoted in ibid., p. 244.
110 Ibid.
111 Alméras, p. 75.

Chapter 4: The League of Nations

1   Gibault I, p. 248.
2   Alméras, p. 80.
3   For a biography of Rajchman, see Marta Aleksandra Balinska, *Une Vie pour humanitaire. Ludwig Rajchman, 1881–1965* (Paris, 1995).
4   Gibault I, p. 247.

5   Vitoux, p. 141.
6   Gibault I, p. 248.
7   Balinska, p. 176.
8   Ibid., p. 180.
9   Alméras, p. 82.
10 Ibid., p. 82.
11 Quoted in ibid., p. 80.
12 Quoted in ibid., p. 81.
13 Ibid.
14 Ibid., p. 81.
15 L.-F. Céline, *La Quinine en thérapeutique*, in *Oeuvres de Louis-Ferdinand Céline*, I (Paris, 1966), p. 631.
16 Ibid., p. 632.
17 Vitoux, p. 142.
18 Ibid.
19 Ibid., p. 150.
20 Quoted in Alméras, p. 82.
21 Letter of 24 February 1925, quoted in Gibault I, p. 256.
22 Letter of 26 February 1925, quoted in Gibault I, pp. 257–8.
23 Ibid., p. 258.
24 Ibid., pp. 258–62, 323–8.
25 L.-F. Céline, 'Louisiane', *Cahiers Céline*, 3, p. 114.
26 Quoted in Gibault I, p. 260.
27 L.-F. Céline, *Romans*, I, pp. 188–91.
28 L.-F. Céline, *Mea Culpa* (Paris, 1936), pp. 14–15.
29 *Cahiers de l'Herne*, p. 151, quoted in Gibault I, pp. 261–2.
30 Henri Mondor, 'Avant-propos', in L.-F. Céline, *Romans*, I (Paris, 1962), p. ix.
31 See Jacques Portes, 'Les Etats-Unis dans les manuels d'histoire et de géographie de la IIIème République (1871–1914)', *Revue d'Histoire Moderne et Contemporaine*, 1981, pp. 196–206.
32 See Claude Fohlen, *La France de l'entre-deux-guerres (1917–39)* (Paris, 1966), pp. 73–88.
33 See Charles S. Maier, 'Between Taylorism and Technocracy', *Journal of Contemporary History*, 5/2 (1970), p. 36.
34 Ibid., pp. 59–60.
35 Quoted in Oliver Targowla, *Les Médecins aux mains sales* (Paris, 1976), pp. 84–5.
36 Antonio Gramsci, 'Americanism and Fordism', in *Selections from the Prison Notebooks* (London, 1971), p. 302.
37 Ibid., p. 310.
38 L.-F. Céline, 'Note sur l'organisation sanitaire des usines Ford à Detroit', *Cahiers Céline*, 3, p. 122.
39 Ibid., pp. 124–5.
40 Ibid., p. 123.
41 Ibid., p. 126.
42 Ibid., p. 129.
43 Ibid., p. 130.
44 Ibid.
45 Alméras, p. 85.

46 L.-F. Céline, 'Notes sur le service sanitaire de la compagnie Westinghouse à Pittsburgh', *Cahiers Céline*, 3, p. 135.
47 Ibid., p. 131.
48 Ibid., p. 132.
49 Ibid.
50 *Cahiers Céline*, 3, p. 136.
51 Alméras, p. 86.
52 *Cahiers Céline*, 3, p. 137.
53 Quoted in Gibault I, p. 263.
54 Ibid., pp. 263–5.
55 Ibid., p. 264.
56 Quoted in Alméras, p. 87.
57 Quoted in Gibault I, p. 266.
58 Alméras, p. 87.
59 Gibault I, p. 267.
60 Ibid., p. 267.
61 Alméras, p. 86.
62 Quoted in Gibault I, p. 270.
63 Ibid., p. 271.
64 Ibid., p. 272.
65 Ibid.
66 Ibid.
67 Ibid., p. 273.
68 Vitoux, p. 153.
69 Quoted in Gibault I, p. 273.
70 Alphonse Juilland, *Elizabeth and Louis: Elizabeth Craig talks about Louis-Ferdinand Céline* (Stanford, CA, 1991), p. 400.
71 Ibid., p. 372.
72 Ibid., pp. 60–1.
73 According to Alphonse Juilland's calculations. See ibid., p. 485.
74 Ibid., p. 485.
75 Alméras, p. 97.
76 Juilland, p. 397.
77 See Colin Nettelbeck (ed.), *Lettres à des amies*, *Cahiers Céline*, 5 (Paris, 1979).
78 Alméras, p. 92.
79 Letter of July 7 1947, in Milton Hindus, *The Crippled Giant: A literary relationship with Louis-Ferdinand Céline* (Hanover, NH and London, 1986), p. 107.
80 Alméras, p. 92.
81 Quoted in ibid., p. 91.
82 Ibid.
83 Quoted in ibid., p. 91.
84 Ibid., p. 92.
85 Ibid., p. 98.
86 Quoted in Gibault I, p. 274.
87 See Paul-Louis Mignon, *Charles Dullin* (Lyon, 1990).
88 *L'Intransigeant*, 1 July 1933, quoted in Vitoux, p. 155.
89 Ibid.
90 Alméras, p. 92.
91 'Note de l'éditeur', L.-F. Céline, *Progrès* (Paris, 1978), unpaginated.
92 Alméras, p. 92.

93 See Nicholas Hewitt, 'Céline and Shakespeare', in Holgar Klein and Jean-Marie Maguin (eds), *Shakespeare and France, Shakespeare Yearbook*, 5 (Lampeter, 1994), pp. 131–46.
94 Gibault I, p. 274.
95 Quoted in ibid., p. 274.
96 L.-F. Céline, *L'Eglise* (Paris, 1952), p. 166.
97 'Entretiens avec Jean Guénot et Jacques Darribehaude', *Cahiers Céline*, 2, p. 164.
98 L.-F. Céline, *Bagatelles pour un massacre* (Paris, 1937), pp. 102–3.
99 Gibault I, p. 275. Marta Belinska, p. 177, also asserts that Céline read the manuscript of *L'Eglise* to Maria Rajchman.
100 Alméras, p. 91.
101 Alphonse Juilland, *Elizabeth and Louis: Elizabeth Craig talks about Louis-Ferdinand Céline* (Stanford, CA, 1991), p. 200.
102 'Sometimes he'd make fun of the Jews: "Oh, he's a cute little Jew!" or "Oh, he's a funny little Jew!"', ibid., p. 201.
103 See Marta Belinska, p. 180.
104 L.-F. Céline, *Bagatelles pour un massacre*, p. 73.
105 L.-F. Céline, *L'Eglise*, pp. 86–7.
106 Ibid., p. 223.
107 Ibid., p. 221.
108 Gibault I, p. 277.
109 Ibid., p. 277.
110 Alméras, p. 97.
111 Vitoux, p. 162.
112 Ibid.
113 *Bagatelles pour un massacre*, pp. 100–1.
114 Gibault I, p. 277.
115 Ibid., p. 278.
116 Ibid., pp. 277–8.
117 Vitoux, p. 165.
118 Ibid.
119 Robert Debré, *Cahiers de l'Herne*, 3, p. 19, quoted in ibid., p. 163.

Chapter 5: Clichy and Montmartre

1 See Jean de Boisline, *Banlieue mon amour* (Paris, 1995), p. 23.
2 Ibid., p. 26.
3 Ibid., pp. 49–50.
4 Berlanstein, *The Working People of Paris*, p. 47.
5 See Donald Reid, *Sewers and Sewermen* (Cambridge, MA, 1991).
6 See Marc Gaillard, *Les Belles Heures de Clichy* (Amiens, 1992), p. 146.
7 See Société Historique et Archéologique de Clichy (SHAC), *Clichy-la-Garenne: Vingt siècles d'histoire* (Paris, 1974), p. 96.
8 Ibid., p. 94.
9 See Gaillard, *Les Belles Heures de Clichy*, p. 146.
10 Ibid., p. 114.

11 See Pierre Caraz, *Mémoire en images: Clichy-la-Garenne* (Joué-les-Tours, 1997), p. 120.
12 Gaillard, pp. 129–30.
13 SHAC, *Clichy-la-Garenne*, p. 96.
14 Gaillard, p. 130.
15 Ibid.
16 SHAC, *Clichy-la-Garenne*, p. 96.
17 See Joseph Bordiga, *Fonctionnement d'une consultation de médecine préventitive pour enfants d'âge scolaire: thèse de médecine* (Paris, 1937); Julius Weber, *Un Centre de triage de la tuberculose, fonctionnement du service et de la consultation de l'Hôpital Beaujon à Clichy, étude critique: thèse de médecine et de doctorat* (Paris, 1937).
18 Gaillard, *Les Belles Heures de Clichy*, p. 148.
19 Ibid., p. 130.
20 SHAC, *Clichy-la-Garenne*, p. 99.
21 Robert de Saint-Jean, *Journal d'un journaliste* (Paris, 1974), p. 109. The entry is for 22 February 1933. *La Garçonne* is the title of the scandalous novel published by the left-wing writer Victor Margueritte in 1922, which describes the quest for sexual independence of a liberated young woman.
22 L.-F. Céline, 'La Santé publique en France', *Monde*, 8 March 1930.
23 Gibault I, p. 280; Vitoux, p. 165.
24 Jeanne Carayon, 'Le Docteur écrit un roman', *Cahiers de l'Herne*, 3, pp. 20–1, translated in Vitoux, p. 167.
25 Gibault I, p. 280.
26 See Theodore Zeldin, *France 1848–1945*, I, *Ambition, Love and Politics* (Oxford, 1973), p. 37.
27 See Jeanne Singer-Kérel, *Le Coût de la vie à Paris de 1840 à 1954* (Paris, 1961), p. 409.
28 Quoted in *Cahiers Céline*, 3, p. 138. The date is given in Gibault I, p. 281.
29 Ibid., p. 138.
30 Ibid.
31 Gibault I, p. 281.
32 See Olivier Targowla, *Les Médecins aux mains sales* (Paris, 1976), p. 24.
33 Ibid., p. 30.
34 Ibid., p. 44.
35 Ibid., p. 121.
36 Quoted in ibid., p. 100.
37 Quoted in ibid., p. 102.
38 P. Desfosses, 'Quelques réflexions sur les Assurances Sociales', *La Presse médicale*, 87 (29 October 1927), p. 1325.
39 F. Jayle, 'Le Congrès des syndicats médicaux de France', *La Presse médicale*, 94 (23 November 1927), p. 1435.
40 Ibid.
41 P. Desfosses, 'La Question des Assurances Sociales', *La Presse médicale*, 3 (11 January 1928), p. 43.
42 See 'Congrès de syndicats médicaux', *La Presse médicale*, 11 (8 February 1928), p. 172.
43 Eugène Briau, 'Assurances sociales et tuberculose', *La Presse médicale*, 3 (11 January 1928), p. 44; 'Assurances sociales et syphilis', *La Presse médicale*, 11 (8 February 1928), pp. 171–2.
44 Briau, 'Assurances sociales et syphilis', p. 172.

45 Dr P. Specklin, 'Les Répercussions des Assurances Sociales sur l'exercice de la médecine', *La Presse médicale*, 5 (16 January 1929), p. 79.

46 L.-F. Céline, 'A propos du service sanitaire des usines Ford à Detroit', *Bulletins et Mémoires de la Société de Médecine de Paris*, 10, Session of 26 May 1928, *Cahiers Céline*, 3, p. 142.

47 Ibid., p. 146.

48 Ibid., p. 151.

49 Ibid., p. 149.

50 Ibid., p. 150.

51 L.-F. Céline, 'Les Assurances sociales et une politique économique de la santé publique', *La Presse médicale* (24 November 1928), p. 1499, quoted in *Cahiers Céline*, 3, p. 155.

52 *Cahiers Céline*, 3, p. 157.

53 Ibid., p. 159.

54 Ibid., p. 160.

55 Ibid., p. 161.

56 Ibid., p. 165.

57 See Guy Thuillier, 'Hygiène corporelle aux XIXe et XXe siècles', *Annales de Démographie Historique* (1975), p. 124.

58 L.-F. Céline, 'La Médecine chez Ford', *Lectures*, 40/4 (1 August 1941), pp. 6–9; 5 (15 August 1941), p. 6; 'Les Idées de L.-F. Céline sur 'la médecine standard'', *Le Concours Médical*, 7 (15 February 1942).

59 See Charles S. Maier, 'Between Taylorism and Technocracy', *Journal of Contemporary History*, 5/2 (1970), p. 59.

60 Vitoux, p. 168.

61 Gibault I, p. 282.

62 Ibid.

63 Florence Gould was a visitor, with Marie Bell, to the apartment in the Rue Girardon during the Occupation.

64 L.-F. Céline, 'Essai de diagnostique et de thérapeutique méthodiques *en série* sur certains malades d'un dispensaire', *Bulletins et Mémoires de la Société de Médecine de Paris*, Session of 22 March 1930, pp. 163–8, reprinted in *Cahiers Céline*, 3, pp. 170–7. Céline's figures of 2200 new patients admitted annually seem fairly reliable. From its opening on 8 January 1929 to 1 January 1934, the 'dispensaire' in the Rue Fanny saw roughly 250,000 patients, while the Assistance Sociale de Clichy, which started off in 1930 with only 1242 cases, saw that number expand to 23,409 by 1934. See SHAC, *Clichy-la-Garenne*, p. 96.

65 *Cahiers Céline*, 3, p. 171.

66 Ibid.

67 Ibid., p. 177.

68 Gibault I, p. 284.

69 Ibid., pp. 283–4.

70 Ibid., p. 285.

71 Ibid., p. 284.

72 Ibid., pp. 285–7.

73 See Robert Poulet, *Mon ami Bardamu*, pp. 91–2. See Gibault I, p. 286.

74 Gibault I, pp. 286–7.

75 Quoted in ibid., p. 287.

76 Poulet, pp. 91–2. See Gibault I, p. 286.

77 Quoted in Gibault I, p. 288.

78   Ibid., p. 289.
79   Quoted in ibid., p. 289.
80   Quoted in ibid., p. 290.
81   Ibid.
82   Letter to Dr Boudreau, 16 July 1929, quoted in Gibault I, p. 290.
83   Jeanne Carayon, 'Le Docteur écrit un roman', *Cahiers de l'Herne*, 3, p. 22, quoted in Vitoux, p. 169.
84   Vitoux, p. 174.
85   Henri Mahé, *La Brinquebale avec Céline* (Paris, 1969), p. 24, translated in ibid., p. 175.
86   Mahé, p. 24.
87   Louis Chevalier, *Montmartre du plaisir et du crime* (Paris, 1980).
88   See Nicholas Hewitt, 'The Geography of Pleasure: Montmartre and Ninteenth-Century Paris', in John Ferris and Jaroslav Machacek (eds), *The European City in the Ninteenth Century* (Prague, 1995), pp. 1–21.
89   L.-F. Céline, *Mea culpa* (Paris, 1936), p. 9.
90   See L.-F. Céline, *Voyage au bout de la nuit*, in *Romans*, I (Paris, 1981), p. 217; Louis Chevalier, pp. 446–52.
91   See Nicholas Hewitt, 'Images of Montmartre in French Writing 1920–1960: "La Bohème Réactionnaire"', *French Cultural Studies*, 4 (1993), pp. 120–43.
92   L.-F. Céline, *Bagatelles pour un massacre*, p. 216.
93   Ibid.
94   L.-F. Céline, *Maudits soupirs pour une autre fois* (Paris, 1985), pp. 135–6.
95   Marcel Aymé, preface to Jean Vertex, *Le Village inspiré* (Paris, 1950), p. 6.
96   Paul Yaki, *Le Montmartre de nos vingt ans* (Paris, 1933), pp. 174–5.
97   Ibid.
98   Géo Cim, *Montmartre mon vieux village* (Paris, 1964), p. 56.
99   Georges Charensol, *D'une rive l'autre*, p. 223.
100   Jean Vertex, *Le Village inspiré*, p. 184.
101   Alméras, p. 101.
102   Gibault I, p. 298.
103   Alméras, p. 101.
104   Alphonse Juilland, *Elizabeth and Louis: Elizabeth Craig talks about Louis-Ferdinand Céline*, pp. 121–3.
105   Ibid., p. 123.
106   L.-F. Céline, letter of 18 June 1930, in *Lettres à Joseph Garcin (1929–1938), Texte établi et présenté par Pierre Lainé* (Paris, 1987), p. 27.
107   Juilland, p. 123.
108   Gibault I, p. 283.
109   Ibid., p. 283.
110   Vitoux, p. 176.
111   Ibid.
112   Ibid. For an annotated edition of *'31' Cité d'Antin*, see Eric Mazet (ed.), *'31' Cité d'Antin* (Tusson, 1988).
113   Alméras, p. 101.
114   Gibault I, p. 297.
115   Vitoux, pp. 176–7.
116   Ibid., p. 177, and Henri Mahé, *La Brinquebale avec Céline*.
117   Ibid., p. 177, and Mahé, *La Brinquebale avec Céline*.
118   See Juilland, ch. 4: 'Elizabeth the Lover', pp. 89–116.

119 Vitoux, p. 177.
120 See Pierre Lainé, 'Préface', in L.-F. Céline, *Lettres à Joseph Garcin*, p. 11; Vitoux, pp. 191–3.
121 Letter of 1 September 1929, p. 17.
122 Ibid., p. 25.
123 Letter of 24 July 1931, p. 48.
124 Letter of mardi (September 1930), p. 31.
125 Letter of 4 August 1930, p. 29.
126 Letter of 15 October 1930, p. 35.
127 See Pierre Lainé, 'Des modèles et de la genèse', in L.-F. Céline, *Lettres à Joseph Garcin*, p. 98.
128 Ibid., p. 101.
129 Ibid., p. 107.
130 Quoted in Lainé, p. 101.
131 Gibault I, p. 292.
132 Philippe Roussin, 'Getting back from the Other World: from Doctor to Author', in Alice Kaplan and Philippe Roussin (eds), *Céline USA*, Special Number of *South Atlantic Quarterly*, 93/2 (Spring 1994), p. 251.
133 Gibault I, p. 292.
134 Ibid., pp. 292–3.
135 Letter to Dr Boudreau of 1 May 1931, quoted in Gibault I, p. 294.
136 Ibid., p. 293.
137 Quoted in Gibault I, p. 293.
138 L.-F. Céline, 'Mémoire pour le Cours des Hautes Etudes', *Cahiers Céline*, 3, p. 189.
139 Ibid., p. 188.
140 L.-F. Céline, 'La Santé Publique en France', *Monde*, 8 March 1930, reprinted in *Céline: Textes et documents*, I (Paris, 1979), pp. 37–50.
141 Ibid., p. 45.
142 See Nicholas Hewitt, *The Golden Age of Louis-Ferdinand Céline* (Leamington Spa, 1987), pp. 29–34.
143 Letter to Henri Mahé, *La Brinquebale avec Céline*, p. 47, cited in Vitoux, p. 195.
144 Vitoux, pp. 202–6.
145 Erika Irrgang, *Cahiers de l'Herne*, pp. 62–4.
146 Gibault I, pp. 300–1.

Chapter 6: *Voyage au bout de la nuit*

1 Leon Trotsky, 'Céline et Poincaré', in *Louis-Ferdinand Céline, L'Herne*, 5 (Paris, 1965), p. 146.
2 Max Descaves, 'Le Dr Georges Duhamel, Prix Goncourt sous un pseudonyme en 1918, aura-t-il un émule tout à l'heure?', *Paris-Midi*, 7 December 1932, pp. 1–2, reprinted in J.-P. Dauphin and H. Godard (eds), *Cahiers Céline*, 1, *Céline et l'actualité littéraire 1932–1957* (Paris, 1976), p. 24.
3 Jeanne Carayon, 'Le Docteur écrit un roman', p. 21.
4 Alphonse Juilland, *Elizabeth et Louis*, p. 123.
5 L.-F. Céline, *Lettres à la NRF*, ed. Pascal Fouché (Paris, 1991), p. 9.
6 Ibid.
7 L.-F. Céline, *Lettres à Joseph Garcin*, p. 50. Letter of 13 December 1931.

8   Ibid., n. 1.

9   Max Descaves, 'Le Dr Georges Duhamel', p. 24.

10 Gibault I, p. 310.

11 Henri Godard, 'Notice', *Romans* IV, pp. 1354–86.

12 Vitoux, p. 186.

13 Gibault I, p. 310.

14 L.-F. Céline, *Lettres à Joseph Garcin*, p. 48.

15 Madeleine Chapsal, 'Voyage au bout de la haine . . . avec L.-F. Céline', *L'Express*, 14 June 1957, reprinted in *Cahiers Céline*, 3, p. 23, quoted in Vitoux, p. 187.

16 André Parinaud, 'L.-F. Céline: "Il faut de la pudeur quand on est romancier"', *Arts*, 12–18 July 1961; 'La dernière interview de Céline', *Almanach de Radio-Télé Luxembourg*, 1962, reprinted in *Cahiers Céline*, 2, p. 189.

17 Elizabeth Porquerol, 'Céline, il y a trente ans', *La Nouvelle Revue Française*, 105 (1 September 1961), reprinted in *Cahiers Céline*, 1, p. 46.

18 Claude Bonnefoy, 'Dernier adieu à sa jeunesse. Quelques semaines avant sa mort L.-F. Céline a raconté l'histoire de ses vingt ans', *Arts*, August 1961, reprinted in *Cahiers Céline*, 2, p. 214.

19 Vitoux, p. 188.

20 Olivier Bernier, *Fireworks at Dusk: Paris in the Thirties* (Boston, 1993), p. 199.

21 Elizabeth Porquerol, 'Céline, il y a trente ans', p. 46.

22 André Parinaud, 'L.-F. Céline: "Il faut de la pudeur quand on est romancier"', p. 189.

23 L.-F. Céline, *Lettres à la NRF*, p. 15.

24 Vitoux, p. 196.

25 Gibault I, p. 311.

26 L.-F. Céline, *Lettres à la NRF*, p. 9.

27 Milton Hindus, *The Crippled Giant*, p. 112.

28 Alméras, p. 110.

29 Vitoux, p. 197.

30 Ibid., p. 198.

31 Paul Vialar, 'L'Histoire extraordinaire de L.-F. Céline', *Les Annales Politiques et littéraires*, 9 December 1932, reprinted in *Cahiers Céline*, 1, p. 34.

32 Max Dorian, 'Céline rue Amélie', in *Louis-Ferdinand Céline, L'Herne*, 3 (Paris, 1963), p. 26.

33 Robert Poulet, *Mon ami Bardamu*, pp. 50–2. See Vitoux, pp. 199–200.

34 Ibid., p. 26.

35 Alméras, p. 111.

36 Ibid., p. 112.

37 Vitoux, p. 200.

38 Alméras, p. 113.

39 See, for example, Elizabeth Porquerol, 'Céline, il y a trente ans', pp. 45–6.

40 Vitoux, p. 201.

41 Ibid.

42 Gibault I, p. 315.

43 Quoted in Vitoux, p. 211.

44 On the 'Goncourt Affair' see, for example: Pierre-Edmond Robert, *Céline et les Editions Denoël* (Paris, 1991); Georges Ravan, *L'Académie Goncourt en dix couverts* (Paris, 1943); Roger Gouze, *Les Bêtes à Goncourt. Un demi-siècle de batailles littéraires* (Paris, 1973).

45 Alméras, p. 119.

46 Vitoux, p. 218.
47 Quoted in ibid., p. 220.
48 Ibid.
49 Ibid., p. 212.
50 Ibid., p. 222.
51 Ibid., p. 213.
52 Ibid., pp. 213, 221–2.
53 Ibid., pp. 212–13.
54 Ibid., pp. 213–14.
55 Trotsky, 'Céline et Poincaré', p. 146.
56 Paul Nizan, *L'Humanité*, 9 December 1932, reprinted in *Louis-Ferdinand Céline*, *L'Herne*, 5, p. 145.
57 See Jean-Pierre Dauphin and Henri Godard, 'Avant-propos', *Cahiers Céline*, 1, *Céline et l'actualité littéraire 1932–57*, pp. 9–10. For a summary of Céline's interviews after the publication of *Voyage au bout de la nuit*, see: Gibault II, pp. 63–6.
58 See, for example, Georges Altman, 'Les "Goncourt" avaient un grand livre, ils ne l'ont pas choisi ... Rencontre avec L.-F. Céline, médecin et auteur de *Voyage au bout de la nuit*', *Monde*, 10 December 1932, reprinted in *Cahiers Céline*, 1, p. 35: 'He's a tall, blonde man, a bit shabby, a bit stooping.'
59 Elizabeth Porquerol, 'Céline, il y a trente ans', p. 44.
60 Robert de Saint-Jean, *Journal d'un journaliste*, reprinted in *Cahiers Céline*, 1, p. 49.
61 Victor Molitor, 'Chez Céline, le sombre flagelleur de l'humanité', *Les Cahiers Luxembourgeois*, 1933, reprinted in *Cahiers Céline*, 1, p. 41.
62 Robert de Saint-Jean, *Journal d'un journaliste*, p. 51.
63 Paul Vialar, 'L'Histoire extraordinaire de L.-F. Céline', *Les Annales politiques et littéraires*, 9 December 1932, reprinted in *Cahiers Céline*, 1, p. 33.
64 Georges Altman, 'Les "Goncourt"', p. 35.
65 Pierre-Jean Launay, 'L.-F. Céline le révolté', *Paris-Soir*, 10 November 1932, reprinted in *Cahiers Céline*, 1, p. 22.
66 Elizabeth Porquerol, 'Céline, il y a trente ans', pp. 45–6.
67 Paul Vialar, 'L'Histoire extraordinaire de L.-F. Céline', p. 32.
68 Pierre-Jean Launay, 'L.-F. Céline le révolté', p. 21.
69 Georges Altman, 'Les "Goncourt"', p. 38.
70 Max Descaves, 'Le Dr Georges Duhamel', p. 24.
71 Alméras, p. 121.
72 Merry Bromberger, 'Le Prix Théophraste Renaudot', *Cahiers Céline*, 1, p. 30.
73 Ibid., p. 31.
74 Elizabeth Porquerol, 'Céline, il y a trente ans', p. 48.
75 Léon Daudet, 'L.-F. Céline: *Voyage au bout de la nuit*', *Candide*, 22 December 1932, quoted in Gibault II, p. 47.
76 For examples of this approach, see Wayne Burns, *Enfin Céline vint* (New York, 1988); James Flynn (ed.), *Understanding Céline* (Seattle, WA, 1984).
77 Pierre-Jean Launay, 'L.-F. Céline le révolté', p. 21.
78 Ibid., p. 22.
79 Merry Bromberger, 'Le Prix Théophraste Renaudot', p. 30.
80 Ibid., pp. 30–1.
81 Ibid., p. 31.
82 Georges Altman, 'Les "Goncourt"', p. 38.

83 Robert de Saint-Jean, '*Journal d'un journaliste*', p. 51.
84 Madeleine Chapsal, 'Voyage au bout de la haine . . . avec L.-F. Céline', *L'Express*, 14 June 1957, reprinted in *Cahiers Céline*, 2, p. 25.
85 See Henri Godard, *Poétique de Céline* (Paris, 1985).
86 Pierre-Jean Launay, 'L.-F. Céline le révolté', p. 22.
87 L.-F. Céline, *Voyage au bout de la nuit*, p. 78. See: Leo Spitzer, 'Une Habitude de style (le rappel) chez M. Céline', *Le Français moderne*, June 1935, pp. 193–208, reprinted in *Les Cahiers de l'Herne*, 1972.
88 See John Sturrock, *Céline: Journey to the End of the Night* (Cambridge, 1990), p. 33.
89 *Voyage au bout de la nuit*, p. 112.
90 Ibid., pp. 8–9.
91 Ibid., pp. 192–3.
92 Ibid., p. 9.
93 Ibid., p. 10.
94 Ibid., p. 139.
95 Ibid., p. 247.
96 Ibid., p. 248.
97 Ibid., p. 51, and Godard, *Romans* I, p. 1293.
98 *Voyage au bout de la nuit*, pp. 41–6.
99 Ibid., p. 366.
100 Ibid., p. 74.
101 Ibid., p. 167.
102 Ibid., p. 5.
103 Ibid.
104 For a full analysis of the novel as a 'Robinsonade', see Nicholas Hewitt, *The Golden Age of Louis-Ferdinand Céline* pp. 65–8.
105 *Voyage au bout de la nuit*, p. 5.
106 Ibid., p. 289.
107 Ibid., p. 437.
108 See Thomas Babington Macaulay, *The History of England from the Accession of James the Second* (London, 1913–15), pp. 563ff.
109 *Voyoge au bout de la nuit*, p. 7.
110 Ibid., p. 505.
111 Ibid., pp. 504–5.
112 Elizabeth Porquerol, 'Céline, il ya trente ans', p. 47.
113 Victor Molitor, 'Chez Céline, le sombre flagelleur de l'humanité', p. 41.
114 Henri Godard, 'Notice', *Romans* I, p. 1223.
115 See, for example, Merry Bromberger, 'Le Prix Théophraste Renaudot', p. 31.
116 Godard, 'Notice', pp. 1224–38.
117 L.-F. Céline, *Bagatelles pour un massacre*, p. 214.

Chapter 7: The 'House of Literature'

1 Gibault II, p. 40.
2 Vitoux, p. 230.
3 Ibid., p. 234.
4 Gibault II, pp. 63–4.
5 Alméras, p. 139.

6   Quoted in Vitoux, p. 230.
7   Letter of 5 October 1933, *Céline: Textes et documents*, 2, p. 53.
8   Letter of June 11 1947 in Milton Hindus, *The Crippled Giant*, p. 98.
9   Eugène Dabit, *Journal intime* (Paris, 1989), p. 257.
10 Ibid., pp. 376–7.
11 Ibid., p. 405. For a detailed, if optimistic, discussion of the relationship between Céline and Dabit, see Pierre-Edmond Robert, *D'un Hôtel du Nord l'autre. Eugène Dabit 1898–1936* (Paris, 1986), pp. 140–4, 179–81.
12 Quoted in Alméras, p. 151.
13 Ibid., p. 135.
14 Letter to Elie Faure, 18 March 1934, *Textes et documents*, 2, p. 58.
15 Letter to Elie Faure, undated, *Textes et documents*, 2, pp. 46–7.
16 Quoted in Vitoux, p. 262.
17 Ibid.
18 Ibid., p. 241.
19 Alméras, p. 145.
20 Ibid., p. 137.
21 Gibault II, pp. 48–9.
22 Alméras, p. 136.
23 Ibid., p. 147.
24 Ibid., p. 144.
25 Ibid., pp. 130–1; Gibault II, pp. 38–9.
26 Gibault II, p. 39.
27 See Pierre Edmond Robert (ed.), *Céline et les Editions Denoël 1932–1948* (Paris, 1991).
28 Vitoux, pp. 226–7; Alméras, p. 131.
29 Gibault II, p. 86.
30 Letter of 9 April 1933 in *Lettres à Joseph Garcin*, p. 53.
31 Letter of 13 May 1933, pp. 55–6.
32 Letter to Cillie Pam ('N'), 8 May 1933, *Cahiers Céline*, 5, p. 101. Céline is careful to give the German titles of both the essay, 'Trauer und Melancholie', and the volume, *Gesammelte Werke, Buch V*.
33 Letter to Evelyne Pollet, July 1933, *Cahiers Céline*, 5, pp. 175–6.
34 Vitoux, p. 238.
35 Ibid., pp. 239–41.
36 'There are two ridiculous characters: the shy young man and the old libertine', *Cahiers Céline*, 2, p. 187, quoted in Gibault II, p. 82.
37 See, for example, Henri Mahé, *La Brinquebale avec Louis-Ferdinand Céline*, p. 27: 'She [Elizabeth Craig] only gave her favours to Louis' old friends and to Louis' young friends, if it amused Louis.' See Vitoux, p. 174.
38 See Alphonse Juilland, *Elizabeth and Louis*, ch. 4; Jean Monnier, *Elizabeth Craig raconte Céline: Entretien avec la dédicatrice de Voyage au bout de la nuit* (Paris, 1988).
39 Letter to Erika Irrgang, 7–9 December 1932, *Cahiers Céline*, 5, p. 44.
40 Alméras, p. 131.
41 Letter to Erika Irrgang, 21 June 1932, *Cahiers Céline*, 5, p. 31, translated in Vitoux, p. 203.
42 Ibid., p. 40, translated in Vitoux, p. 203.
43 Letter to Cillie Pam, week beginning 18 December 1932, *Cahiers Céline*, 5, pp. 87–8.
44 Letter of 15 April 1975 to Colin Nettelbeck, quoted in *Cahiers Céline*, 5, pp. 65–6.

45 Ibid.
46 Letter to Cillie Pam, 21 February 1932, *Cahiers Céline*, 5, p. 144.
47 *Cahiers de L'Herne*, p. 40.
48 Gibault II, pp. 88–9.
49 See Walter Ravez, *Femmes de lettres belges* (Brussels, 1939), pp. 157–162. He comments: 'She has a brain which is able to create' (p. 162).
50 Gibault II, pp. 88–9.
51 Alméras, p. 143.
52 Letter to Cillie Pam, 'début juin, 1933), *Cahiers Céline* 5, p. 104, quoted in Alméras, p. 143.
53 Alméras, p. 143.
54 Quoted in Alméras, p. 155. The English is Céline's original. Much of the composition of *Mort à crédit* took place in a hotel in Saint-Germain-en-Laye.
55 Vitoux, p. 266.
56 Alméras, pp. 154–5.
57 Ibid., p. 156.
58 Letter to Alméras of 1969, quoted in ibid., p. 156.
59 Letter to Robert Denoël, June 1934, *Magazine Littéraire*, no. 116, p. 21, quoted in Vitoux, p. 267.
60 Quoted in Henri Mahé, *La Brinquebale avec Céline*, pp. 101–2, translated in Vitoux, p. 267.
61 Letter to Cillie Pam, 28 August 1934, *Cahiers Céline*, 5, p. 120, translated in ibid., p. 267.
62 Quoted in Mahé, *La Brinquebale avec Céline*, p. 103, translated in ibid., p. 267.
63 Ibid.
64 Milton Hindus, *L.-F. Céline tel que je l'ai vu*, p. 169, translated in Vitoux, p. 267.
65 Milton Hindus, *The Crippled Giant*, p. 126.
66 Alméras, p. 157.
67 See Alphonse Juilland, *Elizabeth and Louis*, ch. 3 'How they met and why they parted', pp. 57–85.
68 Mahé, p. 103.
69 Quoted in Juilland, p. 163.
70 Hindus, *L.-F. Céline tel que je l'ai vu*, p. 169, quoted in Vitoux, p. 267.
71 Tankle was in fact of Russian Jewish origin. See Alméras, p. 158.
72 Ibid., p. 162
73 Vitoux, p. 175.
74 Letter of 17 June 1935 to Karen Marie Jensen, *Cahiers Céline*, 5, p. 230, quoted in Alméras, p. 167.
75 Letter of 14 July 1934, *Textes et documents*, 2, p. 66, quoted in Alméras, p. 167.
76 Gibault II, p. 98.
77 Quoted in Alméras, p. 164.
78 Ibid., pp. 162–3.
79 Letter of '9 [end of winter] 1935' to Karen Marie Jensen, *Cahiers Céline*, 5, p. 228, quoted in Alméras, p. 166.
80 Alméras, p. 166.
81 Ibid., p. 167.
82 Evelyne Pollet, *Escaliers* (Brussels, 1956), p. 40, quoted in Vitoux, p. 239.
83 For a full discussion of this aspect of French inter-war fiction, see Nicholas Hewitt, *Les Maladies du siècle*.
84 See *Journal de l'abbé Mugnier 1879–1939*, 18 January 1933 (Paris, 1985), pp. 531–2.

85 Letter to Elie Faure, 11 August 1934, *Textes et documents*, 2, p. 68.
86 Letter of 18 March 1934, ibid. pp. 58–9.
87 Letter of 22 or 23 July 1935, ibid., p. 73.
88 Letter of 22 July 1935, ibid., p. 71.
89 Ibid.
90 See Tom Kemp, *The French Economy 1913–39* (London, 1972), ch. 6 and 7.
91 Ibid., pp. 96–8.
92 Ibid., p. 109.
93 See Eugen Weber, *Action Française: Royalism and Reaction in Twentieth-Century France* (Stanford, CA, 1962).
94 See Dieter Wolff, *Doriot, du communisme à la Collaboration* (Paris, 1969).
95 See SHAC, *Clichy-la-Garenne*, p. 134; General André Chérasse, *La Hurle. La Nuit sanglante de Clichy: 16 et 17 mars 1937* (Paris, 1983).
96 See Robert Brasillach, *Notre avant-guerre* (Paris, 1981), p. 286.
97 See, for example, letter of 4 August 1930, in *Lettres à Joseph Garcin*, p. 6.
98 'Honneur, gloire, saucisson de Lyon et trompette à la Grosse, Sympathiquement', quoted in Gibault II, p. 121. 'La Grosse' was the hardly flattering name given to Herriot by Léon Daudet in *Action Française*.
99 Alméras, p. 163.
100 Entry for 13 April 1934, *Journal de l'abbé Mugnier 1879–1939*, pp. 540–1.
101 L.-F. Céline, 'Pour tuer le chômage tueront-ils les chômeurs?', *Cahiers Céline*, 3, p. 218.
102 Quoted in Vitoux, p. 241.
103 Alméras, p. 170.
104 Vitoux, p. 257.
105 Letter to Simone Saintu, 16 January 1933, *Cahiers Céline*, 5, p. 22.
106 Letter to Robert Denoël, 3 August 1933, *Textes et documents*, 3, p. 73, quoted in Gibault II, p. 77.
107 Letter to Joseph Garcin, July 1933, in *Lettres à Joseph Garcin*, p. 20.
108 Letter to Robert Denoël, 16 July 1934, *Textes et documents*, 3, p. 83.
109 Alméras, p. 169.
110 Ibid., p. 170.
111 Ibid.
112 See Gibault II, pp. 115–16. On Marie Canavaggia, see Jean Paul Louis (ed.), *Lettres à Marie Canavaggia*, 1: *1936–1947* (Tusson, 1995); 2: *1948–1960* (Tusson, 1995); 3: *Index analytique* (Tusson, 1995).
113 See Jean Paul Louis, 'Introduction', in *Lettres à Marie Canavaggia*, 1, pp. ix–xiii.
114 Quoted in Godard, *Romans* I, p. 1399.
115 Letter of 3 August 1933, *Textes et Documents*, 3, p. 73.
116 Letter of 23 July 1934, *Textes et documents*, 3, pp. 84–5.
117 Quoted in Vitoux, p. 258.
118 Ibid., p. 259.
119 Ibid., p. 258.
120 Quoted in ibid., p. 259.
121 Ibid.
122 Alméras, p. 138.
123 Ibid., p. 139.
124 Letter to Evelyne Pollet, 14 September 1933, *L'Herne*, 1, p. 101.
125 Quoted in Alméras, p. 149.
126 Quoted in Alméras, pp. 148–9.

127 Vitoux, p. 261.
128 L.-F. Céline, 'Hommage à Zola', *L'Herne*, I, p. 170.
129 Ibid., pp. 169–70.
130 Ibid., p. 172.
131 Ibid., p. 171.
132 Vitoux, p. 275.
133 L.-F. Céline, *Maudits soupirs pour une autre fois* (Paris, 1985), p. 136.
134 Vitoux, p. 275.
135 Gibault II, p. 75. For a detailed account of Céline's relationship with Le Vigan, see Claude Beylie and André Bernard: *Robert Le Vigan. Désordre et génie* (Paris, 1996); Pol Vandromme, *Robert Le Vigan, compagnon et personnage de L.-F. Céline* (Kessel-Lo (Belgium), 1980).
136 Gibault, II, p. 109.
137 See Chantal Le Bobinnec, *Gen Paul à Montmartre: Féerie pour Monsieur Jules* (Paris, 1995).
138 Gibault II, p. 110.
139 Ibid., pp. 111–12.

Chapter 8: 1936

1 L.-F. Céline, *Guignol's Band*, I, in *Romans* III (Paris, 1988), p. 85.
2 L.-F. Céline, *Mort à crédit*, in *Romans* I, p. 822.
3 See L.-F. Céline, letter to Little, Brown, dated 12/34, quoted by Alice Kaplan, 'Selling Céline', in Alice Kaplan and Philippe Roussin, *Céline, USA*, p. 398.
4 Entry for 13 April 1934 in *Journal de l'abbé Mugnier 1879–1939*, pp. 540–1.
5 See Theodore Zeldin, *France 1848–1945*, I: *Ambition, Love and Politics* (Oxford, 1973), ch. 12, 'Children', pp. 315–42.
6 Ibid., pp. 522–3.
7 *Mort à crédit*, p. 1062.
8 Ibid., p. 535.
9 Ibid., p. 635.
10 Robert Poulet, *Entretiens familiers avec L.-F. Céline* (Paris, 1958), p. 75.
11 *Mort à crédit*, p. 543.
12 Ibid., p. 544.
13 Ibid., p. 512.
14 Ibid.
15 Quoted in Gibault II, p. 117.
16 Ibid., p. 116.
17 Quoted in Gibault II, p. 117.
18 *Candide*, 11 June 1936, quoted in Gibault II, p. 118.
19 Ibid.
20 Ibid., p. 119.
21 Elie Faure, *Oeuvres complètes* III (Paris, 1964), p. 1127, quoted in Gibault II, p. 118.
22 Quoted in Alméras, pp. 176–7.
23 Letter of 1 June, in Alice Kaplan, 'Selling Céline', p. 401.
24 Alméras, p. 177.

25 Ibid., p. 175.
26 Quoted in Gibault II, p. 120.
27 Ibid.
28 Quoted in Zeldin, *France 1848–1945*, 1, p. 336.
29 Alméras, pp. 177–8.
30 Ibid., p. 178.
31 Quoted in Alméras, p. 178.
32 See Fred Kupferman, *Au pays des Soviets. Le Voyage français en Union Soviétique 1917–1939* (Paris, 1979); Paul Gerbod, 'L'Union Soviétique dans l'opinion française 1917–1941', *Annales du CESERE*, 4, 1981; David Caute, *The Fellow-Travellers: A Postscript to the Enlightenment* (London, 1973).
33 Kupferman, p. 172.
34 Vitoux, p. 295.
35 Gerbod, 'L'Union Soviétique dans l'opinion française 1917–1941', p. 8.
36 Ibid., p. 9.
37 Kupferman, p. 75.
38 See Nicholas Hewitt, '*Mea culpa* et les retours d'URSS', *Céline Etudes: Actes du Colloque International de Paris (1992)* (Tusson and Paris, 1993), p. 160.
39 Quoted in Kupferman, p. 83.
40 Ibid., p. 83.
41 Ibid., p. 74.
42 Gibault II, pp. 129–30.
43 Ibid., p. 132.
44 Quoted in Gibault II, p. 130.
45 Ibid., p. 130.
46 Ibid., p. 131.
47 Letter to Cillie Pam, end July 1936, *Cahiers Céline*, 5, p. 139.
48 See, for example, L.-F. Céline, *D'un château l'autre, Romans* II (Paris, 1974), pp. 18–19.
49 *Voyage au bout de la nuit, Romans* I, p. 113.
50 Gibault II, p. 139.
51 *Bagatelles pour un massacre*, p. 46.
52 *Bagatelles*, p. 332, translated in Vitoux, p. 297.
53 Ibid., pp. 347–8.
54 Vitoux, p. 298.
55 Quoted in Gibault II, p. 137.
56 Ibid., p. 142.
57 Letter to Cillie Pam, October 1936, *Cahiers Céline*, 5, p. 140.
58 Letter to Karen Marie Jensen, 15 October[?] 1936, *Cahiers Céline*, 5, p. 238.
59 Eric Mazet, interview with 'Tinou' Le Vigan, quoted in Claude Beylie and André Bernard, *Robert Le Vigan. Désordre et génie*, p. 145.
60 See *Bagatelles*, p. 362–3.
61 Ibid., pp. 113–22.
62 *Cahiers Céline*, 3, p. 188.
63 Alméras, pp. 178–9.
64 Ibid., p. 180.
65 Letter from Denoël of 28 October 1936, quoted in Alméras, p. 180.
66 Ibid., p. 180.
67 Kupferman, p. 182.
68 Alméras, p. 180.

69 Letter to Karen Marie Jensen, 6 February 1937, *Cahiers Céline*, 5, p. 240, quoted in Alméras, p. 180.
70 Alméras, p. 180.
71 Ibid., p. 181.
72 Gibault II, p. 149.
73 L.-F. Céline, *Mea Culpa, suivi de La Vie et l'oeuvre de Semmelweis* (Paris, 1937), p. 7.
74 Ibid., p. 25.
75 Ibid., p. 18.
76 Ibid., p. 15.
77 Ibid., p. 9.
78 Ibid.
79 Ibid.
80 Ibid., p. 25.

Chapter 9: Anti-Semitism

1   Vitoux, p. 303.
2   Quoted in Vitoux, p. 303.
3   Alméras, p. 182.
4   L.-F. Céline, Letter to Karen Marie Jensen of 2 March 1937, *Cahiers Céline*, 5, p. 242. See Vitoux, p. 304.
5   Ibid., translated in Vitoux, p. 304.
6   Gibault II, p. 122. It is interesting and ironic that the family name Almansor is Spanish in origin and specifically a 'New Christian' name, in other words, Jewish.
7   Alméras, p. 176.
8   Ibid. and Gibault II, pp. 122–3.
9   See Serge Perrault, *Céline de mes souvenirs* (Tusson, 1992).
10 Gibault II, p. 123.
11 Alméras, p. 176.
12 Letter to Karen Marie Jensen, 11 September 1937, *Cahiers Céline* 5, p. 246, quoted in Alméras, p. 182.
13 Ibid.
14 Quoted in Vitoux, p. 304.
15 Ibid., p. 325.
16 Ibid., p. 309.
17 Alméras, p. 191.
18 Gibault II, p. 193.
19 Unpublished text of 12 October 1976, quoted in Gibault II, p. 194.
20 Letter to Albert Paraz, 4 March 1951, *Cahiers Céline*, 6, p. 307, quoted in Gibault II, pp. 194–5.
21 Gibault II, p. 152.
22 Quoted in Vitoux, p. 307.
23 Ibid.
24 Ibid., p. 308.
25 Ibid.

26 Quoted in Vitoux, p. 309.
27 Ibid., p. 301. Béraud's most scandalous polemic was the violently Anglophobic *Faut-il réduire l'Angleterre en esclavage?* (Paris, 1935). For an account of French polemical writing at this time, see Pierre Dominique, *Les Polémistes français depuis 1789* (Paris, 1962), which has a section on Céline, pp. 418–30.
28 This was the interpretation imposed on the pamphlet's title by Emmanuel Mounier in his review, '*Bagatelles pour un massacre*', *Esprit*, 66 (March 1938), reprinted in *Cahiers de l'Herne*, p. 341.
29 'Bagatelles', in *Trésor de la langue française*.
30 Marc Angenot, *La Parole pamphlétaire. Typologie des discours modernes* (Paris, 1982), p. 342.
31 For a detailed analysis of Céline's probable documentation, see Alice Yaeger Kaplan, *Relevé des sources et citations dans 'Bagatelles pour un massacre'* (Tusson, 1987). She refers particularly (pp. 30–5) to his use of the Office de Propagande Nationale, at 4 Rue du Cardinal Mercier, and the Centre de Documentation et de Propagande in the Rue Laugier.
32 Hannah Arendt, *Sur l'antisémitisme* (Paris, 1973), p. 253.
33 Emmanuel Mounier, '*Bagatelles pour un massacre*'.
34 L.-F. Céline, *Bagatelles pour un massacre* (Paris, 1937), p. 164.
35 Ibid., pp. 216–17.
36 Charles Baudelaire, *Mon Coeur mis à nu*, in *Oeuvres complètes* (Paris, 1961), p. 1300.
37 Walter Benjamin, *Charles Baudelaire. A Lyric Poet in an Age of High Capitalism* (London, 1973), p. 14.
38 Alméras, pp. 185–6.
39 Lucien Rebatet, *Cahiers de l'Herne*, p. 44, translated in Vitoux, p. 320.
40 Vitoux, p. 320.
41 Lucien Rebatet, *Cahiers de l'Herne*, p. 45.
42 Alméras, p. 186.
43 Marcel Arland, '*Bagatelles pour un massacre,* par Louis-Ferdinand Céline', *Nouvelle Revue Française*, 293 (February 1938), p. 309.
44 Ibid., p. 309.
45 André Gide, 'Les Juifs, Céline et Maritain', *Nouvelle Revue Française*, 295 (April 1938), p. 634.
46 Emmanuel Berl, *Interrogatoire par Patrick Modiano, suivi de 'Il fait beau allons au cimetière'* (Paris, 1976), pp. 126–7.
47 Vitoux, p. 319.
48 Alméras, p. 189.
49 Quoted in Alméras, p. 188.
50 Ibid.
51 Robert Le Vigan, interview with Roberto Bensaya, 'Bagatelles pour un exil', *La Nation*, 10 August 1969, quoted in Beylie and Bernard, *Robert Le Vigan*, p. 106.
52 Quoted in Gibault II, p. 167.
53 Alméras, p. 188.
54 *Voyage au bout de la nuit*, p. 8.
55 *Mort à crédit*, p. 671.
56 Marcel Jouhandeau, *Le Péril juif* (Paris, 1936), p. 19.
57 Ibid.
58 Gibault II, pp. 157–8. In this context of anti-Semitism in the inter-war years, it is interesting to recall that the apparently innocuous reference to Montaigne

in *Voyage au bout de la nuit* may not be as innocent as it looks. In the 1930s there was considerable speculation in France regarding Montaigne's alleged Jewishness as a descendant of a New Christian Spanish family.

59 See Raymond A. Dior, *Les Juifs, Numéro Spécial, Le Crapouillot* (September 1936). On right-wing anarchism, see Yves Pagès, *Les Fictions du politique chez L.-F. Céline* (Paris, 1994), and François Richard, *Les Anarchistes de droite* (Paris, 1991).

60 Vitoux, pp. 315–17.

61 Philippe Muray, 'Le Siècle de Céline', *L'Infini*, 8 (Autumn 1984), pp. 34–5.

62 See Louis Chevalier, *Classes laborieuses, classes dangereuses à Paris pendant la première moitié du XIXe siècle* (Paris, 1958).

63 Olivier Targowla, *Les Médecins aux mains sales.*

64 Quoted in Alméras, p. 196.

65 L.-F. Céline, *L'Ecole des cadavres* (Paris, 1938), p. 194.

66 Ibid., p. 195.

67 Ibid., p. 197.

68 Ibid., p. 167.

69 Ibid., p. 161.

70 Ibid., p. 166.

71 Ibid., p. 204.

72 Alméras, p. 190.

73 Quoted in Alméras, pp. 190–1. It is Alméras who spotted the highly significant use of the first-person plural which identifies Céline as part of a collective mission.

74 Vitoux, p. 330.

75 Alméras, p. 190.

76 Ibid., pp. 198–9.

77 See Arnold Mandel, *Nous autres Juifs* (Paris, 1978), p. 64.

78 Ibid., pp. 63–4.

79 Vitoux, pp. 322, 328.

80 Henri Mahé, *Brinquebale*, p. 176, translated in Vitoux, p. 323.

81 René Héron de Villefosse, 'Quand Céline séjournait au Canada', *Revue Célinienne*, 3–4, pp. 8–9, quoted in Vitoux, pp. 323–4.

82 Gibault II, pp. 186–7.

83 *D'un château l'autre*, in *Romans* II, p. 246.

84 Vitoux, p. 324.

85 Quoted in Alméras, p. 190.

86 Ibid.

87 Vitoux, pp. 325–6.

88 Quoted in Alméras, p. 194.

89 Merlin Thomas, *Louis-Ferdinand Céline* (London, 1979), p. 156.

90 L.-F. Céline, *L'Ecole des cadavres*, p. 50.

91 Ibid., p. 43.

92 Ibid., p. 51.

93 Ibid., p. 53.

94 Ibid., p. 101.

95 Ibid., p. 102.

96 Ibid., p. 168.

97 Ibid., p. 108.

98 Ibid., p. 79.

99 Ibid., p. 111.
100 Ibid., p. 204.
101 Ibid., p. 205.
102 Ibid., p. 211.
103 Ibid., p. 221.
104 Ibid., p. 16.
105 Ibid., p. 18.
106 Ibid., p. 19.
107 Ibid., p. 20.
108 Ibid., p. 20. Céline's disquiet at his imaginary correspondent is similar in tone to his advice to Henry Miller in a letter written shortly after he read *Tropic of Cancer*. 'Take care to be discreet. More and more discretion! Know how to be wrong – the world is full of people who are right – that's why it's disgusting.' See Brassaï, *Henry Miller, grandeur nature* (Paris, 1975), p. 134. Céline never met his fellow-resident of Clichy, though he continued to read his work, as the correspondence with Hindus confirms. What is important is that the enthusiast who is convinced of his own rightness is dangerous, like the luckless Doctor Bazire in the essay on quinine, because of his passion, but he is also aesthetically inept.
109 See, for example, *L'Ecole des cadavres*, pp. 159–60.
110 Ibid., p. 32.
111 Ibid., pp. 31–2.
112 Ibid., p. 152.
113 Ibid.
114 Ibid., p. 77.
115 Lucien Rebatet, *Les Mémoires d'un fasciste*, 1: *Les Décombres 1938–1940* (Paris, 1976), p. 146.
116 Ibid., p. 223.
117 Alméras, p. 193.
118 Gibault II, pp. 180–4.
119 Ibid., p. 182.
120 Quoted in Gibault II, p. 183.
121 Alméras, p. 198.
122 Marcel Sauvage, *L'Instransigeant*, 23 December 1938, quoted in Alméras, pp. 193–4.

Chapter 10: Phoney War

1 See Henri Godard, 'Notice', in L.-F. Céline, *Romans* III (Paris, 1988), pp. 874–5.
2 Quoted in Godard, p. 874.
3 Ibid., p. 875.
4 Ibid., pp. 877–8.
5 Ibid. and 'Appendice V', pp. 77–9.
6 'L'Histoire de *Casse-pipe* racontée par Céline en 1957' (Récit recueilli par R. Poulet), in *Romans* III, p. 65.
7 See Christine Sautermeister, 'Lecture théâtrale et cinématographique de *Casse-pipe*', in *Céline: Actes du Colloque International de Paris 1979* (Paris, 1980), p. 214; Jean Roman, *Paris 1890s*, p. 59.

8   L.-F. Céline, *Casse-pipe*, in *Romans* III, p. 3.
9   See Godard, 'Notice', in *Romans* III, p. 864.
10 *Casse-pipe*, p. 7.
11 See Jean-Pierre Richard, 'Casque-pipe', *Littérature*, 29 (1978), pp. 3–17.
12 *Casse-pipe*, p. 6.
13 Ibid., p. 4.
14 Ibid.
15 Ibid., pp. 54–5.
16 Ibid., p. 18.
17 *Voyage au bout de la nuit*, p. 287.
18 *Casse-pipe*, p. 60.
19 Ibid.
20 Ibid., p. 55.
21 'Appendice' II, *Romans* III, p. 69.
22 Ibid.
23 Ibid.
24 Ibid., p. 70.
25 Ibid., p. 71.
26 See Godard, 'Notice', in *Romans* III, pp. 878–9.
27 See Jean Crémieux-Brilhac, *Les Français de l'année 40* (Paris, 1990).
28 Vitoux, p. 335.
29 Gibault II, p. 198.
30 Letters to Jean Bonnevilliers, quoted in Gibault II, pp. 199–200.
31 Quoted in Gibault II, p. 200.
32 Ibid., p. 202.
33 Ibid., p. 201.
34 Ibid., p. 205.
35 Vitoux, p. 339.
36 Gibault II, p. 208.
37 Ibid., pp. 208–9.
38 Ibid., pp. 209–10.
39 Letter from Dr Detrieux to the Inspector of the port of La Pallice, 20 June 1940, quoted in Gibault II, p. 211.
40 Quoted in Vitoux, p. 341.
41 Gibault II, p. 212.
42 Ibid.
43 Ibid. pp. 221–2.
44 Letter to Frédéric Empaytaz, 3 November 1940, quoted in Gibault II, p. 22.
45 Letter to Empeytaz, 21 January 1941, quoted in Gibault II, p. 224.
46 Quoted in Gibault II, p. 225.
47 Ibid, p. 224.
48 Ibid., p. 230.
49 Ibid., p. 227.
50 Letter to Empeytaz, 2 February 1943, quoted in Gibault II, p. 228.
51 Ibid., p. 231.
52 Ibid.
53 Ibid., pp. 231–2.
54 See Pierre Assouline, *Gaston Gallimard: Un demi siècle d'édition française* (Paris, 1996), p. 292.
55 Gibault II, pp. 213–14.
56 Ibid., p. 214.

57 L.-F. Céline, *Les Beaux Draps* (Paris, 1941), p. 11.
58 Ibid., p. 13.
59 Ibid., p. 35.
60 *Voyage au bout de la nuit*, pp. 7–8.
61 *Les Beaux Draps*, p. 19.
62 Ibid., p. 44.
63 Vitoux, p. 346.
64 *Les Beaux Draps*, p. 96.
65 See François de Fontette, 'Eléments pour une définition du Juif', *Annales du CESERE*, 5 (1982), p. 21.
66 *Les Beaux Draps*, p. 115.
67 Ibid., p. 197.
68 Ibid., p. 144.
69 Ibid., p. 197.
70 Ibid., p. 137.
71 Ibid., p. 197.
72 Ibid., p. 68.
73 Ibid., p. 162.
74 Ibid., p. 171.
75 Ibid., p. 148.
76 Ibid., pp. 128–9, translated in Vitoux, pp. 349–50.
77 Ibid., p. 205.
78 Ibid., p. 213.
79 Ibid., p. 208.
80 Ibid., p. 187.
81 Ibid., pp. 212–13.
82 Ibid., pp. 208–9.
83 Ibid., p. 217.
84 Ibid., pp. 221–2.
85 Ibid., p. 218.

Chapter 11: The Occupation

1 See Nicholas Hewitt, 'Marcel Aymé and the Dark Night of the Occupation', in Gerhard Hirschfeld and Patrick Marsh (eds), *Collaboration in Occupied France* (Oxford and New York, 1991).
2 Philippe Burrin, *Living with Defeat. France under the German Occupation 1940–4* (London, 1996), p. 117.
3 See the by no means unbiased testimony of Jacques Laurent, *L'Année Quarante. Londres, de Gaulle, Vichy* (Paris, 1965), pp. 92–3. Laurent alleges that between 1940 and 1942, 1300 enemy agents were arrested by the Vichy authorities, 270 of whom were condemned to death and 42 shot.
4 Burrin, p. 91.
5 Ibid.
6 Ibid., p. 87.
7 Ibid.
8 Ibid., p. 89.

9   Ibid.
10   Ibid.
11   See Pascal Ory, *Les Collaborateurs 1940–5* (Paris, 1976), Annexe IV.
12   See: Pierre Drieu la Rochelle, *Fragment de mémoires 1940–1* (Paris, 1982), and *Journal 1939–45* (Paris, 1992).
13   Burrin, pp. 356–7.
14   Ibid., p. 355.
15   See Pascal Ory, *Les Collaborateurs*, pp. 190–200.
16   Ibid., p. 217.
17   Burrin, p. 138.
18   Interview with Madeleine Chapsal, *Cahiers Céline* 2, p. 31.
19   See Nicholas Hewitt, *Literature and the Right in Postwar France. The Story of the 'Hussards'* (Oxford and Washington, DC, 1996), ch. 1.
20   See Gerhard Heller, *Un Allemand à Paris 1940–4* (Paris, 1981), pp. 152–4.
21   See Jacques Adler, *The Jews of Paris and the Final Solution. Communal Response and Internal Conflicts, 1940–4* (Oxford, 1987).
22   See James McMillan, *Dreyfus to De Gaulle. Politics and Society in France, 1898–1969* (London, 1985), p. 134.
23   Burrin, p. 212.
24   See Pascal Ory, *Les Collaborateurs*, ch. 11.
25   Quoted in Gibault II, p. 226.
26   See Arletty, *La Défense* (Paris, 1971), pp. 140–1.
27   Vitoux, p. 358.
28   Gibault II, p. 289.
29   See Drieu la Rochelle, *Journal 1939–1945*, p. 245 (entry for 21 June 1940). Gerhard Heller refers to a letter from Gide to Giono dated 1 October 1940, announcing that the *NRF* will start up again with an editorial team comprising 'Eluard, Céline, Gide and Giono himself' (*Un Allemand à Paris*, p. 42).
30   Alméras, p. 226.
31   Quoted in Gibault II, p. 292.
32   Gibault II, pp. 292–3.
33   Vitoux, p. 358.
34   'Vers le parti unique?', *Au Pilori*, 25 December 1941, p. 2, quoted in Gibault II, pp. 292–4.
35   Gibault II, p. 259.
36   Alméras, p. 220.
37   Ibid., p. 226.
38   See, for example, Vitoux, p. 346.
39   Alméras, p. 265.
40   Letter to Alphonse de Châteaubriant, 14 September 1941, quoted in Gibault II, p. 289.
41   Letter to Karen Marie Jensen, 8 December 1941, quoted in Gibault II, p. 288.
42   Quoted in Gibault II, p. 288.
43   Gibault II, pp. 323–4.
44   Letter to Lucien Combelle (undated), quoted in Gibault II, p. 280.
45   Alméras, p. 243, gives the example of an article for *Je suis partout* of 15 June 1942.
46   See: Henri Godard, 'Chronologie', in L.-F. Céline, *Romans* I, p. LXXV.
47   Quoted in Alméras, p. 222.
48   Quoted in Alméras, p. 227.

49   Quoted in Vitoux, p. 353.
50   Quoted in Alméras, p. 248.
51   See Albert Chesneau, *Essai de psychocritique de Louis-Ferdinand Céline* (Paris, 1971).
52   Vitoux, p. 361.
53   Ibid., pp. 379–80.
54   Alméras, p. 252.
55   Ibid., p. 252.
56   Vitoux, p. 355.
57   Alméras, pp. 232–3.
58   Vitoux, p. 364.
59   Alméras, p. 212.
60   See Jean Cocteau, *Journal 1942–5* (Paris, 1989), p. 32. Cocteau goes on to quote Ernst Jünger's wry comment on the relationship between Epting and Céline: 'It's serious . . . it's like a respectable man falling in love with a dancer. You don't know where it can lead to.' See also Karl Epting, 'Il ne nous aimait pas', *L'Herne*, and Alice Epting-Kullmann's recollections of Céline in *Pariser Begegnungen* (Hanner über Sachingen, 1972), quoted by Hervé le Boterf: 'Louis-Ferdinand Céline, hostile to all social niceties, but who turns up, ten times rather than once, to request favours, in private, for his patients. The father of Bardamu arrives, on a bicycle, dressed in a flea-ridden jacket. He gesticulates, storms and goes into his traditional anti-Semitic routine: "Aren't I right, Madame Epting, when I say that if things continue the way they are, one fine day it'll be the Jews who are dancing on our graves?"' (Hervé le Boterf, *La Vie Parisienne sous l'Occupation*, II (Paris, 1975), p. 194.
61   Vitoux, p. 389.
62   Ibid., p. 383.
63   Gibault II, p. 251. Breker himself, in his memoirs, *Paris, Hitler et moi* (Paris, 1970), makes no reference whatsoever to Céline.
64   Ibid., p. 250.
65   See Heller, *Un Allemand à Paris*, p. 152: 'I was shocked by his anti-Semitic delirium.'
66   Alméras, p. 235.
67   Gibault II, p. 261.
68   Ibid., pp. 261–2.
69   Ibid., pp. 228, 248.
70   Quoted in Gibault II, p. 257.
71   Ernst Jünger, *Journal* I *(1941–3)* (Paris, 1951), p. 95. As Jünger remarked, 'there is in him the look that maniacs have, turned inward, which shines as from the bottom of a hole . . . He tells us how surprised, stupefied, he is that we soldiers are not shooting, hanging, exterminating the Jews – he is amazed that anyone who has a bayonet doesn't make unlimited use of it.'
72   See Gérard Loiseaux, 'Epting, Payr et Céline', in *La Littérature de la défaite et de la Collaboration* (Paris, 1984), pp. 41–54.
73   See Gibault II, p. 268.
74   Vitoux, p. 385.
75   Ibid., p. 376.
76   Gibault II, pp. 254–5. A variant of this story, which substitutes Achenbach for Abertz, retailed to the narrator by one of the alleged participants, Antonio Zuloaga, is to be found in Adry de Carbuccia, *Du Tango à Lily Marlène* (Paris, 1987), pp. 312–15.

77 Alméras, p. 279.
78 Lucien Rebatet, 'D'un Céline l'autre', *L'Herne*, p. 232.
79 Ibid., pp. 233–4.
80 Quoted in Vitoux, p. 381.
81 Ibid.
82 Lucien Rebatet, *Les Mémoires d'un fasciste*, II, *1941–7* (Paris, 1976), p. 103.
83 Gibault II, pp. 271–2.
84 Mahé, p. 224.
85 Robert Champfleury, 'Céline ne nous a pas trahis', *L'Herne*, pp. 246–51.
86 Alméras, pp. 222–3.
87 Ibid., p. 225.
88 Quoted in Gibault II, pp. 248–9.
89 Gibault II, p. 299.
90 Ibid., p. 300.
91 R. Cardine-Petit, 'Une Heure chez L.-F. Céline', *Panorama*, 25 March 1943, quoted in Gibault II, p. 300.
92 Vitoux, p. 374.
93 Gibault II, pp. 237–41.
94 Vitoux, p. 380.
95 Ibid., p. 380.
96 Ibid., p. 381.
97 Alméras, p. 253.
98 'Examples of Wages at Clermont-Ferrand, 1942–1943', in John W. Sweets, *Choices in Vichy France. The French under Nazi Occupation* (New York and Oxford, 1986), pp. 18–19.
99 Alméras, p. 249.
100 Vitoux, p. 371.
101 Quoted in Vitoux, p. 383.
102 Letter to Gen Paul, 26 [unspecified month] 1943, quoted in Gibault II, p. 319.
103 Letter to Gen Paul, postmarked 26 August 1943, quoted in Gibault II, p. 319.
104 Quoted in Vitoux, p. 383.
105 Gibault II, pp. 312–16.
106 Ibid., p. 311–12.
107 Ibid., pp. 316–17.
108 Quoted in ibid., p. 308.
109 Ibid.
110 Alméras, p. 257.
111 Ibid., p. 269.
112 Ibid., p. 329.
113 Ibid., pp. 330–1.
114 Vitoux, p. 371.
115 Gibault II, p. 233.
116 Vitoux, p. 369.
117 Ibid., pp. 372–3, and Frédéric Vitoux, *Bébert, le chat de Louis-Ferdinand Céline*.
118 Vitoux, p. 369.
119 Alméras, p. 276.
120 Vitoux, p. 367.
121 Ibid., p. 362, and Alméras, p. 255.
122 Gibault II, p. 327.
123 Ibid., p. 338.
124 Ibid., p. 343, and Alméras, p. 277.

125   Alméras, p. 254.
126   Ibid., p. 279.
127   Ibid.
128   Ibid., p. 281.
129   Henri Godard, 'Notice', in L.-F. Céline, *Romans* III, p. 949.
130   Ibid., p. 952.
131   Ibid., p. 949.
132   Ibid., p. 950.
133   Quoted in Godard, p. 951.
134   'Synopsis de *Guignol's Band* III', *Romans* III, pp. 763–9.
135   Godard, 'Notice', p. 951.
136   Ibid., p. 953.
137   Ibid., pp. 954–5.
138   Ibid., p. 957.
139   For a description of the manuscripts, see Godard, 'Notice', p. 958.
140   Ibid., p. 1005.
141   Alméras, pp. 274–5.
142   Ibid., p. 275.
143   Ibid.
144   Ibid.
145   Ibid., p. 274.
146   L.-F. Céline, *Guignol's Band*, I, p. 100.
147   Godard, 'Notice', p. 993.
148   *Guignol's Band*, I, p. 87.
149   Ibid., p. 89.
150   Ibid.
151   Ibid., p. 91.
152   Ibid.
153   Jules Vallès, *La Rue à Londres* (Paris, 1951), p. 33.
154   Godard, 'Notice', p. 996.
155   Ibid., p. 996.
156   Jules Vallès, *La Rue à Londres*, p. 103.
157   See Jill Forbes, 'Symbolique de l'espace: le 'Londres' célinien', in *Actes du Colloque International de Paris* 1976, pp. 27–40.
158   See Nicholas Hewitt, 'Céline and Shakespeare', in *Shakespeare Yearbook*, 5 (1994).
159   *Guignol's Band* I, p. 83.
160   Ibid., p. 84.
161   Ibid., p. 85.
162   Robert Poulet, *Entretiens familiers avec Louis-Ferdinand Céline*, p. 75.
163   *Guignol's Band* II, p. 759.

Chapter 12: Exile

1   Jean Galtier-Boissière, *Journal 1940–50* (Paris, 1992), p. 191.
2   Ibid., p. 231.
3   Quoted in Alméras, p. 284.

4 Quoted in Alméras, p. 284.

5 Gibault III, p. 25.

6 Paul Bonny insisted that it was Epting who persuaded Céline to go to Germany in the first place, and that Céline had maintained contacts throughout the Occupation with all levels of the German Embassy staff. See Philippe Alméras, 'Entretien avec Paul Bonny', in L.-F. Céline, *Lettres des années noires* (Paris, 1994), p. 57.

7 Gibault III, p. 27.

8 Vitoux, p. 400.

9 Ibid., p. 401.

10 Gibault III, p. 26.

11 See the book by Luchaire's mistress, Maud de Belleroche, *Le Ballet des crabes* (Paris, 1975), ch. III: 'La Fuite, cette faute de goût. Heil Baden-Baden!', and his daughter's book, Corinne Luchaire, *Ma drôle de vie* (Paris, 1949).

12 Alméras, pp. 284–5.

13 Ibid., p. 285.

14 Ibid., p. 284.

15 Ibid., p. 285. For the correspondence with Paul Bonny, see L.-F. Céline, *Lettres des années noires*, ed. Philippe Alméras.

16 Gibault III, p. 31.

17 Ibid., pp. 32–3.

18 Ibid., p. 33.

19 Vitoux, p. 407.

20 Ibid..

21 Ibid.

22 Gibault III, p. 36.

23 Vitoux, pp. 407–8.

24 Ibid., p. 410; Gibault III, pp. 38–9.

25 Robert Le Vigan, letter to Paraz, 1 February 1950, quoted in Gibault III, pp. 38–9.

26 Gibault III, p. 39; Vitoux, p. 411.

27 Quoted in Vitoux, p. 411.

28 Quoted in Alméras, p. 287.

29 Vitoux, p. 415. Paul Bonny claimed that Céline's subsequent description of Ulm was pure fabrication: 'He never was in Ulm. I told him about Ulm' (see Alméras, 'Entretien avec Paul Bonny', p. 68).

30 Alméras, p. 289.

31 Lucien Rebatet, *Cahiers de l'Herne*, p. 235, translated in Vitoux, p. 416.

32 See Robert Aron, *Histoire de Vichy* (Paris, 1963), pp. 711–35.

33 Vitoux, pp. 419–20.

34 See Corinne Luchaire, *Ma drôle de vie*.

35 Vitoux, p. 420.

36 Ibid., p. 423.

37 Ibid., p. 420.

38 Ibid.

39 Ibid.

40 Reminiscence of Lucette Destouches to Frédéric Vitoux, quoted in Vitoux, p. 420, confirmed by Simone Mitre, 'Céline et de Brinon', *L'Herne*, pp. 244–5.

41 Alméras, p. 291.

42   Letter of 23 June 1949, quoted in Vitoux, pp. 422–3. See also Jean-Louis Tixier-Vignancour, *Des Républiques, des Justices et des hommes: mémoires* (Paris, 1976)
43   Marcel Déat, *Mémoires politiques* (Paris, 1989), pp. 897–8.
44   Vitoux, p. 421.
45   Ibid.
46   Gibault III, p. 58.
47   Quoted in Vitoux, p. 405.
48   Ibid., p. 427.
49   Alméras, p. 292.
50   Gibault III, pp. 61–2.
51   Ibid., pp. 63–4.
52   Ibid., pp. 64–5; Alméras, p. 293.
53   Marcel Déat, 'Extrait du Journal de Marcel Déat', *L'Herne*, p. 254.
54   Marcel Déat, *Mémoires politiques*, p. 898.
55   Lucien Rebatet, *L'Herne*, p. 238.
56   Quoted in Alméras, p. 296.
57   Ibid.
58   Ibid.
59   Letter to J.-L. Tixier-Vignancour, quoted in Alméras, p. 295.
60   Letter to Dr Camus, 30 June 1947, quoted in Alméras, p. 295.
61   Alméras, p. 295.
62   Alméras, p. 294; Gibault III, pp. 68–70.
63   Quoted in Gibault III, p. 70.
64   Alméras, p. 295.
65   Vitoux, p. 431.
66   Alméras, p. 296.
67   Gibault III, p. 74.
68   Ibid., p. 82.
69   Ibid., p. 86.
70   Vitoux, p. 432.
71   Letter to Marie Canavaggia, quoted in Vitoux, p. 433.
72   Lucette Destouches to Vitoux, in Vitoux, p. 436.
73   Ibid., pp. 436–7; Gibault III, p. 76.
74   Vitoux, p. 438.
75   See Godard, 'Chronologie', in *Romans* I, p. LXXIX.
76   See Pierre Assouline, *L'Epuration des intellectuels* (Paris, 1985), p. 63.
77   Gibault III, p. 88. Assouline argues that Denoël, 'equipped with a dossier of press cuttings which had appeared in the *Bibliographie de la France* between 1940 and 1944 . . . intended to prove that everyone had published under the jackboot' (Assouline, *L'Epuration des intellectuels*, p. 78), and that there were strong motives in the publishing industry for having Denoël removed. An author devoted to Denoël, René Barjavel, who investigated the crime with a view to publishing a volume entitled *Les Sept Morts de Robert Denoël*, concluded that the motive was probably merely theft.
78   Letter to Marie Canavaggia, 'Mercredi (décembre 1945)', *Textes et documents*, I (Paris, 1979), p. 89, quoted in Gibault III, p. 88.
79   Gibault III, pp. 93–4.
80   Vitoux, p. 443.
81   Quoted in Alméras, p. 308.
82   Quoted in Helga Pedersen, *Le Danemark a-t-il sauvé Céline?* (Paris, 1975), p. 20.

83   Gibault III, pp. 96–9.
84   Ibid., pp. 96–7.
85   Ibid., pp. 97–8.
86   For full details of Céline's defence against charges of collaboration, see Pedersen, *Le Danemark a-t-il sauvé Céline?*, pp. 80–93.
87   Gibault III, pp. 130–3.
88   Quoted in Gibault III, p. 131.
89   Alméras, p. 321.
90   Ibid.
91   Gibault III, p. 128.
92   Vitoux, pp. 457–8.
93   Quoted in Gibault III, p. 118.
94   Vitoux, pp. 462–3.
95   Quoted in Gibault III, p. 120.
96   Ibid., p. 120.
97   Ibid., p. 121.
98   Vitoux, pp. 474, 478.
99   Ibid., p. 473.
100 See, for example, the list provided by Alméras, pp. 327–8.
101 As Assouline comments, out of three defendants at the trial in the Cour de Justice de la Seine, Sacha Guitry, Mary Marquet and Le Vigan, only Le Vigan was found guilty (see Assouline, *L'Epuration des intellectuels*, p. 102).
102 Vitoux, p. 475.
103 Ibid., pp. 471–2.
104 Ibid., p. 472.
105 Ibid., pp. 472–3.
106 Jean-Paul Sartre, 'Portrait de l'antisémite', *Les Temps modernes* (December 1945), p. 462.
107 The transformation of the denunciator Sartre into 'Jean-Baptiste' may also be at the origin of Camus' attack on Sartre in *La Chute* under the name of 'Jean-Baptiste' Clamence.
108 Vitoux, pp. 477–8.
109 Alméras, p. 324.
110 Ibid.
111 Ibid.
112 For a detailed account of these negotiations, see Gibault III, pp. 137–44.
113 Vitoux, pp. 478–9.
114 Alméras, p. 342.
115 Vitoux, p. 478.
116 Ibid., p. 479. The cover of Helga Pedersen's *Le Danemark a-t-il sauvé Céline?* bears photographs of all the houses on Mikkelsen's estate: 'Fanehuset' certainly looks the most run-down.
117 Letter to Pastor Löchen, undated, *Cahiers de l'Herne*, p. 140, quoted in Gibault III, p. 152.
118 Letter to Dr Camus, 15 June 1948, quoted in Alméras, p. 349.
119 Letter to Le Vigan, of 1950, quoted in Gibault III, p. 152.
120 Letter to Dr Camus, 15 October 1949, quoted in Alméras, p. 356.
121 Gibault III, pp. 151–2.
122 Letter to Le Vigan, undated, quoted in Gibault III, pp. 152–3.
123 Ibid., p. 153.
124 Vitoux, p. 485.

125   Gibault III, pp. 139–40.
126   Ibid., pp. 140–1.
127   Alméras, p. 354.
128   Pierre Monnier, *Ferdinand furieux* (Lausanne, 1979).
129   Vitoux, p. 493.
130   Ibid., p. 494. On post-war French right-wing publishing, see Nicholas Hewitt, *Literature and the Right in Postwar France*, ch. 3.
131   Vitoux, p. 494.
132   Ibid., p. 497.
133   Pierre Monnier, *Ferdinand furieux*, p. 37.
134   Letter to Albert Paraz, 3 December 1948, *Cahiers Céline*, 6, pp. 107–8.
135   Letter to Albert Paraz, 5 April 1952, *Cahiers Céline*, 6, p. 358.
136   Alméras, p. 371.
137   Vitoux, p. 495.
138   Alméras, p. 369.
139   Gibault III, pp. 123–4.
140   Milton Hindus, *The Crippled Giant: A Bizarre Adventure in Contemporary Letters* (New York, 1950), republished as *The Crippled Giant: A Literary Relationship with Louis-Ferdinand Céline*.
141   Milton Hindus, *The Crippled Giant*, p. 47.
142   Alméras, p. 336.
143   See, for example, the letters of 5 and 24 September 1947, pp. 127, 132.
144   Alméras, p. 349.
145   Hindus, p. 44.
146   Alméras, p. 352.
147   Vitoux, p. 484.
148   Ibid., p. 484.
149   See Jean Dubuffet, *Prospectus et tous écrits suivants*, I and II (Paris, 1967), pp. 416–18.
150   Vitoux, p. 490.
151   On Gen Paul and the 'chignole', see J.-P. Crespelle, *Montmartre vivant* (Paris, 1964), pp. 238–9, and André Warnod, *Drôle d'équipe* (Paris, 1960), pp. 18–19.
152   Vitoux, p. 490.
153   Gibault III, p. 179.
154   Vitoux, p. 491.
155   Alméras, p. 357.
156   Vitoux, p. 489.
157   Ibid., pp. 484–5.
158   Gibault III, p. 167.
159   Ibid., p. 184.
160   Vitoux, pp. 489–90.
161   Ibid., pp. 488–9.
162   Gibault III, p. 183.
163   Quoted in Gibault III, p. 214.
164   See Nicholas Hewitt, *Literature and the Right in Postwar France*, pp. 56–7.
165   Gibault III, p. 193.
166   Ibid.
167   Ibid., p. 197.
168   Ibid., pp. 194–7.
169   For a detailed account of Naud's role in Céline's defence, see Frédéric Monnier's edition of the Céline–Naud correspondence, L.-F. Céline, *Lettres à*

son avocat: 118 lettres inédites à Maître Albert Naud (Paris, 1984). See also Naud's own memoirs, *Les défendre tous* (Paris, 1973).

170 See letter of 30 April 1947, in *Lettres à son avocat*, p. 20.
171 Ibid., pp. 22–4.
172 Gibault III, p. 201.
173 See Naud's letter of 13 October 1948, quoted by F. Monnier in *Lettres à son avocat*, p. 74.
174 Quoted in *Lettres à son avocat*, p. 88.
175 See letter of 7 December 1949, p. 89.
176 See *L'Herne*, pp. 483–7, and Helga Pedersen, *Le Danemark a-t-il sauvé Céline?*, pp. 80–93.
177 Gibault III, p. 210.
178 Ibid., p. 206.
179 Quoted in Gibault III, p. 206.
180 Ibid., p. 206.
181 Ibid., p. 207.
182 *Lettres à son avocat*, pp. 86–7.
183 Gibault III, pp. 207–8.
184 Ibid., p. 213.
185 Ibid., pp. 224–9.
186 Ibid., p. 234.
187 Ibid., pp. 242–3. Tixier-Vignancour recounts with some relish how, when the judge in charge of Céline's case was dragged before the Minister, Daniel Mayer, he was asked how he could possibly not have known that Destouches was in reality Céline, and replied: 'Oh, Monsieur le Ministre, in literature, I stopped at Flaubert' (Tixier-Vignancour, *Des Républiques*, p. 227).
188 Vitoux, p. 512.
189 Gibault III, p. 237.
190 See *Lettres à son avocat*, p. 65 (letter of 18 April 1948). In fact, what Albert Naud got was the plaster cast of Céline's right hand from his deathbed, which he accepted with characteristic generosity: 'This hand was to be my only Honorarium, but I write the word with a capital H.' See Albert Naud, *Les Défendre tous*, p. 324.
191 According to François Gibault, Céline's accusations were justified: Mikkelsen, in 1949, was travelling by road from Copenhagen to Paris with a consignment of Céline's gold, which he intended to change in Paris, when he was stopped at the British checkpoint in Germany and the gold, amounting to 8000 crowns, was confiscated. For Gibault, Mikkelsen was too ashamed to ever confess the incident, but considered that, after all he had done for Céline, the writer could hardly complain. See Gibault III, p. 252.
192 Quoted in Helga Pedersen, *Le Danemark a-t-il sauvé Céline?*, p. 179.
193 Mikkelsen's comments on *Féerie pour une autre fois*, quoted in Pedersen, p. 183.

Chapter 13: Meudon

1 Letter to Paul Marteau, 9 July 1951, quoted in Gibault III, p. 256.
2 Vitoux, p. 515.
3 Alméras, p. 382.

4 Vitoux, p. 517.
5 Letter to Paraz, 10 July 1951, in *Cahiers Céline*, 6, p. 345.
6 Ibid, p. 346.
7 Gibault III, pp. 170–1.
8 Alméras, p. 384.
9 Ibid., p. 385. Pierre Monnier remembers that 'Lucette and Ferdinand were taken off in a fine big car with a chauffeur' (Pierre Monnier, *Ferdinand furieux*, p. 191).
10 Vitoux, p. 520.
11 Alméras, p. 386.
12 Ibid., p. 386.
13 Gibault III, p. 265.
14 Alméras, pp. 387–8.
15 Letter to Le Vigan, 27 October 1951, quoted in Gibault III, p. 268.
16 Jean Paulhan, letter of 16 August 1952, in Jeannine Kohn-Etiemble, *226 Lettres inédites de Jean Paulhan* (Paris, 1975), p. 309.
17 Vitoux, pp. 521–2.
18 Ibid., p. 524.
19 Ibid., pp. 524–5.
20 Alméras, p. 388.
21 Gibault III, p. 271.
22 Ibid., pp. 273–4.
23 Alméras, p. 383.
24 Vitoux, p. 526.
25 See the remark already quoted in ch. 12, Ernst Jünger, *Journal* I, *1941–3*, pp. 94–5. According to Nicole Debrie, Jünger later admitted caricaturing Céline. See Nicole Debrie, *Il était une fois . . . Céline* (Paris, 1990), p. 393. See also *Tout Céline*, 4, p. 7.
26 For a full account of the case, see Gibault III, pp. 277–88.
27 Vitoux, p. 523.
28 Ibid., pp. 517–18. Jouhandeau was an important figure in the process of Céline's rehabilitation, but the two writers met only once. Jouhandeau himself described their brief meeting, when he came down from his apartment to shake Céline's hand in Paul Chambrillion's car, and the effect it made on him: 'All the rest of the evening, I remained troubled, overwhelmed, as if after the passing of a comet or after an eclipse,' Marcel Jouhandeau, *Que l'amour est un, Journaliers*, IX (Paris, 1967), pp. 221–2. Jouhandeau, also known for his anti-Semitism and his Collaborationist sympathies, testifies to the success of Céline's self-portrayal as victim: 'In him, I venerated Poverty, the prestige of Martyrdom' (ibid., p. 222).
29 Pierre Monnier, *Ferdinand furieux*, pp. 189–90. See Vitoux, p. 578.
30 Alméras, p. 386.
31 See L.-F. Céline, *Lettres à la NRF*.
32 Letter to Marie Canavaggia, 15 September 1945, quoted by Henri Godard, in 'Notice', in L.-F. Céline, *Romans* IV, p. 1113.
33 Ibid., p. 1115.
34 See Letter to Lucette Destouches, 22 March 1946, quoted by Godard, *Romans* IV, pp. 1115–16.
35 Ibid.
36 See Godard, *Romans* IV, pp. 1117–18.

37 Ibid., p. xviii.
38 Ibid., pp. 565–1082.
39 Ibid., p. 1174.
40 Ibid., p. 1115.
41 Ibid., pp. xiv–xv.
42 Ibid., p. 1112.
43 See Marie-Christine Bellosta, '*Féerie pour une autre fois* 1 et 2: un spectacle et son prologue', *Revue des Lettres Modernes*. 'L.-F. Céline, 3' (1978), pp. 31–62.
44 L.-F. Céline, *Féerie pour une autre fois*, I, p. 111.
45 *Féerie* I, p. 15.
46 L.-F. Céline, *Les Beaux Draps*, pp. 220–1.
47 Ibid., pp. 221–2. The original French word-order, 'où mélodie nous a conduits', is deliberately archaic.
48 See Philip Babock Gove, *The Imaginary Voyage in Prose Fiction* (London, 1961), pp. 116–24.
49 *Féerie* I, p. 171.
50 Ibid., p. 3.
51 *Voyage au bout de la nuit, Romans* I, p. 4.
52 See, for example, *Féerie* I, pp. 54–8.
53 Godard, in *Romans* IV, p. 1187.
54 *Féerie* II, pp. 317, 333.
55 See Marie-Christine Bellosta, '*Féerie pour une autre fois* 1 et 2'; Nicholas Hewitt, 'Le Montmartre de Céline, de *Voyage au bout de la nuit* à *Féerie pour une autre fois*', in *Céline Etudes: Actes du Colloque de Toulouse (5–7 juillet 1990)* (Tusson and Paris, 1991), pp. 101–10.
56 Godard, in *Romans* IV, p. 1178.
57 Ibid., p. 1179.
58 Ibid., pp. x–xi.
59 Ibid., p. xxxi.
60 Ibid., p. xxii.
61 Ibid., p. 1199.
62 Marie-Christine Bellosta, '*Féerie pour une autre fois* 1 et 2'.
63 Quoted in *Romans* IV, pp. 1083–4.
64 L.-F. Céline, Letter to Jean-Gabriel Daragnès, 1948, quoted in *Romans* IV, p. ix.
65 Alméras, p. 394.
66 Godard, in *Romans* IV, pp. 1206–7.
67 Ibid., p. 1205.
68 Ibid., pp. 1210–13.
69 Alméras, pp. 394–9.
70 See Nicholas Hewitt, *Literature and the Right in Postwar France*.
71 L.-F. Céline, *Lettres à la NRF*, p. 204. See also Henri Godard, 'Notice', in *Romans* IV, p. 1354.
72 Letter from Paulhan to Céline, *Lettres à la NRF*, p. 274.
73 Godard, 'Notice', in *Romans* IV, pp. 1363–4.
74 Reprinted in the *Magazine Littéraire*, September 1990.
75 *Romans* III, p. 85.
76 *Entretiens avec le Professeur Y, Romans* IV, p. 498.
77 Ibid., p. 502.
78 Ibid.
79 Ibid., pp. 519–20.

80   Ibid., p. 521.
81   Ibid., p. 534.
82   Ibid., p. 535.
83   Ibid., p. 536.
84   Ibid., p. 539.
85   Ibid., p. 539.
86   Ibid., pp. 541–2.
87   Godard, 'Notice', in *Romans* IV, pp. 1365–6.
88   *Romans* IV, p. 537.
89   *Romans* I, p. 505.
90   Pascal Pia, *Carrefour*, 11 May 1955; Roger Nimier, *Le Bulletin de Paris*, 8 April 1955; Kléber Haedens, *Paris-Presse*, 10 April 1955. See Godard, 'Notice', in *Romans* IV, pp. 1366–7.
91   Alméras, p. 406.
92   Ibid., p. 398.
93   Ibid., p. 411.
94   Vitoux, p. 536.
95   Alméras, p. 413.
96   Ibid.
97   Ibid., p. 412.
98   Ibid., p. 404.
99   Ibid.
100   Robert Poulet, *Mon ami Bardamu*, p. 9.
101   Jean Paulhan, letter of 29 August 1952, in Jeannine Kohn-Etiemble, *226 Lettres inédites de Jean Paulhan*, p. 312.
102   Alméras, p. 400.
103   Ibid., p. 401.
104   Vitoux, pp. 532–3.
105   Ibid.
106   Gibault III, p. 306.
107   Alméras, p. 400.
108   Vitoux, p. 536.
109   See Jean Paul Louis (ed.), L.-F. Céline, *Lettres à Marie Bell* (Tusson, 1991).
110   Gibault III, p. 299.
111   Pierre Monnier, *Ferdinand Furieux*, p. 207, translated in Vitoux, p. 538.
112   Gibault III, p. 303.
113   Letter to Albert Paraz, 9 September 1957, *Cahiers Céline*, 6, p. 429.
114   Gibault III, p. 307.
115   Ibid., p. 300.
116   Ibid., pp. 300–1.
117   Ibid., p. 302.
118   See Henri Godard, 'Notice', in *Romans* II, pp. 978–9.
119   Ibid., pp. 1145–6.
120   Ibid., pp. 1181–2.
121   Louis-Albert Zbinden, 'Miroir du temps', Radio-Télé Suisse Romande (Lausanne), 25 July 1957, reprinted in *Cahiers Céline*, 2, p. 68. The transcription conveys the ungrammatical nature of the original remarks.
122   See Godard, 'Notice', pp. 979–80.
123   Madeleine Chapsal, 'Voyage au bout de la haine … avec L.-F. Céline', *L'Express*, 312 (14 June 1957), reprinted in *Cahiers Céline*, 2, p. 25.
124   Karl Epting, 'Il ne nous aimait pas', *Cahiers de l'Herne*, p. 241.

125 Jeanne Carayon, 'Le Docteur écrit un roman', p. 211.
126 See Godard, 'Préface', in *Romans* II, p. x.
127 L.-F. Céline, *D'un château l'autre, Romans* II, pp. 231–3.
128 L.-F. Céline, *Rigodon, Romans* II, p. 792. As we have seen, according to Paul Bonny, the Ulm episode was pure fabrication: 'He was never in Ulm. I told him all about Ulm' (L.-F. Céline, *Lettres des années noires*, p. 65).
129 *Entretiens avec le Professeur Y*, p. 546.
130 See Godard, 'Préface', pp. xvii–xxiii.
131 See *D'un château l'autre*, pp. 61–87. Céline persistently wrote 'Caron', and in this image is taking up the original title of *Féerie pour une autre fois, La Bataille du Styx*.
132 Lucette Destouches' definition, quoted by Godard, 'Notice', in *Romans* II, p. 1184.
133 Letter to Gaston Gallimard, 18 March 1957, quoted in Godard, 'Notice', p. 979.
134 Gibault III, pp. 314–15; Alméras, p. 418; Vitoux, p. 541.
135 See Godard, 'Notice', p. 1020.
136 See P.-A. Cousteau, 'Quand M. Céline rallie le fumier (doré) du système', *Rivarol*, 20 June 1957; 'D'un râtelier l'autre', *Rivarol*, 11 July 1957.
137 See *Rivarol*, 27 June and 4 July 1957; Lucien Rebatet, 'Céline soi-même', *Dimanche-Matin*, 30 June 1957.
138 See *Cahiers Céline*, 2.
139 Gibault III, pp. 322–3.
140 Vitoux, p. 545.
141 Gibault III, p. 321.
142 Claude Sarraute, 'A propos de son second livre de souvenirs sur la défaite nazie Céline nous dit comment il a fait "bouger la place des mot"', *Le Monde*, 1 June 1960, p. 8, reprinted in *Cahiers Céline*, 2. See Godard, 'Notice', p. 1156.
143 Alméras, p. 423; Gibault III, p. 344.
144 Alméras, pp. 429–30.
145 Ibid., p. 429. In fact, Céline was not eligible for the prize, since it was awarded in rotation to all the arts and had only the previous year been given to a novelist.
146 Ibid., p. 426.
147 Vitoux, pp. 547–8.
148 Letter of 16 July 1971, quoted in Alméras, p. 425.
149 In a letter to André Pulicani in 1950, Céline wrote: 'Le Vigan is in terrible poverty in Buenos Aires, you know! Every week, there arrives a boat-load of Jews from Europe! So . . .' (Letter of 15 December 1950, in L.-F. Céline, *Vingt lettres à André Pulicani, Ercole Pirazzoli, Charles Frémanger, Jean-Gabriel Daragnès, Charles de Jonquières et Albert Manouvriez, Le Lérot Rêveur*, 29 (December 1980), p. 61). The quotation is a fine example of Céline's irreducible anti-Semitism, untroubled by reality, which serves to confirm Arnold Mandel's diagnosis.
150 Letter to Roger Nimier, January 1960, quoted in Godard, 'Notice', p. 1145.
151 Alméras, p. 421.
152 Quoted in Alméras, p. 432.
153 Vitoux, p. 554.
154 Ibid.
155 Ibid., p. 555.
156 See Godard, 'Notice', pp. 1182–3.
157 Vitoux, pp. 556–7.

158 Gibault III, p. 349.
159 Arletty, 'Les Femmes n'ont rien à dire sur Céline', *L'Herne*, p. 273.

Conclusion

1 Philippe Alméras, 'Deux ou trois choses que nous avons appris sur Céline en vingt-cinq ans', in Pascal Fouché (ed.), *L.-F. Céline, 5: Vingt-cinq ans d'études céliniennes*, p. 67.
2 Madeleine Chapsal, 'Voyage au bout de la haine . . . avec L.-F. Céline', p. 25.
3 It is significant that, while Malraux's admiration for Céline extended no further than his first novel, he remained friendly towards him until his death and intervened in an abortive attempt to have Lucette Destouches appointed to the Paris Opera (see Alméras, pp. 428–9).
4 See Nicole Debrie, *Il était une fois Céline*, Willi Szafran, *Louis-Ferdinand Céline: Essai psychanalytique* (Brussels, 1976).
5 Serge André, *L'Imposture perverse* (Paris, 1993), p. 416.
6 See Bettina L. Knapp, *Céline, Man of Hate* (Montgomery, AL, 1974).
7 Letter to Albert Paraz, 1 June 1947, *Cahiers Céline*, 6, p. 22.
8 See Theodor Adorno et al., *The Authoritarian Personality* (New York, 1950).
9 See James Joll, *Three Intellectuals and Politics: Blum, Rathenau, Marinetti* (London, 1960).

Bibliography

1 Bibliographies

For an exhaustive list of all of Céline's writings, the reader is referred to the following:

Dauphin, Jean-Pierre, *Calepins de Bibliographie, 6: L.-F. Céline, I. 1914–1944* (Paris, 1977).

Dauphin, Jean-Pierre and Fouché, Pascal, *Bibliographie des écrits de Louis-Ferdinand Céline* (Paris, 1985).

For lists of studies devoted to Céline, see:

Dauphin, Jean-Pierre, *L.-F. Céline, Essai de bibliographie des études en langue française consacrées à Louis-Ferdinand Céline, Tome 1: 1914–1944* (Paris, 1977).

Krance, Charles, 'Louis-Ferdinand Céline' in Douglas Alden and Richard A. Brooks (eds), *A Critical Bibliography of French Literature*, vol. 6, *The Twentieth Century*, Part I, (Syracuse, NY, 1980), pp. 743–65.

Luce, Stanford and William Buckley, *A Half-Century of Céline. An Annotated Bibliography 1932–1982* (New York and London, 1983).

2 Manuscripts

Most of Céline's manuscripts are in private hands. For accounts of sales at auction of the manuscripts, see the catalogues published by the Bibliothèque L.-F. Céline de l'Université Paris 7: *Tout Céline. Répertoire des livres, manuscrits et lettres de Céline passés en vente 1979–1980* (Paris, 1981); *Tout Céline, 2. Répertoire des livres, manuscrits et lettres de Louis-Ferdinand Céline passés en vente au cours des années 1981 et 1982* (Paris, 1983); *Tout Céline III. Répertoire des livres, manuscrits et lettres de Céline passés en vente au cours des années 1983–1984* (Liège, 1985); *Tout Céline IV. Répertoire des livres, manuscrits et lettres de Céline passés en vente au cours des années 1985 et 1986* (Liège, 1987); *Tout Céline V. Répertoire des lettres et manuscrits de Céline passés en vente au cours des années 1987, 1988 et 1989* (Liège, 1990).

For an illuminating account of reading Céline's manuscripts, see Henri Godard, *Les Manuscrits de Céline et leurs leçons* (Tusson, 1988).

3   Collected Editions of Céline's Works

Oeuvres de Louis-Ferdinand Céline, ed. Jean A Ducourneau. 5 vols (Paris, 1966–9).
Oeuvres de Céline, ed. Frédéric Vitoux. 9 vols (Paris, 1981).
The Pléiade Edition:
    Romans I, introduction by Henri Mondor, chronology by Jean A. Ducourneau (Paris, 1962) (Contains *Voyage au bout de la nuit* and *Mort à crédit*).
    Romans I, ed. Henri Godard (Paris, 1981) (Contains *Voyage au bout de la nuit* and *Mort à crédit*).
    Romans II, ed. Henri Godard (Paris, 1974) (Contains *D'un Château l'autre*, *Nord* and *Rigodon*).
    Romans III, ed. Henri Godard (Paris, 1988) (Contains *Casse-pipe*, *Guignol's Band I* and *Guignol's Band II*).
    Romans IV, ed. Henri Godard (Paris, 1993) (Contains *Féerie pour une autre fois I*, *Féerie pour une autre fois II* and *Entretiens avec le professeur Y*).

4   Books by Céline

La Vie et l'oeuvre de Philippe-Ignace Semmelweis (Rennes, 1924).
La Quinine en thérapeutique (Paris, 1925).
Voyage au bout de la nuit (Paris, 1932) [trans. John Marks, *Journey to the End of the Night* (London and Boston, 1935), Ralph Mannheim, *Journey to the End of the Night* (New York, 1983)].
L'Eglise (Paris, 1933).
Mort à crédit (Paris, 1936) [trans. John Marks, *Death on the Instalment Plan* (London and Boston, 1937), Ralph Mannheim, *Death on the Instalment Plan* (New York, 1971)].
Mea culpa, suivi de Semmelweiss (Paris, 1936) [trans. Robert A. Parker, *Mea culpa and The Life and Work of Semmelweis* (New York, 1937, reprinted 1979)].
Bagatelles pour un massacre (Paris, 1937).
L'Ecole des cadavres (Paris, 1938).
Les Beaux Draps (Paris, 1941).
Guignol's Band I (Paris, 1944) [trans. Frechtman and Nile, New York, 1969)].
Casse-pipe (Paris, 1949).
Féerie pour une autre fois I (Paris, 1952).
Féerie pour une autre fois II: Normance (Paris, 1954).
Entretiens avec le Professeur Y (Paris, 1955) [trans. Stanford Luce, *Conversations with Professor Y* (Hanover, NH, and London, 1986)].
D'un Château l'autre (Paris, 1957) [trans. Carroll and Graf, *Castle to Castle* (New York, 1987)].
Ballets sans musique, sans personne, sans rien (Paris, 1959).
Nord (Paris, 1960) [trans. Delacorte, *North* (New York, 1972)].

Guignol's Band II: Le Pont de Londres (Paris, 1964).
Rigodon (Paris, 1969) [trans. Ralph Mannheim, *Rigodoon* (New York, 1974)].
Progrès (Paris, 1978).
Arletty, jeune fille dauphinoise (Paris, 1983).
Maudits soupirs pour une autre fois (Paris, 1985).
'31' Cité d'Antin, ed. Eric Mazet (Tusson, 1988).

5   Articles by Céline

'Observations physiologiques sur *Convoluta roscoffensis*', *Académie des Sciences*, 1920 (reprinted in CC3, pp. 242–4).
'Prolongation de la vie chez les *Galleria mellonella*', *Académie des Sciences*, 1921 (reprinted in CC 3, pp. 245–6).
'Les Derniers Jours de Semmelweis', *La Presse Médicale*, 25 June 1924, pp. 1067, 1072.
'Note sur l'organisation sanitaire des usines Ford à Detroit', Internal memorandum for the League of Nations, 1925 (reprinted in CC 3, pp. 116–30).
'Notes sur le service sanitaire de la Compagnie Westinghouse à Pittsburgh', Internal memorandum for the League of Nations, 1925 (reprinted in CC 3, pp. 131–6).
'A propos du service sanitaire des usines Ford à Detroit', *Bulletins et Mémoires de la Société de Médecine de Paris*, 10, Session of 26 May 1928, pp. 303–12 (reprinted in CC 3, pp. 137–53).
'Les Assurances sociales et une politique économique de la santé publique', *La Presse Médicale*, 24 November 1928, pp. 1499, 1501 (reprinted in CC 3, pp. 154–66).
'L'infection puerpérale et les antivirus', *La Médecine*, April 1929, p. 309 (reprinted in CC 3, pp. 97–8).
'Note sur l'emploi des antivirus de Besredka en pansements humides', *Bulletins et Mémoires de la Société de Médecine de Paris*, Session of 10 May 1929, pp. 223–4 (reprinted in CC 3, pp. 98–100).
'L'Immunité dans les maladies infectieuses. A propos du livre récent de A. Besredka', *Paris Médical*, June 1929, pp. 537–9 (reprinted in CC 3, pp. 101–9).
'Deux expériences de vaccination en masse et *per os* contre la typhoïde', *La Presse Médicale*, 11 September 1929, pp. 1193–4 (reprinted in CC 3, pp. 167–70).
'La Santé publique en France', *Monde*, 8 March 1930 (reprinted in *Céline. Textes et documents, 1*, pp. 27–49).
'Essai de dignostique et de thérapeutique méthodiques 'en série' sur certains malades d'un dispensaire', *Bulletins et Mémoires de la Société de Médecine de Paris*, Session of 22 March 1930, pp. 163–8 (reprinted in CC 3, pp. 170–7).
'Les Hémorragies minimes des gencives en clientèle', *La Gazette médicale*, 1 November 1931, p. 614 (reprinted in CC 3, pp. 246–8).
'Mémoire pour le Cours des Hautes Etudes', unpublished memorandum, 1932 (reprinted in CC 3, pp. 178–214).
'Pour tuer le chômage tueront-ils les chômeurs?', *Le Mois*, 1 February–1 March 1933, pp. 57–60 (reprinted in CC 3, pp. 215–21).
'Hommage à Emile Zola' in Robert Denoël, *Apologie de 'Mort à crédit'* (Paris, 1936).
'La Médecine chez Ford', *Lectures*, 40/4, 1 August 1941, pp. 6–9; 5, 15 August 1941, p. 6.

'Préface', to Albert Serouille, *Bezons à travers les âges* (Paris, 1944).
'A l'Agité du bocal' in Albert Paraz, *La Gala des vaches* (Paris, 1948).

6 Collections of Articles, Correspondence and Unpublished Fragments

There is currently no collected edition of Céline's correspondence, interviews and articles, althought most of them are to be found in the three following collections:

(a) Les Cahiers de L'Herne

Louis-Ferdinand Céline I, Des témoins, correspondance, inédits, interférences, essais, études, photographies, bibliographie, ed. Dominique de Roux and Michel Thélia (Paris, 1962).
Louis-Ferdinand Céline II (Paris, 1965).
L.-F. Céline, ed. Dominique de Roux, Michel Beaujour and Michel Thélia.
Les Cahiers de l'Herne (Paris, 1972) (a revised and composite edition of I and II).

(b) Les Cahiers Céline

Cahiers Céline I, Céline et l'actualité littéraire, 1932–1957, ed. Jean-Pierre Dauphin and Henri Godard (Paris, 1976).
Cahiers Céline 2, Céline et l'actualité littéraire, 1957–1961, ed. Jean-Pierre Dauphin and Henri Godard (Paris, 1976).
Cahiers Céline 3, Semmelweiss et autres écrits médicaux, ed. Jean-Pierre Dauphin and Henri Godard (Paris, 1977).
Cahiers Céline 4, Lettres et premiers écrits d'Afrique, 1916–1917, ed. Jean-Pierre Dauphin (Paris, 1978).
Cahiers Céline 5, Lettres à des amies, ed. Colin W. Nettelbeck (Paris, 1979).
Cahiers Céline 6, Lettres à Albert Paraz, 1947–1957, ed. J.-P. Louis (Paris, 1980).
Cahiers Céline 7, Céline et l'actualité (1933–1961), ed. Pascal Fouché (Paris, 1986).
Cahiers Céline 8, Progrès, suivi de Oeuvres pour la scène et l'écran, ed. Pascal Fouché (Paris, 1988).

(c) Bibliothèque L.-F. Céline

Céline. Textes et documents 1 (Paris, 1979).
Céline. Textes et documents 2 (Paris, 1982).
Céline. Textes et documents 3 (Paris, 1985).

In addition to these series, Céline's correspondence is to be found in the following separate volumes:

Choix de lettres de l'hiver 1949–1950, ed. Jean Paul Louis (Tusson, 1978).
Ferdinand Furieux: avec trois cent treize lettres de Louis-Ferdinand Céline, ed. Pierre Monnier (Lausanne, 1979).
Lettres des années noires, ed. Philippe Alméras (Paris, 1994).
'Lettres et cahiers de prison', *Magazine Littéraire*, 317 (January 1994), pp. 53–60.
Lettres à Charles Deshayes 1947–1951, ed. Pierre-Edmond Robert (Paris, 1988).
Lettres à Joseph Garcin, ed. Pierre Lainé (Paris, 1987).
Lettres à Marie Bell, ed. Jean Paul Louis (Tusson, 1991).
Lettres à Marie Canavaggia, ed. Jean Paul Louis, I, *1936–1947*; II, *1948–1960*; III, *Index analytique* (Tusson, 1995).
Lettres à la NRF, ed. Pascal Fouché (Paris, 1991).
Lettres à son avocat, ed. Frédéric Monnier (Paris, 1984).
Lettres à Tixier, ed. Frédéric Monnier (Paris, 1985).
Vingt lettres à André Pulicani, Ercole Pirazzoli, Charles Frémanger, Jean Gabriel Daragnès, Charles de Jonquières et Albert Manouvriez, ed. Jean Paul Louis (Tusson, 1980).

Finally, other occasional writings are collected in the Pléiade edition of the novels and in *Préfaces et dédicaces*, ed. Henri Godard (Tusson, 1987).

7 Secondary Works (Albums)

Catalogue de l'Exposition Céline, Musée de l'Ancien Evêché de Lausanne (Lausanne, 1977).
Dauphin, Jean-Pierre and Boudillet, Jacques, *Album Céline* (Paris, 1977).

8 Secondary Works (Books)

Aebersold, Denise, *Céline. Un démystificateur mythomane* (Paris, 1977).
Alméras, Philippe, *Les Idées de Céline* (Paris, 1987).
—— *Céline. Entre haines et passions* (Paris, 1994).
Balta, François, *La Vie médicale de Louis Destouches* (Thèse de Médecine, Académie de Paris, 1977).
Bardèche, Maurice, *Louis-Ferdinand Céline* (Paris, 1986).
Bellosta, Marie-Christine, *Le Capharnaüm célinien ou la place des objets dans 'Mort à crédit'* (Paris, 1976).
—— *Céline ou l'art de la contradiction* (Paris, 1990).
Blondiaux, Isabelle, *Une Ecriture psychotique: Louis-Ferdinand Céline* (Paris, 1985).
Bonnefis, Philippe, *Céline. Le Rappel des oiseaux* (Lille, 1992).
Buckley, William K. (ed.), *Critical Essays on Louis-Ferdinand Céline* (Boston, 1989).
Burns, Wayne, *Enfin Céline vint. A Contextualist Reading of 'Journey to the End of the Night' and 'Death on the Installment Plan'* (New York and Paris, 1988).
Carson, James, *Céline's Imaginative Space* (New York, 1987).
Chantemerle, Isabelle, *Céline* (Paris, 1987).
Chesneau, Albert, *Essai de psychocritique de Louis-Ferdinand Céline* (Paris, 1971).

—— *La Langue sauvage de L.-F. Céline* (Lille, 1971).

Crescuicci, Alain, *Les Territoires céliniens* (Paris, 1990).

Crescuicci, Alain (ed.), *Céline: 'Voyage au bout de la nuit'* (Paris, 1993).

Damour, A.-C. and Damour, J.-P., *L.-F. Céline. Voyage au bout de la nuit* (Paris, 1985).

Dauphin, Jean-Pierre (ed.), *Les Critiques de notre temps et Céline* (Paris, 1976).

Day, Philip Stephen, *Le Miroir allégorique de Louis-Ferdinand Céline* (Paris, 1974).

Debrie, Nicole, *Louis-Ferdinand Céline* (Paris, 1989).

—— *Il était une fois . . . Céline* (Paris, 1990).

Debrie-Panel, Nicole, *Louis-Ferdinand Céline* (Lyons, 1961).

Della Torre, Renato, *Invito alla lettura di Céline* (Milan, 1979).

Del Perugia, Paul, *Céline* (Paris, 1987).

Derval, André, *70 Critiques de 'Voyage au bout de la nuit', 1932–1935* (Paris, 1993).

Flynn, James, *Understanding Céline* (Seattle, 1984).

Fortier, Paul A., *Le Métro émotif de Céline* (Paris, 1981).

François, Jacques, *Contribution à l'étude des années rennaises du docteur Destouches (1918–1924)* (unpublished thesis, Rennes, 1967).

Gibault, François, *Céline 1: 1894–1932: Le Temps des espérences* (Paris, 1977).

—— *Céline, 2: 1932–1944: Délires et persécutions* (Paris, 1985).

—— *Céline, 3: 1944–1961: Cavalier de l'Apocalypse* (Paris, 1981).

Godard, Henri, *Poétique de Céline* (Paris, 1985).

—— *Voyage au bout de la nuit de Louis-Ferdinand Céline* (Paris, 1991).

—— *Céline scandale* (Paris, 1994).

Guénot, Jean, *Louis-Ferdinand Céline damné par l'écriture* (Paris, 1973).

Guisto, Jean-Pierre, *Le Champ clos de l'écriture: Laforgue, Saint-John Perse, Céline* (Valenciennes, 1985).

Hanrez, Marc, *Céline* (Paris, 1961).

Hayman, David, *Louis-Ferdinand Céline* (New York, 1965).

Henric, Jacques and Bailly-Maître-Grand, Patrick, *Louis-Ferdinand Céline* (Paris, 1991).

Henry, Anne, *Céline écrivain* (Paris, 1994).

Hewitt, Nicholas, *The Golden Age of Louis-Ferdinand Céline* (Leamington Spa and New York, 1987).

Hindus, Milton, *The Crippled Giant: A Bizarre Adventure in Contemporary Letters* (New York, 1950) (reissued as *The Crippled Giant: A Literary Relationship with Louis-Ferdinand Céline* (Hanover, NH, and London, 1986; translated as: *Louis-Ferdinand Céline tel que je l'ai vu* (Paris, 1969)).

Holthus, Gunther, *Untersuchungen zu Stil und Konzeption von Célines 'Voyage au bout de la nuit'* (Berne and Frankfurt, 1972).

Huchet, Charles, *'Mort à crédit' de Céline. Une Naissance payée comptant* (Paris, 1993).

Juilland, Alphonse, *Les Verbes de Céline: Première Partie: Etude d'ensemble* (Stanford, CA, 1985).

—— *Elizabeth and Louis. Elizabeth Craig talks about Louis-Ferdinand Céline* (Stanford, CA, 1991).

—— *A Célinian Trove. Elizabeth Craig's Jewelry Box* (Stanford, CA, 1991).

Kaminski, H.-E., *Céline en chemise brune* (Paris, 1938).

Kaplan, Alice Yaeger, *Relevé des sources et citations dans 'Bagatelles pour un massacre'* (Tusson, 1987).

Kaplan, Alice and Roussin, Philippe (eds), *Céline USA* (Durham, NC, 1994).

Knapp, Bettina L., *Céline: Man of Hate* (Montgomery, AL, 1974).

Krance, Charles, *Céline. The I of the Storm* (Lexington, KY, 1992).

Kristeva, Julia, *Pouvoirs de l'horreur. Essai sur l'abjection* (Paris, 1980).

Kunnas, Tarmo, *Drieu la Rochelle, Céline, Brasillach et la tentation fasciste* (Paris, 1972).

Lalande, Bernard, *'Voyage au bout de la nuit'. Céline* (Paris, 1976).

La Querière, Yves de, *Céline et les mots. Etude stylistique des effets de mots dans 'Voyage au bout de la nuit'* (Lexington, KY, 1973).

Latin, Danièle, *Le 'Voyage au bout de la nuit' de Céline. Roman de la subversion et subversion du roman* (Brussels, 1988).

Lavoinne, Yves, *Voyage au bout de la nuit de Céline* (Paris, 1974).

Luce, Stanford, *A Glossary of Céline's Fiction* (Ann Arbor, MI, 1979).

—— *Céline and his Critics: Scandals and Paradox* (Stanford, CA, 1986).

McCarthy, Patrick, *Céline* (Harmondsworth, 1975).

Mahé, Henri, *La Brinquebale aver Céline* (Paris, 1969).

Matthews, J. H., *The Inner Dream: Céline as Novelist* (Syracuse, NY, 1978).

Monnier, Jean, *Elizabeth Craig raconte Céline. Entretien avec la dédicatrice de 'Voyage au bout de la nuit'* (Paris, 1988).

Monnier, Pierre, *Ferdinand furieux* (Lausanne, 1979).

Morand, Jacqueline, *Les Idées politiques de Louis-Ferdinand Céline* (Paris, 1972).

Muray, Philippe, *Céline* (Paris, 1981).

Murray, Jack, *Landscapes of Alienation. Ideological Subversion in Kafka, Céline and Onetti* (Stanford, CA, 1991).

Noble, Ian, *Language and Narration in Céline's Novels: The Challenge of Disorder* (London, 1986).

O'Connell, David, *Louis-Ferdinand Céline* (Boston, 1976).

Ostrovsky, Erika, *Céline and his Vision* (New York, 1967).

—— *Voyeur voyant: A Portrait of Louis-Ferdinand Céline* (New York, 1971).

Pagès, Yves, *Les Fictions de politique chez L.-F. Céline* (Paris, 1994).

Pedersen, Helga, *Le Danemark a-t-il sauvé Céline (1945–1951)?* (Paris, 1975).

Perrault, Serge, *Céline de mes souvenirs* (Tusson, 1992).

Phalèse, Hubert de, *Guide de 'Voyage au bout de la nuit'* (Paris, 1993).

Poulet, Robert, *Entretiens familiers avec Louis-Ferdinand Céline* (Paris, 1958) [reprinted as *Mon ami Bardamu* (Paris, 1971)].

Richard, Jean-Pierre, *Nausée de Céline* (Montpellier, 1979).

Robert, Pierre-Edmond, *Céline et les Editions Denoël* (Paris, 1991).

Rouayrenc, Catherine, *'C'est mon secret': La Technique de l'écriture 'populaire' dans 'Voyage au bout de la nuit' et 'Mort à crédit'* (Tusson, 1994).

Roux, Dominique de, *La Mort de Louis-Ferdinand Céline* (Paris, 1966).

Séebold, Eric, *Essai de situation des pamphlets de Louis-Ferdinand Céline* (Tusson, 1985).

Solomon, Philip H. *Night Voyager. A Reading of Céline* (Birmingham, AL, 1988).

—— *Understanding Céline* (Columbia, SC, 1992).

Smith, André, *La Nuit de Louis-Ferdinand Céline* (Paris, 1973).

Sturrock, John, *Céline. Journey to the End of the Night* (Cambridge, 1990).

Szafran, Willi, *Louis-Ferdinand Céline. Essai psychanalytique* (Brussels, 1976).

Thiher, Allen, *Céline: The Novel as Delirium* (Rutgers, NY, 1972).

Thomas, Merlin, *Louis-Ferdinand Céline* (London, 1979).

Turpin, Jean-Marie, *Le Chevalier Céline, ou la première marche de l'Atlantide* (Paris, 1990).

Vandromme, Pol, *Céline* (Paris, 1963).

—— *Robert Le Vigan, compagnon et personnage de L.-F. Céline* (Kessel-Lô, 1980).

—— *Du côté de Céline, Lili* (Kessel-Lô, 1983).

—— *Marcel, Roger et Ferdinand* (Kessel-Lô, 1984).

Verdaguer, Pierre, *L'Univers de la cruauté: Une Lecture de Céline* (Geneva, 1988).
Vitoux, Frédéric, *Louis-Ferdinand Céline: Misère et parole* (Paris, 1973).
—— *Bébert, le chat de Louis-Ferdinand Céline* (Paris, 1976).
—— *Céline* (Paris, 1978).
—— *La Vie de Céline* (Paris, 1988).
—— *Céline: A Biography*, trans. Jesse Browner (New York, 1994).
Zagadinski, Stéphane, *Céline seul* (Paris, 1993).

9 Secondary Works (Collections of Articles)

Australian Journal of French Studies, XIII 1–2, 1976: *Actes du colloque international d'Oxford, 1975.*
Conference Papers of the Société des Etudes Céliniennes:
  Actes du Colloque International de Paris, 1976 (Paris, 1978).
  Actes du Colloque International de Paris 1979 (Paris, 1980).
  Actes du Colloque International d'Oxford, 1981 (Paris, 1981).
  Actes du Colloque International de la Haye, 1983 (Paris, 1984).
  Actes du Colloque International de Londres, 1988 (Tusson, 1989).
  Actes du Colloque Internationale de Toulouse, 1990 (Tusson, 1991).
  Actes du Colloque Internationale de Paris, 1992 (Tusson, 1993).
Le Bulletin Célinien, 1–46 (Brussels, 1982–6).
La Revue Célinienne, 1–3/4 (Brussels, 1979–81).
Revue des Lettres Modernes, Série L.-F. Céline:
  1 *Pour une poétique célinienne* (Paris, 1974).
  2 *Ecriture et esthétique* (Paris, 1976).
  5 *Vingt-cinq ans d'études céliniennes* (Paris, 1988).

10 Secondary Works (Articles)

Alméras, Philippe, 'L'Amérique femelle ou les enfants de Colomb', *Australian Journal of French Studies*, XIII 1–2 (1976), 97–109.
Arland, Marcel, *'Bagatelles pour un massacre* par Louis-Ferdinand Céline', *Nouvelle Revue Française*, 293 (February 1938).
Bleton, Paul, 'Maximes, phrases et efficace d'un pamphlet', *Actes du Colloque International de Paris, 1979* (BLFC 3), 249–69.
Dunwoodie, Peter, 'Merveilleux, étrange et fantastique dans les romans de Louis-Ferdinand Céline', *Les Lettres Romanes*, 37/1–2 (Feb.–May 1983), 82–111.
Forbes, Jill, 'Symbolique de l'espace: le 'Londres' célinien', *Actes du Colloque International de Paris, 1976* (BLFC 1), 27–40.
Fouché, Pascal, 'Féerie pour un autre Montmartre', *Quinzaine Littéraire* (June 1982), 32–6.
Gide, André, 'Céline, les Juifs et Maritain', *Nouvelle Revue Française* (April 1938).
Hewitt, Nicholas, *'Mort à crédit et* la crise de la petite-bourgeoisie', *Australian Journal of French Studies*, XIII 1–2 (1976), 110–17.
—— 'Céline and Shakespeare', in Holgar Klein and Jean-Marie Maguin (eds), *Shakespeare and France, Shakespeare Yearbook*, 5 (Lampeter, 1994), 131–46.

Kingston, Paul, 'Celine et l'antisémitisme de son époque: aspects de *Bagatelles pour un massacre*', *Actes du Colloque International d'Oxford*, 1981 (BLFC 5), 49–66.

Krance, Charles, 'Semmelweis ou l'accouchement de la biographie célinienne', *Revue des Lettres Modernes, Serie Céline*, 2 (1976).

Mancel, Yannik, 'De la Sémiotique textuelle à la théorie du 'roman': Céline', *Dialectiques, 8* (1975), 45–68.

Mounier, Emmanuel, '*Bagatelles pour un massacre*', *Esprit*, 66 (March 1938).

Muray, Philippe, 'Mort à crédo. Céline, le positivisme et l'occultisme', *Actes du Colloque International de La Haye, 1983* (BLFC 8), 95–116.

—— 'Le Siècle de Céline', *L'Infini*, 8 (Autumn 1984).

Nettelbeck, Colin W., 'Céline devant l'an 40. *Les Beaux Draps* et le début de *Guignol's Band*', *Actes du Colloque International d'Oxford, 1981* (BLFC 5), 67–80.

Out-Breut, Michèle, 'Une Analyse sémiotique de Casse-pipe (II)', *Actes du Colloque International de La Haye, 1983* (BLFC 8), 83–94.

Poli, Jean-Dominique, 'Les Données de mentalité dans les romans et les pamphlets', *Actes du Colloque International de Paris 1976* (BLFC 1), 167–84.

Richard, Jean-Pierre, 'Casque-pipe', *Littérature*, 29 (1978), 3–17.

Robert, P. E., 'Marcel Proust et Louis-Ferdinand Céline: un contrepoint', *Bulletin des Amis de Marcel Proust*, 29 (1979).

Roussin, Philippe, 'Tout dire', *Actes du Colloque International de la Haye*, 1983 (BLFC 8), 117–32.

Sautermeister, Christine, 'Quelques traits caractéristiques du comique de Céline à partir de *Casse-pipe*', *Actes du Colloque International de Paris*, 1976 (BLFC 1), 335–52.

—— 'Lecture théâtrale et cinématographique de Casse-pipe', *Actes du Colloque International de Paris*, 1979 (BLFC 3), 213–22.

Van Zoest, Aart, 'Une Analyse sémiotique de Casse-pipe (1)', *Actes du Colloque International de La Haye, 1983* (BLFC 8), 75–82.

11 Other works consulted

'Congrès de syndicats médicaux', *La Presse Médicale*, 8 February 1928 p. 172. 'Les Assurances Sociales', *La Presse Médicale*, 24 November 1928 p. 1497. 'Les Méfaits des Assurances Sociales et les moyens d'y remédier. D'après Ervin Lick (de Dantzig)', *La Presse Médicale,* 24 November 1928, p. 1498.

Adhémar, Jean, *Imagerie populaire française* (Milan, 1968).

Adler, Jacques, *The Jews of Paris and the Final Solution: Communal response and Internal Conflicts 1940–1944* (Oxford, 1987).

Adorno, Theodor, *The Authoritarian Personality* (New York, 1950).

'Agathon' [Henri Massis and Alfred de Tarde], *Ce que pensent les jeunes gens d'aujourd'hui* (Paris, 1912).

'Agathon' and Mory, Vulfran, *Guidargus: Le Livre politique sous l'Occupation (1940–1944)* (Paris, 1990).

André, Serge, *L'Imposture perverse* (Paris, 1993).

Angenot, Marc, *La Parole pamphlétaire. Typologie des discours modernes* (Paris, 1982).

Antall, József, 'The Life of Ignac Fülöp Semmelweis (1818–1865)', in *Pictures from the Past of the Healing Arts: A Guidebook to the Semmelweis Museum, Library and Archives* (Budapest, 1993).

Arendt, Hannah, *Sur l'antisémitisme* (Paris, 1973).
Ariès, Philippe, *Histoire des populations françaises et de leurs attitudes devant la vie depuis le XVIIIe siècle* (Paris, 1948).
Arland, Marcel, 'Sur un nouveau mal du siècle', *Nouvelle Revue Française*, 125 (1924), 149–58.
Arletty, *La Défense* (Paris, 1971).
Assouline, Pierre, *L'Epuration des intellectuels* (Paris, 1985).
—— *Gaston Gallimard: Un demi-siècle d'édition française* (Paris, 1996).
Aymé, Marcel, 'Avenue Junot', *Je suis partout* (14 August 1943).
—— *Le Passe-Muraille* (Paris, 1943).
—— Preface to Jean Vertex, *Le Village inspiré* (Paris, 1950).
Balinska, Marta Aleksandra, *Une Vie pour humanitaire. Ludwig Rajchman, 1881–1965* (Paris, 1995).
Balzac, Honoré de, *La Cousine Bette* (Paris, 1959). [First published in 1846.]
Barjavel, René, *Journal d'un homme simple . . . vingt ans apres la charette bleue* (Paris, 1982).
Baudelaire, Charles, *Oeuvres complètes,* ed. Y. G. Le Dantec (Paris, 1961).
Belleroche, Maud de, *Le Ballet des crabes* (Paris, 1975).
Benjamin, Walter, *Charles Baudelaire. A Lyric Poet in an Age of High Capitalism*, trans. Harry Zohn (London, 1973).
Béraud, Henri, *Faut-il réduire l'Angleterre en esclavage?* (Paris, 1935).
—— *Le Flâneur salarié, Le Lérot rêveur,* 40 (May 1985).
Bergonzi, Bernard, *The Early H.G. Wells: A Study of the Scientific Romances* (Manchester, 1961).
Berl, Emmanuel, *Interrogatoire par Patrick Modiano, suivi de 'Il fait beau allons au cimetière'* (Paris, 1976).
Berlanstein, Lenard R., *The Working People of Paris, 1871–1914* (Baltimore, MD, and London, 1984).
Bernier, Olivier, *Fireworks at Dusk: Paris in the Thirties* (Boston, Toronto and London, 1993).
Bernanos, Georges, *La France contre les robots* (Rio de Janeiro, 1944).
Beylie, Claude and Bernard, André, *Robert Le Vigan. Désordre et génie* (Paris, 1996).
Bloy, Léon, *Le Salut par les Juifs* (Paris, 1892).
Boisline, Jean de, *Banlieue mon amour* (Paris, 1995).
Bordiga, Joseph, *Fonctionnement d'une consultation de médecine préventitive pour enfants d'âge scolaire* (medical thesis, Paris, 1937).
Brasillach, Robert, *Notre avant-guerre* (Paris, 1981).
Brassaï, *Henry Miller, grandeur nature* (Paris, 1975).
Breker, Arno, *Paris, Hitler et moi* (Paris, 1970).
Briau, Eugène, 'Assurances Sociales et tuberculose', *La Presse Médicale* (11 January 1928), pp. 43–4.
—— 'Assurances Sociales et syphilis', *La Presse Médicale* (8 February 1928), pp. 171–2.
Burrin, Philippe, *Living with Defeat: France under the German Occupation 1940–1944* (London, 1996).
Camus, Albert, *La Chute* (Paris, 1956).
—— *Carnets* (Paris, 1962).
Caraz, Pierre, *Mémoire en images: Clichy-la-Garenne* (Joué-les-Tours, 1997).
Carbuccia, Adry de, *Du Tango à Lily Marlène* (Paris, 1987).
Carco, Francis, *De Montmartre au Quartier Latin* (Paris, 1927).
Carroll, Lewis, *Through the Looking-Glass* (New York, 1960). [First published in 1865.]

Caute, David, *The Fellow-travellers: A Postscript to the Enlightenment* (London, 1973).
Cendrars, Blaise, *L'Or* (Paris, 1924).
Charasse, André, *La Hurle. La Nuit sanglante de Clichy, 16 et 17 mars 1937* (Paris, 1983).
Charensol, Georges, *D'une rive l'autre* (Paris, 1973).
Chevalier, J.-J., *Histoire des institutions et des régimes de la France moderne 1789–1958* (Paris, 1967).
Chevalier, Louis, *Classes laborieuses, classes dangereuses à Paris pendant la première moitié du XIXe siècle* (Paris, 1958).
—— *Montmartre du plaisir et du crime* (Paris, 1980).
Cim, Géo, *Montmartre mon vieux village* (Paris, 1964).
Clarke-Kennedy, A. E., *London Pride: The Story of a Voluntary Hospital* (London, 1979).
Cocteau, Jean, *Journal 1942–1945* (Paris, 1989).
Cohn, Norman, *Warrant for Genocide: The Myth of the Jewish World Conspiracy and the Protocols of the Elders of Zion* (London, 1967).
Conrad, Joseph, *The Secret Agent* (Harmondsworth, 1963). [First published in 1907.]
Crémieux-Brilhac, Jean, *Les Français de l'année 40* (Paris, 1990).
Crespelle, J.-P., *Monmartre vivant* (Paris, 1964).
Crubelllier, Maurice, (with Maurice Agulhon), 'Les Citadins et leurs cultures', in Georges Duby (ed.), *Histoire de la France Urbaine, 4: La Ville de l'âge industriel: le cycle haussmannien* (Paris, 1983).
Dabit, Eugène, *Journal intime* (Paris, 1989).
Daudet, Léon, *Le Stupide dix-neuvième siècle, exposé des insanités meurtrières qui se sont abbattues sur la France depuis 130 ans, 1789–1919* (Paris, 1922).
Déat, Marcel, *Mémoires politiques* (Paris, 1989).
Defoe, Daniel, *The Shortest Way with the Dissenters and Other Pamphlets* (Oxford, 1927). [First published in 1702.]
Desfosses, P., 'Quelques réflexions sur les Assurances Sociales', *La Presse Médicale* (29 October 1927), p. 1325.
—— 'La Question des Assurances Sociales', *La Presse Médicale* (11 January 1928), p. 43.
Dior, Raymond A., *Les Juifs, Numéro Spécial, Le Crapouillot* (September 1936).
Dominique, Pierre, *Les Polémistes français depuis 1789* (Paris, 1962).
Dorgelès, Roland, *Au Beau temps de la Butte* (Paris, 1963).
Drieu la Rochelle, Pierre, *Fragment de mémoires 1940–1941* (Paris, 1982).
—— *Journal 1939–1945* (Paris, 1992).
Drumont, Edouard, *La France juive* (Paris, 1886).
—— *La Fin d'un monde* (Paris, 1892).
Dubuffet, Jean, *Prospectus et tous écrits suivants*, 1 and 2 (Paris, 1967).
Duchartre, Pierre-Louis, and Saulnier, René, *L'Imagerie populaire. Les Images de tous les provinces français du XVe siècle au Second Empire. Les Complaintes, contes et chansons, légendes qui ont inspirè les images* (Paris, 1925).
Dumont, Jean-Marie, *La Vie et l'oeuvre de Jean-Charles Pellerin* (Epinal, 1956).
Eizig, Paul, *The Destiny of Gold* (London, 1972).
Epting, Karl, *Gedanken eines Konservativen* (Bodman and Bodensee, 1977).
Epting-Kullmann, Alice, *Pariser Begegnungen* (Hanner über Sachingen, 1972).
Erikson, Erik H., *Childhood and Society* (Harmondsworth, 1965).
Faure, Elie, *Oeuvres complètes*, III (Paris, 1964).
Fohlen, Claude, *La France de l'entre-deux-guerres (1917–1939)* (Paris, 1966).
Fontette, François de, 'Eléments pour une définition du Juif', *Annales du C.E.S.E.R.E.*, 5 (1982), pp. 15–29.

Fouché, Pascal, 'L'Edition 1914–1992', in Jean-François Sirinelli (ed.), *Histoire des droites en France*, 3 (Paris, 1994), pp. 257–92.

Frank, Nino, *Les Années 30* (Paris, 1969).

Gaillard, Marc, *Les Belles heures de Clichy* (Amiens, 1992).

Galtier-Boissière, Jean, *Journal 1940–1950* (Paris, 1992).

Gerbod, Paul, 'L'Union Soviétique dans l'opinion française 1917–1941', *Annales du C.E.S.E.R.E.*, 4 (1981), pp. 3–26.

Goux, Jean-Joseph, *Freud, Marx. Economie et symbolique* (Paris, 1973).

Gouze, Roger, *Les Bêtes à Goncourt: Un demi-siècle de batailles littéraires* (Paris, 1973).

Gove, Philip Babock, *The Imaginary Voyage in Prose Fiction* (London, 1961).

Gramsci, Antonio, *Selections from the Prison Notebooks*, ed. Quintin Hoare and Geoffrey Nowell Smith (London, 1971).

Griffiths, Richard, *The Reactionary Revolution* (London, 1966).

Guilloux, Louis, *Carnets 1921–1944* (Paris, 1978).

Heller, Gerhard, *Un Allemand à Paris 1940–1944* (Paris, 1981).

Hesnard, A., *De Freud à Lacan* (Paris, 1970).

Hewitt, Nicholas, 'Looking for Annie: Sartre's *La Nausée* and the Interwar Years', *Journal of European Studies*, XII (1982), pp. 96–112.

—— *Les Maladies du siècle: The Image of Malaise in French Literature and Thought in the Interwar Years* (Hull, 1988).

—— 'Marcel Aymé and the Dark Night of the Occupation', in Gerhard Hirschfeld and Patrick Marsh (eds), *Collaboration in Occupied France* (Oxford and New York, 1991), pp. 203–26.

—— 'Images of Montmartre in French Writing 1920–1960: "La Bohème réactionnaire"', *French Cultural Studies*, 4 (1993), pp. 129–44.

—— 'The Geography of Pleasure: Montmartre and Nineteenth-Century Paris', in John Ferris and Jaroslav Machacek (eds), *The European City in the Nineteenth Century* (Prague, 1995), pp. 1–21.

—— *Literature and the Right in Postwar France: The Story of the 'Hussards'* (Oxford and Washington, DC, 1996).

Hodgart, Matthew, *La Satire* (Paris, 1969).

Hoop, Isabelle d', *La Bibliothèque populaire de Clichy, 1872–1924* (Clichy, 1994).

Jamet, Claude, *Images mêlées: La Littérature et le théâtre sous l'Occupation* (Paris, 1947).

—— *Fifi roi* (Paris, 1947).

Jayle, F., 'Le Congrès des Syndicats Médicaux de France', *La Presse Médicale* (23 November 1927), p. 1435.

Joll, James, *Three Intellectuals and Politics: Blum, Rathenau, Marinetti* (London, 1960).

Jouhandeau, Marcel, *Le Péril juif* (Paris, 1936).

—— *Que l'amour est un. Journaliers*, IX (Paris, 1967).

Jouin, Mgr. (ed.), *Le Péril Judéo-Maconnique*, 1: *Les 'Protocoles' des Sages de Sion* (Paris, 1920).

Julian, Philippe, *The Triumph of Art Nouveau. Paris Exhibition 1900* (London, 1974).

Jünger, Ernst, *Journal, I (1941–1943)* (Paris, 1951).

Kaplan, Alice Yaeger, *Reproductions of Banality: Fascism, Literature and French Intellectual Life* (Minneapolis, 1986).

Kargalitsky, J., *The Life of H. G. Wells* (New York, 1966).

Kemp, Tom, *The French Economy 1913–1939* (London, 1972).

Kochan, Lionel, *The Jew and his History* (London, 1977).

Kohn-Etiemble, Jeannine, *226 Lettres inédites de Jean Paulhan* (Paris, 1975).

Kristeva, Julia, *Polylogue* (Paris, 1977).

Kupferman, Fred, *Au Pays des Soviets: Le Voyage français en Union Soviétique 1917–1939* (Paris, 1979).

Laing, R. D., *The Divided Self* (Harmondsworth, 1965).

Lake, Carlton, *Chers papiers: Mémoires d'un archéologue littéraire* (Paris, 1990).

Lanoux, Armand, 'Trois personnages en quête d'une bohème', *Quinzaine Littéraire* '(June 1982), 16–19.

Laurent, Jacques, *L'Année Quarante: Londres, De Gaulle, Vichy* (Paris, 1965).

—— *Les Bêtises* (Paris, 1971).

Le Bobinnec, Chantal, *Gen Paul à Montmartre: Féerie pour Monsieur Jules* (Paris, 1995).

Le Boterf, Hervé, *La Vie parisienne sous l'Occupation*, II (Paris, 1975).

Le Goff, Jacques, 'Au Moyen Age, Temps de l'Eglise et Temps du Marchand', *Annales*, 15 (1960).

Lequin, Yves, 'Les Citadins, les classes et les luttes sociales', in Georges Duby (ed.), *Histoire de la France urbaine, 4: La Ville de l'âge industrielle: le cycle haussmannien* (Paris, 1983).

Leroy, Géraldi, and Roche, Anne, *Les Ecrivains et le Front Populaire* (Paris, 1986).

Loiseaux, Gérard, *La Littérature de la défaite et de la Collaboration* (Paris, 1984).

Lorrain, Jean, *Poussières de Paris* (Paris, 1902).

Luchaire, Corinne, *Ma drôle de vie* (Paris, 1949).

Macaulay, Thomes Babington, Lord *The History of England from the Accession of James the Second*, vol. II, ed. Charles Harding Firth (London, 1913–15).

McMillan, James, *Dreyfus to de Gaulle. Politics and Society in France, 1898–1969* (London, 1985).

Mac Orlan, Pierre, 'La *Folie-Almayer et* les aventuriers dans la littérature', *Nouvelle Revue Française*, 81 (1920), 930–1.

—— *Le Petit manuel du parfait aventurier* (Paris, 1920).

Magraw, Roger, *France 1815–1914: The Bourgeois Century* (London, 1983).

Maier, Charles S., 'Between Taylorism and Technocracy', *Journal of Contemporary History*, V 2 (1970), pp. 27–62.

Malraux, André, *La Tentation de l'Occident* (Paris, 1926).

—— *Les Conquérants*, in *Romans* (Paris, 1947).

Mandel, Arnold, *Nous autres Juifs* (Paris, 1978).

Manoni, Maud, *The Child, his 'Illness' and the Others* (Harmondsworth, 1973).

Margueritte, Victor, *La Garçonne* (Paris, 1922).

Marks, Elaine, *Marrano as Metaphor: The Jewish Presence in French Writing* (New York, 1996).

Mazeline, Guy, *Les Loups* (Paris, 1932).

Melly, George and Woods, Michael, *The Paris of the Surrealists* (London, 1991).

Mercier, Ernest, *Réflexions 1936* (Paris, 1936).

Mignon, Paul-Louis, *Charles Dullin* (Lyons, 1990).

Monod, Jean-Marie, *La Férocité littéraire: De Malherbe à Céline* (Paris, 1983).

Morand, Paul, *1900* (Paris, 1931).

—— *Londres* (Paris, 1933).

Mugnier, Francis, *Journal de l'abbé Mugnier 1879–1939* (Paris, 1985).

Naud, Albert, *Les Défendre tous* (Paris, 1973).

Nimier, Roger, *Le Grand d'Espagne* (Paris, 1950).

Orwell, George, *The Road to Wigan Pier* (Harmondsworth, 1962).

Ory, E., 'Courtes réflexions d'un solitaire sur les Assurances Sociales', *La Presse Médicale* (8 February 1928), p. 171.

Ory, Pascal, *Les Collaborateurs 1940–1945* (Paris, 1980).

—— *Les Expositions Universelles de Paris* (Paris, 1982).

Palmade, Guy P., *Capitalisme et capitalistes français au XIXe siècle* (Paris, 1961).

Paraz, Albert, *Lettres à Pierre Monnier et Pierre Marcot (1949–1951)*, *Le Lérot Rêveur*, 26 (November 1979).

Parrinder, Patrick, *H. G. Wells* (Edinburgh, 1970).

Pauwels, Louis, Mousseau, Jacques, and Feller, Jean, *En français dans le texte* (Paris, 1962).

Poisson, Georges, *Les Hauts-de-Seine, soixante ans avant leur naissance* (Paris, 1986).

Poliakov, Léon, *Histoire de l'antisémitisme, 2: De Voltaire à Wagner* (Paris, 1968).

Pollet, Evelyne, *Escaliers* (Brussels, 1956).

Portes, Jacques, 'Les Etats-Unis dans les manuels d'Histoire et de Géographie de la IIIe République (1871–1914)', *Revue d'Histoire Moderne et Contemporaine*, 28 (1981), 196–206.

Poulet, Robert, *Ce n'est pas une vie* (Paris, 1976).

Quadruppani, Serge, *Les Infortunes de la vérité* (Paris, 1981).

Radine, Serge, *Lumières dans la nuit* (Paris, 1956).

Ravan, Georges, *L'Académie Goncourt en dix couverts* (Paris, 1943).

Ravez, Waler, *Femmes de lettres belges* (Brussels, 1939).

Raymond, Philippe Garnier, *Une Certaine France: L'Antisémitisme 40–44* (Paris, 1975).

Rebatet, Lucien, *Les Mémoires d'un fasciste, 1: Les Décombres 1938–1940* (Paris, 1976).

—— *Les Mémoires d'un fasciste, 2: 1941–1947* (Paris, 1976).

Reid, Donald, *Sewers and Sewermen* (Cambridge, MA, 1991).

Richard, François, *Les Anarchistes de droite* (Paris, 1991).

Rim, Carlo, *Le Grenier d'Arlequin. Journal 1916–1940* (Paris, 1981).

Robert, Pierre-Edmond, *D'un Hôtel du Nord l'autre: Eugène Dabit 1898–1936* (Paris, 1986).

Roman, Jean, *Paris 1890s* (London, 1961).

Sadoul, Georges, *Histoire générale du cinéma, 5: Le Cinéma muet* (Paris, 1975).

Saint-Jean, Robert de, *Journal d'un journaliste* (Paris, 1974).

Sartre, Jean-Paul, 'Portrait de l'antisémite', *Les Temps Modernes* (December 1945).

—— *Situations*, IV (Paris, 1964).

Saulnier, R. and Van der Zee, H. 'La Mort de crédit', *Downa Sztuka Lwów*, II (1939).

Serouille, Albert, *Bezons à travers les âges* (Paris, 1944).

Singer Charles, and Underwood, E. Ashworth, *A Short History of Medicine* (Oxford, 1962).

Singer-Kérel, Jeanne, *Le Coût de la vie à Paris de 1840 à 1954* (Paris, 1961).

Sirinelli, Jean-François (ed.), *Histoire des droites en France*, 3 vols (Paris, 1994).

Société Historique et Archéologique de Clichy (SHAC), *Clichy-la-Garenne. Vingt siècles d'histoire* (Paris, 1974).

Soucy, Robert, *Fascism in France: The Case of Maurice Barrès* (Berkeley, CA, and London, 1972).

Specklin, P., 'Les Répercussions des Assurances Sociales sur l'exercice de la médecine', *La Presse Médicale* (16 January 1929), pp. 78–9.

—— 'Considérations critiques sur les Assurances Sociales. Une solution nouvelle: l'épargne individuelle obligatoire', *La Presse Médicale* (6 March 1929), pp. 305, 10.

Stern, Benhard J., *Social Factors in Medical Progress* (New York, 1968).

Sutcliffe, Anthony, *The Autumn of Central Paris* (London, 1970).

Sweets, John W., *Choices in Vichy France: The French under Nazi Occupation* (New York and Oxford, 1986).

Swift, Jonathan, 'A Modest Proposal', ed. Herbert Davies in *Irish Tracts 1728–1733* (Oxford, 1964). [First published in 1729.]

Targowla, Olivier, *Les Médecins aux main sales* (Paris, 1976).

Thibaudet, Albert, 'Le Roman de l'aventure', *Nouvelle Revue Française*, 72 (1919), 597–611.

Thuillier, G., 'Hygiène corporelle aux XIXe et XXe siècles', *Annales de Démographie Historique*, (1975), pp. 123–30.

Tixier-Vignancour, Jean-Louis, *Des Républiques, des justices et des hommes: Mémoires* (Paris, 1976).

Troyat, Henri, *Un si long chemin* (Paris, 1976).

Vallès, Jules, *La Rue à Londres* (Paris, 1951).

Vallière, P. de, *Honneur et fidélité: Histoire des Suisses au service étranger* (Lausanne, 1940).

Vertex, Jean, *Le Village inspiré* (Paris, 1950).

Warnod, André, *Drôle d'équipe* (Paris, 1960).

Weber, Eugen, *Action Française: Royalism and Reaction in Twentieth-Century France* (Stanford, CA, 1962).

Weber, Julius, *Un Centre de triage de la tuberculose, fonctionnment du service et de la consultation de l'Hôpital Beaujon à Clichy, étude critique* (medical and doctoral thesis, Paris, 1937).

Webster, Nesta Helen, *Britain's Call to Arms: An Appeal to our Women* (London, 1914).

—— *The Surrender of an Empire* (London, 1931).

Wells, H. G., *An Experiment in Autobiography*, 1 (London, 1934).

—— *Kipps* (London, 1961). [First published in 1905.]

—— *The New Machiavelli* (London, 1911).

—— *Tono-Bungay* (London, 1964). [First published in 1909.]

Wilson, Edmund, *Axel's Castle* (London, 1961).

Wolf, Dieter, *Doriot, du communisme à la Collaboration* (Paris, 1969).

Wolf, Nelly, *Le Peuple dans le roman français de Zola à Céline* (Paris, 1990).

Yaki, Paul, *Le Montmartre de nos vingt ans* (Paris, 1933).

Zeldin, Theodore, *France 1848–1945, 1. Ambition, Love and Politics* (Oxford, 1973).

Index

Index